English

For UGC-NET/SLET and Other Competitive Examinations

Neeru Tandon

ATLANTIC

PUBLISHERS & DISTRIBUTORS (P) LTD

Published by

ATLANTIC

PUBLISHERS & DISTRIBUTORS (P) LTD

7/22, Ansari Road, Darya Ganj, New Delhi-110002
Phones : +91-11-40775252, 40775214, 23273880, 23275880
Fax : +91-11-23285873
Web : www.atlanticbooks.com
E-mail : orders@atlanticbooks.com

Branch Office: Chennai
Phones : +91-44-48531784, 28291383
E-mail : chennai@atlanticbooks.com

Disclaimer

- The author and the publisher have taken every effort to the maximum of their skill, expertise and knowledge to provide correct material in the book. Even then if some mistakes persist in the content of the book, the publisher does not take responsibility for the same. The publisher shall have no liability to any person or entity with respect to any loss or damage caused, or alleged to have been caused directly or indirectly, by the information contained in this book.
- The author has fully tried to follow the copyright law. However, if any work is found to be similar, it is unintentional and the same should not be used as defamatory or to file legal suit against the author.
- If the readers find any mistakes, we shall be grateful to them for pointing out those to us so that these can be corrected in the next edition.
- All disputes are subject to the jurisdiction of Delhi courts only.

Printed & bound in India by Atlantic Print Services

Preface

We all want success because nothing succeeds like success. The question before us is: What is the one thing that guarantees success? Is it experience, money, knowledge, education, or training? I feel just one thing out of these cannot guarantee success. One vital element to be incorporated is self-belief. It is a primary factor that gives you the confidence that it is you who can generate the powerful results you want. Positive thinking is another name for this self-belief. Sri A.P.J. Abdul Kalam says in his *Wings of Fire*, "It was in the handling of the crises that arose as a consequence that talent could often be revealed. I later realized by experience, that the best way to prevent errors was to anticipate them." So young friends, if you follow this piece of advice you will be doers, achievers and finally, the winners.

University Grants Commission (UGC) conducts a competitive National Eligibility Test (NET) for Lectureship and Junior Research Fellowship (JRF) for Indian universities. Similarly, various States also conduct such exams (SLET) for recruitment in their universities and colleges. NET-JRF/LS in English is considered a prestigious examination in India. The UGC has made it mandatory for the M.Phil. holders to clear the NET or the State Level Eligibility Test (SLET) to be considered for the post of Lecturer. The move is to ensure the quality of faculty in institutes of higher learning. Among all the subjects of UGC-NET-JRF/LS, English is one of the toughest subjects, because of its vast and multidimensional syllabus. Most of the students find it difficult to qualify the exam, even if they have good basic knowledge and understanding of the subject. Many students have to spend a lot of time in search of the required study material.

This comprehensive book is designed to serve as guide for all the aspirants appearing in UGC-NET/SLET and other competitive examinations with English as a subject. It has been written strictly in accordance with the latest UGC syllabus and pattern. This volume on English contains almost all required information on the subject. The topics are categorically described in an analytical and coherent way. It contains point-wise study material and multiple-choice questions on all the topics covered in the latest UGC-NET/SLET syllabus for all the papers as well as descriptive study matter. The questions have been framed according to the latest techniques and instructions issued by the UGC and state examining bodies. Since this book is for guidance, the students should also consult some more books for detailed study as due to the paucity of space and vastness of syllabus it is not possible to incorporate everything in a single volume. I wish all the best to my readers and seek their comments/views/suggestions for making the book more useful in its subsequent editions. I hope that the features included in this book would help the learners in preparing themselves for these competitive exams.

Syllabus and pattern, model questions, solved papers and practice papers have been provided in the book for better understanding. Answers to the multiple choice questions are also given. Apart from providing pertinent information, these features are aimed at generating discussion which may lead the learners to further sources of information, and which in turn, will make the learning more interesting. This is especially true of the multiple choice questions which may not necessarily appear in the tests as they are. The usefulness of this book would depend upon the creative exploitation of the information available in the book.

Neeru Tandon
(profneerutandon@gmail.com)

Contents

Paper-III: Descriptive Questions

Syllabus and Pattern

PAPER-I

The first paper will be of general nature and it assesses teaching and research aptitude/ability of candidates. This paper is the same for all candidates appearing for the exams. Questions are based on comprehension, analysis, evaluation, structure of arguments, reasoning ability generalization and logical inconsistency. Thinking power and general awareness of the candidates will be under test. Paper-I will be of 2-½ hrs duration. Negative marking will be made for wrong answers in paper-I. UGC has decided to provide choice to the candidates from December 2009 UGC NET onwards. Sixty (60) multiple choice questions of two marks each will be given, out of which the candidate would be required to answer any fifty (50). In the event of the candidate attempting more than fifty questions, the first 50 questions attempted by the candidates would be evaluated.

Syllabus

1. **Teaching Aptitude**
   - Teaching: Nature, Objectives, Characteristics and Basic Requirements;
   - Learner's Characteristics;
   - Factors Affecting Teaching;
   - Methods of Teaching;
   - Teaching Aids;
   - Evaluation Systems.
2. **Research Aptitude**
   - Research: Meaning, Characteristics and Types;
   - Steps of Research;
   - Methods of Research;
   - Research Ethics;
   - Paper, article, workshop, seminar, conference and symposium;
   - Thesis writing: its characteristics and format.
3. **Reading Comprehension**
   - A passage to be set with questions to be answered.
4. **Communication**
   - Communication: Nature, Characteristics, Types, Barriers and Effective Classroom Communication.

5. **Reasoning (Including Mathematical)**
    - Number series; letter series; codes;
    - Relationships; classification.
6. **Logical Reasoning**
    - Understanding the Structure of Arguments;
    - Evaluating and distinguishing deductive and inductive reasoning;
    - Verbal Analogies: Word Analogy—Applied Analogy;
    - Verbal Classification;
    - Reasoning Logical Diagrams: Simple Diagrammatic Relationship, Multi-Diagrammatic Relationship;
    - Venn Diagram; Analytical Reasoning.
7. **Data Interpretation**
    - Sources, Acquisition and Interpretation of Data;.
    - Quantitative and Qualitative Data;
    - Graphical Representation and Mapping of Data.
8. **Information and Communication Technology (ICT)**
    - ICT: Meaning, Advantages, Disadvantages and Uses;
    - General Abbreviations and Terminology;
    - Basics of Internet and E-mailing.
9. **People and Environment**
    - People and Environment Interaction;
    - Sources of Pollution;
    - Pollutants and their impact on human life, exploitation of natural and energy resources;
    - Natural Hazards and Mitigation
10. **Higher Education System: Governance, Polity and Administration**
    - Structure of the institutions for higher learning and research in India; formal and distance education; professional/technical and general education; value education: governance, polity and administration; concept, institutions and their interactions.

PAPER-II

This paper will consist of short questions based on the subject selected by the candidates. Each of these papers will consist of a Test Booklet containing 50 objective type questions (Multiple choice, Matching type, True/False, Assertion-reasoning type). Candidates will have to mark their instructions for filling up the OMR sheet (Optical Mark Reader) provided along with the Test Booklet. Paper-II will be evaluated only in case of those candidates who will be able to secure a minimum of such aggregate marks in Paper-I as may be fixed by the UGC.

Syllabus

1. Chaucer to Shakespeare
2. Jacobean to Restoration Period
3. Augustan Age: 18th Century Literature
4. Romantic Period
5. Victorian Period
6. Modern Period
7. Contemporary Period
8. American and Other Non-British literatures
9. Literary Theory and Criticism
10. Rhetoric and Prosody

PAPER-III

Paper-III will consist of only descriptive questions from the subject selected by the candidate. The candidate will be required to attempt questions in the space provided in the Test Booklet.

I provide you the revised format of Paper-III for NET and SLET in this book.

Whatever may be your subject you also need to read a paragraph and reveal your critical ability to apply knowledge, by answering questions based on the paragraph. You also need to show your ability to expound critically a theme at length with discrimination.

The UGC has restructured the format of Paper-III. The syllabi of all subjects, however, remain unchanged. Paper-III, now consists of four sections.

SECTION–I: Essay writing—two questions with internal choice on general themes and contemporary, theoretical or of disciplinary relevance may be given. The candidate is expected to write up to 500 words for each question of 20 marks (2Q × 20M = 40 Marks). In case the questions are based on electives, the choices should have questions from each elective; otherwise all choices should be of general nature, common to all candidates. In case of science subjects like Computer Science and Applications, Environmental Sciences, Electronic Science etc., two questions carrying 20 marks each may be given in place of essay type questions. The questions in this section should be numbered as 1 and 2.

SECTION–II: Three extended answer based questions to test the analytical ability of the candidate are to be asked on the major specializations/electives. Questions will be asked on all major specializations/electives and the candidates may be asked to choose one specializations/elective and answer the three questions. There is to be no internal choice. Each question will be answered in up to 300 words and shall carry 15 marks each (3Q × 15M = 45 Marks). Where there is no specialization/elective, 3 questions may be set across the syllabus. The questions in this section should be numbered from 3 to 5.

SECTION–III: Nine questions may be asked across the syllabus. The questions will be definitional or seeking particular information and are to be answered in up to 50 words each. For science subjects as mentioned in Section-I, short numerical/computational problems may be considered. Each question will carry 10 marks (9Q × 10M = 90 Marks). There should be no internal choice. The questions in this section should be numbered from 6 to 14.

SECTION-IV: It requires the candidates to answer questions from a given text of around 200-300 words taken from the works of a known thinker/author. Five carefully considered specific questions are to be asked on the given text, requiring an answer in up to 30 words each. This section carries 5 questions of 5 marks each (5Q × 5M = 25 Marks). In the case of science subjects, a theatrical/numerical problem may be set. These questions are meant to test critical thinking, ability to comprehend and apply knowledge one possesses. Questions in this section should be numbered as 15 to 19.

LATEST STRUCTURE OF PAPER-III

Section	Type of Questions	Test of	No. of Questions	Words Per Answer	Words Total	Marks Per Question	Marks Total
I	Essay	Ability to dwell on a theme at an optimum level	2	500	1000	20	40
II	Three analytical/ evaluative questions	Ability to reason and hold an argument on the given topic	3	300	900	15	45
III	Nine definitional/ short answer questions	Ability to understand and express the same	9	50	450	10	90
IV	Text based questions	Critical thinking, ability to comprehend and formulate the concepts	5	30	150	5	25
TOTAL			19	-	2500	-	200

Syllabus

1. Literary Comprehension (with internal choice of poetry stanza and prose passage; four comprehension questions will be asked carrying 4 marks each).
2. Up to the Renaissance
3. Jacobean to Restoration Periods
4. Augustan Age: 18th Century Literature
5. Romantic Period

6. Victorian and Pre-Raphaelites
7. Modern British Literature
8. Contemporary British Literature
9. Literary Theory and Criticism up to T.S. Eliot
10. Contemporary Theory
11. History of English Language, English Language Teaching
12. European Literature from Classical Age to the 20th Century
13. Indian writing in English and Indian Literature in English Translation
14. American and Other non-British English Literatures
15. Literary Theory and Criticism

Negative Marking in UGC NET Paper-I and II

Negative marking at the rate of 25% has been introduced from December 2009 UGC-NET onwards.

For each incorrect answer, 0.5 marks shall be deducted.

For visually handicapped candidates 30 minutes extra time shall be provided separately for Paper I and Paper II. For Paper III 45 minutes extra time shall be provided. They will also be provided the series of a scribe who would be a graduate in a subject other than that of the candidate.

PAPER-I

Teaching and Research Aptitude

1

Teaching Aptitude

"He who ceases to learn cannot adequately teach."—Anonymous

Teaching as professions is divided into many areas of specializations, each requiring different skill—set and methods of training. Some of the major areas of specialization include excellence in communication skills, the ability to hold the attention of young minds, to inspire confidence and finally, the ability to set an example by word and deed. Education can be defined as "the aggregate of all processes by means of which a person develops attributes, attitudes and other forms of behavior of positive value in the society in which he lives." The complete educational process has four important common factors—(i) teacher, (ii) student, (iii) subject-matter, and (iv) setting (context).

Again there are four dimensions associated with a teacher—his competence, his efficiency, his enthusiasm and his morale. These four factors are seen in process of effective classroom interaction.

In the traditional method of teaching, the students do not have the option to select the teaching style according to their aptitude. The learning is incomplete as one teaching style is unacceptable to the learner. The modern teaching method, i.e. the teaching process in the digital mode ends only when the student learns the concept and develops the skill to use it. Classrooms can be made more effective with the aid of animations, video, sound and recorded information. An advantage of the electronic method is that the students can repeat the class at his or her will. If facilitates time management. The assignments, quiz and the feedback can be used to develop the teaching material or improve the teaching aids.

Research suggests that there are eight core competencies that a potential teacher must possess. These are communication skills, intelligence, maturity, perception, persistence, receptivity, social works and teaching interest.

Aptitude, according to Warrior's dictionary, is a condition or set of characteristics regarded as Symptomatic of an individual's ability to acquire with training some knowledge, or skill or set of responses. One must know about the nature, objective, characteristics and basic requirements of teaching.

Learner's Characteristics. While teaching, teacher must know about the type of students, he is catering to, what type of learners they are, whether he is going to teach weak students, slow learners, brilliant students or extra-ordinary focused intelligent group. They need basic knowledge or just a brush up or they require problem solving.

Methods of Teaching. Teachers should know about factors that affects their teaching. There are various methods like lecture, seminars, projects, dictation, assignment or cramming, etc. But when a teacher teaches, he must be sure subject and what will be the best particular subject. For example, science subjects can be expressed or explained through projects or practical methods, while for language one can use langue-phone or assignment method, for literature lecture is useful and for other subjects of humanity even seminars are very useful way of teaching and discussing new concepts or knowledge.

Teaching Aids. Teachers use teaching aids for making teaching within understanding level of students. He may give some notes to students, study material that will help them to understand the subject clearly. Other teaching aids as audio-visual methods like C.D., tapes, maps, etc. are very successful teaching aids.

Factors affecting Teaching. It is true that teacher should be presentable, but it does not matter much, whether his handwriting is very good or not even for that matter students are not really concerned with the degrees of a teacher. What really matter is the subject understanding of the teacher. How well he can explain the subject to students.

Evaluation System. Evaluation system must be objective. If it depends upon person to person, or upon mood of teacher or insufficient knowledge of the teacher or evaluation then it cannot be the real test of student's ability. Evaluation system must be fair.

A conscientious teacher always learns something new, makes it a part of the storage of his knowledge, modifies his views in the light of new facts, reorders his methods and goes to the classroom to acquaint the learners with the new knowledge he has gained.

EXERCISE

1. Which of the following is the main objective of teaching?
   (a) To give information related to the syllabus.
   (b) To develop thinking power of students.
   (c) To dictate notes to students.
   (d) To prepare students to pass the exams.
2. Which of the following is a good method of teaching?
   (a) Lecture and Dictation
   (b) Seminar and Project
   (c) Seminar and Dictation
   (d) Dictation and Assignment.
3. Teacher uses teaching aids for
   (a) making teaching interesting.
   (b) making teaching within understanding level of students.
   (c) making students attractive.
   (d) the sake of its use.
4. Effectiveness of teaching depends on
   (a) qualification of teacher
   (b) personality of teacher
   (c) handwriting of teacher
   (d) subject knowledge of teacher
5. Which of the following is not characteristic of a good Question Paper?
   (a) Objective
   (b) Subjectivity
   (c) No use of vague words
   (d) Reliable.
6. The mean score on any class test is the result of
   (a) dividing the sum of all scores by the number of scores.
   (b) determining the most frequent score.
   (c) adding all the scores and dividing by the most frequent score.
   (d) adding the highest and lowest scores and dividing by two.
7. The least justifiable use of the results of a standardized reading test is to
   (a) identify areas of pupil deficiency.
   (b) evaluate the reading instruction programme.

(c) serve as a basis for report card marks.
(d) serve as the basis for apparent conference.

8. All the following are acceptable goals for dealing with behavior problems in the classroom, except
(a) helping the child to improve his/her self control.
(b) being impersonal and objective.
(c) understanding the offence.
(d) utilizing appeals to children that have personal implications.

9. Of the following, the one situation that will cause the greatest difficulty for a child in the initial stages of reading instruction is
(a) confusion of left and right directionality.
(b) possessing an IQ of 90.
(c) never having attended kindergarten.
(d) being an avid television watcher.

10. Of the following essentials of learning the one that takes preferance over the others is
(a) average intelligence
(b) ability to read
(c) desire to learn
(d) a good teacher

11. A child from a disorganized home will experience the greatest difficulty with
(a) well structured lessons
(b) independent study
(c) programmed instruction
(d) workbooks

12. The term 'identical elements' is closely associated with
(a) group instruction
(b) transfer of learning
(c) similar test questions
(d) the scientific method

13. The evaluation of personality is best made through the use of an
(a) inventory test (b) preference test
(c) survey test (d) projective test

14. The current movement of behavior modification, wherein tokens are awarded for correct answers, is a reflection of
(a) Herbart's Five Steps
(b) Lock's Tabula Rasa
(c) Thorndike's Law of Exercise
(d) Thorndike's Law of Effect

15. When a student's misbehavior persists even after teacher's punishment, the teacher is probably practicing a policy of
(a) retribution
(b) corporal punishment
(c) negative re-inforcement
(d) repression

16. Children's attitude toward persons of different ethnic groups are generally based upon
(a) their parent's attitude
(b) the attitudes of their pear
(c) their sibling's attitude
(d) their religious affiliation

17. Frobel's most important contribution to education was his development of the
(a) vocational school
(b) kindergarten
(c) latin School
(d) play School

18. Teacher tenure laws can best be justified because they
(a) protect teachers whose political views differ sharply with those of the community.
(b) provide for stability of staffing.
(c) allow an experienced teacher to plan creatively.
(d) protect teachers from excessive requirements of principals.

19. The incorrectly associated pair is
    (a) Joseph Lancaster—Contract Plan
    (b) Benyamin Franklin—Academy
    (c) James B Conant—High School
    (d) Elizabeth Peabody—Kindergarten
20. Curriculum makers have the most difficulty when
    (a) there is an inflationary cycle.
    (b) parents are participants.
    (c) teachers unions insist on input.
    (d) the nature of the student population is changing.
21. The educator who advanced the idea of the five formal steps in leaving was
    (a) Rousseau (b) Comenius
    (c) Herbart (d) Froebel
22. "The individual develops through the head, the heart, and the hand", this was the educational philosophy of
    (a) Herbart (b) Pestalozzi
    (c) Froebel (d) Rousseau
23. Martin Luther's greatest contribution to education was his
    (a) translation of the Bible into German.
    (b) advocacy of science curriculum for the universities.
    (c) concept of justification by good works.
    (d) advocacy of church control of schools.
24. Of the following the statement that is least educationally valid is that
    (a) heterogeneous grouping in undemocratic.
    (b) study habits should be taught.
    (c) over learning constitutes a waste of time.
    (d) drill periods should be brief.
25. The trial and error method of instruction is best enhanced by
    (a) role playing
    (b) an audio-visual lesson
    (c) independent study
    (d) programmed instruction
26. All of the following are evidence of a good class audio-visual programme except
    (a) allowing children to decide which educational television programmes they will view in class.
    (b) using globes and maps to teach geographic skills and concepts.
    (c) providing study guides for class viewing of films.
    (d) teacher previewing of all film strips to be shown to the class.
27. An increase in comprehension skill is most likely to result from
    (a) guided silent reading.
    (b) guided oral reading.
    (c) unstructured silent reading.
    (d) the teacher reading to the class.
28. In dealing with a class that is misbehaving, the teacher's least effective course of action is to
    (a) isolate those most responsible for the mis-behaviour.
    (b) ask the advice of his/her grade leader.
    (c) lower the grades of pupils who create the most serious infractions.
    (d) ask the Principal to observe him/her.
29. All of the following are appropriate areas for pupil teacher planning except
    (a) the day's schedule
    (b) the selection of committees
    (c) the sequence in a skill programme
    (d) a class party
30. All of the following are examples of intrinsic motivation except
    (a) encouraging pupils to help develop the aim of a lesson.
    (b) permitting pupils to evaluate each other's answers.

(c) giving short quizzes at the beginning of a lesson.
(d) asking students to contribute to a class resource file.

31. All of the following are descriptive of good teaching except that
(a) creative methods can used to achieve traditional goals.
(b) teachers should allow acting out children to handle manipulative materials.
(c) teachers should refer all children with emotional problems to the guidance counselor.
(d) when given, a punishment should immediately follow the misbehaviour.

32. Of the following activities in a science class, the one with least educational value is
(a) viewing a film strip
(b) constructing a model
(c) reading about a simple experiment
(d) drawing a design

33. The operation of the class library should be the responsibility of
(a) the teacher
(b) volunteer parents
(c) rotating committees of pupils
(d) the School Librarian

34. Group tests that have norms for each grade and that are administered in accordance with uniform procedures listed in a manual of instruction are called
(a) school wide-finals
(b) quizzes
(c) standardized tests
(d) The WALS

35. In comparing the lecture and development lessons, all of the following are true except that
(a) there is more pupil in the development lesson.
(b) slow children drive more benefit from a lecture than brighter children to.
(c) motivation and summary are necessary in both lessons.
(d) the lecture method is more conducive to larger class.

36. A teacher notes poor attendance in class on test day. The teacher should
(a) call the parents of the absentees.
(b) do nothing.
(c) schedule tests throughout the week.
(d) tell the pupils that missing two tests will result in a failing mark.

37. Career education should begin
(a) in the third or fourth grades.
(b) when the child enters junior high school.
(c) in high school economics classes.
(d) when streams are to be divided.

38. To be successful with an overactive child the teacher should
(a) give the child extra written work.
(b) isolate the child from the class.
(c) give the child a pass to bathroom every half hour.
(d) provide the child with purposeful activities that legitimize the need for movement.

39. A class assembly programme best contributes to educational goals when it
(a) features the best singers or actors in the class.
(b) is prepared by the teacher.
(c) is written by the children.
(d) is praised by the parents.

40. While planning to develop the powers of creative thinking, the teacher should allow for all except

(a) failure of an experiment in science.
(b) solving of all problems through use of a well practiced formula.
(c) failure to solve a problem because of insufficient information.
(d) inability to locate a book in Library.

41. All of the following are applicable in good motivation except that it
(a) should be brief.
(b) should be relevant to the pupils.
(c) should always come from the teacher.
(d) should be related to the lesson that follows.

42. Lesson planning should be guided primarily by the consideration of
(a) meeting the needs of the average child in the class.
(b) creating a comfortable class-room environment.
(c) the curriculum goals.
(d) providing students worksheets.

43. A teacher should be catechized for all of the following practices except
(a) undermining the role of the parent.
(b) exercising from leadership.
(c) giving talented students special favour.
(d) becoming overly friendly with student.

44. Individual differences within a class are best handled by
(a) coaching slow children after school.
(b) giving the bright students free reading time .
(c) poor tutoring.
(d) organizing groups for specific purposes.

45. Most educators agree that oral reading
(a) comes naturally to good readers.
(b) requires an audience situation.
(c) is useful for appreciation of poetry.
(d) is only for poor readers.

46. The discovery method of learning is best exemplified by
(a) programme instruction.
(b) team teaching.
(c) mainstreaming.
(d) experimentation in a science laboratory.

47. Major areas of specialization in teaching include except
(a) excellent communication skill.
(b) handsome Personality.
(c) the ability to hold the attention of students.
(d) to instill confidence.

48. How can the classrooms be made more effective?
(a) By using beautiful lights
(b) By decorating them with pictures
(c) With the aid of video sound, animation and recorded information
(d) None of the above.

49. A potential teacher must possess
(a) intelligence, maturity, receptivity and teaching interest
(b) intelligence only
(c) intelligence and handsome personality
(d) None of the above

50. N.C.H.E. stands for
(a) North Central Higher Education
(b) National Commission of Higher Education
(c) National Cooperation of High School Education
(d) National Council on Higher Education

51. If majority of students in your class are weak you should
(a) not care about the intelligent students.
(b) keep your teaching slow.

(c) keep your speed of teaching fast so that students comprehension level may increase.
(d) keep your teaching slow along with some extra guidance to bright pupils.

52. A teacher who is not able to draw the attention of his students should
(a) evaluate his teaching method and improve it.
(b) resign from the post.
(c) find fault in his pupils.
(d) start dictating.

53. A teacher
(a) should introduce the lesson before he starts teaching.
(b) should have command over his language.
(c) should have command over his subject.
(d) All of the above.

54. If students are not able to follow, you should
(a) give them prompt
(b) make the matter easy
(c) illustrate with examples
(d) All of the above

55. Micro teaching is useful to students of
(a) primary classes only
(b) junior classes only
(c) 10 + 2 classes only
(d) higher classes and primary classes both.

56. The greatest important cause of failure in beginning for a teacher lies in the area of
(a) inter-personal relationship
(b) verbal ability
(c) knowledge of the teacher
(d) tight handling of the students

57. The major responsibility with which the School Personnels have been entrusted is that
(a) it harmonizes the needs of the child and demands of the society for the benefit of both.
(b) it makes the child able to get job.
(c) it prepares the school programme according to the need of the child.
(d) All of the above.

58. Classroom discipline can be maintained effectively by
(a) knowing the cause of indiscipline and handling it with stern hand.
(b) providing a programme which is according to the need and interest of the pupils.
(c) by putting on fancy clothes in the classroom.
(d) None of the above.

59. A teacher in the class is
(a) the president of the group
(b) a director of the group
(c) a leader and guide of the group
(d) All of the above

60. Drop outs are more likely to be
(a) unemployed
(b) vulnerable to the requirement of public assistance
(c) engaged in antisocial behavior
(d) All of the above

61. An effective teacher is expected to
(a) encourage the students to make initiative.
(b) reduce the anxiety level of students to moderate level.
(c) to make students feel that education is their need.
(d) All of the above.

62. If a student is constantly rubbing his eyes and is unattentive during blackboard work he is having
(a) adjustment problem
(b) hearing problem
(c) visual problem
(d) All of the above.

ANSWERS

1. (b)	2. (d)	3. (b)	4. (d)	5. (b)	6. (b)
7. (b)	8. (b)	9. (a)	10. (c)	11. (c)	12. (c)
13. (a)	14. (d)	15. (c)	16. (a)	17. (a)	18. (a)
19. (a)	20. (d)	21. (c)	22. (b)	23. (a)	24. (c)
25. (c)	26. (a)	27. (a)	28. (c)	29. (c)	30. (b)
31. (c)	32. (a)	33. (a)	34. (b)	35. (b)	36. (c)
37. (b)	38. (d)	39. (c)	40. (b)	41. (b)	42. (c)
43. (b)	44. (b)	45. (b)	46. (b)	47. (b)	48. (c)
49. (a)	50. (d)	51. (d)	52. (a)	53. (d)	54. (d)
55. (d)	56. (c)	57. (a)	58. (b)	59. (c)	60. (d)
61. (d)	62. (c)				

2

Research Aptitude

Research: Meaning, Characteristics and Types

The word research originally had the same connotation as the words rewrite and redo mean today. Now it is purely a technical term. It means a systematic investigation in a field of knowledge to discover or establish facts or principles. It also means a fresh approach to a subject or interpretation of facts.

"[Research is] a systematic investigation for the purpose of gaining new knowledge. In a broad sense, research is any study that leads to new knowledge for the person doing research."

—*New Standard Encyclopedia*

"[Research is] a studious inquiry or examination, especially critical and exhaustive investigation or experimentation having for its aim the discovery of new facts and their correct information, the revision of accepted conclusions, theories, or lawa in the light of newly discovered facts, or the practical applications of such new or reversed conclusions, theories or laws."

—*Webster's International Dictionary*

Through these definitions we know that research should be systematic. It means that the entire procedure of the investigation is done under certain principles. The word of both kinds of facts, one that famous his hypothesis and the other that goes counter to his assumptions. It follows that the researcher must not be prejudiced or subjective in his observation, experiment, analysis or interpretation nor should he be erratic in the arrangement of facts nor ignore the facts that shalter his postulates or hypothesis.

Research should be a genuine contribution to knowledge. This is possible only when we discover a new fact or interpret a known fact in a new way. It is also that kind of investigation which examines an accepted theory to revise or modify or sometimes reject it. Research can be of applied kind. Here the investigator applies the abstract principles of a theory for practical purposes. In literature, Frud's theory of relativity is applied in the analysis of a literary text.

Types. Nature of research differs from subject to subject. This is because materials and tools of each subject are largely different. Physics, chemistry, botany, zoology and other natural sciences study natural phenomenon. Their basic tools are observation and experiment. They replicate the natural conditions in the laboratory and observe the changes minutely. The social sciences study man and his behaviour. Naturally observation and interview are the important tools that we use in social sciences.

Literature is different from natural sciences or social sciences. When its materials (the object of study) is the creative vities, it applies the tools of social sciences and when the object of study is the text, it applies the tools which are specific to it.

In natural sciences and social sciences we have two kinds of research, basic and applied. Literary Research, because of the duality of its object of study, is of four kinds:

(a) Bibliography, textural criticism
(b) Biographical
(d) Theoretical
(d) Interpretive

Research adds something new to the treasure of knowledge and without it teaching will lose its utility gradually. It has four main objectives:

(a) Advancement of knowledge
(b) Broadening the mind and sharpening the critical insight of the researcher
(c) Creation of a genuine and intellegent interest in subject
(d) Inculation of the sense that the researcher is a member of a collaborative community.

STEPS in Research Writing. (1) Selecting the topic (2) Using the Library for data collection (3) Compiling a working Bibliography.

STEPS

In science, materials are the objects of nature and the tools are scientific instrument. Literary research is equally systematic, methodical and objective, hence scientific. Aristotle applied the same principles in Physics, Politics and Poetics.

Manuscripts and printed books are also material of literary research. In science the basic tools are observation and experiment. The tools of literary research are Bibliography, Note System, scientific tools and textual analysis. We may divide bibliography into four kinds (i) Historical bibliography, (ii) Bibliothecal bibliography, (iii) Enumerative bibliography, and (iv) Practical bibliography. Then Bibliography in general is divided into two main divisions: Primary sources and Secondary sources.

Methods of Research. In other english speaking methodology categorically and Seldom deviates from his critical stance. Even when he is interpreting the facts, he adopts a particular critical approach and method of analysis. In India usually research students mixing two or three approaches, Seldom aware of the fact that their method, a heterogeneous blend, makes their viewpoint vague and blurred.

Every literary work has two aspects, form and content. The creative writer takes the raw material, people and events and imposes a form. Besides researcher organizes the created work in a special way, which is his or her technique.

Wilboy Scott edited an anthology of modern critical texts dividing them into five broad groups—the Moral Approaches, the Psychological Approach, the Sociological Approach, the Formalistic Approach and the Archetypal Approach.

It is also important that the research student should know the difference between the style of an article in a magazine and that of a research paper or a thesis. An article in a magazine is not always exact in referring to the sources of quotations, presentation of facts and distinction between the primary sources and the secondary sources and is more subjective in its approach to the subject.

Research Ethics

The research paper on the thesis demands objectivity, balanced views, exact reference to source and presentation of facts. Researcher must take care of research ethics.

Plagiarism. Plagiarism is borrowing the others without acknowledging them. If a student incorporates a few lines of a writer and does not acknowledge him, he commits plagiarism, which is against the ethics of research. Even when he paraphrases the ideas of others, he can be charged with plagiarism. In all cases plagiarism should be avoided.

Style. As a research paper or a thesis is analytical and argumentative, therefore, its style will considerably differ from that of an average essay, stanza, colloquial words and expressions are to be avoided. Even contractions like won't, shouldn't, I'll or he's are not permitted. The sentences should be balanced, short and precise in expression.

Thesis Writing. Research project carried out with the student's supervisor, normally leading to thesis proposal. Project should make a tangible research contribution. As you discover information and opinions on your topic, you should keep trace of sources that you may use for thesis writing. Create a computer file for this purpose, and enter full information about sources into the file as you proceed with your research when you add sources to your working bibliography, be sure you enter all the publication information needed for the works—cited list. Researchers need to evaluate the quality of any work before using and citing it. In evaluating a book, you might consult Book Review Index and Book Review Digest to see how the book was received by experts in the field of study. In summarizing, paraphrasing, or quoting, keep an accurate record of the pages or other numbered sections. In taking notes, seek to steer a middle course between recording too much and recording too little, in other words, try to be both thorough and concise. Above all, strive for accuracy, not only in copying words for direct quotation but also in summarizing and paraphrasing author's ideas.

Do not expect your first draft to be the finished project. Review and rewriting are always necessary. Then, you may add, eliminate and rearrange material. In later drafts you can concentrate on more mechanical kinds of revision, for more process and economical wording. Finally, correct all technical errors, using a standard writing guide to check punctuation, grammar, and usage and consulting a standard dictionary for the spelling and meaning of words.

Effective writing depends as much on clarity and readability as on content. The organization and development of our ideas, the unity and coherence of your presentation, and your command of sentence structure, grammar and diction are all important considerations.

Paper—refers to a piece of writing, dissertation, essay or monograph in a scholarly way.

Article—means short piece of non-fiction in newspaper etc. It also refers to composition or essay.

Workshop—Teacher's teaching or giving lectures on a special topic.

Seminar—Small class for discussion etc. or short intensive course of study. It also refers to specialists' conference.

Conference—Meeting for discussion, deliberation, meeting, seminar or symposium.

Symposium—is conference, or presentation of collection of essays on particular subject.

Introduction

Always remember that introduction is all about your paper and not about your topic.

Start introduction with a broad basis and then narrow it down to your particular field of study, explaining the rationale behind each step.

With a few key words, generalize the theme in relation to the audience or the subject, whichever suits the topic.

In the introduction, try to inform that reader about the rationale behind the work, justifying why this work is an essential component of research in the concerned field.

The introduction does not have a strict word limit, but it should be as concise as possible.

A good introduction explains how you mean to deal with the topic, and handle the concerned issue. This will motivate readers to read your article/paper.

The introduction is the place to highlight any assumptions, limitations and in the experiment from the start.

The entire introduction should logically end at the research question. The reader, by the end of the introduction, should know exactly what author is trying to achieve with the paper.

The first step to writing a good introduction of the research paper is to do the research/ analysis.

Introduction, being the tricky part of the paper to write, so many authors and researchers prefer to write it last (before writing abstracts), ensuring that they miss no major points.

Avoid technical terms, Avoid abbreviations, Use simple sentences and Avoid common errors of punctuation and grammar.

The Abstract

An abstract is a Brief summary of a longer piece of work, which is usually academic in nature.

As the abstract is published in isolation from the main text, it should therefore stand on its own and be understandable without reference to the longer piece.

It should report the essential facts, and should not exaggerate or contain material that is not there in the paper.

Its purpose is to act as a reference tool, enabling the reader to decide whether or not to read the full text.

It should be used to describe Briefly the purpose and nature of the paper.

Start writing the Abstract with the statement of the paper's purpose, which should be as succinct as possible. If you include background keep this to a minimum.

It should include the Brief details of the research, the analysis carried out the important results obtained.

Use the active rather than the passive voice.

The style of writing should be dense, and sentences will probably be longer than usual.

Cut out any unnecessary words that do not add to the meaning.

The Abstract should generally range between 200-250 words in length.

Abstract is generally written at last, as it's the precise summary of the entire paper.

Literature Review

A literature review is a body of text that aims to review the critical points of current knowledge on a particular topic.

It has to be in the form of a non-quantitative summary and interpretation of research findings reported in the literature.

It should give an overview of what has been said by the key writers, what are the prevailing theories and issues, what is the focus point and what methodologies are used by writers.

It is not in itself primary research, but rather it reports on other findings.

It should be purely descriptive and should provide an assessment of the literature in a particular field.

Literature review is not always critical. It can include both strengths and weaknesses of the writings of particular author.

Literature review should focus on: What themes emerge and what conclusions can be drawn? What are the major similarities and differences between the various writers?

It has to highlight the gaps and inappropriateness of the approach adopted by the particular authors, or raising questions.

Literature review should not be the list and paraphrase, but should add comment and bring out themes and trends.

Literature review should help the author to validate his area of interest, methods and his approach while reviewing other literature.

Literature review should enable narrowing the subject area towards the main topic focus.

Methodology

The methodology section describes your basic research plan.

It usually begins with a few short introductory paragraphs that restate purpose and research questions.

Keep the wording of research questions consistent throughout the paper.

In this section you need to determine the question(s) that you are attempting to answer and the problems faced in finding answers.

Write a very brief introduction to the methodology section as a whole. The introduction should state the goals of the research experiment and should ideally be a single paragraph.

Begin the extended methodology under a new heading. The first part of the extended methodology should address your Research Design, Data (primary/secondary), Variables, Instruments, Procedures and Analysis.

There can be separate paragraphs for each of the elements of methodology.

The methodology material should follow a step-by-step logical sequence.

Methods are not a set of instruction; therefore omit all explanatory information and background—save if for the discussion.

Even when you are sure that your research methods are perfect solution for your research objectives, there can be a possibility that selected method have some drawbacks that can affect the relevancy of your research. These aspects should be also mentioned in methodology section.

Results

The objective is to present the results obtained after doing research.

This can usually be best achieved by presenting the data mainly in Tables and Figures, with the necessary minimum of verbal explanation.

In the text the same data should not be presented in the form of both Tables and Figures.

It is not necessary to include 'raw' data in the results unless they are required.

State each result and discuss it immediately.

Address such questions about the validity and reliability of your measures here.

Technicalities can be included in this section.

Interpret the magnitude of each outcome in a qualitative way; using both your experience of the magnitudes that matter in the research and any published scales of magnitudes.

Discussion

The various results should be drawn together and discussed in relation to previously published data.

Speculation about results obtained in relation to other known facts may also be useful.

In addition, you should discuss the possible theoretical or practical significance of your results and highlight possible areas for future research.

The purpose is to bring the various findings together in an interpretative manner.

The discussion section indicates the degree of accuracy and the significance of the results of the research described.

The discussion is often the difficult part of a paper to write and you should bear in mind that repetition should not be done to emphasize a point.

In this section interpret findings that have been substantiated in the discussion of results and discuss their implications.

The section introduces no new material other than remarks based on these findings. It includes the author's opinions and is written on the basis of the work undertaken in the entire paper.

References

All references cited should be presented in the alphabetical order of the first author, and where necessary by the second and subsequent authors, again using the specified system/format and date citation.

References to journal papers should include the following:

1. Name(s) of author(s) in capitals followed by initials
2. Year of publication in parentheses
3. Title of papers (without capitalization)

4. The full title of the journal in italics (or underlined)
5. Volume number and page numbers.

The correct style of punctuation to use can be seen in the examples set out below. The references should be in single-line spacing within entries and double-spaced between references, as shown:

Dasch, J.M. (1987) "Measurement of dry deposition to surfaces in deciduous and pine canoples." *Environmental Pollution*, 44, 261-277.

Barnard, C.J. and Hurst, J.L. (1996) "Welfare by design: the natural selection of welfare criteria." *Animal Welfare*, 5, 405-433.

Swift S., Stewart G.S. A.B. and Williams P. (1996) "The inner workings of a quorum sensing signal generator." *Trends in Microbiology,* 4, 463-465.

References to booklets and bulletins are laid out in a similar manner to journal papers. However, it is the title of the booklet or bulletin which should be in italics. Where no author's name is given for such publications, the reference in both the text and the Bibliography should be to the adopting organization (e.g. MAFF, FAO, WHO). Only in exceptional circumstances, therefore, will it be necessary to have any anonymous references in the thesis. Specific examples are:

Department of the Environment (1991) Potential effects of climate change in the United Kingdom. HMSO, London

References to books can be of two types, references to a whole book and references to parts of a book. Both should give the name(s) of author(s), date of publication, title of book (in italics), name and location of publisher. References to parts of books should also include the title of the chapter with its pagination, but without capitalization.

Fritshen, L.J. and Gay, L.W. (1979) Environmental Instrumentation, Springer, New York.

EXERCISE

1. A researcher is generally expected to
   (a) study the existing literature in a field
   (b) generate new principles and theories
   (c) synthesize the ideas given by others
   (d) evaluate the findings of a study
2. One of the essential characteristic of research is
   (a) Reliability (b) Generalizability
   (c) Usability (d) Objectivity
3. The Govt. of India conducts census after every 10 years. The method of research used in this process is
   (a) Case study (b) Development
   (c) Survey (d) Experimental
4. An academic association assembled at one place to discuss the progress of its work and future plans. Such an assembly is known as a
   (a) Conference (b) Seminar
   (c) Workshop (d) Symposium
5. An investigator studied the census for a given area and prepared a write up based on them. Such a write-up is called
   (a) Research-paper (b) Article
   (c) Thesis (d) Research-report
6. Hypothesis cannot be stated in
   (a) null and question form terms
   (b) declarative terms

(c) general terms
(d) directional terms

7. Validity of a research can be improved
(a) eliminating extraneous factors
(b) taking the true representative sample of the population
(c) both of the above measures
(d) None of the above

8. Field study is related to
(a) Real life situations
(b) Experimental situations
(c) Laboratory situations
(d) None of the above

9. There is a difference between 'swimming' and 'reading'. Here swimming can notes
(a) Hurried reading
(b) Jumping
(c) Reading abstractly
(d) None of the above

10. In natural sciences and social sciences we have two kinds of research:
(a) Basic and biographical
(b) Basic and applied
(c) Applied and biographical
(d) Bibliographical and biographical

11. Literary research, because of the duality of its object of study, is of four kinds:
(a) Applied, basic, theoretical.
(b) Applied, theoretical, interpretative and biographical.
(c) Bibliography and natural criticism, biographical, theoretical and interpretive.
(d) None of the above.

12. Theoretical research aims to propound a theory of literature or modify and improve an already existing one.
(a) Its true (b) Its false
(c) Cannot say (d) Partly true

13. Which kind of researcher can be compared to the applied research in sciences?
(a) Bibliographical (b) Biographical
(c) Theoretical (d) Interpretive

14. The main function of the university education system is
(a) Teaching (b) Research
(c) Extension (d) All of the above

15. How can you develop your critical insight and avoid being gullible or credulous?
(a) By wide reading
(b) By participating in Seminar and Symposia
(c) Both (a) and (b)
(d) None of the above.

16. "Research should be able to generate in the university a centre of human consciousness perception, knowledge, judgment and responsibility. Research has to be thought of in relation to the whole idea of university. It must aim at establishing a creative front and doing creative work on the contemporary intellectual frontier." who said this?
(a) T.S. Eliot (b) Aristotle
(c) Dr. F.R. Leavis (d) R.S. Crane.

17. What can be the materials of research in science?
(a) Objects of nature (b) Tree and air
(c) Scientific facts (d) Hypothesis.

18. What can be the tools of research in science?
(a) Scientific Instruments, observation and experiment.
(b) Natural phenomenon.
(c) Properties.
(d) All of the above.

19. Literary research is equally systematic, methodical, and objective, hence scientific.

(a) True (b) False
(c) Partly true (d) Partly false

20. The materials of literary research are
(a) manuscripts and printed books.
(b) books written in writer's own hand writing.
(c) only journals, droves.
(d) only newspaper cutting.

21. Bibliography can be divided into many types.
(a) Historical (b) Bibliothecal
(c) Enumerative (d) Practical
Codes:
(a) (b) and (c)
(b) (a), (b), (c) and (d)
(c) (d) and (a)
(d) (a) and (c)

22. Generalized conclusion on the basis of a sample is technically known as
(a) statistical inference of external validity of the research.
(b) data analysis and interpretation.
(c) parameter inference.
(d) All of the above.

23. The final result of a study will be more accurate if the sample drawn is
(a) taken randomly
(b) fixed by quota
(c) representative to the population
(d) purposive

24. Field study is related to
(a) real life situations
(b) experimental situations
(c) laboratory situations
(d) None of the above

25. Attributes of objects, events or things which can be measured are called
(a) qualitative measure
(b) data
(c) variables
(d) None of the above

26. The experimental study is based on the law of
(a) single variable
(b) replication
(c) occupation
(d) interest of the subject

27. An example of scientific knowledge is
(a) authority of the Prophet or great men.
(b) social traditions and customs.
(c) religious scriptures.
(d) laboratory and field experiments.

28. A research problem is feasible only when
(a) it is researchable.
(b) it is new and adds something to knowledge.
(c) it has utility and relevance.
(d) All of the above.

29. Formulation of hypothesis may not be necessary in
(a) survey studies
(b) fact finding (historical) studies
(c) normative studies
(d) experimental studies

30. A good hypothesis should be
(a) precise, specific and consistent with most known facts.
(b) formulated in such a way that it can be tested by the date.
(c) of limited scope and should not have global significance.
(d) All of the above.

31. Logic of induction is very close to
(a) the logic of sampling.
(b) the logic of observation.
(c) the logic of the controlled variable.
(d) None of the above.

32. Which of the following is a primary source of data?

(a) Personal records, letters, diaries, auto-bio-graphics, wills, etc.
(b) Official records—governments, documents, information preserved by social-religious organizations etc.
(c) Oral testimony of traditions and customs.
(d) All of the above.

33. While writing research report a researcher
(a) must not use the numerical figures in numbers in the beginning of sentences.
(b) must arrange it in logical, topical and chronological order.
(c) must compare his results with those of the other studies.
(d) All of the above.

34. Bibliography given in a research report
(a) helps those interested in further researcher and studying the problem from another angle.
(b) makes the report authentic.
(c) shows the vast knowledge of the researcher.
(d) None of the above.

ANSWERS

1. (b)	2. (d)	3. (c)	4. (a)	5. (b)	6. (d)
7. (c)	8. (a)	9. (a)	10. (b)	11. (c)	12. (a)
13. (d)	14. (d)	15. (c)	16. (c)	17. (a)	18. (a)
19. (a)	20. (a)	21. (b)	22. (a)	23. (c)	24. (a)
25. (c)	26. (a)	27. (d)	28. (d)	29. (b)	30. (d)
31. (a)	32. (d)	33. (d)	34. (a)		

3

Reading Comprehension

A comprehension passage contains a number of paragraphs. Every paragraph has a central idea which is expounded with ideas and illustrations and other references. The key sentence that gives the central idea of the paragraph may be at the beginning, middle or end of paragraph. This sentence enunciating the central idea, is otherwise called 'topic sentence'.

The student should approach the passage with an 'open mind'. There is no place for the reader's own opinion, assumptions and prejudices. The crux of the problem is just to understand the writer's point of view.

The passages asked for comprehension are of degree standard. The questions given at the end are usually factual, inferential and critical type. It means that candidates have to infer on the basis of the given facts in the passage. Candidate can write good answers

(i) when they fully grasp the meaning of the passage.

(ii) when they are able to express the meaning of the passage in their own simple, clear and direct English.

(iii) when they clearly understand the questions asked.

Some Important Hints

(i) Read the given passage carefully two or three times, till you understand clearly the theme of the passage.

(ii) Read carefully the questions one by one, and find out whether you fully understand them.

(iii) Now take up the first question, and find out to which part of the passage it refers.

(iv) Then take up the other questions, and find out the parts of the passage they refer.

(v) Now write answers to the questions in Your Own Words. Do not copy the language of the passage. The answers should be brief and to the point.

(vi) Revise your answers, and examine them carefully to see that they are clear and complete. If an answer is too long, you must further compress it.

(vii) Correct all mistakes in spelling, grammar, punctuation, etc.

Example One

I was under the canvas with guns. They smelled clearly of oil and grease. I lay and listened to the rallies on the canvas and the clicking of the car over the rain. There was a little light came through and I lay and looked at the guns. They had their canvas jackets on. I thought they must have been sent ahead from the third army. The bump on my forehead was swallon, and I stopped the bleeding by lying still and letting it coagulate, then picked away the dried blood except over the cut.

1. Who was 'I' in this passage?
   (a) A watchman (b) A soldier
   (c) The author (d) Anybody else
2. The author lay still because
   (a) he secretly wanted to know about the guns.
   (b) he was injured and bleeding.
   (c) he was hiding.
   (d) he hasn't enough space to sit in.
3. In the sentence 'they had their canvas jackets' on the word 'they' stands for
   (a) guns
   (b) the third army
   (c) soldiers
   (d) railway carriages

Ans.: 1. (c); 2. (b); 3. (a)

Example Two

O Time! Who know'st a lenient hand to lay softest on sorrow's wound, and slowly thence (Lulling to sad repose the weary sense). The faint pang stealest unperceived away; On thee I rest my only hope at last, And think, when thou hast dried the bitter tear. That flows in vain O'er all my soul held dear, I may look back on every sorrow past, And meet life's peaceful evening with a smile, As some lone bird, at day's departing hour, Sings in the sunbeam, of the transient shower, Forgetful, though its wings are wet the while, Yet ah! How much this poor heart endure, which hopes from thee, and the alone, a cure?

1. What is the object of the verb 'stealest'?
   (a) Lenient hand (b) Weary sense
   (c) Sorrow's wound (d) The faint pang
2. Give another word for 'transient'.
   (a) Hope (b) Tear
   (c) Bitter (d) Passing
3. To whom or what does thee (L-14) refer?
   (a) Lenient hand
   (b) Sparrow's wound
   (c) Time
   (d) None of the above
4. What type of poem it is?
   (a) Optimistic
   (b) Pessimistic
   (c) Reflective
   (d) None of the above
5. What is 'Life's peaceful evening'?
   (a) Life train
   (b) Cool evening
   (c) Old age
   (d) Stress free atmosphere

Ans.: 1. (d); 2. (d); 3. (c); 4. (a); 5. (c)

Example Three

My mother twisted through and through groaning on a mat.
My father, sceptic, rationalist, trying every curse and blessing.
Powder, mixture, herb and hybrid.

1. Why is the narrator's mother twisting and groaning on a mat?
   (a) She was doing yoga.
   (b) Narrator's mother was groaning because she liked it.
   (c) She was bitten by a scorpion so she was groaning in pain.
   (d) She was psychologically sick.
2. How does the narrator's father move away from his character as a sceptic and a rationalist?

(a) He was a hypocrite.
(b) He wanted to get rid of his wife.
(c) He does not believe in superstition and yet uses herbs and powders to cure his wife of the pain.
(d) None of the above.

3. Give the correct meaning of Sceptic.
   (a) A person who habitually doubts generally.
   (b) Accepted beliefs.
   (c) Symbolizing royal powers.
   (d) None of the above.

Ans.: 1. (c); 2. (c); 3. (a)

4

Communication

Nature, Characteristics, Types, Barriers and Effective Classroom Communication

Communication is the process of transferring information from a sender to a receiver with the use of a medium in which the communicated information is understood both by sender and receiver. Communication requires that all parties understood a common language that is exchanged. There are auditory means, such as speaking, singing and sometimes tone of voice, and non-verbal, physical means, such as body language, sign language, paralanguage, touch, eye contact or the use of writing. Communication is defined as a process by which we attempt to create shared understanding. This process requires listening, observing, speaking, questioning, analyzing and evaluating. Classroom communication is very important in teaching. An important virtue to be developed by teacher is the promotion of competent communication skill. The teacher should be able to communicate in an effective manner by arranging the information emphatically and logically. It is a process, which includes transmission of information, ideas, emotions, skills, knowledge by using symbols, words, pictures, graphs, drawings, illustrations etc. Therefore 'communication' can be defined as 'the interchange of thoughts or ideas'. Effective communication is a prerequisite for the attainment of objectives, more so in educational institutions. All teaching—learning process is carried through the process of communication.

Types of Communication

Language—A language is a tool which is a combination of voice sounds, intonations or pitch, gestures or written symbols which communicate thoughts or feelings. Human spoken and written languages can be described as a system of symbols (lexemes) and the grammars (rules) by which the symbols are manipulated.

Dialogue—A dialogue is a reciprocal conversation between two or more entities. Other than this, other are non-verbal communication, non-human living organisms, animal communication, plants and fungi communication, communication between different species of bacteria etc. Communication stands so deeply rooted in human behaviours and the structures of society that scholars have difficulty thinking of it while excluding social or behavioural events. Aristotle first addressed the problem of communication and attempted to work out a theory of it in *The Rhetoric*. A monologue is also a method of communication. When a child does not speak standard English, the teacher must be able to reach the child on his/her level of understanding and transfer him/her to the standard level of understanding. Effective classroom communication requires the teacher and students to be able to send and receive messages accurately. It states that reorganizing and appreciating communication diversity (culture) allows children to feel good about themselves, and that if the classroom teacher and the speech teacher were to team up, they could coordinate interaction with the students and provide beneficial bilingual and bicultural programmes. It stresses that teacher must understand the nature of language and the nature of dialect differences and then they must decide how to approach the problem—they can recognize 'non-standard' dialect and eradicate it, leave the student language alone, or accept bidialectalism. Classroom should provide a variety of stimuli, provide a secure, comfortable feeling, be adapted to fit the activity, and give some privacy and individuality.

EXERCISE

1. Informal communication network within the organization is known as
   (a) Interpersonal communication
   (b) Intrapersonal communication
   (c) Mass communication
   (d) Grapevine communication
2. T.V. Channel launched for covering only Engineering and Technology subject is known as
   (a) Gyan Darshan (b) Vyas
   (c) Eklavya (d) Kisan
3. In which State the maximum numbers of periodicals are brought out for public information?
   (a) Uttar Pradesh (b) Tamil Nadu
   (c) Kerala (d) Punjab.
4. The main objective of public broadcasting system i.e. Prasar Bharti is
   (a) Information, Entertainment and Education.
   (b) Entertainment, Information and Interaction.
   (c) Education, Interaction and Entertainment.
   (d) Entertainment only.
5. The competency of an effective communication can be judged on the basis of
   (a) personality of communicator
   (b) experience in the field
   (c) interactivity with target audience
   (d) meeting the needs of target audience
6. A group discussion is a form of
   (a) Dyadic communication
   (b) Multiadic communication
   (c) Mass communication
   (d) None of the above
7. Dyadic communication is the transfer of message, from a person
   (a) to another person and vice-versa
   (b) to a group of persons
   (c) to a mass audience
   (d) None of the above
8. Which one of the following is true for informal communication?
   (a) It has a high speed.
   (b) It promotes better high speed.
   (c) It enhances performances of people through the use of grapevine.
   (d) It promotes harmony and resolves many problems.
9. Mass communication
   (a) is meant for delivering messages to the residents of a city.
   (b) does not need technology-based media vehicles.
   (c) is an impersonal tool for delivering information to the masses.
   (d) is more effective than s\dyadic communication so far as reach is concerned.
10. In downward communication, messages
    (a) flow from the bottom to the top of the organization structure.
    (b) flow from the tope to the bottom of the organization structure.
    (c) are meant to be exchanged between the members of the top brass.
    (d) None of the above.

Ans.: 1. (d); 2. (c); 3. (c); 4. (a); 5. (d); 6. (b); 7. (a); 8. (c); 9. (c); 10. (b)

5

Reasoning (Including Mathematical)

Reasoning is the mental (cognitive) process of looking for reasons for beliefs, conclusions, actions or feelings. Psychologists and cognitive scientists tend to study how people reason, which brain processes are engaged, and how the reasoning is influenced by the structure of the brain. Aristotle is, so far as we know, the first writer to give an extended, systematic treatment of the methods of human reasoning. He identified two major methods of reasoning, analysis and synthesis. Aristotle developed what is known as syllogistic logic, which makes it possible to analyze reasoning in a way that ignores the content of the argument and focuses on the form or structure of the argument.

Many problems of practical importance are problem of reasoning about actions. In these problems a course of action has to be found that satisfies a number of specified conditions. A problem of reasoning about actions is given in terms of an initial situation, a terminal situation, a set of feasible actions, and a set of constraints. The task of a problem solves is to find the best sequence of permissible actions that can transform the initial situation into the terminal situation. For UGC-NET, SLET mathematical reasoning we have to read only (a) series completion (b) coding and decoding (c) classification (odd man out) (d) analogical relationship.

EXERCISE

1. Which one of the following belongs to the category of homogeneous data?
   (a) Multi-storied houses in a colony
   (b) Trees in a garden
   (c) Vehicular traffic on a highway
   (d) Student population in a class.
2. In which of the following ways a theory is not different from a belief?
   (a) Verifiability
   (b) Acceptability
   (c) Demonstrability
   (d) Antecedent-consequent.
3. The statement—'Honesty is the best policy' is
   (a) a fact (b) an value
   (c) an opinion (d) a value judgment
4. Which one is like Pillar, Pole and Standard?
   (a) Beam (b) Plank
   (c) Shaft (d) Timber.
5. Following incomplete series is presented. Find out the number which should come at the place of question mark which will complete the series: 4, 16, 36, 64?
   (a) 300 (b) 200
   (c) 100 (d) 150.
6. Find the next number of the sequence 25/7, 50/5, 75/3, 100/1
   (a) 125/11 (b) 125/8
   (c) –125 (d) 125
7. Find the odd one out: T-3, R-4, O-8, H-6, P-2.

(a) T-3 (b) R-4
(c) P-2 (d) H-6.

8. What should be subtracted from six to get 9?
(a) 15
(b) –3
(c) +3
(d) None of the above

9. Find the odd one out: DDFG, NNPQ, WWYZ, RRST, PPRS.
(a) DDFG (b) PPRS
(c) RRST (d) NNPQ.

10. If IS=4, THIS=16, DIFFICULT=81, then what equals WRONG?
(a) 65 (b) 35
(c) 18 (d) 25.

11. Find the odd one out.

(a) 

(b) 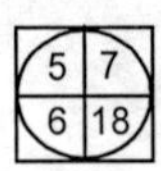

(c) 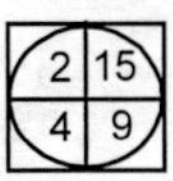

(d) 

(a) (b)
(c) (d)

12. How many perfect squares are there up to 100?
(a) 100 (b) 1000
(c) 10 (d) 5.

13. How many cubic centimeters are there in 1 cubic meter?
(a) 100 (b) 1000
(c) 1000000 (d) 10000000.

14. Of the following statements, there are two statements both of which can not be true but both can be false. Which are these two statements?
(i) All machine make noise.
(ii) Some machine makes noise.
(iii) No machine makes noise.
(iv) Some machines are not noisy.

Codes:
(a) (i) and (ii) (b) (iii) and (iv)
(c) (i) and (iii) (d) (ii) and (iv)

15. Study the argument and the inference drawn from that argument, given below
Argument—Anything that goes up definitely falls down. Helicopter goes up
Inference—So the helicopter will definitely fall down.
What in your opinion is the inference drawn from the argument?
(a) Valid (b) Invalid
(c) Doubtful (d) Long drawn one.

16. Complete the following 7, 3, 6, 7, 5, 11 ——
(a) 15 (b) 16
(c) 4 (d) 18

17. 16/32, 15/33, 17/31, 14/34 ——
(a) 18/30 (b) 13/26
(c) 18/36 (d) 17/25

Direction: Select the words which are related to each-other in one same way as the capitalized words are related to each other.

18. HYGIENE: CLEANLINESS: ?
(a) Soothe: uncover
(b) Deaf: dumb
(c) Awareness: consciousness
(d) Laugh: joke

19. MEANS: METHOD: ?
(a) Teacher: pupil
(b) Air: kite
(c) Smoke: cigar
(d) Elegance: style

20. PAYMENT: SETTLEMENT: ?
(a) Discount: free
(b) Worth: account
(c) Expenditure: spending
(d) Cost: cheap

ANSWERS

1. (a)	2. (b)	3. (d)	4. (a)	5. (c)	6. (c)
7. (c)	8. (b)	9. (c)	10. (d)	11. (d)	12. (c)
13. (c)	14. (c)	15. (d)	16. (b)	17. (a)	18. (d)
19. (d)	20. (c)				

6

Logical Reasoning

The word 'Logical' means consistency in an argument, presentation of facts or expression of ideas or thoughts. It means that one statement should not contradict the other. For example, "A tiger chased me. I ran fast. Sometimes the tiger was ahead of me and sometimes I was ahead of him". The statements are contradictory, so not logical.

Logic is the science of reasoning as expression in language. There are two kinds of logic; deductive and inductive. Deductive logic is concerned with the verification of a generalized statement. It examines consistency in statements and moves from general to particular. Inductive logic moves from particular to general. It observes natural phenomenon or events, establishes cause and effect relationship and then makes a general statement. There are four experimental methods:

(a) Method of Agreement: If two events occur one after another, the preceding event may be the cause of the following event, e.g. pricking of a needle and the ooze of blood or bleeding from the body are two events. The first is the cause of the second event.
(b) Method of Difference: If there are two or more than two events before an event, this method is applied.
(c) Method of Concomitant Variation: If there are two events occurring one after another and rise and fall in the intensity of the preceding event is followed by rise and fall in the succeeding event, the previous event then is cause of the second one.
(d) Method of Residue: It means that when cause and effect relationship is established between preceding and succeeding events, and one is left, the last one is the cause of the reasoning event.

Inductive logic is content-oriented. It is based on facts and data collection. For example:

When I entered the room I found it very cold. The A.C. was on, the fans were revolving with full speed and water was flowing. I tightened the tap and water stopped flowing but the room was still cold. I switched off the fans but there was no respite.

The method of residue says that the A.C. was the cause of the coldness in the room.

Deductive logic is more concerned with form since every argument is expressed by means of language, it pays great attention to logical connection between sentences or prepositions.

(i) Universal affirmative: All men are mortal
(ii) Universal negative: No men are perfect
(iii) Particular affirmative: Some men are honest
(iv) Particular negative: Some men are not laborious

In deductive logic the validity of a conclusion is tested by means of syllogism. A syllogism consists of three prepositions called

Major promise : All crows are black
Minor promise : This bird is a crow
Conclusion : This bird is black

Analogies—Analogy is comparison between two objects or situation of which the first is already known. For example, a child sees the picture of a monkey in his book. When he sees a real monkey on a tree, he immediately connects and calls it to be a monkey by means of analogy. Word analogy is quite common.

7

Data Interpretation

Date will be provided, data based on various interpretative and explanatory questions will be asked.

Four students E, F, G, H appeared in four papers of M.A. final I, II, III and IV. Their marks out of 100 are given below:

Students	**Papers**			
	I	II	III	IV
E	60	81	45	55
F	59	43	51	A
G	74	A	71	65
H	72	76	A	68

Where 'A' stands for absent

Read the above table.

1. Which candidate has secured between 60-55% marks in aggregate?
   (a) E (b) F
   (c) G (d) H.
2. Who has obtained the lowest average in aggregate?
   (a) E (b) F
   (c) G (d) H.
3. Who has obtained the highest average?
   (a) E (b) F
   (c) G (d) H.
4. In which paper the lowest marks were obtained by the candidates?
   (a) I (b) II
   (c) III (d) IV.
5. Which candidate has secured the highest percentage in the papers appeared?
   (a) E (b) F
   (c) G (d) H.
6. In a code, the word ABSTAIN is written as CDQRKP. How will we write the word SAINT in the given code?
   (a) QCKPR (b) KCQRP
   (c) QQPPC (d) RRQCK.
7. The following diagrams represent relationships between members of three groups. Select the diagram which best represents the relationships. LION, COW, ANIMAL.

(a) 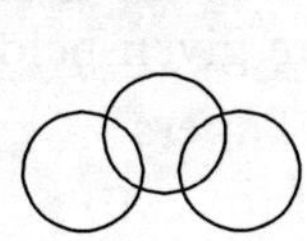 (b) 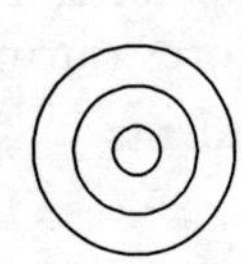

(c) 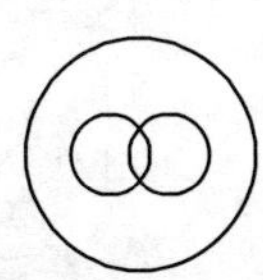 (d) 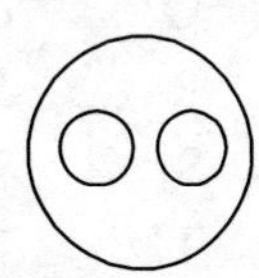

8. The following diagrams show relationship between members of three groups. Select

the diagram which best represent the relationship of furniture, table, chair.

(a)  (b) 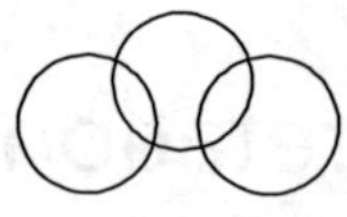

(c) 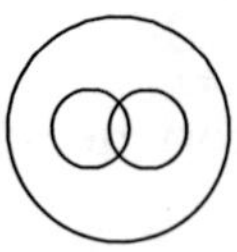 (d) 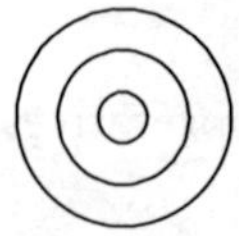

9. If the two big circles represent—animals living on soil and those living in waters, and the small circle stands for the animals who both live on soil and in water, which figure represents the relationships among them?

(a) 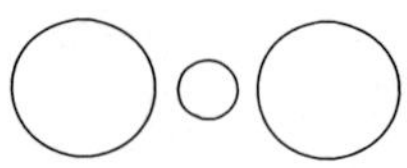 (b) 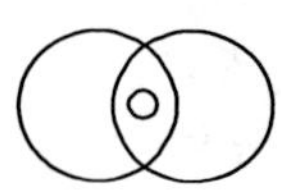

(c) 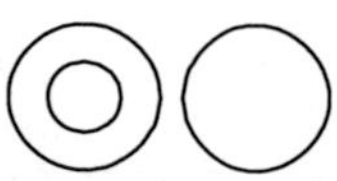 (d) 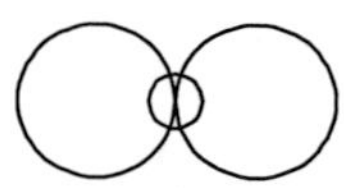

10. Find the odd one out:

(a) 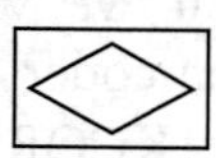 (b) 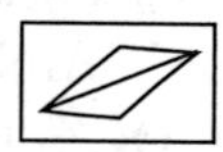

(c) 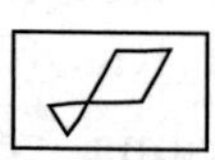 (d) 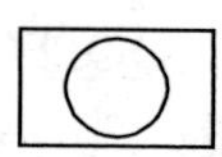

(a) (b)
(c) (d)

Four students O P S T appeared in four papers, I, II, III and IV in a test. Their scores out of 100 are given below:

Students	Papers			
	I	II	III	IV
O	60	81	45	55
P	59	43	51	A
S	74	A	71	65
T	72	76	A	68

where 'A' stands for absent

Read the above table and answer below mentioned questions.

11. Which candidate has secured 60-55% marks in aggregate?
(a) O (b) P
(c) S (d) T.

12. Who has obtained the lowest average in aggregate?
(a) O (b) P
(c) S (d) T.

13. Who has obtained the highest average?
(a) O (b) P
(c) S (d) T.

14. In which paper the lowest marks were obtained by the candidates?
(a) I (b) II
(c) III (d) IV.

15. Which candidate has secured the highest percentage in the paper appeared?
(a) O (b) P
(c) S (d) T.

16. Obesity is a curse of modern times.
(P) As a result, what is lost is the natural goodness of roughage and important nutrients.
(Q) Invariably fat and sugar which cause obesity are added to make food more palatable.
(R) In these days food gets more refined and cooking methods more intricate.
(S) Therefore, there are more obese people today than even before.

That's because today's changed lifestyles often mean less physical exertion and an over indulgence in unhealthy food.

The right combination is
(a) QPRS (b) RPQS
(c) RQPS (d) RPSQ

17. Logic of induction is very close to
(a) the logic of sampling
(b) the logic of observation

(c) the logic of the controlled variable
(d) None of the above.

18. A woman going with a boy is asked by another woman about the relationship between them. The woman replied, "my maternal uncle and the uncle of his maternal uncle is the same". How is the lady related with that boy?
(a) Aunt and nephew
(b) Mother and son
(c) Grandson and grandmother
(d) None of the above.

19. A is the mother of B and C. If D is the husband of C. What A is to D?
(a) Mother (b) Sister
(c) Mother-in-law (d) Aunt.

20. If X is husband of M's sister's mother. What is the relationship between X and M?
(a) Father and son
(b) Grandfather and grandson
(c) Uncle and nephew
(d) None of the above.

Directions: Rahul and Meeta have their birthdays on 29th October and 5th July respectively and the total of their age in years is 11. After two years the ratio in their ages would be 3:2. The wedding anniversary of their parents is exactly in the middle of their birthdays.

21. Rahul's birthday fell on Saturday, on which day did his little sister celebrate her birthday?
(a) Monday (b) Tuesday
(c) Thursday (d) Friday.

22. On which date is their parent's wedding anniversary?
(a) 1st September (b) 3rd September
(c) 29th August (d) 30th August.

23. On which day the same year did the parents celebrate their wedding anniversary?
(a) Monday (b) Tuesday
(c) Sunday (d) Thursday.

ANSWERS

1. (a)	2. (b)	3. (a)	4. (b)	5. (d)	6. (a)
7. (d)	8. (a)	9. (d)	10. (d)	11. (a)	12. (b)
13. (a)	14. (b)	15. (d)	16. (b)	17. (a)	18. (b)
19. (c)	20. (a)	21. (b)	22. (a)	23. (d)	

8

Information and Communication Technology (ICT)

Computers have become indispensable in every field, be it industry, services, research or any other field. Education or teaching is not an exception and thus computers have become integral part of education too.

Main points to be remembered

(a) Internet is a network of many small networks that exist all over the world.
(b) A gateway is a device that connects dissimilar networks.
(c) A backbone is a central interconnecting structure that connects one or more networks.
(d) A set of rules is called protocol.
(e) The TCP is responsible for dividing the file/message into packets (a group of up to 1500 bytes) at source computer and then reassembling them back at destination or recipient computer.
(f) The IP is responsible for handling the address of destination computer.
(g) Internet is not governed by any particular body. It is coordinated by many volunteer organizations like IAB (Internet Architecture Board) IETF (Internet Engineering Task Force) Inter NIC etc.
(h) A WWW client is called a web browser and a WWW server is called web server.
(i) The top-level web page of a website is called home page.
(j) A web portal is a web site hosting many other websites.

Internet—The seeds of Internet were planted in 1969, when U.S. project named ARPANET (acronym for Advanced Research Projects Administration Network). The reason that the Internet works at all is that every computer connected to it users the same set of rules for communication. The communication protocol used by Internet is TCP/IP. The TCP (Transmission Control Protocol) part is also responsible for reassembling the received packets at the destination. The IP (Internet Protocol) part is responsible for handling the address of destination computer so that each packet is routed (sent) to its proper destination. The World Wide Web (WWW) is a set of programs, standards and protocols that allows the multimedia and hypertext files to be created, displayed and linked on the internet. The hypertext transfer protocol (HTTP) is an access method used on Internet. The http generally works in combination with www.

An internet is a network that exists exclusively within an organization and that is based on Internet technology. It delivers an organization's informational resources to each member's desktop quickly and inexpensively but protects the information from unauthorized access. Because an internet is based on Internet Technology, it can have thousands of users across many locations and still be private.

E-mail—The E-mail (Electronic Mail) is sending and receiving messages through computers. The major advantages of E-mail are:

(1) Easy record maintenance
(2) Waste reduction
(3) Low cost
(4) Fast delivery

To visit a site on the Net, you need to supply the address of the site or in other words, its URL to the browser exploring the web is known as Net Surfing. Making the copy of requested web page or file or document on your local computer is called Downloading. E-mail is used to send written messages between individuals or groups of individuals, often geographically separated by large distances. A very convenient and inexpensive way to transmit message, e-mail has dramatically affected scientific, personal, and business communications. An e-mail address has two parts separated by @ ("at") symbol.

(i) *Username*—On the left side of @ separator is the user name. A user name cannot have blanks.
(ii) *Domain name for the host server*—The portion to the right of @ identifies the server or host or network that services your e-mail. It is sometimes also called the e-mail server.

Business travelers using laptops can communicate with others without annoying 'phone tag' session. There are cases where scientists working on the same project never meet; they do all their work through e-mails.

EXERCISE

1. ICT stands for
   (a) Information common technology.
   (b) Information and communication technology.
   (c) Information and computer technology.
   (d) Inter-class technology.
2. Satellite communication works through
   (a) Radar (b) Transponder
   (c) Receptor (d) Transmitter
3. A computer is a machine that works more like a human brain. This definition of computer is
   (a) correct
   (b) incorrect
   (c) partially correct
   (d) partially incorrect
4. ICT includes
   (a) E-mail
   (b) Internet
   (c) Educational Television
   (d) All of the above
5. What was the first Network that was made available?
   (a) DEC Net 1980
   (b) Novell Netware
   (c) IBM m Token Ring 1985
   (d) IBM PC Network 1984.
6. What does the acronym (ISDN) stand for?
   (a) Indian Standard Digital Network
   (b) Integrated Services Digital Network
   (c) Intelligent Services Digital Network
   (d) Integrated Services Data Network.
7. Internet is
   (a) network run by the US Govt.
   (b) a Network run by the United Nations Organizations.

(c) a loose network not owned by anybody but used by all universities and Govt. around the globe.
(d) a commercial information service run by Ziff Davis Co. in US.

8. E-mail programs often
(a) come with local area network software or add-on options or they are independent programs designed to work with a specific network.
b) operate as dependent programs.
(c) Both A and B.
(d) None of the above.

9. A program or software that let you visit different sites on the Net and display their offering on your computer is called
(a) Internet (b) Server
(c) Browser (d) None of the above

10. Net surfing is a term used for which of the following tasks?
(a) Sending mails
(b) Exploring web
(c) Posting messages
(d) None of the above.

11. In an e-mail address, the characters following @ character represent
(a) User name
(b) E-mail recipient
(c) Domain name
(d) None of the above

12. Online textual talk is called
(a) video conferencing
(b) chat
(c) telephony
(d) text phone

13. An internet utility that lets one log on to remote computer systems is known as
(a) Use Net (b) Telnet
(c) FTP (d) Remote Net

14. The online worldwide conversation, known as forum, is also called
(a) FTP (b) Telnet
(c) Usenet (d) All of the above

15. Some of the advantages of E-mail are
(a) low cost (b) speed
(c) waste Reduction (d) All of the above

16. Website is a collection of
(a) HTML document
(b) Graphic files
(c) Audio and video files
(d) All of the above

17. Which of the following protocols is used b WWW?
(a) ftp (b) http
(c) wzc (d) None of the above

18. The communication protocol used by Internet is
(a) HTTP (b) WWW
(c) TCP/IP (d) All of the above

ANSWERS

1. (b)	2. (b)	3. (a)	4. (d)	5. (a)	6. (b)
7. (c)	8. (a)	9. (c)	10. (b)	11. (c)	12. (b)
13. (b)	14. (c)	15. (d)	16. (d)	17. (b)	18. (c)

9

People and Environment

Natural hazards and mitigation

The people are important to develop the economy and society. The people make and use resources and are themselves resources with varying quality. Resources, calamities and disasters are all meaningful only in relation to human beings.

Armed with his greater brain volume, skilled hand, power of abstract thinking, foresight and strong memory he stared interfering with the environment for his own benefits. He has changed natural environment not merely by destroying the habitat but also by transplanting several organisms in a new habitat. He has also disturbed many material cycles of the natural biological community by irrigation, use of chemical fertilizers and disposal of industrial waste. Changing patterns of land use is also the cause of the destruction of the ecosystem. Land use means the land put to a particular use such as forest, farming, construction and wasteland.

Wetland and streams that exist close to industrial areas become dumps of toxic effluents, heavy metals and detergents from the industries. The highly polluted environment of the wetlands limits the population of its organisms.

Deforestation means removal or clearing of forest on account of the human activities. There is a growing fear among ecologists that if suitable remedial measures are not adopted urgently, India will have no forests left by 2030. Its disastrous consequences are reflected in soil erosion and increasing aridity. When trees are felled, and the soil is left exposed, the pounding action of the rain water sweeps away the top soil. The soil is eroded into a muddy stream, leaving the top soil devoid of nutrients.

Construction of dam over big rivers and water reservoirs cast an adverse effect on the environment. A large forest cover is cleared in the construction of dams.

Wars are also a serious threat to the ecosystem. Destructive weapons like missiles and rockets cause the release of poisonous gases in the environment.

Pollution may be defined as an undesirable change in air, water and land that may harmfully affect human life. This can be classified into two kinds:

(1) Air pollution (2) Water pollution

Air Pollution

Air pollutants are products of burning of fuels by people when coal and fossil fuels are burnt, they produce huge quantities of smoke into the environment. Incomplete combustion of the fossil fuels produces carbon monoxide that are reported to cause cancer especially lung cancer in children.

Water Pollution

Disturbs the balance of the ecosystem and causes hazards to the organisms' health. Water becomes polluted by soil erosion leaching of minerals from rocks, decaying of organic matters. Pollutant water in rivers, lakes and ponds is unfit for drinking and harmful to aquatic life.

Exploitation of natural resources—Things essential for living of human and other living organisms like animals and plants are known as natural resources.

Air is the most precious inexhaustible natural resources for all. Water and fuel are next two important resources. Our natural resources are in limited amount to meet the need of growing population. Man is consuming fuels and often natural resources indiscriminately without caring for the consequences. The technological society, using limited assets of minerals and fossil fuels in an uncontrolled manner has made the matter worse. Man's continued unthoughtful actions cause the depletion of natural resources. Today, there is already shortage of water. The situation is similar for other resources like minerals, coals and petroleum.

There could be many causes of depletion of natural resources. Some causes for this are:

- Overuse and irrational use
- Non-equitable distribution
- Technological and industrial development
- Population growth

Large scale felling of trees, deforestation, overgrazing and less rainfall are also responsible for wastage of lots of water.

Energy Resources—On the other hand industrial and technological advancement has had immense pressure on resources particularly energy. Today the chief sources of the energy are conventional fuels like coal, petroleum, petroleum products and natural gas. These all conventional sources of energy are non-renewable resources, they cannot be recycled or regenerated after once exhausted. There is a need to adopt the renewable sources of energy such as solar energy, wind energy and bio-gas. Some of the adverse impacts caused by the depletion of natural resources are:

- Imbalance in nature
- Shortage of materials
- Struggle for existence
- Slacking of economic growth

Shortage of resources world over has accentuated the struggle for existence.

Effect of Pollutants on human life

Effect of Air Pollution—In addition the global warming, air pollution has been held responsible for various health disorders and diseases. It may cause acid rain. It is the term for pollution caused by sulphur and nitrogen dioxide when they combine with atmospheric moisture. This acid formation also takes place when these gases come into contact with rain drops. Emission of hazardous gases causes skin cancer among others. It also affects other organisms terribly. Sulphur dioxide, nitrogen oxide and carbon monoxide diffuse into blood stream which combine with haemoglobin and impede oxygen transport. Chronic bronchitis, lung cancer, bronchial asthma and respiratory allergies are the result.

Water Pollution—Sewage disposal contain many harmful micro-organisms that can cause diseases such as diarrhoea, dysentery and jaundice. Dyes impart colour to water and make it toxic. Wind, rains and rivers are carrears of DDT to agriculture which accumulates in the soil. From the soil, it reaches the plants and form there to the animal and human tissue. Sulphuric acid, an acid waste from coal mines is a serious pollutant that increases the hardness of water and has harmful effects on human beings. Typhoid and paratyphoid fever, bacillary dysentery, cholera, E-coli diarrhoea is caused by Bacterial Pollution. Some diseases are related to the disease carrying insects breeding on water like malaria, filarial, arboviruses, etc. Some diseases are transmitted due to inadequate use of water like conjunctivitis, scabies, ascariasis and shigellosis.

Do you know—Water is a compound of oxygen and hydrogen in the ratio of 8:1 by weight water covers about 71% of the total earth surface. About 95% of the total water on the earth is salty water found in the oceans and seas. It is not fit for drinking or for washing as it is hard. Only remaining 5% is sweet or fresh water found in rivers, lakes, streams, ponds, waterfalls and wells is usable. Let's save water.

Soil Pollution—Due to soil pollution, many diseases like dysentery, cholera, typhoid and paratyphoid are transmitted from soil to people. Temporarily designed landfills become the breeding places of insects and rodents which cause diseases.

Electroplating industry generates wastes of cyanides and battery can cause skin burn and disfigurement.

Health Hazard—Substances that have harmful effect on human and animal health.

DDT—Dichloro-diphenyle trichloro-ethene, chemical that acts as pesticides.

Effluent—Chemical waste discharged from factories.

Bio-accumulation—Increase in the concentration of harmful chemicals in the higher levels of food chain.

EXERCISE

1. Deforestation is
   (a) planting trees in forest
   (b) fire in the forest
   (c) digging pits in the forest
   (d) removal of trees and vegetation from an area
2. Live stock means
   (a) living animal life
   (b) animals for sale
   (c) manufacturing good things in factories
   (d) None of the above.
3. Name the single factor that leads to the destruction of the ecosystem?
   (a) Water logging (b) Kelp
   (c) Exhaustion (d) Deforestation.
4. What is the full form of E.I.A.?
   (a) Environmental Impact Assessment
   (b) Environmental Indian Association
   (c) Energy Indian Atmosphere
   (d) None of the above.
5. Tick the right definition of Pollution.
   (a) An undesirable change in the physical, chemical and biological environment brought by man's activity.
   (b) Problem caused by plastic and other waste material.
   (c) Throwing waste in rivers.
   (d) None of the above.
6. Which one is not non-conventional fuels?

(a) Solar energy (b) Wind energy
(c) Nuclear energy (d) Fossil fuels.

7. Bio-energy is produced from the waste products like cattle dung, human waste, garbage and other organic wastes like weeds, straw of plants.
(a) Its true (b) Its false
(c) Cannot say (d) None of the above

8. Which one does not come under the category of adverse impacts caused by the depletion of natural resources?
(a) Shortage of materials
(b) Slacking of economic growth
(c) Rapid growth of population
(d) Imbalance in nature.

9. Health hazard is
(a) when your life is at risk.
(b) substances that have harmful effect on human and animal health.
(c) when your receive money to remain healthy.
(d) None of the above.

10. Which one is extremely poisonous gas?
(a) Carbon monoxide (Co)
(b) Nitrogen oxide (NO_2)
(c) Sulphur dioxide (SO_2)
(d) None of the above.

11. What do you mean by 'Algal Bloom'?
(a) The nutrients in fertilizers promote the growth of algae that covers a water body and is known as 'Algal Bloom'.
(b) Algal Bloom is a white colour fungus.
(c) It is mining waste due to acid.
(d) None of the above.

12. Which one is not due to Soil Pollution?
(a) Temporarily designed landfills become the breeding places of insects and rodents which cause diseases.
(b) Electroplating industry generates wastes of cyanides and battery can cause skin burn and disfigurement.
(c) Cadmium is transported to the liver through blood from where it is transported to the kidney, accumulate there and paralyses kidney function.
(d) None of the above.

ANSWERS

1. (d)	2. (b)	3. (d)	4. (a)	5. (a)	6. (d)
7. (a)	8. (c)	9. (b)	10. (a)	11. (a)	12. (c)

10

Higher Education System: Governance, Polity and Administration

Central Government is responsible for major policy relating to higher education in the country. It provides grants to the UGC and established Central Universities in the country. The Central Government is also responsible for declaration of Educational Institutions as 'Deemed to be University' on the recommendation of the UGC. State Govts. are responsible for establishment of State Universities and colleges and provide plan grants for their development and non-plan grants for their maintenance. The coordination and cooperation between the Union and the States is brought about in the field of education through the Central Advisory Board of Education (CABE).

There are three principle levels of qualifications with the higher education system in the country. These are:

Bachelor's/Under-graduate level

Master's/Post-graduate level

Doctoral/Pre-doctoral level

National Eligibility Test (NET) is being conducted by the UGC since 1989 for eligibility for lectureship. Around 50,000 students appear for the test every year. Pass percentage is about 50%. Eight State Level Tests have been accredited at par with NET.

"Higher Education is education provided by universities, vocational universities, community college, liberal arts colleges, technical colleges and academic degree providers such as career colleges."

Higher education includes teaching, research and social services activities of universities.

Higher vocational education and training takes place at the non-university tertiary level. Such education combines teaching of both skills and theoretical expertise. Higher education differs from other forms of post-secondary education such as that offered by institutions of vocational education, which are also known as trade schools. Higher vocational education might be contrasted with education in a usually broaden scientific field, which might concentrate on theory and abstract conceptual knowledge.

The UGC of India is not only the long grant giving agency in the country, but also responsible for coordinating, determining and maintaining the standards in institutions of higher education. Apart from UGC here are various professional councils that are responsible for recognizing courses, promoting professional institutes and providing grants to under-graduate programmes. All India Council for Technical Education (AICTE), Distance Education

Council (DEC), Indian Council for Agricultural Research (ICAR), Bar Council of India (BCI), National Council for Teacher Education (NCTE), Rehabilitation Council of India (RCI), Medical Council of India (MCI), Pharmacy Council of India (PCI), Indian Nursing Council (INC), Dentist Council of India (DCI), Central Council of Homeopathy (CCH) and the Central Council of Indian Medicine (CCIM) are the statutory professional councils of India.

Distance Education has redefined the means of education; its goal is to reach larger section of the society through non-formal method.

Higher vocational education and training takes place at the non-university tertiary level. Such education combines teaching of both practical skills and theoretical expertise. Higher education differs from other forms of post-secondary education such as that offered by institutions of vocational education. Higher vocational education might be contrasted with education in a usually broader scientific field, which might concentrate on theory and abstract conceptual knowledge. There are vocational universities in Applied Sciences and Applied Arts.

Higher education in India has evolved in distinct and divergent streams with each stream monitored by an apex body, indirectly of Human Resource Development. The 415 universities/ institutions are mostly funded by the State Governments. However, there are 20 important universities called Central Universities, which are maintained by the Union Government and because of relatively large funding, they have an edge over the others. The engineering education and business schools are monitored and accredited by the All India Council for Technical Education (AICTE).

Apart from these, National Council for Teacher Education (NCTE) controls all the teacher training institutions in the country. Admission to all professional education colleges is done through All-India common admission tests of which the IIT-JEE, IEEF, CAT and CPMT are the most popular ones.

EXERCISE

1. Which are of the following is not considered a part of technical education in India?
   (a) Medical (b) Management
   (c) Pharmaceutical (d) Aeronautical.
2. Which of the following is a Central University?
   (a) Mumbai University
   (b) Calcutta University
   (c) Delhi University
   (d) Madras University.
3. Identify the main principle on which the Parliamentary System operates.
   (a) Responsibility of Executive to Legislature.
   (b) Supremacy of Parliament.
   (c) Supremacy of Judiciary.
   (d) Theory of Separation of Power.
4. The reservation of seats for women in the Panchayat Raj Institutions is
   (a) 30% of the total seats
   (b) 33% of the total seats
   (c) 33% of the total population
   (d) in proportion to their population
5. Match list I with II and select the correct answer:

   List I (Institutions)
   1. Indian Veterinary Research Institute
   2. Institute of Armament Technology
   3. Indian Institute of Science
   4. National Institute for Educational Planning and Administrators

List II (Locations)

(i) Pune (ii) Izzat Nagar
(iii) Delhi (iv) Bengaluru

Codes:

(a) 1 (ii) 2 (i) 3 (iv) 4 (iii)
(b) 1 (ii) 2 (iv) 3 (ii) 4 (iii)
(c) 1 (ii) 2 (iii) 3 (i) 4 (iv)
(d) 1 (iv) 2 (iii) 3 (ii) 4 (i)

6. Education not only conserves the culture of a nation, but about it
   (a) makes the latter rich
   (b) defines the latter
   (c) makes the latter spiritual
   (d) makes the latter mass-oriented and popular.
7. Indian Institute of Advanced Studies is located in
   (a) Shimla (b) Solan
   (c) Dharmshala (d) Chandigarh
8. How many IIM are there in India?
   (a) Six (b) Seven
   (c) Five (d) Eight.
9. Match the following:
   (a) IISC 1. Bangalore
   (b) BARC 2. Trombay
   (c) NDA 3. Pune
   (d) ISM 4. Jharkhand

Codes:	A	B	C	D
(a)	1	2	3	4
(b)	2	3	4	1
(c)	3	4	2	1
(d)	4	3	2	1

ANSWERS

1. (a) 2. (c) 3. (a) 4. (b) 5. (a) 6. (a)
7. (a) 8. (a) 9. (a)

Model Examination Paper

1. Pointing out to a girl a man said "My uncle is the uncle of this girl's uncle". How is the man related with that girl?
   (a) Brother (b) Father
   (c) Father in Law (d) Cousin.
2. If 58 × 12 = 4, 37 × 96 = 5 and 11 × 20 = 2. What is 42 × 12 = ?
   (a) 2 (b) 3
   (c) 4 (d) 5.
3. If the fourth Saturday of a month is the 22nd day, what day is the 13th of the month?
   (a) Tuesday (b) Wednesday
   (c) Thursday (d) Friday.
4. Pointing to Snehal, Mahesh said, 'Her mother's only daughter is my daughter.' How is Mahesh related to Snehal?
   (a) Father (b) Neice
   (c) Sister (d) Uncle
5. One half of the students body at an Indian University Study German and one-third of the others study French. The remaining 600 do not study any foreign language. How many students are there in the University?
   (a) 720 (b) 1100
   (c) 1800 (d) 3600
6. If P's and Q's ages add up to 42 and 42 and P is 10 years junior to R who is 8 years senior to 0. What are the ages of P, Q, R respectively?
   (a) 22 yrs, 20 yrs, 24 yrs
   (b) 20 yrs, 22 yrs, 32 yrs
   (c) 12 yrs, 30 yrs, 32 yrs
   (d) 20 yrs, 22 yrs, 30 yrs.
7. If DUST is called AIR, AIR is called FIRE, FIRE is called WATER, WATER is called COLOUR, COLOUR is called RAIN and RAIN is called DUST then where do fish live?
   (a) Colour (b) Dust
   (c) Water (d) Fire.
8. What percentage of 180.50 is 36.1?
   (a) 20%
   (b) 25%
   (c) 20.50%
   (d) None of the above
9. Which one of the following is not an attribute of research?
   (a) Research is problem oriented
   (b) Research is not inactive
   (c) Research is not a process
   (d) Research is systematic
10. The main purpose of teaching is
    (a) development of thinking power.
    (b) development of resoning power.
    (c) Both A and B.
    (d) Giving information only.
11. Which one of the following is/are educative?
    (a) 16 mm Film Projector
    (b) Tape recorder
    (c) Working pattern of a wind mill
    (d) All of the above.
12. Match List I with List II and select the correct answer from the codes given below the Lists.

List I (Distinguished Ladies)

(a) Jhumpa Lahiri (b) Barkha Dutta
(c) Aparna Dutta (d) Smita Patil

List II (Field of works)

1. Journalist 2. Novelist
3. Filon actress 4. Film Director

Codes:	A	B	C	D
(a)	4	3	2	1
(b)	2	1	4	3
(c)	4	1	3	2
(d)	2	3	4	1

13. Books and documents are the main sources
(a) for data of Historical Research.
(b) for data of Participation Research.
(c) for data of Medical Research.
(d) data for Research going on in Laboratory.

14. The process of transmitting one's problem on Web site is called
(a) Cyber waiting (b) Web Plee
(c) Cyber Rating (d) Web hunting

15. Find the missing number:
16/32, 15/33, 17/34, 14/35
(a) 18/30 (b) 19/36
(c) 19/30 (d) 18/36.

16. Normal telephone line used for internet utility is called
(a) Voice Portal (b) Voice Line
(c) Voice Net (d) Voice Telephone

17. The most important factor in teaching in higher education is to
(a) lead students to the sources of information.
(b) develop a spirit of competition for higher achievement in students.
(c) supply the relevant information to students.
(d) prepare students for the various competitive exams.

18. In which year did U.G.C. become an autonomous body?
(a) 1948 (b) 1988
(c) 1964 (d) 1956.

19. A type of communication which is becoming very important in transmission of data between computer network is known as
(a) Bank networking
(b) Communication network
(c) Satellite area networking
(d) Internal working

20. Maximum threat to the world is from
(a) water Pollution
(b) soil erosion
(c) ozone hole
(d) global warming

21. Which of the following will not hamper effective communication in the class?
(a) A lengthy statement
(b) An ambiguous statement
(c) A precise statement
(d) A statement that allows the listener to draw his own conclusion.

22. In a certain code MENTION is written as LNEITNO. In the same way how is a PATTERN coded?
(a) APTTREM (b) PTAETNR
(c) OTAETNR (d) OTAETRN.

23. Which one of the following is not a correct depiction of emotional intelligence?
(a) Ability to monitor one's own and other's emotions.
(b) Discriminate between different emotions and label them appropriately.
(c) Enhance the cognitive capacity of the individual.
(d) Use emotional information to guide thinking and behavior.

24. A researcher wants to study the future of the BSP in India for the study which tool is most appropriate for him?
(a) Questionnaire (b) Schedule
(c) Interview (d) Rating Scale.

25. The atmosphere of the earth constitutes nitrogen and oxygen gases in the ratio of
(a) 4 : 1 (b) 1 : 2
(c) 1 : 7 (d) 3 : 5.

26. Starting from a point P Satish walked 20 metres towards South. He turned and walked 30 metres. He then turned left and walked 20 metres. He again turned left and walked 40 metres and reached a point. How far and in which direction as the point Q from the point P?
(a) 20 metres West (b) 10 metres East
(c) 10 metres West (d) 10 metres North

27. Mukesh is taller than Rajeev but shorter than Amar. Suman is taller than Mukesh but shorter than Vinay. Who among them will be at the fourth place is they stand in a row in descending order of the height?
(a) Amar (b) Rajeev
(c) Vinay (d) None of the above

28. What should come in place of the question mark in the following letter series?
AYD BVF DRH ? KGL
(a) FMI (b) GMJ
(c) HLK (d) GLJ.

29. ABCD is a square, EPGH is a rectangle, AB = 3, EF = 4, FG = 6. What is the area of the region outside of ABCD and inside EFGH?

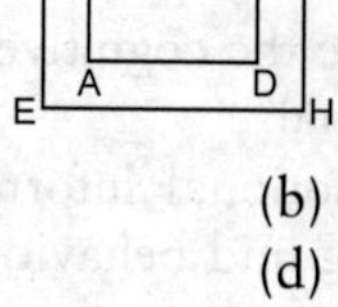

(a) 6 (b) 9
(c) 72 (d) 15.

Directions (Questions 30-32). Given below are two statements I and II followed by two conclusions (1) and (2) considering the statements to be true. Indicate which of the following conclusions logically follows from the given statements by choosing one of the four response alternatives given below the conclusions:

30. **Statements:**
I. All books are stones.
II. All stones are papers.
Conclusions:
1. Some papers are books.
2. Some papers are stones.
Codes:
(a) Only (1) follows
(b) Only (2) follows
(c) Both (1) and (2) follows
(d) Neither (1) nor (2) follows

31. **Statements:**
I. All birds are black.
II. No black is white.
Conclusions:
1. No bird is white.
2. Some birds are not black.
Codes:
(a) Only (1) follows
(b) Only (2) follows
(c) Both (1) and (2) follows
(d) Neither (1) nor (2) follows

32. **Statements:**
I. Some animals are grass eaters.
II. Dog is an animal.
Conclusions:
1. Dogs are grass eaters
2. All animals are dogs
Codes:
(a) Only (1) follows
(b) Only (2) follows

(c) Both (1) and (2) follows
(d) Neither (1) nor (2) follows

33. If the hands of a clock are in perpendicular position what will be the time when they are in the 8-9 position?
(a) $27\frac{3}{11}$ past 8 (b) $32\frac{8}{11}$ past 8
(c) $37\frac{3}{11}$ past 8 (d) $48\frac{2}{11}$ past 8

34. One of the various forms of dialogue between human and computer is termed as
(a) interactivity
(b) biangular dialogue
(c) digital dialogue
(d) human machine dialogue

35. Which of the following agencies is concerned with education and culture?
(a) UNESCO (b) UNICEF
(c) IMO (d) ILO.

36. Full Form of DSS is
(a) data security services
(b) data security systems
(c) data secure software
(d) decision support system.

37. Which diagram represents the relationship between Women, Mothers and Engineers?

(a)  (b) 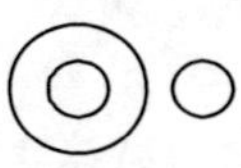

(c)  (d) 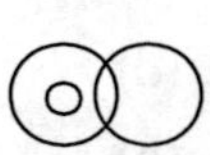

38. Which is the type of 'Research Hypothesis'?
(a) Null hypothesis
(b) Alternative hypothesis
(c) Option
(d) Both (a) and (b).

39. The most important factor in teaching in higher education is to
(a) lead students to the sources of information.
(b) develop a spirit of competition for higher achievement in students.
(c) supply the relevant information to students.
(d) prepare students for the various competitive examinations.

40. The science of communication and control is known as
(a) PERT (b) MIS
(c) Informatics (d) Cybernetics

41. Which one of the following is correctly expressed in respect of motivation of an employee in an organization?

(a) $\text{Motivation} = \frac{\text{Expectancy} \times \text{Instrumentality}}{\text{Valence}}$

(b) $\text{Motivation} = \frac{\text{Valence} \times \text{Instrumentality}}{\text{Expectancy}}$

(c) $\text{Motivation} = \frac{\text{Expectancy} \times \text{Valence}}{\text{Instrumentality}}$

(d) Motivation = Expectancy × Instrumentality × Valence.

42. Which of the following education policy started 10+2+3 programme all over India?
(a) The new education policy
(b) Kothari Commission
(c) Radha Krishna Commission
(d) Gyan Commission.

43. Anant was born 2 years after his father's marriage. His mother is five years younger than his father but 20 years older than Anant. At what age did his father get married?
(a) 35 years (b) 33 years
(c) 23 years (d) 25 years.

44. A told B that C is his father's nephew. D is A's cousin but not the brother of C.

What relationship is there between D and C?

(a) Father (b) Sister
(c) Mother (d) Aunt.

45. If ANOTHER is coded as 7309521, then THORN will be coded as

(a) 95103 (b) 95313
(c) 95013 (d) 95113

46. In the figure, CD is parallel to EF, AD = DF, CD = 4 and DF = 3. What is EF?

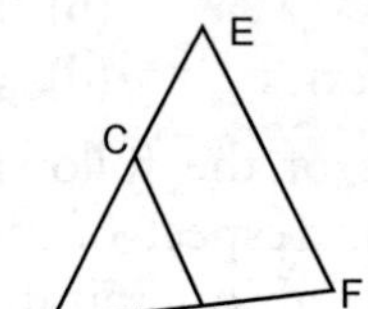

(a) 8 (b) 6
(c) 5 (d) 4.

47. The basic process of communication comprises

(a) Sender→Message→Channel→Receiver
(b) Sender→Receiver→Channel→Message
(c) Receiver→Sender→Message→Channel
(d) Message→Sender→Receiver→Channel

48. Which among the following are the right measures to solve the obstacles in relation to education?

(a) To increase girl schools
(b) To increase and motivate people
(c) To solve economic problems for the people
(d) All of the above.

49. Logic of introduction is very close to

(a) the logic of sampling
(b) the logic of observation
(c) the logic of the controlled variable
(d) None of the above.

50. Match the following:

(A) Tehri Dam 1. Ganga
(B) Sardan Sarovar 2. Vias & Sutlaj
(C) Indira Gandhi Canal 3. Narmada
(D) Nagarjuna Sagar 4. Krishna
5. Bhagirathi

Codes:	A	B	C	D
(a)	5	3	2	4
(b)	5	3	2	1
(c)	5	3	4	2
(d)	5	3	1	2

ANSWERS

1. (b)	2. (--)	3. (c)	4. (a)	5. (c)	6. (d)
7. (a)	8. (a)	9. (c)	10. (d)	11. (d)	12. (b)
13. (a)	14. (b)	15. (d)	16. (b)	17. (a)	18. (d)
19. (c)	20. (c)	21. (c)	22. (c)	23. (d)	24. (d)
25. (a)	26. (c)	27. (d)	28. (b)	29. (c)	30. (c)
31. (a)	32. (b)	33. (a)	34. (a)	35. (a)	36. (d)
37. (d)	38. (d)	39. (a)	40. (d)	41. (d)	42. (a)
43. (c)	44. (b)	45. (c)	46. (a)	47. (a)	48. (d)
49. (a)	50. (a)				

Previous Years' Papers

December 2008

1. 40% of the number is equal to three-fourth of the another number. What is the ratio between first number and second number?
   (a) 15 : 16 (b) 15 : 8
   (c) 9 : 15 (d) 8 : 17
   (e) None of the above.
2. A 360 metre long train crosses a signal post in 18 seconds. What is the speed of the train in km per hour?
   (a) 76 (b) 60
   (c) 64 (d) 72
   (e) None of the above.
3. A and B together can do a piece of work in 4 days. If A alone can do in 6 days. In how many days B can alone complete the same piece of work?
   (a) 12 (b) 8
   (c) 9 (d) 16
   (e) None of the above.
4. What is the compound interest accrued by Ravindra on an amount of Rs. 18000 at the rate of 10 p.c.p.a. at the end of three years?
   (a) Rs. 23498 (b) Rs. 23400
   (c) Rs. 23958 (d) Rs. 23900
   (e) None of the above.
5. A shopkeeper sells a T.V. set on discount of 8% of print price and gains 25%. If print price was Rs. 20000 then, what was the cost price?
   (a) Rs. 13800 (b) 14720
   (c) Rs. 14800 (d) 13720
   (e) None of the above.
6. In a certain code, 'ROAMING' is written as 'APRGOI'. How would 'PLATEAU' be written in the same code?
   (a) AMPTUBE (b) PMAUEBU
   (c) ALPUUAE (d) AMPUUBE
   (e) None of the above.
7. Four of the following five are alike in a certain way and so form a group. Which is the one that does not belong to that group?
   (a) Horse (b) Donkey
   (c) Cow (d) Goat
   (e) Dog.
8. How many meaningful English words can be formed with the letters of the word 'STOP' each using only once in a word but in different sequence, starting with the letter P?
   (a) None (b) Two
   (c) One (d) Three.
9. 'Mother' is related to 'Offspring' in the same way as 'Tree' is related to—
   (a) Sapling (b) Fruit
   (c) Root (d) Stem
10. In a certain code, 'SPRING' is written as '#2%@4=' and GONE' is written as '=74©'. How would SIGN be written in the same code?

(a) #@4= (b) 2@=4
(c) #@=4 (d) #%=4
(e) None of the above.

Directions (Questions 11-15): Read the following passage very carefully and answer the questions given below appropriately. There are certain words in the passage printed in bold letters to lead you to find them out easily in order to help you in answering some of the questions.

I worked as health secretary for about five years from the middle of 1962 to the middle of 1967. Thereafter I worked as finance secretary until the end of 1969. Indiscipline was rampant in the health department. Intense lobbying to secure plum postings was the order of the day. Ministers, legislators, senior officers and other influential people openly pleaded the cause of their protégés. The Health Minister was an honest, well-meaning politician. He approved my proposals to bring about some system and objectively in postings and transfers and put an end to lobbying. But those efforts met with only limited success. Doctors succeeded in getting desired postings by resorting to bribery. On the eve of the elections, the then minister sent down over 100 transfer orders from his camp office. They were in conflict with the guide-lines and quite a few were confusing in as much as two doctors were posted to the same place, or one person was posted to more than one post. I did not carry out the orders. I submitted a note to Chief Minister through the Chief Secretary pointing out why the orders should not be implemented. The Chief Secretary supported me. The Chief Minister decided that the minister's orders should not be implemented. All the doctors who had paid money were disappointed. In several other departments also corruption became widespread. In the works departments corruption had existed since a long time in the matter of awarding contracts. Now bribes were freely offered to secure transfer to particular posts, and even for getting promotions.

As Finance Secretary I found that the finances of the state were in a precarious condition. Financial discipline had evaporated. Long before the advent of the wireless and the telephone, the British had included in the Treasury Code a rule (Rule) empowering collectors to draw money from the treasury to meet emergencies like floods, earthquakes, devastating fires, etc. To my dismay I found that collectors were freely drawing money for all manner of trivial purposes under Rule 27 of the Treasury Code. In one case a collector had drawn money under the rule o buy a staff car for the SDO of another district. All checks and balances had disappeared. There was no accountability and any one could do what he pleased. Resorting to a number of harsh measures I could restore a measure of financial discipline. But the administration continued to be in disarray.

11. How many years did the author work as health secretary?
    (a) He worked as health secretary until the end of 1969.
    (b) He worked as health secretary before he took over as finance secretary.
    (c) He worked as health secretary till the health minister was found to be a man of integrity.
    (d) He worked as health secretary for about five years.
    (e) He did not work as health secretary at all.

12. According to the author what was the order of the day?
    (a) Strict discipline
    (b) Cut throat competition
    (c) Racial discrimination
    (d) Intense lobbying
    (e) None of the above.
13. How did the doctors succeed in getting desired postings?
    (a) Through dedicated service.
    (b) By working in the health minister's constituency.
    (c) By joining hands with the underworld criminals.
    (d) By resorting to sycophancy.
    (e) By resorting to bribery.
14. When the health minister sent down 100 transfer orders from his camp office, how did the author react?
    (1) He immediately obeyed the minister.
    (2) He did not carry out the orders.
    (3) He submitted a note to Chief Minister through the Chief Secretary.
    (a) (1) only (b) (2) only
    (c) (1) and (2) (d) (2) and (3)
    (e) (1) and (3)
15. What happened when the Chief Minister decided that the minister's orders should not be implemented?
    (a) The author was very happy.
    (b) The author arranged a tea party to celebrate his victory.
    (c) The doctors resigned and left the hospitals.
    (d) The health minister submitted his resignation.
    (e) All the doctors who had paid money were disappointed.

Directions: Study the following table carefully and answer the questions given below:

Number of five types of car produced and rejected (for defects) by a company over the years

Car	A		B		C		D		E	
Year	Produced	Rejected	Produced	Rejected	Produced	Rejected	Produced	Rejected	Produced	Rejected
1983	20	2	50	3	15	0.5	80	5	60	4
1984	35	3	45	2	20	0.55	75	4	58	4
1985	15	0.5	40	2.5	17	0.75	58	2	62	3.5
1986	25	0.25	42	2.3	25	1.5	65	3	40	1.5
1987	30	1.5	28	2.5	30	2.0	68	3	45	2
1988	27	1.5	41	2.1	26	1.75	72	3.5	50	2.5

16. In the case of B type car, in which year was the rations of rejection to production the highest among the given years?
    (a) 1983 (b) 1984
    (c) 1985 (d) 1987
    (e) 1988.
17. In the case of E type car, in which year was the ratio of rejection to production the lowest among the given years?
    (a) 1984 (b) 1985
    (c) 1986 (d) 1987
    (e) 1988.
18. What was the difference in number of C type cars rejected between 1984 and 1985?
    (a) 200 (b) 250
    (c) 2000 (d) 2500.

19. The acceptable E type cars in 1985 were what per cent of that of 1984?
(a) 8 (b) 106
(c) 110 (d) 5
(e) None of the above.

20. In the year 1984, in the case of which cars was the rejection below five per cent?
(a) A only (b) B or E
(c) B and C (d) C and D
(e) None of the above.

21. The most realistic attitude towards child's development is that
(a) he can do whatever he wants to do.
(b) he can never make it any way.
(c) he is not born a genius but only with potentialities for becoming one provided certain environmental conditions are met.
(d) he is the master of his fate.

22. The statement that "Even relatively drastic changes in behavior can be effected through the manipulation of environmental influences" is
(a) true (b) false
(c) quasi true (d) it is irrelevant

23. The view that "Emotionality is by the large inherited" is
(a) not acceptable (b) acceptable
(c) realistic (d) unrealistic

24. Which is not true about the development of behavior?
(a) It proceeds from generalized mass activity to specific responses.
(b) It is a gradual and a continuous process.
(c) It varies from child to child and the sequence is not uniform.
(d) It proceeds in a cephalo-caudal and proximo-distal direction.

25. Which of the following is most acceptable generalization about early and special training?
(a) It tends to be uneconomical and wasteful.
(b) It leads to an improvement in performance in certain cases.
(c) It may actually be of great benefit.
(d) All of the above.

26. You want to instill in the pupils of your class the spirit of democracy. Which of the following strategies do you think is most efficient for the purpose?
(a) Organize a discussion on the advantages of democracy over other systems and convince the pupils of its superiority.
(b) Conduct election for a class assembly and give the representatives certain responsibilities.
(c) Maintain a democratic atmosphere in your dealings and make the pupils responsible for class management, sharing duties among themselves.
(d) Invite speakers to the school and make them deliver speeches about world leaders who worked for democracy.

27. Discussion in the class will be most effective if the topic of discussion is
(a) not introduced by the teacher.
(b) started immediately before the start of discussion.
(c) written in the Black Board without introducing it.
(d) informed to the students well in advance.

28. Teacher's communication will be more effective if
(a) the teacher is a master in his subject.
(b) he prepares a good number of instructional aids.

(c) he discusses previous question papers.
(d) he starts from what students already know.

29. The recently launched "Vidya Vahini" is a project related to
(a) school computerization programme.
(b) TV programme related to mass literacy.
(c) establishment of libraries in rural areas.
(d) None of the above.

30. The most critical factor that determines the professional status of a teacher is
(a) unity among teachers
(b) high salary
(c) character
(d) instructional competency

31. Teacher's professionalism may be assessed in terms of all the following commitments except
(a) commitment to the profession and students.
(b) commitment to the colleagues and employer.
(c) commitment to the religion and castes.
(d) commitment to the parents and community.

32. The first important step in teaching is
(a) planning before hand
(b) organizing material to be taught
(c) knowing the background of students
(d) None of the above.

33. Suppose you are an ambitious teacher. You have high deals for class room teaching but your hard labour goes in vain. The reason underlying this problem may be
(a) your teaching level is above the ability level of students.
(b) individual differences among students make your efforts futile.
(c) Both of the above.
(d) None of the above.

34. If a student becomes unconscious in the class what will you do first?
(a) Rushing to the principal's office and canvassing for help impatiently.
(b) Telephoning student's parents and waiting for them.
(c) Giving first aid to him and trying to contact any nearby doctor.
(d) Making arrangement to send him to his home.

35. If you have to teach a blind student along with the normal students, what type of behavior are you expected to exhibit?
(a) Take care of him with sympathy.
(b) Don't give any extra attention because majority of students may suffer.
(c) Arrange the seat in the front row and try to keep your teaching pace according to him without making the other students suffer.
(d) None of the above.

36. Pollution can be
(a) natural
(b) man made
(c) Both (a) and (b)
(d) None of the above

37. Qualitative pollutants are
(a) added by man
(b) naturally occurring
(c) present in the high concentration
(d) None of the above.

38. The country which hosted first *World Earth Summit* (June 1992) on conservation of environment is
(a) India (b) Brazil
(c) Peru (d) Spain

39. Ecological backlash (ecological boomerang) is

(a) production of adverse ecological effect by a previously useful chemical.
(b) production of useful ecological effect by a previously useful chemical.
(c) heat emission due to bomb explosion.
(d) None of the above.

40. When was the Air Prevention and Control of Pollution Act legislated in India?
(a) 1980 (b) 1981
(c) 1982 (d) 1984.

41. Who said: "Persistence of a high order is proclaimed by the protagonist of I am the master of my fate. I am captain of my soul'".
(a) Harlow's invictus
(b) Maslow's invictus
(c) Healye's invictus
(d) None of the above

42. Formal religious education is not desirable as a part of the school curriculum because
(a) teaching of a large number of religious that are there in every society is not possible due to time constraint.
(b) formal teaching of religion is not at all effective.
(c) teachers may not like to teach religion in the schools.
(d) religion is of no value in the context of education of the child.

43. Religious education in some forms is essential because it
(a) develops essential values in children.
(b) provides children with desirable knowledge.
(c) makes good life in a good society.
(d) is the foundation stone on which rests the success of a democratic society.

44. Which is not correct about the school as a social institution?
(a) It has to teach about the social order and its institutions in its instructional activities.
(b) As it stands for the good life in general, it is the critic of society and all its institutions.
(c) It stands for the professional ideals of the community rather than the ideals it practices and tolerates.
(d) It stands for the satisfaction of the needs of the pupils who come for schooling.

45. What does not permit improvement in culture?
(a) Belief in God
(b) Belief in the doctrine of Karma
(c) The historical accidents
(d) Rigid observance of Taboos.

46. In linked list, the successive elements
(a) the number of walks of length k between i^{th} and j^{th} vertex must not occupy contiguous space in memory.
(b) need not occupy contiguous space in memory.
(c) must occupy contiguous space in memory.
(d) None of the above.

47. Linear order in linked list is provided through
(a) the implied position of the node
(b) index number
(c) Pointer
(d) None of the above.

48. The worst case efficient of binary search is
(a) $\log_2, n + 1$ (b) n^2
(c) n (d) None of the above

49. Which property is not expected from a good hashing technique?
(a) Easy to program
(b) Produces keys uniformly distributed over the range

(c) Produces no collisions
(d) All properties are expected.

50. What is not true for linear collision processing?
(a) It may induce more collision
(b) It is easier to program
(c) It requires space for links
(d) All of the above.

ANSWERS

1. (b)	2. (d)	3. (a)	4. (e)
5. (b)	6. (d)	7. (e)	8. (b)
9. (a)	10. (a)	11. (d)	12. (d)
13. (e)	14. (d)	15. (e)	16. (c)
17. (c)	18. (a)	19. (e)	20. (c)
21. (c)	22. (a)	23. (b)	24. (c)
25. (d)	26. (c)	27. (d)	28. (b)
29. (d)	30. (a)	31. (c)	32. (c)
33. (c)	34. (c)	35. (c)	36. (a)
37. (a)	38. (b)	39. (a)	40. (c)
41. (c)	42. (a)	43. (a)	44. (c)
45. (d)	46. (b)	47. (c)	48. (a)
49. (c)	50. (c)		

December 2007

1. Which of the following inventions is pollution free which does not consume much fuel and is less expensive?
(a) Solar oven (b) Soil ship
(c) Bicycle (d) Radio.

2. Insat-2A has a very high resolution radiometer which provides picture of the cloud and the slides appear on TV screen. What is the frequency of its sending pictures of the clouds over the country?
(a) Once everyday
(b) Four times everyday
(c) Eight times everyday
(d) Twice everyday.

3. The cosmic radiation falling on earth from the outer space chiefly consists of three charged particles, electrons, alpha particles and
(a) neutron (b) radsons
(c) protons (d) positrons

4. The atmosphere of the earth constitutes nitrogen and oxygen gases in the ratio of
(a) 4 : 1 (b) 1 : 2
(c) 1 : 7 (d) 3 : 5

5. High Flying trans-sound speed-travelling aircraft and rockets cause maximum damage to which of the following things?
(a) Lonosphere (b) Ozone layer
(c) Aurara Boreasils (d) Stratosphere.

6. What is the average crystal strength of the magnetism of earth?
(a) 50,000 gammas (b) 1000 gammas
(c) 100,000 gammas (d) Not known.

7. The Environment (Protection) Act 1986 was the First Comprehensive Legislation with regard to environmental protection.
(a) True
(b) False
(c) Both (a) and (b)
(d) None of the above.

8. Noise becomes unbearable to human ears when it reaches to the level of
(a) 120 decibel (b) 150 decibel
(c) 200 decibel (d) 100 decibel

9. Which of the following sky-drops has nature or crystal-like structure?
(a) Rain drops
(b) Meteorites
(c) Snow Flakes
(d) None of the above

Direction: Read the passage carefully and answer the question numbers 10-14

Hundred years ago there was much less specialization in work than there is today. One furniture maker would make the whole of a table-indeed, perhaps, all the furniture needed to furnish a house, and he worked in a simple workshop, probably entirely with hand tools. The furniture he made was very good and very beautiful, but it would take him a longtime to make it. The output of one man was, by modern standards, small, and the cost of the furniture relatively high. Only the fairly wealthy could afford a great deal. Most modern furniture is made in factories with the aid of machinery. So nowadays a man working in a furniture factory will, perhaps spend his days mindling one machine which carries out one process only in the making of table legs. A great number of men will be taking part in the various process which go to making the table, and by this division of labour a great many tables will be made in a comparatively short time. A good workman, however should understand all the process which go to make the table, even though he himself actually does only one of them. In the making of more complicated things, such as cars or elaborate pieces of electrical machinery, even this is not possible. It is very likely even that all the processes do not go on in the same factory.

10. Why was the cost of the furniture so high in the past?
    (a) Output was small
    (b) Material was costly
    (c) Artisans were greedy
    (d) None of the above.
11. The artisans of the ancient times did not have
    (a) skill (b) specialization
    (c) markets (d) Both (a) and (c)
12. Production of Furniture is quicker because
    (a) of division of labour
    (b) of machinery
    (c) good conditions of working
    (d) of technology development
13. 'Mindling' in the passage can be replaced by
    (a) thinking of (b) feeling
    (c) taking care of (d) touching
14. Which of the following uses of 'even' are correct?
    (a) The chances of success are even.
    (b) Even a child can do it.
    (c) We will count only even numbers.
    (d) Both (b) and (c).
15. In the following alphabet which letter is seventh to the right of fifteenth letter from the right end?

    A B C D E F G H I J K L M N O P Q R S T U V W X Y Z

    (a) S (b) T
    (c) R (d) H
    (e) None of the above.
16. Starting from a point P Satish walked 20 metres towards south. He turned left and walked 30 metres. He then turned left and walked 20 metres. He again turned left and walked 40 metres and reached a point how far and in which direction is the point q from the point P?
    (a) 20 metres West (b) 10 metres East
    (c) 10 metres West (d) 10 metres North
    (e) None of the above.
17. Two letters in the word ROUBLE have as many letters between them in the word as in the alphabet. Which one of the two comes earlier in the alphabet?
    (a) L (b) O
    (c) E (d) R
    (e) B.
18. Mukesh is taller than Rajeev but shorter than Amar. Suman is taller than Mukesh but shorter than Vinay. Who among them

will be at the Fourth place if they stand in a row in descending order of their height?
(a) Amar
(b) Rajeev
(c) Vinay
(d) Cannot be determined
(e) None of the above.

19. What should come in place of the question mark in the following letter series?
AYD BVF DRH ? KGL
(a) FMI (b) GMJ
(c) HLK (d) GLJ
(e) None of the above.

Directions: Read the following information carefully and answer the questions number 20-22.
(A) There is a family of six persons P, Q, R, S, T and U. They are Engineer, Doctor, Teacher, Salesman, Manager and Lawyer.
(B) There are two married couples in the family.
(C) The Manager is grandfather of U who is an Engineer.
(D) R, the Salesman is married to the lady teacher.
(E) The Doctor S is married to the Manager.
(F) Q is the mother of U and T.

20. How many male members are there in the Family?
(a) Two (b) Three
(c) Four (d) Data inadequate
(e) None of the above.

21. How P is related to T?
(a) Grandmother (b) Father
(c) Uncle (d) Brother
(e) Grandfather.

22. Which of the following is the profession of T?
(a) Manager (b) Salesman
(c) Doctor (d) Engineer
(e) None of the above.

23. In the Figure OR and PR are radii of circles. The length of OP is 4. If OR=2, what is PR? (PR is tangent to circle with center O).

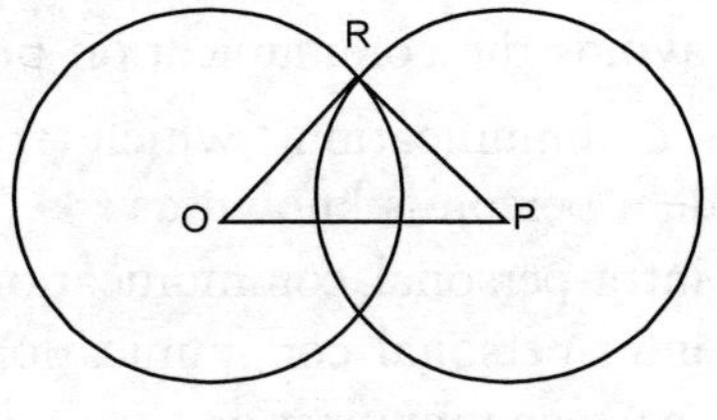

(a) 2 (b) 5
(c) 3 (d) $2\sqrt{2}$

24. ABCD is a square, EFGH is a rectangle, AB = 3, EF = 4, FG = 6. What is the area of the region outside of ABCD and inside EFGH?

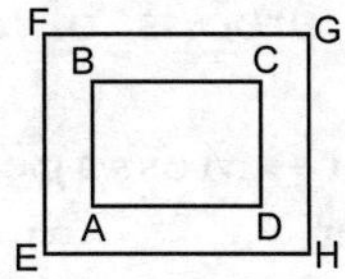

(a) 6 (b) 9
(c) 72 (d) 15.

25.

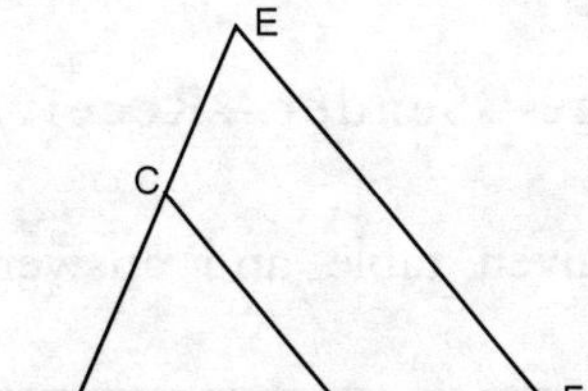

In the figure, CD is parallel to EF, AD = DF, CD = 4 and DF = 3. What is EF?
(a) 8 (b) 6
(c) 5 (d) 4.

26. The process of media messages to be tailored to its format and technology is known as

(a) Perception filter
(b) Media relevancy
(c) Communication clarity
(d) Rhetorics

27. Communicator is the person who
(a) initiates the communication process.
(b) completes the communication process.
(c) controls the communication process.
(d) avoids the communication process.

28. The communication, which transpires inside a person is known as
(a) intra-personal communication.
(b) inter-personal communication.
(c) mass communication.
(d) group communication.

29. Any interruption, which occurs at any point of the communication process is known as
(a) noise (b) barrier
(c) distortion (d) All of the above

30. The basic process of communication comprises
(a) Sender→Message→Channel→Receiver
(b) Sender→Receiver→Channel→Message
(c) Receiver→Sender→Message→Channel
(d) Message→Sender→Receiver→Channel

31. Study the given table and answer the question.

Year	Firm's outlay	Proceeds
1970	3400	4000
1980	3800	4500
1990	4500	5400
2000	7400	8000

Which of the following conclusion is not true?
(a) There has been a steady growth in percentage profit of the firm.
(b) Income of the firm becomes double in 30 years.
(c) Percentage profit in 1990 was 16.6%.
(d) There is 117.65% increase in the expenses of the firm from 1970 to 2000.

32. Which among the following are the right measures solve the obstacles in relation to women education?
(a) To increase girls schools.
(b) To encourage and motivate people.
(c) To solve economic problems for the people.
(d) All of the above.

33. Education administration is
(a) an art
(b) a science
(c) Both (a) and (b)
(d) None of the above.

34. Which commission recommended General School education to be of 10 years?
(a) Mudaliar Education Commission
(b) Kothari Commission
(c) Hunter Commission
(d) All of the above.

35. Which of the following is the chief social determiner of education?
(a) Home (b) School
(c) Family (d) All of the above.

36. Which of the following are elements of education planning?
(a) Problems (b) Builders
(c) Resources (d) All of the above.

37. The main aim of Basic Education is
(a) to be self-dependent and self-sufficient
(b) to depend on the teacher
(c) to depend on the society
(d) None of the above.

38. Which method would you deem suitable for rectifying those students who interrupt the teaching process in the class?
   (a) They should be sent out of the class.
   (b) They should be given harsh punishment in the class itself.
   (c) They should be ignored.
   (d) A complaint should be filed against them with the principal.

39. The job of the teacher is to generate
   (a) affiancing for studies among students.
   (b) confidence in studies among students.
   (c) a belief towards studies among students.
   (d) affect/affiliation for studies among students.

40. As a teacher, what type of behavior of a student would be deemed serious by you?
   (a) Incomplete homework.
   (b) Asking too many questions in the class.
   (c) Talking to other students in the class during the course of a lecture.
   (d) Slightly slow/weak in studies.

41. In the profession of teaching, the most beneficial aspect is
   (a) an opportunity to dominate the children.
   (b) an opportunity to express yourself.
   (c) hefty earning from tution work, besides earnings through salary.
   (d) sufficient number of holidays in a year.

42. A computer's clock-speed is measures in
   (a) megabytes and gigabytes
   (b) nano seconds and pico seconds
   (c) bits and megabytes
   (d) megahertz and gigahertz

43. Machine language and assembly languages are examples of
   (a) high level languages
   (b) low level languages
   (c) high level and low level languages respectively
   (d) None of the above

44. Abhinav was born 2 years after his father's marriage. His mother is five year younger than his father but 20 years older than Abhinav. At what age did his father get married?
   (a) 35 years (b) 33 years
   (c) 23 years (d) 25 years.

45. If $84 \times 13 = 8$, $37 \times 13 = 6$, $26 \times 11 = 6$, then $56 \times 22 = ?$
   (a) 36 (b) 39
   (c) 7 (d) 11

46. If the third day of the month was Monday, then which day will fall on fourth day after 21st?
   (a) Monday (b) Tuesday
   (c) Wednesday (d) Friday.

47. Bibliography given in a research report
   (a) helps those interested in further research and studying the problem from another angle.
   (b) makes the report authentic.
   (c) shows the vast knowledge of the researches.
   (d) None of the above.

48. Survey study aims at
   I. knowing Facts about the existing situation.
   II. comparing the present status with the standard norms.
   III. criticizing the existing situation.
   IV. identifying the means of improving the existing situation.

   Codes:
   (a) I and II both (b) I, II and III
   (c) I, II, III and IV (d) II and III both

49. The experimental study is based on the law of
    (a) single variable
    (b) relication
    (c) occupation
    (d) interest of the subject
50. Logic of introduction is very close to
    (a) the logic of sampling
    (b) the logic of observation
    (c) the logic of the controlled variable
    (d) None of the above

ANSWERS

1. (c)	2. (c)	3. (c)	4. (a)
5. (b)	6. (a)	7. (a)	8. (d)
9. (c)	10. (a)	11. (b)	12. (a)
13. (c)	14. (a)	15. (a)	16. (c)
17. (e)	18. (e)	19. (b)	20. (d)
21. (e)	22. (e)	23. (d)	24. (d)
25. (a)	26. (b)	27. (a)	28. (a)
29. (c)	30. (a)	31. (c)	32. (d)
33. (c)	34. (b)	35. (d)	36. (d)
37. (a)	38. (a)	39. (b)	40. (c)
41. (b)	42. (d)	43. (b)	44. (c)
45. (c)	46. (b)	47. (a)	48. (b)
49. (a)	50. (a)		

EXPLANATION

15. Fifteenth letter from the right end is M and seventh letter to the right of M is S.

16. 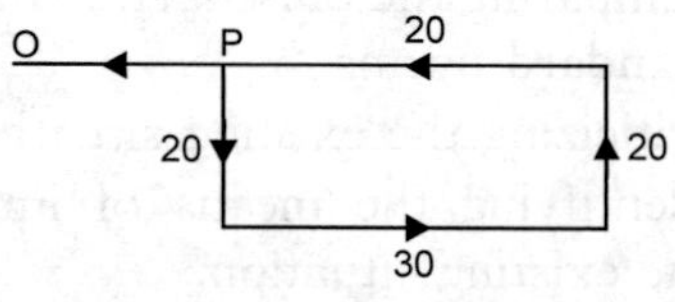

17. Between L and O there are two words in the alphabet and so are in the word ROUBLE. These words U and B out of which B comes earlier in the alphabet.

18. Rajeev < Mukesh < Amar and Mukesh < Suman < Vinay
    ∴ Mukesh will be at the 4th place
19. The sequence in the given series is
    +1, +2, +3, +4 i.e. A, B, D, G, K
    -3, -4, -5, -6 i.e. y, v, R, M, G
    +2 i.e. D, F, H, J, L
    ∴ (?) should be replaced by GMJ
20. (i) S is the lady since she is married to a Manager who is grandfather of U.
    (ii) Q is a lady as she is mother of U and T.
    (iii) R being the salesman is a male.
    (iv) P is a manager as he is grandfather of U. So P is also a male.
    ∴ S is married to P and Q is married to R.
    (v) About U and T, we cannot conclude from the given information whether they are males or females.
22. P is manager, Q is Teacher, R is Salesman, S is Doctor, U is Engineer ∴ T is lawyer.
23. Since the radius to the point of tangency is perpendicular to the tangent, OR must be perpendicular to PR. Therefore, ORP is a right angled triangle, and $(PO)^2 = (OR)^2 + (PR)^2$, then $(PR)^2 = (PO)^2 - (OR)^2$. Thus $(PR)^2 = 4^2 - 3^2$ and $PR = \sqrt{16} - 4 = \sqrt{12} = \sqrt{4}\,\sqrt{3} = 2\sqrt{3}$.
24. Since ABCD is a square, the area of ABCD = 3^2 on 9. The area of rectangle EFGH is length X width of $4 \times 6 = 24$. Thus, the area outside the square and inside the rectangle is 24 – 9 or 15.
28. As CD is parallel to EF, the triangles ACD and AEF are similar. Therefore corresponding sides are proportional. So CD is to EF as AD is to AF. Since AD = DE, AD/AF is ½. Therefore, EF is twice CD or 8.

31. Firm's profit = Revenue – Expenses = 5400 – 4500 = 900
Net percentage profit
= 900, 100/5400 = 16.66%

44. Mother's age = X
Father's age = X + 5
Abhinav age = X – 20 = 10
so X = 30
Mother's age = 30
Father's age = 30 + 5 = 35
Marriage of the Father = 35 – 2 – 10 = 23

45. (8 × 4) – (1 + 3) = 8, (3 +7) – (1 + 3) = 6 and (5 + 6) – 2 + 2 = 7

46. Fourth day after 21 means 25th. It means on 24th it will be Monday.

JUNE 2007

1. In the context of organizational communication which one of the following statements is not correct?
   (a) Organizational communication systems are not affected by how organizations are structured.
   (b) Information on the grapevine is not unidirectional.
   (c) Managers much reconcile the informaility of grapevine communications with the formality of in channel communications.
   (d) Research has shown that nearly 75% of the time, information passed along informally is accurate.
2. Which one of the following is not a correct depiction of emotional intelligence?
   (a) Ability to monitor one's own and other's emotions.
   (b) Discriminate between different emotions and label them appropriately.
   (c) Enhance the cognitive capacity of the individual.
   (d) Use emotional information to guide thinking and behavior.
3. The science of communication and control is known as
   (a) PERT (b) MIS
   (c) Informatics (d) Cybernetics
4. Which one of the following is correctly expressed in respect of motivation of an employee in an organization?
   (a) Motivation = $\frac{\text{Expectancy} \times \text{instrumentality}}{\text{valence}}$
   (b) Motivation = $\frac{\text{valence} \times \text{instrumentality}}{\text{Expectancy}}$
   (c) Motivation = $\frac{\text{Expectancy} \times \text{valence}}{\text{instrumentality}}$
   (d) Motivation = Expectancy × instrumentality × valence
5. Consider the following statements:
   1. The Kothari committee on recruitment policy and selection methods recommended that service allocation on the basis of the civil services examination (written and interview) and the post training test at the National Academy of Administration.
   2. The (First) Administrative reforms commission recommended against the institution of a single civil services examination for all the services covered by it. Which of the statements given above is/are correct?

   Codes:
   (a) 1 only (b) 2 only
   (c) Both 1 and 2 (d) Neither 1 nor 2.

Directions: The following 5 (five) items consist of two statements, one labelled as the 'Assertion' (A) and the others as 'Reason' (R). You are to examine these two statements carefully and select the answers to these items using the codes given below.

Codes:

(a) Both (A) and (R) are true and (R) is the correct explanation of (A).
(b) Both (A) and (R) are true but (R) is not the correct explanation of (A).
(c) (A) is true but (R) is false.
(d) (A) is false but (R) is true.

6. **Assertion (A):** River Kalinadi is an east flowing river in the southern part of India.

   Reason (R): The Deccan plateau is higher along its western edge and gently slopes towards the Bay of Bengal in the east.

7. **Assertion (A):** There are no tea plantations in any African Country.

   Reason (R): Tea plants need fertile soil with high humus.

8. **Assertion (A):** A Jet aircraft moving at mach Number equal to 1 travels Faster at an altitudes of 15 km than while moving at mach number equal to 1 near the sea level.

   Reason (R): The velocity of sound depends on the temperature of the surrounding medium.

9. **Assertion (A):** District Collectors were appointed as the principal census officers of the respective districts to conduct the census of 2002.

   Reason (R): Census is a subject in the union list in the seventh schedule of the constitution of India.

10. **Assertion (A):** The (First) Administrative Reforms Commission's recommendation that a part of the recruitment process to the IAS and other services should be made on the lines of the Method II Examination (used in the U.K. for selection for the civil service) was not acceptable by the Kothari Committee.

    Reason (R): The Kothari Committee considered the element of subjectivity on the part of examiners in the Method II Examination to great to be acceptable.

11. In the human body, which structure is the appendix attached to?
    (a) The large intestine
    (b) The small intestine
    (c) The gall intestine
    (d) The stomach.

12. Consider the following statements:
    1. Same procedures for cadre allocation is used for directly recruited and promotee officers to the all India Services.
    2. Indian Economic Service is included in the central civil services.

    Which of the statements given above are correct?

    Codes:

    (a) 1 only (b) 2 only
    (c) Both 1 and 2 (d) Neither 1 nor 2.

13. The largest coral reef in the world is found near the coast of which of the following countries?
    (a) Australia (b) Cuba
    (c) Ghana (d) Philippines.

14. Who among the following is considered as the inventor of the world wide web (www)?
    (a) Edward Kasner (b) Bill Gates
    (c) Tim Burners Lee (d) Ajij Premji.

15. The dice (each having six faces with each Face having one number from 1 to 6) are rolle(d), what is the number of possible outcomes such that at least one dice shows the number 2?

(a) 36 (b) 81
(c) 91 (d) 116.

16. Five balls of different colours are to be placed in three different colours boxes such that any box contains at least one ball. What is the maximum number of different ways in which this can be done?
(a) 90 (b) 120
(c) 150 (d) 180.

17. Rahul has Five Friends: 3 girls and 2 boys. Rahul's wife also has 5 Friends: 3 boys and 2 girls: In how many maximum number of different ways can they invite 2 boys and 2 girls such that two of them are Rahul's friends and two are his wife's?
(a) 24 (b) 38
(c) 46 (d) 58.

18. Which one of the following non-metals is not a poor conductor of electricity?
(a) Sulphur (b) Selenium
(c) Bromium (d) Phosphorus.

19. Consider the following statements:
1. A Flute of a smaller length produces waves of lower frequency.
2. Sound travels in rocks in the form of longitudinal elastic waves only.

Which of the statements given above is/are correct?

Codes:
(a) 1 only (b) 2 only
(c) Both 1 and 2 (d) Neither 1 nor 2.

20. Consider the following statements:
1. If Magenta and Yellow coloured circles intersect, the intersected area will have red colour.
2. If cyan and magenta coloured circle intersect, the intersected area will have blue colour.

Which of the statements given above is/are correct?

Codes:
(a) 1 only (b) 2 only
(c) Both 1 and 2 (d) Neither 1 nor 2.

21. In which of the following cities is the Global Automotive Research Centre being set-up?
(a) Chennai (b) Hyderabad
(c) Pune (d) Gurgaon.

22. Consider the following statements:
1. In November, 2006 DRDO successfully conducted the Interception test using Prithvi II missile.
2. Prithvi II is a surface to surface missile and can be deployed to guard the metros against air attacks.

Which of the statements given above is/are correct?

Codes:
(a) 1 only (b) 2 only
(c) Both 1 and 2 (d) Neither 1 nor 2.

23. A train complete a journey with a few stoppages in between at an average speed of 40 km per hour. If the train had not stopped anywhere, it would have completed the journey at an average speed of 60 km per hour on average. How many minutes per hour does the train stop during the journey?
(a) 20 minutes per hour
(b) 18 minutes per hour
(c) 15 minutes per hour
(d) 10 minutes per hour.

24. The average salary of 100 employees in an office in an office is Rs. 16,000 per month. The management decided to raise salary of every employee by 5% but stopped a transport allowance of Rs. 800 per month which was paid earlier to every employee. What will be the new average monthly salary?

(a) Rs. 16,000
(b) Rs. 16,500
(c) Rs. 16,800
(d) Cannot be known since data are insufficient.

25. A person has to completely put each of three liquids: 403 litres of petrol, 465 litres of diesel and 496 litres of Mobil oil in bottles of equation size without mixing any of the above three types of liquids such that each bottle is completely filled. What is the least possible number for bottles required?
(a) 34
(b) 44
(c) 46
(d) None of the above

Direction (26-30). Read the passage carefully and choose the best answer for each question.

In a modern computer, electronic and magnetic storage technologies play complimintary roles. Electronic memory chips are fast but volatile (their contents are last when the computer is unplugged). Magnetic tapes and hard disks are slower, but have the advantage that they are non-volatile, so that they can be used to store software and documents even when the power is off.

In laboratories around the world however researches are hoping to achieve the best of both worlds. They are trying to build magnetic memory chips that could be used in place of today's electronic ones. These magnetic memories would be non-volatile; but they would also be faster, able to stand up to hazardous environments more easily. Such chips would have obvious applications in storage cards for digital cameras and music-players; they would enable handhold and laptop computers to boot up more quickly and to operate for longer; they would allow desktop computers to run faster; they would doubtless have military and space-faring advantages too. But although the theory behind them looks solid there are trickly practical problems and need to be overcome.

Two different approaches, based on different magnetic phenomena, are being pursued. The first, being investigated by Gary Prinz and his colleagues at the Naval Research Laboratory (NRL) in Washington, DC; exploits the fact that the electrical resistance of same materials changes in the presence of a magnetic field a phenomenon known as magneto—resistance. For some multi-layered materials this effect is particularly powerful and is, accordingly, called "giant" magneto-resistance (GMR). Since 1997, the exploitation of GMR has made cheap multi-gigabyte hard disks commonplace. The magnetic orientations of the magnetized spot on the surface of a spinning disk are detected by measuring the changes they induce in the resistance of a tiny sensor. This technique is so sensitive that it means the spot can be made smaller and packed closer together that was previously, thus increasing the capacity and reducing the size and cost of a disk drive.

Dr. Prinz and his colleagues are now exploiting the same phenomenon on the surface of memory chips, rather than spinning disks. In a conventional memory chip, each binary digit (bit) of data is represented using a capacitor—reservoir of electrical charge that is either empty or full—to present a zero or a one. In the NRL's magnetic design, by contrast, each bit is stored in a magnetic element in the form of a vertical pillar or magnetisable material. A matrix of wires passing above and below the elements allows each to be magnetized either clockwise or anti-clockwise, to represent zero or one. Another set of wires allows current to pass through any particular element. By measuring an elements resistance you can determine its magnetic orientation, and hence whether it is storing a zero or a one. Since the elements retain their magnetic orientation even when the power is off, the result is non-volatile memory unlike the elements of an electronic memory, a magnetic memory's elements are not easily disrupted by radiation. And compared with electronic memories, whose capacitors need constant topping up, magnetic memories are simpler and consume less power. The NRL researchers plan to commercialise their device through a company called Non-volatile electronics, which recently began to work on the necessary processing and fabrication techniques. But it will be some years before the first chips roll of the production line.

26. In developing magnetic memory chips to replace the electronic ones, two alternative research paths are being pursued. These are approaches based on:
    (a) Volatile and non-volatile memories.
    (b) Magneto-resistance and magnetic tunnel junctions.
    (c) Radiation-disruption and radiation neutral effects.
    (d) Orientation of magnetized spots on the surface of a spinning disk and alignment of magnetic dots on the surface of conventional memory chip.
27. A binary digit or bit is represented in the magneto-resistance based magnetic chip using
    (a) a layer of aluminum oxide
    (b) a capacitor
    (c) a vertical pillar of magnetized material
    (d) a matrix of wires
28. In the magnetic tunnel-junctions (MTJs) tunneling is easier when
    (a) two magnetic layers are polarized in the same direction.
    (b) two magnetic layers are polarized in the opposite directions.
    (c) two aluminium—oxide barriers are polarized in the same direction.
    (d) two aluminium—oxide barriers are polarized in opposite directions.
29. A major barriers on the way to build a full scale memory chip based on MTJs is
    (a) the low sensitivity of the magnetic memory elements.
    (b) the thickness of aluminium oxide barriers.
    (c) the need to develop more reliable and for smaller magnetic memory chips.
    (d) All of the above.
30. A line of research which is trying to build a magnetic chip that can both store and manipulate information is being pursued by
    (a) Paul Freits
    (b) Stuart Parkin
    (c) Gary prinz
    (d) None of the above.
31. Which of the following is not an important consideration in the planning of the development of education in India?
    (a) Equity (b) Quality
    (c) Relevance (d) Religion.
32. Which of the following education policy started 10+2+3 programme all over India?
    (a) The new education policy
    (b) Kothari Commission
    (c) Radha Krishna Commission
    (d) Gyan Commission

33. The association of sea anemone and hermit crab is called as
    (a) Matualism (b) Parasitism
    (c) Symbiosis (d) Commensalism
34. Shannon—weaver index is used to indicate
    (a) biodiversity
    (b) air pollution level
    (c) water pollution
    (d) importance of species
35. In memory allocation, an entry, which is smallest amongst all the entried and equals of a bigger than the required are is selected as
    (a) Worst Fit method
    (b) Best fit method
    (c) First fit method
    (d) None of the above
36. One of the main differences between the responsibilities of a system analyst and a programmer.
    (a) A system analyst is concerned with design of the system whereas a programmer is concerned with computer.
    (b) Programmers deal with computer programs whereas a system analyst deals with many more things such as identifying opportunities for computerization, designing new procedures, selection of equipment, etc.
    (c) Programmers use lower level languages whereas system analysts use higher level language.
    (d) Programmers responsibility is to train systems analysts SPS usage.

Directions: (37–39). At an electronic data processing unit, five out of the eight programme unit, five out of the eight programme sets P, Q, R, S, T, U, V, and W are to be operated daily. On any one day, except for the first day of a month, only three of the programme sets must be the ones that were operated on the previous day. The programme operating must also satisfy the following conditions:

(i) If programme "P" is to be operated on a day, "V" cannot be operated on that day.
(ii) If "Q" is to be operated on a day, "T" must be one of the programmes to be operated after 'Q'.
(iii) If "R" is to be operated on a day, "V" must be one of the programme to be operated after "R".
(iv) The last programme to be operated on any day must be either "S" or "U".

37. Which of the following is true of any day's valid programmes set operation?
    (a) "P" cannot be operated at third place.
    (b) "Q" cannot be operated at third place.
    (c) "T" cannot be operated at third place.
    (d) "R" cannot be operated at fourth place.
    (e) "U" cannot be operated at fourth place.
38. If the programmes sets "R" and "W" are to operated on the first day, which of the following could be the other programmes on that day?
    (a) P, T, U (b) Q, S, V
    (c) Q, T, V (d) T, S, U
    (e) T, S, V.
39. If R is operated at third place in a sequence, which of the following cannot be the second programme in that sequence?
    (a) Q (b) S
    (c) T (d) U
    (e) W.

Qualification	Unemployed Men	Unemployed Women
Journalists	12.5 %	15%
Author	20%	7.5%
Trained-Teachers	15%	22.5%
Postgraduates	22.5%	25%
Graduates	30%	30%

40. According to the survey of 2000, educated unemployed persons in which 1200 were men and 800 women, the following data were collected on the basis of the table. What is the difference in the number of unemployed men and women Journalists?
(a) 20 (b) 30
(c) 40 (d) None of the above.

41. Anant was born 2 years after his father's marriage. His mother is five years younger than his father but 20 years older than Anant. At what age did his father get married?
(a) 35 years (b) 33 years
(c) 23 years (d) 25 years.

Directions: Complete the following series by choosing the best from among the alternative given below each question:

42. NMO, RQS, VUW, ZYA?
(a) DCE (b) BCD
(c) ECD (d) FCD.

43. A told B that C is his father's nephew. D is A's cousin but not the brother of C. What relationship is there between D and C?
(a) Father (b) Sister
(c) Mother (d) Aunt.

44. If ANOTHER is coded as 7309521, then THORN will be coded as
(a) 95103 (b) 95313
(c) 95013 (d) 95113.

45. If 5 × 8 = 28, 3 × 7 = 12, 8 × 6 = 35 then find the value of 13 × 13?
(a) 169 (b) 130
(c) 140 (d) 144.

46. Teachers use aids to make learning
(a) simple (b) easy
(c) take less time (d) interesting.

47. Effecting teaching, by and large, is a function of
(a) teachers scholarship.
(b) teachers honesty.
(c) teachers making students learn and understand.
(d) teachers liking for the job of teaching.

48. A teacher is expected to do all except
(a) participation in community activities.
(b) help pupils to solve their problems.
(c) taking interests in politics.
(d) sponsor clubs and other school affairs.
(e) keeping students records.

49. A researchers wants to study the future of the BSP in India. For the study which tool is most appropriate for him?
(a) Questionnaire (b) Schedule
(c) Interview (d) Rating scale.

50. A teacher is the leader both de Jure and de Facto. He is the authority before the students and so it is his right to lead. While assuming leadership of the students, he would follow some important principles.
(a) Preparation and planning
(b) Creating right atmosphere in the class
(c) Providing opportunities
(d) All of the above.

ANSWERS

1. (a)	2. (b)	3. (d)	4. (c)
5. (a)	6. (d)	7. (d)	8. (b)
9. (b)	10. (c)	11. (a)	12. (b)
13. (a)	14. (c)	15. (c)	16. (b)
17. (d)	18. (a)	19. (d)	20. (c)
21. (a)	22. (b)	23. (a)	24. (a)

25. (d)	26. (b)	27. (c)	28. (a)
29. (c)	30. (d)	31. (d)	32. (a)
33. (d)	34. (a)	35. (b)	36. (b)
37. (c)	38. (c)	39. (a)	40. (b)
41. (c)	42. (a)	43. (b)	44. (c)
45. (d)	46. (d)	47. (c)	48. (c)
49. (a)	50. (d)		

EXPLANATION

15. Number of possible rolled outcomes
$= 1^2 + 2^2 + 3^2 + 4^2 + 5^2 + 6^2$
$= 1 + 4 + 9 + 16 + 25 + 36 = 91$

16. Maximum number of different ways can be done $= 5 \times 4 \times 3 \times 2 \times 1 = 120$

23. Trick

$$\frac{x}{40} - \frac{x}{60} = \frac{3x - 2x}{120} = \frac{x}{120}$$

or, $\frac{x}{120}$ by $\frac{x}{40}$

$$= \frac{x}{120} \times \frac{40}{x} = \frac{1}{3} \text{hour}$$

$$== \frac{1}{3} \times 60 = 20 \text{ minutes per hour}$$

24. The average salary of 100 employees = Rs. 16, 000

$\therefore$ The total salary of 100 employees
$= 100 \times 16{,}000 =$ Rs. 16,00,000

After raise of 5% salary of 100 employees, total salary

$$= \frac{105}{100} \times 16{,}00{,}000 = \text{Rs. } 16{,}80{,}000$$

Total allowance stopped to 100 employees
$= 100 \times 800 =$ Rs. 80,000

$\therefore$ Now, total salary of 100 employees
= Rs. 16,80,000 – Rs. 80,000
= Rs. 16,00,000

$\therefore$ Now, average salary of 100 employees

$$= \text{Rs.} \frac{16{,}00{,}000}{10} = \text{Rs.} 16{,}000$$

25. The least possible number of bottles required for positives of petrol, 465 litres of diesel and 456 litres of Mobil Oil
= H.C.F. of 403, 465 and 496
= 403 | 465 | 1
403
×62 | 403 | 6
372
×31 | 62 | 2
62
× ×
31 | 496 | 16
496
× × ×
= 31

40. $(12.5 \times 1200) / 100 = 150$ men
$(15 \times 800) / 100 = 120$ women
Difference $= 150 - 120 = 30$

41. At the birth time of Anant, age of his mother = 20 years
At the time of marriage, age of his mother $= 20 - 2 = 18$ years
$\therefore$ At the time of marriage, age of Anant father $= 18 + 5 = 23$ years
Marriage of the father $= 35 - 2 - 10 = 23$

42. Every next term in the series starts with a gap of one letter along with some change in the sequence of letters such as, NMO, is For MNO, RQS, is For QRS and So on.

43. A has two cousins C and D. Since C is male so D must be Female (According to the data) and both are the nephew and niece of A's Father.

44. The letters are coded by numbers not to find the answer select the respective number i.e.,

A N O T H E R	→	letters
7 3 0 9 5 2 1	→	code
so T H O R N	→	letters
9 5 0 1 3	→	code

45. (5 – 1) (8 – 1) = 28
(3 – 1) (7 – 1) = 12
(8 – 1) (6 – 1) = 35
Then (13 – 1) (13 – 1) = 144

DECEMBER 2006

1. The most important factor in teaching in higher education is to
   (a) lead students to the sources of information.
   (b) develop a spirit of competition for higher achievement in students.
   (c) supply the relevant information to students.
   (d) prepare students for the various competitive examinations.
2. The main problem for determining educational policy in India is that
   (a) people of higher technical education have unemployment.
   (b) people with higher technical education do not find enough opportunity in India.
   (c) people having higher technical education do not have employment opportunities at all.
   (d) All of the above.
3. In which year did U.G.C. become an autonomous body?
   (a) 1948 (b) 1988
   (c) 1964 (d) 1956.
4. Under which article was the All India Council of Elementary Education established?
   (a) 25th (b) 60th
   (c) 45th (d) 42nd.
5. Plato's theory of educational programme includes
   (a) education for life and not as a preparation for life.
   (b) only fit and elimination of unit.
   (c) denial of validity of mental discipline.
   (d) Plato's science for workers and dialectic for rules.
6. In which year was ISRO (Indian Space Research Organisation) established?
   (a) 1980 (b) 1970
   (c) 1975 (d) 1969.
7. If the greenhouse effect becomes real and melts Polar ice, which one of the following regions will first disappear under water?
   (a) Islands of Kiribati
   (b) Mauritius
   (c) Maldives
   (d) Hawai island.
8. Which pollutant gas is released by cudchewing cattles?
   (a) CO (b) CH_4
   (c) NO_2 (d) CO_2.
9. For maintaining order, insertions in a lexical ordered binary tree can only be performed at
   (a) a leaf level
   (b) a root node
   (c) an intermediate level
   (d) None of the above.
10. Which one of the following in not an input specification for a Batch System?
   (a) Input Record Layout
   (b) Prototype report

(c) Expanded Data Dictionary
(d) Source Document Layout.

11. A structured data type made up of finite collections of ordered elements all of which are of the same date types is a
(a) File (b) Array
(c) Record (d) None of the above

12. A type communication which is becoming very important in transmission of data between computer network is known as
(a) bank networking
(b) communication network
(c) satellite area networking
(d) internal working

13. Eratosthenes measured the size of earth by measuring shadows of bodies in the sun in two cities which were those two cities?
(a) Syracuse and Cairo
(b) Alexandria and Syracuse
(c) Alexandria and Baghdad
(d) Alexandria and Syria.

14. Sometimes secondary pollutants like ozone PAN (proxy acyl nitrate) NHO_3 H_2 SO_4 formed from primary pollutants are more toxic than primary pollutants. This phenomenon of increased toxicity in pollutants is called
(a) Synergism
(b) Greenhouse effect
(c) Eutrophication
(d) Biomagnifications

15. Acid rain is caused by sulphur oxides, nitrogen oxides and hydrochloric acid which are produced by industries, automobiles and thermal power plants using Fossil Fuels. It causes
(a) death of fish due to clogging of their gills by exudation of large amount of mucus caused by solubility and availability for toxic metals like aluminium.
(b) defoliation chlorosis, necrosis of plant foliage.
(c) leaching of mineral salts in soil and decolourisation of red stone of Redfort.
(d) All of the above.

16. Maximum threat to the world is from
(a) water Pollution
(b) soil erosion
(c) ozone hole
(d) global warming

Directions: Study the following table carefully and answer the questions (17-18) give below it.

Number of toys in five types. Manufactured by a company over the years (in 1000).

	Toys				
Years	A	B	C	D	E
2001	200	150	78	90	65
2002	150	18	100	105	70
2003	180	175	92	110	85
2004	195	160	120	125	75
2005	220	185	130	135	80

17. What was the percentage drop on production of A type toys from 2001 to 2003?
(a) 30 (b) 50
(c) 20 (d) 10.

18. What was the percentage (approximate) increase in production of D type toys from 2002 to 2004?
(a) 10 (b) 15
(c) 20 (d) 25.

19. If ABCD is right-angled at A and angle C is 40 and D is the mid-point of BC, then what is angle BDA?

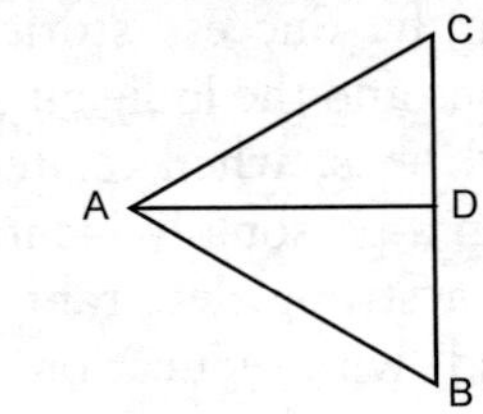

(a) 40º (b) 80º
(c) 90º (d) 50º.

Directions (Question-20): Study the graph and answer the question given below it. The graph represents the temperature of two towns during a week.

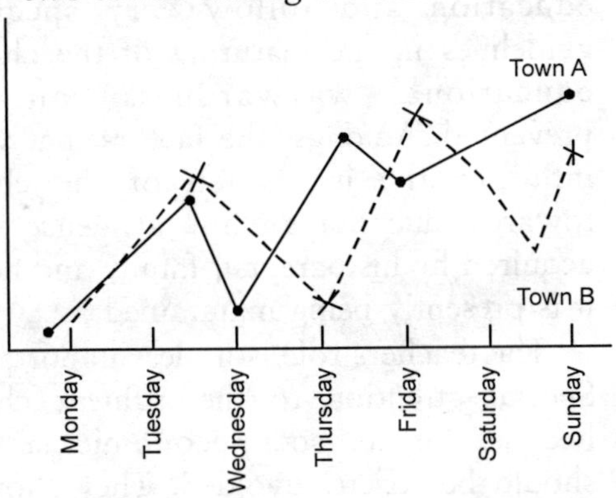

20. In which town is the fluctuation in temperature the highest and between which days?
(a) B-Monday and Tuesday
(b) A-Wednesday and Thursday
(c) B-Thursday and Friday
(d) A-Thursday and Tuesday.

21. The average income of a group of 50 persons working in a factory is calculated to be Rs. 169. It was later discovered that one of the figures was taken to be 134 instead of the correct value 144. The corrected average income will be
(a) 168 (b) 169.50
(c) 170 (d) 169.75.

22. In the following question some number are given which form a series of numbers. Select a number from the given alternatives to continue the series of numbers:
2, 5, 10, 17, 26, 37, ...
(a) 49 (b) 48
(c) 50 (d) 51.

23. In the following question choose one number which is similar to the numbers in the given set 5418, 7320, 4926.
(a) 5490 (b) 3616
(c) 7963 (d) 6216.

24. In this question four groups of letters are given, these of them are alike in a certain way which one is different.
Choose the odd one.
(a) HSIRJ (b) FTGSH
(c) DWEVF (d) ASBYC.

Directions (Question 25)
(i) A, B, C, D, E and F are six members of a family.
(ii) One couple has parents and their children in the family.
(iii) A is the son of C and E is the daughter of A.
(iv) D is the daughter of F who is the mother of E.

25. Which of the following pairs is the parents of the children?
(a) BC (b) CF
(c) BF
(d) Can't be determined
(e) None of the above.

26. Who believes that mass media are primarily moulders of society as well as reflections of it?
(a) George Gerbner
(b) Harold Lasswell
(c) Denis Mcquail
(d) Wilbur Schraman.

27. Which of the following will not hamper effective communication in the class?
    (a) A lengthy statement
    (b) An ambiguous statement
    (c) A precise statement
    (d) A statement which allows the listener to draw his own conclusion.
28. When and where the Mumbai and Kolkata stations inaugurated by the India Broadcasting Company?
    (a) 1927 (b) 1925
    (c) 1928 (d) 1926.
29. Which of the following do not provide entertainment to the targeted audience?
    (a) TV Programes
    (b) Magazines
    (c) Leaflets
    (d) Newspaper features.
30. Independent variable and dependent variable are variables of which method available to communications research?
    (a) Historical Method
    (b) Experimental Method
    (c) Survey Method
    (d) Content Analysis Method.
31. In a certain code MENTION is written as LNEITNO. In the same way how is a PATTERN coded?
    (a) APTTREM (b) PTAETNR
    (c) OTAETNR (d) OTAETRN.

Direction (32-33): Read the passage carefully and choose the best answer for each question.

Children attitudes and behavior patterns are determined primarily from home. If the child develops a hostile attitude towards the parent, then these will be generally protected on to the teachers, the school and, finally, to its inability to profit from education. Parental attitudes towards subjects often influence children's interest in them. Their attitudes towards teachers education influence children significantly. Success stories of uneducated persons and the indigent state of some educated ones, when related to them, especially in a personally identified scenario, will be a strong deterrant to a desire to proceed with education. No matter what the economic stature of the family, the primary factor that will influence the motivational level of the affluent child is the values held by the principal persons in the child's life and it's peers. If the principal persons hold a positive view with respect to the need for education and follow very specific guidelines in the maturing of the child, educational waywardness can be prevented. Amongst the factors that will influence the inclination of the child towards education are how affluence was acquired by his parents / family and how it is presently being maintained.

The teachers role is no less important. Special attention to the affluent child because of its socio-economic status should be strictly avoided. They should motivate the child towards very strong interest in one or more areas of learning. The increased prestige of being a specialist" in the field is a powerful motivator and contributes greatly to self esteem. The pursuits of very deep interests, indicates in the earlier years of education will promote self actualization, the highest level in the hierarchy of human needs.

32. This passage tries to explain that
    (a) the affluent child needs no external motivation.
    (b) the education of the affluent child is not a problem for parents and teachers.

(c) that affluent child will be much influenced by the values held by the important people in his life and his friends.
(d) the parent and teachers together should impart values to the affluent child.

33. From the passage, we can rightly come to the conclusion that
(a) the affluent child cannot be mended in this changing world of complexities.
(b) educational waywardness of the affluent child can be prevented.
(c) children should always be let free discover their own values in life.
(d) the teacher should be aware of the socio-economic standard of the child to hold up values in life.

34. In developing the personality of the affluent child, which of the following factors is most important?
(a) Motivation in more areas of learning.
(b) The teacher-pupil relationship.
(c) Training in the values in life.
(d) Understanding the socio-economic status of the child.

35. A certain amount of money amount to Rs. 720 in 2 years and to Rs. 870 in $4\frac{1}{2}$ years. Find the principal and rate of interest if simple interest is reckoned.
(a) Rs. 500 and 20%
(b) Rs. 600 and 12.5%
(c) Rs. 500 and 15%
(d) Rs. 600 and 10%.

36. A merchant professes to sell rice at the cost price, but uses false weight. He gains 30% in this manner. What weight does he substitute for one kilogram?
(a) 645 1/13 g (b) 750 g
(c) 7693/13 g (d) 800 g.

37. An acrobat climbs a rope stretched from a point 120 metres above the ground to a point on the ground. The angle made by the rope with the ground is 60. Calculate the length of the rope.
(a) 140 m (b) 80 $\sqrt{3}$
(c) 175 m (d) 120 $\sqrt{3}$ m.

Direction (Question 38-39). Read the passage carefully and choose the correct answer for each question.

At 7 a.m. M.S. Ahuja started from his home on his bicycle at a speed of 20 kms per hour. He went two kms west then turned and left and went one km; then he again turned left and covered one km. Unfortunately, his bicycles got punctured so he turned right and had to walk one km at a speed of 5 kms per hour. He got his bicycle repaired which took 5 minutes. Then he turned left and after going for 1 km reached the swimming pool.

38. How far is the swimming pool from M.S. Ahuja's house as the crow flies?
(a) 1 km (b) 2 kms
(c) 3 kms (d) 4 kms.

39. At what time did Ahuja reach the swimming pool?
(a) 7.48 a.m. (b) 7.32 a.m.
(c) 7.42 a.m. (d) 7.38 a.m.

Directions: Certain terms are given below in each question. All are similar in nature except one which is different, pick out the odd one.

40. College, and principle Navy and commander, industry and Director, playground and player, post office and post master.
(a) College and principal
(b) Navy and commander
(c) Playground and player
(d) None of the above.

41. If all the sides of a triangle be increased by 200 percent. What is the corresponding increase in it area?
    (a) 300% (b) 400%
    (c) 600% (d) 800%.
42. The validity and reliability of a research will be at stake when
    (a) the incident was reported after a long period of time from that of its occurrence.
    (b) the author who is the source of information is biased, incompetent or dishonest.
    (c) the researcher himself is not competent enough to draw logical conclusions.
    (d) All of the above.
43. A researcher wants to study the future of the NDA in India. For the study, which too is most appropriate for him?
    (a) Questionnaire (b) Rating scale
    (c) Interview (d) Schedule.
44. There is a debate as to whether teaching is a true profession or not. The most critical factor needed to make teaching a true profession is
    (a) discipline of its own members.
    (b) a longer period of training.
    (c) better spirits among teachers.
    (d) All of the above.
45. If the sample drawn does not specify any condition about the parameter of the population, it is called
    (a) selected statistics
    (b) distribution free statistics
    (c) census
    (d) None of the above.
46. Which of the following is not among the learned motives?
    (a) Reflexes (b) Attitudes
    (c) Habits (d) Interests.
47. Which one of the following statements is correct?
    (a) The teacher should teach well and do nothing else.
    (b) The teachers should teach and do research also.
    (c) The teacher should teach and do research but should concentrate more on research than on teaching.
    (d) The teacher should teach and do research but should concentrate more on research than on teaching.
48. I will appreciate the teacher who
    (a) has strict control over his statements.
    (b) knows the problems of students and helps them.
    (c) is friendly with the students.
    (d) has a charming personality.
49. A good teacher should have
    (a) communication skills
    (b) interpersonal skills
    (c) conceptual clarity
    (d) All of the above.
50. An effective teacher must be
    (a) participative and resourceful
    (b) resourceful and autocratic
    (c) authoritative and resourceful
    (d) resourceful and dominant.

ANSWERS

1. (a)	2. (b)	3. (d)	4. (b)
5. (d)	6. (d)	7. (a)	8. (b)
9. (a)	10. (c)	11. (b)	12. (d)
13. (b)	14. (a)	15. (d)	16. (c)
17. (d)	18. (b)	19. (b)	20. (a)
21. (b)	22. (c)	23. (d)	24. (b)
25. (e)	26. (c)	27. (d)	28. (a)
29. (c)	30. (b)	31. (c)	32. (c)
33. (b)	34. (c)	35. (d)	36. (c)

37. (b) 38. (b) 39. (b) 40. (c)
41. (d) 42. (d) 43. (a) 44. (d)
45. (b) 46. (a) 47. (b) 48. (c)
49. (d) 50. (a)

EXPLANATION

19. It is known that AD = BD = CD. Since the triangle is right angled at A.
Angle ADB = Angles (CAD + ACD)
= 40° + 40° = 80°

20. It is clear from the table that the fluctuation in temperature is the highest between Monday and Tuesday for town B.

21. Total income (First) = 169 × 50= Rs. 8450
Correct total income 8450 + 10 = 8460
Therefore average income = 8460.50
= Rs. 169.50.

22. There is increase by two for the next number from the earlier number 3, 5, 7, 9, 11. Now 37 will increase by 13 i.e. 37 + 13 = 50 is the next number of the series.

23. In each number of a given set, the last two digit number is double the sum of the digits of the first two digit number e.g. in 5418 → 18 = 2 × (5 + 4); 7320 → 20 = 2 × (7 + 3) etc. Thus in 6216, 16 = 2 × (6 + 2).

24. In all other groups. First letter occupies the same position from the beginning and the second second letter occupies from the end.

25. A and F are the parents of the children D and E.

31. The first letter is moved one step backward and the remaining letters are reversed in pairs. Thus, in the same way, the word PATTERN is coded as OTAETNR.

35. 1. Principle + Simple interest for $4\frac{1}{2}$ years = Rs. 870
2. Principle + Simple interest for 2 years = Rs. 720
(1) – (2) gives

Simple interest for $2\frac{1}{2}$ yrs
= Rs. 150
Simple interest for 1 year
= Rs. 150 × 215 = Rs. 60
Simple interest for 2 years = Rs. 120
From (2), we have,
Principal = Rs. 720 – Rs. 120 = Rs. 600
Rate of interest = [Simple interest/ (Principal × no. of years)] × 100
120/600 × 2 × 100 × = 10%.

36. Let Rs. 1 be the cost price of 1 g of rice. In order to gain profit, the merchant uses a false weight which is, say x g less in a kilogram. i.e. instead of 1000 g of rice, he gives only (1000 – x) g of rice.
That means, the price of x g of rice is the profit earned by the merchant.
x/1000 – x = 30/100
100x = 30000 – 3x
130x = 30000
x = 230 10/13 g
The merchant substitutes 769 3/13 g instead of 1000 g.

37. Let PR be the rope and PQ be the pole. In Δ PQR,

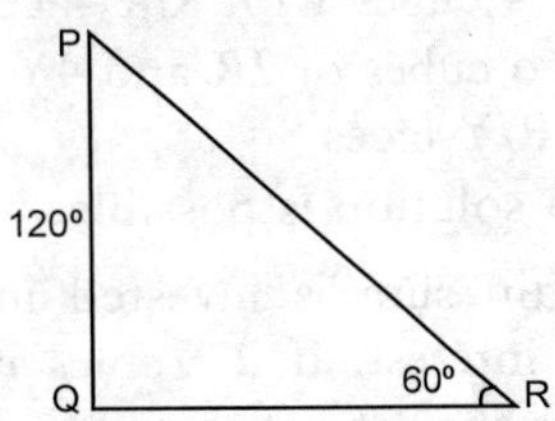

PQ/PR = Sin 60

120/PR = $\sqrt{3/2}$

PR = 120 × 21 √3

= 240 × $\sqrt{3/3}$ = 80 √3 M

Length of the rope = 80 √3 m.

JUNE 2006

1. ABCD is a pattern made up of four one inch cubes with the combinations of red (R) and yellow (y) colours. You are given eight one inch cubes, with four cubes having two opposite faces coloured red and the remaining four cubes coloured yellow. The remaining four cubes have all the six faces divided diagonally into red and yellow triangles. What colour combinations of cubes would be your choice to complete the pattern correctly?

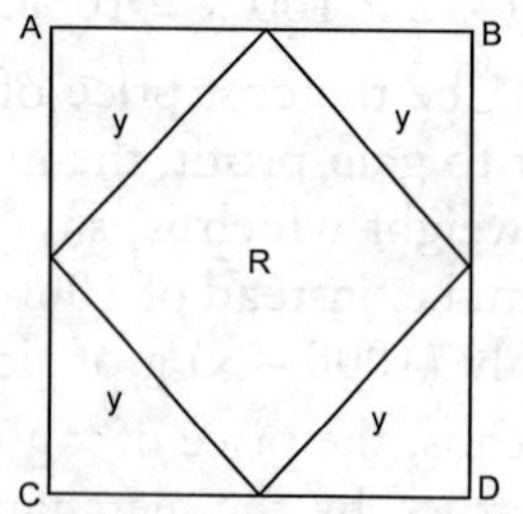

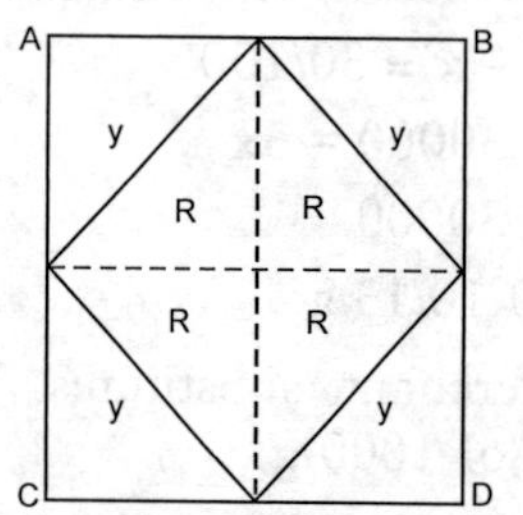

(a) All 4 cubes with 2R and 4 Y faces
(b) All 4 cubes with R/Y faces
(c) Two cubes of 2R and 4Y faces and 2 of R/Y faces
(d) No solution is possible.

2. A certain sum is invested in stocks on simple interest. If it trebles in 10 years. What is the rate of interest?

(a) 18 (b) 20
(c) 22 (d) 25.

3. While travelling in a train, a passenger decided to dry his wet handkerchief by extending it out of the window of his compartment. He thinks that the handkerchief will fly in the same direction in which the train is beading.

(a) The traveller's comprehension is correct.
(b) The traveller's comprehension is only partially correct.
(c) The travelers comprehension is totally incorrect.
(d) Given information is not sufficient for any definite conclusion.

4. **Assertion (A):** Some old persons who live alone are not necessarily lonely or desolate.

Reason (R): Some persons nowadays do become isolated due to neglect by their oncoaring families.

(a) Both A and R are true but totally unrelated.
(b) Both A and R are true but R explains A only partially.
(c) Both A and R are true and R explains A completely.
(d) A is true but R is false.

5. Children of successful and well-to-do parents, often do not perform well in studies why?

(a) Because parents are unable to give enough time and attention to their children.
(b) Because the jobs of successful parents are very demanding in time and effort.
(c) Both (a) and (b) are correct.
(d) Both (a) and (b) are incorrect.

6. A printing company made a mistake in printing calendar dates. Instead of getting printed in sequential order the dates got printed in the reverse order, (as shown in the part of the calendar). If the 30th fall

on a Sunday, on which day will the 2nd fall?

Mon	Tue	Wed	Thu	Fri	Sat	Sun
						30
29	28	27	26	25	24	23
22	21	20	19	18	17	16

(a) Monday (b) Wednesday
(c) Friday (d) Sunday.

7. A red light is fitted on top of a 100 ft high vertical mast located 400 ft to the south-west of the observer at point O. A green light is fitted on top of a 50th high vertical mast located 300 ft to the north west of the observer at point O. What is the distance in feet between?
   (a) The two masts
   (b) The two lights

   A. (a) 450 (b) 500
   (c) 475 (d) None of the above.

   B. (a) 500 (b) 503
   (c) 505 (d) None of the above.

8. A shop gives 10% discount on the purchase of any item. If paid for in cash immediately, a further discount of 12% is given. If the original price of the item is Rs. 250, what is the price of the article if a cash purchase if a cash purchase is made?
   (a) Rs. 200 (b) Rs. 195
   (c) Rs. 198 (d) Rs. 190.

9. A tired research scientist went to bed at 10 o'clock one night after setting his alarm clock one night for noon the following day. When the alarm woke him up, how many hours had he slept?
   (a) 14 (b) 12
   (c) 11 (d) 2.

10. In the figure EF is parallel to BC, FG is parallel to AB, AE is equal to FG = 4, EF = 3, what is BC?

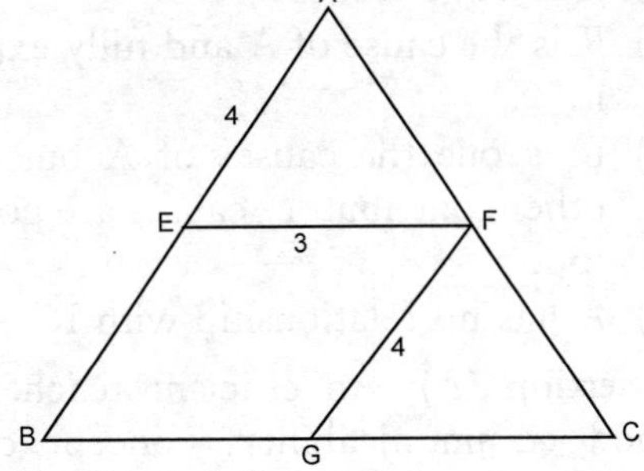

   (a) 7 (b) 6
   (c) 8 (d) 9.

11. Spot the posture that does not belong to the group.
    (a) Sagging shoulders
    (b) Bent head
    (c) Well-planted feet
    (d) Curved spine.

12. **Assertion (A):** 'Hallucinogens' are those intoxicating drugs which cause the image of a stimulus to be seen even in the absence of an actual stimulus.

    Reason (R): 'Hallucinogens' are 'mindaltering drugs' bringing about auto stimulation in the brain.

    Assess the true relationship between A and R:
    (a) A causes R
    (b) R is true cause of A and fully explains it
    (c) R follows from A
    (d) R is the cause of A but does not fully explain it.

13. **Assertion (A):** Some children in today's world are concerned about their uncertain future.

    Reason (R): Implementation of 'Total Nuclear Disarmament Agreement' between super powers is being delayed.

    Judge which of the following is the correct relationship between A and R?

(a) R follows from A.
(b) R is the cause of A and fully explains it.
(c) R is one the causes of A but many other contributory causes are possible too.
(d) A has no relationship with R.

14. **Assertion (A):** An efficient teacher has good communicability, concept clarity and easy approachability.

Reason (R): A teachers task in the classroom is not only to deliver the lecture but also to ensure that it is grasped, understood and absorbed fully by the students.

Decide which of the following explanations gives the true relationship between A and R?

(a) A is explained fully by R
(b) R and A are totally unrelated
(c) R does not explain A at all
(d) R and A are different aspect of two different fields of life altogether.

15. **Assertion (A):** There is a greater chance of solving a problem by insight if every, aspect of the problem has been carefully looked into.

Reason (R): When attention is focused on only one aspect of the problem, correct solution cannot be arrived at.

(a) R explains A fully
(b) R explains A partially
(c) R does not explain A at all
(d) R and A have no connection with each other.

Note: Answer of 16 to 20 is in the explanation form. So no substitute is given in the Booklet.

Direction (Questions 16-20). Read the following passage and answer in your own words. "The world we live in presents an endless variety of fascinating problems which excite our wonder and curiosity. The scientific worker attempts to formulate these problems in accurative terms and to solve them in the light of all the relevant facts that can be collected by observation and experiment such questions as 'what'; 'how'; 'where' and 'when' challenge him to find the clues that may suggest possible replies. Confronted by the many problems presented by, but us say, an active volcano, we may ask: 'what are the laves make of'? How does the volcano work and how is the heat generated? Where do the lavas and gases come from? When did the volcano first begin to erupt and when is it likely to erupt again?

In terms of chemical compounds and elements, the question 'How' refers to processes the way things are made or happen or change. The ancients regarded natural processes as manifestations of energy acting on or through matter. Volcanic eruptions and earthquake no longer reflects the errectic behavior of the gods of the underworld: They arise from the action of the earth's internal heat on and through the surrounding crust. The source of the energy lies in the material of inner earth in many directions. Of course, our knowledge is still incomplete; only the first of the questions we have asked about volcanoes. For example, can as yet be satisfactorily answered. The point is not that we now pretend to understand every thing but that we have faith in the orderliness of natural processes. As a result of two or there centuries of scientific investigation, we have come to believe that nature is understandable in the sense that when we ask questions by way of appropriate observations and experiments, she will answer truly and reward as with discoveries that endure.

16. How does the author describes the task of the scientific worker?

    Ans. The author describes the task of the scientific worker as challenging and very difficult.

17. Why does the author speak about volcanoes?

    Ans. The author speaks about the volcanoes specially active volcanoes which are under the process of operation.

18. What does the question 'How' refers to?

    Ans. The question how refers to processes the way things are made or happen one change.

19. How did the ancients look upon volcanoes and earthquakes?

    Ans. The ancient looked upon volcanoes and earthquakes as the consequence of material processes which are due to the manifestations of energy acting on or through matter.

20. What does the author say about our knowledge of the world?

    Ans. The author says about our knowledge of the world that it is still incomplete.

Directions: The circle graph, drawn here shows the spending of a country on various sports during a particular year. Study the graph and answers the question No. 21 & 22.

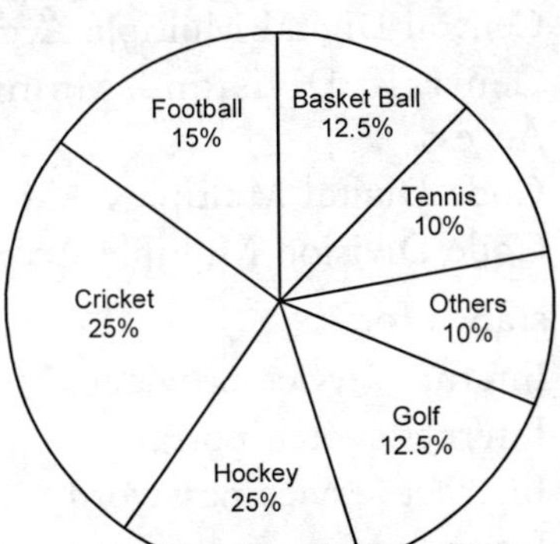

21. The ratio of the total amount spent on football to that spent on hockey is

    (a) 1 : 15 (b) 1 : 1
    (c) 15 : 1 (d) 3 : 20.

22. If the total amount spent on sports during the year was Rs. 1, 20,000,00 how much was spent on basketball?

    (a) Rs. 9,50,000 (b) Rs. 10,00,000
    (c) Rs. 12,00,000 (d) Rs. 15,00,000.

Direction: Study the table and answer the questions 23-25. The following table gives the details of sales for the text books and reference books at primary/secondary/higher secondary/graduate levels.

Year	Primary	Secondary	Higher Secondary	Graduate level
2000	42137	8820	65303	25343
2001	53568	10285	71602	27930
2002	58770	16437	73667	28687
2003	56872	15475	71668	30057
2004	66213	17500	78697	33682
2005	68718	20177	82175	36697

23. What is the growth rate of sales of books at primary school level from 2000 to 2005?

    (a) 29% (b) 51%
    (c) 63% (d) 163%.

24. Which of the categories shows the lowest growth rate from 2000 to 2005?

    (a) Primary
    (b) Secondary
    (c) Higher secondary
    (d) Graduate level.

25. Which categories had the highest growth rate in the period?

    (a) Primary
    (b) Secondary
    (c) Higher secondary
    (d) Graduate level.

26. To whom can you say the ideal teacher?
    (a) The one who is perfect in his teaching the subject.
    (b) The one who is sweet tongued but average in teaching .
    (c) The one who is interested more in general affairs of his college than in teaching work.
    (d) The one who is academically superior, morally the best and produces enlightened students.
27. Which type of question-paper in the following cane valuate students exactly?
    (a) Objective type of question
    (b) Essay type of question
    (c) Short answer type of question
    (d) The mixture of all the above.
28. The problems of which level in education are the most important according to you?
    (a) Of primary level
    (b) Of higher secondary level
    (c) Of higher education
    (d) Of technical education.
29. If two student of your class have quarreled violently and are going to divide the class into two groups what will you do?
    (a) You will not bother at all.
    (b) You will scold the one and favour the other.
    (c) You will suspend your teaching unless they come to terms.
    (d) You will call them, listen to them and pacify them by telling the harms of such conflict.
30. There is likelihood of schools being affected by social ills these days what is your attitudes toward off the ills from your school?
    (a) Pessimistic
    (b) Optimistic
    (c) No concern
    (d) Like other teacher.
31. Which of the following is an education channel jointly run by DD and Indira Gandhi National Open University?
    (a) Animal planet
    (b) Discovery travel & living
    (c) National geographic
    (d) Gyandarshan.
32. What is yellow Journalism?
    (a) News so old that readers are not interested in it.
    (b) Stories that one interesting but less important then hand news, focusing on people as well as facts, include interviews, reviews, articles etc.
    (c) The use of cheaply senstational or unscrupulous methods in newspapers to attract and influence readers.
    (d) None of the above.
33. To which group does Radio Mirchi FM 98.3 belong?
    (a) TV Today Group
    (b) The Times of Indian Group
    (c) The Hindu Group
    (d) Akanksha Publication Group.
34. An advertisement that looks like an article or features is a ....
    (a) advertorial (b) billboard
    (c) display Ad (d) campaign
35. Choose the right expansion for the abbreviation CDMA.
    (a) Central Digital Multiple Access
    (b) Central Division Maintenance Access
    (c) Code Digital Multiplex Aid
    (d) Code Division Multiple Access.
36. ISP stands for
    (a) Internet service provider
    (b) Internet switch portal
    (c) Internet service password
    (d) Internet service plug-in

37. What does DTH stand for?
   (a) Direct to Home
   (b) Delhi Television House
   (c) Documentary Trial Headquarter
   (d) None of the above.
38. HTML is an abbreviation for ....
   (a) Higher Text Mixed Language
   (b) Hyper Terminal Media Link
   (c) Hyper Text Markup Language
   (d) None of the above.
39. A publication that is half the size of the standard newspaper page, is flashy as well as heavily illustrated is called a........
   (a) Tabloid (b) Broadsheet
   (c) Leaflet (d) Brochure
40. A person whose is to re-do stories and write original copies for reporters who send information by telephone..........
   (a) Proofreader (b) Cub
   (c) Reporter (d) Rewriter man.
41. A statistical measure based upon the entire population is called parameter which measure based upon a sample is known as
   (a) Sample parameter
   (b) Inference
   (c) Statistic
   (d) None of the above.
42. A researcher wants to study the future of the BJP in India. For the study which tool is most appropriate for him?
   (a) Questionnaire (b) Schedule
   (c) Interview (d) Rating scale.
43. Atmospheric radioactive window permits thermal radiation of which wavelength to leave the earth?
   (a) 4.3 to 9.3 um (b) 9.5 to 10.6 um
   (c) 7 to 12 um (d) 7.3 to 10 um.
44. General circulation models (GCMs) are use to
   (a) predict climate
   (b) predict cyclones
   (c) study ocean currents
   (d) study effect of temperature on wind.
45. Why recycled plastics one banned for use in keeping met foods?
   (a) They contain chlorine compounds.
   (b) Additives and colouring agents are used in recycled plastics.
   (c) Plastics get degraded into harmful compounds during recycling.
   (d) This use will promote the use to plastics in daily life.
46. In which year Shanti Niketan was converted into Vishva Bharti?
   (a) 1905 (b) 1951
   (c) 1914 (d) 1947.
47. Which of the following commission is called university education commission?
   (a) Mudalior Commission
   (b) Hartogue Committee
   (c) Radha Krishnan Commission
   (d) None of the above.
48. Which among the following are the right measures to solve the obstacles in relation to women education?
   (a) To encourage and motivate people.
   (b) To solve economic problems for the people.
   (c) To increase girl school.
   (d) All of the above.
49. Communication will be effective if it is
   (a) delivered slowly and clearly.
   (b) delivered using appropriate media.
   (c) received as intended by the sender.
   (d) received immediately.
50. The promoter of a product cannot deliver the following to a mass audience currently used media vehicles.
   (a) Information
   (b) Music

(c) Products
(d) He can deliver literally anything through such vehicles.

ANSWERS

1. (b)	2. (b)	3. (c)	4. (b)
5. (c)	6. (d)	7. (b), (d)	8. (c)
9. (d)	10. (b)	11. (c)	12. (b)
13. (c)	14. (a)	15. (a)	16. (*)
17. (*)	18. (*)	19. (*)	20. (*)
21. (b)	22. (d)	23. (c)	24. (c)
25. (b)	26. (d)	27. (d)	28. (a)
29. (d)	30. (b)	31. (d)	32. (c)
33. (b)	34. (a)	35. (d)	36. (a)
37. (a)	38. (c)	39. (a)	40. (d)
41. (c)	42. (a)	43. (c)	44. (a)
45. (b)	46. (b)	47. (c)	48. (d)
49. (d)	50. (c)		

* Answers are given on page 79.

EXPLANATION

1. Alternative (b) is the correct answer. The clue for the answer is given in the question, as pattern can be made with 4 cubes. In order to divide the pattern into four equal parts, draw mental lines from the midpoints of AB, and CD and join them similarly, join straight line. The resulting figure is as given.
2. (b) is the correct choice. If the sum invested is Rs. 100, it trebles in 10 years, so the interest due to 10 yrs is equal to Rs. 300-Rs. 100 = Rs. 200. Thus the interest due on Rs. 100 in 10 yrs = Rs. 200 so that interest on Rs. 100 in 1yr = Rs. 20. Rate of simple interest = 20%.
3. Alternative (c) is correct i.e. the traveller's comprehension is incorrect. The handkerchief will fly in the opposite direction in which the train is heading.
4. (b) is the correct answer because R is neither related to A, nor totally explains A, nor is R false. This leaves us with R explains A partially. If we try to relate A and R in a logical manner we may say that due to the reason of being isolated by their families, such old persons feel lonely or desolate. But this is not so. The assertion only states that some old persons do not necessarily feel lonely but it does not state that they are not the ones who have also been isolated by their families. So R explains A partially.
6. If one looks carefully then it is opponent that in spite of the reverse order of re-emerging, each columns has the break up of number by seven less downwards. The least numbering is going to come, in the Sunday columns. So obviously, the numbers below 16 are 9 and 2 with a difference of 7 days in each number.
8. A 10% discount on Rs. 250 will be Rs. 25. A further discount of 12% is to be made on Rs. 250 minus Rs. 25 = Rs. 225. The discount is Rs. 27. The price paid will therefore be Rs. 225-Rs. 27 = Rs. 198.
9. The alarm goes off at midnight, thus the scientist sleeps for 2 hours.
10. Since EF is parallel to BC and FG is parallel to AB, hence BEFG is a parallelogram. So FG = BE and FG = AE (given). So AE = BE and E is midpoint of AB. Since EF is parallel to BC, F is the mid point of AC. So EF = ½ BC
    BC = 2 EF = 6.
11. This body posture shows determination and readiness for action whereas the other postures depict gloom and passivity.
13. Uncertainty about the future can be due to many causes, i.e. poverty, unemploy-

ment, poor health, parental indifference, natural calamities and men made calamities one such calamities may be nuclear war. Thus 'R' is only one of the causes of A.

15. R explains A fully because to reach a complete and meaningful solution by insight a total grasp over all aspects of the problem is essential.

Notes: Answer of 16 to 20 is in the explanation form so no substitute is given in the booklet.

21. Let the total amount spent be Rs. × Ratio of amount spent on football and of hockey

$$= \frac{15x}{100} = \frac{15x}{100} \Rightarrow 15:15 \Rightarrow 1:1.$$

23. Growth rate % at primary level from 2000 to 2005

$$= \left(\frac{68718 - 42137}{42137} \times 100\right) = 63.1.$$

24. Growth rate at primary level = 63% at secondary level

$$= \left(\frac{20177 - 8820}{8820} \times 100\right)\% = 128\%.$$

at higher secondary level =

$$= \left(\frac{82175 - 65303}{65303} \times 100\right)\% = 25.8\%$$

at graduate level =

$$= \left(\frac{36697 - 25343}{25343} \times 100\right)\% = 44.8\%.$$

DECEMBER 2005

1. The professional requirements of a teacher as explained in the UNESCO publication is/are
   (a) mastery over the subject and competency for teaching.
   (b) innovativeness in approach and teaching strategies.
   (c) justice to the profession.
   (d) All of the above.
2. Effective teaching means
   (a) love, cooperation, sympathy, affection and encouragement given to students.
   (b) corporal punishment given to students at the time of moral offences.
   (c) individualised instruction and open classroom discussion.
   (d) Both (a) and (c).
3. All of the following statements regarding a teacher are correct except that he is/he
   (a) a friend, guide and philosopher.
   (b) teachers what the students do not know.
   (c) the leader of the class.
   (d) changes his attitudes and behavior according to the need of the society.
4. Which of the following provides more freedom to the learner to interact?
   (a) Small group discussion
   (b) Use of film projector
   (c) Viewing countrywide classroom programme on TV
   (d) Lecture by experts.
5. Any effective communication system employs a feedback system in order to
   (a) make the necessary modifications in the process.
   (b) understand more about the content.
   (c) find faults with the sender (the teacher).
   (d) find faults with the receiver (the student).
6. The historical research is different from experimental research in the process of
   (a) replication
   (b) the formulation of the hypothesis

(c) the hypothesis testing
(d) All of the above.

7. The review of the related study is important while undertaking a research because
   (a) it avoids repetition or duplication.
   (b) it helps in understanding the gaps.
   (c) it helps the researcher not to draw illogical conclusions.
   (d) All of the above.
8. A researcher selects a probability sample of 100 out of the total population. It is
   (a) a cluster sample
   (b) a random sample
   (c) a stratified sample
   (d) a systematic sample
9. A researcher divides the populations into PG, graduates and 10 + 2 students and using the random digit table he selects some of them from each. This is technically called
   (a) stratified sampling
   (b) stratified random sampling
   (c) representative sampling
   (d) None of the above.
10. The final result of a study will be more accurate if the sample drawn is
    (a) taken randomly
    (b) fixed by quota
    (c) representative to the population
    (d) purposive

Direction for questions 11 to 12: Study the following passage carefully to answer the questions that follow the passage.

An expert group has sounded a timely warning on what 'environmentally destructive tourism 'will mean to national parks and wildlife sanctuaries and the objectives they are supposed to serve. Given the unique and rare wildlife the country has been endowed with, the rationale for using the resources for attracting tourists from abroad is unassailable. This necessarily postulates that the flora and the fauna should be protected and conserved. As a matter of fact, much of the government's interest in wildlife preservation has traffic on that account. Yet the risk of the revenue earning motivation overrunning the conservation imperatives is very real, the lure of the coveted foreign exchange that goes with this business only serving to enhancing it several folds. Even with the tourists inflow far below the potential, the pressure of visitors is said to have been already felt on the tiger reserves. With the government of India's declared intent to boost tourism quite justified for its own reasons, the need for eliminating the risk assumes a greater sense of urgency. The study team has noted that most of the 41 national parks and 165 wildlife sanctuaries surveyed are open to tourists. The less frequented among them may not require special attention immediately in this respect as much as the ones that are major tourists attraction do. These include the Sanjay Gandhi National Park in Maharashtra, Nandankanan in Orissa, and Bannerghatta in Karnataka. Over a year ago, the India Board for Wildlife expressed concern over the looming danger, and decided that the core areas of national parks and sanctuaries should be kept totally free from biotic disturbances, and the visitors "be permitted to view the wildlife only from areas marked out for the purpose". And now, the expert group has come up with the suggestion that a case by case evaluation be done of the 'capacity' as well as the 'limitations' of all the national parks and wildlife sanctuaries and based on such assessment an area-specific plan for tourists promotion within the safety norms be charted. That this is the most scientific way of doing about the job,. And that there is no time to lose can be readily conceded.

11. Biotic disturbances in the context means
   (a) attacks from other living things, animals etc.
   (b) the disturbances caused by the natives on seeing the strange foreigners.
   (c) the political disturbances causing the closedown of the parks.
   (d) disturbances caused by the wild animals on seeing the tourists.
12. By using the expression "environmentally destructive tourism", the author means
   (a) the preservation of the wild beasts.
   (b) destruction of the wildlife and sanctuaries.
   (c) destroying the attractive sources of wild animals and birds.
   (d) the maintenance of the flora and fauna of the country.
13. To implement the most scientific ways of tourism we should
   (a) get industries and talented persons trained in the field.
   (b) form a commission and plan out how to implement the suggestions.
   (c) send a group of scientists abroad to learn more about tourism.
   (d) spend as much finance as possible to better the suggestions made.
14. George takes 8 hours to copy a 50 page manuscript while Sonya can copy the same manuscript in 6 hours. How many hours would it take them to copy a 100 page manuscript, if they work together?
   (a) $6\frac{6}{7}$ (b) 9
   (c) $9\frac{5}{7}$ (d) 14.
15. If an "anglet" is defined as 1 per cent of 1 degree, then how many anglets are there in a circle?
   (a) 0.36 (b) 3.6
   (c) 360 (d) 36,000.
16. How many multiples of 3 are there among the integers 15 to 105 inclusive?
   (a) 30 (b) 31
   (c) 32 (d) 33.
17. Tom reads at an average rate of 30 pages per hour, while Jan reads at an average rate of 40 pages per hour. If Tom starts reading a novel at 4 : 30, and Jan begins reading an identical copy of the same book at 5: 20, at what time will they be reading the same page?
   (a) 9 : 30 (b) 9 : 00
   (c) 8 : 40 (d) 7 : 50.
18. The price of copper rose by 25 per cent and then fell by 20 per cent. The price after these changes was
   (a) 20 per cent greater than the original price.
   (b) 5 per cent greater than the original price.
   (c) the same as the original price.
   (d) 5 per cent less than the original price.

Directions for questions-19 to 21: Study the line graph below to answer these questions.

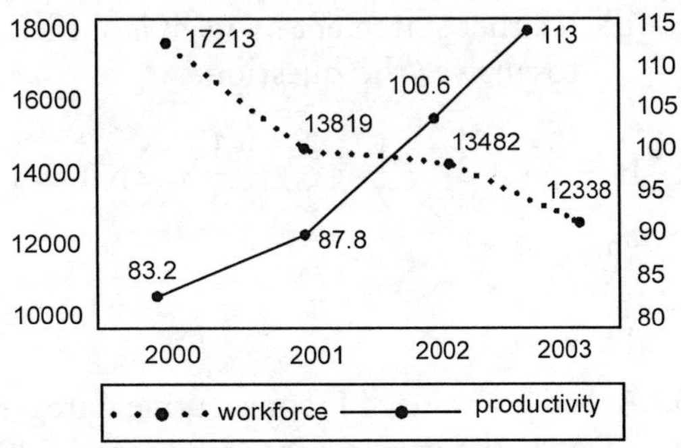

19. By how much percentage has production changed (approximately) in 2003 as compared to its value for 2000?
(a) –3% (b) +5%
(c) 0% (d) +7%.

20. The percentage change in which of the mentioned areas is the highest over the period 2000?
(a) Workforce (b) Productivity
(c) Production (d) Both A and C.

21. Which two variables have moved in the same direction in the mentioned period?
(a) Workforce and productivity
(b) Workforce and production
(c) Production and productivity
(d) None of the above.

Directions for questions 22 to 23. Each of these questions has a problem and two statements numbered I and II. Decide if the I information given in the statement is sufficient for answering the problem. Mark the answer as
(a) if statement I by itself sufficient to answer the question, but statement II by itself is not.
(b) if statement II by itself is sufficient to answer the question, but statement I by itself is not.
(c) if statement I and II taken together are sufficient to answer the question, even though neither statement by itself is sufficient.
(d) if either statement by itself is sufficient to answer the question.

22. If $-\frac{3}{4}x + 3y - \frac{1}{2} = \frac{3}{2}y - \frac{1}{4}x$, what is the value of x?
(a) $y^2 = 4$
(b) $y = 2$.

23. A list contains 11 consecutive integers. What is the greatest integer on the list?
(a) If x is the smallest integer on the list, then $(x + 72)^{1/3} = 4$.
(b) If x is the smallest integer on the list, then $1/64 = x^{-2}$.

Directions for questions 24 to 25. Study the given information carefully and answer the questions that follow.
(i) There are seven books one each on Psychology, Hindi, English, Sociology, Economics, Education and Accountancy, lying on a table one above the other.
(ii) Sociology is on the top of all the books.
(iii) Accountancy is immediately below education which is immediately above Sociology.
(iv) Economics is immediately above Psychology but not in the middle.
(v) Hindi is immediately below psychology.

24. Economics is between which of the following books?
(a) Accountancy and Education
(b) Psychology and Hindi
(c) English and Psychology
(d) Psychology and Sociology.

25. Which three books are between Accountancy and Hindi?
(a) English, Economics and Psychology
(b) Economics, Psychology and Education
(c) Economics, Psychology and Hindi
(d) Cannot be determined.

26. In a certain code, '247' means' spread red carpet'; '236' means' dust one carpet' and '234' means 'one red carpet'. Which digit in that code means 'dust'?
(a) 2 (b) 3
(c) 5 (d) 6.

27. At a farm, there are hens, cows and bullocks, and keepers to look after them.

There are 69 heads less than legs; the number of cows is double of that of the bullocks; the number of cows and hens is the same and there is one keeper per ten birds and cattle. The total number of hens plus cows and bullocks and their keepers does not exceed 50. How many cows are there?

(a) 10 (b) 12
(c) 14 (d) 16.

28. A bus starts from city X. The number of women in the bus is half of the number of men. In city Y, 10 men leave the bus and five women enter. Now, the number of men and women is equal. In the beginning, how many passengers entered the bus?

(a) 15 (b) 30
(c) 36 (d) 45.

Directions for questions 29 to 30: In each of the following questions, a statement is given, followed by two conclusions. Mark the answer as

(a) if only conclusion I follows;
(b) if only conclusion II follows;
(c) if either I or II follows; and
(d) if neither I nor II follows.

29. **Statement:** Morning walks are good for health.

Conclusions: I. All healthy people go for morning walks.

II. Evening walks are harmful.

30. **Statement:** The best way to escape from a problem is to solve it.

Conclusions: I. Your life will be dull if you don't face a problem.

II. To escape from problems, you should always have some solutions with you.

31. Who called his mass communication theory as "cultivation of dominant image patterns"?

(a) Donald L. Shaw
(b) Maxwell McCombs
(c) Davidson
(d) George Gerbner

32. Who classified his theories on the basis of world's national media systems?

(a) Siebert et al (b) Sandra Ball
(c) Nelvin De Pleur (d) George Gerbner.

33. "The Times of India" came into being with the amalgamation of which of these papers?

(a) The Standard and The Telegraph
(b) The Bombay Times and The Courier
(c) The Standard and The Courier
(d) Both (a) and (b).

34. Who is known as the 'father of Indian Cinema'?

(a) Torney
(b) J.F. Madan
(c) Dada Saheb Phalke
(d) Natraj Mudaliar.

35. Which media would be ideal to attract the attention of children to sell chocolates to them?

(a) Radio
(b) Newspapers
(c) TV (advertisements)
(d) Leaflets.

36. Function of School Cabinet is

(a) to make law/rules for the protection of school.
(b) to make law/rules related with mental hygiene.
(c) Both (a) and (c).
(d) None of the above.

37. Which of the following activity is related with school organization?

(a) Physical development related activity.
(b) Literary activity.

(c) Cultural and beautification related activity.
(d) All of the above.

38. Which of the following are elements of education planning?
(a) Problems (b) Builders
(c) Resources (d) All of the above.

39. In which year Gurukul System was established?
(a) 1902 (b) 1901
(c) 1905 (d) 1911.

40. Who was the founder of Shanti Niketan?
(a) Dayanand
(b) Raja Ram Mohan Roy
(c) Rabindra Nath Tagore
(d) None of the above.

41. Do the position of earth's north magnetic pole and south magnetic pole coincide respectively with the north pole and the south pole?
(a) Yes
(b) No
(c) Not yet determined finally
(d) They lie at the opposite poles.

42. Our earth rotates from
(a) West to East (b) East to West
(c) South to North (d) North to South

43. Who was the astronaut last to the leave the moon?
(a) Eugene Cerran
(b) Harrison Schmitt
(c) Neil Armstrong
(d) Edwin Aldrin.

44. Most natural satellites go round their planets in the same direction as the planets go round the Sun. In exceptional cases, a planet possessing four satellites rotates in the retrograde motion. Which is that planet?
(a) Mercury (b) Saturn
(c) Jupiter (d) Mars.

45. Which man-made object on the earth was found visible from the moon?
(a) Empire State Building, New York
(b) Eiffle Tower, Paris
(c) The Great Wall of China
(d) Statue of Liberty, New York.

46. A secure site protects you from ....
(a) sending information to an unscrupulous site.
(b) sending information that can be harvested from the internet by a third party.
(c) buying junk you don't really want.
(d) All of the above.
(e) None of the above.

47. Your history file lists all pages you've visited ....
(a) within the number of days for which your browser is set up to save history.
(b) in your entire life time.
(c) with conviction.
(d) more than four times.
(e) None of the above.

48. Which among the following countries used the cryogenic rocket technology for the first time?
(a) Great Britain (b) Russia
(c) USA (d) France.

49. Our GSLV space vehicle uses a cryogenic engine with liquid oxygen as the propellants because the boiling point of liquid hydrogen is very low. What is it?
(a) –50° C (b) –210° C
(c) –253° C (d) –273° C.

50. Who located the site of the north magnetic pole?
(a) William Gilbert
(b) Hans C. Oersted
(c) R.E. Amundsen
(d) None of the above.

ANSWERS

1. (d)	2. (c)	3. (b)	4. (d)
5. (a)	6. (d)	7. (d)	8. (b)
9. (b)	10. (c)	11. (a)	12. (b)
13. (b)	14. (a)	15. (d)	16. (d)
17. (d)	18. (c)	19. (a)	20. (b)
21. (b)	22. (b)	23. (a)	24. (c)
25. (a)	26. (d)	27. (b)	28. (d)
29. (d)	30. (b)	31. (d)	32. (a)
33. (d)	34. (c)	35. (c)	36. (c)
37. (d)	38. (d)	39. (a)	40. (c)
41. (b)	42. (a)	43. (a)	44. (c)
45. (c)	46. (b)	47. (a)	48. (c)
49. (c)	50. (c)		

EXPLANATION

14. Time taken by both for 100 pages = 1/16 + 1/12 = 7/48 or 48/7 = 66/7 hrs.

15. 1 anglet = 0.01? or 1? = 100 anglets. So 360 degrees = 360 × 100 = 36,000 anglets.

16. 15 = 3 × 5 and 105 = 3 × 35. Number of integers = 35 – 3 + 1 = 33.

17. No. of pages read by Tom in 50 min = 30 × 5/6 = 25. Jan gains 10 pages every hour, so he will gain 25 pages in 2.5 hrs. Hence v time = 5 : 20 + 2 : 30 = 7 : 50.

18. Let the price be 100. Then it becomes 125 after discount of 20% it becomes 125 × 0.8 = 100. We see that there is no change between the two.

19. Production in 2003 = 12.3 × 113 + 1390 (000). Production in 2000 = 17.2 × 83.2 = 1431. We see that it has decreased over the period, by about 3%.

20. We notice that productivity is increasing from 83.2 to 113, which the highest change.

21. Visual question: Workforce and production had declined over the years.

22. From I, we get 2 values of y, hence it is insufficient. In II we get y = 2 from which x can be found out.

23. From II we get 2 values of x, but from I we get only I value, hence I is sufficient.

24. The order of the book we get is: Sociology, Education, Accountancy, English Economics, Psychology, Hindi.

26. Note that 2, 3 and 4 are recurring, so 6 must be dust.

27. Number of heads = H + C + B + K. Number of legs = 2 H + 4C + 4B + 2K. Hence H + 3C + 3B + K = 69. Also C = 2B and C = H and K = (C + B + H)/10. Solving the equations, we get C = 12, H = 12, B B = 6 and K = 3. The sum can also be done by substituting the choices.

28. M – 10 = W + 5 and W = 1/2 M. Solving the 2 equations we get M = 30 and W = 15.

29. We cannot conclude either I or II from the given statement.

30. Since the best way to escape from a problem is to solve it, then you must have solutions in order to escape from problems.

PAPER-II

Objective Types Questions

11

Chaucer to Shakespeare (1440-1625)

Chaucer lived through the reigns of two kings, Edward III and Richard II and saw the beginning of a third, that of Henry IV. In his times English became the language of the law courts and of Parliament. The great plague or Black Death had devastated the land, and labour shortage, low wages, and high taxation to meet the cost of the French wars had greatly increased the misery of the masses. The poll-tax levied by Richard II led directly to the Peasants 'Revolt', to the social and political troubles of the times were added religious troubles caused by a corrupt church. The general corruption in the church roused John Wycliff to a fury of reform through his pamphlets and preachers. The three main poets of this period are Chaucer, Langland, and Gower.

Important writers and their works:

WRITERS	WORKS
Geoffrey Chaucer (1340-1400)	*The Romaunt of the Roses*
	The Book of the Duchess
	Troilus and Crieseyde
	The Legend of Good Women
	The Canterbury Tales
William Langland (1330-86)	*Piers the Plowmnan*
	A Treatise on the Astrolate
John Barbour (1320-95)	*Bruce*
Wyclif's–Bible (1380)	
John Gower (1330-1408)	*Speclum Meditantis*
	Vox Calmantis
	Confessio Amantis
Robert Hennyson (1429-1508)	*Moral Fabillis of Esope*
	Orphens and Eurydice
	Robene and Makyne
	Garmond of Gude Ladies
William Dunbar (1460-1530)	*Goldyn Targe*
	Thrissil and Rois
	Dance of the Seven Deidlie Synnis
	Lament for the Makaris

Gavin Douglas (1474-1522)	*The Police of Honour*
	King Hart
	Conscience
John Lydgate (1370-1451)	*The Falls of Princes*
	The Temple of Glass
	Story of Thebes
	London Lick Penny
Thomas Occleve (1368-1450)	*Regement of Princes*
	The Complaint of Our Lady
	Occleve's Complaint
Edmund Spenser (1552-99)	*The Shepheards Calender*
	The Runs of Time
	The Tears of the Muses
	Mother Habberd's Tale
	The Ruins of the Muses
	Amoretti
	Epithalamion
	Prothalsmium
	A view of the Present State of Ireland (Prose)
	The Faerie Queene
Sir Philip Sidney (1554-86)	*Astrophel and Stella*
	Ar Cadia
	Apologie for Poetrie
	The Harmonie of the Church
John Donne (1573-1631)	*Of the Progress of the Soul*
	Songs and Sonnets
	Aire and Augels
	A Nocturnall Upon S Lucies Day
	A Valediction: Forbidding Mourning
	The Extasie
	The Pseudo—Martyr
	Ignatius His Conclave
	Devotions
	Death's Duell
Robert Greene (1588-92)	*Alphonsus, King of Aragon*
	Frrer Bacon and Frier N Bongey
	Orlando Furnioso

Thomas Nash (1567-1601)	*Summer's Last Will and Testement*
	The Uncomfortable Traveller
Thomas Lodge (1558-1625)	*The Wounds of Civile War*
	Rosalynde
	Legacie
Christopher Marlowe (1564-93)	*Tamburlaine the Great*
	The Jew of Malta
	Edward II
	Doctor Faushis
	The Tragedy of Dido
	The Massacre of Paris
George Peele (1558-98)	*The Araygnement of Paris*
	The Old Wives' Tale
	The Love of King David and Fair Bethasabe
William Shakespeare	*Venus and Adonics*
	The Rape of Lucree
	The Passionate Pilgrim
	Henry VI
	Richard III
	The Comedy of Errors
	Titus Andronicus
	The Taming of the Shrew
	Love's Labour Last
	Romeo and Juliet
	A Midsummer Night's Dream
	The Two Gentlemen of Verona
	King John
	Richard II
	The Merchant of Venice
	Henry IV
	Much Ado About Nothing
	Henry V
	Julius Caesar
	The Merry Wives of Windsor
	As You Like It
	Hamlet

	Twelfth Night
	Troilus and Cressyede
	All Well That Ends Well
	Measure for Measure
	Othello
	Macbeth
	King Lear
	Antony and Cleopatra
	Timon of Athens
	Coriolanus
	Pericles
	Cymbeline
	The Winter's Tale
	The Tempest
	Henry VIII
Thomas Kyd (1558-94)	*The Spanish Tragedie*
	Cornelia
Ben Jonson (1573-1637)	*Every Man in His Humour*
	Every Man out of His Humour
	Cynthia's Revels
	The Poetaster
	Volpone, or the Fox
	The Alchemist
	Silent Woman
	Bartholomew Fayre
	The Devil is an Ass
	The Staple of News
	Sejanus his Fall
	Cat line his Conspiracy
	The Masque of Beauty
	The Masque of Queens
	Obron, The Fairy Prince
	Underwoods (lyrics)
John Webster (1578-1634)	*The White Devil*
	The Duchess of Malfi

Francis Beaumount (1584-16)	*The Faithful Shepherdess*
and John Fletcher (1579-1625) (jointly wrote)	*The Devil's Law Case*
	A Kind of No King
	The Night of the Burning Pestle
	The Scornful Lady
	The Maid's Tragedy
George Champman (1559-34)	*The Blind Beggar*
	The Tragedy of Chabot
	All Fcols
	Eastward Hoe
Thomas Malone (1394-1471)	*Morte de'Arthur*
John Fisher – (1459-1535)	*The Ways of Perfect Religion*
Roger Ascham (1515-68)	*Toxophulus*
	The Schoolmaster
John Lyle (1554-1606)	*Euphues the Anatumy of Wit*
	Euphues and his England
Samuel Daniel (1562-1619)	*Chrest Victorie Triumph*
Robert Burton (1577-1640)	*The Anatomy of Melancholy*
Francis Bacon (1561-1626)	*Essays 9 (three editions)*
	The Advancement of Learning
	The History of Henry VII
	Apophthegms
	The New Atlantis
	Novum Organum
	Sylva and Sylvarum
Sir Thomas Mox (1478-1535)	*Utopia*
	The Life of John Picus
	The Historie of Richard III

William Langland

Langland, the traditional author of Piers' Plowman is the last great poet to writer in the Anglo-saxonal literature verse. He was born about 1332 in the Western part of England near the Malvern hills. Then he shifted to London. Here he made his living as a beggar singing Psalms for the souls of the dead and wrote his poems. The famous *The Vision of Piers the Plougman* is a huge poem of illiterative verse divide into a large number of a passus' or Cantos—A, B, and C. The cantos then develop the allegony. A lovely lady the holy church, appears and tells the dreams to seek the Truth (God). On his asking what is Truth, she tells him it is love. Two other character are then introduced, Falsehood and Lady Meed. A marriage between the two is proposed but is opposed by Theology. Lady Meed confesses her sins to a friar and is promised salvation is then denounced by the author. The king then proposes to marry Meed to his knight, conscience, but conscience objects and denounces the Lady. So Reason is called and after a long argument in which Wit, Wisdom and Wrong take part he decides that no mercy should be shown to Wrong and that every god deed should be rewarded. The king is so pleased with Reason that he decides to keep him always as his councellor. The scene changes to the field of folk and Reason asks them to seek saint Truth the reoebtebt Crowd decide to start on their pilgrimage in search of Truth, but no one knows the way at this point appears Piers. Phowman after whom the poem is named. He promises to lead company after he has ploughed his half acre of land. He asks everybody to work hard at his job, and those who refuse are made to work by hunger. As they are about to start on the journey, Piers receives from truth the Pope's pardon covering not only Piers and his heirs but all who helped Piers ploughing and sowing. The poem in its first version ends here with the poet's passionate plea that only good works can obtain salvation and not pardens. The rest of the poem comprising the second and third versions is the sequel to the first and contains the triple vision of Dowel (Do-Well), Dobet (Do-better) and Dobest (Do-best).

Some critics have bestowed high praise on Piers the Plowman, and so far as the matter of the poem is concerned, the praise is justified. It is a frankly didactic poem concerned with religious reform. He attacks social and political inequalities and as his hew is a ploughman, save have called him a revolutionary. His aim was not to destroy society but to improve and purify its moral life. The poem has vigour, intensity, and sincerity, and because the author spoke for the people, it became immediately popular and remained till 16th century.

Critics criticized the poem for its Literary ment. The author's handling of the dance of the dream or vision, but a number of visions, so it becomes difficult to follow the rambling come of the plot. On the whole the poem has little attraction for the modern reader except a few lively descriptions and dialogues.

Gower (1332-1408)

Gower was a typical poet of the time who wrote in three languages: French, Latin and English. His French works consist of some fifty ballades or love songs and one huge poem *Speculum Meditantis*, a long sermon in verse on the immortality of the age. His Latin work Vox clamantis is concerned with Wat Tyler's Rebellion of 1381. His English work, *Confessio Amentis*, is an enormous poem of 14000 Octosyllabie lives. He says he wrote this at the instance of king Richard who had complained that nobody wrote in the English tongue. The subject is Love. The poet approaches Venus, the goddess of Love, who asks him to make his confession to her priest, Genius. Before hearing tells him stories to illustrate the seven deadly sins and then subdivisions so that the poet may know if he is guilty and confess accordingly.

The stories drawn from classical and medieval sources are curious and interesting and some of them are borrowed by Chaucer. Gower shows power and fluency of narration, but is too long-winded and' hopelessly dull. He lacked vivacity, charm, humour—qualities which Chancer possessed in an eminent degree.

Geoffrey Chaucer

Chaucer is not merely the first English poet of any importance, the father of English poetry' he is one of the greatest poets England has ever produced. The chief characteristics of Chaucer's Poetry, thus, are the products either of his own native genius or of his contact with the early

Renaissance of Italy. These two influences moulded so harmoniously in him that he succeeded where his contemporaries Langland and Gower had failed, in giving a new direction of English poetry. He was a pioneer who set a pattern for later poets, and is therefore, rightly called the father of English poetry. In the first place, he gave new subjects to English poetry, drawn partly from Italian literature. Partly from Latin. Partly from the popular tales of the day, partly, and this is the most importance of all, from the English life which he sant around him. Secondly, he also introduced new methods of handling them. In his hands the metrical sentence began to assume variety, balance and modulation. He was the first to make use of the heroic couplet. Thirdly, he transformed a dialect into a capable vehicle of poetry more suited to the native genius than scholastic Latin or the French of Paris of Stratford at Bow. He introduced a collopwal tone, a conversational note, which had all the freshners and vigom of the soil in it. In the fourth place, as a natural consequence of the conversational note, he brought into English Poetry an inexhaustible humour, which permeated all his work lent to it a peculiar charm, but was never noisy or forced. In the fifth place, he revolutionized the art of narration. He is a conscious and forthright artist who 'conveys the effect of rapid action in a few vivid strokes, and fills his pages with a series of pictures as bright and glittering as the illuminations in a medieval manuscript.

We have no certain evidence of the dates of Chaucer's works. The invention of printing was to come some forty years after his death and in his time publication of books as we know it today was unknown.

Chaucer's works can be divided into three periods. French, Italian and English. In the first or *French Period*—he wrote *ROMAUNT OF THE ROSE*, *The Book of the DUCHESS*, *The Parliament of Fowls* and a few minor poems, mostly lyrics. In the second or *Italian period* he wrote *Troilus and Cressida*, *the House of Fame* and *the Legend of Good Women*. In the third or *English period* he wrote *The Canterbuty Tales*.

Before English period Chaucer had been merely a borrower, a translator or adapter. He had been a slave to the allegorical convention and his own native genius had found vent only in occasional flasher of realism and humour in his dream allegories. Two of these—*The House of Fame* and *The Legend of Good Women*: he left unfinished, the former one presumably because he found it too artificial for his taste and latter because he found it monotonous. Then suddenly his native genius suppressed so long broke forth from its bondage and found full and unhampered expression in *the Canterbury Tales*. He conceived the idea of a pilgrimage to bring together an assorted company of people as letters of those tales. He ushered in the era of modern literature and established himself as the greatest European poet of his time, leaving for behind the contemporary poetry of France and Italy on which he had been nourished.

The Prologue: The Prologue is at once the most original and the most significant part of *the Canterbury Tales*. It begins with the description of the pleasant season of April. Chaucer describes his meeting at the Tabard Inn in southwork with 'Wel hyne-and Twenty'people. The poet soon becomes one of their company and arranges to ride out with them the next morning. Then follows a description of the pilgrims. It covers about seven hundred lines and is by far the most important part. The wide range of the characters, representing almost all the classes of English humanity except the very highest and the lowest, and the poet's keen observation and geographical portrayal of the physical and moral features of each pilgrim, have combined to make the Prologue a valuable document of the social history of 14th century England. This description is followed by the suggestion of the Host that each one of them tell two stories on the way to Canterbury and another two on the journey back, and that he who told the best tales should have a supper.

The generally accepted belief is that the Prologue was composed in or about the year 1387, and that some of the tales were written afterwards. The most distinctive feature of the Prologue is its originality. The Canterbury pilgrims have been described with such vividness and realism that scholarship is now busy searching 14th century England, rather than the books which Chaucer might have read, for the originals of these portraits in the Prologue.

The theme of the Prologue is simple as well as dramatic. The manner in which the poet brings together the pilgrims and makes the Host put forward his scheme is truly dynamic and dramatic. Chaucer's great power of characterization is then brought out in the sketches of his fellow pilgrims, who. Limited broadly to the middle class, represent a fairly comprehensive portion of English society. The military profession has three representatives in the Knight, his Squire and his Yeoman. The predominant ecclesiastical class has as many as eleven representatives—a Prioress with her Chaplain and three Priests, a Monk, a Friar, a Paroner, a Summones, a Poor Parson, and a clerk of oxford. Then we have the liberal professions represented by a Man of the Law, a Doctor of Physic, and the Poet himself. Finally, running down the social scale, we have the Franklin and the guildsman representing agriculture, the five guildsmen representing the crafts, a Merchant, a Shipman, a Reve, a Manciple, a cook, a Miller, the Wife of Bath and the Host.

The Prologue, is thus, almost a picture gallery of contemporary England. Every portrait, in which, has been well and graphically done. The elements of local colour, individual character portraiture, nature description and the natural humour combine to make it a unique work in the English poetry of those early times. Chaucer's superts power of characterization, like his all pervading humour, humour, provides a valuable gift to posterity. He did not only introduce modern humour in English poetry, but also opened a new road that had for its distinction the hitherto inaccessible recesses of the human heart and mind.

Chaucer displays a peculiar unity in diversity while handling his several characters in the Prologue to Canterbury Tales. The Prologue has rightly been called the first act in the drama of the Tales. The portrait of the pilgrims in the Prologue may be supposed to be static in so far as they lack movement and development. But in spirit the different pilgrims are themselves essentially dynamic characters, revealing themselves in dress, habits and action assigned to them. Their individual vitality in the tales is convincing; they reveal themselves fully and dynamically in the tales and in the link connecting the tales where they are seen quarrelling, arguing and making jokes and comments. The mere mention of a particular class, trade or profession was enough to bring before the eyes of the people a complete picture of the members belonging to it. Considered collectively those 29 Pilgrims are 'an epitome of the age': It is accepted that Chaucer's pilgrims are at once types and individuals true to their own age and representative of humanity in general.

The Canterbury Tales happen to be associated with a Pilgrimage to the tomb of Thomas A. Becket. Such pilgrimages, as this, were one of the outstanding features of the social life of the middle ages. The pilgrims enjoy complete liberty on their way to Canterbury. The jolly host of the Tabard, Harry Bailly, gives them hearty welcome and a supper of his best-good victual and strong drink to match and to beguile the tedium of the journey he made. The proposal that each member of the party shall tell two tales on the way to Canterbury, and two on the way back; and that the one who tells the best tale shall be treated by all the rest to a supper on their return to be Tabbard Inn.

But in reality the work is merely a fragment of twenty-four tales. We have the chivalrous epic of the Knight and the clerk's beautiful account of the patient Griselda's wifely devotion balanced in strange contrast by the coarse farcical stories of the Miller and the Reeve. Chaucer takes his raw material from many different sources. His finest work as a narrative poet is the Knights Tale, which is herok in subject, chivalrom in sentiment, and romantic in tone.

Chaucer was not in any sense a poet of the people. He was a court poet, who wrote for cultured readers and a refined society. The great vital issues of the day never inspired his verse. Though he holds the mirror up to the life of his time, the dark underside of it is nowhere reflected by him. It is significant that his only mention of the peasants' revolt is in the form of a humorous reference in the Nonnes Priestes Tale of the Cock and the Fox. He was an easy-going, genial, tolerant nature, and nothing of the reformer went to its composition. Little touched by the religions or social movements, he responded readily to the influence of Italian humanism, and it is though him that its free secular spirit first expresses itself in our poetry. It Wyclif was 'the morning star of the Reformation', Chaucer may be called 'the morning star of the Renaissance'.

Prose of Chaucer's Age: Chaucer's own few prose writings-such as his translation of Boethius and his Treatise on the Astrolabe-are not important. Wyclif's Bible is an interesting example of vigorous artless English. But the great prose work of this period is the singular volume which goes by the title *The Travels of Sir John Maundeville*. The fact that the supposed Maundeville describes a bird which could carry an elephant away in its claws, a Phoenix, and a weeping crocodile, a valley in which devils were jumping etc. will show that this book is at least amusing; while, even though it is only a translation, it keeps its place as the first English Prose Classic.

Fifteenth Century: With Chaucer English literature made we enter upon a long barren period of its history. Little affected by the Labours of Wyclif, religion continued to degenerate and there was little enough to inspire and much to repress literary genius. Nearly all the poets tried to walk in Chaucer's footsteps and, with little of his genius, labored to reproduced his matter and style. Of there, *Thomas Occleve*, and *John Lydgate* were very voluminous. *William Dunbar* was the greatest British poet between Chaucer and Spenser. He is known for his graceful allegorical poem *The Thistle* and *The Rose* and *Dance of the Seven Deadly Sins*. The other names are Stephen Hawes (1475-1530) and John Skelton (1460-1529). As a metrist Skelton neglected newic verse and abandued it in favour of short irregular the known as 'Skeltonics'. Scottish poets did much to bring the love of nature into later English literature. It can not be ignored that ballad literature in general became increasingly popular in the century after Chaucer's death.

Meanwhile more promising work was being done in 15th century Prose than in verse. Wyclif had failed to shake, when he set out his arguments in English instead of Latin, and his *Repressor of Overmuch Blamming for the Clergy* and his *Boke of Faith*, must be mentioned as landmarks in the history of our prose. But the great prose *Morte Darthur* by *Sir Thomas Malory*. The Morte Darthur holds a high place in literary history, not only on account of its intrinsic interest, but also because it has been a well-spring of inspiration to many modern poets, such as Mathew Arnold, Swinburne, Willeam Morris, and pre-eminently Tennyson. In style, it is artless, for Malory pays little attention to grammar, and his sentence structure is often faulty.

William Tyndale's *English New Testement* (1525), *The Complete English Bible of Miles Coverdale* (1535) and Cromwell's *Great Bible* (1539) reflect the steady growth of popular interest in the scriptures during the years immediately preceding the Reformation, while they exerted great influence in the development of a standard English prose.

Wyatt and Surrey are the chief poets represented in a collection of 'Songs and Sonnets' by various authors, which is commonly known, from the name of its publishers, as *Tottel's Miscellany*. Published in 1557, this work deserves special mention in any history of English Literature for it distinctly marks the dawn of the new age.

The whole period extending from the accession of Elizabeth in 1558 to the death of James I in 1625. Then 67 years fall naturally into three divisions—the first 21 years of the queen's reign; the 24 years between the publication of Spenser's Shepheardes Calender and her death, and the 22 years of the reign of James I. Strictly speaking, it is of course to the first two divisions only that the term Elizabethan should be applied, while the proper designation for the third is Jocobean.

Drama in 15th Century: Drama grew out of the religious ceremony of the church. Arresting episodes from the life of Christ and Gospel stories were illustrated in which the performers acted the story in dumb shows, mostly acted on Christmas and Easter. Gradually drama broke away from the service of the church.

The Mysteries and the Miracles: Plays grew out in the 14th century. The mysteries dealt with subjects taken from the Bible and the miracles with the lives of Saints. Both seriousness and laughter characterize these plays. Seriousness is represented by the figures of God and his angles and the comic element is revealed through Noah's wife and satan'. These plays gave to Englishmen a taste for theatrical shows and prepared the ground for the Elizabethan drama of a later date. In origin the English mystery plays have borrowed much from the French plays of a similar type, but fundamentally they breathed of the native soil.

In the mystery and miracle, serious and comic elements are interwoven. Now they part. *The Morality* was didactic and dealt in abstractions and allegory. The characters embodied certain qualities that types. Sivi, Grace, Rependance, Perseveratice, Seven Deadly Sins, Good and Bad Angels, Everyman etc. Devil held a prominent place in the miracle plays. Thus, the writer of Morality plays linked the drama with contemporary reality. In Moralities we come across, for the first time, the tragic soil struggle, the secret of progression of character and the delineation of conflicting passions, which the marked features of Shakespearean tragedy. *Everyman* is considered as the best morality play. The Interlude was a late product of the dramatic development of Morality play. The Interlude was far superior to Morality. Johar Heywood was the most gifted writer of the Interlude. His 'The Four P's' and 'Johan Johan' are memorable interludes.

Influence of Renaissance: The influence of Renaissance reached England quite late as late as the end of the 15th century. A number of social, political, religious and national forces nurtured and strengthened it in England. The Renaissance was an intellectual rebirth which 'showed itself in the effort of the individual to free himself from the rigid institutions of the Middle ages, fendalism and the Church, and to assert his right to love, to think and to express himself in accordance with a more flexible secular code (Moody and Lovett). This, Renaissance as Symbols points out, 'denotes the whole transition from the Middle Ages to the modern world: The revival of classical learning is a factor of immense importance in Renaissance. Renaissance began in Italy with Petrach, Boccaccio, Giolte, Nicolo, Pisano, Raphel, Leonardo, Michelangelo, Pieco della Mirandola and Medicis. It made classic literature and art the basis of a new literature and a new art. It began a new worship of beauty, knowledge and statesmanship. Old, ecclesiasticism was paganised, nuditily in sculpture and painting was accepted. The invention of printing which took place in Germany gave a new impetus to the revival of learning. Germany became the home of Reformation, Luther began it in 1517 when he attacked the power of the church and pope. Reformation, as time went on, produced a moral reaction against the worldly spirit of Renaissance; but in long run it ushered in an era of religious liberty and freedom of thought. In Italy Renaissance influenced through the senses, in Germany it influenced through the intellect. Renaissance, thus, was the result of three impulses:

1. The inspiration derived from the revival of classical learning.
2. The stirring of man's imagination by the great voyages of discovery.
3. The spirit of religious reformation which began in Germany.

Renaissance reached England quite late in the beginning of the 16th century and it came to its full splendor in the latter days of Elizabeth caxton's printing press, set up in 1476, provided books abundantly to the people of England. The revival of classical learning not only expanded the intellectual and emotional horizon of the writers but also influenced the technique and mode of expression.

The Age of Shakespeare (1558-1625)

The Age of Shakespeare, known as the golden age of literature, extends from the accession of Elizabeth in 1558 to the death of James I in 1625. It was an era of peace, of economic prosperity, of stability, of liberty and of great explorations. The main characteristics are:

1. Political Peace and Stability
2. Social Contentment
3. Religious Tolerance
4. The Queen's Popularity and the Upsurge of Patriotism
5. Expansion of both mental and geographical horizons.
6. Foreign Travels and Fashions
7. Backwardness of the Age due to Superstitions, ghosts, witness, fancies, charms & omens.

Poetry (1568-1603)

The poetry of the Elizabethan era represents the spirit of conquest and self-glorification, humanism and vigorous imagination, emotional depth and aerial graces.

The main characteristics are as under:

1. High conception of poetry as a dignified and evaluated form of literary expression.
2. The spirit of Independence from the set rules of poetic composition, grammar and prosody.

3. Varied poetical forms like lyric, elergy, ode, sonnet etc. were attempted.
4. Love poetry, Patriotic poetry, philosophical poems and Satrical poems are the main divisions of poetry.
5. The poetic production was of great and original beauty and is known for its originality.

Sir Philip Sidney (1554-86)

As a man of letters Sidney is remembered for *Arcadia* (1590) a prose romance, *Apology for Poetry* (1580), and *Astrophel and Stella* (1593), a collection of Sonnets.

Astrophel and Stella—These Sonnets reveal Sidney's love for Penelope is Stella. These Sonnets are the first direct expression of personal feeling and experience in English poetry. We find in his Sonnets much of the conventional material of the Italian sonneteers, and over fantastic imagery, intimacy, familiarity melody, fine notes of passion and unforgettable phrases. For example:

> "My true-love hath my heart, and I have his,
> By just exchange one to the other given
> I hold his dear, and mine he cannot miss,
> There never was a better bargain driven."

> "Less brilliant than Marlowe, less witty than Lyly, inferior to Spenser in glamour, and excelled by many a contemporary song-writer in deftness of fancy, he (Sidney) has produced a body of work which for its versatile excellence places him in the foremost rank of his time."
>
> —Rickett

Edmund Spenser (1552-99)

A close friend of Sir Philip Sidney and Sri Walter Raleigh, Spenser is a typical representative of his age. His poetry combines the best of both the Renaissance and Reformation. He is rightly called 'the poet's poet', because all great poets—Milton, Donne, Dryden, Pope, Wordsworth, Shelley, Keats, Tennyson, the aforesaid qualities which make him a Titan in non-dramatic poetry. His main poetic are given below.

1. *The Shepherd's Calendar*—(1579) for the first time brings to English poetry the richness, the warm pictorial quality, and sense of amplitude. The poet show remarkable skill in dealing with various old- time metres in a fresh and masterly way.
2. *Miscellaneous Poems*—In 1591 Spenser collected his smaller poems, and published them. "Mother Hubbard's Tale", "Ruins of Time", "The Tears of the Muses", The Fate of the Butterfly are poems worth mentioning. The names of his collection are "Complaints", "Amorelti", "Epithalamion", "Prothalamion", "Fan Hymns" etc.
3. *The Faerie Queen*—The Faerie Queen appeared in instalments. The first three books were published in 1589-90, and the second three books appeared in 1596. Two cantos and two odd stanzas of Book 1609. Spenser projected twelve books but completed only six books celebrating Holiness, Temperance, Chastity, Friendship, Justice and Courtesy. The fragment of the seventh book deals with constancy. The first three books are by far the best. Arthur is the central character in Faeric Queene. He appears at critical moments and marries Gloriana, the Queene of the Fairyland in the end.

It is one of the most remarkable allegories in the Renaissance poetry. Faerie Queene is an ethical allegory in which the noble powers of the human soul struggling towards union with God, and warring against all the forms of the evil are rich in imaginative ornament. It is also known as religious allegory. As religious allegory it represents the work of true Religion in rescuing Humanity from the power of great dragon, Satan Spenser identifies true religion with Protestanism, and the enemies of True Religion are the enemies of England. So the two lines of allegory run together and the poem becomes at once the medium of the poet's moral teaching and his reading of contemporary events and moments. In the first three books the shadowy Faiery Queene sometimes represents the glory of God and sometimes Elizabeth. The excess of symbols and want of human touch, languidity of narration and abstract characters make the allegory confused, inconsistent and obscure Spenser does not excel either as an allegorist or as a writer of romance, but he is incomparable as a showman of peageants. His consummate descriptive power is seen at its best in the faerie Queene—picture-gallery. Spenser also appears as a matchless painter in words. His word-pictures are colourful, concrete, vird and beautiful. He is a great colourist. As we read the Faierie Queene, a beautiful panorama of fleeting images and pictures rises before our eyes. He has also painted a wonderful gallery of pictures of men and women representing a cross-section of English life.

Spencer's contribution to poetic style, diction and versification is memorable. He coined new words, imported many from France and Italy, and saved many obsolete words from oblivion. Spenser evolved a true poetic style which the succeeding generations of English poets used. He is truly the poet maker, who inspired others to achieve greatness in the field. No man contributed so much to the transformation of style and language as Spenser, for not only did he deliberately endeavour at reform, but by the charm of his diction he made the new manner popular and fruitful.

The introduction of Spenserian stanza which has been admired by countless critics and imitated by all poets since its introduction, is his most remarkable contribution. This is a nine-line stanza running ababbcbcc, the last line being what is called an Alexandrine, or line of six limbic feet, instead of five. The Faerie Queene, is not a medieval romance but a romantic epic. It combines the prominent features of both a romance and an epic. The treatment of the subject is in the grand style suitable for an epic. The language is dignified and sublime. Charles Lamb has rightly called him 'the poet's poet'. Dryden freely acknowledged that Spenser had been his master in English, and adds that 'no man was ever born with a greater genius or more knowledge to support it': Wordsworth praises Spenser as the embodiment of nobility, purity and sweetness. He is also known as the "Second Father of English Poetry", because it was he, and not Chaucer, who gave to the poets not only of his own age but of all ages, a high and noble conception of their calling.

His Limitations: Macaulay, first of all, pointed out that Spenser is difficult to read. The modern reader "loses himself in the confused allegory of the Fairie Queene, skips all but the marked passages, and softy closes the book in gentle awareness".

Even the best of his longer poems, while of exquisite workmanship and delightfully melodious, generally fail to hold the reader's attention. The very melody of his verses sometimes grows monotonous.

Christopher Marlowe and George Chapman: *The Hero and Lender* was left incomplete due to Marlowe's untimely death. It was completed by George Chapman. The profuse use of imagery, the richness of decoration and purple patches cloy the readers. Besides completing *Hero and Lender*, Chapman also translated *Iliad* (1611) and *Odyssey* (1613) and composed some sonnets.

William Shakespeare: Shakespeare also composed sonnets and two narrative poems—"Venus and Adonis" (1593) and "The Rape of Lucrece" (1594). Shakespeare's sonnets are the most precious pearls of Elizabethan lyricism, some of them unsurpassed by any lyricism. The majority of the sonnets were written probably in 1594, when Shakespeare had gained the patronage of the Earl of Southampton. He preferred the Spenserian pattern, consisting of three decasyllabic quatrains, each rhyming alternately, and rhyming couplet to conclude. Thomas Thorpe printed a collection of 154 sonnets of Shakespeare in 1609. It was dedicated to a certain 'Mr W.H.' and to a 'Dark Lady'. His sonnets reveal an emotional crisis in his life. The autobiographical note is strongly marked in them.

Henry Constable: Constable's sonnets are remarkable for melody, beauty and Spenser's sensuous charm.

Daniel: Daniel was endowed with a lyric quality of a brilliant order. He was influenced by foreign poets. His collection of sonnets, known as Delia, is based on the conventional theme of love. He wrote sonnets without conviction and without a real mistress to sing. The language of his sonnets is pure and versification is correct.

Drayton: His sonnet sequence Idea symbolizes the polonic idea of beauty, which was notably familiar to Du Bellay in France and to Spenser in England. He wrote 52 Sonnets. He for the first time imparted dramatic sense to sonnet writing, but his sonnets suffer from artificiality and lack of true passion.

Other Minor Sonneteers: The other sonnet writers were translators and poor imitators of Petrarch and Ronsard. Lodge's Phillis, Fletcher's Tears of Fancy, Percy's Celia, Lynch's Dillia and Smith's Choloris are poor in stuff and purely imitative in character.

John Donne: A new kind of poetry was beginning with John Donne (1573–1631) whose work belongs essentially to the time of James. Donne, who was a celebrated divine and preacher, wrote songs, sonnets, marriage poems, elegies and satires. His historical importance lies in the fact that he initiated the 'metaphysical' school of poetry. He was also a satirist. He wrote five satires which expose the legislators. His satire is bitter, pointed and original. He expresses his resentment against injustice and corruption of the age. He also satires the uncertainly and misplaced zeal of the age of matters of religion. Donne adopted Horatian method of anecdotal narrative in satire. He employs an informal, conversational, racy and nervous style. His poems are all intensely personal and falls naturally into three division:

(i) Amorous Poetry (A Valediction, Forbidding Mouring Extasie)
(ii) Religion Poems (A Hymn to God the Father; Holy Sonnets)
(iii) Satirical Poems (of the Progress of the Soul).

Ben Jonson: As the creator of the comedy of Humours, Ben Jonson was the foremost satirest of his age. The spirit of satire also looms large in the three collections of his poetry. *Epigrammes*, *The Foriest*, *Underwoods*. Ben Jonson is the real founder of the comedy of manners after Restoration period. Jonson's intellectualism realism and classicism influenced the literary development during the 17th century. He is the pioneer of neo-classicism.

Other names are Joseph Hall, John Marston and George Wither. William Brown, Giles Fletcher, Phineas Flethcer are other minor poets. Viscount St. Albans in 1621. He was found guilty of taking bribes and was subjected to a huge fine and exiled from court and office . He spent the last five years of his life in the pursuit of scientific and literary works.

Bacon's Essays (1561-1626): Bacon's essays are full of practical wisdom designed to help in the successful conduct of life. It is frankly worldy wisdom without any pretence worldly wisdom without any pretence of idealism. He was a practical Psychologist with a sound knowledge of human nature. But it is their style more than their matter which makes these essays so memorable. The essays are in the form of short pithy sayings or maxims, each of which may itself be expanded into an essay. Many of his statements sound like proverbs. e.g. 'Reading maketh a full man, conference a ready man, and writing an exact man', 'He that hath wife and children hath given hostages to fortune', 'Revenge is a kind of wild justice' etc. Such weighty sentences are scattered throughout the Essays and are supported by quotations from the ancients mostly Latin. He also uses words in their Latin meaning and his sentences are marked by balance and antithesis.

The title, *ESSAYS*, may have been suggested by Montaingne's *ESSIS* which had appeared around 1580. The Frenchman is pre-eminently personal and discursive while Bacon is impersonal and aphoristic. There is only one essay of Bacon's that 'On Gardens', which is personal and reveals his delight in gardens.

A minor literary work of Bacon's is the *New Atlantis*. It is just another Utopia, which describes an Bacon's is the *New Atlantis*. It is just another Utopia, which describes an imaginary island in the pacific inhabited by scholars and scientists. The book which was published incomplete after Bacon's death is really an off short of his philosophical speculations. His principle philosophical works are the *Advancement of Learning* in English and the *Novum Organum* in Latin. In the *Advancement of Learning* the author discusses the various methods of advancing knowledge which he divides into history, poetry and philosophy. In Novum Organum he expounds the inductive method of acquiring accurate knowledge.

Bacon, a versatile thinker and writer, thought that his Latin works would become immortal, while his English works would not last long. It is sheer irony that Bacon is remembered today by dirt of his English works, while his Latin works have fallen into oblivion. His Essays in English, ten in number, appeared in 1597. The second edition (1612) and the third edition (1625) raised the number to thirty eight and fifty eight respectively. They contain utilitarian wisdom and are written in lucid, clear and aphoristic style. Bacon began the vogue of essay writing in English and so is known as the Father of English Essays. Alexander Pope very succinctly summed up Bacon's character in the following couplet:

> "If Part allure thee, think, how Bacon shined,
> The Wisest, the brightest and the meanest of mankind."

Bacon, the Wisest of Mankind: He, first of all, expounded the philosophy of Induction which as earned for him the title of the Father of Modern Science, though his contributions to science stand at zero. Bacon was the first to insist that 'knowledge is power'. Bacon's one pursuit was the advancement of knowledge. He lived for it and died for it.

Bacon, the Brightest of Mankind: Bacon's position as one of the originators of English prose is controversies, because he thought that no work written in vernacular has lived beyond its age. He wanted to make an appeal to the vital intellectual hierarchy of Europe and not to confine his ideas to English readers who were not intellectually advanced enough to appreciate his Bright and high ideas.

Bacon, the Meanest of Mankind: Bacon has been called the meanest of mankind because of his relations with Essex, a patron and sincere friend of Bacon. Bacon, at the instigation of the Queen, conducted the case against his friend, Essex and concluded it with his execution. Bacon always suppressed his real opinions and jumped in tune with the wishes of the king, exploited all kinds of flattery to open the gateway for a higher ruse. His conduct might be base, but his motive was noble. Bacon is meanest because of his corrupt record at the Lord chancellor. A philosopher like Bacon who should have shown a God like is difference was found guilty of the most unbecoming flattery.

Bacon's Misuse of Power: Bacon was also found guilty of misusing his official position and power. His granting of monopolies was a false charge as he had not favoured individuals but nations.

Bacon aimed at advancing human happiness by removing ignorance and by prompting knowledge. In the words of Selby, "Bacon is one of the most interesting figures of this age. He represents its deep patriotism, its high aims, its lofty enthusiasm", Bacon was certainly the wisest and the brightest' intellectual.

BACON AS THE FATHER OF ENGLISH ESSAYS

Bacon is the first great English writer who in the words of Hugh Walker, is the first English essayist, as he remains for sheer mass and weight of genius, the greatest: His Essays have won him a place apart and are a source of his fame with the world at large. As an essayist Bacon is not friendly, confidential, intimate and familiar with the reader. His essays are for the most part detached and impersonal and there is nothing on them to mark the tragedy of his life: He dealt with life with its problems in a chalty gossiping manner but tried hard to provide solutions. Bacon's attitude to life, the conditions of his time and the frame of his mind compelled him to conceal rather than reveal his personality gossiping manner but tried hand to provide solutions. Bacon's attitude to life, the conditions of his time and the frame of his mind compelled him to conceal rather than reveal his personality in his essays. Bacon took the form from Montaigne, but filled it with material drawn from his own mind. Bacon surpassed all his contemporaries in the capacity to utter pregnant thoughts on almost any theme. He was short of time and thrifty of his thoughts and his literary material. There is a neatness and ordered compactness which distinguish his essays, which are occasional and discursive, containing detached thoughts, written down as they occur. The astonishing range of topics of Bacon's essays is his great attraction; along with the clean sententious English.

Bacon was the first English essayist who employed a style that is conspicuous for lucidity, clarity, economy, precision, direction, masculinity and mathematical placenness. His images and figures of speech are simple and clearly illustrate his ideas. Flexibility, wit and fun are his notable characteristics. Bacon was a distinguished rhetorician. His command of phrase was extraordinary. As a thinker and stylist, Bacon is the pioneer of rational and scientific thinking, and of lucid and clear style.

MULTIPLE CHOICE QUESTIONS

1. Chaucer was born in
   (a) 1320 (b) 1340
   (c) 1300 (d) 1375
2. Chaucer's poetic period may be divided into how many periods?
   (a) Two, French and English
   (b) Three, French, Italian and English
   (c) Only English
   (d) None of the above
3. How many pilgrims are there in Chaucer's Canterbury Tales?
   (a) 29 (b) 27
   (c) 28 (d) 31
4. In which period of Chaucer's poetic career was the Prologue to the Canterbury Tales was written?
   (a) French
   (b) Italian
   (c) English
   (d) None of the above.
5. Chaucer's Canterbury Tales, is written in
   (a) iambic pentameter or heroic verse (with the rhymes running in verse, ten syllables and five accents each).
   (b) seven iambic pentameter lines rhyming ababec (seven line stanza).
   (c) blank verse.
   (d) None of the above.
6. Chaucer began his works by composing
   (a) Love lyrics (b) Ballads
   (c) Roundels (d) All of the above
7. In which poem does Chaucer speak of his life 'as an hermyte'?
   (a) Divine Comedia
   (b) The Parliament of Fowls
   (c) Somunium Scipionics
   (d) The Mouse of Fame.
8. Chaucer reflects—in his works
   (a) Sentimentalism (b) Romanticism
   (c) Real life (d) All of the above
9. In is said that Chaucer borrowed the story of Troilus Criseyde from another Writer's account. Whom did he borrow it from?
   (a) Baccaccio (b) Petarch
   (c) Dante (d) Jean de Meung.
10. The framework of the Canterbury Tales resembles that of
    (a) Petrarchan complications
    (b) Boccaccio's decameron
    (c) Wy Cliffe's works
    (d) None of the above
11. Which dialect did Chaucer opt for from out of the ones in use in his time?
    (a) The Southern
    (b) The East Midland
    (c) The Nothern
    (d) The Kentish
12. Which of the following is not a distinctive feature of Chaucer's diction?
    (a) All lines have the same number of syllables.
    (b) They have a rhyme-pattern.
    (c) Use of alteration and repetition.
    (d) All the above are the features of the diction.
13. Which of Chaucer's works has been termed by S.D. Neil as a novel in verse?
    (a) The Canterbury Tales
    (b) The Parliament of Fowls
    (c) The Book of the Duchess
    (d) The House of Fame.
14. What is the reward suggested by Harry Baily, the host of the pilgrims and the judge of the stories, for the best story told by the pilgrims?
    (a) The best story teller was to be made the poet Laureate.
    (b) The rest of a pilgrims were to offer a supper to him.

(c) No reward.
(d) None of the above.

15. 'The Well of English undefiled'. What quality of Chaucer does the phrase refer to?
(a) His diction
(b) His linguistic competence
(c) His overdance of foreign influences
(d) None of the above.

16. Why did Long call The Prologue to the Canterbury Tales 'The Prologue to modern fiction'?
(a) Because of its lack of poetic quality
(b) Because of its narrative unity
(c) Because of its formlessness
(d) None of the above.

17. Here's God's plenty, who is Dryden referring to?
(a) Shakespeare (b) Spenish
(c) Marlowe (d) Chaucer

18. Name the longest Tale in *The Canterbury Tales*.
(a) The Wife of Bath's Tale
(b) The Franklin's Tale
(c) The Knight's Tale
(d) The Cook's Tale.

19. How many tales were actually planned by Chaucer for him Canterbury Tales, and hint many could actually be completed?
(a) 120 planned, 20 completed
(b) 124 planned, 24 completed
(c) 20 planned, 20 completed
(d) 134 planned, 34 completed

20. Harry Baily is a character in Chaucer's
(a) Troilus and Criseyde
(b) Prologue to the Canterbury Tales
(c) The Physician's Tale
(d) The Pardoner's Tale

21. The name of Shakespeare's wife was
(a) Anne Hemingway
(b) Caroline
(c) Anne Hathway
(d) Percy Hathway

22. Hamlet belongs to
(a) the first period of Shakespeare's dramatic career.
(b) the second period of Shakespeare's dramatic career.
(c) the third period.
(d) the fourth period.

23. Who said that in *Hamlet* we see a great, on almost enormous intellectual activity, and a proportionate aversion to real action conquest upon it?
(a) Bradley (b) E.K. Cambers
(c) Mrs. Jamson (d) Cderidge.

24. The plot of *Hamlet* is borrowed from
(a) the legend of Almet
(b) a French translation of the Almet
(c) Nash's preface
(d) All of the above.

25. How Hamlet escaped his death at the hands of English?
(a) By substituting other orders for the execution of Rosencrants and Guildenstern.
(b) By jumping into the sea.
(c) By tearing the sealed letters.
(d) None of the above.

26. How the Queen dies?
(a) Claudius offers her the Poisoned cup.
(b) She unknowingly drinks from poisoned cup which Claudius has prepared for Hamlet.
(c) He wants to show Laertes down.
(d) None of the above.

27. The love of Ophelia for Hamlet is
(a) merely a show
(b) external

(c) profound and sincere
(d) All of the above.

28. A dramatic device, in which a particular character of the play, takes to itself, something all alone, is called
(a) Synonymous (b) Phonetics
(c) Solioguy (d) None of the above.

29. The play *Hamlet* can also be regarded as a battle of
(a) Wits
(b) Intellects
(c) Wits or of intellects
(d) None of the above.

30. 'The play within the play' was invented by the Hamlet
(a) to catch the conscience of the king
(b) to catch the conscience of Hamlet
(c) to entertain the king
(d) All of the above.

31. What was the name of Shakespeare's mother?
(a) Curey Arew (b) Lucy Ardew
(c) Mary Ardew (d) None of the above.

32. The meaning of 'Anon' is
(a) soon (b) coming Soon
(c) reply to a call (d) None of the above.

33. Who said 'Brenty is the soul of wit'?
(a) King (b) Polonius
(c) Queen (d) Hamlet.

34. How many times does the ghost appear in the play Hamlet?
(a) 3 (b) 4
(c) 5 (d) None of the above.

35. Why was Ophelia not given a Christian burial?
(a) Because she was unmarried.
(b) Because she was not a Christian.
(c) Because she died an unnatural death.
(d) Because she was in love with Hamlet.

36. Unity of action requires that the play
(a) should contain one main central interest or motive.
(b) should not have sub-plots or under-plots.
(c) should have a single plot.
(d) None of the above.

37. Who has been robbed of his dukedim in the Tempest?
(a) Sebartiati (b) Antonio
(c) Prospero (d) Alunso

38. When Prospero came to the exchanged island, what was the age of his daughter Miranda?
(a) Three years (b) One year
(c) A few months (d) Ten years.

39. Who is Hymen?
(a) The goddess of marriage
(b) The god of marriage
(c) The goddess of rainbow
(d) The god of rainbow.

40. The first English tragedy is
(a) Gorbodic
(b) Edward II
(c) Gew of Malta
(d) The Spanish Tragedy

41. Ariel is reminiscent of Shakespeare's earlier fairies in
(a) Hamlet
(b) Macbeth
(c) Pericles
(d) A Midsummer's Night's Dream

42. The Key-notes of *The Tempest* are
(a) Forgiveness and freedom
(b) Revenge
(c) Revenge and freedom
(d) All of the above.

43. Only one of the following poets belonged to the second, phase of middle English literature. Identify him.

(a) William Langland
(b) Philip Sidney
(c) Spenser
(d) Chaucer

44. Piers the Plowman is a _____ Poem.
(a) allegory (b) clergy
(c) visionary (d) prophet

45. The 'Crede of Piers Plowman' is a Satire against
(a) doctors (b) prioress
(c) merchants (d) friars

46. The lovely lady in the I cants of the Piers the Plowman symbolisis
(a) The court (b) The Holy church
(c) The politicians (d) None of the above.

47. The Piers the Plowman first appeared in 1632. The next 30 years were years of disperate social conditions. These conditions led to a rebellion. Which rebellion?
(a) The Hundred years War
(b) The War of the Roses
(c) The Peasant Rebellion of 1381
(d) The Battle of Against court

48. What is common among Fairy Queene, Divine comedy and Pilgrim's Progress?
(a) They are religion
(b) They are political
(c) They are great allegories
(d) They are novels

49. Who said 'My Master Spenser'?
(a) Drydens (b) Cowley
(c) Thomas (d) None of the above.

50. In which of his works does Spenser celebrate his love for Elizabeth Boyle whom he married Lalis?
(a) Amoreth (b) Prothalmion
(c) Epithalmion (d) None of the above.

51. The wife of Bath was
(a) lame (b) deaf
(c) blind (d) None of the above.

52. Which of Chaucer's works celebrates Saurt Valentine's Day?
(a) The Canterbury Tales
(b) The Book of the Duchess
(c) The House of Fame
(d) The Parliament of Fowls

53. Which language had an indeclinable impact on Chaucer?
(a) Latin (b) Greek
(c) French (d) Roman

54. The verse in *The Canterbury Tales* consorts of
(a) alliterative lines
(b) rhymed lines
(c) unrhymed lines
(d) alternative lines rhyming

55. How many women characters figure in Prologue?
(a) 1 (b) 2
(c) 3 (d) 4

56. Which work of Chaucer is called 'a Psychological novel'?
(a) *The Canterbury Tales*
(b) *Troilus and Crysede*
(c) *Legend of Good Women*
(d) *The House of Fame*

57. The Piers the Plowman Langland saw a series of visions. What was the first vision that he saw?
(a) The vision of seven Deadly sins.
(b) The vision of a Field Full of Folus.
(c) The vision of Lady Bribery.
(d) The vision of Man's Moral and Spiritual life.

58. How many Cantos on there in Langland's Piers the Plowman?
(a) Five (b) Six
(c) Seven (d) Eight

59. The first canto of Piers the Plowman deals with
   (a) the vision of Holy church
   (b) Lady meed
   (c) Falsehood
   (d) Seven deadly Sins
60. *Confessio Amantis* is a great English work written by
   (a) John Gower
   (b) Geoffrey Chaucer
   (c) William Langland
   (d) None of the above.
61. Which work of John Gower is inspired by the Peasant's Revolt of 1881?
   (a) Confessio Amantus
   (b) Vox Clamantis
   (c) Speculum Meditantis
   (d) None of the above.
62. In Vox clamantis consists of ______ books
   (a) five (b) six
   (c) seven (d) eight
63. Who translated Higden's Polychronicon?
   (a) John Wyclif (b) John of Trevisa
   (c) Langland (d) Gower
64. Due of the first Englishmen to challenge the authority of the Catholic church was
   (a) John Wyclif (b) Chaucer
   (c) Malory (d) None of the above.
65. Who is known as 'father of English prose?'
   (a) John Gower (b) John Wyclif
   (c) Chaucer (d) Langland
66. Who were Lorrards?
   (a) Poor Priests of the Church of England.
   (b) Poor Priests of the Roman catholic church.
   (c) The followers of Wyclif.
   (d) The pilgrims of Chaucer's Age.
67. Wyclif's The Prible is a translation of
   (a) Greek Texts (b) Latin Texts
   (c) Hebrew Texts (d) Arabic Texts
68. *Regement of Princes* is a work of
   (a) John Lydgate
   (b) Thomas Occleve
   (c) John Walton
   (d) Alexander Barclay
69. Who among the following poets wrote a famous poetry mourning the death of Chaucer?
   (a) Occleve in 'The Governail of Princess'
   (b) Lydgate in 'Fallas of Princess'
   (c) James I of Scotland in 'The King's Quair'
   (d) William Dunbar in the 'Thistle and the Rose'.
70. Which poet introduced 'Eclogues (Pastoral Poems) to England?
   (a) Alexander Barclay
   (b) John Skelton
   (c) Gawin Douglas
   (d) Robert Henrysm
71. Who has the credit of being the most voluminous poet of medieval England?
   (a) John Lydgate
   (b) Thomas Occleve
   (c) Stephen Hawes
   (d) Alexander Barclay
72. Which work of Skelton is an elaborate set piece in praise of himself?
   (a) Magnificance
   (b) Garland of Laurel
   (c) The book of Philip Sparrow
   (d) The Bowge of Court
73. Robert Henryson is a Scottish poet of the
   (a) 13th century (b) 14th century
   (c) 15th century (d) 16th century
74. Who is known as the Chaucer of Scotland?
   (a) William Dunbar
   (b) Robert Henryson
   (c) John Lydgate
   (d) Gavin Dougles

75. The poem 'The cuckoo and the Nightingale' has been written by
(a) William Dunbar
(b) John Skelton
(c) Hawes
(d) Anonymous writer

76. Name the first English Printer?
(a) William Caxton
(b) Holinshed
(c) John Dewey
(d) None of the above.

77. Caxton's Printing press was set up in
(a) 1475 (b) 1476
(c) 1477 (d) 1478

78. Which was the first printed English book?
(a) The Book of Historyes of Jason
(b) The Recuyell of the Historye of Troye
(c) Morte d' Arthur
(d) The fame sonnes of Aymon

79. Which is the first book in English in poetic prose?
(a) *Confessio Amantis*
(b) *Nun's Priest's Tale*
(c) *Morted' Arthur*
(d) *Vex Clamantis*

80. Which of the following is the earliest version of Bible?
(a) William Tyndales English New Testament.
(b) Miles Coverdales's English Bible.
(c) Cromwell's Great Bible.
(d) King James Authorised version of the Bible.

81. The vogue of the lyric was inaugurated by
(a) Wyatt
(b) Henry Howard
(c) Thomas Sackville
(d) Sir Thomas Moor

82. Who is known as the connecting Link between Chaucer and Spenser?
(a) Henry Howard
(b) Thomas Sackville
(c) Roger Ascham
(d) Sir Thomas Wyatt

83. The characters represent abstract qualities in
(a) Morality Plays (b) Mystery Plays
(c) Social Play (d) Interludes

84. The Betraying of Christ is a
(a) Miracle Play (b) Morality Play
(c) Social Play (d) Political Play

85. The Morality play *Everyman* belongs to the
(a) 14th century (b) 13th century
(c) 15th century (d) 16th century

86. *The Merry Play* is written by
(a) John Heywood
(b) John Rastell
(c) Sir Thomas Moor
(d) None of the above.

87. Miracle Plays were based on
(a) stories from the Bible
(b) stories from the Lives of the Saints
(c) concepts of Christian theology
(d) None of the above.

88. Blank verse was used for the first time for dramatic purposes in
(a) Jocasta
(b) Gorboduc
(c) Spanish Tragedy
(d) None of the above

89. Gorbuduc, the first regular tragedy in English was written by
(a) Thomas Sackville
(b) John Heywood
(c) Thomas Norton
(d) Sackville & Norton

90. The earliest known religious play is
   (a) *Noah*
   (b) *Nativity*
   (c) *Adam*
   (d) None of the above

91. Which is the first periodical, manuscript, newspaper that figured in Europe?
   (a) Gazatta
   (b) The Rambler
   (c) Times supplement
   (d) Paston letters

92. Shakespeare died during the region of
   (a) Mary (b) James II
   (c) Charles II (d) Elizabeth

93. Who is at once the child of the Renaissance and the Reformation?
   (a) Spenser (b) Sidney
   (c) Kyd (d) Nashe

94. The word 'Sonnet' is derived from _____ word 'Sonetto'.
   (a) English (b) Greek
   (c) Latin (d) Italian

95. Who competed Marlowe's Hero and Leanders'?
   (a) Shakespeare (b) Chapman
   (c) Ben Jonson (d) Heywood

96. Tamburlaine is the story of
   (a) a sailor
   (b) a French soldier
   (c) a Roman soldier
   (d) a Scythian Shepherd

97. 'Marlowe's mighty lines' first came into Elizabeth's drama with
   (a) Tamburlaine (b) Edward II
   (c) Dr Faustus (d) None of the above.

98. Marlowe's *The Jew of Malta* is a dramatic presentation of
   (a) a king
   (b) a duke
   (c) a scholar
   (d) Machavillian Man

99. Thomas Kyd was the founder of
   (a) romantic comedy
   (b) romantic tragedy
   (c) satire
   (d) dramatic romance

100. Who gave the name 'Sporting kyd' to Thomas kyd?
   (a) Shakespeare (b) Ben Jonson
   (c) Marlowe (d) John Lyly.

101. The first picasque novel is
   (a) *The life of Jack Wilton*
   (b) *Terrors of Night*
   (c) *Anatomy of Absurdity*
   (d) None of the above.

102. Chaucer has been criticized for presenting an incomplete picture of his times, because
   (a) he overemphasizes the rights of the lower class.
   (b) he exaggerate the courtly benevolence.
   (c) he writes for the court and cultivated.
   (d) he supports the Lollardy and the Peasant Revolution too fervently.

103. *The Ways of Perfect Religion* was written by
   (a) John Wycliffe (b) John Fishes
   (c) John of Trevise (d) Lydgate

104. Who has been called the first of the modern pacifists?
   (a) Tyndale (b) Ascham
   (c) Mox (d) Survey

105. Who introduced the Sonnet form to England?
   (a) Petarch (b) Wyatt
   (c) Spenser (d) Shakespeare

106. Who made the first use of the unrhymed ten syllabled line English poetry through his translations of virgil?

(a) Thomas Wyatt
(b) Thomas Sackville
(c) The Earl of Survey
(d) None of the above

107. An alternative name for Lyly's Euphues is
(a) Bestiary
(b) The unfortunate Travellor
(c) The Winter's Tale
(d) The Anatomy of Wit

108. One of the dominant characteristics of Sidney's Arcadia is
(a) Pathos
(b) Pathetic fallacy
(c) Euphuision
(d) Concrete imageries

ANSWERS

1. (b)	2. (b)	3. (a)	4. (c)	5. (a)	6. (a)
7. (d)	8. (c)	9. (a)	10. (b)	11. (b)	12. (c)
13. (a)	14. (b)	15. (c)	16. (b)	17. (d)	18. (c)
19. (b)	20. (a)	21. (c)	22. (c)	23. (d)	24. (d)
25. (a)	26. (b)	27. (c)	28. (c)	29. (c)	30. (a)
31. (c)	32. (c)	33. (b)	34. (a)	35. (c)	36. (a)
37. (c)	38. (a)	39. (b)	40. (a)	41. (d)	42. (a)
43. (a)	44. (a)	45. (d)	46. (b)	47. (c)	48. (c)
49. (c)	50. (a)	51. (b)	52. (d)	53. (a)	54. (b)
55. (c)	56. (b)	57. (b)	58. (c)	59. (a)	60. (a)
61. (b)	62. (a)	63. (b)	64. (a)	65. (b)	66. (c)
67. (b)	68. (b)	69. (a)	70. (a)	71. (a)	72. (b)
73. (c)	74. (a)	75. (d)	76. (a)	77. (b)	78. (b)
79. (c)	80. (a)	81. (a)	82. (b)	83. (a)	84. (b)
85. (c)	86. (a)	87. (a)	88. (b)	89. (c)	90. (c)
91. (a)	92. (d)	93. (a)	94. (d)	95. (b)	96. (d)
97. (a)	98. (d)	99. (a)	100. (b)	101. (a)	102. (c)
103. (b)	104. (c)	105. (b)	106. (c)	107. (d)	108. (b)

12

Jacobean to Restoration Periods (1625-1700)

This entire period was dominated by the civil war, which divided the people into two factions, one lays to the king and the other opposed to him. The began when James I, who had recoined the right of royalty from an Act of Parliament, gave too much premium to the Divine Right and began to ignore Parliament which had created him. The Puritans, who had become a potent force in the social life of the age, heralded the movement for constitutional reforms.

The reign of James I (1603-25) is known as Jacobean age. This was the period in prose writings of Bacon, Divine's sermons, and the king James translation of the Bible. It is known for the major writings by other notable poets and playwrights including Divine, Ben Jonson, Drayton, Beaumont and Fletcher, Websty, Chapman, Middleton and Massinger. The first half of the 17th century is known as the *Puritan Age*, for Puritanism was the dominant force during this period. It is also called the Age of Milton, for Milton was the greatest poet of the period. It is also called the Age of Milton, for Milton was the greatest poet of the period. As first king James I and then Charles I ruled England during these years, it is also referred to as the *Jacobean Age* or the *Caroline Age* (adjective from Charles)—It is an age of transition. By this time the Renaissance impulse has exhausted itself, the Elizabethan exuberance and optimism have been succeeded by a mood of apprehension, disillusionment and defeat. It is important that the Jacobean age remained upto mid-17th century. During this period, criticism of the Church and the court increasingly became more vocal and widespread and resulted ultimately in the civil war and the beheading of Charles.

WRITERS	WORKS
John Milton (1608-74)	*L 'Allegro* (1632)
	II Penseroso (1632)
	Comus (1634)
	Lycidas (1637)
	Paradise Lost (1667)
	Paradise Regained (1671)
	Sainson Agonistes (1671)
	Ode on the Morning of Christ's Nativity (1629)
	Oh, Shakespeare (1630)
	Oh Arriving at the Age of Twenty Three (1631)
	Of Education (1644)
	Aeropagitica (1644)
	History of Britain (incomplete)

Thomas Middleton (1570-27)	*The Changeling* (1624)
	Women Beware Women (1622)
	The Witch
	The Spanish Gipsy (1623)
	The Raoring Girle, or Moll Cutpurse
Thomas Dekker (1572-1632)	*Old Fortunatus* (1599)
	The Shoemaker's Holiday (1599)
	Satiromastix (1602)
	The Virgin Martyr (1620)
Thomas Heywood (1575-1650)	*A Woman Killed with Kindness* (1603)
	The English Travellor (1633)
	The Captives (1624)
	King Edward the Fourth (1597)
	The Royall King and the Loyall Subjects (1602)
George Herbert (1593-1633)	*The Temple* (1633)
	Affliction
	Easter Wings
	The Collar
	Man
Richard Crashaw (1613-49)	*Steps to the Temple* (1646)
	Comen Deo Nostro (1652)
	The Infant Mortyrs
	A Letter to the Cpunters of Denbigh
Henry Vaughan (1622-95)	*Poems* (1646)
	Olar Iscanus (1651)
	Silex Suntillans (1650)
	The Retreat
Abraham Cowley (1618-67)	*Pyramus and This be* (1628)
	Constantia and Philetus (1630)
	The Darideis (1656)
	The Mistress (1647)
	Pindarigne Odes
Thomas Carew (1594-1639)	*Poems* (1640)
Sir John Locke (1632-1704)	*Concerning the Human Understanding*
Sir Thomas Brown (1605-82)	*Religio Medici* (1642)
	Vulgar Errors (1646)

	Hydriotaphia: Urn Burial (1658)
	The Garden of Cyrus (1658)
	Christian Morals
Thomas Hobbes (1588-1679)	*Leviathan* (1651)
Sir William Temple (1628-99)	*Memoirs* (1691)
Jeremy Taylor (1613-67)	*The Liberty of Prophesying*
	Holy Living (1650)
	Holy Dying (1651)
Thomas Fuller (1608-61)	*The History of the Holy War* (1639)
	The Curch History of Britain (1655)
	The Worthies of England (1662)
	Good Thoughts and Bad Times (1645)
John Dryden (1631-1700)	*The Wild Gallant* (1663)
	The Rival Ladies (1663)
	The Indian Emperor (1665)
	Essay of Dramatic Poesy (1668)
	Tyrannick Love (1669)
	The Conquest of Granda (1669-70)
	Aureng – zeb (1675)
	All for Love or The World Well Lost (1678)
	Absalem and achitophel, Second part (1682)
	Don Sebastian (1690)
	Cleomenus (1692)
	Love Triumphant (1694)
William Congreve (1670-1729)	*The Old Bachelor* (1693)
	The Double Dealer (1693)
	Love for Love (1695)
	The Way of the World (1700)
	The Mourning Bride (1697)
Thomas Otway (1651-85)	*Alcibiades* (1675)
	Don Carlos (1676)
	The Orphan (1680)
	Venice Preserved (1682)
Samuel Butler (1612-80)	*Hudibras* (1663)

Chief Literary Trends of the Age

(1) Dominance of Satire
(2) Realism in Love—Poetry
(3) Development of New Style
(4) The Metaphysical Trend
(5) Abundance of Religious Poetry
(6) A Unique Element of Epic Poetry
(7) Prose of Matter Rather than Manner
(8) Logical and Straight Forward Style
(9) Degeneration of drama.

John Milton (1608-74): About eight years before Shakespeare's death John Milton was born in London on December 9, 1608. Milton, though a Puritan, was a classicist and humanist. He delighted in everything that pleased his eyes, and was a passionate lover of beauty. His early poems exhibit all that has best in Elizabethan literature. His first poem "On the Morning of Christ's Nativity", though married by conceits and inequalities of style, is the high waterman of lyric poetry in England. L'Allegro and II Penseroso are two distinguished poets of the Herton period. Both the poems written by Milton are autobiographical Comus marks a distinct stage in the development of Milton's mind. Besides these Milton wrote in a fragmentary masque called Arcades, several Latin poems and his famous Sonnets. He wrote his Sonnets on the themes of patriotism, duty, music, subjects are "On His Decreased Wife, to the Nightingale", "The Massacre in Piedmont" and "On His Blindness".

Most of Milton's prose was written during the middle period of his life (1640-60), when he was busy with public affairs. His prose works either deal with his personal business or public interests. In all they consist of 25 pamphlets, of which 21 are in English and 4 are in Latin. In 1644, he wrote a rather poor tract oF Education. His tracts on divorce were occasioned when his wife deserted him. Aeropagitica, a great and impassioned treatise on the freedom of the press, stands apart.

Milton's finest poetry was written when at the age of 44 he because blind. *Paradise Lost* and *Paradise Regained* and *Samson Agonists* were written during this period. *Paradise Lost* is an immense classical epic in 12 books. The scene of action is universal space. The time represented is Eternity. The characters are God and His creatures. In form it follows the strict unity of the classical epic. In theme it deals with the fall of man, but by means of introduced narratives it covers the rebellion of Satan in Hearen, the celestial varfare, and the expulsion of rebels. It is full of classical allusions and contains similies of the Homeric type, saturated with Milton's classical learning.

Paradise Regained is a sequel to the *Paradise Lost.* It opens with the journey of Christ into the wilderness after his baptison, and its from books descube the temptation of Christ by Satan, and the answers and victory of the Redeemer.

Samson Agonists is a choral drama, after the Greek model. It has threefold unity of time, place and action, and therefore, it achieves a concentration. Its verse is the blank verse of Elizabethan tragedy, with inevitable Miltonic adaptations. Samson in his blindness is described.

John Milton was the greatest English poet after Shakespeare W.H. Hudson remarks. "In him we have a wonderful union of intellectual power and creative power, both at their highest. He is also a consummate literary artist, whose touch is as sure in delicate detail as in vast general effects."

Milton was a superb poetic artist. To Milton poetry was not a mere intellectual exercise and diversion, it was something solemn. Sacred and sublime. Poetry comes only from divine inspiration, which is possible. Milton's own poetry is sublime and majestic. He lived a life of purity and austerity, and his poetry bears the unmistakable stamp of the nobility of his character, wordsworth wrote, 'There hadst voice whose sound was like these.'

Milton lived beauty in all its manifestations. He was extracted by the beauties of external nature. L' Allegro and II Penseroso testify to his love of nature and music. In prose IV of Paradise lost, Milton has nicely described the beauty of Adam and Eve, in whose looks divine the image of their Maker Shoni'.

Period of his life and during the later period of his life and his religions zeal almost kills his humanism. The Puritan spirit represents spiritual discipline, moral austerity, other wordly outlook, religious zeal and moral earnestness. The avowed aim of *Paradise Lost* is "to justify the ways of God to men". Its theme is Biblical and is directly traceable to the Purtan element in Milton. The subject of *Paradise Regained* resembles that of Comus. The theme of Samson Agonistes is also Biblical and is imbedded with moral earnestness.

Milton drank deep at the springs of classical learning. He wrote Latin prose as freely as he wrote English. He wrote Greek tragedy (The Samson Agonister), the pastoral elegy (Lycidas) and the Ode (Ode on the Nativity of Christ). The dignity of his style was built on classical models. He was fond of classical allusions, His diction is stamped with dignity, sublimity and stateliness. In his poetic style we inevitably find the imprint of a cultured mind, a lofty soul and an artistic conscience. Mathew Arnold remarks, "In the sure and flawless perfection of his rhythm and diction, he is as admirable as Virgil or Dante, and in this respect he is unique amongst us. No one else in English literature, possesses the like distinction..." as a poetic artist Milton is never careless or slipshod. There is hardly a line in his poetic work which is unpoetical hardly a word which is superflows. The artistic excellence charactenses his entire poetry from Ode to Nativity to Samson Agonistes. The appreciation of Milton's poetry has been rightly called 'the last reward of consummate scholarship'. Milton's style, says Raleigh is not a loose-flowing garment but is tightly fitted to the thought. 'He packs his meaning in the fewest possible words', says Raleigh, and we may add in 'the most musical language'. He again says 'of all the English styles Miltons is best entitled to the name of classics'. Tennyson called Milton 'God – Gifted organ voice of England' and 'mighty-mouthed inventor of harmonies'. Milton takes the first place among the masters of English music. He deftly adopted his metres to poetic forms. As a aversifier, Milton mended the loose dramatic blank verse of Elizabethan dramatists and made of it a worthy epic metre.

Richard Crawshaw (1613-49): Richard's Crawshaw's best work is in *Steps to the Temple* (1646). Some of his poems are secular but he is at his best in his religious poems. His poetry is noticeable for striking but fantastic conceits, for its religious fire and fervom. It is emotional rather than thoughtful. In many of his odes we find ganty extravagances and senscious decorations, an undisciplined raptune and mytic imagery. His poetry is mainly lyrical. His poem 'The Flaming Heart', was a great success.

Henry Vaughan (1622-93): His books include *Poems* (1646), *Olor Iscanus* (1651), *Silex Scintillans* (1650) and *Thalia Rediviva* (1678). In the beginning Vaughan composed secular poems under the influence of Ben Jonson. They are *Poems* and *Silex Scientillions.*

Vaughan like Crawshaw was at heart a mystic. His work never rises to the heights attained by Crawshaw, but he had a considerable gift for fantasy and used it to decorate his serious poetry. His poems reveal his good intellectual power and originality.

Abraham Cowley (1618-67): Cowley distinguished himself as a classical scholar. He was a man of versatile literary interests , who wrote poems, plays, essays, and histories. He wrote an epical romance *Pyramus* and *This be* (1628) at the age of ten, and two years late he wrote *Constantia and Philatus*. His well known poems are "The Mistress" (1647), a collection of love poems, "The Davide Is" (1656) and the "Pinderic Odes". Cowley is important as a transitional poet of this period. He was the last of the metaphysical posts and in many respects he foreshadows the English classicists. He deserved to be numbered among the disciples of Dorine. His knowledge of the ancients whom he imitated, entitles him to be considered a humanist. With all his piety, his fantasy, his conceits and his pindarism, Cowley is, first of all, an intellectual. He is wholly neither with the song writers, nor with the clear and virorons satinsts of the new age. But as the harbinger of Dryden and Pope, his work has a historical importance that must not be overlooked.

Andrew Marvell (1621-78): Marvells's poems which were circulated in manuscript during his life, have been described says Edward Albert, as the finest flower of serious and secular verse. His work has the subtlety of wit, the passionate argument and learned imagery of the metaphysical, combined with the clarity and control of the classical followers of Johnson and gracefulness of Cavaliers. His rhythms are flexible, his melody delicate. He loved nature and the freshness of gardens and sincerity.

Marvell combined like Milton the Renaissance. Senseriousness and Humanism with Puritanism. His poems deal with the theme of nature, as 'Garden', 'Upon the Hill', love as 'The gallery', 'To His Coy Mistress', and patriotism, as Horation Ode upon Cromwell's Return from Ireland.

Robert Herrick (1591-1674): Robert Herrick's two volumes of poems "The Noble Numbers" (1647), and "Hesperides" (1648) are collections of short poems, both sacred and profane. His lyrical power is characterized by freshness, passion and felicity of expression. It is also meditative and observant. His poetry shows strong influence of Ben Johnson and the classics. To Anthene, To Julia and cherry Ripe are his best known shorter pieces.

Richard Lovelace (1618-58): Lovelace's "Lucasta" (1649) contains some of his finest lyrics, such as To Althea from Prison and To Lucasta, going to the Wars. His poems are simple and sincere, and free from the cynicism of his day. His poems are careless in workmanship, full of affected wit and gallantry, and often rendered obscure by extravagant and grotesque conceits.

Sir John Suckling (1609-42): Suckling's Ballad upon a Wedding and why so pale and Wan, Fond Lover reflect his gaity, generosity and wit. He is witty and humourons. His laughter is not coarse and cytical, cut is of pleasant and mercucial quality.

Edmund Waller (1606-87): Throughout his life, Edmund wrote verse, but only occasional verse. Smoothness, elegance, corrections, a certain studied grace, coldness of feelings, polish and refinement, distinguish his poetry. The wit of metaphysical poets recurs in Waller, but is alternated, diluted and purified. His well known poems—"The Bird", "Go Lovely Rose" and "On a Girdle" are models in this genre. His imagery is clear and well sustained. In his political and patriotic poems and in rhymed couplets in ten syllables, he is dignified and lofty. The fine verse he wrote towards the end of his life to express the serenity which accompanies old age might serve as text for an examination into the birth of classical qualities in literature.

Denham (1615-69): The other pioneer of classicism was John Denham who was highly praised by Pope. He is the unrivalled pioneer of regulated and correct poetry. Denham's *Cooper's Hill* (1642) and *Windson Forest* were written in the heroic couplet. His poetry is remarkable for proportion, wit, balance, order, neatness and clarity. Pope was highly influenced by him.

Jeremy Taylor (1613-67): He is remembered for his collections of sermons. *The Liberty of Prophesying* (1647), *Holy Living* (1650) and *Holy Dying* (1651) deserve mention as fine specimens of religious prose. In his writings hi is find of quotations and allusions and of florid, rhetorical figures such as simile, exclamation, and apostrophe, and his language is abundant, melodies and pleasing.

Thomas Fuller (1608-61): Another divine, wrote serious historical books, *The History of the Holy War* (1639), dealing with the Crusader, and *The Church History of Britain* (1655). His pamphlets include *Good Thoughts in Bad Times* (1645) and *An Alarm to the Countries of England and Wales* (1660). His memorable work is *The Worthies of England*, published posthumously in 1662. His works reveal his original and penetrating mind, with and humour. His style is accurate and sententious. His dry autitheatrical humour appealed strongly to Coleridge and Elia.

Abraham Cowley (1618-67): The famous essayist. Cowley cultivated a form of essay more intimate and confidential, though less profound, weighty and philosophical than the Baconian. As a prose writer his output is slender. It consists of a mere handful discourses and prefaces. His essays are noticeable for intimacy, and simple sincere self-revelation. They are the friendly chat of a thoughtful and reflect spectator of life. His essay Of Myself is the finest of his composition.

James Howell (1594-1666): Howell's Epistalae Hoe is a collection of familiar letters, domestic and foreign, partly historical, political and philosophical, Howell's style is simple, famitias and easy, rapid and clear in narrative, humorous or pathetic according to the occasion. Howell anticipated the periodical essay and he has been spoken of as a journalist before the time of journalist.

Sir Thomas Browne (1605-82) Browne's prose work, though small in size, are of great literary interest. *Religio Medici* (1635), his confession of faith, is a curious mixture of religious faith and scientific skepticism. *Pseudodoxia Epidemica or Vulgar Errors* (1646) shares the same mental inconsistency. Hydrotophia or Urn Burial contains Browne's reflection on human mortality. It is considered to be his masterpiece.

Browne deserves a Proper place among the essayists of the seventeenth century. His writings are collections of independent papers which the author has chosen to need as chapters. "He is in finish soul and substance an essayist from start to finish', says Hugh Walker. Browne takes his readers into his confidence in the same artless and undisguised manner as the immortal Montaigue. His style is Pedantic, ornate and strongly Latinized, sometimes to the limit of obscurity. Dr. Johnson speaks of Brown's style as 'a tissue of many languages'.

John Dryden (1631-1700): John Dryden was the first of the new, as Milton was the last of the elder school of poetry. For forty years he abundantly produced literary works of every kind-poems, plays and prose works Dryden was a representative poet of his age. "Heroic Stanzas" (1659) was a series of heroic stanzas on the death of Cromwell. It is his first poem of any consequence. "Astraea Redux" (1660), a poem in celebration of Charles II's return, marks the beginning of the new age and an advance in his poetical craftsmanship. *Annus Mirabilis* (1667) contains topical interest. It gives a spirited account of the Great Fire and shows Dryden's metrical case and flexibility. *Absalom and Achitophel* (1681) is a fine, finished satire. The Satire itself written in mockery of the Popish plot and the Exclusion Bill, attacked Shaftesbury as Achitophel, was kind to Monmouth as Absalom. In the second part of *Absalom and Achitophel* (1682) Dryden contributed a violent attack on Shadw'll, giving him the name of Og. *The Fables* (1699) reveals Dryden's narrative skill. As a lyric poet Dryden's fame rests on the animated song for *St. Cecilia's Day* (1687) and *On Alexander's Feast* (1697). Both these melodies verse and a varied and powerful style.

Dryden is an exceptionally correct and dignified poetic craftsman. He has a master of select and polished diction. His faculty of placing words both in poetry and prose is wonderful. Admiring his craftsmanship, Dr Johnson wrote; "Dryden found of English brick and left it marble." Dryden's well-known Essay on Dramatic Poetry is the model of the new prose. His prose-style is characterized by cleaners, vigom, a wonderful felicity of phrasing, and a colloquial ease which preserves a literary distinction. His prose is nearly always stons, flexible and delightfully straightforward. Saintsbury writer: "Considering what he started with, what he accomplished, and what advantages he left for his successors, he must be pronounced, without exception, the greatest craftsman in literature."

Dryden perfected the heroic couplet which was to occupy for many years the place of the accepted measure of serious English poetry. As a poetic craftsman he is original. Dryden's poetry is characterized by 'a splendid intellectuality and a manly vigour of style'.

Dryden's poetry is intellectual, satirical and realistic. He is a poet of reason and good sense. In his poetry passion and imagination are subordinated to intellect. So his poetry is prosic in character. He heralded the neoclassical age in literature. He is famous for his play like the *Indian Emperor*, *Tyrannic Love*, *Aurengzebe* and *All for Love*.

Samuel Butler (1612-80): Butler is a remarkable figure in the poetic development of the Restoration. *Hudibras* is undoubtedly the greater satire outside Dryden's *Absalom and Achitophel* and remains the masterpiece of satire in the grotesque manner. Butler's Hudibras, a pointed satire on Puritans, Lias published respectively in 1663, 1664 and 1668.

John Bunyan (1632–1704): During the Restoration period Bunyan alone contests the supremacy of Dryden as a prose writer. Bunyan's religious autobiography, Grace Abounding was the work of his captivity and it appeared in 1660. The first part of the *Pilgrim's progress* belongs to a second imprisonment in 1675. In 1680 Bunyan's *The Life and Death of Mr. Badman*, a curious little story, and in 1682 *The Holy War*, an allegory appeared.

Kipling called Bunyan 'the father of the novel'. He may not be the creator or the father of English novel but he is decidedly a pioneer of English novel. Bunyan's dialogues are natural, real and life like. His sense of humour comes out in general casual recounters met with by Christian on his journey. Bunyan was a belated Puritan in the Restoration period. What beauty was to Spenser, and power to Marlowe, righteousness was to Bunyan. We can rightly call him a 'genuine child of Renaissance in a Puritan framework.'

Thomas Hobbes – Hobbes, a great political thinker, opposed the Divine Right Theory. He is before Dryden the first of all our prose writers whose style may be said to be uniform and correct, and adopted carefully to the subject on which he wrote. His treatise, the Leviathan (1651) declared that the origin of all power was in the people, and that the end of all power was the end of the common weal.

Thomas Otway (1651-85): Otway wrote *Alcibiodes* (1675), *Don Carlos* (1676). *The Orphan* (1680) and *Venice Preserv'd* (1682). The first two plays are written in blank verse. This powerful tragedy is noticeable for the note of deep pathws, a calmness of tone and utter obsence of rent. *Venice Preserv'd* is Otway's best work.

William Congreve (1670-1729): Congreve is the best finest writer of the comedy of manners. He wrote all his comedies before he was thirty. He was a good classical scholar and interested in translation his poems and translations impressed the dramatist, poet and critic John Dryden, who included some of them in a collection of miscellaneous poems called Examen Poeticum (1693). In 1692 Congreve's novel *Incognita* was published; its plot was worked out on the lines of dramatic models, and the following year he finished his first play, *The Old Bachelor*. *The Way of the World* (1700) is considered by common consent as a work of art and as a pure comedy of manners. It deserves especial consideration as a comedy by don't of its many artistic excellences, such as flashes of wit and brilliant, sparkling dialogues.

Congreve's style is suffered with subtle irony. There is subdued tone of gaiety in his dialogue, touched off by wit. Albert wrotes "Congreve is undoubtedly the greatest of the Restoration comedy writers. In his work the comedy of manners reaches perfection." "His plays are a faithful reflection of the upper-class life of his day, but their undoubted immorality is saved from being objectionable by brilliant art, a hard finish and a total lack of realism. In the artificial society which he depicts, moral judgement would be out of place."

George Etherege (1635-91): His three plays are *The Comicical Revenge or Love in A Tub* (1664), *She Wou'd of the Cou'd* (1668), and *The Man of the Mode or Sir Fopling Flutter* (1676). His plays established the comedy of manners, and paved the way for Congreve. He paints a true picture of the graceful, heatless and licentious upper classes of the period. The prose dialogue is natural and brilliant, and its light, any grace conceals some deficiency of plot and construction.

Sir John Vanbrugh (1664-1726): His best three comedies are *The Relapse* (1696), *The Provok'd Wife* (1697) and *Confederacy* (1705). In his first two plays Vanbrugh employs all the familiar puppets of the Restoration comedy, the fops and the fools being treated with more naturalness. *The Confederacy* breaks fresh ground as it was considered the best play of the period in construction, characterization and dialogue.

George Farquhar (1678-1707): A man of versable genious, George Farq when was in turn a clergyman, an actor and died when he was 29 years old. His plays are *Love and a Bottle*, *The*

Constant Couple, *Sir Harry Wildair*, *The Inconstant*, *The Way to Win Him*, *The Recrubiting Officer* and *The Beaux*, *Stratagem*. In the last two plays Farquahar, in the words of Edward Albert, "added something new to Restoration comedy, in taking his material from a wider life than the polite upper class depicted by Congrave, and his characters people. His dialogue lacks the polish and two sustained wit of Congreve."

Lord Halifax—Halifax, an outstanding figure in the House of Lords, was an eminent orator and writer of political tracts. His small volume called *Miscellanies* contains a number of political tracts. His style is simple and straightforwardness.

MULTIPLE CHOICE QUESTIONS

1. Who wrote *Way of the world*?
   (a) Dryden
   (b) Congreve
   (c) Dekker
   (d) Richard Crawshaw
2. Milton's *Paradise Regained* was published in
   (a) 1674 (b) 1667
   (c) 1671 (d) 1681
3. What was the main cause of the collapse of drama in the age of Milton?
   (a) The civil disturbances and closing of the theatres in 1642.
   (b) Strong opposition of the Puritans.
   (c) Both (a) and (b).
   (d) None of the above.
4. The name of Milton's wife is
   (a) Catherine Woodcock
   (b) Mary Powell
   (c) Elizabeth Minshull
   (d) All (a) (b) and (c)
5. Which sonnet is not written by Milton?
   (a) *On His Deceased Wife*
   (b) *To The Nightingale*
   (c) *The Masscure in Piedmont*
   (d) *Blindness is a curse*
6. *Paradise Lost* has how many books?
   (a) Twelve (b) Thirteen
   (c) Ten (d) Two
7. Milton wrote twenty five pamphlets, they are
   (a) all in English
   (b) all in Latin
   (c) 21 in English and 4 in Latin
   (d) 4 in English and 21 in Latin
8. The main theme of *Paradise Lost* is
   (a) Saton's revenge
   (b) the war of God and Satan
   (c) man's disobedience and his fal
   (d) the description of satan
9. *Samson Agonistes* by Milton is a
   (a) choral drama.
   (b) made after the Greek Model.
   (c) example of threefold unity of time, place and action.
   (d) All of the above.
10. Who wrote about Milton, 'Thou hadst voice whose sound was like these'?
    (a) Coleridge
    (b) William Wordsworth
    (c) Keats
    (d) Shelley
11. The term 'metaphysical as applied to poetry was first used by
    (a) Dr Johnson (b) Donne
    (c) Saintsbury (d) Aristotle
12. Who said about metaphysical poets that "they played with thoughts as the Elizabethans had played with words"?
    (a) Ben Johnson
    (b) Sir Walter Raleigh
    (c) Sir Walter Scott
    (d) Dryden

13. Metaphysical poetry may be classified into two broad divisions of
    (a) amorous and religious verse
    (b) religious and anti-religious verse
    (c) Both (a) and (b)
    (d) None of the above.
14. Who is not a metaphysical poet of 17th century?
    (a) John Divine
    (b) George Herbert
    (c) Richard Crawshaw
    (d) Thomas Fuller
15. Richard Crawshaw's best work is
    (a) *Iscanus*
    (b) *The Temple*
    (c) *Steps to the Temple*
    (d) None of the above.
16. 'To His Coy Mistress' was written by
    (a) Andrew Marvell
    (b) Richard Lovelace
    (c) Sir John Suckling
    (d) Abraham Cowley
17. 'Fond Lover' was written by
    (a) Andrew Marvell
    (b) Sir John Suckling
    (c) Richard Lovelace
    (d) None of the above.
18. Highly praised by Pope, John Denham is the unrivalled pioneer of regulated and correct poetry. He wrote
    (a) *Cooper's Hill*
    (b) *Windson Forest*
    (c) Both (a) and (b)
    (d) None of the above.
19. *Religio Medici* is written by
    (a) Sir Thomas Fuller
    (b) Sir Thomas Browne
    (c) Lord Halifax
    (d) William Temple
20. The two big political parties emerged in the Restoration period are
    (a) The Whings and the Tories
    (b) Tories and Whistem
    (c) Royal power and divinily
    (d) None of the above
21. Name the first poem by Dryden written at the age of 18.
    (a) An elegy on the death of young lord Hastings
    (b) Heroic stanzas
    (c) Astraea Redux
    (d) Absalom and Achitophel
22. Which poet does not belong to the Restoration period?
    (a) John Oldham (b) Bishop ken
    (c) Dryden (d) John Gay
23. The main causes of the Rise of Prose in the Restoration age
    (a) the Growth of Science
    (b) rise of Journalism
    (c) french Influence
    (d) All of the above.
24. Who called Bunyan 'the father of the novel'?
    (a) Kipling (b) Dryden
    (c) Edward Albert (d) Lord Halifax
25. Name two diarists of the Restoration period.
    (a) John Tilloston and Samuel pepys
    (b) John Evelyn and cudworth
    (c) Samuel Pepys and John Eyelyn
    (d) None of the above.
26. What is the characteristic of the Restoration comedy of Manners?
    (a) Intellectual and Refined Tone
    (b) Presentation of Aristocratic London society
    (c) Sex and Licentiosness
    (d) All of the above.

27. Who has written 'Love for Love'?
    (a) Congreve (b) Vanbrugh
    (c) Dryden (d) None of the above.
28. Who was restored to the throne of England in 1660?
    (a) Charles I (b) Charles II
    (c) James (d) Harold
29. Dryden's Mac Flecknoe has been written in
    (a) blank verse
    (b) free verse
    (c) heroic couplet
    (d) Spenserian Stanza
30. Each line of a heroic couplet is
    (a) an Iambic pentameter
    (b) a trochaic pentameter
    (c) an Iambic tetrameter
    (d) an anapestic pentameter
31. The lady of light was the nick name of
    (a) Milton (b) Donne
    (c) Vaughan (d) None of the above.
32. Which Milton's poem is based on patience?
    (a) *Paradise Regained*
    (b) *L' Allegro*
    (c) *Paradise Lost*
    (d) *On his Blindness*
33. Milton's "On his blindness" is a/an
    (a) Epic (b) Elegy
    (c) Sonnet (d) Blank verse
34. "Lycidas" of Milton is an/a
    (a) Epic (b) Masque
    (c) Comedy (d) Elegy
35. In "Lycidas", the King has been presented as a
    (a) poet
    (b) shephered
    (c) priest
    (d) None of the above.
36. Which poet helped Milton in writing when he became blind?
    (a) Andrew Marvell
    (b) Henry Vaughan
    (c) Donne
    (d) None of the above.
37. Milton's "Comus" was published in
    (a) 1634 (b) 1644
    (c) 1654 (d) 1664
38. Puritanism has Milton as its
    (a) Singer (b) Preacher
    (c) Playwright (d) Priest
39. Which Milton's work is without a trace of Puritanism?
    (a) "L' Allegro"
    (b) "Pensireso"
    (c) Both (a) and (b)
    (d) None of the above.
40. Burton's great and only literary achievements the Antony of Melacholy is
    (a) Satirical
    (b) Melancholical
    (c) Religious
    (d) Characteristic of time
41. The masterpiece of Thomas Browne is
    (a) "Hydriotaphia"
    (b) "The Garden of Lyrus"
    (c) "Religio Medice"
    (d) "Vulgur Errors"
42. The most popular of Bunyan's works is
    (a) The Pilgrims Progress
    (b) The Holy War
    (c) The Holy city
    (d) The Life and Death of Mr. Badman
43. Bunyan's style was influenced by
    (a) Bible (b) Fairie
    (c) Queene (d) Eupheus
44. Fuller's most considerable work "The Worthies of England" was published by
    (a) his son (b) his father
    (c) his brother (d) his friend

45. Walton's most famous work "The Complete Angler" was published in
(a) 1603 (b) 1623
(c) 1633 (d) 1653

46. "The Preacher" is the sub-title of
(a) "Ecclesiastical" (b) "Ezekiel"
(c) "Haggai" (d) "St. Mathew"

47. The New Testament opens with
(a) "St. Mattew" (b) "St. Mark"
(c) "Philemon" (d) "Hebrews"

48. Who told Job to "curse God and die"?
(a) His wife (b) His neighbour
(c) His sons (d) Satan

49. In "Genius", Abel was a
(a) shepherd (b) farmer
(c) horse keeper (d) mason

50. In "Genius", God called the dry level
(a) desert (b) earth
(c) air (d) mountains

51. How many books are there in the Bible?
(a) 66 (b) 60
(c) 50 (d) 46

52. Medieval Europe knew the Bible in
(a) Latin (b) French
(c) Greek (d) English

53. William Tyndale translated the "New Testament" from
(a) Greek (b) Latin
(c) French (d) English

54. James I of England appointed 47 scholars to produce an English version of the Bible in
(a) 1600 (b) 1610
(c) 1604 (d) 1620

55. The "Old Testament" was originally written in
(a) Hebrew (b) Latin
(c) Greek (d) English

56. The New Testament was translated into Middle English in
(a) 16th Century (b) 15th Century
(c) 14th Century (d) 12th Century

57. The script of The Old Testament was
(a) Latin (b) French
(c) Russian (d) Greek

58. Which of the following statements is true about the rule of Oliver Cromwell?
(a) Oliver Cromwell, a puritan, has suppressed too many natural impulses.
(b) Oliver Cromwell has brought about many economic reforms for the welfare of England.
(c) Oliver Cromwell encouraged the English dramatists and he made significant contribution towards the development of English drama.
(d) None of the above.

59. The period in English history after 1660 is called
(a) Restoration period
(b) Elizabethan period
(c) Jocabean period
(d) Victorian period

60. Which of the following statements is true about the Restoration period in England?
(a) Released from restraint, society abondered the decencies of life and the reverence for law and plunged into excusers more unnatural than had been the restraints of Puritanism.
(b) King Charles II was a role model of social morality and human behaviour.
(c) None of the above.

61. In the later part of the 17th century, England witnessed the rise of two political parties. What are these two political parties?
(a) The Whites and the Rects
(b) The lords and the commons

(c) The Whigs and the Tories
(d) The communals and the seculars.

62. Why does Jocabean Age is also known as Caroline Age?
(a) On the name of a beautiful Lady Caroline.
(b) Caroline was the mistress of Milton.
(c) Caroline term is an adjective taken from Charles I, the ruler of the period.
(d) None of the above.

63. What are the main aims of Puritan movement?
(a) Religious liberty (b) Civil Liberty
(c) Purity of Life (d) All of the above

64. Who was the founder of 'Metaphysical' School of poetry?
(a) George Herbert (b) John Donne
(c) George wither (d) John Marston

65. Which of the following is called the Father of English criticism?
(a) Dr. Johnson (b) John Dryden
(c) Longinus (d) Mathew Arnold

66. Which of the following has not been authored by Dryden?
(a) Hudibras
(b) Religio Laici
(c) The Hind and the Panther
(d) The Modal

67. In Dryden's 'Mac Flecknoe' Mac means
(a) Father of (b) Son of
(c) Teacher of (d) None of the above.

68. The plays of William Congreve are known as
(a) Comedy of humours
(b) Comedy of manners
(c) Farce
(d) Comedy of errors

69. William Congreve was a
(a) Restoration dramatist
(b) Gothic novelist
(c) Jocabean dramatist
(d) Augustan Satirest

70. The display of Wit forms an important part of which of the following dramas?
(a) Shakespearean comedy
(b) Shakespearean tragedy
(c) Restoration comedy
(d) Jocabean drama

71. 'A Woman killed with Kindness' was written by one of the most important exponents of domestic drama named
(a) John Webster
(b) Thomas Heywood
(c) Thomas Middleton
(d) Philip Massenger

72. "For God's sake hold thy tongue and let me love" such abrupt beginnings are characteristic of
(a) Ben Jonson (b) John Donne
(c) Shakespeare (d) Spenser

73. 'The Elegie' in praise of John Donne was written by
(a) Henry Vaughan
(b) Thomas carew
(c) Abraham Cowley
(d) Andrew Marvell

74. Milton's 'Comus'is a drama called
(a) Force (b) Masque
(c) Romance (d) Revenge tragedy

75. Who called Milton 'the mighty-mouthed inventor of harmonies?'
(a) Arnold (b) Dryden
(c) Johnson (d) Tennyson

76. Thomas Browne, the greatest prose writer of the Puritan age, was by profession
(a) a cobbler (b) a doctor
(c) a hunter (d) a pamphleteer

77. Poetry in the Restoration period was predominantly
(a) Lyrical (b) Satirical
(c) Sentimental (d) Philosophical

78. An important element in Dryden's satire is his dexterity in handling the
(a) Blank verse
(b) Sonnet form
(c) Heroic couplet
(d) None of the above.

79. 'Grace Abounding' is the autobiography of
(a) J. Collier (b) A. Cowley
(c) John Milton (d) John Bunyan

80. Dryden emphasized three virtues for which the poet should arose admiration which of the following is not one of them?
(a) Valour (b) Justice
(c) Duty (d) Love

81. What does Dryden mean by the term 'concernment'?
(a) Duty (b) Sanity
(c) Comparison (d) Infaluation

82. Dryden's All for Love is a transitional play, showing the features of both, the heroic play and the
(a) sentimental tragedy
(b) sentimental comedy
(c) restoration comedy
(d) comedy of humours

83. Who wrote comedies such as Love in a Bottle and the Recruiting officer in the Restoration Age?
(a) Otway (b) Wycherley
(c) Vangbungh (d) Farquhar

84. Sir Thomas Browne's Religio Medici became an immediate success. It was translated into Latin, French, German, Dutch and Italian and was reprinted about eight times during the author's life-time. What is the theme of the work?
(a) The religion of a doctor.
(b) Doctors are not atheists.
(c) Religion is not incompatible with Science.
(d) All of the above.

85. The first regular English Journal was started in 1622 by
(a) Thomas Arches (b) Nicholas Burne
(c) Addeson and Steel (d) Both (a) and (b)

86. Who said of *Paradise Lost* that Milton was the Devil's party without knowing it?
(a) Lamb (b) Coleridge
(c) Arnold (d) None of the above.

87. Whom does Milton indict in *Paradise Lost* as 'the sons of Belian flown with insolence and wine?"
(a) The Anglican clergy
(b) The opponents of the common wealth
(c) The cavalier poets
(d) All of the above.

88. Which is the metre used in *Paradise Lost*?
(a) Alexandrine
(b) Hexameter of the Aenied
(c) Pentameter of Blank verse
(d) None of the above

89. 'Comus' by Milton is
(a) a forceful plea for freedom of the press.
(b) a mosque preaching the ultimate triumph of virtue over the evil.
(c) a political tract advocating the cause of the common wealth.
(d) None of the above.

90. Which of the following is not true?
(a) L'Allegro strikes a positively anti-Puritan note.
(b) II Penseroso has definite Christian associations.
(c) The two companion poems are the poems of joy.
(d) None of the above.

91. The Source of *Paradise Lost* chiefly lies in
(a) Classical epic
(b) The Bible

(c) Anglo-Saxon Chronicles
(d) Old English Texts

92. Milton's Poetic Style is usually regarded as
(a) Plam and simple (b) Classical
(c) Grand (d) Ornamental

93. "In Milton, there is always an appearance of effort, in Shakespeare, scarely any". This remark has been made by
(a) Dr Johnson (b) Dryden
(c) William Hazlett (d) Mathew Arnole

94. The view 'Better to reign in Hell than to serve in Heaven' has been expressed in *Paradise Lost* by
(a) Milton (b) Adam
(c) Beelzebub (d) Satan

95. Milton's *Paradise Lost* is written in
(a) Heroic couplet
(b) Spencerian stanza
(c) Free verse
(d) Blank verse

96. Which of the following romantic poets was greatly influenced by Milton's style and manner?
(a) Wordsworth (b) Byron
(c) Shelley (d) Keats

97. Milton is criticized as
(a) an egotistic poet
(b) a humourless poet
(c) too allusive
(d) All of the above.

98. In Book III of *Paradise Lost* Satan comes to the earth where does he alight first?
(a) In the Garden of Eden
(b) On the Sun
(c) On mount niphates
(d) None of the above.

99. Who directs Satan to the earth in *Paradise Lost*?
(a) Sun (b) Gabriel
(c) Ragheal (d) Uriel

100. Milton's poetic career can be divided in from periods. Given below are the periods and the years. Match them.
(a) Cambridge period (i) 1932-38
(b) Harton period (ii) Upto 32
(c) Journalistic period (iii) 1660-71
(d) Poetic achievement (iv) 1640-60

Codes:	A	B	C	D
(a)	(iv)	(iii)	(ii)	(i)
(b)	(ii)	(i)	(iv)	(iii)
(c)	(iii)	(iv)	(i)	(ii)
(d)	(iv)	(ii)	(iii)	(i)

101. Which term is used to describe Milton's poetic art?
(a) Miltonic suplimits
(b) Hellenic Spiril
(c) Miltonic Renaissance
(d) Miltonic style

102. Satan's Fall in *Paradise Lost* is
(a) an act of sacrifice
(b) an assertion of free will
(c) violation of religious laws
(d) political revolt

103. Satan reduced (tempted)
(a) Adam (b) Eve
(c) Angels (d) None of the above.

104. The phrase 'grand parent' refers to
(a) Adam and Eve (b) Rebel angels
(c) Beelzebub (d) Milton himself

105. 'Mother of Mankind' refers to
(a) Eve
(b) Eve's mother
(c) First woman on earth
(d) None of the above.

106. Satan remained tossing upon the lack of fine in Hell.
(a) Nine days (b) For a week
(c) For one night (d) A fort night

107. Arch-fiend is the phrase used for
(a) Beelzabub (b) God
(c) Satan (d) Motoch

108. Fallen angels compared to
   (a) the sea weeds on the Red sea
   (b) the sand on the Red sea
   (c) the mud on the Red sea
   (d) the grass on a mountain

109. Who headed the Puritan Govt. that was formed after the hanging of Charles I?
   (a) Chomwell
   (b) James II
   (c) Charles II
   (d) None of the above.

110. *Vulgar Errors* is written by
   (a) John Lily (b) Thomas Leyd
   (c) Milton (d) Thomas Browne

111. John Donne fell in love with the niece of Lord Egerton named
   (a) Anne mox (b) Fanny Burny
   (c) Celia (d) None of the above

112. "Here lies my wife, here let her rest! Now she is at rest, and so am I!" This was a proposed epitaph to be engraved on the tomb of his wife. Who was that poet?
   (a) Phillip Massigner (b) John Donne
   (c) John Dryden (d) Milton

113. 'The Elegie' in praise of John Donne was written by
   (a) Thomas carew
   (b) Henry Vaughan
   (c) Andrew Marvell
   (d) Abraham Cowley

114. What could be another name for Renaissance?
   (a) The New Learning
   (b) The Reformation
   (c) The Protestanism
   (d) Humanism

115. Milton's *Comus* is an
   (a) elegy (b) masque
   (c) ballad (d) epic

ANSWERS

1. (b)	2. (c)	3. (c)	4. (d)	5. (d)	6. (a)
7. (c)	8. (c)	9. (d)	10. (b)	11. (a)	12. (c)
13. (a)	14. (d)	15. (c)	16. (a)	17. (b)	18. (c)
19. (b)	20. (a)	21. (a)	22. (d)	23. (d)	24. (a)
25. (c)	26. (d)	27. (a)	28. (b)	29. (c)	30. (a)
31. (a)	32. (c)	33. (c)	34. (d)	35. (b)	36. (a)
37. (a)	38. (a)	39. (c)	40. (d)	41. (a)	42. (a)
43. (a)	44. (a)	45. (d)	46. (a)	47. (a)	48. (a)
49. (a)	50. (b)	51. (a)	52. (a)	53. (a)	54. (c)
55. (a)	56. (c)	57. (d)	58. (c)	59. (a)	60. (a)
61. (c)	62. (c)	63. (d)	64. (b)	65. (b)	66. (a)
67. (b)	68. (b)	69. (a)	70. (c)	71. (b)	72. (b)
73. (b)	74. (b)	75. (d)	76. (b)	77. (b)	78. (c)
79. (d)	80. (b)	81. (c)	82. (a)	83. (d)	84. (d)

85. (d)	86. (d)	87. (c)	88. (c)	89. (b)	90. (b)
91. (b)	92. (c)	93. (b)	94. (d)	95. (d)	96. (d)
97. (d)	98. (c)	99. (d)	100. (b)	101. (a)	102. (b)
103. (b)	104. (a)	105. (a)	106. (a)	107. (c)	108. (a)
109. (a)	110. (d)	111. (a)	112. (c)	113. (a)	114. (a)
115. (b)					

13

Augustan Age: 18th Century Literature

The Augustan Age is sometimes called the Classic Age and sometimes the Age of Pope of English literature. The epithet 'classic' denotes that the poets and critics of this age believed that the works of the writers of classical antiquity presented the best of models and the ultimate standards of literary taste. They had little faith in the promptings and guidance of individual genius, and much in laws and rules imposed by the authority of the past. When in 1706 Walsh wrote to Pope: "The best of the modern poets in all languages are those that have nearest copied the ancients", he expressed concisely the principle of classicism. The other epithet, 'Augustan', was applied in the first instance as a term of high praise, because those who used it really believed that as the Age of Augustan was the golden age of Latin Literature, so the Age of Pope was the golden age of English literature. It serves to bring out the analogy between the English literature of the first half of the eighteenth century and the Latin Literature of the days of Vergil and Horace. In both cases men of letters were largely dependent upon powerful patrons. In both cases a critical spirit prevailed.

The literature of this era was Partly new and Partly a continuance of that of the Restoration. Though manners were coarse politics scandalously corrupts, and the general tone of societal brutal, the England of the early eighteenth century witnessed a resolute attempt in the direction of moral regeneration.

IMPORTANT WRITERS AND THEIR WORKS

WRITERS	WORKS
Alexander Pope (1688-1744)	*An Essay in Criticism* (1711)
	Windosor Forest (1713)
	The Pope of the Lock (1712)
	Eloisa to Aberland
	Elegy to the Memory of an Unformate Lady of the charactors of women an essay on Man
	The Dunciad
Mathew Prior (1664-1721)	*The Town and Country Mouse* (1687)
	Alma or The Progress of the Mind (1718)
	Solomon on the Vanity of the World (1718)
	The Chameleon, The Thief and the Cordelies.
	To Chole
John Gay (1685-1732)	*Fables* (1727)

	The Beggar's Opera (1728)
	The Rural Sports (1713)
	The Shephered's Week (1714)
	What d' ye call it (1715)
	Trivia or The Art of Walking the Streets of London (1716)
Edward young (1683-1765)	*Last Day* (1714)
	The Force of Religion (1714)
	The Love of Fame (1725-28)
	The Complaint or Night Thoughts on Life, Death and Immorality (1742)
Samuel Garth (1661-1719)	*The Dispensary* (1699)
William Somerville (1675-42)	*The Chase*
Lady Winchilsea (1661-1720)	*The Spleen* (1720)
	The Prodigy (1706)
	Miscellany poems (1713)
Thomas Parnell Prose (1679-18)	*The Hermit*
	Daniel Defoe-Robinson Crusoe (1719)
	Duncan Campbell, Memoires of a Caralier, captain singleton (1720)
	Moll Flanders (1722)
	Roxane (1724)
	A New Voyage Round the World (1725)
Jonathan Swift (1667-1745)	*The Battle of Books* (1704)
	A Tale of A Tub (1704)
	The Battle of Books
	The Gulliver's Travels
Sir Richard Steele (1672-1729)	*The Funeral* (1701)
	The Lying Lover (1703)
	The Tender Husband (1705)
	The Conscious Lovers (1722)
	The Tatler (1709)
	The Guardian (1713)
Joseph Addison (1672-1719)	*The Spectator*
	The Vision of Mirza
	Public credit

	The Campasign (1704)
	Cato (1703)
	Rosamond (1707)
	The Drummer (1715)
Dr Samuel Johnson (1709-84)	*London* (1738)
	The Vanity of Human Wisher (1749)
	The Life of Savage (1744)
	The Lives of the Poets (1781)
	Dictionary of the English Language (1753)
	Shakespeare (1765)
	A Journey to the Western Islands of Scotland (1775)
	The Rambler, Rasselas, A Prince of Abyssinia (1759)
James Thomson (1700-48)	*The Seasons* (1730)
	Liberty (1736)
	The Castle of Indolence (1748)
	Sophonisba (1729) (Play)
	Alfred (1740)
Oliver Goldsmith (1728-74)	*The Traveller* (1764)
	The Deserted Village (1770)
	The Hermit
	Elegy on the Death of a Mad Dog
	The Good Natured Man (1768) Play
	She Stoops to Conquer (1773) Play
	The Citizen of the World (1759)
	The Vicar of Wakefield (1766)
Thomas Gray (1716-71)	*Ode on a Distant Prospect of Eton College* (1747)
	Elegy written in a country churchyard (1751)
	Pindaric Odes (1757)
William Collins (1721-59)	*Oriental Eclogies* (1742)
	Ode to Evening
	Ode to the popular superstitions of the Highlands
	Odes to Simplicity
	To Fear

	To the Passions
	How Sleep, The Brave (Short elegies)
William Cowper (1731-1800)	*The Progress of Error, Truth, Table, Talk etc.*
	The Task (1785)
	On the Receipt of My Mother's Picture
William Blake (1757-1827)	*Poetical Sketches* (1783)
	The Book of Thel (1790)
	The French Revolution (1791)
	America Europe (1793-94)
George Crabbe (1754-1832)	*The Library* (1781)
	The Village (1783)
	The Borough (1810)
	Tales (1812)
Mark Akenside (1721-70)	*An Epistle to Curio* (1744)
	The Pleasures of the Imagination (1744)
Christopher Smart (1722-70)	*Song to David*
William Shenstone (1714-63)	*Levities or Pieces of Humour*
	The School Mistress (1742)
Robert Burns (1559-96)	*A Found kess and then we Sever*
	The Jolly Beggers.
Samuel Richardson (1689-61)	*Pamela or Virtue Rewarded* (1740)
	Clarissa Harlowe (1748)
	Sir Charles Grandison (1754)
Edmund Burke (1729-97)	*A Vindication of Natural Society* (1756)
	A Philosophical Inquiry (1756)
	American Taxation (1774)
	A Letter to a Noble Lord (1795)
James Boswell (1740-95)	*The Life of Samuel Johnson* (1791)
Henry Fielding (1707-54)	*Joseph Andrews* (1742)
	A Journey from this World to the Next (1743)
	Jonathan Wild the Great (1743)
	Tom Jones (1749)
	Amelia (1751)
	Voyage to Lisbon
Tobias Smollett (1721-71)	*The Adventures of Roderick Random* (1748)
	The Adventures of Peregrine Pickle (1750)
	The Expedition of Humphry Clinker (1771)

Lawrence Sterne (1713-68)	*Tristram Shandy* (1767)
	A Sentimental Journey Through France and Italy (1768).
Bishop Percy (1729-1811)	*Religues of Ancient English Poetry*
Adam Smith (1723-90)	*The Wealth of Nations* (1776)
Richard Brinsley –	*The Rivals* (1744)
Henry Mackenzie (1745-1831)	*The Man of Feeling* (1771)
William Godwin (1756-1836)	*Political Justice* (1793)
	Caleb Williams (1794) A novel
Miss Fanny Burney (1752-42)	*Evelina* (1778)
	Cecilia (1782)
	Camilla (1796)
	The Wanderer (1814)
Harace Walpole (1717-97)	*Castle of Otronto* (1764)
Mrs. Anne Rad cliffe (1764-32)	*The Mysteries of Udolpho* (1794)
	The Italian (1797)
William Beckford (1760-1844)	*The History of the Calign, Vatheck* (1786)
Mathew Prior (1664-1721)	*Alma: Or the Progress of the Mind* (1718)
	Solomon on the Vanity of the World (1718)
R.B. Sheridon (1751-1816)	*St. Patrick's Day*
	A Trip to Scarborough (1776)
	The School for Scandal (1777)
	The Critic: or a Tragedy Rhearesed (1779)
John Arbuth not (1667-1735)	*Memoirs of Martinus Scriblerus* (1709)
	The History of John Bull (1712)
	The Art of Political Lying
Lord Bolingbroke (1678-1751)	*A Letter to Sir William Wyndham*
	A Letter on the Spirit of Patriotism
	Alciphrm or the Minute Philospher
Joseph Butler (1692-1752)	*Analogy of Religion*

General Characteristics of the Age

1. The Rise of the Political Parties (the Whigs and the Tories). The Whig Party stood for the Pre-eminence of personal freedom and the Tony Party supported the view of royal Divine Right. The torries who mostly belonged to the landed classes, objected to the foreign wars because they had to pay taxes to prolong it, while the Whings, consisting largely of the trading classes, favoured the continance of war, as it contributed to their ideologies and programmes both the political parties felt the necessity of utilizing the services of literary men, and the politicians bribed the authors to join one or the other of political camps. Consequently, most men of letters show a strong political bias. The politics of the period helped to make it an age of political pamphleteering, and periodicals. The rise of periodical writing allowed great scope to the talent of prose writers of the time and helped the development of prose. Hence, we find in this age the clear and simple prose style used in the periodical essay and journalism. Albert said, "It was the golden age of political pamphleteering and the writers made the most of it."

2. Rise of Clubs and Coffee Houses. The coffee houses becomes the centres of fashionable and public life. A Whig would never go to a Tory Coffee House and vice-versa. John Dennis said, "Books were seldom judged on their merits, the praise or blame being generally awarded according to the political principles of then authors." The coffee houses were the popular haunts of prominents writers and they figure prominently in the writings of the day. The discussions in coffee houses took place in polished, urbans, elegant, easy and lucid style.

3. The New Publishing Houses. The rising interest in politics compled with the decline of drama, resulted in a remarkable increase in the size of the reading public. Many people took interest in publishing works of the time. They employed writers of the period.

4. The Rise of the Middle Class and the New Morality. Emergence of a powerful middle class, which was associated with the nobility in the exercise of power and political influence, and directed culture. It was a period of comfortable aristrocratic rule in which the middle classes, especially the rich rulers. The predominance of the middle class made it an age of tolerance, moderation and common sense. The powerful dominance of the middle classes led to moral regeneration in the 18th century.

5. An Age of Prose and Reason. Poetry itself became prosaic as it was not used for creative works of imagination, but for essays, satires and criticism. The graceful elegance of Addison's essays, the terse vigour of Swift's satires, the artistic finish of Burke's orations-these have no parallel in the literary history of the 18th century.

6. Predominance of Satire. The prevalence of Satire, which resulted from the unfortunate union of politics with literature, is an important literary characteristic of this age. A satirist is like a labourer who clears away the ruins and rubbish of an old house before the architect and builders begin on a now and beautiful structure.

7. The Classical Age. The classical writers of the 18th century regarded the old English writers with contempt and indifference. They were guided by reason, good sense and wit, they wanted order and balance, and every kind of excess and irregularly was abhorrent to them. They were classics, because they claimed the formal classical qualities of moderation, tolerance and good sense. Summing the classicism of the Age of Pope, W.J. Long writes: "The general tendancy of literature was to look at life critically, to emphasize intellect rather than imagination, the form writers strove to repress all emotion and ethusiams, and to use only precise and elegant methods of expression. This is what is often meant by the 'classicism' of the ages of Pope and Johnson. It refers to the critical, intellectual spirit of many writers, to the fine polish of the heroic couplets is the elegance of their prose, and not to any resemblance which their work bears to true classic literature."

Good Sense. Good sense is one of the literature of this period. In the words of W.H. Hudson: "Good sense became the ideal of the time, and good sense meant a love of the reasonable and the useful, and a hatred of the extravagant, the mystical and the visionary."

Literature of the Town. The range of the literature of the period is strictly limited. It is a literature of the town and the fashionable upper circles of the city of London. Pope, Addison Steele, Bruke and all other writers of this period deal only with urban themes. Steele and temperament, show remarkable interest in the middle classis, and thus, broadess the scope of literature, which prior to them was strictly confined to fashionable and aristocratic circles.

Artificial and Conventional style. The poets of the period deftly cared for form and took all pains to polish and refine the poetic style. It "led to the establishment of a highly artificial and conventional style, which presently became Sterotyped into a regular traditional poetic diction."

Dominance of the Heroic Couplet. Heroic couplet dominated in poetry. This metre produced a close, clear and pointed style, as we shall note in the poetry of Pope. Its epigrammatic terseness provided a suitable medium of expression to the kind of poetry which was then popular. In the long run the heroic couplet outlived its utility as it 'was bound to grow monotonous, and that it was too narrow and inflexible'.

Alexander Pope (1688-1744). Pope was independent, and had no profession, but literature. Pope received very little school education, but he privately studied English books. He acknowledged Dryden as his poetic master, though much of French poet are critic. The publication of *Essay on Criticism* and *The Rape of the Lock* of Homer were so successful financially that he bought a Villa at Twickenham, on the Thames. He died in 1744 and was buried at Twickenham.

Essay on Criticism **(1711)** is also written in heroic Couplet. It seems up the art of poetry as taught first by Horace. Boilean and other 18th century classicists.

The Rape of the Lock, a masterpiece of its kind, was first published in 1712, and then in 1714. It was soon after this that voltaine called him 'the best poet of England, and at present, of all the world'. The Rape of the Lock is a mock-heroic poem, in which the mockery arises from 'the contrast between the sublimity of the Style and what the 18th century called the meanners of the occasion. "It is a classic of drawing-room poetry. It is modeled after Boilean's Le Lutrin, a satire on the French clergy, and La secchia Rapita (stolen Pruckel) a famous Italian satire on the petty causes of the endless. Italian wars. It is an authentic expression of the artificial life of the age of its cards, parties, toiletterin, laptogs, tea-drinking, snuff-taking, and idle vanities." It is not only a satire on society, it is also a wilty periods of the heroic style in poetry.

The translation of the Iliad and the Odyssey—the former made single-handed, the latter with much help from others—represents the labours of Pope's second period. The real difficulty by in fact that neither he nor his age could understand or enter into the spirit of Humer or the Humeric world. His public, however, wanted neither a scholarly nor a faithful version of the Greek poems, but a readable, drawing-room rendering of them in accordance with the taste of their own time. This was given to them by pope. As Gibbon afterwards said, his translation has every ment except fidelity to the original.

Then Pope dedicated himself completely to satiric and didactic poetry. The principal works of this period are: Satires and Epistles of Horace Imitated, The Prologue to there—the Epistle to

Dr. Arbuthnot—is specially valuable as the most frankly personal of all Pope's writings. It contains among other well-known passages the famous character study of Addison under the names of Atticus.

An Essay on Man—a poem in form epistles a defence of the moral government of the universe. The Essay is hopelessly confused and self-cantrodictory. But it contains many passages which are justly famous, and are still often quoted, for their rhetorical beauty and power.

Pope's merits and defects are those of the classical school. He had neither the imaginative power nor the depth of feeling without which great poetry is impossible. Nor was he a great printer. But he was the very embodiment of the kind of intelligence which was cultivated and admired. He was also, and adroit literary craftsman, and the neat, compact, antithetic, and epigrammatic style of writing which was the classical ideal, assumed perfection in his hands. After Shakespeare he is the most frequently quoted of English poets.

"Who shall decide when Doctors disagree?"
"A little learning is a dangerous thing".
"And fools rush in where angels fear to treat"
"To err is human, to forgive divine'.
"The proper study of mankind if man'.

Dr. Johnson was once asked whether Pope was a poet, he replied; "If Pope be not a poet, where is poetry to be found". He is a poet according to the 18th century poetic standards. In fact he was not a poet, but a versifier in an age of Prose. His influence dominated the poetry of this age, and many foreign writers. like Wordsworth he could not appreciate the beauties of nature. His poetry is town poetry, strictly limited to the fashionable society of London. As a metrest, Pope is wholly restricted to the heroic couplet. Pope's couplet is characterized by correction and finish.

OTHER POETS OF THE PERIOD

Malthew Prior's (1664-1721) first work is a parody of Dryden's The Hind and the Panthew, entitled the *Town and Country Mouse* (1687). It was written in collaboration with Charles Montagu. His other works are *Alma*, or *The Progress of the Mind* (1718), and *Solomon on the Vanity of the World* (1718).

John Gay (1685-1732) is best remembered for his fables (1727) which is collogcial easy, octosyllabic, and the *Beggar's Opera* (1729) which is a famous play. It contains some pretty songs and much genuine humour. Gay's chief poetic works are *The Rural Sports* (1713), written in the heroic couplet. The Shepherd's Work, *what d' ye call it* (1715), a postral farce, and *Triviel is The Art of Walky the Streets of London* (1716) a Witty parody of the heroic style. Gay mirrors the manners and outward show of his age.

Edward Young (1683-1765) wrote various kind of poetry. His *Last Day* written in the heroic couplet. He is remembered for the complaint or Night Thoughts on Life, Death and Immorality, which is written in the blank verse. It was occasioned by the death of his wife. It is a lengthy poem of sententious reflection and shows considerable technical skill in the management of the blank verse, but it is handicapped by a stilled theatrical phraseology. It anticipates the 'Churchyard School' of poetry.

Samuel Garth's (1661-1719) *The Dispensary* (1699) is a satire on the society of Apothecaries. It is written in the couplet.

William Somerville (1675-1742) wrote *The Chase*, a gloomy and somber poem, imitating the 'Churchyard School' of poetry.

Linda Winchilsea (1661-1718) stood to some extent for the new spirit. Some of her poems are "The Spleen" (1701), "A Poems" (1713), containing, a Nocturnal Reveria. She had the gift of producing smooth and melodious verse, and had a discerning eye for the beauties of nature. Wordsworth singled her out as a remarkable poet.

Thomas Parnell (1679-1718) made a notable break with the trends of the 18th century poetry. His best work is contained in the Hermit. He shows skill as a versifier, and he has a genuine regard for nature.

PROSE

The Age of Pope, is the age of prose in the real sense. Dryden is the first great pioneer of modern prose. His ease, force, vigour, clearness and intellectuaility imparted a really true prosaic character to his writings. Dryden's Essay on Dramatic Poetry was undoubtedly a model of the new prose.

The periodical essay was the peculiar product of the 18th century. It was not published in book form like other types of essays, as the essays of Bacon, but it was published in journals and magazines which appeared periodically. It had an inherent social purpose. It aimed at improving the manners and morals of the people and hence, it is also termed as the 'social essay'. The increasing interest in the political affairs, the establishment of prose in the 18th century. Daniel Defoe, Jonathan Swift, Sir Richard Steele and Joseph Addison are the some great writers of the periodical essay in the age of Pope.

Daniel Defoe (1661-1731). As a pioneer in journalism as well as in the novel Defoe enjoys an important place in English literature. The germs of the periodical essay are found in Defoe's Review, which at first appeared weekly, then twice, and later thrice a weak. Its main aim was to acquaint the English people with the thoughts of Defoe on international politics and on commerce. The greatly The Tatler and The Spectator Defoe's works of fiction are called 'fictitious biographies'. Leslic Stephen calls them 'history minus the facts'. His major works are *Robinson Crusoe* (1719), *Duncan Compell* are *Robinson Crusoe* (1719), *Duncan Campbell Memories Flanders*, *A Journal of the Plague Year*, *Colinel Jackque* (1722) and *Roxana* (1724) and a *New Voyage Round the World* (1725).

Jonathan Swift (1667-1745). Swift was 'the most original prose writer of his time-the man of genius among many men of talent'. He wrote a few papers for the Tatler and The Spectator. The Journal to Stella was written in the years 1710-13. Swift is known for his Drapier's Letters (1724). He also contributed to Sheriden's Dublin periodical The Intelligences.

Swift's humour was far too grim and sardonic. Hugh walker points out that Swift's intellect was too massive for the essay', and we look for the real swift on the lager convas of 'Gulliver' or 'A Tale of a Tub'.

Swift's *The Battle of Books* (1704) and *A Tale of A Tub* (1704) take rank among the finest prose satires in English literature. The theme of the former is the dispite between ancient and modern authors, and the latter is a satire on the Dissenters and even the Church of England. In 1726, Swift's inventive genius, his fierce satire, and his cruel indignation with life, not written from only literary motive, but rather fate and human society. Swift deftly used all fable, irony etc. as instruments of his Satire this style is terse, lucid, simple, direct, vigorous and suggestive. He deftly uses "proper words in proper place, and carefully avoids the use of big, bombastic and high sounding words".

Sir Richard Steele (1672-1729); Steele, an original genius, founded The Tatler on April 12, 1709. It appeared three times a week. At the beginning it was practically written by Steele alone. Steele wrote under the pseudonym of Mr. Bickerstaff, which he borrowed from Swift. Addison also began to contribute to the Tatler. The Tatler became immensely popular but it was discontinued on Jan 2, 1711. Steele had contributed one hundred and seventy papers to it when it came to an end. Steele was the originator of The Tatler and joined with Addison in creating The Spectator in Steele suggested the idea of the Spectator and his club, The human figure of the Spectator and his club. The human figure of the spectator surrounded by his club of representatives of various grades and classes of society, was an immense improvement on The Tatler's crude machinery of the coffee houses, and its Shadowy figure of Bickerstaff. Herein consists the superiority of The Spectator. The Spectator would lose its charm without Sir Roger, Sir Andrew, will Honeycomb and the Spectator himself.

Steele's papers have sincerity, frankness and genuine autobiographical touches. In the short span of four years in which Addison and Steele worked together the periodical essays was established as one of the most important form of literature.

Joseph Addison (1672-1719). He was a great social critic and reformer who brought about a revolutionary change in the quality of life in contemporary England through his contributions to The Spectator, a periodical which he founded in collaboration with Sir Richard Steele. He was, indeed, an informed observer, a judicious critic of manners and characters. His task was to recover the people out of that desperate state of vice and folly into which the age had fallen. It was his task, 'to enliven morality.' In order to create a rational standard of conduct the shameless licence and shallowness of restoration manners. In the field of politics Addison perceived the absurdity of the party system. He regarded it as the parent of hypocrisy and self-deception Addison also exposed the trifles which engaged the attention of fashionable women. He ironically laughed at the follies and foibles of ladies. There is an inherent moral purpose in Addison's social criticism. In all Addison advocated moderation and tolerance, and was the enemy of enthusiasm.

Addison is a genial humourist. His humour is humane, serene and impartial, and reflects the nobility of his temperament. He knew how to use ridicule without abusing it. He was the gentle satiris. He good humouredly exposed only minor lapses and small sins against society. His power of ridiculing keenly without malignity is of course best shown in his character of Sir Rogis de coverly. Addison's style is noticeable for neatness and lucidity of expression. He represents in this manner, 'our indispensable 18th century'. Addison took great care to select words from a rich stock and was careful not to weary his readers by repetition of the same sound. He polished and balanced his phrases until the rhythm was perfect. He used metaphors to impart clarity to his style. According to Dr. Johnson Addison's prose is the model of the middle style'...whoever wishes to attain an English style familiar but not coarse, and elegant but not ostentations, must give his days and nights to the volumes of Addison.

DRAMA

The drama of Pope's age is almost a blank. The days of the brilliant and exotic flower of Restoration comedy was over. Addison's Cato is the only noteworthy work in the field of tragedy. It was an attempt to introduce to the English stage the decorous and rhetorical drama of the French School. Steele's The Constant Lover is so overweighted with ethical purpose as to be, in spite of occasional humour, insipid and dull. Steele's comedy does not amuse, it preaches. So, he became the founder of that highly genteel, didactic and vapid kind of play which is known as sentimental comedy, and which became popular in the age of Jonson. George Lillo (1693-1739) established a 'domestic drama' or form of tragedy, the characters and incidents of which were to be taken from common life instead of from romance or history. His famous works are London Merchant and Fatal Curiosity.

Dr. Johnson—The greatest English man of letters between Pope and Wordsworth, Samuel Johnson was born at Lichfield, in 1709. In 1738 he published a poem called *London*, and formed a connection with Cave's Magazine, to which for a number of years he regularly contributed the parliamentary reports. He produced the *Vanity of Human Wishes* (1749) and a tragedy, *Irene* (1737), on the new. Classical model, and in March 1750, started a periodical, The Rambler in imitation of The Spectator, which appeared on Tuesdays and Saturdays till March 1752, all save five members being from his won pen. Dr. Johnson was the acknowledged dictator of contemporary literature. Smotllet called him. 'the great charm of literature'. His poems are written in the heroic couplet and abrund in personifications and other tricks that belong at to the poetic diction of the age of Pope. In their didacticism, their formal, rhetorical style, and their adherence to the closed couplet they belong to the Psendo-classic poetry.

Chur Chill (1731-64). He was a satirist and his best work The Rosciad and social figures of the time. It is written in the heroic couplet and is obviously modeled on Pope's The Dunciad.

Oliver Goldsmith (1728-74). Goldsmith's first poem, "The Traveller" (1764) is written in the heroic couplet and deals with his wonderings through Europe. It contains a series of descriptions and criticism of the places and peoples of which he had experience.

Goldsmith uses simple and clear language. The couplet is melodious and polished. In the *Deserted Village* (1770) Goldsmith deals with the memories of his youth and the pathetic note is more freely expressed. Goldsmith's The Hermit and the witty Elegy on the Death of a Mad Dog are remarkable for sentimentatism and the blending of humour and pathos. Goldsmith's poetry represents the poetic tradition of Pseudo-classicism so far as the use of the heroic couplet and the stilled and pompous phraseology is concerned. Goldsmith's treatment of nature and rural life, note of human sympathy and simplicity of expression are the characteristics of the new poetry.

MULTIPLE CHOICE QUESTIONS

1. John Dryden was born on the
   (a) 7th August 1632
   (b) 8th August 1631
   (c) 9th August 1631
   (d) 10th August 1631

2. The name of John Dryden's father was
   (a) Pyramus Dryden
   (b) Eramus Dryden
   (c) Earnest Dryden
   (d) None of the above.

3. Dryden was conferred the Post Graduate degree by the Archibishop of Canterbury, on the recommendation of
   (a) Queen Elizabeth
   (b) James I
   (c) James II
   (d) None of the above
4. The great Plague broke out in London in
   (a) 1665 (b) 1666
   (c) 1565 (d) 1566
5. An Essay on Dramatic Poesy was published in
   (a) 1662 (b) 1664
   (c) 1666 (d) 1668
6. Dryden's last play was
   (a) *Triumphant*
   (b) *Absalim and Achitophel*
   (c) *The Hind and the Panther*
   (d) *Satires of Jusenal and Persius*
7. Dryden mainly wrote
   (a) plays (b) prose
   (c) poetry (d) All of the above
8. Jaine describes the poetic genius of Dryden as 'Preminently robust and
   (a) romantic
   (b) unromantic
   (c) beautiful
   (d) None of the above
9. "Absalom and Achitophel", "the Medal" and "Mac Flexmoe" are
   (a) religious poems
   (b) political poems
   (c) socio-Political poems
   (d) political Religion poems
10. Dryden wrote a didactic work thesis called
    (a) Macl Fleknoe
    (b) Alexnader Feast
    (c) Religiolaici
    (d) None of the above
11. Dryden himself produced a play whose name was
    (a) *Aurengzebe*
    (b) *Hind and the Panther*
    (c) *Sir Martin Marshall*
    (d) None of the above
12. Dryden's last and heroid tragedy was
    (a) *Hind and the Panther*
    (b) *Aurangzebe*
    (c) *Sir Martin Marshall*
    (d) None of the above
13. The most original comic drama of Dryden was
    (a) *The Wild Gallant*
    (b) *Sir Martin Marshall*
    (c) *The Kind Creeper*
    (d) None of the above
14. *The Rival Ladies* and *Secret Love* are his
    (a) comedies (b) romances
    (c) tragedies (d) tragic-comedies
15. Gray's Odes 'On Spring' and 'Hymn to Adversity' were written in
    (a) the first stage of his poetic career
    (b) the second stage of his poetic career
    (c) the third stage of his poetic career
    (d) the fourth stage of his poetic career
16. Gray's The Elegy Written in a country churchyard marked the transition for Gray fron the classicism of ________ to romanticism.
    (a) Raman School
    (b) France School
    (c) Popeah School
    (d) None of the above
17. The Progress of Poesy belongs to
    (a) the first stage
    (b) the second stage
    (c) the third stage
    (d) the fourth stage

18. The second period of Gray's poetic career is truly _____ in nature.
    (a) transitional
    (b) non-transitional
    (c) semi transitional
    (d) None of the above.
19. Gray wrote mainly to please
    (a) Andeenia (b) Readers
    (c) Himself (d) All of the above
20. During Gray's life time only _____ poems were published
    (a) thirteen (b) thirty
    (c) thirty-nine (d) None of the above
21. Gray's poetry has rich rhythmical harmony and solemn ______ effect.
    (a) lyrical (b) musical
    (c) rhythmical (d) emotional
22. The interest in the life of humble is essentially
    (a) a romantic trait (b) sympathetic
    (c) a poetical spirit (d) All of the above
23. Progress of Poesy is a
    (a) beauteous poem
    (b) imaginative poem
    (c) narrative poem
    (d) All of the above
24. The Ode deals with
    (a) single phrase (b) double phase
    (c) several phrase (d) All phases
25. The Pindaric Ode consists of
    (a) one parts (b) two parts
    (c) three parts (d) four parts
26. The Progress of Poetry consists of
    (a) three triads (b) four triads
    (c) six triads (d) None of the above
27. In the poem 'The progress of Poesy' the poet invoices
    (a) the spirit of progress
    (b) Aedian Lyre
    (c) Juno
    (d) Irisis
28. Muse is supposed to live
    (a) in Heaven (b) on Himalyas
    (c) on Alps (d) on Helicon
29. The temple of Goddess venus is situated at
    (a) Idalia (b) Arolia
    (c) Hesperia (d) None of the above
30. Eyphrosyne is one of the three goddesses of
    (a) Art (b) Music
    (c) Light (d) Diane
31. The horrors of night are dispelled by the
    (a) Sun (b) Moon
    (c) Light (d) Diane
32. The God of poetry and music is
    (a) Apollo (b) Cupid
    (c) Jupiter (d) Mars
33. The Band is one of the
    (a) famous ode of Gray
    (b) two Sister Odes
    (c) most musical ode
    (d) All of the above
34. 'The Band' deals with an episode in
    (a) Welsh history (b) Greek history
    (c) Egyphan history (d) Roman history
35. The bard laments the death of his dead
    (a) relatives (b) friends
    (c) brother (d) comradis
36. Edward III is compared with the
    (a) rising sun (b) rising moon
    (c) setting sun (d) None of the above
37. When Johnson's translation of a French version 'voyage to Alyssinia' was published?
    (a) 1731 (b) 1725
    (c) 1733 (d) 1734

38. In 18th century art was a part of ordinary life and trade; whose words are these?
    (a) Teveyuan (b) Johnson
    (c) Reynolds (d) None of the above
39. The Humanitarian spirit of which century expressed itself in other spheres of social life?
    (a) 18th (b) 19th
    (c) 20th (d) None of the above
40. Who was pre-eminently a prose writer in the age of prose?
    (a) Emerson (b) Johnson
    (c) Emily Dickenson (d) Shakespeare
41. Johnson reputation was increased by ____, which Johnson published in 1749.
    (a) Journey to Abyssinian
    (b) The Vanity of Human Wishes
    (c) Both of these
    (d) None of the above
42. When was Johnson's 'Dictionary of English Language' published?
    (a) 1755 (b) 1759
    (c) 1758 (d) 1785
43. What is the name of Milton's sister?
    (a) Anne (b) Emity
    (c) Maria (d) None of the above
44. John Dryden was married at
    (a) Lady Elizabeth Howard
    (b) Mary Howard
    (c) Virginia Howard
    (d) None of the above
45. John Dryden was buried at
    (a) West minister abbey
    (b) Eastminister Abbey
    (c) Northampton
    (d) None of the above
46. Dryden wrote ______ plays.
    (a) 26 (b) 17
    (c) 37 (d) 27
47. What was the sub-title of 'All for Love'?
    (a) The Lost World
    (b) The World Well Lost
    (c) The world Lost
    (d) None of the above
48. Jonathan Swift was a cousin of
    (a) John Dryden (b) Thomas Swift
    (c) Samuel Johnson (d) William Minto
49. Swift called truest, 'The most virtous friend of
    (a) Stella (b) Selia
    (c) Sophia (d) Stephen
50. Swift frustration due to poverty and dependence made him an
    (a) imbittered person
    (b) bittered person
    (c) embiltered person
    (d) ambittered person
51. Swift followed the style of Lucian's 'True History' in
    (a) *A Tale of Tub*
    (b) *Gulliver's Travels*
    (c) *The Travel Books*
    (d) *The Charm*
52. Swift Pindark Ode was published in the
    (a) Ahenian Mercury (b) Athenian Mars
    (c) Ahenian Venus (d) Athenian Earth
53. Swift addressed his poem 'cadenum and vanessa' to his beloved.
    (a) Cadenum (b) Vanessa
    (c) Dingley (d) Stella
54. A Vehemence and ability of Mind, a curious imagery, a vivacity of diction was displayed in
    (a) *Gulliver Travels*
    (b) *The Travel Books*
    (c) *The Charm*
    (d) *A Tale of Tub*
55. _____ is a tale of an imaginary seaman's experiences.

(a) *The Charm*
(b) *Gulliver Travels*
(c) *A Tale of Tub*
(d) *The Travel Books*

56. In the first book of *Gulliver's Travels* Gulliver's Ship wrecked at
(a) Lilliput (b) Hilliput
(c) Dilliput (d) Jolliput

57. Swift's pamphlet was criticized by William wotton and
(a) Addison
(b) Richard Bentley
(c) Levis
(d) Sir William Temple

58. 'The Battle of Books' is in the form of an
(a) Prose (b) Poetry
(c) Epic (d) Letter

59. According to John Misery' The Battle of the Books is a
(a) Passion (b) Fairy
(c) Horror (d) Fantasia

60. The Episode of the Spider and the bee is taken from the
(a) Temple's essay (b) Spider essay
(c) See essay (d) Church essay

61. Henry Fielding remarried his maid named
(a) Helen Christen (b) Mary Christen
(c) Mary Daniel (d) Helen Daniel

62. In the Age of Pope which kind of poetry dominated the other kinds?
(a) Epic poetry (b) Lyric poetry
(c) Satiric poetry (d) Romantic poetry

63. "True wit is nature to advantage dressed what oft was thought, but never so well expressed". This couplet is a famous quote firm
(a) Swift (b) Pope
(c) Dryden (d) Shakespeare

64. The character Atticus is a caricature of
(a) Addison (b) Steele
(c) Johnson (d) Bacon

65. Which of the following pre-romantic poets wrote the seasons?
(a) Collins (b) Gray
(c) Thomson (d) Goldsmith

66. Thomas's 'Castle of Indolence' has been written in
(a) Blank verse (b) Free verse
(c) Spenserian stanza (d) Sonnets

67. When poem by Cowper, written in blank verse contains the famous line 'God made the country and man made town'?
(a) The Task
(b) The Village
(c) Songs of Experience
(d) The deserted village

68. The vision of Mirza and Public credit are popular allegories by
(a) Goldsmith (b) Addison
(c) Steele (d) Johnson

69. Who called Addison's prose as 'Attic' and 'Asiatic'?
(a) Johnson (b) Steele
(c) Arnold (d) Addison himself

70. Sir Roger de coverley, the imaginary old man of Coverlay papers is a
(a) City merchant
(b) Army officer
(c) Rich man-about-town
(d) Tory country spuine

71. Besides Roger, which of the following characters is/are also associated with Addison?
(a) Sir Andrew Freeport
(b) Captain sentry
(c) Will honeycomb
(d) Both (a) and (b)

72. Besides Marlowe, who else wrote a tragedy by the name Tambertaine?
(a) Addison (b) Steele
(c) Gay (d) Nicholas Rowe

73. The History of a Young Lady is the subtitle of
(a) Moll Flanders
(b) Pamela
(c) Clarisse
(d) None of the above

74. Who rapes clarissa in Richardson's novel?
(a) Belford (b) Howe
(c) Lovelace (d) All of the above

75. Which 18th century critic has criticized Paradise Lost for its lacking in human interest?
(a) Dr. Johnson (b) Mathew Arnold
(c) Oliver goldsmith (d) Richard Steele

76. Who said, 'A book should help us either to enjoy life or to endure it?"
(a) Boswell (b) Pope
(c) Dr. Johnson (d) Addison

77. Who wrote 'A Sentimental Journey?'
(a) Toblas Smollett (b) Lawrence Sterne
(c) Henry fielding (d) Jane Austen

78. Who are the 'four Wheels of the Novel Wain", as Sainstbury calls them?
(a) Richardson, Fielding, Golding, Sterve
(b) Fielding, Richardson, Smollett, Johnson
(c) Smollett, Sterve, Burney, Golding
(d) Richardson, Fielding, Smollett, Sterve

79. Which of his novels is called 'a comic epic in prose' by Henry Fielding?
(a) Joseph Andrews (b) Tom Jones
(c) Amelia (d) Boswell

80. Who praised Addison's style as 'the model of the middle style?'
(a) Alexander Pope (b) Jonathan Swift
(c) Dr Samuel (d) Broswell

81. Pope translated was introduced by
(a) Otway
(b) Sir William Davenant
(c) Corneille
(d) Dryden

82. The heroic tragedy was introduced by
(a) Otway
(b) Sir William Davenant
(c) Corneille
(d) Dryden

83. The transitional poets replaced the Neo-classical Heroic couplet by
(a) the four lined stanza
(b) Spenserian stanza
(c) the heroic quatrain
(d) All of the above

84. Who is considered to be the first literary philosopher?
(a) George Berkeley
(b) Arbuthnot
(c) Addison
(d) None of the above

85. What is a Picaresque novel?
(a) A novel whose hero is a Villain
(b) A novel whose hero is a knight
(c) A novel whose hero is a wandering rogue
(d) A novel whose hero is subordinate to the heroine

86. *Nightmare Abbey* is a novel by
(a) Peocock (b) Walpole
(c) Austen (d) None of the above

87. The term neo-classical in English literature means
(a) a new kind of literature.
(b) an old and outdated literature.
(c) the work of the writers of classical antiguity presented to the poets and critics of the age the best of models and the ultimate standards of literary taste.
(d) literature of classical writers.

88. Pope's *The Rape of the Lock* has been written in
(a) Spensarian Stanza (b) Blank verse
(c) Free verse (d) Heroic couplet

89. 'Moral Epistles' was written by
(a) Pope (b) Swift
(c) Goldsmith (d) Steele

90. The term 'bathos' was first used by
(a) Pope (b) Shakespeare
(c) Dryden (d) Arnold

91. Which of the following was a patron by Jonathan Swift?
(a) William Wolton (b) William Temple
(c) Queen Anne (d) James I

92. Who said; I heartly hate and detest that animal called mean"?
(a) Orwell (b) Swift
(c) Eliot (d) Pope

93. Roxane is a fiction by
(a) Steele (b) Johnson
(c) Defoe (d) Sterne

94. Who has been hailed as "the master of illusionist"?
(a) Richardson (b) Sterne
(c) Defoe (d) None of the above

95. Addison's the Drummer is
(a) An opera (b) A masque
(c) A tragedy (d) A prose-comedy

96. The age of Dr. Johnson is also known as
(a) the age of romanticism
(b) the age of transition
(c) the age of Victorianism
(d) Modern age

97. The poet who succeeded Dryden as Laureate was
(a) Pope (b) Shadwell
(c) Dr. Johnson (d) Flethcer

98. 'Ode on solitude' is one of the earliest productions of which of the following great names?
(a) Dryden (b) Milton
(c) Pope (d) Swift

99. 'Music is inarticulate poetry', who has said this?
(a) Pope (b) Dryden
(c) Milton (d) Cowley

100. Irene is a rhetorical tragedy by
(a) Dryden (b) Jonson
(c) Johnson (d) None of the above

101. Sheridan is famous for his
(a) Pastrols (b) Tragedies
(c) Comedies (d) Allegories

102. Who has written *The Rivals* came out in?
(a) 1770 (b) 1775
(c) 1781 (d) 1785

103. Which periodical was brought out by Daniel Defoe?
(a) Review
(b) The Edler
(c) The Morning News
(d) The Observer

104. *Cato* by Joseph Addison is a
(a) novel (b) comedy
(c) tragedy (d) romance

105. *The Rape of the Lock* is written in
(a) Three cantos (b) Four cantos
(c) Five cantos (d) Six cantos

106. Who said 'The proper study of mankind is man'?
(a) Ben Jonson (b) Shakespeare
(c) Dryden (d) Pope

107. 'The Seasons' by James Thomson is written in
(a) Spenserian Stanza
(b) Heroic couplet
(c) Blank verse
(d) Ottava Rima

108. 'Tom Jones' by Fielding appeared in
(a) Eighteen books (b) Twelve books
(c) Eight books (d) Six books

109. Who wrote the famous novel *Tristam Shandy*?
   (a) Laurance sterve (b) Fielding
   (c) Smollett (d) George Eliot

110. Who is the most important writer of the Pindaric Odes in English?
   (a) Keats (b) Shelley
   (c) Gray (d) Dryden

111. Who wrote the *Wealth of Nations*?
   (a) Jonathan Smith (b) Adam Smith
   (c) Thomas Percy (d) Sheridan

112. Who was Samuel Johnson's biographer?
   (a) Mackenzie (b) Boswell
   (c) Brook (d) Walpole

113. Boswell wrote a series of articles for
   (a) The London Club
   (b) The London Herald
   (c) The London chronicle
   (d) The London Magazine

114. Edmund Broke is considered the backbone of
   (a) Whigs (b) Tones
   (c) Extremists (d) Moderates

115. William Cowper is best known for his
   (a) elegies (b) satires
   (c) short poems (d) None of the above

116. Which is the first book in English in poetic prose?
   (a) *Confession Amantis*
   (b) *Nun's priest's Tale*
   (c) *Morte d'Arthur*
   (d) *Vox clamantis*

117. Bacon became a member of Parliament is
   (a) 1500 (b) 1584
   (c) 1561 (d) 1556

118. Bacon wrote in which two languages?
   (a) Latin and English
   (b) French and Arabic
   (c) German and English
   (d) English and English

119. Bacon's History of Henry VII appeared in
   (a) 1600 (b) 1620
   (c) 1622 (d) 1559

120. New Atlantis is modeled in
   (a) More's Otopia
   (b) Johnson's Epigramme
   (c) Marlowe's Hero and Leander
   (d) None of the above

121. Which work of Bacon was left incomplete due to his sudden death?
   (a) Sylvia Sylvarum
   (b) Novuum organum
   (c) New Atlantis
   (d) None of the above

122. Who called Bacon the first essayist, as he remains for Sheer mars and weight of genius?
   (a) Dr. Johnson (b) Ben Johnson
   (c) High Walker (d) Shakespeare

123. Bacon's general conception of essay was borrowed from
   (a) Seneca (b) Montaigne
   (c) Hugh Walker (d) Hooks

124. Who called Bacon's style an index of the emergence of the modern world?
   (a) Dryden (b) Johnson
   (c) Pope (d) L.C. Knights

125. Which writing of Bacon is philosophical?
   (a) Essays
   (b) The Advancement of Learning
   (c) New Atlantis
   (d) None of the above

126. The only essay Bacon which is personalies
   (a) Of Death (b) Of susperstition
   (c) Of Ambition (d) Of Gardens

127. Which work of Bacon is another Utopia?
   (a) Advancement of Learning
   (b) New Atlantis

(c) Novum organum
(d) None of the above

128. Which of the four chief dialects that flourished in the pre-Chaucerian period became the standard English in Chaucer's time?
(a) The Northern
(b) The Southern
(c) The East-Midland
(d) The West-Midland

129. Who wrote *The Parliament of Fouls*?
(a) William Langland
(b) Sir David Lyndsay
(c) James – I
(d) Geoffrey Chaucer

130. The origin of English drama is attributed to
(a) the Lituogu, a religious ceremony of the Church
(b) Chaucer
(c) the ballad
(d) the royal jesters

131. The literary genre, the ecologue, is attributed to
(a) John Skelton
(b) Alexander Barclay
(c) William Dunbbar
(d) Stephen Hawes

132. *La Mala Regele* by Thomas Occleve is a satire on
(a) poverty (b) superstition
(c) fanaticism (d) morality

133. 'Utopia' is also known by the name
(a) an unknown Island
(b) a strange land
(c) a world of imagination
(d) the kingdom of nowhere

134. The greatest shortcoming of 15th century poetry was
(a) immoral note
(b) poor versification
(c) poverty of themes
(d) All of the above

135. English New Testament appeared in
(a) 1523 (b) 1525
(c) 1528 (d) 1531

136. English New Testament is a work of
(a) William Tyndale
(b) John Wycliff
(c) John Barbour
(d) Stephen Hawes

137. Which is known as the first real English comedy?
(a) Jocasta
(b) The four P's
(c) Roister Doister
(d) London Lack Penry

138. The first real English comedy was written by
(a) Nicholas udall (b) Erasmus
(c) Drayton (d) Mills Coverdale

139. Who was the first to use the blank verse in English drama?
(a) Sackville (b) Marlowe
(c) Shakespeare (d) Thomas kyd

140. Spenser's 'Shepherd's Calender' contains three principle themes—Love, Poetry and
(a) Religion (b) Art
(c) Diplomacy (d) Chivalry

141. 'The Fairy Queene' follows are the style of
(a) Virgil's Achneid
(b) Dante's Divine comedy
(c) Sir Philip Sidney's Arcadia
(d) Aristo's Orlando Furioso

142. Sir Philip Sidney's 'Arcadia' is a prose romance containing several

(a) allusions (b) cantos
(c) ecologues (d) fallacis

143. *Mother's Bombic* is a comedy written by
(a) John Lyly (b) Gosson
(c) Thomos Nashe (d) J. Kyd

144. Who called Francis Bakon jestingly 'Little Lord Keeper?
(a) The Prince (b) The King
(c) The Queen (d) All of the above

145. 'The New Atlantis' by Francis Bacon is a/an
(a) unfinished novel (b) unfinished poem
(c) drama (d) essay

146. 'Unmarried men are best friends, best masters, best servants, but not always best subjects.' Who wrote this?
(a) A.G. Gardiner (b) Francis Bacon
(c) Charles Lamb (d) Shakespeare

147. 'There is nothing good or bad, thinking makes it so'. In which Shakesperean play does this line occur?
(a) Julius Caesar (b) Hamlet
(c) As you like it (d) King Lear

148. Which of the following marks the beginning of Shakespeare's success?
(a) Sonnets
(b) The Merchant of Venice
(c) Venus and Adonics
(d) Love Labour's Lost

149. Who said, 'Shakespeare has only heroines and no heroes?'
(a) Eliot (b) Ruskin
(c) Johnson (d) Arnold

150. *The Unfortunate Traveller* by Thomas Nashe is a typical
(a) revenge play
(b) picturesque novel
(c) love tragedy
(d) pastoral romance

151. Who is referred to as the pioneer of picturesque novel in English?
(a) Thomas Leyd (b) Thomas Nashe
(c) Thomas Lodge (d) John Lyly

152. Who among the following wrote only tragedies?
(a) Thomas kyd (b) Shakespeare
(c) Marlowe (d) Cowley

153. One of the University Wits who was killed in a tavern at the age of 29 was
(a) Greene (b) Lyly
(c) Kyd (d) Marlowe

154. Who is considered as Shakespeare's master in tragedy?
(a) Robert Burton
(b) Marlowe
(c) Thomas kyd
(d) None of the above

155. Who coined the phrase Marlowe's mighty line?
(a) Samuel Jonson (b) Ben Jonson
(c) Matthew Arnold (d) Shakespeare

156. Who wrote 'Anatomy of Melancholy'?
(a) Christopher Marlowe
(b) George Peele
(c) Thomas kyd
(d) Robert Burton

157. Which is believed to be the first important revenge tragedy?
(a) *Gorboduc*
(b) *Hamlet*
(c) *The Spanish Tragedy*
(d) *Tamburlaine*

158. Thomas Middleton's *The Witch* influenced Shakespeare to write a play. The name of that play is
(a) *A Mid Summer Night's dream*
(b) *Macbeth*
(c) *Hamlet*
(d) *Othello*

ANSWERS

1. (c)	2. (b)	3. (d)	4. (a)	5. (d)	6. (a)
7. (d)	8. (b)	9. (d)	10. (c)	11. (d)	12. (b)
13. (c)	14. (d)	15. (a)	16. (c)	17. (c)	18. (a)
19. (c)	20. (a)	21. (b)	22. (a)	23. (b)	24. (c)
25. (c)	26. (a)	27. (b)	28. (d)	29. (a)	30. (d)
31. (a)	32. (a)	33. (b)	34. (a)	35. (d)	36. (c)
37. (b)	38. (a)	39. (a)	40. (b)	41. (b)	42. (a)
43. (a)	44. (a)	45. (a)	46. (d)	47. (b)	48. (a)
49. (a)	50. (c)	51. (b)	52. (a)	53. (b)	54. (b)
55. (d)	56. (a)	57. (b)	58. (c)	59. (d)	60. (a)
61. (c)	62. (c)	63. (b)	64. (a)	65. (c)	66. (c)
67. (a)	68. (b)	69. (c)	70. (d)	71. (d)	72. (d)
73. (c)	74. (c)	75. (a)	76. (c)	77. (b)	78. (d)
79. (a)	80. (c)	81. (b)	82. (b)	83. (d)	84. (a)
85. (c)	86. (a)	87. (c)	88. (d)	89. (a)	90. (a)
91. (b)	92. (b)	93. (c)	94. (c)	95. (c)	96. (b)
97. (b)	98. (c)	99. (b)	100. (c)	101. (c)	102. (b)
103. (c)	104. (c)	105. (c)	106. (a)	107. (a)	108. (c)
109. (d)	110. (d)	111. (d)	112. (a)	113. (c)	114. (c)
115. (b)	116. (a)	117. (c)	118. (a)	119. (c)	120. (c)
121. (b)	122. (d)	123. (b)	124. (d)	125. (b)	126. (c)
127. (d)	128. (a)	129. (b)	130. (a)	131. (d)	132. (b)
133. (b)	134. (a)	135. (c)	136. (a)	137. (a)	138. (a)
139. (d)	140. (c)	141. (a)	142. (c)	143. (a)	144. (b)
145. (b)	146. (d)	147. (b)	148. (b)	149. (d)	150. (c)
151. (d)	152. (b)	153. (b)	154. (d)	155. (c)	156. (b)
157. (c)	158. (b)				

14

Romantic Period

Chronology of Important Dates

1770	-	Birth of Wordsworth
1771	-	Birth of Scott
1788	-	Byron's birth
1789-99	-	French Revolution
1798	-	Lyrical Ballads
		Landor's Gebin
1799	-	Campbell's Pleasures of Hope
1800	-	Death of Cowper
		Edgeworth's Castle Rack rent
1805	-	Scott's Lay of the Last Minstrel
1807	-	Byron's Hours of Idleness
		Moore's Irish Melodies
		Wordsworth's Intimations of Immortality
		Lamb's Tales from Shakespeare
1808	-	Scott's Marmion
1809	-	Quarterly Review founded
		Byron's Childe Harold
1810-13	-	Coleridge's Lectures on Shakespeare
1811	-	Jane Austen's *Sense and Sensibility*
1812	-	Jane Austen's *Pride and Prejudice*
1813	-	Shelley's Queen Mab
1814-31	-	Waverle Novels
1814	-	Wordsworth's Excursion
		Scott's Waverly
1816	-	Shelley's Alastor
1817-20	-	Keat's Poems
		Blackwood's Magazine
		Death of Jane Austen

		London Magazine
		Coleridge's Biographia Literaria
1818	-	Byron's Beffo
1818-20	-	Shelley's Prometheus
1819	-	Keats' Eve of St. Agnes
1819	-	Byron's Don Juan
		Scott's Ivanhoe
		Shelley's The Cenci
1820	-	Keats' Hyperion
		Shelley's Adonais
		Byron's Cain
		De Quincey's Opium Eater
1822	-	Death of Shelley
1821-23	-	Lamb's Elia
1824	-	Byron's death
1832	-	Death of Scott
		Death of Crabbe
1834	-	Death of Coleridge
1844	-	Thomas Campbell's death
1850	-	Death of Wordsworth

Romantic Period

Romantic period is also known as The Age of Wordsworth or the Renaissance of Wonder (1798-1850). The term 'Romantic Revival' is applied to the splendid outburst of literature in the age of Wordsworth. The word 'revival' indicates a return to literature of those romantic qualities which had characterized the literature of the Elizabethan Age. There was a natural revolt against the classical spirit of the eighteenth century which gave rise to artificiality in poetry, both in regard to subject matter and style. Hence the literary movement, known as the Romantic Revival, was on the one hand a revolt against the classical creed of the eighteenth century, and on the other a revival of the Romantic spirit of the Elizabethan age. W.J. Long says, "The essence of Romanticism was that literature must reflect all that is spontaneous and unaffected in nature and in man, and be free to follow its own fancy in its own way".

The term 'Romanticism' has been variously defined by various critics. Heine calls it "the reawakening of Middle Ages...a passion flower blooming from the blood of Christ". Victor Hugo defines it as 'liberalism in literature'. Goethe says, 'Romanticism is disease, classicism is health'. George sand calls it "emotion against reason". To Herford romanticism stands for 'Liberty of imagination'. C.M. Bowra contradicts those critics who regard it as an expression of insubstantial dreams. He says: "The romantics were not content to dream, to fashion illusions. They insisted, their creations must be real".

Cemmenting on the difference between classicism and romanticism Stoddard remarks:

"Classicism is born of law; it is nourished by authority, its ideals are known.... The cardinal notion of romanticism is not acceptance but rejection, Romanticism rejects the literal and seeks the allegorical, it leaves the seen and searches the unseen, it casts aside the evident and seeks a symbol of deeper thought," To Wats Dunton, it is 'the renaissance of wonder'. Pater calls it the 'addition of strangeness to beauty'. Abercrombie stresses the subjective element of romanticism. He writes: "Romanticism is a withdrawal from outer experience to concentrate on inner experience." Summing up the main traits of romanticism, F.L. Lucas says: "Remoteness, the sad delight of desolation, silence and the supernatural, winter and dreariness, vampiric love and stolen trysts, the flowering of passion and the death of beauty, Radcliffe horrors and sadistic cruelty, disillusion, death and madness: the Holy Grail, the battles on the Border, the love of the impossible; are the main characteristics of romanticism." Legious and Cazamian emphasize both the emotional and call it "an accentuated predominance of emotional life, provoked and directed by the imaginative vision." To Rickett, "Romanticism, generally speaking, is the expression in terms of art of sharpened sensibilities, heightened imaginative feeling...."

In order to conclude all the definitions, we came across these following elements:

1. Love for nature
2. Simplicity and a revolt against all artificiality
3. An expression of the inner urges of the soul of the artist
4. Spontaneous outflow of powerful feelings
5. Extraordinary expression of the wonder, mystery and beauty of the universe
6. Expression of the inherent dignity and nobility of man
7. An interest in the past and experiment with old meteres and poetic forms
8. Freedom of Imagination
9. Regeneration of Poetic style

The Influence of French Revolution on Romanticism

The French Revolution of 1789 sent a thrill of fresh life through the whole civilized world. It ushered in an era of democratic ideas of liberty, brotherhood and the rights of man. The background to English Romantic Movement was furnished by the French Revolution as a historical event. This was the end of the old order of suppression and tyranny and the beginning of the new order based on the democratic ideal of liberty, equality and fraternity. The Revolution proclaimed the natural rights of man and the abolition of class distinctions. Patriotic clubs and societies multiplied in England, all asserting the doctrine of liberty, equality and fraternity, the watchwords of Revolution. The third phase of Revolution is known as the military phase or the Age of Napolean.

Romanticism largely began as a reaction against the prevailing Enlightenment ideals of the day. Inevitably, the characterization of a broad range of contemporaneous poets and poetry under the single unifying name can be viewed more as an exercise in historical compartmentalization than an actual attempt to capture the essence of the actual 'movement'. Indeed, the term "Romanticism" did not arise until the Victorian period. Nonetheless, poets such as William Wordsworth were actively engaged in trying to create a new kind of poetry that emphasized intuition over reason and the *pastoral* over the urban, often eschewing modern forms and language in an effort to use 'new' language. Romantic poetry referred to the natural aspects of the world, focusing on the feelings of sadness and great happiness. An early exponent was Robert Burns, who is generally classified as a proto-Romantic poet and influenced Wordsworth and Samuel Taylor Coleridge. Burns's *Poems, Chiefly in the Scottish Dialect* was published in April 1786 and included "The Two Dogs," "Address to the Deil," "To a Mountain Daisy," and the widely anthologized "To a Mouse."

Wordsworth himself in the Preface to his and Coleridge's *Lyrical Ballads* defined good poetry as "the spontaneous overflow of powerful feelings," though in the same sentence he goes on to clarify this statement by asserting that nonetheless any poem of value must still be composed by a man "possessed of more than usual organic sensibility (who has) also thought long and deeply". Thus, though many people seize unfairly upon the notion of spontaneity in Romantic Poetry, one must realize that the movement was still greatly concerned with the pain of composition, of translating these emotive responses into the form of Poetry. Indeed, Samuel Taylor Coleridge, another prominent Romantic poet and critic in his *On Poesy or Art* sees art as "the mediatress between, and reconciler of nature and man". Such an attitude reflects what might be called the dominant theme of Romantic Poetry: the filtering of natural emotion through the human mind in order to create art, coupled with an awareness of the duality created by such a process.

The movement was, in a sense, formalized with the joint publication by Wordsworth and Coleridge of *Lyrical Ballads* in 1798. The work emphasized what would become the key tenets of Romanticism, namely the reconciliation of man and nature, alongwith an attempt to abandon the low language of 18th century English poetry and to attempt to convey poetic ideas via a common vernacular. Their work is deeply rooted in the tradition established by Edmund Spenser and John Milton. They, along with William Blake believed that they were reviving the true spirit of English poetry by pursuing the "romance" and the sublime that was lost since Milton.

John Keats, Percy Bysshe Shelley, and Lord Byron then comprised the latter half of the movement, largely continuing in the same tradition, though deviating slightly into more metaphysical matters.

Perhaps due to the perceived personal nature of Romantic poetry (one which the Romantic Poets themselves are not entirely innocent of encouraging), there has often been a fascination with the lives of the Romantic poets. This view is often reinforced by the imagery conjured up in contemporary discourse because a number of them died before reaching thirty, notably Percy Bysshe Shelley and John Keats (25). This has led to a conflation of the lives of the Romantic poets with the poetry itself.

The "Big Six" of English romantic literature pertains to the six figures who are historically supposed to have formed the core of the Romantic movement of late 18th and early 19th century England. The term, though widely used as an easy term for the canonical Romantic poets, is just as widely known to be both anachronistic and unduly exclusive. Reconstructing centered around Leigh Hunt. Although chronologically earliest among these writers, William Blake was a relatively late addition to the list; prior to the 1970s, romanticism was known for its "Big Five."

For some critics, the term establishes an artificial context for disparate work and removing that work from its real historical context") at the expense of equally valid themes (particularly those related to politics.)

The six authors are, in order of birth and with an example of their work:

- William Blake – *The Marriage of Heaven and Hell*
- William Wordsworth – *The Prelude*
- Samuel Taylor Coleridge – *Rime of the Ancient Mariner*
- George Gordon, Lord Byron – *Don Juan*
- Percy Bysshe Shelley – *Prometheus Unbound*
- John Keats – *Ode on a Grecian Urn*

Major Romantic Poets of the World

- Armenia: Varand
- Brazil: Álvares de Azevedo, Castro Alves, Casimiro de Abreu, Goncalves Dias
- Denmark: Nikolaj Frederik Severin Grundtvig, Adam Gottlob Oehlenschlager, Hans Christian Andersen, Soren Kiekegaard
- England: William Blake, George Gordon Byron, Samuel Taylor Coleridge, Percy Bysshe Shelley, William Wordsworth, John Keats
- France: Alphonse de Lamartine, Victor Hugo, Theophile Gautier, Alfred de Musset, Charles Baudelaire
- Georgia: Nikoloz Baratashvili
- Germany: Novalis, Heinrich von Kleist, Clemens Brentano, Joseph von Eichendorff, Achim von Arnim
- Hungary: Sandor Petofi
- Ireland: Thomas Moore
- Italy: Giacomo Leopardi, Ugo Fosocolo, Alessandro Manzoni
- Montenegro: Petar II Petrovic Njegos
- Poland: Three Bards (Adam Mickiewicz, Juliusz Slowacki, Zygmunt Krasinski, Cyprian Kamil Norwid)
- Portugal: Alexandre Herculano, Almeida Garett, Antonio Feliciano de Castilho
- Romania: Mihai Eminescu
- Russia: Golden Age of Russian Poetry—Aleksandr Pushkin, Mikhail Lermontov, Fyodor Tyutchev, Evgeny Baratynsky
- Scotland: Robert Burns, Joanna Baillie, Walter Scott
- Serbia: Branko Radicevic, Dura Jaksic, Laza Kostic, Jovan Jovanovic Zmaj
- Slovakia: Janko Kral'
- Slovenia: France Preseren
- Spain: Gustavo Adolfo Becquer, Jose de Espronceda, Rosalia de Castro, Jose Zorrilla, Jacint Verdaguer
- United States: Henry Wordsworth Longfellow, Ralph Waldo Emerson.

The Romantic Period: 1798-1837

The Romantic Period (sandwiched between the French Revolution & the beginning of Queens Victoria's reign) was characterized largely by a belief in the primacy of the imagination. A reliance and emphasis upon nature was the cornerstone of the writers and artists from this brief, but rich time period in English literature. No figure stood out as greatly from this time period than William Blake (1757-1827), who is considered as being the first of the Romantics, Spontaneity and human impulse were considered to be good by him, as long they belonged to the individual and weren't anyone else's—conformity to social norms was condemned by the Romantics. Reason only existed on the periphery of energy, which was the heart of his philosophy, and characterized this literary period. This is best exemplified in Blake's "The Marriage of Heaven and Hell") and reason is created, with sensual desire and impulses serving as the driving force in this noteworthy work, with reason (the "heavenly" metaphor) existing only as a secondary factor.

William Wordsworth and Samuel Coleridge must be mentioned as being "first generation" Romantics, along with Blake, with their 1798 collaborative work, "Lyrical Ballads" being a beacon and benchmark for this era. Wordsworth's "Lines Composed a Few Miles from Tintern Abbey," "Intimations on Mortality," "The Prelude" & Coleridge's "The Rime of the Ancient Mariner" are all examples of essential works contained in this volume, which many point to as being the actual start of the Romantic period itself. The best way to categorize the collaborative contributions Wordsworth & Coleridge is to remember that Wordsworth made the natural seem supernatural and that Coleridge portrayed the supernatural as being natural truths.

A movement such as this was driven by certain political and social milestones that were occurring as well, such as: (1) the French Revolution & (2) the rise of Industrialism. These factors served as the driving forces behind writers such as Thomas Paine's "Rights of Man" (written in 1791 as a response to infamous pro-establishment politician Edmund Burke's *Reflections on the Revolution in France)* and Mary Wollstonecraft's "A Vindication of the Rights of Women," in terms of relating this spirit of imagination and reaffirmation between nature and the soul, expressed via the newfound freedom and thinking of the masses over the gentry classes that gave rise to the French Revolution, just across the French Channel, in the first place.

The group of poets who came to be known as the second generation of Romantics included the following George Gordon, Lord Byron (1788-1822), Percy Bysshe Shelley (1792-1822), and John Keats (1795-1821). They all wrote sonnets, odes, and epics dealing with nature. Byron's epic, *Don Juan,* and his autobiographical *Childe Harold's Pilgrimage,* both were exemplary of his melancholic state, along with his witty and irreverent style exemplifying his contempt for others from this time period, such as Coleridge and Wordsworth themselves. Shelley's sonnets and odes, such as "Ode to the West Wing", were characterized by their sensory imagery, emphasizing natural beauty. Keats' poetry, unlike Byron's, was not inspired by depressive states, rather it was focused on intensity—regardless of the emotional from that it came in, (love, pain, or otherwise). Keats' "Ode to a Nightingale," "Ode on a Grecian Urn," and "Ode on Melancholy" are exemplary of this style of writing. What must be noted is that all of these "second generation" Romantics all died tragically young, with the "first generation" Romantics—Coleridge and Wordsworth outliving them. What these figures all had in common was that they highlighted the imperfections of man, via an emphasis upon human emotion and natural themes. They all sought to bring their ideas to the literary forefront, because these ideas—to them—were hidden in the background previous to the 1800s, for far, too long without being completely explored.

The Transcendentalist movement was a reaction against 18th century rationalism and a manifestation of the general humanitarian trend of 19th century thought. The movement was based on a fundamental belief in the unity of the world and God. The soul of each individual was though to be identical with the world—a microcosm of the world itself. The doctrine of self-reliance and individualism developed through the belief in the identification of the individual soul with God.

Unlike many European groups, the Transcendentalists never issued a manifesto. They insisted on individual differences—on the unique viewpoint of the individual. American Transendental Romantics pushed radical individualism to the extreme. American writers often saw themselves as lonely explorers outside society and convention. The American hero—like Herman Melville's Captain Ahab, or Mark Twain's Huck Finn, or Edgar Allan Poe's Arthur Gordon Pym—typically faced risk, or even certain destruction, in the pursuit of metaphysical self-discovery. For the Romantic American writer nothing was a given. Literary and social conventions, far from being helpful, were dangerous. There was tremendous pressure to discover an authentic literary form, content, and voice—all at the same time. It is clear from the many masterpieces produced in the three decades before the U.S. Civil War (1861-65) that American writers rose to the challenge.

WILLIAM WORDSWORTH (1770-1850)

Born in 1770 at Cockermouth Cumberland. In 1802 he married Mary Hutchinson. During his stay in the Lake District he composed some of his finest poems –"Michael", "The Old Cumberland Beggar", "She Dwelt Among the Untrodden Ways", "Strange Fits of Passion and Nuttings". The first book of the Recluse tells of his settlement in the Lake District. He finished his long autobiographical poem, *The Prelude* in 1805-06 but it was posthumously published in 1850. It records his development as a poet. In 1807 two volumes of his poetry were published. Some of the finest poems of these volumes are "The Solitary Reaper", "The Green Linnet", "I Wandered Lonely as a Cloud", "Ode on the Intimations of Immortality", "Resolution and Independence", "Ode to Duty" and some sonnets.

After the publication of *The Excursion* in 1814 Wordsworth's poetical power was on the wane. His later poems—"The White Doe of Rylstone" (1815) "The Waggoner" (1819), "Peter Bell" (1819), and "Yarrow Revisited" (1835) mark the decline in an increasing degree. He was made Poet Laureate in 1843 after Southey's death. He died in 1850. He expounded his theory of poetry and poetic diction in the Preface to the second edition of the Lyrical Ballads (1800).

Four Stages in Wordsworth's Poetic Development

Wordsworth gave an account of the growth of his mind in *The Prelude* or Growth of a Poet's Mind and Tintern Abbey.

First Period—His early intercourse with natural objects developed in him a calmness and tranquility of soul.

"The visible scene would enter unawares into his mind, With all its solemn imagery".

Second Period—Period of senses, the young poet drank in the beauty of nature with the passion of a lover.

"The sounding cataract haunted me like a passion, the tall rock".

Third Period—The stage of 'dizzy joys' and 'aching raptures' came to an end with his experience of human sorrow and suffering in France. 'He heard the still, sad music of humanity', and his love of nature became linked with the love of man.

Fourth Period—The final stage was the period of the soul, when the poet's love of nature became reflective, mystical and spiritual. He felt in nature, a presence' that disturbed him with 'the joy of elevated thoughts'.

Characteristics of Wordsworth's Poetry:

1. Imagination
2. Nature
3. Human Life
4. Mysticism
5. Poetic Art
6. Limitations: Inequality, Limited Range, Excessive Egoism, Deficiency in Poetic Style
7. Moral Value of Wordsworth's poetry.

SAMUEL TAYLOR COLERIDGE (1772-1834)

S.T. Coleridge was born in 1772 in Devonshire. He was the youngest of the thirteenth children of the Vicar of Ottery St. Mary. The French Revolution appealed to him and he welcomed it in some early poems. In 1797 Coleridge met Wordsworth and planned the joint publication of the Lyrical Ballads. He died in 1834, and was buried in Highgate Church. His poetic output is slender. His best poetry was composed between two years 1797-98. The most noteworthy of Coleridge's poems is the *Rime of Ancient Mariner*.

Coleridge wrote the first part of 'Christabel' in 1797 and second part was added to it in 1800. 'Kubla Khan,' written in 1798 is a fragment painting, a gorgeous oriental dream picture. His other memorable poems composed during 1798 are 'Frost at Midnight' and 'France: An Ode.' In 1802 he wrote his famous ode 'Dejection'.

Coleridge as a Romantic Poet

Coleridge is one of the chief protagonists of Romantic poetry. Chief qualities are-

(a) Mystery and supernaturalism
(b) Love of nature
(c) Dreaminess
(d) Coleridge's Metrical Art
(e) Limitations of Coleridge's Poetry:
    (i) Lack of actuality
    (ii) Smallness and Incompleteness of poetic work.

SIR WALTER SCOTT (1771-1832)

- The Father of the Historical novel in English Literature
- Translated some of the German ballads into English
- Represents the romantic love for the revival of the past
- Ministrelsy of the Scottish Border-His first Collection (1802-03)
- The lay of the last Minstrel (1805)
- Marmion (1808)
- The lady of the Lake (1810)
- Chief lyrical poet between Burns, Blake & Shelley.

LORD BYRON (1788-1824)

- Born in 1788, Byron published his first collection of poems, Hours of Idleness in 1807
- Byron said "I woke up one morning and found myself famous"
- His strong individually
- Byron is the most subjective
- His wit and satire
- His love of Nature
- His Interest in the Present
- Passion for Liberty and Rebellinous spirit
- His Lyricism
- His style is noticeable for conversational ease and naturalness of expression
- Displays an epigrammatic wit and great vivacity
- Byron's greatest contribution to English remark poetry was the addition of passion

P.B. SHELLEY (1792-1822)

- The eldest son of Sir Timothy Shelley who born at Field Place in Sussex on August 4, 1792.
- He was physically fragile uncommon boy, violent in his likes and dislikes, but gentle and courteous.
- He wrote a pamphlet, entitled 'The Necessity of Atheison', which caused considerable fiction with the authorities of the universities.
- He fell in love with Harriet Westbrook, eloped with her to Edinburgh and married her.
- After separation from Harriet who later committed suicide Mary Godwin, daughter of William Godwin.
- He wrote "Queen Mab" (1813), "Alastor" (1815).
- Prometheus unbound (lyrical drama) 1819.
- Adonais, Epipsychidion (1821).
- On July 8, 1822 he was drowned in the sea.
- Hellas (a verse drama) appeared in 1822.
- As a romantic poet Shelley's finest poetry is an expression of his unquenchable desire for 'what is not', for the unreliable and the unknown.

- His Revolutionary Idealism.
- Transcendentalism.
- Shelley, the poet of the future.
- Shelley, the poet of visions.
- The Prophetic Note in Shelley's poetry.
- Shelley-on Effectual Angel.
- Shelley, the poet of Nature.
- Shelley, the poet of Love.
- Shelley's Lyricism.
- His romantic poetic style is reflective of his nature and is full of uncontrollable passion and energy.
- His style glows with passion and music and abundance of imagery.

JOHN KEATS (1795-1821)

- John Keats was born in 1795 in London.
- In 1817 the first volume of his poems appeared.
- In 1818 he published Endymion.
- He said, "I think I shall be among the English poets after my death".
- His two poems "I stood Tip Toe Upon A Hill" and "Sleep and Beauty"—show the influence of Spenser and Leigh Hunt.
- He is known for his pictorial quality.
- Keats' great odes—"To a Nightingale", "On a Grecian Urn", "To Psyche", "On Melancholy", "To Autumn"—were nearly all written in 1819.
- His Odes are the monumental contribution to Romantic poetry.
- As a sonneteer Keats ranks with the greatest English poets.
- Edward Albert remarks, "of the Sixty one sonnets some ten, including On First Looking into Chapman's Homer, When I have fears, and Bright Star are worthy to be ranked with those of Shakespeare."
- "English Romanticism attains in Keats the final stage of progress".
- Keats was the pure poet, with an in exhaustible capacity for joy and for creating beauty for its own sake.
- In the poetry of Keats are united all the different elements of Romanticism—love of nature, sensuousness and pictorial quality, supernaturalism and medievalism, Hellenism and a mystic worship of Beauty .
- Sensuousness and Concretenss.
- "Keats as a poet is abundantly and enchantingly sensuous"—Arnold.
- Keats is called a poet of senses because in his poetry the sensuous appeal is most intense and all pervading:
  (i) because his emotions are immediately excited to senses
  (ii) because his poetry is full of sensuous imagery.

- Keats' early poem is blatantly sensuous, but the poetry of his maturity is penetrated with sentiment and intellectualism.
- Beauty is Truth and Truth Beauty.
- His Hellenism.
- 'Keats was a Greek'—Shelley said.
- Medievalism.
- Keats Loved nature for her own sake and not for the sake of any other idea.
- Keats, a poet of Beauty.
- 'A thing of beauty is a joy forever'.
- Keats found beauty in life with all its sufferings and tears.
- His humanity.
- His Poetic Art – Keats was a conscious artist and his poetry is marked by its artistic workmanshop.
- Keats hardly expresses a thought or feeling in abstract terms: his thoughts leaps up into visual forms.
- Keats employed various kinds of metres and stanza forms in his poetry.
- His Negative capability.
- The Odes of Keats are the ripest fruits of the poetic genius.
- Lowell says "Wordsworth has influenced most of the ideas of the successful poets; Keats its form".

OTHER POETS: ROBERT SOUTHEY (1774-1843)

He is remembered for "Joan of Arc" (1798), "Thalba, the Destroyer" (1801), "The Curse of Kehama" (1810), and "Roderick, the Last of the Goths" (1814).

* All these poems are romantic in theme, straightforward and unaffected in style.
* His prose work include "The History of Brazil, The History of Peninsular War" (1823-32) and "The Life of Nelson".

LEIGH HUNT (1784-1859)

* Keats was greatly influenced by him.
* His memorable work is the *Story of Rimini* (1816).
* Hunt is seen at his best in the shorter pieces, The Nile and Abou Ben Adhem.
* He developed the story properly. His prose works include "Men, Women and Books", "Autobiography", "Tom Town" etc.

THOMAS MOORE (1779-1852)

* He is an Irish poet, who is best remembered for his *Lalla Rookh* (1817), an oriental romance, written in the Scott—Byron manner.
* Also known for his, Irish Melodies'.
* *The Twopenny Postbag* (1813), *The Fudge Family in Paris* (1818) and *Fables for the Holy Alliance* (1823) are his political Satires.

THOMAS CAMPBELL (1717-1844)

He edited The New Monthly Magazine from 1820 to 1830.

- His 'Pleasures of Hope' written in heroic couplet contains many beautiful descriptions of nature.
- His other poems are "Gertrude of Wyoming" (1809), "The Pilgrim of Glencoe" (1842), "Ye Mariners of England" and "The Battle of Baltic".

THOMAS HOOD (1799-1845)

He is mainly remembered for his humorous poems which show his mastery over verbal wit and funning.

* "The Dream of Ergene Aram"
* "The Song of the Shirt"
* "The Bridge of Sighs"
* "Fair Inez"
* "Ode to Melancholy"
* "Silence" (Sonnet)

SAMUEL ROGERS (1763-1855)

He wrote "The Pleasures of Memory" (1792) in the 18th century poetic manner. His "Columbus" (1812) and "Jacqueline" (1842) are in the Byronic manner.

Other poets who deserve mention are T.L. Beddoes, John Clare, James Hogy and Eboneza Elliott.

PROSE IN THE ROMANTIC AGE

- The rise of modern review and magazine is the main feature of the age.
- *The Edinburgh Review* (1802) was established by Jeffers, Sydney Smith and others (Whigs).
- *The Quarterly* was started as the mouthpiece of Tory party by William Giffard and Lockhart.
- *Edinburgh Magazine* was launched in 1817 by Wilson, Lockhart and Hoggy. It was followed by *London Magazine* and *Fraser* (1830).
- Nearly all men of letters regularly contributed to these periodicals. Most of the prose writers of the time were essayists.

PROSE WRITERS: CHARLES LAMB (1775-1834)

Says W.J. Long, "Of all our English essayists he is the most lovable, partly because of his delicate, old fashioned style and humour, but more because of that cheery and heroic struggle against which shines like a subdued light in all his writings."

- In 1807 he and his sister co-authored *Tales from Shakespeare*. His reputation as a critic rests on Specimens of English Dramatic poets, who lived About the Time of Shakespeare (1808).
- Lamb's first essay appeared in The London Magazine in 1820 under the name of Elia. The first volume of essays was published as Essays of Elia in 1823, and the second under the title *The Last Essays of Elia* in 1833.

- Charles Lamb is known as the prince among English essayists. His wisdom, his humanity, his intimate personal revelations, his love of the past, his reminiscences, his genial humour, his profound pathos and his style have endeared Lamb as an essayist. Major qualities are as under:
  (a) Autobiographical Element in the Essays of Elia
  (b) Lamb's Nobility of Nature
  (c) Lamb's Humour and Pathos
  (d) Lamb's Humanity
  (e) The Reminiscent Charm of the Essays of Elia
  (f) Lamb's Style
  (g) Lamb's Art of Essay writing.

WILLIAM HAZLITT (1778-1830)

From 1814 until his death William Hazlitt contributed to The Edinburgh Review, The Examiner, The Times and The London Magazine.

- Hazlitt's critical prose is superb. He has been called 'the critic's critic'.
- Hazlitt as an essayist is second only to Charles Lamb.
- He lacks the gentleheartedness and uniformity, geniality and good humour of Elia. However his essays are remarkable for the following characteristics.
  (i) Wide range and variety
  (ii) Autobiographical element
  (iii) Custo and Joy
  (iv) Hazlitt's personal style
  (v) Hazlitt a master of aphorism.

THOMAS DE QUINCEY (1785-1859)

- De Quincey is a voluminous writer of great versatility.
- The most illuminating of De Quincey's literary work is Literary Reminiscences, which contains brilliant appreciations of Wordsworth, Coleridge, Lamb, Shelley, Keats, Hazlitt and Landor.
- His admirable distinction between the literature of knowledge and the literature of power has been widely accepted.
- Of his autobiographical sketches the best known is his confessions of An English Opium Eater (1821).
- De Quincey successfully attempted to create a new style which combines the best elements of prose and poetry.
- He was a purist in style and he took great pains to select right words for the right place. But he cared more for the sounds of words than for their sense. His language is highly figurative.

NOVEL IN THE ROMANTIC AGE

The novel showed the most marked development during this period. This was largely due to the work of Scott and Jane Austen, who respectively established the historical and domestic types of novel.

SIR WALTER SCOTT (1771-1832)

- Scott wrote historical novels known as 'waverly novels' with great haste. It contains 27 novels and five tales.
- His novels appealed to a wide circle and entirely captured the fancy of the day.
- Historical realism is part of Scott's fiction.
- Endowed with the creative energy of imagination, Scott made the reader feel the glamour of the places and the actuality of the past.
- Scott often takes liberties with facts and alters them.
- Despite his love for historical realism, Scott never freed himself from the influence of the marvelous.
- The historical novel had its origin in the Gothic romance, and in giving it a new orientation Scott did not remove its original traits.
- Scott's novels are on a vast scale, covering a wide range of action.
- With the exception of the Bride of Lammermoor, the element of love in his novels is generally pale and feeble.
- In Scott's novels scene is an essential element in the action. He knew Scotland and loved it.
- Scott was the first novelist to recreate the past. He could successfully recreate his men and women drawn directly from Scottish life, which he knew well.
- Scott's humour is racy, full-blooded, and always genial and wholesome.
- Scott could not portray complex characters.

JANE AUSTEN (1775-1813)

- Jane Austen, the daughter of a Hampshire clergyman, was born in 1775 at Steventon.
- She passed her life very quietly, cheerfully, in the doing of small domestic duties.
- Her first novel *Pride and Predudice* is a fine example of domestic comedy.
- Her novels are all much the same, yet subtly and artistically different.
- She has been called 'the pure novelist'.
- She did for the English novel what the Lake poets did for the English poetry—she simplified and refined it making it a true reflection of English life.
- Her limited range became her strength. Great human passions and purposes of life were beyond her range. Themes of personal relationships fascinated her.
- The visible structure of Jane Austen's novels may be flimsy enough, but their foundations drive deep down into the basic principles of human conduct.
- She was neither a social philosopher, nor a romancer. She was mainly interested in the comedy of human nature.
- Her novels might be called novels of manners because they depict like the comedies of Congreve the manners, customs, and follies of her limited social circle.
- Jane Austen is a gentle humorist. She was not a satirist because she did not possess the savage and stinging characteristic of Swift. She brilliantly used irony in social comedies.

- As a humorist, Austen has no moral purpose. She wrote primarily to entertain, but her comic view of life was so fundamental to her that all her novels are soaked in it.
- Love and Marriage form an important element in Jane Austen's vocation for women. She realized that husband and wife should be spiritual counterparts of each other. A perfect marriage is fundamentally a perfect friendship.
- Jane Austen's art of characterization has not been excelled by any writer. Her special charm as a novelist lies, not in any greater insight into character, but in the impracticality with which she individualism and differentiates them.
- All her characters are living, breathing realities. She shows them compounded with faults and virtues like real human beings.
- Her novels have an exactness of structure and a symmetry of form.
- All her stories are faultlessly constructed, every character and every incident is necessary for the development of plot.
- Her style is natural and unaffected, clear and careful. The structure and movement of sentences is neat and brisk. She had complete mastery over dialogue.
- She imparted realism to English novel in an age of Romanticism.
- She pioneered the comedy of manners successfully and introduced dramatic element.
- She wrote from the feminine point of view.

OTHER NOVELISTS OF THE PERIOD

Maria Edgeworth (1767-1849)
John Galt (1779-1839)
W.H. Ainsworth (1805-82)
George P.R. James (1801-60)
Charles Lever (1806-72)
Thomas Love Peocock (1785-1866)

MULTIPLE CHOICE QUESTIONS

1. Wordsworth was popularly known as the poet of
   (a) Mining districts
   (b) Waverly region
   (c) The Lake districts
   (d) Lancashiri region
2. The Romantic age is also known as the
   (a) age of Pope
   (b) age of Dryden
   (c) age of Johnson
   (d) age of Wordsworth
3. Who gave the Romantic period the title of the Renaissance of Wonder in poetry?
   (a) William Wordsworth
   (b) William Blake
   (c) Theodox Watts
   (d) Professor Herford
4. After whom did Wordsworth become the Poet Laureate of England?
   (a) Robert Southey (b) John Dryden
   (c) Sir Walter Scott (d) S.T. Coleridge
5. Who wrote the Ode to France under the influence of the French Revolution?

(a) S.T. Coleridge
(b) William Wordsworth
(c) P.B. Shelley
(d) William Blake

6. Wordsworth's *Preface to the Lyrical Ballads* was
(a) a separate supplement to the Lyrical Ballads.
(b) a rejoinder to Coleridge's Biographia Literaria.
(c) the preface to the first edition of the Lyrical Ballads.
(d) the preface to the second edition of the Lyrical Ballads.

7. 'If Winter comes, can spring be far behind'? This is the concluding line of
(a) *The Cloud*
(b) *The Eve of St. Agnes*
(c) *Ode to the West Wind*
(d) *Prometheus Unbound*

8. 'Poets are the unacknowledged legislators of the world' who said this?
(a) William Wordsworth
(b) P.B. Shelley
(c) Thomas Carlyle
(d) John Keats

9. In 1802 Wordsworth got married to his cousin
(a) Mary Pierci
(b) Mary Wollstonecraft
(c) Mary Godwin
(d) Mary Hutchinson

10. 'The Prelude' by Wordsworth is
(a) a Philosophical poem
(b) a Metaphysical poem
(c) an Autobiographical poem
(d) a Historical poem

11. 'We are laid asleep in body and become a living soul'. In which of Wordsworth's poem does this line occur?
(a) The Excursion (b) The Prelude
(c) Rainbow (d) Tintern Abbey

12. William Wordsworth wrote a sonnet on
(a) Milton (b) Pope
(c) Ben Johnson (d) Spenser

13. Biographia Literaria is written by
(a) William Blake (b) Thomas Carlyle
(c) S.T. Coleridge (d) Wordsworth

14. 'Descriptive Sketches' is a poem written by
(a) William Blake
(b) William Collins
(c) William Cowley
(d) William Wordsworth

15. According to Wordsworth Rime of the Ancient Mariner was based on a dream of Coleridge's friend.
(a) Robert Southey (b) Cruishank
(c) Dr. Salnaidim (d) None of the above

16. Shelley writes in Adonais "A Portion of the loveliness which one he made more lovely." Who does 'he' refer to in these lines?
(a) John Keats
(b) William Wordsworth
(c) S.T. Coleridge
(d) Himself

17. Wordsworth believed that the language of poetry should be
(a) complex (b) urbanized
(c) colloquial (d) simple

18. Who said, 'Poetry is the spontaneous overflow of powerful feelings recollected in tranquility?
(a) T.S. Eliot (b) Byron
(c) Coleridge (d) Wordsworth

19. 'Abundantly and enchantingly sensuous', who attributed this phrase to Keats?
(a) Arnold (b) Lamb
(c) T.S. Eliot (d) P.B. Shelley

20. The great decade of Wordsworth's poetry was from
    (a) 1791 to 1801 (b) 1797 to 1807
    (c) 1798 to 1808 (d) 1795 to 1805
21. In the first stage, Wordsworth's love for nature was like that of a
    (a) animal (b) mystic
    (c) poet (d) child
22. "Beauty is Truth, Truth is Beauty: That is all ye know on earth, that is all ye need to know". These lines are from one of the famous odes of Keats. Name that Ode.
    (a) Ode to Autumn
    (b) Ode to a Nightingale
    (c) Ode to Psyche
    (d) Ode on a Grecian urn
23. Who opposed Wordsworth's views on poetry?
    (a) Shelley (b) Blake
    (c) Byron (d) Coleridge
24. 'River Dudden' by Wordsworth is a
    (a) series of elegies (b) series of satires
    (c) series of ballads (d) series of sonnets
25. 'The Thorn' by William Wordsworth consists of
    (a) twelve stanzas
    (b) twenty stanzas
    (c) twenty one stanzas
    (d) twenty two stanzas
26. Nature poem imbued with Wordsworth's Philosophy and mysticism is
    (a) Tintern Abbey
    (b) The Thorn
    (c) Ode to Duty
    (d) Ode on the intimations of Immortality
27. 'Wordsworth had his passion for nature fixed in his blood'. Who said this for Wordsworth?
    (a) De Quincey (b) Coleridge
    (c) Cazamian (d) Walter Scott
28. French Revolution is a poem composed by
    (a) Wordsworth (b) Shelley
    (c) Keats (d) Scott
29. The doctrine that identifies God with the universe is
    (a) Naturalism (b) Pantheism
    (c) Mysticism (d) None of the above
30. From whom did the Romantic poets get the idea 'Return to Nature'?
    (a) Garrod (b) Cobbelt
    (c) Roussean (d) De Quincey
31. 'Let Nature be your teacher', these words are from
    (a) 'The Thorn'
    (b) 'The Tables Turned'
    (c) 'The Prelude'
    (d) 'Daffodils'
32. Wordsworth's Theory of 'poetic diction' was propounded in
    (a) Poetic volumes
    (b) The Prelude
    (c) Preface to Lyrical Ballads
    (d) Biographia Literaria
33. 'The World is Too Much' with US is a/an
    (a) Epistle (b) Sonnet
    (c) Elegy (d) Ballad
34. 'Lectures on Shakespeare' was published in 1849 by
    (a) Rousseau (b) Locke
    (c) S.T. Coleridge (d) Byron
35. In addition to being a poet Coleridge was also a
    (a) dramatist (b) critic
    (c) essayist (d) novelist
36. Who among the following had called Wordsworth a moral eunuch?
    (a) Byron (b) Browning
    (c) Shelley (d) Arnold

37. Who emphasized the use of the language really used by man for poetry?
(a) Coleridge (b) Shakespeare
(c) Chaucer (d) Wordsworth

38. Byron's letters were published after his death by his friend
(a) Thomas Moore
(b) Thomas Carlyle
(c) George Herbert
(d) Alexander pope

39. Shelley eloped with a married woman named
(a) Clair Clairmont
(b) Hariet West brook
(c) Hary Garriet
(d) Maria Weston

40. I woke up one morning and found myself famous'. Who commented this on his sudden success as a poet?
(a) Milton (b) Shelley
(b) Byron (d) Keats

41. Who among the following is known for his Hellenic spirit?
(a) John Keats (b) Lord Byron
(c) P.B. Shelley (d) Robert Southey

42. "Our Sweetest songs are those that tell of Saddest thoughts." Who composed these famous lines?
(a) Keats (b) Shelley
(c) Byron (d) Wordsworth

43. On whose grave is this epitaph engraved? 'Here lies one whose name was writ in water'.
(a) John Keats
(b) P.B. Shelley
(c) Robert Southey
(d) William Shakespeare

44. Keats' brother, Tom, died of the same disease Keats was suffering from. Name that disease.
(a) Carcinoma (b) Bronchitis
(c) Asthema (d) Consumption

45. Which of the following works of Keats is a narrative romance composed in pentameter couplets?
(a) Bright Star (b) Human Seasons
(c) Lamia (d) Ode to Autumn

46. Rebecca is a character in Scott's
(a) 'Rob Roy'
(b) 'Ivanhoe'
(c) 'The Antiquity'
(d) 'The Heart of Midlothian'

47. Which poem of Sir Walter Scott written in 1810 made him famous throughout England and Scotland?
(a) 'Revely'
(b) 'The Lord of the Isle'
(c) 'The Lady of the Lake'
(d) 'Marmion'

48. 'The Life of Napolean' is a biography written by Scott in
(a) seven volumes
(b) nine volumes
(b) eleven volumes
(d) twelve volumes

49. Name the novel written by Scott in 1814 which brought him immediate and grand success and whose authorship was kept as a secret by the novelist.
(a) *Guy Mannering* (b) *Old Morality*
(c) *The Antiquity* (d) *Waverley*

50. Which is Thomas De Quincey's best known work?
(a) Confession of an Opium Eater
(b) The English Mail Coach
(c) Joan of Arc
(d) Murder considered as one of the Fine Arts

51. Besides being an essayist, De Quincey was also a

(a) Poet (b) Playwright
(c) Biographer (d) Critics

52. The Quarterly Renew was founded in 1809 by
(a) Jon Gay (b) John Galt
(c) John Murray (d) John Keats

53. Southey is always remembered for his
(a) Epics (b) Odes
(c) Ballads (d) Elegies

54. Robert Southey was made the Poet Laureate in
(a) 1810 (b) 1811
(c) 1812 (d) 1813

55. *Theodoric* by Thomas Campbell was written in
(a) Ottava rime (b) Closed couplet
(b) Blank verse (d) Terza rime

56. *Lord Uliin's Daughter* by Thomas Campbell is a
(a) Ballad (b) Lyric
(c) Epic (d) Sonnet

57. Who has been called the last of the romantic mistrels?
(a) Thomas Moore
(b) Thomas Campbell
(c) Thomas Hood
(d) Thomas Kyd

58. Leigh Hunt adopted free form of verse by rejecting
(a) Spenserian stanza (b) Terza rime
(c) Classic couplet (d) Blank verse

59. *Evelina* is a famous novel of
(a) Jane Austen (b) Fanny Burney
(c) Jane Eyre (d) Jane Porter

60. Shelley died by
(a) drinking poison
(b) drowning himself
(c) hanging himself
(d) None of the above

61. 'Season of mists and mellow fruitfulness'.
(a) To Blossom
(b) Ode to the West Wind
(c) Ode to Autumn
(d) Tintern Abbey

62. The novels of Sir Walter Scott deal with scenes in
(a) Faulkland (b) Switzerland
(c) Ireland (d) Scotland

63. Which of the following women writers is from Romantic movement?
(a) Fanny Burney
(b) Maria Edgeworth
(c) Susan Ferries
(d) Jane Porter

64. Who was it that defined romanticism as addition of strangeness to beauty?
(a) Wordsworth (b) Walter Pater
(c) William Blake (d) Charles lamb

65. Coleridge's 'The Rime of the Ancient Mariner' is a
(a) Sonnet (b) Ode
(c) Elegy (d) Ballad

66. Wordsworth has written a poem Ruth. Who has written a novel under the same title?
(a) Charles Dickness
(b) George Meridith
(c) Charlotte Bronte
(d) Elizabeth Gaskell

67. Which poet has been described by Mathew Arnold as a beautiful but in effectual angel beating in the void his luminous wings?
(a) Byron (b) Shelley
(c) Keats (d) Blake

68. Keats abandoned his poem 'Hyperion' because it contained traces of an excessive influence of

(a) Milton (b) Shakespeare
(c) Spenser (d) Pope

69. The first fruit of Wordsworth's genius was seen in the 'Lyrical Ballads'. This was published in
(a) 1798 (b) 1799
(c) 1800 (d) 1801

70. Which of the following poems was not composed by Wordsworth?
(a) 'Frost at Midnight'
(b) 'Ode on the Intimations of Immortality'
(c) 'The Prelude'
(d) Lines written on few miles above Tintern Abbey.

71. To the elder group of Romantic poets belonged.
(a) Wordsworth, Coleridge and Scott
(b) Wordsworth, Coleridge and Southey
(c) Wordsworth, Coleridge and Keats
(d) Wordsworth, Coleridge and Shelley

72. "Bliss was it is that down to be alive. But to be young was very heaven?" Here Wordsworth is referring to
(a) Elizabethan age
(b) Commonwealth period
(c) French revolution
(d) Augustan age

73. The total member of poems included in 'Lyrical Ballads' is
(a) 23 (b) 24
(c) 25 (d) 26

74. Who said about Wordsworth, "His poetry is the reality his Philosophy is the illusion"?
(a) T.S. Eliot (b) John Ruskin
(c) Arnold (d) Byron

75. "I see in Wordsworth the Natural Man rising up against the spiritual Man continually and then he is no poet but a philosopher at Enemity against all true poetry or Inspiration". Who said this?
(a) William blake
(b) Coleridge
(c) Hazlitt
(d) None of the above

76. Wordsworth's purpose in 'Lyrical Ballads' was to
(a) make the familiar, unfamiliar
(b) make the unfamiliar familiar
(c) Both (a) and (b)
(d) None of the above

77. Which is the last poem of 'The Lyrical Ballads'?
(a) Tintern Abbey (b) The Excursion
(c) An Evening Walk (d) Daffodils

78. Which one of Coleridge poems was included in 'Lyrical Ballads'?
(a) 'The Rime of the Ancient Mariner'
(b) 'Christable'
(c) 'Kubla khan'
(d) All of the above

79. Who was opium-addicted?
(a) Wordsworth (b) Coleridge
(c) Keats (d) Southey

80. To which age did Charles Lamb belong?
(a) The Augustan Age
(b) The Age of Transition
(c) The Romantic Age
(d) The Victorian Age

81. Charles Lamb also wrote a play named
(a) Dream children (b) John Wood Will
(c) South Sea house (d) The Cenci

82. Hugh Walker has called lamb
(a) the Prince of Essayist
(b) a Pathetic figure
(c) a third role writer
(d) None of the above

83. In Lamb's essay 'Valentine's Day' Valentine was a

(a) King (b) Bishop
(c) Steele (d) None of the above

84. Who is an 18th century author, essayist and painter? One of his paintings is Still in National Portrait Gallery ____.
(a) Addison (b) Bacon
(c) Hazlitt (d) Thackery

85. Hazlitt wrote essays which may be termed as ____.
(a) Aphoristic (b) Personal
(c) Periodical (d) Allegorical

86. *The Round Table* is a ____ by Hazlitt.
(a) play
(b) essay
(c) lecture
(d) collection of essays

87. Hazlitt was unpopular mostly for his
(a) arrest for debt
(b) political views
(c) his passion for his Landlord's daughter
(d) temper was Irish

88. The Indian Juggler is an example of Hazlitt's style ____.
(a) Discursive (b) Oratorical
(c) Prolix (d) Copious

89. Hazlitt pays a handsome tribute to Coleridge in the essay ____.
(a) *My First Acquaintance With*
(b) *The Plain Speaker*
(c) *The Indian Jugglers The Poets*
(d) None of the above.

90. Blake's songs of Innocence is about ____?
(a) the joys of childhood in a natural and protected world
(b) the pastoral world
(c) Both (a) and (b)
(d) None of the above

91. 'Pity would be no more if we did not make somebody poor'. Who wrote these lines?
(a) Wordsworth (b) Coleridge
(c) Shelley (d) Blake

92. In which of his works, Blake denounced the subordination of women?
(a) *Songs of Experience*
(b) *The book of Citizen*
(c) *Visions of the Daughters of Albion*
(d) *He Did Not Denounce*

93. Blake is a
(a) communist (b) socialist
(c) conservative (d) symbolist

94. Blake is concerned with feelings, emotions and instincts, so his poetry is full of ____.
(a) imagination
(b) ideal views
(c) supernatural things
(d) blessings

95. Who made the cryptic remark that 'Milton was of the Devil's party without knowing it'?
(a) Cowper (b) Blake
(c) Arnold (d) Dr. Johnson

96. Which poem of Blake is a ballad about bed time?
(a) Laughing song (b) A cradle song
(c) Nurses song (d) Infant joy

97. Child is the central figure in
(a) 'Songs of Innocence'
(b) 'Little Blake Boy'
(c) 'The lamb'
(d) 'The Green'

98. In which poem Blake passes satire on church?
(a) 'The Lily'
(b) 'The Garden of Love'
(c) 'Sun Flower'
(d) 'To Tirgah'

99. What was the popular name of Byron?

(a) Broken Soul (b) Broken Sealer
(c) Broken Dandy (d) Broken Feasta

100. What is the another name of Satan?
(a) Grafton (b) Asmodeus
(c) Michael (d) Lucifer

101. In which from Byron's 'The vision of Judgement' has been conceived?
(a) Conceived in an allegorical form
(b) Conceived as mock heroic
(c) Conceived as a dream vision
(d) Conceived as a mock epic

102. Who as per Christian belief, are cherubs?
(a) Subtle and bright bodies angels.
(b) An order or class of heavenly beings symbolizing divine wisdom and justice.
(c) The second highest order of angels.
(d) Angels spinning the thread of man's life.

103. What is your estimate of the poem 'The Vision of Judgment' by Byron?
(a) It is a perfect mock epic, unparalled in English literary history.
(b) It is a masterpiece of verse satire in the English language.
(c) It is a masterpiece of burlesque of a fellow poet's poem.
(d) It is a poem extolling the king so much so that it gives him a place among the blessing in the heaven.

104. What was the name of Byron's wife?
(a) Jame Dsabella
(b) Anna Isabellea
(c) Augusta Leigh
(d) Claire Claviment

105. Who is known as brother poet of Byron?
(a) Gambas (b) Shelley
(c) Jane Williams (d) Leigh Hunt

106. What are the three classical unities?
(a) Unity of consent, unity of joy and unity of sorrow.
(b) Unity of place, unity of time and unity of action.
(c) Unity of source, unity of means and unity of time.
(d) Unity of taste, unity of harmony.

107. Which novel of Jane Austen has been considered to be the best from literary point of view?
(a) *Northanger Abbey*
(b) *Emma*
(c) *Mansfield Park*
(d) *Sensefield Park*

108. To which age did Jane Austen belong?
(a) Modern age (b) Age of transition
(c) Romantic age (d) Victorian age

109. Who has been called 'Prose Shakespeare' by Macaulay?
(a) Thomas Hardy
(b) Charles Dickens
(c) Jane Austen
(d) William Golding

110. Jane Austen's subject matter for his novels is _______.
(a) human nature (b) frustration
(c) revenge (d) None of the above

111. Which novel of Jane Austen was in form of Letters?
(a) *Mansfield Park*
(b) *Emma*
(c) *Northanger Abbey*
(d) *Elinor and Marrianne*

112. How many novels did Jane Austen write?
(a) Six (b) Eleven
(c) Sixteen (d) Twenty three

113. Jane Austen was contemporary to
(a) Thomas Hardy
(b) Sir Walter Scott
(c) Charles Dickens
(d) Oscar Wilde

114. Austen's two novels were published posthumously. They are

(a) *Pride and Prejudice* and *Mansfield Park.*
(b) *Emma* and *Persuation.*
(c) *Persuation* and *Sense and Sensibility.*
(d) *Northanger Abbey* and *Persuation.*

115. The novels of Walter Scott deal with scenes in
(a) Scotland (b) Ireland
(c) Switzerland (d) America

116. The phase, Waverly novels is associated with ______
(a) Henry Fielding
(b) Jane Austen
(c) Walter Scott
(d) None of the above

117. Which literary period has been called a homogenous period?
(a) Romantic (b) Puritan
(c) Victorian (d) Edwardian

118. Literary Reminiscenes is the most illuminating critical work of
(a) William Hazlitt
(b) Thomas De Quincey
(c) Leigh Hunt
(d) Lord Byron

119. Which poem of Keats highly impressed Shelley?
(a) 'Ode to a Nightingale'
(b) 'Hyperion'
(c) 'I had a Dove'
(d) 'To Autumn'

120. Who died of fever?
(a) Byron (b) Keats
(c) Shelley (d) None of the above

121. A Byronic hero is he who is
(a) vain and melancholy
(b) cynical
(c) finds no good in life or love or anything
(d) All of the above

122. Which work of Keats deal with the murder of a lady's lover by her two wicked brothers?
(a) Endymion (b) Hyperion
(c) Lamia (d) Isabella

123. Adonis is an elegy in
(a) Shakespeare (b) Dryden
(c) Keats (d) Wordsworth

124. Keats volume of poems was dedicated to
(a) Spenser (b) Fanny Browne
(c) Leigh Hunt (d) Wordsworth

125. Which is Shelley's autobiographical poem?
(a) 'Alastor' (b) 'Queen Mab'
(c) 'Adonis' (d) 'The Cenci'

ANSWERS

1. (c)	2. (d)	3. (c)	4. (a)	5. (a)	6. (d)
7. (c)	8. (b)	9. (d)	10. (c)	11. (d)	12. (a)
13. (c)	14. (d)	15. (b)	16. (a)	17. (d)	18. (d)
19. (a)	20. (b)	21. (d)	22. (d)	23. (d)	24. (d)
25. (b)	26. (d)	27. (a)	28. (a)	29. (b)	30. (c)
31. (b)	32. (c)	33. (b)	34. (c)	35. (b)	36. (c)
37. (d)	38. (a)	39. (b)	40. (c)	41. (a)	42. (b)

43. (a)	44. (d)	45. (c)	46. (b)	47. (c)	48. (b)
49. (d)	50. (a)	51. (d)	52. (c)	53. (c)	54. (d)
55. (b)	56. (a)	57. (a)	58. (c)	59. (b)	60. (b)
61. (c)	62. (d)	63. (b)	64. (b)	65. (d)	66. (d)
67. (b)	68. (a)	69. (a)	70. (a)	71. (b)	72. (c)
73. (a)	74. (b)	75. (a)	76. (a)	77. (a)	78. (a)
79. (b)	80. (c)	81. (b)	82. (a)	83. (d)	84. (c)
85. (b)	86. (d)	87. (c)	88. (a)	89. (a)	90. (c)
91. (d)	92. (c)	93. (d)	94. (a)	95. (b)	96. (c)
97. (a)	98. (b)	99. (c)	100. (d)	101. (c)	102. (b)
103. (c)	104. (b)	105. (b)	106. (b)	107. (b)	108. (c)
109. (c)	110. (a)	111. (d)	112. (a)	113. (b)	114. (d)
115. (a)	116. (c)	117. (c)	118. (b)	119. (b)	120. (a)
121. (d)	122. (d)	123. (c)	124. (c)	125. (a)	

15

Victorian Period

The Victorian Age, also known as the Age of Tennyson in English literature, witnessed an unprecedented change and progress in all spheres of life. The literature of this period, wonderfully rich and varied in personal quality, embodies the spirit of the age. The chief characteristics of Victorian period are as under:

1. An Era of Material Affluence
2. An Era of Peace
3. Prosperity and Progress
4. The New Education
5. Victorian Compromise
6. Social unrest, Social Purpose and Realism
7. Advance of Democratic Ideals
8. The Impact of Science
9. Revival of Interest in the Past
10. Idealism and Pessimism

POETRY

Alfred Lord Tennyson (1809-92)

Lord Tennyson became Poet-Laureate in succession to Wordsworth. At the age of seventeen he brought out poems by two Brothers in Collaboration with his elder brother, Charles. His poems, chiefly lyrical was published in 1830.

His longer poem 'The Princess' (1847) deals with the theme of 'the new woman in a seriocomic' manner. It is written in blank verse but contains several beautiful lyrics.

In 'Memoriam' (1850) a philosophic poem, was inspired by the death of the poet's friend, Arthur Henry Hallam.

It is an elegy which contains meditations on life and death.

Tennyson, the most representative poet of his age, reflects in his best poetry the restless spirit of the progressive Victorian Age. Tennyson is the most complete embodiment of the Victorian spirit of compromise. To him love is a domestic sentiment.

Tennyson also championed the cause of women's progress and education in 'The Princess'.

His poem 'Locksley Hall' is full of the restless spirit of 'young England.'

In his political opinions Tennyson believed in a compromise between aristocracy and democracy.

The thing that most impresses Tennyson is the spectacle of order in the universe.

His nature poetry is original and bears the impact of contemporary science. It is seen in the minuteness and exactness of his observation.

Tennyson's landscape painting shows that he was endowed with the exactitude of the botanist and the delicate sensibility of the artist. His nature poetry is intellectual.

Tennyson is a great and gifted poetic craftsman. His poetic style shows remarkable variety, which harmonises with the variety of his themes.

Tennyson attained high excellence in every king of poetry—the song, the idyll, the dramatic monologue, the dialect poem, the descriptive or 'pageant' poem, the ballad, the war-ode, the threnody, the epic narrative, and the drama.

He is also unsurpassable in handling the English metres. He skillfully employed blank verse.

Rickett wrote about Tennyson, "As a word paintes of typical English scenery, as the exponent of the simple emotions of everyday life, he holds a treasured and honourable place. His delicacy and melodies and utterance, will always endear him to English men and women."

Robert Browning (1812-89)

It was the example of Shelley and Byron which inspired him to dedicate his life to poetry, in the hope of making some striking contribution to the progress of intellectual freedom and the perfection of man.

His earliest work 'Pauline' appeared in 1833, followed by 'Paracelsus' (1835), *Stafford* (play-1837), 'Sordello' (1840) and 'Bells and Pomegranates' (1846) etc.

In 1846 Browning married Elizabeth Barrett, the poetess, whose works had strongly attracted him.

His last volume 'Asoland' was published in 1899. The same year he died and was buried in Westminster Abbey.

Browning's Optimism is his message and also his philosophy of life.

He believes that salvation can be attained by the assertion of will and passion in right channels.

Browning is a poet of hope which lies optionism was a result of experience. He finds all things good through virtue is the best.

Browning's firm faith in the existence of God, who is all pervading, benign and all powerful, is the main source of his optimism. In Pippa passes he says

God is in his Heaven
All is right with the world.

The chief characteristic of Browning's poetry is his firm connection that life is worth living.

Browning is an ardent singer of the glory of love between man and woman. The object of love in his poems is not an imagined goddess but a real woman. Browning, like Donne, is the poet of wedded love.

His love poetry is intensely realistic in character. The imagery of his love poetry is of suburban streets, straws, medicine bottles, pliowos, window blinds etc.

All love poems of Browning whether dealing with cases of successful love of failure in love end on a note of optimism and triumph.

Browning also treats love as a philosophic principle which harmonises and unifies all beings. A life devoted to love is an ennobling life and leads man higher and higher.

Browning's genius was essentially dramatic but due to his profound interest in depicting human soul and psyche he could not be a successful dramatist. So he attempted the monologue form.

Psychological insight, analytical subtlety, and power of dramatic interpretation among the main features of Browning's dramatic monologues.

Browning did not invent the dramatic monologue but he made it especially his own. He composed beautiful monologues with intense lyrical intensity on love theme.

Browning's monologues are remarkable for psychological depiction of human characters. Cazamian calls his monologues 'Studies in practical psychology'.

Browning is a gifted poetic craftsman. He is matchless in writing dramatic monologues. He often seems to be careless of music and melody. He invented a large variety of verse forms and used them with consummate skill.

Obscurity is a serious drawback in Browning's poetry. It arises to some extent from his preoccupation with soul dissection or psychological analysis.

His style is, often, telegraphic. His stupendous learning and findness for Latin quotations and expressions further complicate matters for his readers. The language at his command was a poor instrument to render effectively and with the same speed of thought.

Browning is an original poet. He was astonishingly great but also astonishingly faulty, and his faults have come in the way of the appreciation of his real greatness.

Mathew Arnold (1822-83)

Arnold was also a distinguished prose writer and literary critic. His poetry places him in a different state.

According to Garrod, Arnold is the greatest elegiac poet in our language, not in virtue of merely thyrsis, but in virtue of the whole temper of his Muse.

His elegiac spirit is like that of Gray rather than that of Milton, or Shelley or Tennyson. Even the personal elegies, in which the poet laments the death of some close relative or friend, runs astrong note of impersonal grief over the miserable destiny of human life. The subject of Rugby chapel is his own father; in a Southern Night it is his brother, in Westminister Abbey and thyrsis, his most intimate friends.

Arnold's poetry is an expression of his inherent pessimism and loveliness.

His elegies are expression of his inner grief. Various factors combined to make him a frustrated individual; his uncongenial occupation, contemporary conflict between science and religion, the conflict in his own soul and above all his thoughtful temperament.

But Arnold is never hopeless. He feels' man can come out triumphant out of chaos and gloom, if he strives to know his soul. The self-dependence is Arnold's panacea for curing 'His strategic disease of modern life'.

Arnold vchemently criticized the rising spirit of modernity in all spheres of contemporary life in his poetry.

Arnold was a born classicist, a lover of shapeliness, restraint clarity and lucidity. He disliked eccentricity, arbitrariness, and self-will which romanticism encourages. Despite his minate love for classicism and his reaction against romanticism, Arnold could not wholly keep the romantic element out of his poetry.

Love of nature is present as an essence in all his work. But he loved nature in her quienter and more subdued moods. As a poet of nature, Arnold is best when he is melancholy.

Arnold was a great and gifted poetic artist, who took great pains in polishing and perfecting the rhythm of his poems.

He is really a classic so far as his felicitous phraseology, the crystalline perfection of his lines, his fastidious workmanship and lucidity of expression are concerned. His lyrical facility, which reaches the point of singing, is arrested by thinking.

A.H. Clough (1819-61)

Clough was an intimate friend of Arnold, whose Thyrsis is a noble monody on clough's death.

His first long poem 'The Bothie of Toperna-vuolich' (1848), 'Amours de Voyage' (1849) and 'Dipsychus' (1850) are charged with much of the deep seated unrest and despondency.

James Thomson (1834-82)

Thomson's 'The City of Dreadful Night' strikes a note of unrelieved pessimism.

The gloom and depression that envisage the poem are due largely to the many poem disappointments he had suffered, intensified by his constitutional intemperances.

Edward Fitzgerald (1809-88)

Fitzgerald is remembered for his translation of the Persian work, The Rubaiyat of Omar Khayyam. His translation has the force and beauty of an original work.

No English writer has expressed so beautifully the Epicurean philosophy as Fitzgerald. The translation is remarkable for its artistic beauty and its fine sincerity of utterance.

Fatalism is an important element in Fitzgerland's pessimism.

THE PRE-RAPHAELITE MOVEMENT IN ENGLISH POETRY

The Pre-Raphaelite poets drew their inspiration from the works of Italian painters before Raphael.

The celebrated Pre-Raphaelite Brotherhood was founded in 1848 by three painters, Holman Hunt, John Millais and Rossetti and one sculptor Thomas Woolner.

The qualities of Pre-Raphaelite poetry are as under:

- An extension of romantic Revival
- Medievalism
- Art for Art's sake
- Picturesquences
- Love for symbolism

- Music and melody
- Conclusion
- The Pre-Raphaelite poets

Dante Gabriel Rossetti (1828-82)

Rossetti, the eldest of the Pre-Raphaelite school of artists and poets, was himself both painter and poet.

His poetical work consists of two slender volumes, *Poems* (1870) and *Ballads and Sonnets* (1881).

Rossetti's poetry is sensuous, picturesque and impassioned like that of Keats.

Rossetti is a great melodist. He carefully chose words for their melodious and musical quality. His style is also marked by abundant use of symbols.

William Morris (1834-96)

William Morris, a man of versatile genius, produced a great amount of poetry and was one of the most conspicuous figures of Mid-Victorian Literature.

He was considered as 'poet, artist manufacturer, and socialist author of *The Earthly Paradise*'.

Morris's first volume of poetry, *The Defence of Guenevere and other poems* (1858) reveals his strong love of beauty of colour, sound and scenery, and his passion for the medieval.

The Life and Death of Jason (1866) is a long narrative poem on a familiar theme.

The Earthly Paradise (1866-70) is a collection of twenty-four tales on various subjects of classical and medieval origin.

A.C. Swinburne (1837-1909)

Swinburne was a prolific poet of the Pre-Raphaelite School.

'Altanta in Colydon' (1865), an attempt at an English version of an ancient Greek tragedy, was his first considerable effort in poetic form.

It is remarkable for musical style, tuneful and impetuous movement, a cunning metrical craftsmanship, and a mastery of melodious diction.

Music, melody and picturesquences are the outstanding qualities of his poetry.

- Other Poets
- E.B. Browning (1806-61)
- Christina Georgina Rossetti (1830-94)
- A.E.O Shaughnessy (1844-81)
- Coventry Patmore (1823-96)
- Alexander Smith (1830-67)
- Robert Buchanan (1841-1901)
- Sir Edwin Arnold (1832-1904)

VICTORIAN PROSE

The prose literature of Victorian Era is immensely rich and varied. Historical prose was abundantly written.

Scientific treatises also attained Literary rank. As regards the development of prose style, Carlyle and Macaulay developed the middle style. Ruskin and Peter cultivated ornate style Stevenson's style, is modern.

Thomas Carlyle (1795-1881)

Carlyle was a versatile thinker and writer who successfully wrote on philosophy, history, criticism and biography. His earliest work consisted mainly of translations, essays and biographies. Rickett, said, "The greatest personality in criticism and essay during the earlier part of the era was Thomas Carlyle."

The most readable of Carlyle's longer works is *Heroes and Hero Worship* (1840), which deals with certain leaders in the fields of religion, poetry, war and politics. It is an interesting study to compare this work with the *Representative Men of Emerson*. The latter looks upon the world as governed by ideals, which belong not to individuals but to humanity. When some man appears in whom the common ideal is written large, other men follow him because they see in him a truth which they revere in their own souls. So the leader is always in the highest sense a representative of his race. But Carlyle will have nothing of such democracy; to him common men are stupid or helpless and must be governed from without. Occasionally, when humanity is in the slough of Despond, appears a hero, a superman, and proceeds by his own force to drag or drive his subjects to a higher level. When the hero dies, humanity must halt and pray heaven to send another master.

It is evident before one has read much of *Heroes* that Carlyle is at heart a force-worshiper. To him history means the biography of a few heroes, and heroism is a matter of power, not of physical or moral courage. The hero may have the rugged courage of a Cromwell, or he may be an easy-living poet like Shakespeare, or a ruthless despot like Napoleon, or an epitmon of all meanness like Roussiau; but if he shows superior force of any kind, that is the hallmark of his heroism, and before such an one humanity should bow down. Of real history, therefore, you will learn nothing from *Heroes;* neither will you get any trustworthy information concerning Odin, Mahomet and the rest of Carlyle's oddly consorted characters. One does not read the book for facts but for a new view of old matters. With hero-worshipers especially it ranks very high among the thought-provoking books of the past century.

Of the historical works of Carlyle the most famous is the *The French Revolution* (1837). On this work Carlyle spent much heart-breaking labor, and the story of the first volume shows that the author, who made himself miserable over petty matters, could be patient in face of a real misfortune. Moreover, if furnishes a striking example of Carlyle's method, which was not historical in the modern sense, but essentially pictorial or dramatic. He selected a few dramatic scenes, such as the storming of the Bastille, and painted them in flaming colors. Also he was strong in drawing portraits, and his portrayal of Robespierre, Danton and other actors in the terrible drama was astonishingly vigorous, though seldom accurate. His chief purpose in drawing all these pictures and portraits was to prove that order can never come out of chaos save by the iron grip of a governing hand. Hence, if you want to learn the real history of the French Revolution, you must seek elsewhere; but if you want an impression of it, an impression that burns its way into the mind, you will hardly find the equal of Carlyle's book in any language.

Carlyle's wife was a brilliant but nervous woman with literary gifts of her own. She had always received attention; she expected and probably deserved admiration; but so did Carlyle, who expected also to be made the center of all solicitude when he called heaven and earth to witness against democracy, crowing roosters, weak tea and other grievous afflictions. After her death (in London, 1866) he was plunged into deepest grief. In his Reminiscences and Letters he fairly deifies his wife, calling her his queen, his star, his light and joy of life, and portrays a companionship as of two mortals in a Paradise without a serpent. All that is doubtless as it should be, in a romance; but the unfortunate publication of Mrs. Carlyle's letters and journals introduced a jarring note of reality. A jungle of controversial writings has since grown up around the domestic relations of the Carlyles,—impertinent, deplorable writings, which serve no purpose but to make us cry, "Enough, let them rest in peace" Both had sharp tongues, and probably both were often sorry.

From the moors the Carlyles went to London and settled for the remainder of their lives in a house in Cheyne Row, in the suburb of Chelsea. There Carlyle slowly won recognition, his success being founded on his *French Revolution*. Invitations began to pour in upon him; great men visited and praised him, and his fame spread as "the sage of Cheisea". Then followed his *Cromwell* and *Frederick the Great,* the latter completed after years of complaining labor which made wreck of home happiness. And then came a period of unusual irritation, to which we owe, in part at least, Carlyle's railings against progress and his deplorable criticism of England's great men and women,—poor little Browning, animalcular De Quincey, rabbit-brained Newman, sawdustish Mill, chattering George Eliot, ghastly-shrieky Shelley, once-enough Lamb, stinted-scanty Wordsworth, poor thin fool Darwin and his book (The Origin of species, of which Carlyle confessed he never read a page) which was wonderful as an example of the stupidity of mankind.

Such criticisms were reserved for Carlyle's private memoirs. The world knew him only by his books, and revered him as a great and good man. He died in 1881, and of the thousand notices which appeared in English or American periodicals of that year there is hardly one that does not overflow with praise.

In the home at Cheisea were numerous letters and journals which Carlyle committed to his friend Froude the historian. The publication of these private papers raised a storm of protest. Admirers of Carlyle, shocked at the revelation of another side to their hero, denounced Froude for his disloyalty and malice; whereupon the literary world divided into two camps, the Jane Carlyleists and the Thomas Carlyleists, as they are still called. That Froude showed poor taste is evident; but we must acquit him of all malice. Private papers had been given him with the charge to publish them if he saw fit; and from them he attempted to draw not a flattering but a truthful portrait of Carlyle, who had always preached the doctrine that a man must speak truth as he sees it. Nor will Carlyle suffer in the long run from being deprived of a halo which he never deserved. Already the crustiness of the man begins to grow dim in the distance; it is his rugged earnestness that will be longest remembered.

We have followed literary custom rather than individual judgement in studying Dickens, Thackeray and George Eliot as the typical Victorian novelists. On Dickens, as the most original genius of the age, most people are agreed; but the rank of the other two is open to question. There are critics besides Swinburne who regard Charlotte Bronte as a greater genius than

George Eliot; and many uncritical readers find more pleasure or profit in the Barchester novels of Anthony Trollope than in anything written by Thackeray. It may even be that the three or four leading novels of the age were none of them written by the novelists in question; but it is still essential to know their works if only for these reasons: that they greatly influenced other story-tellers of the period, and that they furnish us a standard by which to judge all modern fiction.

To treat the many Victorian novelists adequately would in itself require a volume. We shall note here only a few leading figures, naming in each case a novel or two which may serve as an invitation to a better acquaintance with their authors.

The Bronte sisters, Charlotte and Emily, made a tremendous sensation in England when, from their retirement, they sent out certain works of such passionate intensity that readers who had long been familiar with novels were startled into renewed attention. Reading these works now we recognize the genius of the writers, but we recognize also a morbid, unwholesome quality, which is a reflection not of English life but of the personal and unhappy temperament of two girls who looked on life first as a gorgeous romance and then as a gloomy tragedy.

Charlotte Bronte (1816-55) was perhaps the more gifted of the two sisters, and her best-known works are *Jane Eyre* and *Villette. The Date of the Latter Novel* (1853) was made noteworthy by the masterpiece of another woman novelist, Mrs. Elizabeth Gaskell (1810-65), who was the exact opposite of the Bronte sisters,—serene, well-balanced, and with a fund of delicious humor. All these qualities and more appeared in *Cranford* (1853), a series of sketches of country life (first contributed to Dicken's *Household Words)* which together form one of the most charming stories produced during the Victorian era. The same author wrote a few other novels and an admirable Life of Charlotte Bronte.

Charles Reade (1814-84) was a follower of Dickens in his earlier novels, such as *Peg Woffington*; but he made one notable departure when he wrote *The Cloister and the Hearth* (1861). This is a story of student life and vagabond life in Europe, in the stirring times that followed the invention of printing. The action moves rapidly; many different characters appear; the scene shifts from Holland across Europe to Italy, and back again; adventures of a startling kind meet the hero at every stage of his foot journey. It is a stirring tale, remarkably well told; so much will every uncritical reader gladly acknowledge. Moreover, there are critics who, after studying *The Cloister and the Hearth*, rank it with the best historical novels in all literature.

Anthony Trollope (1815-82) began as a follower of Thackeray, but in the immense range of his characters and incidents he soon outstripped his master. Perhaps his best work is *Barchester Towers* (1857), one of a series of novels which picture with marvelous fidelity the life of a cathedral town in England.

Another novelist who followed Thackeray, and then changed his allegiance to Dickens, was Bulwer Lytton (1803-73). He was essentially an imitator, a follower of the market, and before Thackeray and Dickens were famous he had followed almost every important English novelist from Mrs. Radcliffe to Walter Scott. Two of his historical novels, *Rienzi* and *The Last Days of Pompeii*, may be mildly recommended. The rest are of the popular and somewhat trashy kind; critics jeer at them, and the public buys them in large numbers.

One of the most charming books of the Victorian age was produced by Richard Blackmore (1825-1900). He wrote several novels, some of them of excellent quality, but they were all overshadowed by his beautiful old romance of *Lorna Doone* (1869). It is hard to overpraise such a story, wholesome and sweet as a breath from the moors, and the critic's praise will be unnecessary if the reader only opens the book. It should be read, with *Cranford*, if one reads nothing else of Victorian fiction.

Two other notable romances of a vanished age came from the hand of Charles Kingsley (1819-75). He produced many works in poetry and prose, but his fame now rests upon *Hypatia*, *Westward Ho*! And a few stories for children. *Hypatia* (1853) is an interesting novel dealing with the conflict of pagan and Christian ideals in the early centuries. *Westward Ho*! (1855) is a stirring narrative of seafaring and adventure in the days of Elizabeth. It has been described as a "stunning" boys' book, and it would prove an absorbing story for any reader who likes adventure were it not marred by one serious fault. The author's personal beliefs and his desire to glorify certain Elizabethan adventurers lead him to pronounce judgment of a somewhat wholesale kind. He treats one religious party of the period to a golden halo, and the other to a lash of scorpions; and this is apt to alienate many readers who else would gladly follow Sir Amyas Leigh on his gallant ventures in the New World or on the Spanish Main. Kingsley had a rare talent for writing for children (his heart never grew old), and his *Heroes* and *Water Babies* are still widely read as bedtime stories.

Of the later Victorian novelists, chief among them being Meredith, Hardy and Stevenson, little may be said here, as they are much too near us to judge of their true place in the long perspective of English literature. Meredith, with the analytical temper and the disconnected style of Browning, is for mature readers, not for young people. Hardy has decided power, but is too hopelessly pessimistic for anybody's comfort,—except in his earlier works, which have a romantic charm that brightens the obscurity of his later philosophy.

In Robert Louis Stevenson (1850-94) we have the spirit of romance personified. His novels, such as *Kidnapped* and *David Balfour*, are stories of adventure written in a very attractive style; but he is more widely known, among young people at least, by his charming Child's Garden of Verses and his *Treasure Island* (1883). This last is a kind of dime-novel of pirates and buried treasure. If one is to read stories of that kind, there is no better place to begin than with this masterpiece of Stevenson. Other works by the same versatile author are the novels, *Master of Ballantrae*, *Weir of Hermiston* and Dr. Jekyll and Mr. Hyde; various collections of essays, such as *Virginibus Puerisque* and *Familiar Studies of Men and Books*; and some rather thin sketches of journeying called *An Inland Voyage* and *Travels with a Donkey*.

John Ruskin (1819-1900)

The prose of Ruskin is a treasure house. Nature portrayed as everyman's Holy Land; descriptions of mountain or landscape, and more beautiful descriptions of leaf or lichen or the glint of light on a breaking wave; appreciations of literature, and finer appreciations of life itself; startling views of art, and more revolutionary views of that frightful waste of human life and labor which we call political economy,—all these and many more impressions of nature, art and human society are eloquently recorded in the ten thousand pages which are the work of Ruskin's hand.

LIFE. The early training of Ruskin may explain both the strength and the weakness of his work. His father was a wealthy wine merchant, his mother a devout woman with puritanic ideas of duty. Both parents were of Scottish and, as Ruskin boasted, of plebeian descent. They had but one child, and in training him they used a strange mixture of severity and coddling, of wisdom and nonsense.

The young Ruskin was kept apart from other boys and from the sports which breed a modesty of one's own opinion; his time, work and lonely play were minutely regulated; the slightest infringement of rules brought the stern discipline of rod or reproof. On the other hand, he was given the best pictures and the best books; he was taken on luxurious journeys through England and the Continent; he was furnished with tutors for any study to which he turned his mind. When he went up to Oxford, at seventeen, he knew many things which are Greek to the ordinary boy, but was ignorant of almost everything that a boy knows, and that a man finds useful in dealing with the world.

There were several results of this early discipline. One was Ruskin's devotion to art, which came from his familiarity with pictures and galleries; another was his minute study of natural objects, which were to him in place of toys; a third was his habit of "speaking his mind" on every subject; a fourth was his rhythmic prose style, which came largely from his daily habit of memorizing the Bible. Still another result of his lonely magnificence, in which he was deprived of boys' society, was that his affection went out on a flood tide of romance to the first attractive girl he met. So he loved, and was laughed at, and was desperately unhappy. Then he married, not the woman of his choice, but one whom his parents picked out for him. The tastes of the couple were hopelessly different; the end was estrangement, with humiliation and sorrow for Ruskin.

At twenty-four he produced his first important work, *Modern Painters* (1843), which he began as a defense of the neglected artist Turner. This controversial book led Ruskin to a deeper study of his subject, which resulted in four more volumes on modern painting. Before these were completed he had "fairly created a new literature of art" by his *Seven Lamps of Architecture* and *Stones of Venice*. He was appointed professor of fine arts at Oxford; he gave several series of lectures which appeared later as *Lectures on Architecture and Painting*, *Michael Angelo and Tintoret*, *Val d'Arno* and *The Art of England*.

By this time he was renowned as an art critic; but his theories were strongly opposed and he was continually in hot water. In his zeal to defend Turner or Millais or Burne-Jones he was rather slashing in his criticism of other artists. The libel suit brought against him by Whistler, whom he described as a coxcomb who flung a pot of paint in the face of the public, is still talked about in England. The jury (fancy a jury wrestling with a question of art!) found Ruskin guilty, and decided that he should pay for the artist's damaged reputation the sum of one farthing. Whistler ever afterwards wore the coin on his watch chain.

Works of Ruskin. The works of Ruskin fall naturally into three classes, which are called criticisms of art, industry and life, but which are, in fact, profound studies of the origin and meaning of art on the one hand, and of the infinite value of human life on the other.

The most popular of his art criticisms are *St. Mark's Rest* and *Mornings in Florence*, which are widely used as guidebooks, and which may be postponed until the happy time when, in Venice or Florence, one may read them to best advantage. Meanwhile, in *Seven Lamps of Architecture* or *Stones of Venice* or the first two volumes of *Modern Painters*, one may grow acquainted with Ruskin's theory of art.

His fundamental principle was summarized by Pope in the line, "All nature is but art unknown to thee." That nature is the artist's source of inspiration, that art at its best can but copy some natural beauty, and that the copy should be preceded by careful and loving study of the original,—this was the sum of his early teaching. Next, Ruskin looked within the soul of the artist and announced that true art has a spiritual motive, that it springs from the noblest ideals of life.

The beauty of Ruskin's style, its musical rhythm or cadence, its wealth of figure and allusion, its brilliant coloring, like a landscape of his favorite artist Turner,—all this is a source of pleasure to the reader, entirely aside from the subject matter. That this superb eloquence was devoted not to personal or party ends, but to winning men to the love of beauty and truth and right living, is the secret of Ruskin's high place in English letters and of his enduring influence on English life.

Summary. The age of Victoria (1837-1901) approaches our own so closely that it is still difficult to form an accurate judgment of its history or literature. In a review of the history of the age we noted three factors, democracy, science, imperialism, which have profoundly influenced English letters from 1850 to the present time.

Our study of Victorian literature includes (1) The life and works of the two greater poets of the age, Tennyson and Browning. (2) The work of Elizabeth Barrett, Matthew Arnold, Rossetti, Morris and Swinburne, who were selected from the two hundred representive poets of the period. (3) The life and the chief works of the major novelists, Dickens, Thackeray and George Eliot. (4) A review of some other novelists of the age, the Brontë Sisters, Mrs. Gaskell, Anthony Trollope, Blackmore, Kingsley, Meredith, Hardy and Stevenson. (5) The typical essayists and historians, Macaulay, Carlyle, Ruskin, with a review of other typical groups of writers in the fields of religion, history and science.

T.B. Macaulay (1800-89)

Macaulay contributed a number of essays to The Edinburgh Review. His essays are of two kinds-those dealing with literary subjects and those dealing with historical studies, including his famous essays on Lord Clive and Warren Hastings.

He contributed five biographes to the Encyclopedia Britannica.

His magnium opus History of England in five volumes is a remarkable work.

He had a firm faith in the 'Happy materialism' of his age.

His style is energetic, vivid and picturesque. It has a boundless fertility of illustration. His vocabulary is copious and expressive.

Matthew Arnold (1822-88)

Matthew Arnold's prose works are large in bulk and wide in range. Essays in Criticism (1865-89) contains the finest of his critical work, which stamped by wide scholarship and careful thought.

He showed a reaction against Romanticism and advocated a return to the classical spirit, To him 'poetry is the criticism of life'!

According to Arnold the critic should bring the 'best' from all branches of knowledge and should make it prevail.

'Culture Anarchy' (1869) and 'Literature and Dogma' (1873) are his major works.

His style is perfectly liked, essay and rhythmical.

W.H. Pater (1839-94)

Water Horatio Pater was a distinguished critic and stylist.

His first essays appeared in book form as 'studies in the History of Renaissance' (1873) and are concerned chiefly with art.

'Imaginary Portraits' (1887) deals with artists; and 'Appreciations' (1889) is on literary themes. *Marius, the Epicurean* (1885) is a remarkable Philosophical novel.

Pater represented the school of aesthetic criticism.

In his 'Essay on Style in Appreciations' he gives importance to beauty of expression.

THE OXFORD MOVEMENT

Cardinal Newman was the pioneer of the Oxford or Tractarian Movement. The other stalwarts of this movement were John Keble, W.G. Ward and Edward Bouverie Pusey.

John Kebly (1792-1866), the professor of poetry at Oxford, gave the emotional atmosphere of the movement, and Newman provided its dialectics.

Defining Oxford Movement Gates writes that it was "in its essence and attempt to reconstruct the English Church in harmony with the romantic ideal".

The Oxford movement stimulated religious feelings all over the country. It was a strong protest against, the materialism and utilitarianism of the Victorian Age.

R.L. Stevenson (1850-94)

Stevenson, like Montaine and lamb, is personal and intimate.

Stevenson brought the story element to essay writing. He was a great observer of man and nature and he could write brilliant and charming essays even in the most trivial scene or even in Street or in country.

Stevenson was a moralist too. He is profoundly ethical and a skilled stylist.

VICTORIAN NOVEL

The Victorian Age in English Literature is remarkable for the development of the novel. The novelists of this era are Dickens, Meredith, Thackeray, Hardy, George Eliot, The Bronte Sisters. Great Writers chose this form for self-expression. Dickens was the first to introduce the novel of social reform. Thackeray used novel to express 'a conscious, considered criticism of life'. The Victorian novel reflected all the complex forces which influenced the contemporary age. In its very variety and treatment of matter, therefore, the Victorian novel is the index of the many-sided interests.

Charles Dickens (1812-70)

Dickens was the first novelist who possessed extreme sensibility with which he felt the sufferings of the poor, an intense imagination with which he depicted pictures of their lives, and aroused the conscience of the people.

He is among the greatest humorists of the world.

He is the pioneer of realism in 19th century novel. His best characters are portraits from life, and the life that he knew best was lower class life.

Dickens is a novelist with a purpose.

Dickens attacked the abuses in the existing system and throughout he considered himself as the champion of the weak, the outcast and the oppressed.

Dickens could vividly describe every detail of manners, appearance, dress and other external details of his characters.

Humour and Pathos is present in his writings from the very beginning. His humour arises from the heart and not from the lips. His humour is 'broad, humane and creative'.

His novels have no organic unity, they are full of detachable episodes, characters who serve no purpose in furthering the plot.

He is one of the masters of prose in his own way.

His style is often too much mannered. At its best Dickens' style is neither polished nor scholarly, but it is clear, rapid and workmanlike.

According to Hugh Walker, is the most original novelist of England.

Other Novelists

Charles Kingsley (1819-75)
Charles Reade (1814-84)
Edward Lytton Bulwer (1803-73)
Benjamin Disraeli (1804-81)
Wilkie Collins (1824-89)
W.M. Thackeray (1811-63)
Anthony Trollope (1815-82)
Samuel Butler (1835-1902)
George Meredith (1828-1909)
Thomas Hardy (1840-1928)
Elizabeth C.Gaskell (1810-65)
George Eliot (1819-80)

The Regional Novel and Thomas Hardy

Hardy was a prolific and versatile novelist and poet belongs more to the twentieth century than the 19th century.

His novels have the following qualities.

(a) Hardy's Wenex
(b) Hardy and Nature
(c) Hardy's Pessimism is his philosophy of Life
(d) Hardy's superb characterization
(e) His plots are well built and symmetrical

(f) Hardy was a great stylist. His is an admirable style, clear straightforward, unprententious

(g) He is a great regional novelist of the 19th century.

Victorian Drama

Victorian literature was far behind in drama and theatre. Arnold wrote 'In England we have no drama at all', says Arnold. The first half of the 19th century was almost completely barren from the dramatic point of view.

The influence of contineneta1 dramatists brought about a revolutionary change in British drama. Ibsen, Hebbel, Duan, Angler, Gorky, Strindberg and many other made memorable contribution to the rise of realistic drama in England.

Major Names

1. Henrik Ibsen
2. T.W. Robertson
3. Henry Arthur Jones
4. A.W. Pinero.

MULTIPLE CHOICE QUESTIONS

1. How old was Queen Victoria when she ascended the throne?
   (a) 15 years (b) 17 years
   (c) 18 years (d) 21 years
2. Who is known as the most representative poet of the Victorian age?
   (a) Robert Browning (b) Lord Tennyson
   (c) Mathew Arnold (d) Thomas Hardy
3. In 1830, Tennyson published his first collection of poems entitled
   (a) 'Poems'
   (b) 'Poems Chiefly Lyrical'
   (c) 'Dramatic Lyrics'
   (d) 'The Princess'
4. 'Love your enemy, bless your haters said the greatest of the great'. Who said this?
   (a) Browning (b) Tennyson
   (c) Milton (d) Carlyle
5. Tennyson's received the Chancellor's prize in the year 1829 for the poem
   (a) 'Timbuctoo' (b) 'Maud'
   (c) 'Princess' (d) 'Ulysses'
6. 'For men may come and men may go but I go on forever.' This extract occurs in Tennyson's
   (a) 'The Brook' (b) 'Idle tears'
   (c) 'Ulysses' (d) 'Crossing the Ben'
7. 'Pauline' is a work of
   (a) Mathew Arnold
   (b) P.B. Shelley
   (c) Robert Browning
   (d) Alfred Lord Tennyson
8. 'The Old order Changeth, yielding place to new, and God fulfils himself in many ways'. This is an extract from Tennyson's
   (a) The cup (b) Morte d'Arthur
   (c) Harold (d) Enoch Arden
9. Verse dramas like 'Queen Mary' and 'Becket' were written by
   (a) Robert Browning
   (b) Alfred Lord Tennyson
   (c) Elizabeth Barret Browning
   (d) A.H. Clough
10. Browning was denounced for his obscurity when in 1840 he composed

(a) 'Sordello'
(b) 'The Ring and the Book'
(c) 'Pauline'
(d) 'Fra Lippo Lippa'

11. Which of the following by Robert Browning is a children's poem?
(a) 'Asolando'
(b) 'Fra Lippo Lippi'
(c) 'The Pied Piper of Hamelin'
(d) 'The Lost Leader'

12. 'God's in His heaven. All's right with the world.' These lines appear in Robert Browning's
(a) 'The Last Ride Together'
(b) 'Porphyria's lover'
(c) 'Rabbi Ben Ezra'
(d) 'Pippa Passes'

13. 'Fra Lippo Lippa' is a/an
(a) elegy
(b) dramatic monologue
(c) allegory
(d) dramatic romance

14. The longest poem in the English language written by Robert Browning is
(a) 'Sordello'
(b) 'The Last Ride Together'
(c) 'Evelyn Hope'
(d) 'The Lost Leader'

15. 'Who knows but the world may end tonight'. This line occurs in
(a) 'Porphyria's Lover'
(b) 'Rabbi Ben Ezra'
(c) 'The Last Ride Together'
(d) 'My Last Dutchess'

16. 'Poetry is a criticism of life.' Poet who preached this is
(a) Robert Browning
(b) Matthew Arnold
(c) Lord Tennyson
(d) A.H. Clough

17. "Rabbi Ben Ezra is the embodiment of all that is deepest in Browning's philosophy of religion and morality" who said this?
(a) Cazamion (b) Leigh Hunt
(c) Hugh Walker (d) Rickett

18. Browning is considered as the father of
(a) love poems
(b) dramatic monologue
(c) closet dramas
(d) poetic plays

19. The Oxford Movement during the Victorian period started in the early
(a) 1830s (b) 1840s
(c) 1850s (d) 1860s

20. Rugby Chapel by Arnold is written on the death of his
(a) friend (b) daughter
(c) father (d) wife

21. 'The Princess' (1847) is written by Tennyson in a
(a) romantic style
(b) mock-heroic style
(c) epic style
(d) comic style

22. The 'Last Poem' which Tennyson wrote in anticipation of his death is
(a) The Dreamer (b) Lockley Hell
(c) Maud (d) Oenone

23. Elizabeth Gaskell wrote a historical novel named
(a) *Sylvia's Lover* (b) *Cransford*
(c) *Cousin Phyllis* (d) *North and South*

24. Thackerey was born in
(a) London (b) England
(c) Italy (d) India

25. Which novel of Thackeray brought him universal acclaim as a novelist?
(a) *Esmond* (b) *Vanity fair*
(c) *The Newcomers* (d) *Pendennis*

26. In which of Thackeray's novels the protagonist is an Indian Army officer?
    (a) *The Newcomers*
    (b) *Diamond*
    (c) *Barry Lyndon*
    (d) *Rebecca and Rewena*
27. Which work of Thackeray is a comic-romantic children's Story?
    (a) *Barry Lyndon*
    (b) *Rebecca and Rewene*
    (c) *The Rose and the Ring*
    (d) *Ivanhoe*
28. In which novel of Dickens does Sir Leicester Deadlock appear?
    (a) *Bleak House* (b) *American Notes*
    (c) *Hard Times* (d) None of the above
29. What is the sub-title of Dickens's Oliver Twist?
    (a) The Posthumous Papers
    (b) The Parish Boy's Progress
    (c) Our Mutual Friend
    (d) Little Dorrit
30. Victorians considered Dickens as their family novelist because he avoided
    (a) romance (b) sex
    (c) pathox (d) violence
31. Dickens' *A Tale of Two Cities* shows considerable influence of Carlyle's
    (a) Sarter Resartus
    (b) Felix Holt
    (c) Life of John Sterling
    (d) The French Revolution
32. *Wuthering Heights* is a novel written by
    (a) Emily Bronte (b) Charlotte Bronte
    (c) Anne Bronte (d) George Eliot
33. The Biography of Charlotte Bronte was written by
    (a) Mrs. Browning (b) Mrs. Gaskell
    (c) Mrs. Shelley (d) Mrs. Cowley
34. Who became the first professor of fine arts at Oxford in 1870?
    (a) Trollope (b) Thomas Carlyle
    (c) Disraili (d) John Ruskin
35. Name the Journal in which *The Blessed* was published.
    (a) The Germ (b) The Critic
    (c) The Egoist (d) The Review
36. Walter Pater belonged to
    (a) Pre-Raphaelitic School
    (b) Metaphysical School
    (c) Romantic School
    (d) Classical School
37. *Rubaiyat of Omar Khayyam* was translated by
    (a) John Ruskin (b) Walter Scott
    (c) John Keats (d) Fitzgerald
38. Omar Khayyam was a poet from
    (a) Turkey (b) Greece
    (c) Persia (d) India
39. 'Take the cash and let the credit go', is a doctrine of
    (a) Plato (b) Aristotle
    (c) Sophocles (d) Omar Khayyam
40. A Scottish essayist, philosophic and historian of the Victorian Age is commonly known as the dictator of the period. Who is he?
    (a) Thomas Carlyle
    (b) John Ruskin
    (c) Anthony Trollope
    (d) Rudyard Kipling
41. To which journal did Macaulay contribute regularly?
    (a) Edinburgh Review
    (b) Quarterly Review
    (c) Reflector
    (d) Gentleman's Magazine

42. Which of the following is not a novel by Trollope?
(a) *Can You Forgive Her?*
(b) *The Eustance Diamonds*
(c) *Phineas Finns*
(d) *The Professor*

43. The Professor of poetry at Oxford who is considered as the father of the Oxford Movement in England is
(a) G.K. Chesterton
(b) Henry Newman
(c) John Keble
(d) Charles Kingsley

44. *Apologia Pro Vita Sira* is the spiritual autobiography of
(a) Henry Newman (b) Lewis Caroll
(c) John Keble (d) Lockhart

45. The Leader of the Decadent Movement, he joined hands with Henry Highland in bringing out a periodical. The Yellow Book. Identify him from among the following:
(a) Aurey Beardsley (b) Arthus Symons
(c) Oscar Wilde (d) Earnest Dowson

46. *The Princess* (1847) is written in a
(a) Romantic Style (b) Epic Style
(c) Mock-heroic Style(d) Comic Style

47. Who propogated the idea of 'high seriousness' and 'grand style' in poetry?
(a) Byron (b) Spenser
(c) Arnold (d) Scott

48. Alfred Tennyson was appointed Poet Laureate in
(a) 1855 (b) 1850
(c) 1854 (d) 1857

49. Which novelist of the Victorian age, besides Dickens, is known for his brilliant irony and social spirit?
(a) Thackeray (b) Kingsley
(c) G.K. Chesterton (d) Huxley

50. Identify the last Victorian poet.
(a) Dante Gabriel Rossetti
(b) Swinburne
(c) Mrs. Browning
(d) Alfred Tennyson

51. In poems such as Fra Lippo Lippi and Andrea Del Sarto, Browning reflects his love for
(a) Greece (b) Spain
(c) Italy (d) None of the above

52. Who expressed aptly the sense of Victorian predicament in the following lines—"Between two worlds, one dead, The other powerless to be born"?
(a) Tennyson (b) Browning
(c) Arnold (d) Hopkins

53. From which poem of Tennyson following lines been taken. "There lives more faith in honest doubt Believe one, than in half the creed."
(a) In Memoriam
(b) Maud
(c) The Idylls of the King
(d) Dora

54. Identify the poet about whom it can be said that he is the greatest poet among English critics and the greatest critic among English poets.
(a) Coleridge (b) Dryden
(c) Arnold (d) Dr. Johnson

55. Which novelist of the Victorian age besides Dickens, is known for his brilliant irony and social spirit?
(a) Thackeray (b) Kingsley
(c) Chesterton (d) Huxley

56. Thomas Hardy was born on
(a) July 2, 1840
(b) July 2, 1842
(c) July 7, 1840
(d) July 7, 1842

57. One of Hardy's forefather was
   (a) the Mayor of Jersey
   (b) the governor of Jersey
   (c) Mayor of Trafalgar
   (d) the Governor of Trafalgar
58. Hardy took a keen interest in
   (a) The Plays of Shakespeare
   (b) Homer
   (c) Tennyson
   (d) None of the above
59. Hardy became a novelist and poet to
   (a) quench his literary thrust
   (b) to meet the rising expenses of his first wife
   (c) to become master minded in this field
   (d) None of the above
60. Hardy's first novel in print way was
   (a) *Under the greenwood tree*
   (b) *A pan of blue eyes*
   (c) *Desperate Remedies*
   (d) *The Return of the Native*
61. Heathcliff appears in the novel of
   (a) Charlotte Bronte (b) Anne
   (c) Emily Bronte (d) Patrick Bronte
62. Whose death brought end of an era?
   (a) Tennyson (b) Browning
   (c) Arnold (d) Gray
63. The first independent volume of Tennyson's poems, which appeared in 1830 is
   (a) Poems, chiefly Lyrical
   (b) The Miller's Daughter
   (c) The Lover's Tale
   (d) The Princess
64. Who pronounced Tennyson to be the first poet since Lucretius who understood the draft of Science?
   (a) Mill (c) Huxley
   (b) Arnold (d) Fitgerald
65. Which Victorian novelist acted as assistant editor of the Westminister's Review?
   (a) Charles Dickens (c) George Eliot
   (b) Charlotte Bronte (d) Emily Bronte
66. Which work of George Eliot was a Wordsworth story told in prose as well as a novel?
   (a) Adam Bede
   (b) Silas Marner
   (c) The Mill on the Floss
   (d) Middlemarch
67. Who advocated 'disinterestedness' in literary criticism?
   (a) T.S. Eliot
   (b) Aristotle
   (c) Mathew Arnold
   (d) None of the above
68. Which one of the following poems is the most difficult and obscure, written by Robert Browning?
   (a) 'Sordello'
   (b) 'The Pied Piper'
   (c) 'The Lost Leader'
   (d) 'The Lost Mistress'
69. The following line comes in which poem of A Tennyson. 'To strive to seek, to find, and not to yield'.
   (a) 'Maud' (b) 'Ulysses'
   (c) 'In Memorium' (d) 'Locksley Hall'
70. Which poem of Arnold contains these lines: "Hath neither Joy, nor love, nor light, Nor certitude, Nor peace, Nor peace, Nor help for pain?"
   (a) 'Dover Beach'
   (b) 'The Scholar Gypsy'
   (c) 'Rugby Chapel'
   (d) None of the above
71. The longest poem in the English language, written by Robert Browning is
   (a) 'The Last Ride Together'
   (b) 'The Ring and The Book'

(c) 'The Lost Leader'
(d) 'Evelyn Hoe'

72. Who wrote 'The Cry of the Children?'
(a) Robert Browning
(b) Elizabeth B. Browning
(c) Alfred Tennyson
(d) P.B. Shelly

73. Who said about Shakespeare: "Others abide our question. Thou art free. We ask and ask–Their smilest and art still, out topping knowledge?"
(a) Robert Browning
(b) Alfred Tennyson
(c) Mathew Arnold
(d) Clough

74. Mathew Arnold's 'Culture and Anarchy' is a revolt against
(a) politics (b) Manchesterdom
(c) poverty (d) ruler

75. George Eliot wrote under the Pseudoym of a man. Who was the man?
(a) G.H. Lewes (b) G.B. Shaw
(c) G. Tillotson (d) W. Alless

76. Identify the novelist who is known as 'a novelist of civilization'.
(a) Thomas Hardy (b) George Eliot
(c) Henry James (d) Virginia Woolf

77. Life Charlotte Bronte, one of best biographies is written by
(a) Mrs. Gaskell (b) Charles Reade
(c) Anthony Trollope (d) George Eliot

78. Ruskin's English may be called
(a) Johnsonian (b) Shakespearean
(c) Chaucerean (d) Spenserian

79. In the last decade of the 19th century the comedy of manners was revived in the works of
(a) Wilde (b) Jones
(c) Pinero (d) All of the above

80. Who produced a collection of plays, *Plays Pleasant and Unpleasant*, in 1898?
(a) Gladstone (b) Galsworthy
(c) G.B. Shaw (d) Henrik Ibsen

81. Who wrote the *Cloister and The Hearth* (1861) one of the best historical novels of Victorian age?
(a) Charles Reade
(b) Thackeray
(c) George Eliot
(d) Anthony Trollope

82. Who wrote Essays on Milton?
(a) Carlyle (b) Macaulay
(c) Charles Reade (d) Mrs. Gaskell

83. Who criticized the Pre-Raphaelite poetry severely in his essay. The Fleshly School of Poetry—D.G. Rossetti?
(a) A.H. Clough
(b) Robert Buhanan
(c) Hugh Walker
(d) Mathew Arnold

84. The Oxford Movement in the Victorian period started in the year
(a) 1830s (b) 1840s
(c) 1850s (d) 1860s

85. The professor of poetry at oxford who is considered as the father of the Oxford Movement in England is
(a) G.K. Chesterton
(b) Henry Newsman
(c) John Keble
(d) Charles Kingsley

86. Verse dramas like Queen Mary and Becket were written by
(a) Robert Browning
(b) Elizabeth B. Browning
(c) Alfred Tennyson
(d) W.C. Macready

87. 'Ramola' is a turning point in the career of
    (a) Charlotte Bronte (b) Mrs. Gaskell
    (c) George Eliot (d) Emily Bronte

88. The adjective 'Spasmodic' was given to the poets by
    (a) D.G. Rossetti
    (b) W.E. Aytoun
    (c) Tennyson
    (d) T. Young Simpson

89. Both Arnold and Aristotle appeared to be
    (a) enamoured of poetry
    (b) fed up of poetry
    (c) impressed by poetry
    (d) oblinum of lyrical poetry

ANSWERS

1. (c)	2. (b)	3. (b)	4. (a)	5. (a)	6. (c)
7. (c)	8. (b)	9. (b)	10. (a)	11. (c)	12. (d)
13. (b)	14. (d)	15. (c)	16. (b)	17. (c)	18. (c)
19. (a)	20. (c)	21. (d)	22. (b)	23. (a)	24. (d)
25. (b)	26. (a)	27. (c)	28. (a)	29. (b)	30. (b)
31. (d)	32. (a)	33. (b)	34. (d)	35. (a)	36. (a)
37. (d)	38. (c)	39. (d)	40. (c)	41. (b)	42. (d)
43. (c)	44. (b)	45. (a)	46. (c)	47. (c)	48. (b)
49. (a)	50. (c)	51. (c)	52. (c)	53. (a)	54. (c)
55. (a)	56. (a)	57. (b)	58. (a)	59. (-)	60. (c)
61. (c)	62. (b)	63. (a)	64. (b)	65. (b)	66. (c)
67. (c)	68. (a)	69. (b)	70. (a)	71. (b)	72. (b)
73. (c)	74. (b)	75. (a)	76. (b)	77. (a)	78. (a)
79. (d)	80. (c)	81. (a)	82. (b)	83. (b)	84. (a)
85. (c)	86. (c)	87. (c)	88. (b)	89. (d)	

16

Modern Period

Chronology of Important Dates

1900	-	Beginning of the Modern Age
1903	-	Death of W.E. Heuley
1903-08	-	Hardy's Dynasts
1907	-	Birth of W.H. Auden
1909	-	Hardy's Time's Laughing Stocks
1910	-	W.B. Yeats' 'The Green Helmet and Other Poems'
1919	-	Yeats' 'The Wilde Swans at Coole'
1921	-	Lawrence's 'Women in Love'
1922	-	Eliot's 'The Waste Land'
		Joyce's 'Ulysses'
1925	-	Eliot's 'The Hollow Man'
1928	-	Lawrence's 'Lady Chatterley's Lover'
1929	-	Bridge's 'Testament of Beauty'
1930	-	Death of Bridges
		Shaw's 'The Apple Cart'
1932	-	A Huxley's 'Brave New World'
1933	-	Death of Galsworthy
1936	-	Kipling's Death
1940	-	Auden's 'Selected Poems'
		Yeats' 'Last Poems and Plays'
1941	-	Death of James Joyce
		Death of Virginia Woolf
1942	-	De La Mare's 'Collected Poems'
1944	-	T.S. Eliot's 'Four Quarters'
		De La Mare's 'Collected Rhymes and Verses'
1945	-	Orwell's 'Animal Farm'
1946	-	Spender's 'Poems of Dedication'
1948	-	Robert Greves' 'Collected Poems'
1949	-	Auden's 'The Shield of Achilles'
		Fry's 'The Lady is Not for Burning'

1950	-	Death of G.B. Shaw
		Death of Bridge
1951	-	Spencer's 'World Within a World'
1952	-	Dylan Thomas' 'Collected Poems'
1953	-	Death of Dylan Thomas
1954	-	Day Lewis' 'Christian Eve'
1958	-	C.P. Snow's 'The Affair'
1960	-	Auden's 'Homage to Clio'
		Day Lewis' 'The Buried Day'
1961	-	Elizabeth Jennings 'My Sad Captains'
1962	-	Elizabeth Jennings 'Song For a Birth or a Death'
1964	-	Kathleen Raine's 'The Hollow Hill'
1968	-	George Barker's 'The Golden Chains'
1969	-	Vernon Scannell's 'Epithets of War'
1971	-	John Silkin's 'Crow Wakes'
1973	-	Richard Hughis' 'The Wooden Shepherdess George Mann's Shrapnel'

MODERN PERIOD

Modern period refers to the literature written since the beginning of World War I in 1914. The poets include Yeats, Frost, Eliot, Wallace, Stevens, Auden, Robert Graves, Robert Lowell and Dylan Thomas; the novelist; Conrad, Joyce, Lawrence, Virginia Woolf, E.M. Forster, Ernest Hemingway, F. Scott Fitzgerald and William Faulkner; the dramatists, G.B. Shaw, Sean O' Casey, Eugene O'Neill, Tennessee Williams, and Samuel Beckett; and the critics, T.S. Eliot, I.A. Richards, F.R. Leavis, Lionel Trillin, and the American New Critics.

This period transformed the whole fabric of private and social life and outlook of the English nation. Thinkers like Shaw, Samuel Butler and Wells assumed the role of social heretics and iconoclasts, and men and women generally showed an extraordinary enthusiasm for reform. The new age was an age of ideas and opinions and free enterprise in propounding them, were the essence of the new spirit of intellectual liberalism that dominated the thinkers of the time. The complete decline of feudalism and full ascendancy of democracy changed the entire scenario of Europe. The social change and the rise of democracy and liberalism gave new content to the creative writers. As a result of change in the content of literature, new forms and techniques were invented. Realism, impressionism, symbolism, expressionism, dadaism and surrealism were the main styles in both art and literature. These new techniques and styles are the salient feature of modernism. France was the leader of modernism and England soon followed it pound and Eliot in poetry and James Joyce and Virginia Woolf in novel were the first in the modernist movement. In drama Shaw and Galsworthy followed the social realism of the Norwegian dramatis, Henrick Ibsen. For the sake of convenience we can divide the entire century into two halves: The period of modernism and the period of post-modernism.

Poetry was continued to be written in the traditional style till the publication of Eliot's *The Love Song of Alfred J. Prufrock* and Other poems. The Edwardians and the Georgians failed to express the spirit of the age. The Imagists and the War poets, especially Wilfred Owen and Isaac Rosenberg, wrote a new kind of poetry which we may call modern.

The novel was given its form by Henry James. Joseph Conrad soon followed him. Virginia Woolf rejected Wells, Galsworthy and Bennet because they did not notice the inner reality. Wolf and Joyee rejected the traditional way of writing the novel and developed a technique called the stream of consciousness technique or interior monologic Shaw and Galsworthy rentalised the British drama that had remained in coma throughout the 19th century.

The modern age is also known as The Age of Interrogation and Anxiety. The following traits distinguish the modern era:

(i) Anxiety and Interrogation
(ii) Art for Life's save
(iii) Growing interest in the Poor and the Working classes
(iv) Impact of Socioeconomic conditions on Literature
(v) Psychology and Literature
(vi) Impact of Socioeconomic conditions in Literature
(vii) The Influence of Radio and Cinema
(viii) Printing was multiplied and cheapened
(ix) The invention of locomotive and telegraph, rapid and cheap intercommunication
(x) Boom of pornographic literature.

Modern literature has been produced in the new milieu. It is the literature of challenge and of the reconstruction of new values. Scott James writes: "The writings, expressive of many temperaments, reveal the intellectual atmosphere in which G.B. Shaw, H.G. Wells, Arnold Benett, John Galsworthy, G.K. Chesterton, Harley Graville Barker and Graham Greene were to find then essential and necessary milien. In one sense men were being made in their time, in another they were making it. Against this background, too, we must set quieter and more reflective spirits, like Henry, Norman Douglas and a number of poets."

It was an exciting age for writers—"an age which marked a definite break with the past, a challenge to authority, an assertion of the right to be anarchistic in thought and in form-romantic, realistic, passionate—a self-conscious age when writers were intensely critical of the composition of society, and were beginning to be critical of the individual soul."

Modern Poetry

Modern poetry depicted that the poet was no longer a singer of beautiful dreams expressing himself in Sweet words. The poet's job in the modern age is to express the chaos and the changing scenario of life and society around him. T.S. Eliot's 'Wasteland' was both 'a demonstration and a manifests of what the new poetry wanted to do and could do'. The main characteristics of modern poetry are as follows:

The reaction against Victorianism had begun.

The best poets of the period were seeking for models.

The poetry of the first two decades of the 20th century is the poetry of transition from Victorianism to modernism.

Modern poetry is the poetry of experience, dominated by the image of a city.

Imagism—The imagists, under the influence of T.E. Hulone and G.M. Hopkins, brought about a revolution in poetic technique.

Imagists insisted on the use of hard, dry and precise visual images.

The new poetic revolution pioneered by T.S. Eliot and Ezra pound was an 'Anglo-American' achievement:

Transitional Poets	–	Alfred Austin
		W.E. Henley
		John Davidson
		William Watson
		Francis Thompson
		Robert Bridges
		A.E. Housman
The War Poets	–	Rupert Brooke
		Wilfred Owen
		Sregfried Sassoon
		Charles Sorley
The Georgian Poets	–	Walter de La Mare
		W.H. Davies
		John Masefield
		James Elory Flecker
		Edward Thomas
		Ralph Hodgson
		W.W. Gobson
		John Drinkwater
		Harold Monro
		Alfred Noyes
		G.K. Chesterton
		Lascelles Abercrombia
The Oxford Poets	–	W.H. Auden
		Stephen Spender
		Cecil Day Lewis
		Louis Mac Neice

Michael Roberts for a while organized these poets, then, the leadership passed to W.H. Auden.

They remain associated in the History of English poetry as 'the four Musketeers of the Oxford Movement:

Oxford movement is also known as 'the modern movement' and 'the new country movement.

The Neo Romanticism

Dylan Thomas (1814-53) is the pioneer of neo-romantic poetry. His works include 'Eighteen Poems' (1934), 'Twenty Five Poems' (1936), 'Deaths and Entrances' (1946), 'Collected Poems' (1952) and 'Milk Wood' (1953).

George Barker is another such important poet. His works include 'Thirty Preliminary Poems' (1933), 'Eros in Dogma' (1944), 'News of the World' (1950), 'The True Confession of George Barker' (1950) and 'Collected Poems' (1957). His poetry mainly deals with human suffering and guilt.

The Apocalyptic Movement

The poets of the Apocalyptic Movement centre on the individual and not the community.

J.F. Hendry and Henry Treece, who edited 'The New Apocalypse' (1940) and 'The White Horseman' (1941) were the pioneers of this poetic movement.

Nicholas Moore, G.S. Fraser, Tom Scott and Vernon Watkins were other prominent members of this group.

The Apocalyptic poetry is obscure.

This movement was opposed to the political affinities of Auden and his group.

It expressed hatred of the Machine Age and proclaimed its faith in the individual as the hope for humanity.

New Poets Nine in Number

D.J. Euright's 'Authology Poets of the Fifties' (1950) and Robert Conquest's 'Anthology' (1956) brought nine new poets to notice.

They were John Wain, Kingsley Amis, John Holloway, Donald Davie, D.J. Enright, Philip Larkin, Thomas Gunn, Robert Conquest and Elizabeth Jennings.

The majority of these young poets belonged to working class or lower middle class and all of them were educated in Oxford or Cambridge University.

Other Poets of the 20th Century

Roy Campbell (1901-57)
William Empson
Ruth Pitter
Kathleen Raine
Edwin Muir
Alum Lewis
Roy Broadbent
Laurence Durrell

Alan Ross
Sir John Betjeman
Virnon Scannell
John Silicon
F.T. Prince
J.P. Fletcher
J.H. Shibbs
Edward Milne

Kathleen Nott

Anne Riddler

Randolph Stoove

George Mann Macbeth

Modern Prose

Modern prose writers try hard to achieve simplicity and clarity of expression.

The written language of to-day is much nearer the spoken language than it ever before was before.

Journalism, novel writing, autobiography, biography, travel literature, and the essay continue to live and grow.

Modern essayist has imparted new dimensions to the development of prose style.

Among the eminent essayists we have

G.K. Chesterton (1874-1936)

Hilaire Belloc (1870-1953)

E.V. Lucas (1868-1983)

A.G. Gardiner (1865- 1946)

Robert Lynd (1879-1949)

Max Beerbohm (1872-1956)

W.H. Hudron (1841-1972)

C.M. Doughly (1843-1926)

Lord Bertnant Russell (1872-1970)

Among the Literary Critics we have

A.C. Bradley

Sir Walter Raleign

W.P. Ker

George Saintsbury

Edmund Gosse

Edward Dowden

Sir Arthur Quiller-Couch

John Dover Wilson

Aldous Huxley

Lytton Strachey

T.E. Lawrence

I.A. Richards

F.R. Leaves

E.K. Chambers

G.B. Harrison

Wilson Knight

William Empson

J.B. Priestley

Modern Fiction

Modern Fiction surpassed poetry and drama and became the only form which attracted readers of varied tastes and temperaments.

Variety and complexity of themes appealed modern readers.

Modern Science fiction was introduced by H.G. Wells.

Because of technological and scientific advances, space exploration and the threat of nuclear and germ warfare, there has been a tremendous increase in science fiction.

Realism is the central point. The modern novel presents the doubts, uncertainties, frustrations and anxieties of the modern man. It is therefore pessimistic in tone.

The modern novel contains a large-scale criticism and condemnation of contemporary values and of civilization.

Frank treatment of Love, Sir and marriage in modern novel.

The psychology of Sex and Psychological theories Frend and Havelock Ellis, new biological theories and methods of birth control influenced the writing.

The modern novel has evolved a serious art form, which is compact and integrated. There is no place for moralizing or didactic role in modern novel. Henry James and Courad evolved techniques which revolutinized the form of the novel.

The direct and loose biographical method of narration was abandersed in favour of an indirect and oblique narration.

Novels translated from foreign languages have influenced contemporary fiction. The effect of Kafke, Mann and Gide has continued over many years.

Gunter Grass, Heinrick Froll, Alberto Morasio and the Russians Pasterneck and Solzhenilsy Jean Paul Sartre, Albert Camus and Simone de Beauvoir exercised great influence on contemporary English novel.

The Publication of paperback volumes advent of television, novels in the form of serials and films increased the demand of novel.

Eminent Novelists of the 20th century

Joseph Conrad (1857-1924)

George Moore (1852-1933)

H.G. Wells (1886-1946)

John Galsworthy (1867-1933)

Arnold Bennett (1867-1931)

Rudyard Kipling (1865-1936)

E.M. Forster (1879-1970)

W.S. Maugham (1874-1965)

Aldous Leonard Huxley (1894-1963)

Hugh Walpole (1884-1941)

D.H. Lawrence (1885-1930)

The Stream of Consciousness Novel

'Stream of consciousness' was first used by William James in Principles of Psychology to denote the chaotic flow of impressions and sensations through the human consciousness.

It is also called the subjective novel or the Psychological novel.

The stream of consciousness technique was influenced by the symbolism of the French poets and the novelist, Marcer proust, and by the writings of William James and Henry Burgson.

Dorothy Richardson, James Joyce and Virginia Woolf's contribution to the development of the Stream of consciousness technique is noteworthy.

Dorothy Richardson's first novel *Painted Roofs* (1915) was the first novel written in the Stream of consciousness technique.

Joyce's first work *The Dubliners* (1914) a collection of short stories, is based on the life of the Dubliners *A Portrait of the Artist As a Young Man* (1916) has Dublin as its setting. *Ulysses* (1922) is Joyce's masterpiece.

Virginia Woolf adopted the Stream of consciousness technique in *Jacob's Room* (1922). She deftly uses the device of internal monologue to reveal the consciousness and Psychic conditions of Jacob. *Mrs. Dalloway* (1925), *To the Lighthouse* (1927), *The Waves* (1931) by her are the significant development in the stream of consciousness technique.

Novel after 1950

The writers of the new generation deal with the new psychological problems arising from the bizarre and contradictory nature of an affluent society which is discontented with itself. The novelists use a mixture of realism, cynicism, dark comedy, shrewd comment and satire to express their search for stability and basic values.

Major Novelists

Graham Green
Evelyn Waugh
Henry Green
George Orwell
Sir Charles Percy Snow
William Golding
Lionel Polis Hartley
Anthony Powell
H.E. Bates
John Masters
Lawrence Durrell
Joyce Cary
A.F. Johnstone Wilson
William Cowper
Miss Mondoch
Alah Silbiroe

Modern Drama

The Development of Theatres gave a new direction to the evolution of drama in the 20th century.

The most important of the theatrical developments was the creation of the Irish National Theatre in Dublin, W.B. Yeats and J.M. Synge contributed much to the development of Irish theatrical movement.

Foreign dramatists—Ibsen, Strindberg, Anton Chechor, Tolstoy, Gorkey, Brecht and others–influenced the development of modern drama.

Expressionism was the boldest experiment in drama which was not concerned with society but with man.

The influence of Samuel Beckett was important on drama. It was under his influence that the Absurd Drama came into being.

The arrival of cinema constituted a new threat to the theatre. A revolutionary change came in Playwriting when television appeared. Writers like Alun Owen, Clive Exton and John Mortimen wrote for the small screen rather than for the public stage.

The Realistic Drama—also known as the naturalistic drama or the problem play, presents a real picture of life J.M. Barrie, John Galsworthy, G.B. Shaw, James Birdie its development others contributed to its development.

The Revival of the Poetic Drama

At the Abbey Theatre, Yeats endeavoured to revive poetic drama. But it was T.S. Eliot who firmly established the tradition of poetic drama in the 20th century.

Stephen Philis wrote poetic plays including *Paola and Frances* (1900), *Herod* (1901) *Ulysses* (1902). The *Son of David* (1904) and *New* (1906).

Among other writers of poetic drama

- John Masefield
- Gorden Bottomley
- James Elory Flencher
- Lascellus Flecuer
- John Drink Water

Drama, according to Eliot, expresses the depth of human soul, Eliot says: 'The human soul, in intense emotion, strives to express itself in verse.' He assists that 'the greatest drama is poetic drama, and dramatic defects can be compensated by poetic excellence'.

Eliot holds that the craving for poetic drama is permanent in human nature.

The Murder in the Cathedral (1935) is his first full length poetic play.

THE WRITERS AND THEIR WORKS

WRITERS	WORKS
Joseph Conrad (1857-1924)	*Almayer's Folly* (1985)
	An Outcast of the Islands (1896)
	The Nigger of the "Narcissus" (1897)
	Lord Jim: A Tale (1900)
	Youth—A Narrative (1902)
	Heart of Darkness (1902)
	Nostrono—A Tale of the Sea Board
	The Secret Agent (1907)
	The Shadow Line (1917)
	Suspense—A Napoleonic Novel (1925)
Herbert George Wells (1866-1946)	*The Time Machine* (1895)
	The Wonderful Visit (1895)
	The Island of Dr. Moreau (1896)
	The Invisible Man (1897)
	The War of the Worlds (1898)
	When The Sleeper Walks (1899)
	The First Men in the Moon (1901)
	The Food of the Gods (1904)
	Kipps (1905)
	Experiment in Autobiography (1935)
	Marriage (1912)
	The Contemporary Novel (1911)
	The History of Mr. Polly (1900)

James Joyce (1882-1941)	*Dubliners* (1900)
	A Portrait of the Artist as a Young Men (1916)
	Ulysses (1922)
	Finnegans Wake (1939)
Virginia Woolf (1882-1941)	*The Voyage Out* (1941)
	Jacob's Room (1922)
	Mrs. Dalloway (1925)
	To the Light House (1927)
	The Waves (1931)
	Flush (1933)
	The Years (1937)
	Orlando a Biography (1928)
	The Common Reader (1925)
	Roger Fry (1940)
	The Death of the Moth (1942)
	Between the Acts (1941, unfurnished)
	Mr. Bennet and Mrs. Brown (1924), an essay
	A Room of One's Own (1929), feminist essay
Samuel Butler (1835-1902)	*Life and Habit* (1877)
	Evolution Old and New (1879)
	Unconscious Memory (1880)
	Luck or Cunning as the Means of Organic Modification? (1887)
	The Trapansese Origin of the Odyssey (1893)
	The Authoress of the Odyssey (1897)
	Alps and Sanctureis of Piedmont and the Canton Ticino (1881)
	Shakespeare's Sonnets Reconsidered (1899)
	Ex Voto (1888)
	Essays on Life, Arts and Science (1904)
	The Note Books of Samuel Butler (1912)
	The Way of All Flesh (1903)
	Butler also translated into prose-Iliad in 1898 and Odyssey in 1900
George Moore (1852-1933)	*A Modern Lover* (1883)
	A Mummer's Wife (1885)
	A Drama in Muslin (1886)
	Spring Days (1888)

	Esther Waters (1894)
	Evelyn Innes (1898)
	Many Inventions (1893)
	The Jungle Book (1894)
	Captains Courageous (1897)
	The Day's Work (1898)
	Kim (1901)
	Just so Stories for Little Children (1902)
	Puck of Pook's Hill (1906)
	Rewards and Fairies (1910)
	Debits and Credits (1926)
	Limits and Renewals (1932)
	The Seven Seas (1896), Poetry
	The Five Nations (1903), Poetry
	Barrack-room Ballads (1892), Poetry
	Departmental Ditties (1886), Poetry
Edward Morgan Forster (1879-1970)	*Where Angels Fear to Trend* (1905)
	The Longest Journey (1907)
	A Room with a View (1908)
	Howards End (1910)
	A Passage to India (1924)
	The Celestial Omnibus (1911) Short Stories
	The Story of the Siren (1920), Short Stories
	The Eternal Moment (1928), Short Stories
	Aspects of the Novel (1927), a Critical Work
	Abinger Harvest (1936), a Critical Work
	Two Cheers for Democracy (1951), a collection of essays
Aldous Leonard Huxley (1894-1963)	*The Burning Wheel* (1916)
	The Defeat of Youth (1918)
	Leda (1920)
	Eyeless in Gaza (1936)
	Crome Yellow (1921)
	Antic Hay (1929)
	Those Barren Leaves (1925)
	Point Counter Point (1928)
	Brave New World (1932)
	After Many a Summer (1939)

	Time Must Have a Stop (1944)
	Sister Teresa (1901)
	The United Field (1903)
	The Lake (1905)
	The Brook Kerith, A Syrian Story (1916)
	Heloise and Abelard (1921)
	Confession of a Young Man (1888)
	Memoirs of My Dead Life (1906)
	Hail and Farewell! Ave (1911)
	Salve (1912)
	Conversations in Ebury Street (1924)
George Robert Gissing (1857-1903)	*Demos, a Story of English Socialism* (1886)
	Thyzra (1887)
	The Neither World (1887)
	New Grub Street (1891)
	The Private Papers of Henry Ryecroft (1303)
	Charles Dickens, a Critical Study (1898)
	By the Jonian Sea (1901)
	The Emancipated (1890)
	The Old Women (1893)
	Eve's Ransom (1895)
Enoch Arnold Bennett (1867-1931)	*The Old Wives' Tale* (1908)
	Clayhanger (1910)
	Hilda Lessways (1911)
	These Twain (1916)
	Riceyman Steps (1923)
	Sacred and Profane Love (1905)
	Buried Alive (1908)
	The Pretty Lady (1918)
	The Love Match (1922)
	The Truth about an Author (1903)
	The Author's Craft (1914)
Rudyard Kipling (1865-1936)	*Tales from the Hills* (1888)
	Soldiers Three (1888)
	The Phantom Rickshaw (1888)
	Wee Willie Winkie (1888)
	Life's Handicap (1891)
	The Perennial Philosophy (1946)
	The Devils of Loudun (1952)

V.S. Naipaul (b. 1932)	*The Mystic Masseur* (1957)
	A House for Mr. Biswas (1961)
	The Mimic Man (1967)
Graham Greene (1904-91)	*Battlefield* (1934)
	England Made Me (1935)
	Brighton Rock (1938)
	The Power and the Glory (1940)
	The Heart of the Matter (1948)
	The End of the Affir (1951)
	The Quiet American (1955)
	A Burnt-Out Case (1961)
	The Commedians (1966)
	Travels with my Aunt (1969)
	May We Borrow Your Husband? (1967), Short-fiction
	Shades of Greene (1976), Short Stories
	A Gun for Sale (1936), Short Stories
	The Ministry of Fear (1943), Short Stories
	The Third Man (1950), Short Stories
	Our Man in Havana (1958)
Charles Percy Snow (Lord Snow) (1905-80)	*Strangers and Brothers* (1940)
	Time of Hope (1949)
	The Masters (1951)
	The New Men (1954)
	The Conscience of the Rich (1958)
	Corridors of Power (1964)
	The Two cultures and the Scientific Revolution (1959), a Lecture
Kingsley Amis (b. 1922)	*Lucky Jim* (1954)
	That Uncertain Feeling (1955)
	I Like it Here (1958)
	Take a Girl Like You (1960)
	Girl, 20 (1971)
	The Anti-Death League (1966)
William Gerald Golding (b. 1911)	*Lord of the Files* (1954)
	The Inheritors (1955)
	Pincher Martin (1956)
	Free Fall (1959)

	The Scorpion God (1971)
	The Spire (1964)
George Orwell (Erichugh Blair) (1903-50)	*Keep the Aspidistra Flying* (1936)
	Burmese Days (1934)
	The Road to Wigan Pier (1937)
	Animal Farm (1945)
	Nineteen Eighty Four (1949)
I.A. Richards (1893-1979)	*Principles of Literary Criticism Practical Criticism*
	Coleridge on Imagination
	The Foundation of Aesthetics
	(With C.K. Ogden & James Wood)
	The Meaning of Meaning (With Ogden)
F.R. Leavis (1895-1978)	*New Bearings in English Poetry* (1932)
	For Continuity (1933)
	The Great Tradition (1948)
	The Common Pursuit (1952)
	Revaluation (1936)
	Education and the University (1944)
	D.H. Lawrence: Novelist (1955)
David Jones (1895-1979)	*The Anathemata* (1952)
	In Parenthesis (1937)
	The Sleeping Lord (1974)
Evelyn Waugh (1903-66)	*Sword of Honour*
Anthony Powell (b. 1905)	*The Music of Time* (1951)
John Wain (b. 1925)	*Hurry on Down* (1953)
John Braine	*Room at the Top* (1957)
	Life at the Top (1957)
	The Jealous God (1965)
Alan Sillitoe (b. 1928)	*Saturday Night and Sunday Morning* (1958)
Angus Wilson	*The Wrong Set* (1949), *Short Stories* (1913-91)
	Such Darling Dodos (1950), Short Stories
	Old Men at the 200 (1961), Short Stories
	No Laughing Matter (1967)
	If By Magic (1973)
	The Middle Ages of Mrs. Eliot (1959)
	Late Call (1964)
Anthony Burgess (b. 1917)	*Malayan Triogy*
	Time for a Tiger (1956)

	The Enemy in the Blanket (1958)
	Beds in the East (1959)
	A Clockwork Orange (1961)
Iris Murdoch (b. 1919)	*Under the Net* (1954)
Muriel Spark (b. 1918)	*Memento Mori* (1959)
	The Prime of Miss Jean Brodie (1962)
Dorris Lessing (b. 1919)	*The Grass is Singing* (1950)
	Children of Violence Martha Quest (1952)
	A Proper Marriage (1954)
	A Ripple from the Storm (1958)
	Land Locked (1965)
	The Four Gated City (1969)
	The Golden Note Book (1962)
Margared Drabble (b. 1939)	*Millstone* (1965)
	The Needle's Eye (1972)
J.G. Farrell (1935-79)	*The Siege of Krishnapur* (1973)
	(Based on Indian Mutini)
William Butler Yeats (1865-1939)	*The Wanderings of Oisin* (1889)
	The Wind Among the Reeds (1899)
	The Shadowy Waters (1900)
	The Green Helmet and Other Poems (1910)
	Responsibilities (1914)
	The Wild Swans at Coole (1919)
	The Tower (1928)
	The Winding of Heart's Desire (1894)
	Poems (1933)
	DRAMAS:
	The Countess Cathleen (1892)
	The Land of Heart's Desire (1894)
	The Shadowy Waters (1900)
	Cathleen in Haulihan (1902)
	On Baile's Strand (1904)
	The Hour-glass (1904)
	Deirdre (1907)
	The Resurrection (1913)
	At the Hawk's Well (1917)
	The Only Jealousy of Emer (1919)
	Calvary (1921)

	The Cat and the Moon (1926)
	Ideas of Good and Evil (1903), Prose
	Calvary (1921)
	The Cutting of an Agate (1912),
	Prose A Vision (1925), Prose
Gerald Manley Hopkins (1844-89)	*Spring God's Grandeur*
	The Caged Skylark
	Felix Rendal
	Pied Beauty
	Inversnaid
	Harry Plougman
	The Wreck of the 'Deutschland'
	The Windhover
	Spelt from Sibyl's Leaves
	That Nature Heraditean Fire
T.S. Eliot (1888-1965)	*Gerontion*
	Prufrock and Other Observations (1917)
	The Waste Land (1922)
	The Hollow Men (1925)
	Ash Wednesday (1930)
	Four Quartets (1944)
	Sweeney Agonistes (1927), a drama
	The Rock (1934), a drama
	Murder in Cathedral (1935), a drama
	The Family Reunion (1939), a drama
	The Cocktail Party (1949), a drama
	The Confidential Clerk (1953), a drama
	The Elder Statesman (1958), a drama
	The Sacred Wood (1920), essays
	The Idea of a Christian Society (1939)
	What is a Classic? (1945)
	For Lancelot Andrewes (1928)
	The Use of Poetry and the Use of Criticism (1933)
	Elizabethan Essays (1934)
	After Strange Gods (1934)
	Points of View (1941)
Wystan Hugh Auden (1907-73)	*The Orators* (1932)
	Look Stranger (1936)

	New Year Letter (1941)
	The Age of Anxiety (1948)
	Collected Shorter Poems (1950)
	The Poet's Tongue (1935)
	Verse (1938)
Stephen Spender (1909-77)	*Poems* (1933)
	Vienna (1934)
	The Still Centre (1939)
	Ruins and Visions (1942)
	Collected Poems (1955)
	The Distructive Element (1935), a critical work
	Poetry Since (1947)
	World Within World (1951), autobiography
Dylan Marlais Thomas (1914-53)	*18 Poems* (1934)
	Twenty-five Poems (1936)
	The Map of Love (1939)
	The Deaths and Entrances (1946)
	Under Milk Wood (1954), a verse play
C. Day Lewis (1909-72)	*Transitional Poem* (1929)
	From Feathers to Iron (1931)
	The Magnetic Mountain (1933)
	A Time to Dance (1935)
	Overtures to Death and Other Poems (1938)
	Word Over All (1943)
	Poems (1948)
	The Georgics of Virgil (1940), a translation
	The Friendly Tree (1936), a novel
	Starting Point (1937), a novel
	Child of Misfortune (1939), a novel
	Hope for Poetry (1934), criticism
	Poetry for You (1945), criticism
	The Poetic Image (1947), criticism
Louis Macneice (1907-63)	*The Earth Compels* (1938)
	Autumn Journal (1939)
	Plant and Phantom (1941)
	Spring Board (1944)
	Holes in the Sky (1948)
Dame Edith Sitwell (1887-1964)	*The Sleeping Beauty* (1924)

	Troy Park (1925)
	Collected English Eccentrices (1933)
	Aspects of Modern Poetry (1934)
	Street Songs (1942)
	The Songs of the Cold (1945)
Ezra Pound (1885-1972)	*The Pisan Cantos* (1948)
	Hugh Selwyn Mobberly (1920)
Robert Bridges (1844-1930)	*The Growth of Love* (1876)
	Promethes the Fire Giver (1883)
	Errors and Psyche (1885)
	Poems in Classical Prosody (1903)
	DRAMAS:
	The Feast of Bacchus (1889)
	Palicio (1890)
	The Christian Captives (1890)
	The Return of Ulysses (1890)
	Achilles in Scyros (1890)
	The Humours of the Court (1893)
	Nero Port I and II (1885 & 1894)
John Masefield (1878-1967)	*Ballads and Poems* (1910)
	The Everlasting Mercy (1911)
	The Widow in the Bye Street (1912)
	The Daffodil Fields (1913)
	Lollingdon Downs (1917)
	Dauber (1913)
	Reynard the Fox (1919)
	Right Royal (1920)
	The Land Workers (1943)
	Midsummer Night (1928)
	End and Beginning (1934)
	Wondering (1943)
John Millington Synge (1871-1909)	*The Shadow of the Glen* (1903)
	Riders to the Sea (1904)
	The Well of the Saints (1905)
	The Tinker's Wedding (1907)
	The Playboy of the Western World (1907)
Henry Arthur Jones (1851-1929)	*The Silver King* (1882)
	Saints and Sinners (1884)

	The Temper (1893)
	The Liars (1897)
	Judah (1890)
	Mrs. Dane's Defence (1900)
John Galsworthy (1867-1933)	*The Country House* (1907), a novel
	Fraternity (1909), a novel
	The Patrician (1911), a novel
	The Dark Flower (1913), a novel
	The Free Lands (1915), a novel
	Beyond (1917), a novel
	Saint's Progress (1919), a novel
	Maid in Waiting (1931), a novel
	Flower Wilderness (1932), a novel
	The Man of Property (1906), a novel
	The Forsyte Saga (1922), a novel
	A Silver Box (1906) a drama
	Strife (1909), a drama
	Justice (1910), a drama
	The Skin Game (1920), a drama
	Loyalties (1922), a drama
	Escape (1926), a drama
	The Inn of Tranquility (1912)
Oscar Wilde (1856-1909)	*The Sphinx* (1894), Poetry
	The Ballad of Reeding Gaol (1998), Poetry
	Lord Arthur Savile's Crime (1887), Prose
	The Canterville Ghost (1887), Prose
	The Happy Prince and the other Tales (1888), Prose
	The Picture of Dorian Gray (1890), a novel
	De Profundis (1897)
	Vera, or the Nihilists (1880), a drama
	The Duchess of Padua (1883), a drama
	Salome (1892), a drama
	Lady Windermere's Fan (1892), a drama
	A Woman of No Importance (1893), a drama
	An Ideal Husband (1895), a drama
	The Importance of being Earnest (1895), a drama
Sean O' Casey (1884-1964)	*The Shadow of a Gunman* (1923)

	Juno and the Polycock (1924)
	The Plough and the Stars (1926)
	The Silver Tassie (1929)
	Within the Gates (1933)
	The Star Turns Red (1940)
	Red Roses for me (1946)
	Oak Leaves and Lavender (1946)
	Cockadoodle Dandy (1949)
William Somerset Maugham (1874-1965)	*A Man of Honour* (1903)
	Lady Frederick (1907)
	Mrs. Dot (1908)
	Jack Straw (1908)
	Home and Beauty (1919)
	The Circle (1921)
	The Constant Wife (1927)
	For Services Rendered (1932)
	Caesar's Wife (1919)
J.B. Priestley (1894-1984)	*Dangerous Corner* (1932)
	Time and the Conways (1937)
	I Have Been Here Before (1937)
	An Inspector Calls (1946)
	When We are Married (1938)
	A Severed Head (1964)
Harold Pinter (b. 1930)	*The Birthday Party* (1958)
	The Dumb Waiter (1960)
	The Care Taker (1960)
	A Night Out (1961)
	The Home Coming (1969)
	Old Times (1971)
	Silence (1969)
Arnold Wesker (b. 1932)	*Chickens Soup with Barley* (1960)
	Roots (1960)
	I Am Talking About Jerusalem (1960)

MULTIPLE CHOICE QUESTIONS

1. The voluminous book *Outline of History* has been written by
   (a) Rudyard Kipling
   (b) Samuel Butler
   (c) H.G. Wells
   (d) James M. Barrie

2. The term 'Imagism' is associated with which of the following?
   (a) T.S. Eliot (b) F.R. Leavis
   (c) Ezra Pound (d) D.H. Lawrence
3. Eric Blair is the original name of which of the following writers?
   (a) Henry James (b) James Joyce
   (c) George Orwell (d) D.H. Lawrence
4. Which of the following authors was born in India?
   (a) James Joyce (b) Henry James
   (c) T.S. Eliot (d) George Orwell
5. In Kipling's *The Plain Tales From The Hills*, the 'Hills' stands for which of the fillowing cities?
   (a) Mussoorie (b) Nainital
   (c) Ooty (d) Shimla
6. William Somerset Maugham was born in which of the following countries?
   (a) India (b) England
   (c) France (d) Ireland
7. Which of the following is a contemporary of James Joyce?
   (a) Dawel Defoe (b) Thomas Hardy
   (c) Henry Fielding (d) Virginia Woolf
8. Which one is a true comedy of manners and one of the best plays of Somerset Maugham?
   (a) *Mrs. Dot*
   (b) *Jack Straw*
   (c) *The Circle*
   (d) *The Constant Wife*
9. Which of the following novels of Joyce was banned for obscenity?
   (a) *Finnegans Wake*
   (b) *Dubliners*
   (c) *Ulysses*
   (d) *A Portrait of the Artist as a young man*
10. Virginia Woolf was the daughter of an eminent critic who was he?
    (a) Matthew Arnold
    (b) John Ruskin
    (c) Sir Leslie Stephen
    (d) None of the above
11. In which of the following novels of Virginia Woolf does a character change his sex?
    (a) *Mrs. Dolloway*
    (b) *To the Light House*
    (c) *Orlando*
    (d) None of the above
12. Which of the following essay of Virginia Woolf is on feminism?
    (a) *A Room of One's Own*
    (b) *Roger Fry*
    (c) *The Death of the Moth*
    (d) *The Moment*
13. E.M. Forster's 'A Passage India' is about
    (a) the Indian great mythologies
    (b) Hinduism
    (c) Gandhian thought
    (d) the relationship between the English and the native Indians
14. Which critic introduced the terms, a 'flat character' and a 'round character'?
    (a) T.S. Eliot (b) Arnold Keltle
    (c) Mathew Arnold (d) E.M. Forster
15. A flat character is
    (a) a single idea or quality
    (b) a type or two-dimensional
    (c) one without much individualizing details
    (d) All of the above
16. A round character is
    (a) a complex one
    (b) represented with subtle particularly
    (c) uncomparable to a person in real life
    (d) All of the above

17. The novels of the inter-war years (1918-39) are characteristic of
(a) expressionism
(b) allusive style and formlessness of life
(c) discontinuity of time
(d) All of the above

18. *Darkness at Noon* (1941) was written by
(a) George Orwell (b) William Golding
(c) Authony Gurgen (d) Arthur Koestler

19. The poem 'If' was written by
(a) Rudyard Kipling
(b) T.S. Eliot
(c) G.M. Hopkins
(d) None of the above

20. R.L. Stevenson is popular for, what is known as
(a) adventure fiction
(b) epistolary novel
(c) gothic fiction
(d) None of the above

21. The characters of 'Henry James' novels are
(a) Illiterates
(b) Intellectuals
(c) Middle class workers
(d) None of the above

22. Who called Henry James "the Victorian of fine consciousness"?
(a) John Gross (b) R.L. Stevenson
(c) Thomas Hardy (d) Joseph Conrad

23. Rudyard kipling was awarded the Nobel Prize in the Year.
(a) 1905 (b) 1907
(c) 1909 (d) None of the above

24. The novelist who embraced Drawn's theory completely is
(a) H.G. Wells (b) Samuel Butley
(c) Joseph Courad (d) None of the above

25. The term 'neo-romanticism' can be associated with
(a) W.H. Auden (b) Ezra Pound
(c) T.S. Eliot (d) Dylan Thomas

26. Who used the novel as a means of social propaganda?
(a) Samuel Butler (b) H.G. Wells
(c) John Galsworthy (d) All of the above

27. The phrase 'Religion by the Blood' is associated with
(a) D.H. Lawrence
(b) Virginia Woolf
(c) E.M. Forster
(d) None of the above

28. Which of the following is a characteristic of James Joyce's style?
(a) Broken narrative
(b) New private vocabulary
(c) Sardonic humour
(d) All of the above

29. James Joyce perfected the following:
(a) Science fiction
(b) Magical realism
(c) Stream of consciousness
(d) None of the above

30. The phrase 'Stream of Consciousness' was used by—in his 'Principles of Psychology' (1890).
(a) Sigmund Frend (b) William James
(c) C.G. Jung (d) James Joyce

31. "A cynic is a man who knows the price of everything and the value of nothing". Who wrote this?
(a) Oscar Wilde
(b) H.G. Wells
(c) D.H. Lawrence
(d) None of the above

32. Who described himself, "my face looks like a wedding cake left out in the rain"?

(a) Dylan Thomas
(b) T.S. Eliot
(c) W.H. Auden
(d) None of the above

33. "Asking a working writer what he thinks about critics is like asking a lamp-post what it thinks about dogs." Who wrote this?
(a) Ezra Pound
(b) George Orwell
(c) John Osborne
(d) None of the above

34. The term 'New Critics' was used for the first time by
(a) T.S. Eliot
(b) William Empson
(c) J.E. Spingarm
(d) None of the above

35. Which is true of 'epiphany'?
(a) Means Manifestation.
(b) Sudden revelation while observing commonplace object.
(c) Was adopted by James Joyce to mean secular experience.
(d) All of the above.

36. An epistolary novel is one in which
(a) there is no plot
(b) there is discursive narrative
(c) the narrative is conveyed entirely by
(d) None of the above

37. Kunstlerroman—
(a) is an Artist novel.
(b) represents the development of the artist/novelist into maturity.
(c) is about the artist's achievement of the mastery .
(d) All of the above.

38. Who is the writer of *Experiment in Autobiography*?
(a) H.G. Wells
(b) James Boswell
(c) Salman Rusdie
(d) None of the above

39. What is common between Boris Pasternak and Jean Paul Satire?
(a) They were Russian Sartre
(b) They declined the Nobel Prize
(c) Their writings were proscribed
(d) They died on the same date

40. An anti-novel is one in which there is _____
(a) no plot
(b) no characterization
(c) no relations of time and space
(d) All of the above

41. T.S. Eliot was awarded Nobel Prize for Literature in the year
(a) 1947 (b) 1948
(c) 1947 (d) 1950

42. Which of T.S. Eliot's poems is based in a musical pattern?
(a) The Waste Land (b) Ash Wednesday
(c) The Rock (d) Four Quarters

43. Who said that "The Waste Land is a cross-word puzzle of synthetic literary chronology" and "spurious verbal Algebra"?
(a) Chinweizu
(b) Wyndham Lewis
(c) Ezra Pound
(d) None of the above

44. Who was it that viewed The Waste Land the Longest poem in the English language because of its profundity, perplexity and density of poetic allusions, myths and meaning?
(a) Ezra pound
(b) Wyndham Lewis
(c) William Empson
(d) None of the above

45. *The Waste Land* was dedicated to
(a) Camae (b) James Frazer
(c) Ezra Pound (d) Jessie Weston

46. Who said that "the complexity of the modern poetry is the result of the complexity of the modern life?"
(a) Stephen Spender
(b) W.B. Yeats
(c) T.S. Eliot
(d) None of the above

47. G.B. Shaw was awarded the Noble Prize for Literature in the year
(a) 1920 (b) 1922
(c) 1925 (d) 1930

48. The writer of the *Essay*, *Hamlet* and *His Problem* is ______
(a) Matthew Arnold (b) Ben Jonson
(c) T.S. Eliot (d) F.R. Leavis

49. *World Within World* is an autobiography of
(a) Stephen Spender (b) W.H. Auden
(c) C. Day Lewis (d) T.S. Eliot

50. Who said, "For art's sake alone I would not face the toil of writing a single sentence"?
(a) T.S. Eliot (b) G.B. Shaw
(c) S. Spender (d) None of the above

51. What is The Fifth Column?
(a) The only play written by Hemingway
(b) Radio and TV
(c) Chuchil's autobiography
(d) None of the above

52. Aldius Huxley's title 'Brave New World' is borrowed from Shakespeare's
(a) The Tempest
(b) Hamlet
(c) Measure for Measure
(d) None of the above

53. The term 'Science Fiction' was coined by
(a) Ernest Ackerman
(b) J.R.R. Talkein
(c) Kurt Vannegat
(d) None of the above

54. The name of only play by James Joyce is
(a) *Pigmalion* (b) *Ulysses*
(c) *Exiles* (d) *Finnegan's Wake*

55. Who said "An archaeologist is the best husband any woman can have the older she gets, the more interested he is in her"?
(a) Agathe Christsie
(b) Ezra Pound
(c) G.B. Shaw
(d) None of the above

56. Who is known as "a classical in literature, royalist in politics and anglo catholic in religion"?
(a) T.S. Eliot (b) Ezra Pound
(c) M. Arnold (d) W.B. Yeats

57. 'The Seven Types of Ambiguity' was written by
(a) F.R. Leavis
(b) I.A. Richards
(c) William Empson
(d) None of the above

58. The Bloomsbury Group, a literary club, was founded by
(a) Ezra Pound (b) W.B. Yeats
(c) Virginia Woolf (d) None of the above

59. The New Critics believe in
(a) the view of autonomy of literature
(b) psychological approach
(c) Both (a) and (b)
(d) None of the above

60. The error of evaluating a poem by its emotional effects is known as
(a) International fallacy
(b) Pathetic fallacy

(c) Affective fallacy
(d) None of the above

61. The phrase 'Collective unconscious' is associated with
(a) Sigmund Frend
(b) C.G. Jung
(c) Both (a) and (b)
(d) None of the above

62. The Poem 'Against Romanticism' was written by
(a) Ezra Pound
(b) T.S. Eliot
(c) Kingsley Amis
(d) None of the above

63. Who among the following is associated with New Criticism?
(a) I.A. Richards
(b) Cleanth Brooks
(c) David Daiches
(d) None of the above

64. Octavia Paz received Nobel Prize in
(a) 1990 (b) 1991
(c) 1944 (d) 1956

65. G.B. Shaw with 'Life force' specifically in
(a) Man of Destiny
(b) Man and Superman
(c) Joan of Arc
(d) Pignation

66. In James *The Portrait of a Lady* who is the Lady?
(a) Mrs. Touchett
(b) Isabel Archer
(c) Henrielta Stackpde
(d) None of the above

67. *Just So Stories* is a story collection by
(a) Kipling (b) Poe
(c) Mark Twain (d) Tennyson

68. Forster is a novelist difficult to assers: he can be easily overestimated or underestimated. This quotation about Forster is from which of the following critics?
(a) Walter Allen (b) Diane Neil
(c) E. Elbert (d) Fredrick Karl

69. In Forster's Howard's End, Howard's End is the name of a
(a) house (b) town
(b) bridge (d) road

70. 'Religion by the Blood' is a phrase which is associated with
(a) James Joyce (b) Conrad
(c) Virginia Woolf (d) D.H. Lawrence

71. Which of the following women was instrumental in Launching Lawrence as a writer?
(a) Jessica Chambers
(b) His mother, Lydie
(c) Friede weekly
(d) None of the above

72. Which of the following novels of D.H. Lawrence is a sequal to his novel *The Rainbow*?
(a) *Women in Love*
(b) *Sons and Lovers*
(c) *Lady Chatterley's Lover*
(d) *The White Peacock*

73. Sons and Lovers may be taken as
(a) an autobiographical novel
(b) expression of the political convictions of the author
(c) a criticism of the contemporary society
(d) None of the above

74. Which of the following novels of Huxley is inspired by the message of Bhagwat Geeta?
(a) *The Brave New World*
(b) *Time Must have a Stop*
(c) *The Perennial Philosophy*
(d) *Crome Yellow*

75. Graham Green's 'May We Borrow Your Husband' is a collection of
(a) essays (b) poems
(c) short Stories (d) novels

76. By Profession, Conrad was a
(a) doctor (b) sailor
(c) teacher (d) priest

77. Who called Henry James the 'Victorian of fine consciousness?'
(a) Joseph Conrad (b) James Joyce
(c) G.M. Hopkins (d) E.M. Forster

78. In Joyce's Ulysses each episode coincides with which of the following classical books?
(a) *Virgil's Aenid*
(b) *Dante's Divine Comedy*
(c) *Homer's Odyssey*
(d) None of the above

79. Look Back in Anger is a classical because
(a) it was an attack on British complacency
(b) it shook the foundation of pro-aristocracy governance
(c) it was taken as a revolt
(d) it awakened the policy makers from their slumber

80. The 'Theatre of Absurd' is linked with
(a) Sartre (b) Samuel Beckett
(c) Osborne (d) Wesker

81. Who succeeded Queen Victoria after her death in 1901?
(a) George V (c) Edward V
(b) Edward VI (d) Edward VIII

82. Which important bill was passed in 1914?
(a) Home Rule Bill Act
(b) National Insurance Act
(c) Franchise Act
(d) Atlantic Flow Act

83. Sherlock Holmes was introduced to the readers in 1887 by Sir Arthur Conan Doyle in
(a) *The Exploits of Brigadier General*
(b) *Mican Clarke*
(c) *A Study in Scarlet*
(d) *The Lost World*

84. *Where Angelo Fear to Tread* is a novel of
(a) Joseph Conrad
(b) Somerset Maugham
(c) D.H. Lawrence
(d) E.M. Forster

85. Verse de Libre means
(a) blank verse (b) no verse
(c) free verse (d) courtly verse

86. He was greatly attracted by the theories of Walter Scolt and found himself adopted as the mentor of the aesthetic movement. Who is 'he' here?
(a) George Moore (b) Oscar Wilde
(c) R.L. Stevenson (d) H.G. Wells

87. In 1895 Oscard Wilde had to go to jail for two years. He was charged of
(a) immoral homosexual conduct
(b) rape
(c) theft
(d) None of the above

88. Oscar Wilde Waste was a
(a) Decadent (c) Socialist
(c) Tory (d) Whig

89. Name the work of Oscar that he wrote serving a jail term.
(a) *De profunids* (b) *The Sphinx*
(c) *Intentions* (d) *Rouchne*

90. 'Impression De Theatre' by Oscar Wilde is a
(a) Prose work (c) Poetry work
(b) Fiction (d) Biography

91. 'An Ideal Husband' and 'A Woman of No Importance' by Oscar Wilde are the
    (a) romances (b) tragedies
    (c) comedies (d) satires
92. Who wrote the elegy Wordsworth's Grave?
    (a) William Watson (b) Satiny Dobell
    (c) Alexander Smith (d) Oscar Wilde
93. One of the most influential of Oscar Wilde's plays was written in French and was translated into English in 1894 by Lord Alfred Douglas. Name that play.
    (a) *Vera*
    (b) *Salome*
    (c) *The Dutchess of Padua*
    (d) *The Mirror of the Sea*
94. Which of the following is a Novella?
    (a) Almayer's Folly
    (b) Under the Western Eyes
    (c) Nostromo
    (d) The Nigger of the Narcisscal
95. Robert Bridges started his career as a
    (a) diplomat (b) barister
    (c) teacher (d) surgeon
96. Which novelist was known as the literary bad boy of the Victorians?
    (a) Samuel Butler (b) George Meredith
    (c) Charles Dickens (d) Henry Newman
97. Who is the author of Shakespeare's Sonnets Reconsidered?
    (a) George Moore (b) W.B. Yeats
    (c) Samuel Butler (d) G.R. Girsing
98. George Moore was a
    (a) Scottish Poet
    (b) Irish novelist
    (c) Italian playwright
    (d) American novelist
99. 'Veramilda' and 'Worbarton' by George Robert Gissing are
    (a) Psychological novels
    (b) Romantic novels
    (c) Historical novels
    (d) Picturesque novels
100. G.B. Shaw was greatly impressed by the Norweigian dramatist
    (a) Wilson (b) Nicen
    (c) Gibsen (d) Ibsen
101. Bernard Shaw got the Nobel Prize for literature in 1925 for
    (a) *Man and Superman*
    (b) *Saint Joan*
    (c) *Pygmalian*
    (d) *The Apple Cart*
102. One of Shaw's plays deals with the problem of phonetics and pronunciation. Which of the following is that play?
    (a) *Pymalion* (b) *Condide*
    (c) *Major Barbara* (d) *Apple Cart*
103. Yeats was greatly influenced by the Oxford Scholar
    (a) Walter Pater (b) George Moore
    (c) D. Rosselti (d) A. Swinburne
104. W.B. Yeats awarded the Nobel Prize for literature in
    (a) 1921 (b) 1922
    (c) 1923 (d) 1924
105. Who wrote the popular poem 'Sea-Fever'?
    (a) W.H. Devies
    (b) W.B. Yeats
    (c) John Masefiled
    (d) Walter De La Mare
106. Ezra Pound was a/an
    (a) Irish playwright
    (b) American playwright
    (c) American novelist
    (d) American poet
107. The credit of igniting the spark for writing in John Galsworthy goes to

(a) Ada, the wife of his cousin
(b) Arthur, his cousin
(c) his father
(d) his mother

108. Whose models of problem plays did Galsworthy follow in writing his plays?
(a) T.W. Robertson (b) Henry Jones
(c) Arthur Pinero (d) Henrick Ibsen

109. John Galsworthy published some of his works under the pseudonym of
(a) John Wilson (b) John Perkins
(c) John Sinjohn (d) John Squire

110. Which of the following is not a children's story by Walter De La Mare?
(a) *The Riddle*
(b) *The Magic Jacket*
(c) *The Duck Cheese*
(d) *A Child's Play*

111. T.S. Eliot was awarded the Nobel Prize for literature for his
(a) *Four Quarters*
(b) *Portrait of a Lady*
(c) *The Waste Land*
(d) *The Love Story of J.A. Purfrock*

112. Who propounded the imagist theory of poetry?
(a) T.S. Eliot (b) Ezra Pound
(c) John Ruskin (d) Rupert Brooke

113. Name the modern poet who translated the Bhagwat Gita in collaboration with Swami Prabhavanandan.
(a) Stephen Spender
(b) C.D. Levis
(c) Christopher Isherwood
(d) W.H. Audey

114. The first English newspaper devoted exclusively to women's interest which was founded in 1903 is
(a) Daily Mail (b) Daily Express
(c) Daily Mirror (d) Daily Vision

115. Which playwright called his own plays a sardonic comedy?
(a) G.B. Shaw
(b) Somerset Maugham
(c) Ibsen
(d) T.S. Eliot

116. Which group of poets did Robert Graves join but left it soon after?
(a) Pre-Raphaelites poets
(b) Elizabethan poets
(c) Georgian poets
(d) Aesthetic poets

117. Which novel of E.M. Forster published posthumously as a homosexual theme?
(a) *The Longest Journey*
(b) *Howards End*
(c) *A Passage to India*
(d) *Manrica*

118. Identify the playwright and novelist who wrote forty seven plays and twenty eight novels in addition to an opera libretto, television and radio serials.
(a) Hugh Walpole
(b) Graham Greene
(c) William Golding
(d) J.B. Priestly

119. Edwin Muir is chiefly known for his
(a) critical work
(b) historical plays
(c) oicturesque
(d) None of the above

120. Virginia Woolf was the daughter of a famous literary critic
(a) Harold Pinter
(b) George Herbert
(c) Leslic Stephen
(d) Edward Thomson

121. D.H. Lawrence was a pioneer of
(a) stream of consciousness novel
(b) psychoanalytical fiction

(c) psychological fiction
(d) imagism in fiction

122. D.H. Lawrence was greatly influenced by
(a) Freud (b) Marx
(c) Darwin (d) Aristotle

123. Hopkins was made poet laureate in
(a) 1915 (b) 1913
(c) 1920 (d) 1929

124. Hopkins was nicknamed
(a) Skin (b) Tommy
(c) Willy (d) Harry

125. Robert Bridges outstanding contribution to poetry lies in
(a) sensuous images
(b) metaphors
(c) rhyme scheme
(d) metrical innovation

ANSWERS

1. (d)	2. (c)	3. (c)	4. (d)	5. (d)	6. (c)
7. (d)	8. (c)	9. (c)	10. (c)	11. (c)	12. (a)
13. (d)	14. (d)	15. (d)	16. (d)	17. (d)	18. (d)
19. (a)	20. (a)	21. (b)	22. (d)	23. (b)	24. (b)
25. (d)	26. (d)	27. (a)	28. (d)	29. (c)	30. (b)
31. (a)	32. (c)	33. (c)	34. (c)	35. (d)	36. (c)
37. (d)	38. (a)	39. (b)	40. (d)	41. (b)	42. (d)
43. (b)	44. (a)	45. (c)	46. (c)	47. (c)	48. (c)
49. (a)	50. (b)	51. (a)	52. (a)	53. (a)	54. (c)
55. (a)	56. (a)	57. (c)	58. (c)	59. (a)	60. (c)
61. (b)	62. (c)	63. (c)	64. (a)	65. (c)	66. (b)
67. (a)	68. (a)	69. (a)	70. (c)	71. (a)	72. (a)
73. (a)	74. (c)	75. (c)	76. (b)	77. (a)	78. (c)
79. (a)	80. (b)	81. (d)	82. (a)	83. (c)	84. (d)
85. (c)	86. (b)	87. (a)	88. (a)	89. (a)	90. (b)
91. (c)	92. (a)	93. (b)	94. (d)	95. (d)	96. (a)
97. (c)	98. (b)	99. (c)	100. (d)	101. (b)	102. (a)
103. (a)	104. (c)	105. (c)	106. (d)	107. (a)	108. (c)
109. (c)	110. (d)	111. (c)	112. (b)	113. (c)	114. (c)
115. (b)	116. (c)	117. (d)	118. (d)	119. (a)	120. (c)
121. (b)	122. (a)	123. (b)	124. (a)	125. (d)	

17

Contemporary Period

Most of the readers equate the term postmodern literature with contemporary literature. The term postmodern literature is used to describe certain tendencies in post-world war literature. It is both a continuation of the experimentation championed by writers. If the modernism period (relying heavily, for example, on fragmentation, paradox, questionable narrators etc.) and a reaction against Enlightment ideas implicit in Modernist Literature. Postmodern literature like postmodernism as a whole, is difficult to define and there is little agreement on the exact characteristics, scope and importance of postmodern literature.

Contemporary literature is literature with its settling generally after World War II. The somewhat malleable term of contemporary literature is usually applied with a post 1960 cutoff point.

Towards the end of the century, electronic literature developed as a genre due to the development of hypertext and latest the World Wide Web.

The best-selling works of the 20th century are estimated to be *Quotations From Chairman Mao* (1966, 900 million copies), *Harry Potter and the Philosopher's Stove* (1997, 120 million copies) *And Then There Were None* (1939, 115 million Copies) and *The Lord of the Rings*, (It was also voted 'book of the century' in various surveys.

The genre classification of contemporary literature represents certain texts written during and after 1960. There are also other requirements for a text to classify as contemporary literature; the text should be of a class distinguishable by a high standards of writing; be it beauty, composition style, significance.

The current definition of 'literature' seems to have narrowed somewhat and is largely defined now as it is taught within the context of English; incorporating poetry, theatre and dramatic performance, essays and fictional prose.

It is within this category of English Literature that contemporary literature represents literature produced from 1960 to the present day. However, it certainly doesn't represent all written works that fall within this time period and indeed, there is more to contemporary literature than merely a time period. There are also stylistic issues and issues with personal subjectivity that cause certain classifications within and omissions from this genre to be contested.

Reasons that have been given for outcasting certain texts from the classification of contemporary literature are things like poor grammar and syntax and inconsistent or poorly constructed character and storylines. There is also a belief that certain genre fiction (such as romance and sci-fi) is generally outcast from the realism of 'literature' however that is extremely disputable.

Contemporary British Authors

Peter Ackroyd
Martin Amis
J.G. Ballard
Julian Barnes
Anita Brookner
A.S. Byatt
Angele Carter
Caryl Churchitt
Ted Hudges
Kazuo Ishiguro
Philip Larkin
Doris Lessing
Salman Rushdie
Will Self
Graham Swift
Fay Weldon
Jeanette Winterson

Common Themes and Techniques

Irony, Playfulness, Black humour
Intertextuality
Pastiche (to combine, or paste together multiple elements)
Metafiction
Poioumena (specific type of metafiction)
Historiograhic metafiction
Temporal distortion
Magic realism
Technouculture and hyperreality
Paranoia
Maximalism
Minimalism
Different Perspectives

List of Contemporary British Authors (at the Virginia Public Library)

Adams, Douglas (1952)
Aldiss, Brian W. (1925)
Amis, Martin (1949)

Bainbridge, Berye (1934)
Ballard, J.G. (1930)
Banur, Ian (1954)
Barker, Pat (1943)
Barnes, Julian (1946)
Baxter, Sstephen (1957)
Bennett, Alan (1934)
Boyel, William (1952)
Burgen, Anthony (1917)
Byatt, A.S. (1936)
Chatwin, Bruce (1940)
Clarke, Arthur C. (1917)
Clarke, Susanee (1959)
Drabble, Margaret (1939) *The Gates of Irony*
The Peppered Mouth
The Red Queen
The Seven Sisters
A Summer-Bird Cage
The Witch of Exmoor

Fforde, Jasper (1961)
Fitzgerald, Penelope (1916) — *The Gate of Angels* (1990)
Human Voices (1999)
The Means of Escape (2000)

Fleming, Ian
Forsyth, Frederick
Gaiman, Neil
Hamilton, Peter. F. (1960)
Harris, Robert (1957)
Horn by, Nick (1957)
Le, Carre, John (1931)
Lessing, Doris (1919) *Ben, In the World*
The Fifth Child
The Grass is Singing
Love Again
The Marriages between Zones Three, Four & Five
The Sweetest Dream

Lodge, David (1935)
McEwan-Ian (1948)
Mortimer, John Clifford (1923)
Murdock, Iris (1919) — *The Green Knight*
Jackson's Dileimme
The Sea, the sea
The Unicous
A Word Chilg
Myerson, Julie (1960)
Naipaul, V.S. (1932) — *Half a life*
Pratchett, Terry (1948)
Pym, Barbare (1913)
Robinson, Derek (1932)
Rowling, J.K. (1965) — *Harry Potter Series*
Rushdie, Salman (1947) — *East, West Stories*
Fury
The Ground Beneath Her Feet
The Moor's Last Sign
The Satanic Verses
Shaw, Bob (1931)
Smith, Michael Marshall (1965)
Smith, Zadie (1976)
Spark, Muriel (1918)
Stewart, Mary (1916)
Swift, Graham (1949)
Townsend, Sue (1946)
Weldon, Fay (1931)

MULTIPLE CHOICE QUESTIONS

1. Who began his literary career with two volumes of short stories. The writers Sat (1919) and Such Darling Dodas (1950)?
   (a) Emile Zola (b) Moupassant
   (b) Angus Wilson (d) Iris Murdoch
2. What is Muriel Spark's auto-biography entitled as?
   (a) *Vox Ego Sum Amoris*
   (b) *Curriculum Vitae*
   (c) *A Fairly Honourable Defeat*
   (d) *Moments Mori*
3. Larkin's first volume of poetry which was published in 1945 was
   (a) 'The Whitsun Weddings'
   (b) 'The North Ship'
   (b) 'High Windows'
   (d) None of the above

4. Who is the author the 'Female Eunuch' that provided a Shimulus to the development of a newly outspoken and often provocative feminism in the 1970s?
   (a) Harold Pinter (b) Germaine Greer
   (c) Stevie Smith (d) Alan Sillitoe
5. Who wrote the *Wide Sargasso Sea* (1966) which can be said partly to be a rethinking of Mr. Rochester's account of his courtship and marriage as given in Jane Eyre?
   (a) Barbara Pym (b) Jean Rhys
   (c) Angele Carter (d) John Fowle
6. Who is the author of Live Like Pigs, a play about the resettlement of gypsies in a housing-estate, which explores anti-social behavior?
   (a) Arnold Wesker (b) Harold Pinter
   (c) Joe Orton (d) John Arden
7. Harold Pinter's relatively recent plays *One for the Oad* (1984), and *Mountain Language* (1988) are insistently concerned with acts of interrogation and with
   (a) Adultery
   (b) Language
   (c) Pattiness of values
   (d) All of the above
8. Who is the authors of the plays *Owners* and *Cloud Nine*?
   (a) David Hare (b) Trevor Griffin
   (c) Caryl Churchill (d) Howard Brenton
9. In which year was the annual Booker Prize established?
   (a) 1959 (b) 1969
   (c) 1979 (d) 1989
10. 'Amsterdam', a somewhat diagrammatic and dispiriting study of euthanasia, published in 1998, was authored by
    (a) Ian Mc Ewan (b) David Lodge
    (c) Alasdair Gray (d) James Hogg
11. In which year did Paul Heyse receive the Nobel Prize?
    (a) 1909 (b) 1910
    (c) 1911 (d) 1908
12. Who received the Nobel Prize for literature in 1995?
    (a) Dario Fo (b) Wole Soyinka
    (c) S. Heaney (d) Sartre
13. When did Rushdies 'Midnight Children' appear?
    (a) 1980 (b) 1981
    (c) 1982 (d) 1984
14. In which year was the Irish National Theatre Society founded?
    (a) 1901 (b) 1902
    (c) 1903 (d) 1904
15. The writer of the novel *Brideshead Revisited* is
    (a) Evelyn (b) Golding
    (c) Conrad (d) Joyce

ANSWERS

1. (c)	2. (b)	3. (c)	4. (b)	5. (b)	6. (d)
7. (b)	8. (c)	9. (b)	10. (a)	11. (b)	12. (c)
13. (b)	14. (c)	15. (a)			

18

American and Other Non-British Literatures

American literature had a long period of apprenticeship. It furnished and made errors like all the other literatures of the world. It imitated the style and subject matter of European writers, thus having the major influence of Europe upon it. American literature begins with the first English colonies at Psymouth and Proston. Until 1900, American literature could not decide whether to wear a grave frock coat or a rough hickory shirt.

Like other national literatures, American literature was shaped by the history of the country which produced it. The growth of American literature is bound up with the growth of America as a nation. The historical factors influenced the growth of American literature in various ways. American writers were really European writers living in America. American literature developed its own standards. American literature has been enriched by the myriad cultural traits which go to make America.

Historical Perspective

1603	Accession of James I
1607	Settlement of Virginia
1609	Separatists go the Holland
1620	Settlement of Plymouth by Separatist Pilgrims
1630	Settlement of Massachusetts Bay
1632	Maryland Chartered
1633	Land in power over all England
1635	Connecticut founded
1636	Providence settled
1649-60	Commonwealth in England: Puritans in Power
1660	The Restoration
1663	Carolina Chartered
1664	New Jersey and New York established
1675-76	King Philips War and Bacon's Rebellion
1681	Pennsylvania Chartered
1684	Massachusetts charter revoked
1689	Revolt against Andros
1689-97	King William's War against the French
1702-13	Queen Arina's War

1732	Georgia Charterd
1734	Beginning of the Great Awakening
1755	Deportation of Acadians
1756-63	French and Indian War
1760	Accession of George III

The study of American literature in the colonial time is the study of literature in isolated partitions. American literature, gives each colony or to each group its own literary accent. The English language that prevailed in all the colonies was the English language that had been brought from England in the 17th century. William J. Long narrated that there were three reasons due to which colonists could not write good books during the colonial period. They are lack of literature, lack of culture and lack of nationality.

According to Geoffrey Moore, the American literature of the colonial Period can be divided into six main categories which are as follows:

1. Accounts of Exploration and Colonization
2. Histories and Narratives of Settlement
3. Diaries, and First-hand Descriptions of Events
4. Sermons
5. Books of Theological and Political Exposition and Argument
6. Satirical work on Liberal Tendencies.

Despite the increased activity in poetry and the drama and the beginning of a native tradition of the novel, however, the major energies of the Americans in the last three decades of the 18th century went not into creative literature but into politics and controversy. The late 18th century in fact, was a great age of American prose and in the newspapers and magazines, which sprang up in every city of importance between 1780 and 1800 there appeared essays on American politics and society. The great social movement gave rise to numerous newspaper and magazines, with their poems, satires, essays stories—a bright and varied array compared with the colonial product more significant of the new social life are the crude plays of Reyall Tyler and William Donlag, which were immensely popular in the new playhouses, and the romances of Charles Brockden Brown, which at the close of this period mark the beginning of the American novel. America's first newspaper 'The Boston News' was issued in 1704 and soon a number and weeklies of this period, though poor and imitative in nature gave ample proof of the fact that the people were taking an interest in cultural and literary affairs instead of being engrossed in material needs. New classes like the gentlemen, statesmen and soldiers were now created.

The tide of national sentiment that swept over America produced in its wake a genuine interest in belles-lettre in literature that was not merely informational or utilitarian. The writers were more self conscious and the spread of education created on enlighted public who were ready for finer literature.

In the case of the short story the usual 'time lag' noticed between the appearance of a new literary genre in England and its imitation in America, is not seen. The short story had a relatively even start in international competition, as it was largely dependent upon the magazines. Benjamin Franklin seems to have been one of the pioneers in this field.

The first quarter of the 19th century witnessed a number of changes in the American literary scene. Romanticism meant a break away from the rigid restraints of classicism. In America too there appeared an immense variety of literary gernes and verse forms such as blank verse, octosyllabic lines, the Spenserian Stanza, the sonnet, the ode, the lyric and the metrical romance. With the romantic movement nature became very important in American literature. There was a romantic idealism or transcendentalism, which emerged after 1830 in the works of Emerson, Thoureak, Margaret Fulter and William Ellery Channing. Transcendentalism was truly a liberating force of the period and it definitely was a blessing to literature as it gave to American literature not only a new significant aesthetic theory, but also two of its major artists—Emerson and Thoreau.

American Poetry

William Cullen Bryant (1794-1878) dominates the poetry of the entire united States Prior to the first genuine success of Longfellow and Poe, just as Irving and Cooper dominate the purpose of the period. Byrant was quite legitimately the first American. This fact has won for him the title 'The Father of American Poetry'.

Bryant's poetry reflects the finest features of this glorious movement. Yet he is not altogether free from classicism. In fact Bryant exhibits a blending of classical and romantic qualities. It was the poem Thantopsis' published in 1817 in the North American Review' that won Bryant a reputation as a poet, Bryant is undoubtedly a moralist who finds in nature much that inspires didactic reflections. He is marked by unusually flexible metrical patterns. He avoided structural complications by using simple quatrains, blank verse, or unspecialized couplets. Byrant has been called several things, American Wordsworth, a belated representations of new England Puritanism and 'A Stately moralist in verse'.

We get a proper sense of William Cullen Bryant's greatness a poet when we recall what Emerson has said of him, "He is our native, sincere, original, patriotic poet.... He is original because he is sincere a true painter of the face of the country and of the sentiments of his own people".

Washington Irving

Washington Irving (1783-1859) reveals himself as inheritor of the literary qualities of both the classical and the romantic periods. Irving's work 'Knickerbocker's History of New York' (1809) a mock-heroic chronicle of the old dutch colony was his famous work. Irving's leaning towards satire was something he owed to the influence of the classicists. Irving made use of his sharp satire in his attack on English writers. In style also Irving is unmistakably classical. Irving's genius was quite individual. The appearance of the work was preceded by a series of intriguing advertisements in a New York paper, asking about the whereabouts of a mythical Dutch historian, Diedrich Knickerbocker. Washington Irving is in the words of Marcus Cuincliff 'The first man of letters from the United States to win an international reputation'. He loved his fellow-human beings and was interested in watching them and reproducing their manners and characters in words. But those who insist on originality of plot in a short-story may criticise Irving. His *Rip Van Winkle* and its companion piece *The Legend of Sleepy Hollow* both drive then plot from German folk tales. His stories are rich in local colour. His stories are different from the tightly structured stories of Poe or Hawthrone. His stories are leisurely and discursive. Irving has a charming way of taking the reader into his confidence. His style is also a great factor that accounts for his popularity as a story teller. The easy rhythm of the sentences, and the mild occasional relief of a pleasantry are delightful features of Irvings writings. His intrinsicment and the fact that he was the first in the field, and also his influence on other writers have made Poe declare that Irving was the most deservedly eminent among all the pioneers of American literature.

When Edgar Allen Poe appeared on the literary scene the Puritan prejudice against fiction had gone. Poe has established himself as an expert in the field of stories of ratiocination. Though in his poems Poe professed to care very little for it, he had a genuine interest in science as is evident from his scientific or pseudo-scientific narratives of marvelous adventure. He was the first among American writers to formalize the technique of the short story, seeking totality of effect through compression, immediately and finally Poe was the first to develop a new fiction of psychology analysis and his portraits of abnormal or self destructive states contributed much to greater masters like Dosteouske. Poe's stories therefore are a landmark in the development of American fiction.

Edgar Allen Poe was the first American literary critic to express the aesthetic tradition in art.

When James Fenimore Cooper (1789-1851) appeared on the scene of American literature, the novel was already in existence. It was by sheer accident that Cooper started novel-writing. His wife challenged him to make good the boast and the result was the first novel *Precaution* (1820), a novel depicting English society. It contained plenty of moral element and sentiment. Between 1820 and 1826, Cooper wrote a number of novels all depicting romantic.

Major Writers of America

1. Washington Irvin
2. James Fenimor Cooper
3. Edgar Allan Poe
4. Ralph Waldo Emerson
5. Henry David Thorean
6. Nathaniel Hawthorne
7. Herman Melville
8. Mark Twain
9. Emily Dickenson
10. Edger Allan Poe
11. Walt Whatman
12. Ralph Waldo Emerson
13. Henry Wadsworth Loryfellow
14. William Dean Howells
15. Stephen Crane
16. Jack London
17. Theodox Dreser
18. Henry James
19. Edith Wharton
20. Ezra Pound
21. Edgar Lee Masters
22. Carl Sandbing
23. Robert Frost
24. Cummings
25. Hart Crane
26. Archibald Macbeish
27. William Carlos Williams
28. Wallace Stevens
29. Thodox Roethke
30. Earnest Hemingway
31. John Dos Parris
32. John Steinbeck
33. William Faulkner
34. Thomas Wolfe
35. Eugene O' Neil
36. Tennesse Williams

37. Edward Albee
38. Arthur Miller
39. Saul Bellow
40. John Updice

MULTIPLE CHOICE QUESTIONS

1. A young homosexual who hates the world he can't live in and the one he resides in, appears in Edward Albee's
   (a) *The Zoo Story*
   (b) *The Death of Bessia Smith*
   (c) *The Sandbox*
   (d) *The American Dream*
2. Name the playwright who wrote *Who is Afraid of Virginia Woolf* in 1962.
   (a) George Arnold (b) Edward Albee
   (c) James Bryce (d) Robert Frost
3. Which of the following is a poetical autobiography of Bronson Alcott's youth?
   (a) The Doctrine and Discipline of Human Culture
   (b) Table Talk
   (c) New Connecticut
   (d) Tablets
4. Name the writer who was encouraged by Carl Sandburg and Floyd Dell to publish his first book *Windy Macpherson's Sin* in 1916.
   (a) John Andre
   (b) Bess Streeter Aldrich
   (c) Anderson Sherwood
   (d) Walt Whitman
5. *Poor White* (1920) is a novel by Anderson about
   (a) Mid-east (b) Mid-west
   (c) Mid-south (d) Mid-north
6. Which was the first novel of James Baldwin?
   (a) *Another country*
   (b) *Tell Me How Long The Trains Been Gone*
   (c) *Go Tell it on the Mountain*
   (d) *Giovanni's Room*
7. Which of the following book of Saul Bellow presents a Kalfica Like atmosphere?
   (a) *Henderson the Ram King*
   (b) *The Salimmer's Planet*
   (c) *The Dean's December*
   (d) *The Victim*
8. Who got the Nobel Prize for literature in 1976?
   (a) Robert Frost (b) Ergenio Montale
   (c) Robert Anderson (d) Saul Bellow
9. Which of the following is a collection of short stories by Saul Bellow?
   (a) *The Dangling Man*
   (b) *Mosby's Memoirs*
   (c) *The Victim*
   (d) *The Adventures of Angie March*
10. Name the novel of Pearl S. Buck which she wrote in 1931 and for which she got the Pultizer Prize.
    (a) *The Good Earth*
    (b) *The House of Earth*
    (c) *Son*
    (d) *A House*
11. What was the pen name of Pearl S. Buck?
    (a) Pearl Lennis (b) Pearl Walsh
    (c) Pearl Ellison (d) Pearl Bergson
12. Who got the Nobel Prize for literature in 1938?
    (a) Pearl S. Buck (b) Sinclair Lewis
    (c) Engene O' Neill (d) Robert Frost
13. What is the real name of Mark Twain?
    (a) Samuel Lionel Clemens
    (b) Samuel Mark Clemens

(c) Samuel Langtorne Clemens
(d) Samuel Taylor Clemens

14. "I never saw a moor
I never saw the sea;
Yet I know I how the heather looks,
And what a wave must be."
Who wrote the above lines?
(a) T.S. Eliot
(b) Walt Whitman
(c) William Faulkner
(d) Emily Dickenson

15. Who wrote the famous naturalistic novel *Invisible Man*?
(a) Ralph Ellison (b) Ralph Emerson
(c) S. Eddy (d) Leon Edel

16. R.W. Emerson was an essayist and
(a) lawyer (b) novelist
(c) poet (d) playwright

17. William Faulkner was awarded the Nobel Prize for Literature in
(a) 1949 (b) 1950
(c) 1951 (d) 1952

18. Who wrote his first novel *This Side of Paradise* in 1920 when he was still a trainee in the army?
(a) William Faulkner (b) Thomas Farrell
(c) F.S. Fitzgerald (d) Ralph Ellisin

19. 'A Masque of Reason' by Robert Frost is a/an
(a) critical essay (b) verse drama
(c) ballad (d) epic

20. Robert Frost was awarded the Pultizer Prize
(a) only once (b) twice
(c) thrice (d) four times

21. Who was invited by President John F. Kennedy to recite his patriotic poem 'the Gift Outright' at the inaugural ceremony?
(a) E.E. Cummings
(b) Robert Frost
(c) Theodox Dressier
(d) Thelma Howard

22. Which of the following is a satirical play by Francis Scolt Fitzgerald?
(a) *The Beautiful and Damned*
(b) *The Vegetable*
(c) *The Crack-Up*
(d) *The Price was High*

23. Which American novelist committed a suicide by gunshot in 1961?
(a) Paul Blackburn
(b) Earnest Hemingway
(c) Theodex Dressier
(d) None of the above

24. The Old Man and The Sea' recounts the 84 days adventure of
(a) Matadors (b) Santiago
(c) The author (d) Philip

25. Identify the story collection by Henry James out of the following:
(a) *The Wheel of Time*
(b) *The Wheel of Home*
(c) *The Other House*
(d) None of the above

26. Arthur Miller was a famous
(a) poet (b) playwright
(c) novelist (d) critic

27. Name the play by Arthur Miller which has only one long act and its theme is based on individual guilt.
(a) *The Crucible*
(b) *Incident of Victory*
(c) *All my Sons*
(d) *After the Fall*

28. Which was the first play written by O'Neill's in 1913-14?

(a) *Bound East for Cardiff*
(b) *The Moon*
(c) *Beyond the Horizon*
(d) *The Web*

29. Which play of Irwin Shew depicts the feelings of a woman dreaming of the life of her unborn son?
(a) *Slege*
(b) *Sons and Soldiers*
(c) *Retreat to Pleasure*
(d) *Children from their Games*

30. Who wrote the following about novel writing?
"......every great novel must first of all be based on a profound sense of moral value, and then constructed with a classical unity and economy of means."
(a) Beyamin Franklin
(b) Edith Wharton
(c) E. Hamingway
(d) None of the above

31. Who said 'Give me liberty, or give me death?'
(a) Abraham Lincoln
(b) Patrick Henry
(c) George Washington
(d) John F. Kennedy

32. Which one is Sylvia Plath's novel?
(a) *Ariel* (b) *The Bell Jaiz*
(c) *The Colossus* (d) *Catch-22*

33. Who translated Oman Khayyam into English?
(a) Edward Fitzgerald
(b) Scott Fitzgerald
(c) Edgar Fawcet
(d) Ford Madox Ford

34. Name the mathematician and philosopher who was awarded the Nobel Prize for literature in 1950.
(a) Bertrand Russell (b) Aldons Huxley
(c) William James (d) James Joyce

35. What techniques are characteristic of Walt Whitman?
(a) Sprawling lines and cataloguing technique.
(b) Straightforwardness.
(c) Ornamental and elaborate.
(d) Use of monosyllables.

36. Emerson, Thoriu and Whitman represented which aspects of American Romanticism?
(a) Individualism and optimism, a bright picture
(b) Emotions rather than intellect
(c) Naturalness
(d) Spontaneity

37. American transcendentalism stands for
(a) romantic distrust of the intellect and exaltation insight.
(b) reality can be apprehended through spiritual insight.
(c) german philosophers and English interpreters.
(d) metaphysical justification.

38. American literature after 1890 shows
(a) the complexity and changes in the nature of American life.
(b) the world wars.
(c) economic depression leading to introspection.
(d) emergence of a wide reading public.

39. American literature besides fiction achievements significance in
(a) general prose-writing
(b) history, biography, criticism, social-political writing
(c) journalism
(d) argumentative writings, debate etc.

40. Who were the first American orators?
(a) Preachers (b) Priests
(c) Lay Leaders (d) Politicians

41. Which literary work helped Abraham Lincoln become American President?
(a) Aunt Phillis's Cabin
(b) Moby Dick
(c) Walden
(d) Uncle Tom's Cabin

42. The American folklox consists of
(a) British folklox.
(b) combination of British, French and Spanish.
(c) Indian and Negro folklores in combination with European traditions.
(d) Chinese and Asian.

43. Emerson called Edgar Allen Poe
(a) a jingle man
(b) a great lyrical poet
(c) a great American poet
(d) None of the above

44. Who called poet a great lyric poet?
(a) W.B. Yeats (b) Emerson
(c) Longfellow (d) Whitman

45. Which of Emerson's works has this entry; "Little things are often filled with great beauty"?
(a) Nature
(b) American Scholar Lecture
(c) Harvard Dignity School
(d) Journal for March 1852 Address

46. Who said of Thoreau's poems that 'the rhyme and marjoram are yet not honey'?
(a) R.W. Emerson
(b) Nathaniel Hawthorne
(c) H.D. Thorean
(d) Herman Melville

47. Nathaniel Hawthorne is a writer of
(a) Prose (b) Fiction
(c) Plays (d) Drama

48. Emily Dickenson had literary affinity with
(a) Emerson (b) Thorean
(c) Melville (d) Whitman

49. Who wrote "I find ecstasy in living"?
(a) Whitman (b) Longfellow
(c) Frost (d) Dickenson

50. Dickenson's poetry can be best described as
(a) Confessional poetry
(b) Poetry of recluse
(c) Celebration of democracy
(d) American dream

51. What part of American geography did Whitman include in his representative American poem?
(a) Sea Coasts
(b) Lakes
(c) Priaries
(d) Great oceans, its mountains and it illimitable prairies

52. How best Whitman's 'Passage to India' can be described.
(a) a transcendental poem. Envisioning the spiritual unification and fulfillment man.
(b) a poem to celebrate achievement of mankind.
(c) scientific-sociology record of America.
(d) glorification of American life.

53. Who called Theodox Dreiser's *An American Tragedy* a harrowing novel?
(a) Irving Rabbit (b) I.A. Richards
(c) F.R. Leavis (d) Wilson Knight

54. James revealed his mastery of realistic fictional technique in
(a) Portrait of a Lady
(b) The Bostonians
(c) The American
(d) The Princess Cassamassion

55. Wharton's stories and novels have been widely compared with
    (a) Henry James (b) Henry Adams
    (c) Gertrude Steen (d) John Steinbeck
56. Ezra Pound was well versed in
    (a) Greek literature
    (b) Ancient-Indian scriptures
    (c) Egyptian literature
    (d) Anglo-Saxon, Italian Chinese literatures
57. Pound has translated extensively from
    (a) French (b) Italian
    (c) Greek (d) Chinese
58. Why Pound was called an 'imagest'?
    (a) He used imagery.
    (b) He subscribed to the need of direct treatment of the thing, to use a word only which has a direct relevance, to compose in the sequence of musical phrase.
    (c) New fashion in poetry.
    (d) No ornamentation or good ornamentation.
59. Which poem is one of the first to make Ezra Pound famous?
    (a) 'A Virginal'
    (b) 'A Pact'
    (c) 'Contos'
    (d) 'Ballad of the Goodly Fere'
60. Who wrote 'Chicago'?
    (a) Carl Sandburg
    (b) Wallace Stevens
    (c) Edgar lee Masters
    (d) Archibald Macleish
61. Which group of poets are called 'Chicago Poets?'
    (a) Carl Sanburg, Vachel Lindsay; Edgar Lee, Harvet
    (b) Robert Frost, Edgar Allen Poe, Emerson
    (c) William Carlos William, E.E. Cummings, Archibald
    (d) Archibald, Carl Sandburg, Edgar Allen Poe.
62. Frost was called the first American poet
    (a) who achieved world recognition
    (b) who can be labeled a real master-poet
    (c) depicted American landscape
    (d) who enlogized shoemaking
63. In which poem Frost wrote 'Good fences make good neighbours'?
    (a) Reluctance
    (b) Mending wall
    (c) The Posture
    (d) In Hardwood Groves
64. What did Frost say in 'The Gift Outright'?
    (a) The historical past of Americans.
    (b) The task ahead before the nation.
    (c) The role of Americans in the Post II World War era.
    (d) The ambiguous relationship of Americans with the land and freedom. Giving gift which was already theirs—the hard way.
65. Hart Crane belongs to which part of America?
    (a) Boston (b) New York
    (c) Ohio (d) Philadelphia
66. What other poetic features are achievements of Hart Crane?
    (a) Music
    (b) Metaphor
    (c) Logical employment of words
    (d) Combination of music and metaphor
67. Theodore Roethke is close to W.B. Yeats in
    (a) Visionary Strain
    (b) Vision of Life

(c) Understanding of life characteristics
(d) Great sensibility

68. Hemingway reached the height of his creativity in *A Farewell to Arms and For Whom the Bell Tolls* which were
(a) love poems (b) romantic plays
(c) war novels (d) satirical plays

69. Fitzgerald in his works concentrated particularly upon
(a) love
(b) satirising society
(c) the aristocracy of wealth
(d) None of the above

70. Which of Fitzgerald's works was left unfurnished?
(a) *The Last Tycoon*
(b) *The Crack-up*
(c) *Tender is the Night*
(d) *The Great Gatsby*

71. John Steinback was awarded the Nobel Prize for Literature in
(a) 1960 (b) 1962
(c) 1965 (d) 1970

72. Which work brought John Steinback Success?
(a) *Long Valley*
(b) *Tortilla Flat*
(c) *In Dubious Battle*
(d) *Of Mice and Men*

73. William Faulkner received the Nobel Prize in
(a) 1920 (b) 1925
(c) 1950 (d) 1960

74. Who wrote Thomas Woolfe's biography?
(a) Elizabeth Nowell
(b) John Dos Passos
(c) Ernest Hemingway
(d) F. Scott Fitzgerald

75. As a writer, Woolfe's most precious asset was
(a) imagination (b) freedom
(c) love (d) foresight

76. Eugene O' Neil is an American playwright of
(a) the 19th century
(b) the 20th century
(c) Post-second World War
(d) None of the above

77. In the Hairy Ape O' Neill presents
(a) realism
(b) symbolism
(c) realism with symbolic expression
(d) None of the above

78. 'Lazarus laughed' is O Neill's
(a) symbolic drama
(b) religious chorus
(c) tribute to Christian character
(d) poetic drama

79. O' Neill was influenced by
(a) Greek tragedies
(b) Ibsen and Strindberg
(c) Shakespeare
(d) None of the above

80. Name the poet who got the Pulitzer Prize in 1961 for his 'Collected Poems' published in 1953
(a) Edward Fitzgerald
(b) Conrad Alken
(c) John Steinbeck
(d) Norman Mailer

81. Edward Albee (Franklin) is a
(a) novelist (b) poet
(c) critic (d) playwright

82. Who said "All souls have a personal identify with God and abide in Him"?
(a) Courad Alken
(b) A.B. Streeter

(c) Louisa May Alcott
(d) Amos Bronson Alcott

83. 'Winesburg, Ohio' (1919) by Anderson is a
(a) Novel (b) Poetry collection
(c) One-out Play (d) Short-Story

84. Issae Asimor was a
(a) Russian (b) Hungarian
(c) Polish (d) Dutch

85. Who among the following is a science fiction writer?
(a) Irving Babbit (b) James Baldwin
(c) Issac Asmov (d) Conrad Alken

86. Which prize was awarded to Bellow's 'Humbold't Gift'?
(a) Nobel Prize
(b) Booker Prize
(c) Pulitzer Prize
(d) National Book Award

87. Saul Bellow received Novel Prize for Literature in
(a) 1976 (b) 1967
(c) 1987 (d) 1997

88. An early American writer who exercised a great influence on Cooper, Poe and Hawthrone was
(a) Charles Brockden Brown
(b) Pearl S. Buck
(c) Paul Bowle's
(d) None of the above

89. Which novel of Pearl S. Buck describes about the scientists working on the atom bomb?
(a) *The Hidden Flower*
(b) *Dragor Seed*
(c) *Command the Morning*
(d) *The Promise*

90. Which of the following novels of Bernard Malamud won National book Award as well as the Pultizer Prize?
(a) *The Fixer* (b) *The Natural*
(c) *The Tenants* (d) *A New Life*

91. Bob Smith is the central figure in Eugene O' Neill's play titled
(a) *The Iceman Cometh*
(b) *A Farewell to Arms*
(c) *The Hairy Ape*
(d) *Gold*

92. Name the play of Eugene O' Neill which fused symbolism, poetry and the affirmation of a pagan idealism in an ironic tragedy of modern materialism.
(a) *The Great God Brown*
(b) *Strange Interlude*
(c) *The Fountain*
(d) *The Emperor Jone*

93. In 'Strange Interlude O' Neill attempted to create a dramatic technique using the stream-of-conciousness method in a nine-act tragedy of frustrated desire which prize did he get for it?
(a) Booker Prize
(b) Nobel Prize
(c) Pulitzer Prize
(d) National Book Prize

94. Edger Allan Poe, on the death of his parents, was taken into the home of a Richmond merchant named
(a) Joseph Allan (b) John Allan
(c) William Allan (d) Marcos Allan

95. 'The Gift of the Mage', 'A Retrived Reformation' 'The Furnished Room' and 'After Twenty' years are the famous stories of
(a) Leo Tolstoy (b) Ayan Rand
(c) John Steinbeck (d) O' Henry

96. Which play of Irwin Shaw depicts the feelings of a woman dreaming of the life of her unborn son?
(a) *Siege*
(b) *Sons and Soldiers*

(c) *Retreat to Pleasure*
(d) *Children from their games*

97. 'American Harvest' (1942) is an anthology by
(a) Allen Ginsberry (b) Wallace Stevens
(c) Allen Tale (d) Archibald

98. Which American author wrote a book on V.S. Naipaul in 1972?
(a) Lawrence Thompson
(b) Leon Uris
(c) Paul Theroux
(d) John Updike

99. Who wrote *Walden*, *Excursions*, *The Maine Wood* and *A Yankee in Canada*?
(a) Lionel Trilling
(b) John Reuben Thompson
(c) Bernard Malmud
(d) Henry David Thourean

100. Henry David Thourean died of
(a) chicken Pox (b) tuberculosis
(c) heart-attack (d) drowning

101. Identify the auto-biography of Edith Wharton.
(a) *The Spark*
(b) *A Backward Glance*
(c) *Here and Beyond*
(d) *The Mother*

102. Who wrote the 'Leaves of Grass' one of the classics of world poetry?
(a) Walt Whitman (b) Robert frost
(c) T.S. Eliot (d) Emily Dickenson

103. Which nobel of John Steinback won him Pultizer Prize and is considered the chief cause of the Nobel Prize he was conferred in 1962?
(a) *The Grapes of Wrath*
(b) *Tortilla Flat*
(c) *Of Mice and Men*
(d) *Burning Bright*

104. Who wrote 'The Necessary Angel' in 1951 which contains seven essay on 'Reality and the Imagination'?
(a) Ezra Pound (b) Ayan Rand
(c) J.C. Ransom (d) Wallace Stevens

105. Identify the autobiography of Sherwood Eddy.
(a) *A Pilgrimage of Ideas*
(b) *I Have Seen God Do it*
(c) *Man Discover God*
(d) *Eighty Adventure Years*

106. Novels such as *Sound of Honour*, *Decline and Fall* and *Scoop* were written by
(a) P.G. Wodehouse
(b) George Orwell
(c) Christopher Isherwood
(d) Evelyn Waugh

107. Who worked as a journalist of 'The Timed' from 1926 to 1930?
(a) Evelyn Waugh
(b) Angus Wilson
(c) Graham Greene
(d) Stephen Spender

108. Identify the novel of Iris Murdoch that has a religious theme.
(a) *The Sacred and Profana Love Machine*
(b) *Henry and Cato*
(c) *The Time of the Angels*
(d) *Nuns and Soldiers*

109. Which is the first volume of autobiography by Dorris Lessing?
(a) *The Golden Notebirr*
(b) *African Laughto*
(c) *Under My Skin*
(d) *London Observed*

110. We get a glimpse of the powerful personality of W.H. Auden in the autobiography of

(a) Christopher Isherwood
(b) Evelyn Waugh
(c) Stephen Spender
(d) W.H. Auden

111. Stephen Spender, W.H. Auden, C. Day Lewis and Louis Macneice formed a very influential group of left-wing writers in the 1930s alongwith a novelist and playwright named ________
(a) Christopher Isherwood
(b) Christopher Fry
(c) William Golding
(d) Anthony Burgess

112. The theme of 'The Temple' by Stephen Spender, a novel that was written almost fifty years before its publication is
(a) Polygamy (b) Polyandry
(c) Homosexuality (d) All of the above

113. When did Harold Pinter receive the Nobel Prize for literature?
(a) 2002 (b) 2003
(c) 2004 (d) 2005

114. Which of the following is a One-act Play by Harold Pinter?
(a) *The Basement*
(b) *Silence*
(c) *Night School*
(d) *The Handmaids Tale*

115. Who was awarded the Nobel Prize 1972?
(a) Pablo Neruda (b) Heinrich Boll
(c) Patrick white (d) Eyvind Johnson

116. Who wrote his detective novels under the Pseudoname Nicholas Blake?
(a) Noel Coward (b) Robert Bold
(c) Cecid Day-Lewis (d) Brendor Behan

117. Samuel Beckett was conferred the Nobel Prize for literature in
(a) 1965 (b) 1969
(c) 1974 (d) 1981

118. Who wrote the famous play *A Man For All Seasons* in 1960?
(a) Samuel Beckett
(b) Kingsley A miss
(c) Malcolm Bradbury
(d) Robert Bolt

119. Name the first play written by Christopher Fry.
(a) *The Boy with a Cart*
(b) *A Phoenix too Frequent*
(c) *The First Born*
(d) *Thor, with Angels*

120. William Golding got the Booker Prize for his novel
(a) *Close Quarters*
(b) *Lord of the Flies*
(c) *The Spire*
(d) *Rites of Passage*

121. When did William Golding got the Nobel Prize for literature?
(a) 1983 (b) 1984
(c) 1985 (d) 1982

122. Christopher Isherwood's novel which expresses 'an autobiographical treatment of sexual problems' is
(a) *A Single Man*
(b) *Meeting by a River*
(c) *Mr. Norris Changer*
(d) *Goodbye to Berlin*

123. V.S. Naipaul got the Nobel Prize for literature in
(a) 1999 (b) 2000
(c) 2001 (d) 2005

124. Name the first published novel of Margaret Drabble.
(a) *The Waterfall*
(b) *A Summer Bird-Cage*
(c) *The Middle Ground*
(d) *The Realms of Gold*

125. Thomas Dylan was a
(a) biographer (b) novelist
(c) essayist (d) poet

126. *The Map of Love* (1939) and *Death and Eubances* (1946) are the literary works of
(a) V.S. Naipaul (b) C.D. Lewis
(c) Thomas Dylan (d) J.M. Barrie

127. Which of the following is a novel by Allan Sillitoe?
(a) *Key to the Door*
(b) *A Start in Life*
(c) *The Flame of Life*
(d) *Out of the Whirlpool*

128. David Lodge joined a University on 1976 as professor of Modern English Literature. It is
(a) Birmingham (b) Dublin
(c) New York (d) Liverpole

129. Which of the following is a play by Agatha Christie?
(a) *Murder in Mesopotamia*
(b) *Appointment Death*
(c) *Absent in the Spring*
(d) *Witness for the Prosecution*

130. John Osborne's pungently observant and equally spiteful autobiography is
(a) That Time
(b) A Better Class of Person
(c) A Bond Honoure
(d) The Unnameable

131. Who was George Orwell?
(a) Novelist (b) Playwright
(c) Story-teller (d) Dramatist

132. 'They fuck you up, your mum and dad." This is the opening line of Larkin's poem
(a) 'To The Sea'
(b) 'Church Going'
(c) 'This Be The Verse'
(d) 'Annus Mirabilis'

133. This playwright started writing under 'nom de plume' and died at a very going age of thirty four. Which writer is being referred to here?
(a) John Fowles
(b) Terence Ratigan
(c) Joe Orton
(d) Arthur Miller

134. Who began her literary career in 1985 with the publication of Oranges Are not the Only Fruit, a wity, perceptive study of a provincial childhood in a women dominated confines of an evangelical Christian Sell?
(a) Rebecca West
(b) Elizabeth Bowen
(c) Barbara Pym
(d) Jeanette Winterson

135. Who wrote 'The Last Testerment of Oscar Wilde?'
(a) Alvisdair Gray (b) Brian Friel
(c) Peter Ackroyd (d) Ian McEvan

136. Who is the central character in Salman Rushdies famous novel *Midnight's Children*?
(a) Abdul Gaffar (b) Saleem Sinal
(c) Meera Menor (d) None of the above

137. Identify the novel of Salman Rushdie which has been interpreted by many Muslims as his deliberate blasphemy.
(a) *The Ground Beneath His Feet*
(b) *Sour Sweet*
(c) *The Moor Last Sign*
(d) *Satanic Verses*

138. In 1999, which writer was chosen as the 'British Personality of the Millennium' by listeners to a popular news programme?
(a) Shakespeare (b) Wordsworth
(c) T.S. Eliot (d) Bernard Shaw

139. The play *Rosencrantz and Guildenstern Are Dead*, was written by
(a) Arnold Wesker (b) Tom Stoppard
(c) Harold Pinter (d) Joe Orton

140. What is the real name of George Orwell?
(a) Eric Blair (b) Eric Ambler
(c) Eric Evans (d) Smith

141. Who is the movement poet?
(a) Philip Larkin (b) Ted Higher
(c) T.S. Eliot (d) W.H. Auden

142. The Oxford Movement which was led by the teachers was essentially
(a) religious movement
(b) a literary movement
(c) a political movement
(d) a social movement

143. The term neo-romanticism can be associated him
(a) Ezra Pound (b) T.S. Eliot
(c) Thomas Dylan (d) W.H. Auden

144. The 'Auden Group' of poets consists of W.H. Auden, Stephen, Cecil Day Lewis and
(a) Louis Mc Neice
(b) Dylan Thomas
(c) Keith Douglas
(d) William golding

145. Who is regarded as the father of the neo-romantic poetry of the 1940s?
(a) W.H. Auden
(b) Thomas Dylan
(c) Christopher Isherwood
(d) Christopher Fry

146. The Anthology Some Imagist poets was published in 1915 by
(a) Ezre Pound (b) Army Lowell
(c) William Carlos (d) None of the above

147. Which of the following group of poets does not belong to the 20th century?
(a) Pre-Raphaelites (b) Imagism
(c) New Signatures (d) Geogians

148. Edgar Allen Poe's 'Eureke' is a
(a) Poem (b) Play
(c) Short-Story (d) Prose-poems

149. Who is the author of 'Zipzag Way'?
(a) Anita Desai
(b) Kiran Desai
(c) Anubha Chauhan
(d) Shashi Deshpande

150. Christopher Isherwood has collaborated in the translation of the great Indian Classic
(a) The Ramayan
(b) The Mahabharata
(c) The Gita
(d) The Rig Veda

151. Which writer has won the 'PEN's Asian Poetry Prize?'
(a) Shiv K. Kumar
(b) Kamala Das
(c) Nissim Ezekiel
(d) A.K. Ramanujan

152. Which is the latest book of verse of Shiv K. Kumar?
(a) *Articulate Silences*
(b) *Cobwebs in the Sun*
(c) *Woolgathering*
(d) *Woodpeckers*

153. Shiv K. Kumar has described Sleeplessness caused by one's wife's infidelity in which poem?
(a) Inscomnia (b) Rape
(c) Bedroom (d) The Ring

154. Which poet has described his poetry as a 'totally impressionistic recording of subjective responses'?
(a) Adel Jussawalla
(b) Keki N. Daruwalla

(c) A.K. Ramanujan
(d) Kamala Das

155. "Cultivating an extreme austerity in style... his poems are so few but they are marble images of integrity". Here 'his' refers to
(a) Arun Kolatkar
(b) R. Parthasarthy
(c) Nissim Ezekiel
(d) A.K. Ramanujan

156. Who among the following poets is a doctor by Profession?
(a) Arun Kolaticar (b) Gieve Patel
(c) K.N. Daruwalla (d) J. Mahapatra

157. Which work of Mahapatra won him the Sahitya Academi Award in 1981?
(a) The False Start (b) Relationship
(c) Close the Sky (d) Waiting

158. Arun Kolatkar is a bilingual poet who writes both in
(a) Marathi and English
(b) Bengali and English
(c) English and Punjabi
(d) Marathi and Punjabi

159. The poem 'Tribute to Pape' has been composed by
(a) Mamta Kalia (b) Kamala Das
(c) K.N. Daruwalla (d) Kolaticas

160. Which author has written stories relating to Famine Stricken Bengal?
(a) Sunity Devi (b) Cornelia Sorabji
(c) Ela Sen (d) C.T. Ramabai

161. Attiah Hosain wrote a collection of short stories.
(a) *Phoenix led and other stories*
(b) *A Garland of Stories*
(c) *Shadow on the wall*
(d) *Gifts of Passage*

162. Who has written the collection of short stories came for a Coffee, please?
(a) Malathi Rao
(b) Margaret Chatterji
(c) Juliette Banerjee
(d) Vasantha Ravindras

163. Which story of Khwaja Ahmad Abbas describes the flight of pavement of wellers in Bombay?
(a) *Cartoon*
(b) *One Thousand Nights*
(c) *Wheat and Roses*
(d) *The Black Sun*

164. The recent collection of stories *A Bride for the Sahib* has been written by
(a) M.R. Anand (b) R.K. Narayan
(c) Khushwant Singh (d) Raja Rao

165. Cleopatra is a character in Aurobindo's play
(a) *Perseus the Deliverer*
(b) *Rodogune*
(c) *Vasavadutta*
(d) None of the above

166. Which dramatist writes his plays first in Kannada and their translates them into English?
(a) Vijay Tendulkar (b) Girish Karnad
(c) Tagore (d) None of the above

167. Which play of Kannada is a commentary on our own society and its politicians and officials?
(a) Naga-Mandala (b) Yayati
(c) Tughlaq (d) Hayavadana

168. Which play of Asif Currimbhoy centres round the Bengal nexalite movement?
(a) The Refugee (b) Inguilab
(c) The Miracle Seed (d) Mansoon

169. Which novel by Bhabani Bhattacharya as a 'modern fable of India at the time of Independence'?

(a) *Music for Mohini*
(b) *So Many Hungers*
(c) *A Goddess Named Gold*
(d) None of the above

170. Which novel depicts the Chinese invasim of 1962?
(a) *Music for Mohini*
(b) *Shadow from Ladakh*
(c) *So Many Hungers*
(d) *He Who Rides a Tigs*

171. Which novel of Anita Desai is considered to be 'an epic on Calcutta'?
(a) *Bye-Bye Blackbird*
(b) *Voices in the City*
(c) *The Village By the Sea*
(d) *In Custody*

172. Which novel of Anita Desai has been described as a 'four dimensional piece'?
(a) *Cry, the Peacock*
(b) *Clear Light of Day*
(c) *In Custody*
(d) *Voices in the City*

173. The novel *Hullabaloo in the Guava Orchard* has been written by
(a) Anita Desai
(b) Kiran Desai
(c) Shashi Deshpande
(d) Nayantara Sehgal

174. Which novel of Anita Desai has been considered "more individual less generalized and conventional than her earlier fiction"?
(a) *Cry, the Peacock*
(b) *In Custody*
(c) *Voices in the City*
(d) *Clear Light of Day*

175. Who is the Central character in Anita Nair's novel *Ladies' Coupe*?
(a) Janaki (b) Akhilendeswari
(c) Margaret (d) Prabha

176. Unweiling India is a well known work of
(a) Manju Kapur (b) Anees Jung
(c) Geeta Mehta (d) Shobha De

177. Anees Jung is a muslim woman from
(a) Hyderabad (b) Lucknow
(c) Kashmir (d) Delhi

178. Which novel deals with the theme of lesbianism?
(a) *Difficult Daughters*
(b) *A Marked Woman*
(c) *Storm in Chandigarh*
(d) *Roots and Shadows*

179. Who is untouchable in *The God of Small Things*?
(a) Esthappen (b) Velutha
(c) Father Mulligan (d) Pappachi

180. The title of Bharati Mukherjee's novel *The Holder of the World* is after the name of a Mughal emperor, who is he?
(a) Aurangzeb (b) Shahjahan
(c) Akbar (d) Humayun

181. Who is the first Asian writer to win as individual Pulitzer Prize, America's ultimate literary accolade?
(a) Saul Bellow (b) E. Hemingway
(c) Jhumpa Lahiri (d) Pearl S. Buce

182. Which novel of Taslima Nasreen is written in loving memory of all who have left their nation and migrated to other countries like herself?
(a) *Lajja* (b) *Fera*
(c) *Shodh* (d) None of the above

183. *Forever Free* is a novel written by
(a) Raji Narasimhan
(b) Taslima Nasreen
(c) Jhumpa Lahiri
(d) Geeta Mehta

184. 'An Unfinished Autobiography' is a well-known work of

(a) Nayantara Sehgal
(b) Indira Goswami
(c) Shobha De
(d) Jhumpa Lahiri

185. *Lihaaf*, a popular novel, written before independence, is a work of
(a) Shobha De
(b) Ismat Chugtai
(c) Anita Desai
(d) Shashi Deshpande

186. Padma is the central character in the novel of Rushdie's
(a) *Shame*
(b) *The Satanic Verses*
(c) *Midnight's Children*
(d) *Grimus*

187. Who has translated Rajinder Singh Bedi's Urdu novel *Ek Chadar Maili Si* into English as *I Take This Woman*?
(a) Arun Joshi (b) Khushwant Singh
(c) Shashi Tharoor (d) Ruskin Bond

188. Which novel won Chaman Nahal Sahitya Akademi Award?
(a) *The English Queens*
(b) *Azadi*
(c) *Into Another Dawn*
(d) *My True Faces*

189. *An Equal Music* is the novel written by
(a) Amitabh Ghosh (b) Vikram Seth
(c) Vikram Chandra (d) Salman Rushdie

190. Which two authors have been described as 'Terrible Twins' of Indian-English fiction?
(a) Salman Rushdie and Vikram Seth
(b) Vikram Seth and Shashi Tharoor
(c) Shashi Tharoor and Salman Rushdie
(d) Arun Joshi and Vikram Seth

191. Which work of Ved Mehta is autobiographies of
(a) *Face to Face*
(b) *Delinguent Chacha*
(c) *Fly and the Fly*
(d) *The New Theologian*

192. The Partition of India and the consequent trauma of the East Bengali Psyche is focused in Amitabh Ghosh's
(a) *The Countdown*
(b) *The Shadow Lines*
(c) *The Calcutta Chromosome*
(d) *In an Antique Land*

ANSWERS

1. (a)	2. (b)	3. (c)	4. (c)	5. (b)	6. (c)
7. (d)	8. (d)	9. (b)	10. (a)	11. (b)	12. (a)
13. (c)	14. (d)	15. (a)	16. (c)	17. (b)	18. (c)
19. (b)	20. (c)	21. (d)	22. (b)	23. (b)	24. (b)
25. (a)	26. (b)	27. (b)	28. (d)	29. (b)	30. (b)
31. (a)	32. (b)	33. (b)	34. (a)	35. (a)	36. (a)
37. (a)	38. (a)	39. (b)	40. (a)	41. (d)	42. (c)
43. (a)	44. (a)	45. (d)	46. (a)	47. (b)	48. (a)
49. (d)	50. (a)	51. (d)	52. (a)	53. (a)	54. (a)
55. (a)	56. (d)	57. (d)	58. (b)	59. (d)	60. (a)

61. (a)	62. (b)	63. (b)	64. (d)	65. (c)	66. (d)
67. (a)	68. (c)	69. (c)	70. (b)	71. (b)	72. (b)
73. (c)	74. (a)	75. (b)	76. (b)	77. (c)	78. (d)
79. (a)	80. (b)	81. (d)	82. (d)	83. (b)	84. (a)
85. (c)	86. (c)	87. (a)	88. (a)	89. (c)	90. (a)
91. (c)	92. (a)	93. (c)	94. (b)	95. (d)	96. (b)
97. (c)	98. (c)	99. (d)	100. (c)	101. (b)	102. (a)
103. (a)	104. (d)	105. (a)	106. (d)	107. (c)	108. (c)
109. (c)	110. (c)	111. (a)	112. (c)	113. (d)	114. (b)
115. (b)	116. (c)	117. (b)	118. (d)	119. (a)	120. (d)
121. (a)	122. (a)	123. (c)	124. (b)	125. (b)	126. (c)
127. (d)	128. (a)	129. (d)	130. (b)	131. (a)	132. (c)
133. (c)	134. (d)	135. (c)	136. (b)	137. (d)	138. (a)
139. (b)	140. (a)	141. (a)	142. (a)	143. (c)	144. (a)
145. (b)	146. (b)	147. (a)	148. (d)	149. (a)	150. (b)
151. (b)	152. (c)	153. (a)	154. (b)	155. (b)	156. (b)
157. (b)	158. (a)	159. (a)	160. (c)	161. (a)	162. (a)
163. (b)	164. (d)	165. (b)	166. (b)	167. (c)	168. (b)
169. (b)	170. (b)	171. (b)	172. (b)	173. (b)	174. (b)
175. (b)	176. (b)	177. (a)	178. (b)	179. (b)	180. (a)
181. (c)	182. (b)	183. (a)	184. (b)	185. (b)	186. (c)
187. (b)	188. (b)	189. (b)	190. (a)	191. (a)	192. (b)

19

Literary Theory and Criticism

The word 'criticism' is derived from the Greek root Krinei which means 'to judge', and the term kritikos means 'a judge of literature'. The Greek term originated as early as in the fourth century. The term criticism, as applied to the study and analysis of a body of literary writing, developed only in the seventeenth century in Europe, and later, became a term used in common parlance accepted as being authoritative. In fact it encompasses three distinguishable fields of inquiry-literary theory, literary history, and literary (or evaluable) criticism retaining the original Greek sense.

Literary Theory lays down Principles of literature, its categories and criteria and describes the features and forms that make up a literary work. It is a systematic account of the nature of literature. Literary criticism deals with the understanding and appreciation of specific works and authors. Due to various reasons the word criticism has come to be replaced by more comprehensive terms as theory (just theory and not literary theory), culture studies etc. In this sense, the origins and history of literature, its nature and function, and its relationship to our life and society. Literary history and literary criticism enrich each other, and there can be no separation between the two.

Classical literary criticism takes its origin from classical philosophy. It was in the early fourth century, mostly from out of the views held by Plato and Aristotle who, for the first time, made a sustained and systematic inquiry into the nature of art and its modes of existence.

Aristophanes (circa 450-385 BC), the Greek poet, may be singled out as one who, for the first time, spoke of the rights and duties of the poet. He took upon himself the role of a social reformer and satirist. He is generally thought to be one of the founding fathers of ancient literary criticism. His play *Frogs* is the earliest attempt at practical criticism in which the playwright weighs the merits of Aeschylus and Euripdes as stylists.

Plato (circa 429-347 BC) Plato was the first to expound a theory of art in general terms, and his views have exerted a strong influence on every generation of thinkers who came after him. He was a philosopher and a poet rolled into one. In his dialogue form, one finds the truth and science of philosophy coexviting with the beauty and art of poetry. Ironically Plato banishes all poets from his ideal state. He exiles poets on two grounds. The first is the metaphysical and, the second, ethical Plato regarded the study of morals as basic, and wanted all arts to be guided by moral principles value, truth, and social significance of literature, we find that there is a storehouse of knowledge available in Plato. It is with him that Literary criticism truly begins. He firmly established criticism and placed it on a high pedestal. Poetry is not just a matter of words and technique, but is a lofty and mysterious creation of man.

Aristotle (384-322 BC) Aristotle was an academic, a man of letters, a naturalist, and, in the words of Eliot, 'a perfect critic'. Aristotle owed his philosophical career to his great master

Plato. Rhetoric and Poetics contain the literary criticism of Aristotle, and both works are his lecture notes. Apart from the Bible, no other work has appeared in more editions than poetics. There are wide disagreements among them about the full meaning and implications of these terms and concepts: mimesis, katharsis, humaritia and spoudaios.

Mimesis—The most commonly accepted English equivalent of this Greek term is imitation. Whereas for Plato imitation implies copying and hence, trivial and insignificant, it is creative and dynamic for Aristotle. The artist imitates things as they ought to be, and so, art is a free and voluntary activity of the human consciousness, free from any utilitarian motives. Mimesis also implies the active mode of constructing an art object according to universal from is imparted to the works. Aristotle gave a new dimension to the word 'imitation'. It does not mean photographic reproduction. It is often said that drama holds the mirror upto nature. Poetic imitation, for Aristotle, is an imitation of inner human action.

Katharsis—This is a key word in Aristotle occurring only twice in Poetics. It occurs in chapter 6 in which tragedy is defined as "an imitation of an action that is serious, complete, and of a certain magnitude, in language embellished with each kind of found in separate parts of the play; in the form of action, not or narrative, through pity and fear effecting the proper purgation (Katharsis) of these emotions."

Aristotle's theory of Katharsis may be considered to be his reply to Plato's charge against tragedy that it devitalizes our emotions. Pity and fear describe a process of moral and imaginative identification with the agent. When we come out of this involvement, we find ourselves inwardly transformed and feel a sense of release and serenity. It may mean at therapentic, moral, structural and intellectual level. In the sense Katharsis is translated as purgation. It means that by presenting the emotions of pity and of the excesses of these emotions. The purpose audience by disciplining it, and refining it by removing the excesses.

As a religious metaphor, Katharsis suggests 'the sense of purification'. In tragedy we realize that the good, virtuous, and innocent people may be destroyed, but the values of goodness, virtue, and innocence remain sound and serene. Tragedy leads to an awakening. Katharsis is also a kind of 'insight experience'. The result of Katharsis is emotional balance, or equilibrium. It involves restoration of emotional health. Aristotle sees art not as being harmful as Plato does, but as being beneficial, either as therapy, or a moralizing agent, or as a release from guilt, or as a supreme form of learning.

Hamartia—or tragic flaw derives its meaning etymologically from archery. It means 'to miss the mark', 'to err or fail'. In the Gospel according to St. John, the term means 'sin'. The Protagonist commits a moral error, and for this, he received his punishment. The tragic flaw occurs when he applies the laws that operate in the fendal world to the family by demanding a profession of love from his daughters. Aristotle's view of tragedy is for more sophisticated than a melodramatic notion.

Spoudaios—(noble character) For Aristotle, character is what determines moral choice. Tragedy, imitates noble character, and comedy base character. Aristotle never even once said that someone of the common mould can not be a tragic hero. The nobility referred to in Poetics is morally determined, and not socially construed. Aristotle devolves fourteen chapters for a full discussion of the tragic spirit. He spells out the elements which are the different components of a tragedy. Hierarchically, they are plot, character, thought, diction, spectable and song.

Character is that which reveals moral purpose. Aristotle holds that with respect to the requirements of art "a probable impossibility is to be preferred to a thing improbable and yet possible".

Aristotle discovered that pity and fear are the two emotions which arouse tragic feelings in humans. The tragic emotions unite the other concepts, and a wholesome theory of tragedy is built. Pity and fear demand the tragic hero to be noble; only then his fall from happiness to misery arouses in us these emotions.

The rebirth of Poetics took place in the twentieth century. Much of modern criticism derives from Aristotle. Poetics has only twenty-six chapters. The first five are introductory chapters, the next eight, diction and the next four are on the epic, and the very last one deals with problems in criticism. Lyric poetry is completely ignored, only the epic and the comedy are given only sketchy treatment.

HORACE (ALLIAS QUINTUS HORATIUS FLACCUS) (65-68 BC)

The greatest Roman poet-critic, Horace lived at a peaceful time conducive to discussion about art. Virgil, Ovid and Horace belonged to the age that is now called the Angustan Age. Horace is more practically oriented though less philosophical than Aristotle. According to him a writer should exercise judgement in his choice of words, for words have personality, and are subject to the laws of change. Poets, for him, are born as well as made. The ultimate goal of poetry is to instruct and afford pleasure. Western criticism has accepted this Horation dictum as an unwritten truth. The romantic critics did not have much use for Horace. Horace was read and discussed the Renaissance.

The importance and gravity of classical rhetoric as found in Horace is felt in three areas. Motication to compose, the moral issues that govern a work and the factors relating to the style of composition. Horace's positive achievements cannot easily be ignored. He asserts the supremacy of Greek literature, and this is an opening of a new phase in criticism. His conception of imitation meant a recreation. For the attainment of the best results, he lays down a set of principles. His book *The Ars Poetica* is a nice document that gave a new direction to critical thought.

Longinus (1 To 3 Century AD)

The third member of the 'Classical Triumvirate of Criticism' besides Aristotle and Horace, is Longinus. In the domain of Greek thought, he is second only to Aristotle. The emphasis of Longinus is on the literature of power. For him literature is not propaganda, not a sermon, not entertainment. It is vision. Its function is sacramental. We are lifter out of ourselves and carried to a new realism of experience and perception, and filled with ecstasy as if we ourselves had created what we see and hear. Our reaction to the truly sublime is directed not by the power of discursive reason, but by intuition and insight.

Building upon his theory of sublimity, Longinus classifies the five sources of sublimity—

1. Capacity for great thought and a firm grasp of ideas,
2. Inspired emotion and strong passion: these two characteristics, amplitude of mind,
3. Figures of speech and a proper construction of figures,

4. Noble diction,
5. The effect of dignity and elevation, the power to integrate and fuse the elements so as to give them a tone of sublimity.

Longinus was the first critic to talk extensively about the impact of poetry on the readers. This has led to 'reception aesthetics' and reader-response theories. His work 'on sublimity forms the bedrock of western critical thought'.

LITERARY CRITICISM IN THE RENAISSANCE

The term 'Renaissance' is of Italian origin, meaning 'rebirth' or 'reawakening'. It stands for the historical rebirth of literary and cultural movements in the 14th, 15th of 16th centuries. Initially the movement started in France, Germany, England and other countries of Europe.

There was a revival in the study of arts and literature, sparked by an interest in Greek and Roman literature of the Classical Age.

Literary criticism during the Elizabethan age in England was not as rich and diversified as the criticism in Italy and France during the same period. The greatest and the most important work of this age is, of course, Sidney's 'Apologie for Poetry'. Thomas Wilson's 'Art of Rhetoric' (1553) is probably the first work of criticism in the English language. Roger Ascham's 'Schoolmaster' (1568) and Richard Tottel's 'Tottel's Miscellany' (1559) are two other important works. The second phase was a period when attention was paid to the metrics and metrical patterns in poetical composition. 'Art of English Poesic' (1589) by Mary Webb are the earliest works on classification of meter. The third stage is the stage of philosophical criticism of this period are Sir Philip Sidney's 'Apologie for Poetry' (1583), Thomas Campion's 'Art of English Poesy' (1602) and Samuel Daniel's 'Defence of Works' were in the nature of defences against the attacks of the Puritans on poetry, and the classicists on versification.

The fourth stage belonged to the first half of the seventeenth century, and Ben Johnson, the Elizabethan dramatist, was the important figure during this period. Johnson was a classicist, if Sidney defended poetic art, Johnson taught it.

The fifth stage opens up a new dimension in English literary criticism when the French come on the scene, some of its characteristics features were:

1. a devotion to the national cause
2. commitment to classicism in a pure form, and
3. the faith that art should imitate nature.

John Dryden, the poet laureate, became the presiding genius of this period.

Sir Philip Sidney. Sidney is the first critic-and a critic of lasting significant-representing all that is superlative in Renaissance criticism. According to Ben Johnson, he was the 'one in whom all the Muses met'. It was from the Italians that Sidney borrowed the concept of the dramatic unities, the poet as second creator, and tragedy as evoking and winning our admiration. He drew from Horace the idea of the poet being the seer, and the notion of the twin function of poetry. His work was published in two separate editions, 'The Defence of Poesie' by William Ponsonby and 'An Apology for Poetrie' by Henry Olney.

Apologie happens to be the first English text, complete and comprehensive, propounding a set of principles on the art of literature. The form or plan of Apologic conforms to the rhetorical principle of construction. Apologie falls into seven broad divisions:

1. Exordium
2. Narration, describing the antiquity of poetry
3. Proposition, that poetry is imitation
4. Division-Religious, Philosophie, Imitative
5. Proof
6. Regutation, and
7. Peroration

Sidney offers a definition of poetry—a poet is the maker, and poetry is the art of representation. "Poesy therefore is an art of imitation, for so Aristotle termed it in his word mimesis, that is to say, a representing, counterfeiting or figuring forth – to speak metaphorically, a speaking picture, with this end to teach and delight" (146). He classified different categories of poetry, and adds that metre is not necessary for poetry. Poetry is proved to be superior to history and philosophy.

The credit for introducing Aristotelianism should go to Sidney. Sidney may be regarded as the first dramatic critic. His conception of tragedy is an amalgam of medieval notions, and Aristotle's doctrine as interpreted by the Italian critics. Sidney's Apologie can make no claim to originality. Critical doctrines gathered from a variety of sources have been given a recognizable shape and order. By focusing attention on the shortcomings of contemporary literature, his Apologie stimulated interest in the art of writing as a discipline to be consciously and carefully cultivated.

But many of his sentences are long, loose, and often Chimsy. The rules of syntax and grammar are not always respected. But Sidney's prose bears the stamp of his personality.

John Dryden (1631-1700). John Dryden was such an influential personality in so many spheres of learning that the period 1660 to 1700 is rightly called the Age of Dryden. He was a poet, dramatist, translator, critic, all rolled into one. Dr. Samuel Johnson called John Dryden 'the father of English criticism'. T.S. Eliot echoed the same sentiment when he said that Dryden was 'positively the first practitioner of comparison and analysis in the history of criticism'. Much of Dryden's criticism is found in his prefaces. Dryden uses the term 'examen' for critical analysis, and this term was originally used by the French playwright, Corneille. When Dryden wrote prefaces to his plays, he practiced dramatic criticism that was descriptive in nature. The most relevant works of Dryden are 'Defence of an Essay of Dramatic Poesy', 'A Parallel of Poetry and Painting', 'Preface to Fables Ancient and Modern', and 'An Essay of Dramatic Poesy'.

Of Dramatic Poesy deals with major issues in drama: the ancients versus the moderns, the French versus the English, blank verse versus heroic verse. Dryden's tolerance and impartiality are evident in the entire Essay. He favours and defends the genre tragicomedy, rejects the addiction to the unities. His basic faith in the mimetic form of art, and the Horation function of literature is unshakeable itself with the language and style of poets, except for his famous evaluations of Shakespeare and Chaucer. Aristotle, Horaic and Longinus were the major influences on Dryden.

Alexander Pope (1688-1744). Pope aimed largely at improving the literary taste, and establishing exacting standards for literary compositions. His criticism is spread over *An Essay on Criticism* (1711), *Preface to Shakespeare* (1725) *Art of Sinking* (1727-8), *Epistles to*

Angustur (1733), *Preface to the Translation of the Iliad* (1715), and his letters. Pope is not in favour of the conceits of the metaphysical. Poetry of commonsense is the best for man. Pope's use of poetic diction, and use of Scatological words can be justified as Pope was no blind adherent to the rules of composition. He admits that rules are useful in so far as they lead us to the works of great writers of all time, but they must be set aside if they are cramping and wooden to the extent of being dogmatic.

Four classifications of Pope's use are noticeable

1. to refer to all mental and intellectual faculties taken together 'so vast is art, so narrow human wit'.
2. to refer to the gift of the poet, the poet's genius.
3. to refer to the quality of ingenuity in a poet.
4. to refer to the poetic imagination.

In fact Pope's Essay is not a new system, or a new exposition of a view of poetry and criticism, but it constitutes a cultural continuum. There are countless saws and maxims which he has contributed to the English language. External truths are presented in an epigrammatic and terse style. Pope's demands of a critic are beyond the reach of ordinary practitioners.

A little learning is a dangerous thing,
Drink deep, or taste not the Pierian Spring,
There shallow drafts intoxicate the brain,
And drinking largely sobers us again.

He felt that he must possess a level of scholarship almost impossible for the common critic to acquire, he should not practice criticism unless he has established himself as a first rate poet.

Samuel Johnson (1709-84). He is the most widely known figure among the Augustans. His range of reading was phenomenal; he had an insatiable appetite for books. Anti-intellectualism in most characteristic of Johnson. Criticism was a subordinate activity to creative imaginative literature. In Rambler 208, he says, "Criticism, in my opinion, is only to be ranked among the subordinate and instrumental arts." He believed in a direct relationship between life and literature. Religious and moral structures were strongly embedded in his Psyche. There are people who strongly believe that modern criticism starts with Johnson. His greatest work in criticism 'Lives of Poets' alone bears ample testimony to the greatness of his grant among criticism. Johnson literally believed that the aim of criticism is to establish laws with which to estimate excellence in works. Johnson, the lexicographer felt that linguistics was both descriptive and perspective. His first dictionary in the world built on historical principles. (The Dictionary of the English languages). The best of Johnson, his magnum opus, is his lives. The lives of the poets are arranged in the order of the dates of their death. These essays follow a set pattern of a threefold division; biography, character and criticism. English new classical criticism has Dryden at the beginning, Pope in the middle and Johnson at the end. As a confirmed Tory in political belief, he had no sympathy for anything that went along with the Whig belief. Johnson's greatness as a critic has been confirmed by many generations that came after him. As an editor, he was perhaps the first person to establish the principles for sound textual criticism. He was short-sighted and had no eye for beauty in nature and no ear for music. He was nourished strictly on neoclassical thought. Johnson practiced criticism in the Age of Prose. He attacked Milton's 'Lycidas' because the emotions it expresses were insincere. He was in favour of poetic justice when he preferred a happy ending to king lear, little realizing that a tragic end to the play is an emotional necessity.

William Wordsworth. The literary theory of Wordsworth came to be written between the years 1798 and 1815. During this period Wordsworth wrote the *Preface to Lyrical Ballads*, *The Three Part Essay upon Epitaphs* and the *Prefaces to The Excursion* (1814) and *To The Poems* (1815) Wordsworth pleads for the retention of the common speech in poetry. He says, "Good poetry is the spontaneous overflow of powerful feelings, it takes its origin from emotion recollected in tranquility." Wordsworth says that the greater portion of a good poem does not differ from prose as far as the use of language and the order of words go, but the use of metre adds charm and intensifies feelings and emotions. He uses a 'selection' of the language of the rustics, and when this selection is removed, Wordsworth's theory does not work. The literary criticism of Wordsworth is the manifesto of the British Romantic Movement. It effects a formal break with the neoclassical tradition. He rejects the diction of 18th century poetry. His naturalism and emotionalism are quite well known. Wordsworth dismissed elevated vocabulary which excluded the trivial. He disliked personification, pathetic fallacy, periphrasis, inversions, antithesio use of classical mythology, conceits, hyperbole, and rustic speech are hard to define. His own poetic models were Spenser and Milton. For him, poetry is the release of personal emotions.

Wordsworth's theory regarding the spontaneous overflow of powerful feelings is not applicable to all poets in general, and sometimes, even to his own poems. His theory lacks a formal system, because it is mostly occasional; but it is original and not derivative as Shelley's Defence, and quite different from the mere obiter dicta of the other romantics as for example, Keat's Letters. The ultimate value of Wordsworth's Preface lies in the major shift it helped to effect in the emphasis from the relationship between the poem and the reader to that between poet and poem; in other words from critical evaluation and judgement to the creative process itself. Rene Wellek demonstrates that Wordsworth's theory is built on the premise of neoclassicism.

Samuel Taylor Colerdige (1772-1834). Coleridge's achievement as a literary critic is massive, and matchless. Both as a literary critic and as a speculative philosopher, Coleridge is rated as the highest in England. For I.A. Richards, Coleridge is the founding father of all modern criticism. Many of the key terms in his metaphysics are derivatives from German thought. He called himself, 'a High German transcendentalist'. Coleridge built up a systematic epistemology based on a unified method, a method by which creative imagination works. He employs 'the distinction between fancy and imagination as value-based'. 'Imagination' is the 'esemplastic' power, the power that is capable of unifying or building into one imagination is not only a reproductive faculty but is also recreative. Fancy merely assembles and juxtaposes images without transforming them whereas imagination. Moulds them into a new whole. Coleridge's philosophy of organic formalism needs to be distinguished from mechanical formalism.

Coleridge took a holistic look at the poet, his faculty, and his work with its impact on the reader. A true poet is a whole man, ideal in every way, possessing sensibility, philosophic wisdom. Genius and imagination are higher than talent and fancy Coleridge rates the fundamental unity in the poet's mind as the highest faculty, and distinguishes different types of poetic gifts. He does not recognize the distinction between the poet and poetry. Whereas for Wordsworth, 'metre is but an adventitions aid to composition,' Coleridge defends metre in convincing terms. Metre must be organic and not a mere ornament. He insists on unity in a poem; he is a formalish first and last, and does not even bother about questions regarding the value of a cook of literature, Coleridge's key terms are unity and wholeness. In chapter XVII of Biographia Literaria, he reiterates that he adopts with full faith the Aristotelian dictum that 'poetry, as poetry, is essentially ideal. It was Coleridge who introduced the philosophic method in English criticism. According to Herbert Read, Coleridge made criticism into a Science'. Coleridge deferred from the neoclassical school of criticism as practiced by Johnson. All through his life, Coleridge was interested in studying the process of artistic creation.

Matthew Arnold (1822-88). Arnold belongs to the Victorian era. He felt it was his duty to awaken the nation from the shipor into which it had fallen, that he must create a climate for the creative artist to function properly, and the people must be brought to an awareness of the best that is written and thought.

As a true democrat, powered by the spirit of nationalism, Arnold preached his social philosophy of culture (sweetness and light) as the only cure for the spreading all that affected national life. The Arnoldian concept of culture lays stress on the harmonious development of human nature. Culture is not just personal equipment, but a social force leading to social progress. Culture is described by Arnold in the first essay 'Sweetness and Light' in Culture and Anarchy as having its origin in the love of perfection; it is a study of perfection. In the words of Eliot, Arnold's 'study of Poetry' is a classic in English criticism. It is true that Arnold, in the words of Eliot, is a propagandist for criticism. It is equally true that his essays constitute, according to leavis, high pamphleteering. But for Arnold greatness in poetry and genuineness in poetry are one and the same. In Leavis's view, 'we read Arnold gave importance to the unity, wholeness and totality of a work of art'.

Again, for Arnold, poetry that does not possess 'truth and high seriousness'—that which gives to our spirits which they can rest upon-cannot be ranked as great poetry. He has his notions of moral seriousness in his concept of high poetry. "The best poetry is what we want, the best poetry will be found to have a power of forming, sustaining, and delighting us, as nothing else can". The first prose work of Arnold was the *Preface to the Poems* of 1853. He rejected the poetry of the Romantics and the Elizabeth. Arnold rated the English romantic very low in comparison with their continental counterparts. Arnold's views were a reaction to the ideals that romanticism preached. He called Shelly 'a beautiful and ineffectual angel beating in the void hes luminous wings in vain.' Arnold considered both literatures and religion as two indivisible parts of culture. Creative theory was not Arnold's forte. Evaluation of literature was his speciality. His famous phrase 'Literature is a criticism of Life' has meant many things to many people.

T.S. Eliot (1888-1965). In 1919, Thomas Stearns Eliot wrote a very important essay, 'Tradition and the Individual Talent'. It appeared in two instalments in the journal *The Egoist*, which is an invaluable document so far as literary criticism in our time is concerned. His view of tradition is negative in so far as it distrusts novelty or originality, or any kind of revolution or individualistic attempt, and it is positive in that it recommends that the poet should have a sense which makes a writer traditional. The writer should be conscious of the dead writers; the conscious present is but an awareness of the past. The poet must subordinate himself to this tradition, because it is more important than himself, and his personality as a poet. In the essay 'The Function of Criticism', Eliot says that the problem of criticism is one of establishing order. A critic must listen to his inner voice alone. He practices the method of evaluator or judicial criticism, and does not indulge in close analysis of texts as recommended by the New Critics. He is a follower of Arnold, creating an audience for him. Eliot has the readers of his own poetry in his mind when he evaluates other poets particularly the dead ones.

Eliot's essays written during the 1920s and the 1930s helped in changing the course of English Literature history considerably. Eliot replaced the critical orthodoxy of Arnold. For him there has been a decline in English poetry from Shakespeare and Milton to the eighteenth century, with the possible exception of Wordsworth.

In many ways, Eliot has proved himself to be the most important critic of our century. His concept of the impersonal theory of poetry, unified sensibility, his emphasis on the perfection of the spoken idiom for poetry, and his formulae, are all invaluable aids to the understanding and appreciation of poetry. He maintained three types of criticism: creative criticism, historical criticism, and proper criticism. He does not approve of interpretation and judicial criticism. The aim of criticism is 'the return to the work of art with improved perception'. In his essay, 'Religion and Literature', Eliot observes: 'Literary criticism should be completed by criticism from a definite ethical and theological standpoint.... The greatness of literature cannot be determined only literary standards: In his essay 'Hamlet and his Problems', Eliot describes his 'objective correlative'—"The only way of expressing emotion in the form of art is by finding an objective correlative." Eliot always held the view that poetry should approximate to the spoken language as it is spoken during the poet's lifetime. That's why on of the common language and Dryden's language 'which restored English verse to the condtion of speech'. He maintained that Milton corrupted the language by subjecting it to 'a peculiar kind of deterioration' and wrote 'English like a dead language.' He did not favour the poetic prose of the nineteenth century. While he seems to favour prosaic style in poetry, he attacks poetic style in prose. The entire criticism of Eliot deals with poetry of drama (poetic drama) which he tried his best to revive and defend.

Eliot's contribution to the criticism of the novel is not noteworthy. He admired Joyce and he said that "*Ulysses* is a book quite as Irish in material as a book can be, but a book so significant in the history of the English of that I must take its place as a part of the tradition, of that language".

George Watson's estimate of Eliot's achievement runs thus, "Eliot made English criticism look different, but in so simple sense. He offered it a new range of rhetorical possibilities, confirmed it in its increasing contempt for historical processes, and yet reshaped its notion of period, by a handful of brilliant institutions."

In his well known preface to *For Lancelot Andrews* (1928), Eliot openly described himself as a classicist in literature, a royalist in politics, and an Anglo-Catholic in religion.

T.S. Eliot and I.A. Richards are jointly associated as pioneers of the movement of New Criticism. Both of them were among the most influential critics of the twentieth century, only Eliot was descriptive and Richards theoretical.

I.A. Richards (1893-1979). Ivor Armstrong Richards is often referred to as the critical consciousness of our age. John Crowe Ranson begins his book *The New Criticism* with the remark that any discussion of the New critics must start with Dr. Richards, Marry others have the same opinion that he is the creator of modern criticism. He had many things—poet, dramatist, speculative philosopher; but primarily he was a Psychologist and semanticist.

Richard says that the aesthetic state is not any different from the ordinary state in our life. Poetry organizes our impulses and attitudes and mind. Art in general and literature in particular is valuable for us in this sense that it integrates our activities, resolves our mental conflicts and tension, and leads us to a liberated state. Richard calls this harmonized state, this balancing of conflicting impulses, 'synaesthesis'.

Richard's psychologism shows that he is not concerned with the poetic object per se enclosing a certain structure in itself, but only with our responses to the object. The poem is the reader's response to it. Such confessedly open subjectivism leads his to the conclusion that poetic language is ambiguous plurisignant, open to different and diverse meaning Richards along with C.K. Ogden expounded a theory of language. They distinguished between two uses of languages the referential and the emotive. Poetry communicative feelings and emotions, and has nothing to do with meaning or knowledge. Richard's Psychological theory effective communication and worthlessness of the experience with reference to chosen poems in his Practical Criticism is unverifable.

Theories of Criticism

Classical Criticism—Literary criticism is nearly as old as literature. It means understanding and appreciative literature. Classical literary criticism takes its origin from classical philosophy. It was in the early fourth century, mostly from out of the views held by Plato and Aristotle who, for the first time, made a sustained and systematic inquiry into the nature of art and its shape as an independent discipline Aristophanes, the Greek poet, spoke of the rights and duties of a poet. Plato gathered the odds and ends of proto-criticism and articulated them in a coherent manner.

Medieval Criticism—The literary criticism of the medieval period has not been an area of much research and scholarship. By and large, medieval criticism followed the system of classifying literature under the heads of grammar, restoric and logic. The Medieval Age developed a systematic poetic grammar. Great works of antiquity of the Pagan Age, and critical commonplace were made the objects of study and meditation. Horace had a clear influence on the Middle ages, but not Longinus. A considerable amount of medieval criticism dealt with biblical criticism and mysticism and allegorical readings of works. The poets were theologians and their poetry was the overflow of moments of inspiration. Medieval theory was based on a divine plan in which the function of literature was supposed to help an individual to became a better Christian. Though the Middle Ages were by and large a dark period, there are some works which will tell us that these were the ones that prepared the ground for Renaissance thought.

Renaissance Criticism—Literary criticism during the Renaissance was up against a major task of justifying imaginative literature. Many Renaissance scholars successfully answered these charges by blanking the artist and not the art. Renaissance criticism took upon itself the primary duty of writing and reconciling the best elements in Aristotle and Horace, and establishing criticism as an independent field of study. Among Renaissance critics, the following stand out prominently for students of English literature: Pebarch, Scaliger, Minturno, Boccacio and the Italian commentators, Robertello and Castelvetro. J.E. Spingarn's pioneering work *Literary Criticism in the Renaissance* (1899) raises some fundamental questions.

English Neoclassical Criticism—Despite the variety and disparity of writing it is possible to see a unified development in English criticism from Dryden to Johnson. The English neoclassical criticism shows a preference for the Roman rather than the Greek, Horace rather than Aristotle. Neoclassical criticism was concerned with what poets ought to do rather than what they might do or have done. Discussion on art, artist, work and audience centred on the issues of rules and the end results. In it the methodology for the analysis and discussion of works was drawn from the tradition of the rhetoric where the end is persuation rather than pleasure. Art was a set of rules by which nature was imitated, or even improved but dependent on nature as 'the universal light', the ultimate source.

Romantic Criticism—It was Thomas Carlyle she used the terms 'romanticism', 'romantic' and 'romanticist' with reference to the Germans, and in the books and treatises, the term came into vogue in England in the 1850s the French Revolution, with its slogan of liberty, equality and fraternity, fuelled and planted in the minds of people fresh impulses demanding social and political reforms. The writings of Rousseau, William Godwin and Mary Wollstonecraft who pleaded for the vindication of the rights of women influenced public opinion. Concepts such as truth, nature, god and plenitude were redefined. In the domain of literary criticism too, the impact of the changed attitudes was conspicuously noticeable.

Philosophy of Kant and Coleridge and the other of Aristotle known as Formalist Critics and Genre critics.

Russian Formalism—The best achievements of the Russians lie in the novel, and the short story. As for criticism, the second and the third decades of the 20th century noticed a lively debate in Russia on matters relating to poetic art and its understanding but the major breakthrough came about in the form of Russian formalism. It was a major reaction against the biographical determinism, and the posivism of the 19th century. The Russian formalists staveel attacking the historical, sociological, and other extrivisic approaches to literary study. They vehemently opposed the symbolists for whom language was only a medium. It was an attempt to create an independent science of literature which studies literary material specifically. For them, the function of art is to 'make us see things, not to know them.' Russian formalism can be seen as a forerunner to structuralism. The two concepts defamiliarisation and retardation are quite fundamental.

Archetypal Criticism—Archetypal criticism marks the transition from New Criticism to Structuralism. It can be by cultural anthropologists. The most influential book in this respect is *The Golden Bough*, (12 volumes) by the Cambridge anthropologist James Frazer. Among the most noteworthy practitioners of archetypal criticism are Leslie Fiedler, Frances Fergussim, Richard Chase, Philip Wheelwright, Wilson Knight & Mand Boduin. Northrop Frye (1921-91) is one critic who is known as its founding father. Three of his works, *Fearful Symmentry* (1947), *Anatomy of Criticism* (1957) and *Fables of Identity* (1963), stimulated a deeper interest in the study of myths. In his much-anthologised essay, The Archetyper of Literature, Frye expresses his dissatisfaction with New Criticism. His view of life, and his view of literature are one and the same.

Structuralism Criticism—Structuralism has affected many disciplines such as philosophy, anthropology, and literary criticism. Structuralism divides the world into two units; the visible, or payable, or observable and the invisible or underlying. Structuralism excludes both the author and reality as points or reference for interpretation. The structuralism method consists in an analysis of the 'immanent' structures of work. It is an attempt to catch the force of the text, its power, and reduce the possibilities of boredom. It is an aesthetic based on the pleasure of the text. The reader makes explicit the conventions of reading structuralism refutes the Aristotelian 'mimetic' criticism that believes that literature is the imitation of reality. Structuralism rejects the Romantic 'expessive' criticism which views literature as the expression of the feelings of a creative artist. Structuralism replaces the atomism and individualism of New Criticism by its trust in and reliance on universatism.

Deconstruction—All texts, literary and non-literature are made of language. Meanings always proliference in endless ways. Normal traditional interpretation do not recognize the conflicting ideologies of the text. A deconstructive reading looks for meanings in the text that theme in traditional interpretations. The text itself does not resolve the tensions in them into a unity or harmony. We should be alive to this, if we modes of thinking. In a strict sense, nobody ever deconstructs a texts, it deconstructs itself.

Meanings are always disseminated and any deconstructive reading of a text catches a fleeting moment of this dissemination. Barbara Johnson said, "Deconstruction is not synonymous with destruction...it is in fact much closer to the original meaning of the word analysis, which etymologically means 'to undo'—a virtual synonym for 'to deconstruct'". The deconstruction of a text does not proceed by random doubt or arbitrary subversion, but by the careful teasing out of warring forces of significances within the text itself. If anything is destroyed in a deconstructive exponent of deconstruction.

New Historicism—New historicism dismisses the eschatological, or telecological connotations of traditional historians. New historicism is, therefore, historicist rather than historical. It is interested in history-as-text, that is, history as recorded and represented in different documents, which form its texts. Our subjectivity too is shaped by, and shapes, culture. One constitutes the other. New historicism deconstructs the traditional distinction between history (thought to be factual) and literature (thought to be functional). History is another text even as literature is; literature is another cultural artifact, even as history is, and it can tell us something about the social life of the times when they were written. Louis Montrose's famous definition of new historicism is that it centres upon both the historically of the text, and the textuality of history. Old historicism limited itself either to studies about the life of the author's order to know his intentions, or to historical periods to knowthe spirit of the age in which the work was written. New historicism draws from Derrida's view that every aspect and feature of reality is textualised. There is nothing outside the text.

Cultural Materialism—Cultural Materialism and new historicism have several affinities. The former is overfly British and the other overfly American. Cultural criticism is an outgrowth of Marxisan. It includes popular art, fiction and even television. In his notes towards the Definition of Culture—Eliot describes culture as that which makes life worth living. Cultural materialism is apparently Marxist, according to which culture can never transcend material forces and relations of production. Raymond Williams, who was the 'pied-piper' of his generation, gave it its name. Its prime argument is that the culture of the working classes is never taken into consideration in highbrunt criticism of literature. It is considered inferior culture. All cultural productions reveal the role of culture in the circulation of power. Cultural materialism subvert and undreminer the power grid. New historicism and cultural criticism help us in many ways in strengthening our understanding of literature. They help us to see how literary texts participate in the circulation of discourses.

Postcolonial Criticism—As a discipline Literary studies, postcolonialism emerged during the late 1980s or rather in the early 1990s of the last century. The nomenclature 'post-colonialism' is used to refer "to all the culture affected by the imperial process from the moment of colonisation to the present day". Postcolonialism examines and analysis the aftermath of colonization and the effects of colonial oppression. In other words, it analyses the literature that was affected by the imperial process, the literature that grew in response to colonial domination. Cultural colonization still exists, and there has been no complete decolonization. Much of postcolonical identity. Postcolonial, or third phases which can be termed as 'adopt'. Any discussion of postcolonialism cannot afford to by pass these basic issues: the conception and representation of the empire, nationalization and globalization, its relationship with post modernism and feminism, the play and place of language, material practices and control of production.

Reader-Response Criticism—Richards can be called the forerunner of reader-response (also called audience-oriented) criticism. Based on Phitosophic grounds, there can be another route to 'reader-response criticism' justifies what this criticism means, but the fact is that it is not just the response that matters; it is the analysis of how we respond to a given text that matters. In the context of literary studies, it is still evolving and it helps us to understand our own reading processes. It believes that the meaning of a text is contained in the text, and it is not the product of the author or the reader. The reader is absent when the writer writes, and the writer is normally absent when the reader reads. The general theory of the school is classified into four sections: transactional reader-response theory, affective stylistics, subjective reader-response theory and psychological reader-response theory.

Feminist Criticism—By way of redressing the balance, feminist criticism seeks to challenge traditional notions and establish, instead, the perspectives and experiences of women which had been marginalized for ages and ages. The two axious on which feminism is built are (1) gender difference is the foundation for structural inequality between men and women by which women suffer sympathetic social injustice and (2) the inequality between the sexes is not the result of biological necessity, but is produced by cultural construction of gender differences. Feminist theory, broadly, chooses two areas to tackle these issues and develop what critics call a 'criticism of their own'- woman as reader, and woman as writer. While most feminist critics are wary of the frame works in theory built by patriarchy they are quick to seize upon those elements which suit them, like the Psychoanlytic, Marxist and deconstructionist theories.

Psychoanalytic Criticism—The psychoanalytic view of human behaviour is relevant to our experience of Literature. Psychoanalysis is defined as a form of mental therapy which aims to come mental disorders by investigating the interaction of the conscious and unconscious elements of the mind. Much has been taken from Sigmund Frend, who gave his ideas the name psychoanalysis in 1896, Psychoanalytic criticism can be comeniently divided into three phases. The first two belong to the early or classical phase, and the third to the poststructuralist phase. Jacques Locan called 'the French Frend' is a French Psychoanalyst. What Locan was interested in is re-writing, re-interpretating classical Frendian Psychoanalysis in the light of post-structuralist theories. Locan uses linguistic and literary traditions unlike Frend.

Psychoanalytic criticism, whether Frendian or Locanian, helps us in our critical assessment of literary works in many ways. It can be author, text based, or reader-based. Critics must often resort to Psychoanalysis is also used in the writings of literary biographics which are called Psycho-biographies. One finas word Psychoanalytic criticism is neither verifable nor falsifiable.

Marxist Criticism—The German philosopher Karl Marx and the German sociologist Friendrich Engels are the founding fathers of this school of criticism. Marxist criticism is not interested in solving individual problems, or attaining individual salvation. Marxism foregrounds economic realitities of human culture. Marxist Literary theories do not constitute a school. To understand how Marxism Literary theorists have applied these concepts in relation to literature. They can be classified under five headings—

(1) **The Reflection Model**—Literature is understood as reflecting the reality outside it. Literature creates a functional world which is a reflection of the real world.

(2) **The Production Model**—The French Marxist Pierre Macherey developed this theory. Literary composition is seen as productive labour in which materials are turned into end products.

(3) **The Greek Model**—The Rumanian sociologist, Lucien Goldmann, developed this model. The literary work is not to be understood as the expression of the author's self, or his individual genius, but the expression of the social class.

(4) **The Frankfurt School**—of Marxism promoted by Theodox Adorno rejects the formal view a says that Art has its our format laws.

(5) **The Bakhtinian view of Marxism**—treats literature as a social practice, rather than as a form of knowledge. This language based model has opened up several possibilities of rethinking Marxism in the light of the post. Saussurean view of the world.

Hermeneutics—The word 'hermeneutics' comes from a Greek word which means 'to say' or 'to explain', and thus, also 'interpretation'. The term refers both to the theory and the practice of interpretation. The principal function of hermeneutics is to bring to light some work that is obscure and foreign to one's tongue. There is no hermeneutic school of criticism as such, nor does the term stand for any particular brand of interpretation. The oldest tradition in hermeneutics involves Biblical exercises. There is the legal hermeneutics concerned with the understanding and interpretation of the law, and the phicological hermeneutics which is concerned with the preservation of classical texts. As a subject of philosophical enquiry, hermenteutics has occupied the best of minds like Dilthy, Heidegger, Godamer, etc. Hermeneutic thought gets into a blind alley, and it cannot enter into any productive dialogue with poststrucuralist views on language. Deconstructive criticism maintains that it is impossible to unveil, or reach out to the meaning of a text; the text has no meaning at all.

American Criticism—In a strict sense, literary criticism can be sent to have come of age in the U.S. only in the 20th century. George Santayana coined the phrase 'the genteel tradition' to describe the tendency that prevailed in criticism. As a classicist in taste, he depended more on evaluating a literary work on moral grounds, than on analyzing or explaining it. He combines technical philosophy with literary criticism. Two writers of the period who stand out prominently are also two of the greatest American writers: Ralgh Waldo Emerson and Edger Allan Poe. Emerson's essay, The American Scholar, acclaimed as the inaugural address of the declaration of American literary independence, was published in *The Democratic Review* and Poe's *The Philosophy of Composition*. White Emerson, the transcendentalist, busied himself with laying the foundations for the establishment of an American tradition free from the European influence, Poe took up the aesthetics of the form and content of poetry.

Henry James, one of the most distinguished American novelists of all time, was the first to break away from the provincialism that marked the writings of his contemporaries. He was the first to introduce realism and the genre novel of manners in American fiction.

African-American Criticism—African-American history and culture had been deliberately and consistently excluded from American education and literary history. African-American criticism is as old as American criticism itself. Its genesis can be located in the earliest writings which seek to contest the prevailing belief that the writings of the African-Americans are inferior in quality to those of the others. Langston Hughes, Sora Neil Hurston, Richard Wright, Ralph Ellison, James Baldwin were a few major writers. Writers began to feel that they should use their black culture to their advantage. It was their duty to portray the blacks as human. Protest literature came to an end during the 1960s with the growth of 'black aesthetics' (Black is beautiful). A new era in interpretation of black literature was ushered in with the publication of Afro-American Literature: *A Reconstruction of Instruction* (1978). Using the methods of rhetorical analysis and intertextuality, advocated by post structuralism, the reconstructionist critics re-interpreted African-American classics. A semiotic study of literature was made by Henry Louis Gates, Jr. which approached African-American works based upon purely aritistic considerations.

Black women's writings have now emerged full scale-as diasponic feminist literature. African-american scale-as diasponic feminist criticism analysis their problems. 'Suspended Woman', assimilated woman, emergent woman and liberated woman are some categories of their representation writers like Alice Walker and Toni Morrism bring home the black experience most convincingly by foregrounding it. African-American criticism also engages in a revisionary reading of white American writers.

British Criticism—In the 20th century, British criticism may be said to start roughly from the second decade of the century, when modernism in arts emerged in many countries of Europe. In England, the year 1922 represents the annus mirabills of modernism with the publication of The Waste Land and Ulysses. The symbolist movement of French origin did have an impact on England. The School of English was established in Oxford in 1894. When I.A. Richards appeared on the scene, literary studies took a different shape altogether.

At the time Walter Raleigh and Sir Arthur Quiller Couch were occupying positions of Prominence in the two citadels of learning, criticism came into its own in the universities at the beginning of the twentieth century. A.C. Bradley was the best known critic whose *Shakespearean Tragedy* (1904) was a Bible for Indian students. A few other critics merit our consideration. Oliver Elton produced a large body of writing, but is remembered mostly for his survey of *English Literature* (1928). It contains a series of direct and personal judgements on literary works. For him, it is the primary work of the critic to redefine the classic and thus he performs adequately. The others are Walton Paton Ker, Herbert Grierson and H.W. Gavod.

It is true that the changes in the outlook on the theory and criticism took place under the benign influence of T.S. Eliot, I.A. Richards and their disciples. F.R. Lewis not merely inherited, but took upon himself the role of the torchbearer of the humanistic tradition earlier initiated by his spiritual predecessor Arnold in the 19th century. Lewis did not hold any of the critics who had preceded him in high esteem, Aristotle not exempted. His only concession was given to Mathew Arnold. Literary criticism must be humanistic for him. In the history of criticism, he has a firm place, a place as firm as that of his preceptor, Mathew Arnold.

F.W. Bateson, a scholar critic and bibliographer who edited Essays in Criticism and William Empson, whom Frank Dermode called 'the chief English literary critic of the century' are two other well-known British literary critics. With the arrival of New Criticism, the distinction between British and American criticism ceases to exist. And now, all get subsumed into what goes by the grandiose name 'Theory'.

Formalist Criticism—The formalist criticism of America should not be confused with the Russian formalism which is based on modern linguistics. The American Yvor Winters, R.P. Blackmur, Robert Heilman, Alen Tate, Cleanth Brooks and W.K. Wimsatt followed Ransom's aesthetics broadly. These critics negated the Victorian and neotiumanist emphasis on the moral uses of literature, the historical tradition and the biography of the author as necessary background for the study of a literary text.

What is important for the formalist critic is a close reading of the text in terms of its form (metre, stanza, rhyme and rhythm) and the materials (simite, metaphor, imagery, allusion and symbol) it is made of.

The New-Aristotelians/The Chicago School of Critics—The basic difference between the formalists and the neo-Aristotelians lies in their principles of critical analysis and concept of the nature of art. The Chicago critics follow Aristotle when they say that knowledge is based on systematic analysis of the objects of nature. They follow the Aristotelian system of classification of knowledge based on the nature of subject under study.

MULTIPLE CHOICE QUESTIONS

1. Arnold was opposed to
   (a) romanticism (b) classicism
   (c) sensuousness (d) philistinism
2. Who said, 'Poetry is a criticism of life under certains'?
   (a) Wordsworth (b) Coleridge
   (c) Keats (d) Arnold
3. In which text does Arnold say that poetry is superior to history?
   (a) 'Keats'
   (b) 'Milton'
   (c) 'Wordsworth'
   (d) 'The study of Poetry'
4. Where did Keats write, "That if poetry comes not naturally as the leaves to a tree, it had better not come at all"?
   (a) The Eve of St. Anes
   (b) Endymion
   (c) Letter to John Taylor
   (d) La Belle Dame saws Merci
5. Arnold was the first English critic to insist on the necessity of
   (a) dialectical criticism
   (b) comparative criticism
   (c) functional criticism
   (d) classical criticism
6. What factors are essential in a plot?
   (a) A grand opening
   (b) Balanced in form
   (c) A beginning, middle and end
   (d) All of the above
7. In a plot according to Politics there should be self explanatory beginning, middle must follow naturally to the catastrophe and the end should be
   (a) naturally related to the beginning.
   (b) related to the beginning and middle.
   (c) casually related to something that.
   (d) appropriate, went before beginning and middle.
8. According to Aristotle what points are important in a character? First goodness, secondly appropriateness, thirdly true to life and lastly
   (a) truthful (b) magnificent
   (c) powerful (d) consistency
9. In a plot of tragedy the hero's fortunes move from happiness to misery because of
   (a) fate (b) tragic flaw
   (c) wrong judgement (d) human failings
10. Who can be a tragic hero?
    (a) A perfectly good human.
    (b) A good man with human failings like error of judgement or a flaw.
    (c) A good man with certain weakness over which he has no control.
    (d) Ill-fated man.
11. Horacis greatest works in criticism are contained in
    (a) Odes (b) Epistles
    (c) Ars Poetica (d) Satires

12. Ars Poetica is Horacis treatise on art of poetry which contains
    (a) stray views on poetry.
    (b) basically an epistle.
    (c) significant deliberation on poetry.
    (d) random observation on poetry but they are significant statements of a great poet.
13. Horacis concept of poetry is based on
    (a) disenchantement with the Alexandrian and the old Latin models.
    (b) the enlightened poets turned to revival of the ancient Greek tradition in place of Alexandrian and old Roman models.
    (c) the new-found splendor was great.
    (d) there is a significant relationship between the theory and practice of the new-found splendor of ancient Greeks.
14. Horace emphasized the nature of poetry and said it must be pleasure giving. Is it true?
    (a) True
    (b) False
    (c) True but didn't Plato say the same
    (d) Partially true
15. Sublimity has been defined as
    (a) excellence of language
    (b) uplifting effect
    (c) intensity of thought
    (d) grandeur of thought and intensity of feeling expressed in appropriate language.
16. How did Longinus explain the sublime?
    (a) As something more than what is good for instruction delight and persuasion.
    (b) More for the soul.
    (c) Uplifting spirit.
    (d) A certain destination and consummate excellence in expression.
17. Longinus believed that stately thoughts belong to the
    (a) stately minds
    (b) genius
    (c) mind trained for the purpose
    (d) loftiest minds
18. What are the chief figures which make for sublimity?
    (a) Chetoric
    (b) Emotion
    (c) Rapid flow
    (d) Rhetorical question, asyndeton, hyperbaton and piriphrasis
19. What is the role of arrangement of words in a composition for sublimity?
    (a) It blends thought, emotion and figures in a harmonius whole in which harmony plays a significant role.
    (b) Harmony.
    (c) Dignity.
    (d) Logic and good taste.
20. Longinus as a critic can be best defined as
    (a) a classicist
    (b) a classicist with moral bent of mind
    (c) suker of perfection
    (d) a classicist in taste, romanticist in temper and an idealist at heart
21. Plato attacked poetry because he believed
    (a) poets had a bad influence of social morality.
    (b) poetry is based on copy of the appearances and not reality.
    (c) poets aroused emotions and desires which served no social purpose.
    (d) poetry was based on irrational frenzy.
22. What is Plato's concept of organic unity?
    (a) One complete whole
    (b) Complete in itself
    (c) A coherent whole in which every part is relevant

(d) He believed that art is like a living organism, a complete coherent whole in which every part has relevance to each other and the whole.

23. Plato desired that poetry should have
(a) a structure
(b) form and style
(c) a moral purpose
(d) austerity

24. Plato believed that poetry should have
(a) decorum, order, austerity and restraint.
(b) a definite form.
(c) little experimentation.
(d) no deviation from the declared path of decorum.

25. "It is not rhyming and versing that maketh a poet, no more that a long gown maketh an advocate." Who has said this?
(a) Shakespeare (b) Marlowe
(c) Spenser (d) Sidney

26. Sir Philip Sidney had a strong urge for reviving the canons of criticism of
(a) Longinus (b) Aristotle
(c) Dr. Johnson (d) Bacon

27. Dryden as a critic
(a) favoured romantic qualities
(b) favoured classical qualities
(c) synthesized classical and romantic qualities
(d) approved of neither classical nor romantic qualities

28. Who is the founder of descriptive criticism in English?
(a) Sidney (b) Ben Jonson
(c) Dryden (d) Dr. Johnson

29. Dryden calls comedy "a representation of human life in inferior persons and low subjects:" In this regard he followed
(a) Horace (b) Aristotle
(c) Plato (d) Longinus

30. Pope was a great critic of the age of
(a) Prose
(b) Reason
(c) Prose and reason
(d) Augustan literature

31. Which poet has observed 'Men not afraid of god, afraid of one'?
(a) Dr. Johnson (b) Dryden
(c) Pope (d) Addison

32. In Sidney's *An Apology for Poetry*, the Romans have a word for poets?
(a) Maker (b) Creator
(c) Vates (d) Prophets

33. Sidney is not in favour of
(a) comedy (b) tragedy
(c) tragis-comedy (d) All of the above

34. In Greek literature, the word 'pot' means
(a) maker (b) prophet
(c) teacher (d) All of the above

35. Who said this? "This judge of poets is only the faculty of poets"
(a) Sidney (b) Dryden
(c) Ben Jonson (d) Pope

36. Johnson gave to comedy
(a) structure and coherence
(b) a firm plot
(c) clear characterization
(d) All of the above

37. The Latin meaning of 'humours' is
(a) mood (b) character
(c) liquid (d) comedy

38. Which of the following humours is also called 'yellow bile'?
(a) Blood (b) Choler
(c) Philgm (d) Melan choly

39. Dryden's *An Essay of Dramatic Poesy* is a work of
(a) interpretative criticism
(b) legislative criticism

(c) comparative criticism
(d) Textual criticism

40. Dryden with all his critical allurement of classical love was unconsciously a forerunner of
(a) romantic criticism
(b) neo-classicism
(c) objective criticism
(d) None of the above

41. Alexandar Pope has an undying craving to conform to the laws of
(a) neo-classical tenacity
(b) prose and reason
(c) nature
(d) None of the above

42. Which poet was from his birth of constitution tender and delicate?
(a) Pope (b) Milton
(c) Dryden (d) Collins

43. 'The end of writing is to instruct, the end of poetry is to instruct by pleasing'. Who has said this?
(a) Wordsworth (b) Dr. Johnson
(c) Coleridge (d) Arnold

44. Dr. Johnson gave a new interpretation to the term of
(a) imagination
(b) fancy
(c) imitation
(d) Photographic reproduction

45. Dr. Johnson observes: "Poetry is an imitation of particular, with which it deals, but, through it, the universal." This definition of poetry occurs in
(a) Lives of the Poets
(b) Preface to Shakespeare
(c) Rambler
(d) None of the above

46. Which of the unities Dr. Johnson found justified by reason?
(a) Unity of time (b) Unity of place
(c) Unity of action (d) All of the above

47. Who has written Dictionary of English Language first ambitious attempt at an English lexicon?
(a) John Dryden (b) Dr. Johnson
(c) Joseph Addison (d) James Boswell

48. Wordsworth's *Preface to the Lyrical Ballads* is a landmark because
(a) he makes a critical statement for the new romantic poetry.
(b) he explains his own poetry.
(c) he declares a departure from the classical mode of poetry.
(d) presents the romantic ethics.

49. Wordsworth and Coleridge defined poetry as an "overflow of powerful feelings" but it was tempered by saying that it was
(a) emotion recollected in tranquility
(b) assertion of emotion
(c) own feeling and personification of nature
(d) rationalization

50. Where has Wordsworth written the following? "I have never given way to my own feeling in personifying natural objects without bringing all that I have said to a rigorous after-test of good sense."
(a) *Preface to the Lyrical Ballads*
(b) Essays
(c) "Letter" to W.R. Hamilton
(d) Prelude December 23, 1829

51. Who called Coleridge the 'meditor' between Germany and England?
(a) T.S. Eliot (b) Rene Wellik
(c) Cleanth Brooks (d) I.A. Richards

52. For Coleridge 'a poem is not a machine, and you cannot write it off'. Who said this?
(a) George Watson (b) Rene Wellik
(c) F.R. Leavis (d) None of the above

53. Coleridge was influenced in his critical thoughts by
(a) Immanuel Kant (b) Hegal
(c) Spinza (d) German ethics

54. Coleridge's criticism is
(a) descriptive (b) textual
(c) ligistative (d) idealistic

55. Whose poetry struck Coleridge as remarkable, what he say?
(a) Magnificent language
(b) Harmony between theme and style
(c) Delightful thought
(d) The union of deep feeling with profound

56. Who has written this in appreciation of poetry? "Poetry turns all things to loveliness, it exalsts the beauty of that, which is beautiful, and it adds beauty that which is most deformed, it marries exultion and horror. Grief and pleasure, eternity and change, it subdues to union under its yoke all irreconcilable things. It transmutes all that it touches."
(a) Byron (b) Wordsworth
(c) Shelley (d) Keats

57. Shelley is in the tradition of
(a) Sidney (b) Plato
(c) Dryden (d) Dr. Johnson

58. Who said? "Poetry is a criticism of life under certains".
(a) Wordsworth (b) Coleridge
(c) Keats (d) Arnold

59. John Keats, according to Mathew Arnold was deficient in the area of
(a) moral interpretation
(b) romance
(c) farsightedness
(d) natural beauty

60. Who said? Arnold's outlook is "honest and frank and often penetrating".
(a) Cazamian (b) Eliot
(c) Richards (d) Johnson

61. There is plenty of ironic banter in
(a) "The study of poetry"
(b) "Essays in Criticism"
(c) "The Functions of Criticism at the Present Time"
(d) None of the above

62. Literary themes are dealt in Pater's
(a) Appreciations
(b) Pall Mall
(c) Guardian
(d) Imaginary Portraits

63. In his essay on style in Appreciations, Pater gives importance to
(a) love
(b) romance
(c) joy
(d) beauty of expression

64. Which travel sketch is considered Lawrences' best?
(a) Twilight in Italy
(b) Sea and Sardinia
(c) Morning in Mexico
(d) Etruscan Places

65. According to Lawrence the basis of human sensuality was
(a) Thoracic gangolion
(b) The lumbar gangolion
(c) Cardiac plexus
(d) Solar plexus

66. In his major criticism Lawrence makes a distinction between
(a) knowledge and instinct.
(b) sensitive mind and intellectual awareness.
(c) education and ignorance.
(d) intuition and the mind, instinct of the body and intellect of the mind.

67. Which one of the following phrases has been coined by T.S. Eliot?
 (a) Art for Art's sake
 (b) Suspension of disbelief
 (c) Objective correlatice
 (d) Touchstone method
68. The phrase 'Objective Correlative' was first used by Eliot in his
 (a) Essay on 'Hamlet'
 (b) Essay on 'Macbeth'
 (c) Essay on 'King Lear'
 (d) Essay on 'Othello'
69. The phrase 'dissociation of sensibility' was first used by Eliot in his
 (a) Essay of 'Hamlet'
 (b) Metaphysical poets.
 (c) Frontiers of Criticism
 (d) Tradition and Individual Talent.
70. Which of the following critical works has not been authored by F.R. Leavis?
 (a) The Meaning of Meaning
 (b) The Great Tradition
 (c) New Bearings in English Poetry
 (d) Revaluation
71. Which of the following novelists has been mentioned in Leavis' The Great Tradition?
 (a) Thomas Hardy (b) Joseph Conard
 (c) Jane Austen (d) George Eliot
72. In which category can you keep the criticism of F.R. Leavis?
 (a) Ontological criticism
 (b) Historical criticism
 (c) Biographical criticism
 (d) Comparative criticism
73. Richards, *The Meaning of Meaning* was written in collaboration with whom?
 (a) T.S. Eliot (b) C.K. Ogden
 (c) R.P. Blackmur (d) Wiliam Empson
74. Who is the author of the book *Coleridge on Imagination*?
 (a) I.A. Richards (b) F.R. Leavis
 (c) L.K. Ogden (d) Games Wood
75. "A poet in our time is a semi-barbarian in a civilized community." This line may be associated with which of the following critics?
 (a) T.S. Eliot
 (b) I.A. Richards
 (c) F.R. Leavis
 (d) Thomas Love Peacock
76. Jacques Derrida was an Algerian born intellectual
 (a) French (b) American
 (c) British (d) Swiss
77. The "New Criticism" in America was influenced by
 (a) T.S. Eliot and I.A. Richards
 (b) Coleridge
 (c) Irving Babbitt
 (d) None of the above
78. The tenets of "New Critics" in America are
 (a) close examination of the texts themselves.
 (b) close examination of the texts, analyzing style and imagery.
 (c) a poem as an organic whole.
 (d) technical criticism.
79. The "New Critics" like Yovr Winters and Cleanth Brooks believed that a poem can be "experienced" as a work of art by
 (a) the accurate sensibility of the critic.
 (b) the integrity and knowledge of the critic.
 (c) scholarly critic with the help of scientific methodology.
 (d) the acuteness of the individual sensibility and knowledge of the semantics.

80. Brooks has mainly used his critical tool on
   (a) poetry (b) prose
   (c) short stories (d) fiction

81. The Southern movement was primarily Ograrian but also included
   (a) aesthetics
   (b) aesthetics and interpretation of difficult poetry
   (c) political issues, like industrialization
   (d) a moral agenda

82. What did Ransom declare about Brook's *Modern Poetry and Tradition* (1939) and *The Well Wrought Urn* (1947)?
   (a) Great works of criticism
   (b) A great modern critic
   (c) A true American critic
   (d) The best living interpreter of difficult verse.

83. Who is the author of *The Sacred Wood*?
   (a) F.R. Leavis (b) T.S. Eliot
   (c) I.A. Richards (d) James Wood

84. Who wrote the book *The Principles of Literary Criticism*?
   (a) William Empson (b) I.A. Richards
   (c) T.S. Eliot (d) Cleanth Brooks

85. Which of the following books was written by I.A. Richards in collaboration with C.K. Ogden and James Wood?
   (a) The Foundation of Aesthetics
   (b) The Meaning of Meaning
   (c) Coleridge on Imagination
   (d) The Principles of Literary Criticism

86. Which theory was applied to the whole gamut of arts and social sciences, including linguistics anthropology, political science, even architecture?
   (a) Theory of Imagination
   (b) Theory of Poetry
   (c) Theory of Deconstruction
   (d) Theory of Dramatic Pleasure

87. He was an outstanding scholar, critic and leader of
   (a) New humanist movement
   (b) Aesthetics movement
   (c) New Romantic movement
   (d) None of the above

88. What is Brooks' contribution in the Well Wrought Urn?
   (a) He has used his critical tools disterously in analysis of a number of poems, especially Keats' Odes.
   (b) His analysis is personal but very deep.
   (c) He has studied the imagery in these poems and highlighted its patterns.
   (d) He has discussed mostly the works of Augustan poets like Alexander Pope and John Dryden.

89. Which book Brooks wrote with W.K. Wimsatt during his days at Yale University?
   (a) Literary Criticism: A Short History
   (b) An Approach to Literature
   (c) Understanding Fiction
   (d) Understanding Poetry

90. Who has written "The Double Agent"?
   (a) R.P. Warren (b) Cleanth Brooks
   (c) Kenneth Burke (d) R.P. Blackmur

91. R.P. Blackmur combined in his criticism the techniques of George Santayana, I.A. Richards, William Empson, T.S. Eliot and Henry James. What was the result?
   (a) Aestheticism and a moral conception of literature.
   (b) A minute dissection of the style, form, diction and structure for proper evaluation of a literary work.
   (c) Not much different from other critics.
   (d) Destruction of a work of literature.

92. Lionel Trilling was associated with Literary magazine like:
   (a) The Keyson Review and Partisan Review
   (b) Southern Review
   (c) Transition
   (d) The Literary Criterion
93. Who has written *Matthew Arnold* (1939) and *E.M. Forster* (1943) with acumen?
   (a) Cleanth Brooks (b) Yvor Winters
   (c) Lionel Trilling (d) Allen Tate
94. The Liberal Imagination and the opposing self are Trilling's
   (a) creative Writings
   (b) essays
   (c) critical Writings
   (d) social writings expressing the need for moral climate
95. John Crowe Ranson was a
   (a) poet (b) critic of poetry
   (c) critic (d) poet-critic
96. The names of J.C. Ranson, Allen Tate and R.P. Warren are taken together in a particular context. What is this context?
   (a) Members of the fugitive-Agrarian group at vanderbilt
   (b) The group called New Critics
   (c) Southern literature
   (d) Mid-west literature
97. In the World's Body Ranson asserts
   (a) failure of science to achieve the body that is in poetry.
   (b) poetry sustains more than science.
   (c) science has not lived up to man's exceptions.
   (d) poetry is more real than the virtual reality of science.
98. In the 'New Criticism' what was the need of the times?
   (a) A balanced critic
   (b) Adherence to the tenets of New Criticism
   (c) Giving importance to the tradition
   (d) An antological critic (based on the philosophy concerned with the nature of being).
99. What was the lacuna in Chaucer's poetry according to Arnold?
   (a) Truth
   (b) Fluidity of movement
   (c) High seriousness
   (d) Heroic subject matter
100. Who held that "Form is everything. It is the secret of life"?
   (a) Eliot (b) Wilde
   (c) Shaw (d) Auden
101. Who said that "No man was ever yet a great poet with out being at the same time a profound philosopher"?
   (a) Wordsworth (b) Coleridge
   (c) Arnold (d) T.S. Eliot
102. What was the view of Dr. Johnson on Shakespeare?
   (a) A ruthless, urban and sublime poet
   (b) A pathetic, tender and domestic poet
   (c) A rhapsodic, violent and exuberant poet
   (d) None of the above
103. What was Dr. Johnson's opinion on language of poetry?
   (a) It should be the language of the learned.
   (b) It should be an universal language.
   (c) It should be a sublime poetic language.
   (d) None of the above.
104. "Criticism as a distinct form of creation and enjoyment consists of asking and answering rational questions about literature." Who said this?

(a) Plato (b) Horace
(c) Pope (d) Abercrombic

105. Which novel of Oscar Wilde was a product of aesthetic movement?
(a) *De Profoundis*
(b) *An Ideal Husband*
(c) *Lady Windermac's*
(d) *The Picture of Durian Gray*

106. The aesthetes brought out a periodical named as
(a) Yellow Book (b) Red book
(c) Pink Book (d) Green Book

107. What should be the ideal age of the poet according to Plato in Laws?
(a) Less than thirty years
(b) More than thirty years
(c) Less than fifty years
(d) More than fifty years

108. Who was the first English critic who endeavoured to define the limits or art and taste in his essays on 'Pleasures of Imagination?'
(a) William Hazlitt
(b) Joseph Addison
(c) De Quencey
(d) None of the above

109. Name the author among the aesthetes who was the chief pursuer of beauty.
(a) George Moox (b) Lionel Johnson
(c) W.B. Yeats (d) Walter Pater

110. Whose biography did Richard Aldingdon write in 1950 which was named 'Portrait of a Genius'?
(a) D.H. Lawrence
(b) Lawrence of Arabia
(c) T.S. Eliot
(d) Virginia Woolf

111. Which English poet translated the 'Ion' and was deeply impressed by it?
(a) Byron (b) Pope
(c) Sidney (d) Shelley

112. Who wrote the critical essay 'Apologie for Poetry?'
(a) P.B. Shelley
(b) John Dryden
(c) Sir Philip Sidney
(d) William Wordsworth

113. Apologie for poetry was written in 1595 in response to Gosson's pamphlet
(a) The School of Thought
(b) The School of the Abuse
(c) The School of Poetry
(d) The School of Lyricism

114. Regarding which of the following did Aristotle say 'In Poetics' that in having passed through many phases, reached its natural form, and there it shopped?
(a) Poetry (b) Philosophy
(c) Tragedy (d) Comedy

115. Who was the tutor to young Alexander the Great?
(a) Aeschylus (b) Socrates
(c) Plato (d) Aristotle

116. In Poetics, Aristotle writes "in a simpler and restrictive sense the action of a tragedy is not longer than"
(a) twelve hours (b) eighteen hours
(c) one day (d) five day

117. According to Aristotle tragedy has three external elements-Spectacle, lyrical song and
(a) character (b) thought
(c) diction (d) plot

118. 'Aspects of the Novel' in a critical work by E.M. Forster which is based on the Clarke Lecturer that is delivered in the
(a) Oxford University
(b) Cambridge University

(c) London University
(d) Chicago University

119. Which of the following terms, as used by Aristotle, means a sudden turn?
(a) Peripeteia (b) Mimesis
(c) Anagnorisis (d) Megethos

120. Which critical work of E.M. Forster is known for its conversational style, aspects of narratology, and flat and round character?
(a) Two Cheers for Democracy
(b) Abinger Harvest
(c) Aspects of the Novel
(d) The Eternal Moment

121. Which of the following in Aristotelian vocabulary means the plot?
(a) Megethos (b) Muthos
(c) Ethos (d) Phobon

122. Pope's 'Essay on criticism' is an example of
(a) Classical criticism
(b) Romantic criticism
(c) Applied criticism
(d) None of the above

123. Thomas Gray, Bishop Percy, Thomas Warton and Bishop Hurd were the early romantic critics of the
(a) Romantic period
(b) Augustan period
(c) Elizabethan period
(d) Victorian period

124. According to Aristotle, 'imagination', 'symbol' and 'parodox' are the characteristics of
(a) tragedy (b) comedy
(c) poetry (d) art

125. Who according to Matthew Arnold was an imperfect disciple of Shakespeare, for he had an excess of natural magic, not enough moral profoundity, while Shakespeare had both qualities to the full?
(a) Wordsworth (b) Tennyson
(c) Keats (d) None of the above

126. Who was called by Arnold a "beautiful and ineffectual angel, beating in the void his luminous wings in vain"?
(a) Byron (b) Keats
(c) Shelley (d) Carlyle

127. Identify the work of Mikhail Bakhtin
(a) Freudians
(b) The Path in Rome
(c) The Birth of Tragedy
(d) Advertisement

128. Who are the two great 'classics of our prose' according to Arnold?
(a) Bacon and Johnson
(b) Addison and Lamb
(c) Hazlitt and Johnson
(d) Dryden and Pope

129. Arnold defines poetry as the
(a) Criticism of life
(b) Criticism of society
(c) Criticism of morality
(d) None of the above

130. Which of the following is a criticism of art by John Berger?
(a) Permanent Red
(b) The Success and Failure of Picaso
(c) A Painter of our Time
(d) Ways of seeing

131. George Bernard Shaw was greatly influenced by the theory of an essential 'Life force' of
(a) John Berger (b) Henri Bergson
(c) Roland Barthes (d) Hilane Belloc

132. The most famous writer of the heroic couple is

(a) Dryden (b) Chaucer
(c) Pope (d) Spenser

133. Who used two types of texts: 'Readerly' and 'Writerly'?
(a) Michail Bakhtin (b) Hilaire Belloc
(c) Hobbas (d) Roland Banthas

134. Which of the following was defined by Coleridge as "a mode of memory emancipated from the order of time and space"?
(a) Primary imagination
(b) Fancy
(c) Secondary imagination
(d) All of the above

135. Rousseau is associated with
(a) French Revolution
(b) American War of Independence
(c) Russian Revolution
(d) None of the above

136. The theory of Catharsis is associated with
(a) Aristotle (b) Dryden
(c) Plato (d) Sidney

137. Who wrote 'In defence of poetry?'
(a) T.S. Eliot (b) Keats
(c) Yeats (d) Shelley

138. Which one is not a part of the proverbial 'three unities'?
(a) Unity of Time (b) Unity of Purpose
(c) Unity of Place (d) Unity of Action

139. In which metre is Shelley's 'Ode to the West Wind' Writter?
(a) Spensarian stanza (b) Ottava Rima
(c) Terza Rima (d) Blank verse

140. In which class can we place Spenser's 'Shepherd's Calender'?
(a) Pastoral (b) Romance
(c) Epic (d) Eulogy

141. The word dialogue is derived from 'dialogos' which is a
(a) German word (b) French word
(c) Latin word (d) Greek word

142. Who said: Poets are the unacknowledged legislators of the word?
(a) Byron (b) Shelley
(c) Keats (d) Coleridge

143. Who wrote the Preface to the Getanjali?
(a) W.B. Yeats (b) T.S. Eliot
(c) W.H. Auden (d) Philip Larkin

144. Who wrote 'Poetry is the spontanious overflow of powerful feelings'?
(a) Herrick
(b) Wordsworth
(c) Aristotle
(d) None of the above

145. Which one is not a romantic characteristic?
(a) A conscious adherence to set rules
(b) Spontaniety
(c) An impression of strangerness
(d) An atmosphere of wonder

146. Who is the writer of 'Culture and Society?'
(a) Cleanth Brooks
(b) T.S. Eliot
(c) Butrand Russell
(d) Raymond Williams

147. The thirteenth century vercular poem which has been called the earliest literary criticism is
(a) Tieresias
(b) Ennead
(c) Ulixes
(d) The Owl and the Nightingale

148. 'Prographia Literature' is a miscellaneous work of autobiography, literary criticism and

(a) Biography (b) Psychology
(c) Philosophy (d) All of the above

149. Harold Bloom is a leading member of the so-called
(a) Oxford School of literary criticism
(b) Cambridge School of literary criticism
(c) London School of literary criticism
(d) Yate School of literary criticism

150. Nicolas Boilean's mock epic which inspired and influenced Pope to write 'The Rape of the Lock' is
(a) Le Putrin (b) Le Lutrin
(c) Le Sutrin (d) Le Zutrin

151. A French poet is believed to be the real originator of Surrealism. Who is he?
(a) Flanbert (b) Andre Breton
(c) Nicolas Boilean (d) Henri Bergson

152. Who has written 'Irony as a Principle of Structure'?
(a) Catherine Carswell
(b) William Brown
(c) Cleanth Brooks
(d) A.S. Byatt

153. For which work was Helene Cixous awarded her Ph.D. degree?
(a) Le Rive do La Meduse
(b) The Exile of James Joyce
(c) The Newly Born Woman
(d) Portrait de Dosa

154. In the Freudian context 'conciousness' is associated with
(a) individual's perception of reality
(b) awareness of the surroundings
(c) enlightenment view of individualism
(d) individual's role in society

155. Who wrote 'Structuralist Poetics', 'The Pursuit of Signs' and 'On Deconstruction'?
(a) Ford Madsa (b) Carrington
(c) Anthony Conron (d) Jonathan Culler

156. What is the sub title of Arnold's 'Culture and Anarchy'?
(a) An Essay in Political and social Criticism.
(b) An Essay on Political Anarchy.
(c) An Essay on Political and Social values.
(d) None of the above.

157. Who wrote 'Poetry is a Sword of Lightning ever Unsheathed?'
(a) Wordsworth (b) Dryden
(c) Eliot (d) Shelley

158. Dryden's dialogue, published in 1688, that is considered the most important for his general literary theory, was titled
(a) An Essay of Dramatic Poesey
(b) Defence of an Essay of Dramatic Poesey
(c) Essay of Heroic Plays
(d) Aurangzebe

159. Which among the following critics did not believe in the authority of ancient classics?
(a) Wordsworth (b) Dryden
(c) Pope (d) Johnson

160. Which of the following poets made a fortune by translating Homer?
(a) Spenser (b) Shelley
(c) Dryden (d) Pope

161. Who is believed to have said, "That which does not concern the common man is to no significance"?
(a) Voltaire (b) Rousseau
(c) Locke (d) Southey

162. Who is stated to have said, 'Criticism is the art of interpreting art?'
(a) Dryden (b) Arnold
(c) Walter Pater (d) Eliot

163. Who is primarily associated with the term 'objective correlative?'

(a) Shelley (b) Sandburg
(c) Eliot (d) Hardy

164. Who wrote 'The Lives of the Poets'?
(a) Boswell (b) Hazlitt
(c) Macaulay (d) Dr. Johnson

165. Who wrote 'The Interpretation of Dream'?
(a) Mary (b) Jung
(c) Frend (d) Darwin

166. Who wrote 'Principles of Literary Criticism' in 1924?
(a) I.A. Richards (b) F.R. Leavis
(c) A.G. Gardiner (d) Kennith Brook

167. Who said 'Language is primarily an auditory system of symbols'?
(a) Bloach (b) Franz Boas
(c) Sapir (d) Whitney

168. Tetra meter comprises a line with
(a) three lambs (b) two lambs
(c) five lambs (d) four lambs

169. Who among the following was not a critic?
(a) M. Arnold (b) Ruskin
(c) Dryden (d) Tennyson

170. "Literature always anticipates life. It does not copy it but moulds it to its purpose" was said by
(a) Oscar Wilde (b) Coleridge
(c) Ezra Pound (d) Aristotle

171. Who was defined essay as 'receptack for detached thoughts' and as 'dispersed meditations?'
(a) Addison (b) Steele
(c) Shakespeare (d) Bacon

ANSWERS

1. (d)	2. (d)	3. (d)	4. (c)	5. (b)	6. (d)
7. (d)	8. (d)	9. (b)	10. (b)	11. (c)	12. (d)
13. (b)	14. (a)	15. (d)	16. (d)	17. (d)	18. (d)
19. (a)	20. (d)	21. (a)	22. (d)	23. (b)	24. (a)
25. (d)	26. (b)	27. (c)	28. (c)	29. (b)	30. (c)
31. (c)	32. (c)	33. (c)	34. (a)	35. (c)	36. (d)
37. (c)	38. (b)	39. (b)	40. (a)	41. (c)	42. (a)
43. (b)	44. (a)	45. (b)	46. (c)	47. (b)	48. (a)
49. (a)	50. (c)	51. (b)	52. (a)	53. (a)	54. (a)
55. (c)	56. (c)	57. (a)	58. (d)	59. (a)	60. (a)
61. (a)	62. (a)	63. (d)	64. (c)	65. (d)	66. (d)
67. (c)	68. (a)	69. (b)	70. (a)	71. (a)	72. (a)
73. (c)	74. (a)	75. (b)	76. (a)	77. (a)	78. (b)
79. (d)	80. (a)	81. (b)	82. (d)	83. (b)	84. (b)
85. (a)	86. (b)	87. (a)	88. (a)	89. (a)	90. (d)
91. (b)	92. (a)	93. (c)	94. (c)	95. (d)	96. (a)

97. (a)	98. (d)	99. (c)	100. (b)	101. (b)	102. (c)
103. (b)	104. (d)	105. (d)	106. (a)	107. (c)	108. (b)
109. (d)	110. (a)	111. (d)	112. (c)	113. (b)	114. (a)
115. (d)	116. (c)	117. (c)	118. (b)	119. (a)	120. (c)
121. (b)	122. (b)	123. (c)	124. (a)	125. (c)	126. (c)
127. (a)	128. (d)	129. (a)	130. (b)	131. (b)	132. (c)
133. (d)	134. (b)	135. (a)	136. (a)	137. (d)	138. (b)
139. (c)	140. (a)	141. (d)	142. (b)	143. (a)	144. (b)
145. (a)	146. (d)	147. (d)	148. (c)	149. (d)	150. (b)
151. (b)	152. (c)	153. (c)	154. (a)	155. (d)	156. (a)
157. (d)	158. (a)	159. (a)	160. (d)	161. (b)	162. (c)
163. (c)	164. (d)	165. (c)	166. (a)	167. (c)	168. (d)
169. (d)	170. (a)	171. (d)			

20

Rhetoric and Prosody

> The art of using language so as to persuade or influence others, the body of rules to be observed by a speaker or writer in order that he may express himself with eloquence.
>
> —*Oxford English Dictionary*

Rhetoric, the art of persuasive communication, has long been recognized as the systematization of natural eloquence. According to this tradition, the first writers of rhetoric-books observed situations in real life where eloquence succeeded, analysed the resources used by such speakers, and developed a teaching method which could impart those skills.

Vickers in Defence of Rhetoric

Rhetoric deals with the study of the elements of language, especially metre, that contribute to rhythmic and acoustic effects in poetry. The basis of 'traditional' prosody in English is the classification of verse according to the syllable stress of its lines. Effects such as rhyme scheme, alliteration and assonance further influence a poem's sound meaning. Non-metrical prosoding study is sometimes applied to modern poetry. Prosody, can be defined as the theory of versification that which creates poetic design and patterning is prosodic. It includes principles and practice of meter, rhyme and stanza. However, something like rhyme is also frequently claimed as a rhetorical dance. So things like alliteration, consonance and assonance are rhetorical as well as prosode.

"The analysis and description of meters; metrics; the patterns of accent in a language is prosody."

There is a complete overlap between prosody and rhetoric, with no particular defining like between them. Prosody is basically a matter of repetition: a thing has to repeat in older for there to be a pattern. But repetition, in turn, is one of the strongest strains of rhetoric.

In his Rhetoric, Aristotle defined rhetorical discourse as the art of discovering all the available means persuasion in any given case and focused his discussion on the various ways in which the orator deploys devices for achieving intellectual and emotional effects on an audience that are needed to persuade them to accede to his point of view.

Later classical rhetoricians concurred with this definition of rhetoric as the art of persuading an audience and (still following Aristotle's lead) analysed the text of a rhetorical discourse into 'invention' (the finding of arguments or proofs) 'disposition' (the arrangement of such matter and rhythms that will most effectively express this material).

Rhetoric and Syntax: A lot of rhetorical terms refer to syntactic patterns. Asyndeton, for example, refers to an absence of connecting particles between clauses, while polysyndeton refers to a profusion of connecting particles between clauses. W.B. Yeats, again, provides clear examples of how this syntactic kind of rhetoric works in a poem. Looking through Yeats's late poems, we find that he is enamoured with the conjunction 'or'. For example, in 'Lapis Lazuli':

'Every accidental crack or dent
Seems a water-course or an avalanche'

Or lofty slope: Through this rhetorical technique, the poem's referential basis becomes multitudinous. The conjuction 'or' basically binds things together while denoting their separateness. Indeed, Yeats often binds two alternatives together as if they did express one thing, his rhythm counter-pointing his sense: 'Some moralist or mythological poet', 'fashion or mere fantasy', 'A Starlit or a moonlit done', 'nothing can be sole or whole'.

Here the conjuction 'or' because it expresses alternatives, is more specifically termed a disjunctive, but Yeats' use of it might be termed 'inclusive disjunction' because he allows that all alternatives are simultaneously possible. Yeats thus welds alternatives together into units of inclusive disjunction, and this rhetorical gimmick has the effect of making the substantive foundation of his poems seem fissiparous. Through this ambivalent play with conjuction-disjuntion. Yeats generates semantic instability whilst rhetorically affecting a rhetorically suspend the reader between closure and multiplications open-endedness.

Rhetoric and Post-structuralism

Traditional idea of rhetoric basically imply that it is something done to a language which is already there; an extra level of design and manipulation which makes language more dynamic and interesting, in various ways.

Post-structuralists, as you know, claim that language is fundamentally constitutive of our sense of reality. In this respect, rhetorical plays upon linguistic structures are not secondary flourisher, but one hugely powerful indicators of the provisionality and indeterminancy of our grasp of reality. According to contemporary rhetoric, we mediate and understand reality primarily through linguistic figuration. And so, rhetoric becomes something much more philosophical, a kind of fundamental study of knowledge.

Rhetorical Questions: Rhetoric can help make a poem at once more playful and more direct. Rhetorical question refers to a question for which no answer is expected or necessary. W.B. Yeats, for one, is almost obessed with posing rhetorical questions in his verse, Keats also uses it in 'Ode to a Nightingale' and other poems too. Rhetorical question is used to achieve an emphasis stronger than a direct statement. It is mostly used in persuasive discourse and tends to impact an oratorical tone to a speech. Shelley's 'Ode to the West Wind' closes with the most famous rhetorical question in English—'O Wind.

If Winter cames, can Spring be far behind?'

Cadence: The rise and fall produced by the alteration of couder and soften syllabus in accentual tongues. It shows the flow of the language.

Circumlocution: A round about way of saying things. Another term which has a similar meaning is periphrasis. An example of this is found in Shakespeare's *Hamlet* where Polonius gives a round about explanation of Hamlet's madness.

Consonance: Harmony of sound or the mutual fitness between sound and sense. It is opposed to dissonance. In prosody consonance also comes for the use (at line-ends) of different vowel sounds followed by the same consonants, e.g. rat-hit; good, blood, add-read etc.

Use of Caesura: A kind of pause or break, in a line of verse. It helps in producing musical effect. The artistic use of caesure is one of the surest tests of a writer's skill. Milton has used this device most skillfully.

Enjambment: The carrying or 'running on' of the sense of a like of verse into the text line. Its opposite is end-stopping in which each line is a thought unit and ends with a punctuation mark.

Elegiac Stanza: A stanza of four lines of iambics. The rhyme scheme is generally ab ab. It is used in Gray's Elegy written in a country churchyard also.

Metre

Metre is the name for the regular or nearly regular, sound patternings of verse. In English, metre has very often been a matter of accenting or stressing words, or parts of words, in a line composed of a fixed number of syllables. Because some syllables are accented and some not, a notation has been arrived at to denote a stressed syllable _'_ and an unstressed syllable _˘_.

The rhythm of a line is determined by the number of stresses. So a dimeter has two, a trimester three, a tetrameter four, a pentameter five and a hexameter six. Sometimes the term 'foot' is introduced to distinguish the units of verse in which the stressed syllable occurs. So a dimeter is also described as a two-foot line and so on.

The exact character of a metre is shaped by the patterned arrangement of stressed and unstressed syllables. It is still customary to use the Classical names for these. The full description of a metre combines the number of stresses with the patterning of stressed and unstressed syllables. Metres create different effects. Iambic metres are suitable for the expression of thought and recollection. The movement from an unstressed to a stressed syllable suggests the clarification of thought. Troachau metres often sound firm and settled. William Blake's 'The Tyger' bursts on us with assertive power: "Tyger! Tyger! burning bright".

English metres one very rarely entirely regular. The ear likes variation, and the mind and heart recognize that there are times when the pulse of the poem requires a departure from the pattern of successes. Furthermore, not every stress is of equal weight. A word is not just material; its meaning is going to in a line, and that will be reflected in the weight of its stress. Another factor is performance: a reader is free to choose how to emphasize some of the stresses according to the relative importance he or she then us they have.

English is considered a stress-timed language, unlike French, which is a syllable-timed language. In poetry, stressed and unstressed syllables are often put together in specific syllables are often put together in specific patterns. In poetry these patterns are called meter, which means 'measure', The meters you find in poetry are the same ones as we use in everyday speech. The main difference is that in speech these patterns tend to occur spontaniously and without any special order; in poetry they are usually carefully chosen and arranged.

There are four main meteres—iambic, trochain, dactylic and anapestic. A fifth kind of meter is called Spondaic and consists of two consequtive along stressed syllables, and a sixth is called 'Pyrrhic' this is a metrical foot having two short or unaccented syllables. In addition, there are two even lesser-known meters, amphibrach, (it has a short-long-short pattern-delicious) and amphimacer—a long- short-long (eighty-eight).

If the meter of a poem seems to fall into none of the above categories, it may simply have an irregular or impredicterble meter that does not follow any set pattern.

The Rhythms of Poetry

The rhythm in poetry is both complex and simple. It is still an area in which critics are for from satisfied that an descriptive language study, new terms and methods of analysis are being invented

The Iambus: The iambic foot contains an unaccented first syllable and an accented second syllable.

Detail confér

The Trochee: The trochaic first contains an accented second syllable.

Spélling máster

The Dacty: The dactylic foot begins with an accented syllable which is followed by two unaccented syllables.

Family technical

The Anapest: The anapestic foot begins with two unaccented syllables which are followed by the accented syllable.

Unreformed non be liéF

Line: Lines give poems shape. Grammar determines whether a poetic line is end-stopped or run-on. The end of an end-stopped line is co-terminus with a syntactic unit; it coincides with the end of a clause or sentence. Hence punctuation marks close an end-stopped line.

A run-on-line is one in which the line is not co-terminus with a grammatical unit, and this effect is called an enjambment, and a run-on-line is called an enhambed line. The sentence organizes meaning, and the line is an artistic arrangement, often dependent on rhythm and syllable count.

English poets have usually adopted either an eight-syllable or a ten-syllable line. The eight syllable line is found in the ballerd tradition. The pithy, trimmed down, direct style finds the short line an appropriate form of expression also used for humourous and light verse the ling line is suited to poems on serious, elevated topics. Wordsworth writes in a ten-syllable line and John Milton uses it to present the drama of the Fall in Paradise Lost. Poets have also written in twelve syllables (hexameter) but hexameter is better used as a variation, as in the last line of the Stanza Edmund Spensh used in The Fairy Queene, Keats used the hexameter for the final line of his stanza in The Eve of St.

A metric line is named according to the number of feet composing it.

Manometer	:	one feet
Dimeter	:	two feet
Trimester	:	three feet
Tetrameter	:	four feet
Pentameter	:	five feet
Hexameter	:	six feet (an Alexandrine is a line of six iambic feet)

Heptameter	:	seven feet (a fernateener is a line of seven iambic feet; it tends to break into a unit of four feet followed by a unit of three feet)
Octameter	:	eight feet

Caesura: A Caesura is simply a pause. Absence of sound is also an important element of poetry. When reading a line of poetry, we are often obliged to pause. This is because there is a caesura a break in the line (indicated by II). The caesura dramatizes the emotional life of the poem; it checks the pace and allows the reader to recollect and ponder. It often marks a change in tone; the line might become more ardent, more wistful or more longing. Caesures often influence the close of a line, stanza or poem. Some caesures are quite long, others are very short. Normally, there is a fairly long caesura at the end of every line of poetry. There is usually also a very short caesura after every foot.

Stanza Form: Lines form stanzas. There are various kinds and forms of stanzas. Usually the stanza of given poem are marked by a recurrent rhyme scheme or otherwise.

Monostich: A poem or stanza with one line is called a monostich.

Couplet: The couplet is two consecutive rhyming lines. When the lines are written in iambic pentameter (lines of ten syllables with a heavier stress falling on the even syllables) they are called heroic couplets.

The couplet has a self-affirming quality. What is said in the first line is developed and concluded in the second. By the time the rhyming word is reached, the reader might feel that the point of the couplet has been established.

Triplet: The terct or tercet of triplet, is a stanza of three lines with a single rhyme. The lines may be of same length or of varying lengths. It is not a popular form. P.B. Shelley used terza rima-an Italian form invented by Dante Alighieri. Thomas Hardy, Philip Larkin etc. have used it. The difference between a triplet and terza Rima is very basic. Terza rima is composed of tarcets which are interlinked, in that each is joined to the one following by a common rhyme-aba, bcb, cdc and so one.

The Quatrian: A quatrain is a four line stanza. It is popular being used in ballads and lyrical verse.

Hexastich: A poem of six lines is called Hexastich.

Heptastich: A poem of seven lines is called Heptastich.

It is employed with various metres and rhyme schemes. Handled well, the quatrain is economical: arguments, stages in stories or emotions can be framed neatly and held together harmoniously by various rhyme patterns.

Rhyme Royal: It is a seven line, iambic pentameter stanza rhyming ab abbcc.

Ottava Rima: It has eight lines. It rhymes c b a b a b c c. like terza rima and the sonnet. It was brought from Italian into English by Sir Thomas Wyatt. Byron discovered it in a new sense in his satiric poem Don Juan.

Sonnets: Sonnets have fourteen lives. They are distinguished by the way their rhymes divide them up. The Petarchan sovinet has an eight-line section (Octave) followed by a six-line one (sesetet). The Shakespearean sonnet consists of four quatrains concluded by a couplet.

In the Petrachan Sonnet, the poet explores an idea or experience in the octave and than comes to a conclusion in the sestet. Sestets often begin: and but,' for', if', 'then' or 'thus'. The Shakespearian sonnet can present the stages of an argument or elaborate a single idea. In both cases the closing couplet is important either for confirming or, as in Sonnet 130, countering the argument.

Limerick: A poem which normally has five lines. It is also known as Doggerel. Silly, trivial poetry. A humorous poem may belong to a set form. A limerick has an a a bb a rhymes scheme; the first two and last rhymes are trimester, the third and fourth, dimeter. It is usually dactylic.

Spenserian Stanza: Spenserian stanza is a still longer form devised by Edmund Spenser for The Fairy Queene-nine lines, the first eight iambic pentameter and the last iambic hexameter (an Alexandrine) rhyming a b a b b c b c c.

French Stanza Forms: Many forms have been imported from France like the Rondeau, the Villanelle and the Triolet, containing intricate repetitions of rhymes and lines, which have been used mainly, but not exclusively, for light verse. Poets like W.H. Auden, William Empson Dylan Thomas etc. have used it.

Mechanical And Organic Form: S.T. Coleridge coined the term 'mechanical form' for strict adherence to a form, and 'organic form' for the way some poets allow their thoughts and feelings to mould and alter the form.

Blank Verse: Unrhymed iambic pentameter.

Free Verse: The argument in favour of organic form leads to free verse or verse libre. Free verse is now very popular, perhaps in part because it gives a sense of freedom from form and consequently, of sincerity. But the sense of freedom is an illusion. All verse has form; otherwise it would not be verse. So free verse can not mean lines free from any of the disciplines of verse. Some poets writer in syllabics lines that have the same number of syllables but no regular metrical patterns. Other poets dispense with line-to-line regularity, making each line work in its own terms. It means that the lines are given shape by clusters of sounds (alliterations, assonances), repetitions and rhythmical units.

Walt Whitman, regarded as one of the founders of free verse, is unmistakable rhythmical.

Rhyme – (rime)

Rhyme Schemes: Rhyme schemes-the pattern of rhymes in a series of lines. Rhyme is the effect created by matching sounds at the end of words. Ordinarily this includes the last accented vowel and the sounds that follow it, but not the sound of the preceding consonants.

Masculine And Feminine Rhyme: Masculine rhyme falls on one syllable; fat, cat, repair, affair. Feminine or double rhyme includes two syllables, of which only the first is stressed, better, shelter, pleasure, treasure.

Triple Rhyme: Triple rhyme is often reserved for light verse and doggerel. It involves three syllables-Practical, Tactical.

Interlaced Rhyme and Enclosed Rhymes

A B A B is an example of interplaced rhyme most long stanzas use it. The effect is to make the poem press forward in anticipation of the next rhyme. Poems thus interlaced often close, as many sonnets do, with a rhyming couplet.

Enclosed rhyme occurs when a couplet is contained in another rhyme. For example, contained in Browning's 'Meeting at Night', two rhymes enclose a couplet.

Rhyme works both forwards and backwards. Forwards because in rhyme, and backwards because we have to remember the previous word in order to hear the rhyme.

A line can be intensified with internal rhyming. This occurs when the word at the end of the line rhymes with an earlier word in the same line.

Comic verse often depends on rhyme. The rhymes make a ghastly accident sound neat and clean. The regularity of the rhymes lends an inappropriate, and therefore funny, smoothness to the event. Perhaps the disparity between the harmonies of rhyme and calamitons events is why comic poetry so often depends on rhyming.

Perfect And Imperfect Rhymes: If the correspondence of the rhymed sounds is exact, it is called perfect rhyme, or else 'full' or true rhyme. Until recently almost all English writers of serious poem have limited themselves to perfect rhymes.

Sounds

Poetry uses some of the features of language in heightened ways. This includes the sounds of words. Much of the time, the sounds of words don't matter. Cadence is the movement and usually the change in the pitch of the voice towards a close cadences can be steady, falling or rising. Our voices rise at the end of a question and often fall when we deliver bad news. This means that cadence is a smaller to tone and also, therefore, of meaning.

Alliteration: Alliteration is the repetition of consonants. The effect in the poetry is created by the regularity of the alliteration. When alliteration is irregular, readers might get the feeling that the poet's preoccupation with his or her subject occasionally punctuates the line in the form of the repeated consonants. It gives a sense of continuity.

Assonance: Assonance is the repetition of a vowel sound. The rules of alliteration apply to assonance also. There are two important things. First assonance (like rhyme) can depend on whether a vowel sound is long or short. There is assonance on the short vowel 'can' and the long vowel 'day; second, assonance often works on a small scale.

Texture: Texture of a poem is depend upon the combined physical effects of lines, caesuras, rhythms, cadences and sounds. A crucial factor is the density of the sounds. When alliteration is combined with strong rhythms, the texture of the verse is often rough and abrasive. The textures are often this and even airy.

The texture of poems is strongly shaped by the arrangement of syllables. A series of monosyllabic words can be stark and even aggressive in their erocation of bleakness. The combination of monosyllabic and polysyllabic words in a poem creater emotionally significant changes in tone as well as texture.

Inversion: The figure of speech in which words are presented out of them naturally or expected order in.

Of arms and a man I sing.

Onomatopoeia: Formation of words to represent natural sounds. A most effective device in appealing to the sense of sound.

Buzzing of the bees

Whirring wings

Apostrophe: The figure of speech in which the absent are addressed as though they were present, the living as well as dead, objects as well as human beings.

The Simile: A directly expressed comparison shown with the help of words—'like' and 'as'.

The Metaphor: A comparison which is implied rather than stated. It does not contain the words like or as.

Personification: The figure of speech in which we give human qualities to inhuman things or objects.

The wind sings a sweet song.

Hyperbole: International exaggeration. Something is said in a heightened tone to create a particular effect.

OTHER LITERARY TERMS

ALLUSION	A reference to another text or event.
AMBIGUITY	Something suggesting more than one meaning or interpretation.
ANONYMOUS	'Without a name', indicates that an author of a work is not known.
ANTITHESIS	A direct contrastor opposition.
ANTONYM	A word opposite in meaning to another.
COCOPHONY	Bad-sounding
CLICHÉ	A tired expression that has lost its original power to surprise because of overuse.
CONNOTATIONS	The implied meanings of a word, its overtones and associations over and above its literal, dictionary meaning.
CONSONANCE	Repetition of inner or end consonant sounds, e.g.
CONTEXT	The verbal or physical surroundings of a text.
DENOTATION	The basic dictionary meaning of a word without any of its associated meanings.
ELLIPSIS	Omission, a leaving out of something, which is nevertheless still implied.
ENJAMBEMENT	(Or run on lines) In enjambement the grammatical sense runs from one line of poetry to the next without pause or punctuation, opposite of end-stopped line.
EUPHEMISIN	An attractive substitute for a harsh or unpleasant word or concept, a less direct way of referring to something potentially offensive.
EUPHONY	'Good-sounding'-melodious.

EXPLETIVE	An unnecessary word or phrase used as a filler in speaking or writing ('you know') oras an aid to metrical regularity in verse ('oh') an exclamation or oath.
EXPLICATION	An explanation, analysis, or interpretation of a text.
GENRE	A certain form or style of writing. e.g. Poetry, novel, essay, drama etc.
IRONY	Irony is the perception of a clash between appearance and reality, between seems and is, or between ought and is. Irony falls mainly into three categories—verbal, dramatic and situational.
LITERARAL MEANING	The precise plain meaning of a word or phrase in its simplest, original sense.
LITOTES	A kind of irony, the assertion of something by the denial of its opposite, 'Not bad'. 'This is no small matter'.
LYRIC	A poem, brief and discontinuous emphasizing sound and pictorial imagery rather than narrative or dramatic movement.
METATHESIS	Interchanging of letters, sounds or syllables within a word.
METONOMY	'Substitute meaning' an associated idea names the item: Mixed Metaphor – changed or contradictory metaphors in the same discourse.
MONOLOGUE	A text recited by one person alone.
NEOLOGISM	A newly coined word.
PARADOX	"Other than what you expect. An apparently untrue or self-contradictory statement or circumstance that proves true upon reflection or when examined in another logic.
PARODY	A parody imitates the serious manner and characteristic features of a particular literary work. The term parody is often used synonymously with the more general term Spoof, which makes fun of the general particular work or author.
PARALEPSIS	Mention of desire to omit something in order to emphasize it. Also known as apophasis.
PARALLELISM	The comparison of things by placing them side-by-side, a one to one correspondence of form, meaning, or both in a text.
POETIC LICENSE	The liberty taken by a poet who achieves special effects by ignoring the conventions of prose.
POINT OF VIEW	The vantage point from which a story is told or an account given I, or he/she, er.
PUN	A figure of speech involving a play on two or more words them necessary, also called pleonasm, tautology etc.

REFRAIN	A set sphrase or chorus recurring throughout a song or poem, usually at the end of a stanza or at some other regular interval.
SATIRE	Literature that ridicules vices and follies.
SCANSION	A system for analyzing and marketing poetical meters and feet.
SOUND SYMBOLISM	A relationship between the sound structure an/or qualities of a word and its referent.
SYNECDOCHE	Reference to something by just a part of it.
SYNONYM	A word that means the same or almost the same as another.
TONE	An author's revealed attitude toward his or her subject or audience, sympathy, longing, amusement, shock, sarcasm etc.
UNDERSTATEMENT	An ironic minimizing of a fact in order to emphasize it, meiosis.
ZEUGMA	The technique of using one word to yoke two or more others for ironic or amusing effect, achieved when at least one of the yoked is a misfit.

Style

Style is the body to which thought is the soul, and through which it expresses itself. A good style is one that is suitable for its purpose. The role of the writer is to impart information. For him there is scarcely any choice: the facts are there, and he has merely to state them. But as soon as he wishes to interest or amuse, persuade or sudden, a writer has to select his facts. Good style is mainly a matter of the perfect use of contrast and similarity, the new and the old.

The varieties of style are infinite. Fashions in style, as in dress, change gradually; the new and the old overlap, and there are always some who do not follow the fashion at all.

The most primitive style in the world is the simple-sentence style. In it each idea is given equal prominence, because each is expressed as it arises, without any attempt to connect it formally with what presedis. It is a style with the minimum of dependent clauses, a style simple and straightforward, each idea being linked with the preceding by and or some equivalent.

The Detailed Style: The very earliest prose makes little use of detail; when an author has to express his ideas labouriously in a language not yet supplied by use for artistic purposes and with figures unaccustomed to writing; he is content with the more important facts. But at a rather later stage, when the resources of the language have been explored by pioneers and the writer has ready to his hand a whole host of phrases, we find an extreme fondness for detail and, too often, a lack of discrimination in its choice. Given a sense of proportion in the writer, the love of detail is, of course, an advantage. In the hands of Shakespeare and Keats, Gibban and Macaulars, Tennyson and Rossetti, it adds colour and body without being carried, save in rare cases, to the point of exaggeration. Keat's St. Agnes' Eve would lose all its beauty if it were stripped of its detailed descriptions. For this exuberant delight in small things is of the very stuff of English romanticism—and romanticism sits more easily on our race than classicism.

Whenever the nation has renewed its youth, has looked out upon the world with a fresh zest-as in the great Renaissance which culminated under Elizabeth, the romantic revival of the late 18th century, the Pre-Raphaelite movement—we find again the concrete rather than the abstract style, the detailed rather than the general.

The Exuberant Style: The medieval love of detail, like its Renaissance counterpart often goes with a love of words for their own sake. It is only mastery of the instrument and our familiarity with the language—that varies.

Use of Tags: Another result of the inadequate command of language is the use of stock phrases fill up a line or make a rime.

Ballad Style: Perhaps it is the ballad which makes the most lavish use of these conventional fragments, for the literary other medieval verse from lay in story and situation rather than nicety of expression. For this reason and because of its early connection with dancing, the ballad seems to us the quintessence of medieval naivete. We find the continual use of repetition in phrase and incident, the preference of monologue and dialogue to reported speech and often and often to reported action. Seem to full of marked oddities that there is little wonder that 18th century poets thought ballad-forging the easiest of tasks—little worder, too, that they proved mistaken.

Spenserian or Simple Aesthetic: For the Spenserian style is the style of a lover of beautiful sights and sounds, rather than that of a thinker of profound thoughts. For example, in the Faeriec Queeni what strikes us is the easy, unhasting, writing paci—a pace largely due to the mere. The stanza-form flows on, rime answering and anticipating rime, so that there seems no natural stopping place until we reach the slight backward swirt and pause of the last line. Thomson, in The Castle of Indolence, and Keats are the best-known among those who have learnt Spenser's lesson Shelley, in The Revolt of Islam and Adonais, never quite succeeds in catching Spenser's urbane leisurelinessy, Tennyson, though he often captures Spenser's grace, does not use his metre and has a deeper note.

Conventional Amorist Style: The Elizabethan sonneteers adopt another style-the conventional amorist. Some of them go so far as to borrow both sentiments and phrasing from foreign poets; nearly all of them address similar calmly perfernd appeals to similar inexorable mistresses. The lady's eyes are always stens, her cheeks always roser, her lips always cherries.

In various forms the conventional amorist style is found throughout civilsed literature.

Conceited Style: With the Elizabethans style is generally 'conceited' that is to say, a figure of speech, or 'conceit' is twisted and turned and squeezed till the last drop of sense is extracted. Conceits were not confirmed to love poems; they are found almost everywhere in Elizabethan verse. Shakespear's early plays, especially Richard II, are full of them.

Metaphysical Style: The ordinary metaphors and similes had become commonplace; they were to the man with an imagination what plain, unfigurative speech is to us. For the weakness of the metaphysical poet was that, when his imagination failed to work, he used his ingenuity instead. Donne is the master of this style.

The Hyperbolic Style: This extravagance in language, then, lacks the charm of the earlier Elizabethan excesses, because it is less spontaneous. Beginning with Marlowe and Kyd, this hyperbolic style remains characteristic of Elizabethan drama to the end. With this the Elizabethans had re-discovered the possibilities of language; it is for them no longer a mere mechanical means for the expression of ideas; it is clay to be modeled into quaint shapes, a toy to be played with.

Euphuism: This is as evident in prose as in verse. We get Euphism with its elaborate cross-alliteration, its plays on words, its antitheses, its mechanically balanced sentences, its endless comparisons drawn from 'unnatural natural history'.

Arcadianism: We get Arcadianism, with its rather labored elegance, its compound words, its comparisons of the natural to the artificial etc.

The Pregnant or Epigrammatic Style: Bacon for the use of this style. His main characteristics are a laconic brewing, a stately harmony, a full mind, a free use of antithesis, of 'conceits', and an abruptness which does not attempt to make a natural transition from one idea to another. This epigrammatic style was taken up and modified by the writers of characters who supplied it, gave it a more familiar tone, and increased the number and audacity of the conceits, until they come to write what may almost be called metaphysical prose.

Architectural Prose: These ran an under-current of less eccentric prose. One stream in this undercurrent was a prose which in vocabulary and in sentence structure owed a great deal to Bacon, but more to Latin-the architectural prose.

The Plain Style: There are several varieties of the Restoration plains style. Dryden's verse, masculine and sonorous, often antithetical, the gentlemanly style of his prose, full of a cultured common-sense and an easy mastery of the language.

Miltonic Grand Style: Milton's Grand style the severity and finished outline of Spenser the use of the sentence-paragraph but that his sentence-paragraph is not like Spenser's sentence-stanza, a loose-joined ambling pad. We notice the variety of pause-a variety partly learnt from the Elizabethan drama in its best days, partly due to his classical studies, but largely the result of his own genius. Milton's fondness for Latin-derived words-often used in their classical sense rather than in the sense they been in English. In Milton's hands this adds dignity to the verse, but it is a dangerous method for minor poets, who may easily fall into such depths of bathos.

The Later Plain Style: Dryden commanded many metres and a multitude of rhythmical effects; Pope used heroic couplet. To Dryden's school of study, common-sense, plain English succeded a still plainer style-the style of swift. Alongside this was the style of Addison, a style intended for an audience largely composed of gentle women. In Addison's own hands the effort was delightful; but after him it became in careless hands a prose marked by all the faults of uncultured colloquialism. Sentence-structure became slipshod, vocabulary unselected, grammatical accuracy itself was neglected, and the conception of the sentence as a phrase in prose-music was entirely lost. All this is not generally true of the greater-writers, such as Fielding and Sterne; but it is true of the mass of controversial and periodical writing.

Johnsonian Style: The Law of Contrast acted again and we had the Johnsonian style. His style was apt to be mechanically balanced and like himself, rather heavy. But even at its worst, it was a corrective to the prevailing faults of the age.

Whimsical Style: By the time Scott died, English prose had almost achieved the infinite variety of the Eizabethan period. There was the whimsical style of lamb, which owed something to many writers—especially to Browne—but yet remained intensely original, allusive, humorous, pathetic, full of quaint imaginings and irrelevant relevancies.

True Classical Style: There is Landor's style, which aims at leisure of Greek art, but avoids the narrowness and artificiality of the 18th century pseudo-classic.

Dickensian Style: Somewhat akin to Carlyle's style in mastery of the grotesque and in force is Dickens's; but in Dickens's prose there is nothing of the merely eccentric. Whereas Carlyle's influence on style has been almost wholly bad-even Meredith learnt as many faults as virtues from him-Dickens has formed a good model for hundreds of beginners and has taught much to many, such as Chesterton, who are not beginners.

Comic Verse: Keats brought back the Spenserian pictorial power and in Hyperion, the stately march of Milton; Byron, in his most characteristic work, gave us what is still our best comic verse.

The Shorthand Style: Browning's realism is many-sided, not a mere choice of realistic detail. Browning writes as he thinks. Browning made it his business first of all to become more fully conscious of the contents of his own or his characters' mind, and then to express his new knowledge in the abrupt, colloquial style natural to those who are thinking aloud.

Futurist Style: The futurist writer disintegrates the language completely, using mathematical and musical signs, dispensing with stops, inventing onomatopoeic words, writing, say, to represent a child falling and being comforted.

Journalese: Among the many highly individuals styles in our highly individual literature, lack of space has compelled the neglect of many great names, there is one style, associated with no great nature, which can not be overloaded, so characteristic of our age is it – the Journalistic style. It has its origin in the conditions of the modern press, conditions which oblige hundreds of people to write at great speed in an arresting manner of matters of which they are more or less ignorant.

Acatalectic: A line of verse which is metrically complete and carries through the basic pattern. It is opposed to catalectic which stands for a line lacking a syllable of its last foot. The following two lines illustrate this point:

"Hamlet cries his mother's tainted.

Gertrude nearly falls down, faint."

In the first line all feet are complete. Hence it is called Acatalectic. In the second line the last foot of one syllable. Hence it is called Catalectic.

Acrostic: Acrostic is a composition generally in verse, in which certain letters (initial, middle or end) or successive lines form words when put together.

Alexandrine: A line of verse containing six iambic feet, generally used as the last line of the Spenserian stanza. (e.g. Spenser's The Faerie Queene). It has derived its name from Alexandre Paris, an old French poet who used this verse. According to some, it is called Alexandrine after some poems of 12th and 13th centuries written in this pattern about Alexander the Great. In English poetry, its best illustration is to be found in Robert Bridge's Testament of Beauty.

Anapaest: A metrical foot consisting of two short syllables followed by a long syllable; prosodically represented as VV-. The word underneath forms an anapaest foot. It is generally used for swift movement. Shelley is very fond of this metre (Skylark).

Antonomasia: A figure of speech in which a proper noun is used instead of a common, e.g. a Machiavelli for a crafter politician or a Napoleon for a good general.

Ballad Metre: A four-line stanza, with rhyme at the end of the second and fourth lines. It is composed of iambic tetrameter and trimester.

MULTIPLE CHOICE QUESTIONS

1. The meaning of Boroque is
   (a) serious literature with serious meaning
   (b) dull, prosaic and boring literature
   (c) luxurious and extravagant literature
   (d) literature dealing with Bar dancers
2. What is a Caesura in Poetry?
   (a) A pause in a line of verse dictated by the metres.
   (b) A pause in a line of verse not dictated by the metres but by the natural rhythm of the language.
   (c) Any pause, any gap in poetry.
   (d) None of the above.
3. What is an eclogue?
   (a) It comes before Prologue
   (b) It comes after prologue
   (c) A short pastoral poem in which shepherd converse with one another
   (d) None of these
4. What is Epistle?
   (a) Letter in prose
   (b) Play in poetic-prose
   (c) Story in poetry
   (d) Letter in verse
5. What is a monody?
   (a) A poem of mourning, spoken by one person only.
   (b) A poem in a drama in prase of one character.
   (c) Another word for monologue.
   (d) None of the above.
6. What is the rhyming pattern of Spenserian Stanza?
   (a) Abccd bcca (b) A b c aabbbb
   (c) Ababbcbcc (d) None of the above
7. What is Threnody?
   (a) A Greek lyre, usually a choral dirge for singing in praise of the dead.
   (b) It is related with thesis play.
   (c) A Greek Play.
   (d) None of the above.
8. What is Acatalectic?
   (a) A line of verse which is metrically complete and carries through the basic pattern.
   (b) A composition, generally in verse.
   (c) A line of verse containing six-iambic feet.
   (d) None of the above.
9. The 'heroic' couplet is written in
   (a) Iambic pentameter
   (b) Dactylic hexameter
   (c) Italian stanza
   (d) None of the above
10. The opposite of Acatalectic is
    (a) Accent (b) Acrostic
    (c) Alliteration (d) Catalectic
11. Purple Passage means
    (a) a sudden fall in style.
    (b) a passage written in grand style.
    (c) a passage dealing with description of colours.
    (d) a sudden heightening of style, which makes a section of work stand out among the rest.
12. The feet of two syllables in which the unstressed syllable precedes the stressed one is called
    (a) anapaestic (b) iambic
    (c) trochaic (d) None of the above
13. The stress placed upon certain syllables of a line is
    (a) punctuation (b) acrostic
    (c) accent (d) None of the above
14. What determines the metre in English verse?
    (a) The arrangement of accented and unaccented syllable.

(b) Lines of the poem.
(c) Number of words used in the poem.
(d) All of the above.

15. What is anti-climax?
(a) Gradual or sudden disappearance or reversal of expectations.
(b) Another name of climax.
(c) It is a figure of speech.
(d) None of the above.

16. What is the feet of three syllables called in which two unstressed syllables precede the stressed one?
(a) Trochaic (b) Anapaestic
(c) Dactylic (d) Iambic

17. What is Anthithesis?
(a) A regular metre.
(b) A figure of speech in which opposition of ideas is emphasized by balance of sharply contrasting words.
(c) It comes before thesis.
(d) None of the above.

18. A literary device in which the same vowel sounds are followed by different consonant sounds, is called
(a) assonance (b) aphorism
(c) antonyms (d) antonomasia

19. What is Bathos?
(a) It is a figure of speech in which there is a sudden collapse of high expectancy.
(b) Used to produce tragic effect.
(c) Another name for Pathos.
(d) Opposite of Pathos.

20. Unrhymed verse in iambic pentameter is called
(a) anapaest (b) alliteration
(c) blank verse (d) tragedy

21. What is the rhyming pattern of Pope's Essay on Man?
(a) A b c a (b) A b b a
(c) A b (d) A a

22. Two successive syllables with approximately equal light stresses constitute a
(a) Invective (b) Romantic
(c) Pyrrhic (d) Socratic

23. A rhetorical device aiming at high-sounding and inflated writing is known as
(a) Bombast (b) Caesura
(c) Cadence (d) All of the above

24. Decasyllabic is
(a) a line consisting of five syllables
(b) a line consisting of eight syllables
(c) a line consisting of ten syllables
(d) a line consisting of twelve syllables

25. Harsh and inharmonious rhythm, sometimes used for producing special effects in poetry is known as
(a) dissonance (b) consonance
(c) couplet (d) None of the above

26. A couplet consisting of two dissimilar lines is known as
(a) stich (b) catalectic
(c) distich (d) None of the above

27. Explain Disyllabic.
(a) The objective used for a word or metrical foot containing two syllables.
(b) Metrical foot containing ten syllables.
(c) Combination of iambic pentameter and a couplet.
(d) None of the above.

28. Doggerel is used for
(a) dignified verse
(b) undignified verse
(c) verse having a rough rhythm
(d) Both (b) and (c)

29. The third part of Pindaric Ode is called
(a) Strophe (b) Anti-strophe
(c) Epode (d) All of the above

30. A figure of speech which stands for a pleasant way of referring to something unpleasant like death is known as
    (a) euphemison (b) epode
    (c) euphony (d) All of the above
31. Smooth flow of sound produced by the careful selection and arrangement of words is known as
    (a) euphony
    (b) euphemism
    (c) Both (a) and (b)
    (d) None of the above
32. A line which has an unstressed syllable at its end is
    (a) Masculine Rhyme
    (b) Falling Rhyme
    (c) Feminine Rhyme
    (d) Feminine Ending
33. What is Feminine Rhyme?
    (a) It occurs when the rhyme is in two syllables.
    (b) It is also called double rhyme.
    (c) Both (a) and (b).
    (d) None of the above.
34. What is Foot?
    (a) Human organ.
    (b) A unit of syllables determining the metre of a line of verse.
    (c) A general term for poetry.
    (d) The musical flow of language.
35. Hendecasyllabic is
    (a) a fix metre for elegy.
    (b) a line of verse containing eleven syllables.
    (c) a line of prose using a definite pattern.
    (d) a line used in rare poetry.
36. A line of verse containing seven feet is known as
    (a) heptameter (b) hexagon
    (c) septametre (d) head Rhyme
37. Heroic Quatrains is
    (a) the iambic Pentameter in pairs
    (b) rhyming lines
    (c) a dominant verse
    (d) a stanza of four iambic pentameters, having the first line rhyming with the third and second with the fourth.
38. A line of verse with an additional syllable at the end is known as
    (a) hypermetrical (b) hyperbola
    (c) hypersyntia (d) hypersyllble
39. When a syllable within the line rhymes with the final syllable, it is known as
    (a) Ordinary Rhyme (b) Internal Rhyme
    (c) Middle Rhyme (d) Both (b) and (c)
40. What is Masculine Rhyme?
    (a) Known as single rhyme, it occurs when the rhyme is in the last syllable.
    (b) It is used by men poets only.
    (c) It is used to describe the character of a brave hero.
    (d) None of the above.
41. Two syllables, the first accented and the second unaccented is known as
    (a) dactylic (b) troctiatic
    (c) anapaestic (d) tribrach
42. A line of verse having one foot only is
    (a) monologue (b) monosyllable
    (c) monodrama (d) monometer
43. Monosyllable is
    (a) a word having one syllable
    (b) a line of poem having one feet
    (c) Both (a) and (b)
    (d) None of the above
44. What is Pararhyme?
    (a) When rhyme is used in the complete paragraph.
    (b) When in a para no rhyme is found.
    (c) When rhyme is used at the end of the para.

(d) A type of rhyme which the vowel sounds of the accented syllables in the rhyming words are different, the consonant sounds, both before and after the vowels, are the same.

45. A sequence of five feet, or a verse of that length is called
(a) pentapody (b) periphrasis
(c) peroration (d) personification

46. Poeticisms is
(a) words that are normally used in poetry and not in prose.
(b) when a group of a particular poetry is formed.
(c) when poets use their own way of writing .
(d) Both (b) and (c)

47. What is Quintain?
(a) A stanza of five lines
(b) A stanza of four lines
(c) A stanza of seven lines
(d) A stanza of eight lines

48. Rhyme-Royal is
(a) rhyme used to describe a royal persona.
(b) a stanza of fourteen foot.
(c) a stanza of seven five-foot lines in iambic metre.
(d) a stanza having rhyme of its own type.

49. What is Sextain?
(a) Any stanza of six lines
(b) Another word for sixain
(c) The last six lines of the sonnet
(d) Both (a) and (b)

50. Verse which is measured by the number of stresses rather than by the number of syllables in a line is known as
(a) Sprung verse
(b) Sprung rhythm
(c) Spondee
(d) Spensarian stanza

51. The meaning of Bathos is
(a) intentional, ludicrous descent from the exalted to the commonplace.
(b) unintentional, ludicrous descent from the exalted to the commonplace.
(c) Both (a) and (b).
(d) sudden rise to an exalted style from the commonplace.

52. What is an eclogue?
(a) A poem expressing lament or sorrow.
(b) A short pastoral poem in which shepherds conversion with one another.
(c) A short lyric describing an incident of deep sorrow like death.
(d) None of the above.

53. Epistle is a
(a) letter in verse (b) story in verse
(c) play in verse (d) essay in verse

54. The chief four type of composition are argumentation description, narration and
(a) expression (b) summation
(c) exposition (d) extention

55. What is the device called by which a writer expresses almost the opposite meaning to what he ostensibly speaks?
(a) Paradox (b) Conceit
(c) Irony (d) Understatement

56. What is the rhythming pattern of Pope's *An Essay on Man*?
(a) Aa (b) Abab
(c) Ab (d) Ababc

57. A reference to characters and events of mythology means
(a) allusive (b) allegory
(c) alexandrine (d) affective

58. By alexandrine we mean
(a) ugly sounds
(b) model of excellance

(c) a twelve syllable iambic line used in old French poem
(d) None of the above

59. An ecologue is a/an
(a) poem expressing lament or sorrow
(b) short pastoral poem in which shepherds comerse with one another
(c) short lyric
(d) None of the above

60. Affective fallacy was used by American critics, Wimsatt and
(a) Beardsley (b) Ezra Pound
(c) T.S. Eliot (d) L. Durrell

61. Aphasia denotes
(a) poetic diction
(b) lighter writings
(c) ludicrous situations
(d) language disorder

62. Belles Letteres means
(a) beautiful letter writing
(b) beautiful hand writing
(c) lighter writing in prose
(d) masterpiece works

63. 'Negative capability' is a term associated with
(a) Coleridge (b) Keats
(c) Tagore (d) Shelly

64. Humanism is most pronounced in
(a) Romanticism (b) Renaissance
(c) Classicism (d) Neo-classicism

65. What is meant by 'sing-song tone?'
(a) A happy tone
(b) A rash or flourishing tone
(c) A boring childish tone
(d) None of the above

66. A monody is a poem
(a) of mourning, recited by one person only.
(b) of praise of one individual by another.
(c) about oneself, one's own thoughts and ideas.
(d) written in a singular metrical pattern.

67. To get the complete meaning of a poem antological criticism puts emphasis on
(a) the texture (b) the structure
(c) the narrator (d) Both (a) and (b)

68. What is a 'Sestina'?
(a) The other name for a sonnet
(b) The old English word 'Siesta'
(c) A courtly wit
(d) A complex French lyrical form

69. What is that device by which non-human and non-living nature is credited with human emotions?
(a) Parody
(b) Pathetic fallacy
(c) Unification of sensibility
(d) Objective correlation

70. What is the term used to mean a sudden change of fortune in a play or story?
(a) Hamartia (b) Catharsis
(c) Nemesis (d) Bathos

71. A play which is usually written to be read rather than acted or performed is called a/an
(a) comic play (b) melodrama
(c) closet drama (d) interlude

72. A pause in a line of verse necessary for the natural rhythm of the language is known as
(a) an acrostic (b) an allusion
(c) an assonance (d) a caesura

73. Spondaic foot contains two
(a) stressed syllables
(b) unstressed syllables
(c) stressed or unstressed syllables
(d) different syllables

74. Mysteries were generally based on
   (a) historical themes
   (b) human tragedy
   (c) biblical themes
   (d) lives of ogres

75. Alliteration is the repetition of speech sounds in a sequence on nearby words, usually applied to
   (a) consonants only
   (b) vowels only
   (c) Both (a) and (b)
   (d) None of the above

76. Which is not one of the essential characteristics of prose drama?
   (a) Plot (b) Characters
   (c) Dialogues (d) Rhyme

77. 'Interior monologue' is most prominently connected with
   (a) comedies
   (b) tragedies
   (c) stream of consciousness technique
   (d) tragic-comedy

78. The successive syllables with approximately equal light stresses constitute a
   (a) Spondee (b) Pyrrhic
   (c) Trochaic (d) Dactylic

79. What do you call a language that appear smooth, pleasant and musical to the ear?
   (a) Euphony (b) Cocophony
   (c) Melody (d) Harmony

80. A satire is a literary device that
   (a) uses laughter as a weapon
   (b) works as a corrective of human voice and folly
   (c) ridicules the failing than the individual
   (d) All of the above

81. 'Pun' is a play on words that are similar
   (a) in sound but diverse in meaning
   (b) in meaning but diverse in sound
   (c) Both in sound and meaning but with different spellings
   (d) None of the above

82. What is meant by tropes in rhetoric?
   (a) A figure of speech
   (b) Metaphonical language
   (c) Implicit metaphor
   (d) A decided extension of change in the standard meanings of words.

83. An unintelligible speech, meaningless sound inarticulate chalter is known as
   (a) Gibberish (b) Elision
   (c) Esoteric (d) Empathy

ANSWERS

1. (c)	2. (b)	3. (c)	4. (d)	5. (a)	6. (c)
7. (a)	8. (a)	9. (a)	10. (d)	11. (d)	12. (b)
13. (c)	14. (d)	15. (a)	16. (b)	17. (b)	18. (a)
19. (a)	20. (c)	21. (d)	22. (c)	23. (a)	24. (c)
25. (a)	26. (c)	27. (a)	28. (d)	29. (c)	30. (a)
31. (a)	32. (d)	33. (c)	34. (b)	35. (b)	36. (a)
37. (d)	38. (a)	39. (d)	40. (a)	41. (b)	42. (d)
43. (a)	44. (d)	45. (a)	46. (a)	47. (a)	48. (c)

49. (d)	50. (a)	51. (b)	52. (b)	53. (a)	54. (c)
55. (c)	56. (a)	57. (a)	58. (c)	59. (b)	60. (a)
61. (d)	62. (c)	63. (b)	64. (b)	65. (c)	66. (a)
67. (d)	68. (d)	69. (b)	70. (a)	71. (c)	72. (d)
73. (a)	74. (c)	75. (a)	76. (d)	77. (c)	78. (b)
79. (a)	80. (d)	81. (a)	82. (d)	83. (a)	

Solved Papers

DECEMBER 2008

1. With whom did Byron go on a long journey to Portugal, Turkey, Spain etc.?
   (a) Shelley (b) Coleridge
   (c) Hobhouse (d) Leigh Hunt
2. In which work does the character Medora exist?
   (a) Manfred
   (b) Don Juan
   (c) Childe Harold's Pimgrimage
   (d) Corsair
3. Who wrote the following Lines (in 1816): "Every feeling hath been shaken; Pride, which not a world could bow, Bows to thee-by thee forsaken Even me soul forsakes me now"?
   (a) Shelley (b) Keats
   (c) Byron (d) Southey
4. Byron wrote: "Maid of Athens, Ere We Part" in
   (a) 1807 (b) 1810
   (c) 1813 (d) 1815
5. Whom did Byron address when he wrote (while departing from England in April 1816):
   "Here's sigh to those who love me,
   And a smile to those who hate;
   And whatever sky's above me,
   Here's a heart for every fate!"
   (a) Shelley
   (b) Hobhouse
   (c) (His friend) (Tom Moore)
   (d) Keats
6. Which of the following sequences is correct?
   (a) Vanity Fair, Henry Esmond, Middlemarch, The Return of the Native.
   (b) Henry Esmond, Vanity Fair, Middlemarch, The Return of the Native.
   (c) Middlemarch, The Return of the Native, Vanity Fair, Henry Esmond.
   (d) The Return of the Native, Middlemarch, Vanity Fair, Henry Esmond.
7. Queen Victoria's reign, after whom the Victorian period is named, spans
   (a) 1833-1901 (b) 1837-1901
   (c) 1840-1905 (d) 1842-1905
8. Pre-Raphaelite poetry is mainly concerned with
   (a) narrative and style
   (b) narrative and nature
   (c) form and design
   (d) form and value
9. The concept of "mad woman in the attic" can be traced to
   (a) The Tenant of Wildfell Hall
   (b) Villette
   (c) Wuthering Heights
   (d) Jane Eyre
10. Who among the Victorians is called "the prophet of modern society"?
    (a) Ruskin (b) Carlyle
    (c) Macaulay (d) Arnold

11. Albert Camus was a French existentialist. Given below is the list of his novels. Identify the novels not written by him.
    (a) *The Trial, The Castle*
    (b) *The Plauge, The Outsider*
    (c) *The Renel, The Myth of Sisphus*
    (d) None of the above

12. The author of *Portrait of India* is
    (a) V.S. Naipaul
    (b) N.C. Chaudhary
    (c) Ved Mehta
    (d) EM. Forster

13. *Revenue Stamp* is the autobiography of
    (a) Dalip Kaur Tiwana
    (b) Amrita Pritam
    (c) Shivani
    (d) Shobha De

14. Which of the following novels came under burning criticism and, even threats?
    (a) *The Suitable Boy*
    (b) *Sanatic Verses*
    (c) *The Great Indian Novel*
    (d) *English August*

15. Who wrote *My True Faces*, *Azadi*, *Into Another Dawn*, *The Crown And the Lioncloth*?
    (a) Sudhir Ghose
    (b) Khushwant Singh
    (c) Manohar Malgonkar
    (d) Chaman Nahal

16. In which of his books does Carlyle discuss "the condition-of-England question"?
    (a) *Sartor Resartus*
    (b) *On Heroes, Hero-worship, and the Heroic in Poetry*
    (c) *Chartism*
    (d) *French Revolution*

17. When was the First Folio of Shakespeare's plays published?
    (a) 1623 (b) 1603
    (c) 1634 (d) 1599

18. Who said that *Hamlet* is "most certainly an artistic failure"?
    (a) Ben Jonson (b) Dr. Johnson
    (c) T.S. Eliot (d) L.C. Knights

19. Which of the following comedies was attacked by Steele in *The Spectator*?
    (a) The Man of Mode
    (b) The Country Wife
    (c) The Double Dealer
    (d) The Way of the World

20. Whose style was praised by Dr. Johnson as "elegant but not oustentatious, familiar but not ostentatious, familiar but not coarse"?
    (a) Dryden (b) Fielding
    (c) Addison (d) Goldsmith

21. Wordsworth presents his views on the nature and function of poetry first in
    (a) The 'Preface' to the 1800 edition of the Lyrical Ballads
    (b) The 'Advertisement' appended to the first edition of the Lyrical ballads
    (c) A separate supplement
    (d) A letter to Dorothy

22. The dictum that Life imitates Art is expounded by
    (a) John Ruskin (b) Walter Pater
    (c) Oscar Wilde (d) Matthew Arnold

23. F.R. Leavis's 'great tradition' of the English novel does not include
    (a) Jane Austen (b) Thomas Hardy
    (c) George Eliot (d) Joseph Conrad

24. 'Structuralism' was first employed in the study of
    (a) Psychoanalysis (b) Anthropology
    (c) Literature (d) Linguistics

25. The lines "Stern Daughter of the Voice of God, O Duty!" illustrate
    (a) synecdoche (b) antithesis
    (c) apostrophe (d) interrogation

26. A novel tracing the development of the artist is known as
    (a) Bildungsroman
    (b) Erziehungsroman
    (c) Kunstleroman
    (d) Graeco Roman
27. *Bhowani Junction* is written by
    (a) Paul Scot
    (b) John Masters
    (c) Bhabani Bhattacharya
    (d) Amitav Ghosh
28. *Archeology of Knowledge* is written by
    (a) Aristotle
    (b) Roland Barthes
    (c) Jean Francois Lyotart
    (d) Michel Foucault
29. "When I consider how my light is spent ...." is an example of
    (a) Synecdoche (b) Hyperbole
    (c) Metonymy (d) Pun
30. Who among the following is not a Marxist critic?
    (a) Christopher Williams
    (b) Raymond Williams
    (c) Terry Eagleton
    (d) Victor Shkolovsky
31. During which king's reign in England did the Hundred Year's war start?
    (a) Henry III (b) Edward III
    (c) Henry IV (d) Richard III
32. In which year did Henry V land in France?
    (a) 1411 (b) 1412
    (c) 1415 (d) 1416
33. Who is proverbially known having called Gandhi the "naked fakir"?
    (a) Churchill (b) Queen Victoria
    (c) Hitler (d) Stalin
34. Who was Gandhiji's mentor in Russia?
    (a) Stalin (b) Lenin
    (c) Gorki (d) Tolstoy
35. Who said about Vivekananda? "I have gone through his words very thoroughly and after having gone through them, the love that I had for my country became thousand fold."
    (a) Tagore
    (b) Nehru
    (c) Gandhi
    (d) Subhash Chandra Bose
36. Hume was the greatest philosopher of century.
    (a) Sixteenth (b) Seventeenth
    (c) Eighteenth (d) Nineteenth
37. The biography of which of the following was not written by Izaac Walton?
    (a) Donne (b) Johnson
    (c) Wotton (d) G. Herbert
38. When was the King's Bible or the Authorized Version published?
    (a) 1611 (b) 1610
    (c) 1614 (d) 1608
39. King James' Bible possesses the excellence of prose of
    (a) 15th century
    (b) 16th century
    (c) 17th century
    (d) sweetness of all ages
40. Who is said to be the first to translate the Bible into English direct from original Hebrew and Greek texts?
    (a) William Tyndale (b) Reynolds
    (c) Crammer (d) Parker
41. Who wrote: "*Mysteries of Udolpho*"?
    (a) Mrs. Radcliffe
    (b) Horace Walpole

(c) Virginia Woolf
(d) Proust

42. Which of the following is a woman novelist?
(a) Hardy (b) Conrad
(c) Trollope (d) George Eliot

43. Who among the following is known as Christopher North?
(a) Francis Jeffrey (b) Lockhart
(c) John Wilson (d) Gibbon

44. By what name was Shelley called by the boys at school?....... Shelley
(a) Mad (b) Happy
(c) Redoubtable (d) Genius

45. In which of Shelley's poems do the following lines exist: "While yet a boy, I sought for ghosts, and sped through many a listening chamber, cave and ruin?"
(a) Alastor
(b) Queen Malc
(c) Revolt of Islam
(d) Hymn to Intellectual Beauty

46. Where was Shakespeare born?
(a) London
(b) Lanscaster
(c) Stratford-on-Avon
(d) Dublin

47. Uriah Heep is a character in
(a) David Copperfiel
(b) Ivanhoe
(c) The Christmas Carol
(d) Nicholas Nickleby

48. Which play is said to be written by Shakespeare in collaboration with (probably) Marlowe?
(a) *Tempest*
(b) *Titus Andronicus*
(c) *Love's Labour's*
(d) *Winter's Tale*

49. In which of the following plays of Shakespeare is a King assassinated?
(a) *Macbeth* (b) *Hamlet*
(c) *Othello* (d) *Julius Caesar*

50. Louka is a character in
(a) *The Apple Cart*
(b) *Arms and the Man*
(c) *Pygmalion*
(d) *The Devil's Disciple*

ANSWERS

1. (c)	2. (d)	3. (c)	4. (b)
5. (c)	6. (a)	7. (b)	8. (c)
9. (c)	10. (d)	11. (a)	12. (c)
13. (b)	14. (b)	15. (d)	16. (c)
17. (a)	18. (c)	19. (b)	20. (c)
21. (b)	22. (a)	23. (b)	24. (b)
25. (c)	26. (c)	27. (b)	28. (d)
29. (c)	30. (d)	31. (b)	32. (c)
33. (a)	34. (d)	35. (c)	36. (c)
37. (b)	38. (a)	39. (d)	40. (a)
41. (a)	42. (d)	43. (c)	44. (a)
45. (d)	46. (c)	47. (a)	48. (b)
49. (a)	50. (b)		

JUNE 2008

1. For Mathew Arnold 'a poetry of revolt against moral ideas' is
(a) a poetry of immorality
(b) a poetry of acceptance of life
(c) a poetry of revolt against life
(d) a poetry of revolutionary ideas

2. Who called Wordsworth 'the lost leader'?
(a) Byron
(b) Tennyson
(c) Browning
(d) Matthew Arnold

3. The Gothic novel is satirized in
   (a) *The Mysteries of Udolpho*
   (b) *Northanger Abbey*
   (c) *Mill on the Floss*
   (d) *The Heart of Midlothian*
4. Carlyle's Sartor Resartus is
   (a) an autobiography
   (b) a fictive biography
   (c) a biography
   (d) a fictive autobiography
5. Who wrote the book *Road to Xanadu*?
   (a) A. Herbert Read (b) Hasil Wiley
   (c) J.L. Lowes (d) Coleridge
6. Don Juan by Byron is
   (a) a heroic narrative
   (b) a epic satire
   (c) a long ballad
   (d) a sonnet sequence
7. On whose real-life experiences is based?
   (a) Alexander Selkrick
   (b) Dontel Defoe
   (c) Gulliver
   (d) Christian
8. The repetition of similar vowel sounds is called
   (a) alliteration (b) onomatopoeia
   (c) assonance (d) head rhyme
9. Which of the following plays by G.B. Shaw attacks Darwinism?
   (a) *You Never Can Tell*
   (b) *Back to Methuselah*
   (c) *Man and Superman*
   (d) *St. Joan*
10. Who wrote *The Defence of Lucknow*?
    (a) E.M. Forster
    (b) Lord Tennyson
    (c) Rudyard Kipling
    (d) John Dryden
11. The theme of Browning Paracelsus is
    (a) search for excellence in art
    (b) search for knowledge
    (c) search for success in love
    (d) search for worldly well-being
12. Who first attacked most prominently the Restoration Comedy for its immorality?
    (a) Dr. Johnson (b) Jeremy Collier
    (c) Macaulay (d) Addison
13. Whose style was praised by Dr. Johnson as "elegant but not ostentatious, familiar but not coarse"?
    (a) Dryden (b) Goldsmith
    (c) Cowley (d) Addison
14. John Bunyan's The Pilgrim's Progress is
    (a) a symbolic narrative
    (b) a historical narrative
    (c) an allegory
    (d) a fable
15. "The Spider and the Bee" episode occurs in
    (a) *A Tale of a Tub*
    (b) *Gulliver's Travels*
    (c) *The Battle of the Books*
    (d) *Journal of Stella*
16. W.H. Auden wrote "Homage to Clio." Which discipline is she the Muse of?
    (a) Poetry (b) Dancing
    (c) History (d) Learning
17. The theme of Bacon's *The New Atlantis* is
    (a) pursuit of knowledge
    (b) discovery of the new world
    (c) advancement of science
    (d) democratic political philosophy
18. Ben Johnson is a
    (a) Jacobean dramatist
    (b) Reformation dramatist

(c) Restoration dramatist
(d) Elizabethan dramatist

19. According to Longinus, the most important source of the sublime is
(a) elevated language
(b) a vigorous treatment of emotions
(c) a clever use of figures
(d) a lofty cast of mind

20. Which one of the following is an 'artificial' comedy?
(a) The Birthday Party
(b) The Cocktail Party
(c) The Way of the World
(d) Volpone

21. *Pamela* is
(a) a picaresque novel
(b) a Gothic novel
(c) a novel of ideas
(d) an epistolary novel

22. Which is the first English tragedy?
(a) *The Spanish Tragedy*
(b) *Gorboduc*
(c) *Cato*
(d) *The Battle of Alcazar*

23. T.S. Eliot uses the term 'objective correlative' in
(a) The Function of Criticism
(b) Tradition and the Individual Talent
(c) The Frontiers of Criticism
(d) Hamlet and His Problems

24. Utilitarianism identified 'what is good' with
(a) what is true
(b) what is morally right
(c) what makes for happiness
(d) what is beautiful

25. Who among the following is not an imagist?
(a) W.B. Yeats (b) Amy Lowell
(c) T.E. Hulme (d) Ezra Pound

26. The Suffragette movement was a movement for
(a) social reform
(b) redress of sufferings
(c) women's rights
(d) children's rights

27. The Decline and Fall of the Romantic Ideal was written by
(a) Edward Gibbon (b) L.C. Knights
(c) F.L. Lucas (d) Graham Hugh

28. Who calls poetry "the breathe and finer spirit of all knowledge"?
(a) Wordsworth (b) Coleridge
(c) Shelley (d) Keats

29. Aldous Huxley writes about his visit to India in
(a) *Eyeless in Gaza*
(b) *The Doors of Perception*
(c) *Mortal Coils*
(d) *Jesting Pilot*

30. 'The Growth of a Poet's Mind' is the subtitle of
(a) *The Rime of the Ancient Mariner*
(b) *Lyrical Ballads*
(c) *The Prelude*
(d) *Kubla Khan*

31. Lady Bracknell is a character in
(a) *Lady Windermere's Fan*
(b) *An Ideal Husband*
(c) *A Woman of No Importance*
(d) *The Importance of Being Earnest*

32. In which of the following plays Shakespeare attacks the Puritans?
(a) *Richard II*
(b) *Twelfth Night*
(c) *The Merchant of Venice*
(d) *The Comedy of Errors*

33. Who said that Shakespeare has in his comedies only heroines and no heroes?
(a) Carlyle (b) Hazlitt
(c) Ben Jonson (d) Ruskin

34. Milton's Aeropagitica is a defence of
(a) reason against imagination
(b) freedom to form unions
(c) freedom of thought
(d) freedom of expression

35. 'Metaphyscal conceit' is basically
(a) a simile
(b) a metaphor
(c) a symbol
(d) None of the above

36. Who said: "It is not enough that Aristotle has said so, for Aristotle drew his models to tragedy from Sophocles and Euripedes and if he had seen ours, might have changed his mind"?
(a) Coleridge (b) Sidney
(c) Johnson (d) Dryden

37. Thyrsis commemorates
(a) Arthur Hugh Clough
(b) Arthur Hallam
(c) John Keats
(d) Edward King

38. The correct title of William Langland's whole poem is
(a) 'The Piers Plowman'
(b) 'Piers the Plowman'
(c) 'The Vision of Piers the Plowman'
(d) 'The Books of Pier's the Plowman'

39. *Utopia* was written by
(a) John Bunyan
(b) Sir Thomas Malory
(c) Sir Thomas More
(d) Cardinal Wolsey

40. The authorised version of the Bible appeared in
(a) 1573 (b) 1595
(c) 1611 (d) 1660

41. Who introduced the sonnet form in English for the first time?
(a) Chaucer (b) Wyatt
(c) Milton (d) Surrey

42. The *Mystery Plays* were based on
(a) stories from the Bible
(b) stories from the lives of the saints
(c) marvelous happenings and events
(d) concepts of Christian theology

43. The Astrophel and Stella sonnets were composed by
(a) Wyatt and Surrey
(b) Sir Philip Sidney
(c) Spenser
(d) Shakespeare

44. Who complained that Spenser "write no language"?
(a) Johnson (b) Ben Jonson
(c) Dryden (d) Lamb

45. 'Affective fallacy' is defined as the error of judging
(a) a work by its effects on the reader
(b) a work by the intention of the author
(c) inanimate objects as animate
(d) a work by affections aroused

46. Doctor Faustus in Marlowe's play is
(a) a headstrong physician
(b) a calculating gentleman
(c) an introspective ascetic
(d) a heartless sensualist

47. Who is Dryden's *An Essay of Dramatic Poesy* says that "there is no theatre in the world has anything so absurd as English tragic-comedy"?
(a) Eugenius (b) Crites
(c) Neander (d) Lisideus

48. According to Coleridge, in poetry, metre is
(a) a necessary condition
(b) not a necessary condition
(c) a super condition
(d) a mere ornament

49. The title of Robert Burton's well-known book is
    (a) *The Anatomy of Melancholy*
    (b) *Religio Medici*
    (c) *Religion of Protestantism*
    (d) *A Country Parson*
50. Which one of the following is a Movement Poet?
    (a) Louis MacNeice (b) Thom Gunn
    (c) Sylvia Plath (d) E.E. Cummings

ANSWERS

1. (c)	2. (c)	3. (b)	4. (d)
5. (c)	6. (b)	7. (a)	8. (c)
9. (b)	10. (c)	11. (b)	12. (b)
13. (d)	14. (c)	15. (c)	16. (c)
17. (b)	18. (a)	19. (d)	20. (c)
21. (d)	22. (b)	23. (d)	24. (c)
25. (a)	26. (c)	27. (c)	28. (a)
29. (d)	30. (c)	31. (d)	32. (b)
33. (d)	34. (d)	35. (a)	36. (d)
37. (d)	38. (c)	39. (c)	40. (c)
41. (b)	42. (a)	43. (b)	44. (b)
45. (a)	46. (a)	47. (d)	48. (d)
49. (a)	50. (b)		

DECEMBER 2007

1. Who said the following words: "Indo Anglian literature is a curious phenomenon with a fairly long history?"
    (a) P.P. Mehta
    (b) V.K. Gokak
    (c) K.S. Srinivas lyengar
    (d) M.K. Naik
2. To whom did Thomas Moore say the following words: "How shall we rank three upon glary's page?"
    (a) Thomas Hume
    (b) Sir Walter Raleigh
    (c) Wilberforce
    (d) Newman
3. Who is the writer of *The King Emperor's English*?
    (a) Narain
    (b) Khushwant Singh
    (c) Anand
    (d) Naik
4. *Literature and Authorship in India* is written by
    (a) Iyengar (b) Naik
    (c) Anand (d) Narain
5. *One Thousand and One Nights* was written by
    (a) Tarashankar Bandopadhyaya
    (b) S.K. Ghosh
    (c) Anand
    (d) Khushwant Singh
6. *Indian Detective Stories* was written by
    (a) S.K. Ghosh (b) S.B. Bannerjee
    (c) Narain (d) Raja Rao
7. Who wrote: "English as an Indian literary medium wore an artificial look, especially when it was realized that the mother tongue satisfied the inner urge for expression better than any other medium?"
    (a) Anand (b) Gokak
    (c) Naik (d) B.J. Wadia
8. Who is the writer of the following line: "Thoughts that breathe and works that burn?"
    (a) Shelley in 'Defence of Poetry'
    (b) Gray in 'The Progress of Poetry'
    (c) Wordsworth in 'Preface to Lyrical Ballads'
    (d) Johnson in 'The Lives of Poets'
9. Who is the writer of the following words: "English literature has benefited a great deal from translations that brought to England the best 'freights of worth that other countries had to offer?'

(a) Legouis and Czamian
(b) Courthope
(c) Baker
(d) Hugh Walker

10. Who has written the following words: "The Authorized Version of the Bible is but a translation and yet, it is an English classic."
(a) Naik (b) Gokak
(c) Iyengar (d) Anand

11. Who is generally known as the father of Bengali fiction?
(a) Bankim Chandra Chatterjee
(b) Tagore
(c) R.C. Dutta
(d) Sarat Chandra Chatterjee

12. 'Nalinaksha' is a character in
(a) *Anand Math*
(b) *Gora*
(c) *The Wreek* by Tagore
(d) *The Deliverance* by Sarat Chandra Chatterjee

13. Who wrote the romance *Binaca* or *The Young Spanish Maiden*?
(a) Tagore (b) Toru Dutt
(c) Bannerjee (d) Mrs. Ghoshal

14. Of which of the following novel of Anand, Lal Singh is not the hero?
(a) *The Village*
(b) *Across the Black Waters*
(c) *The Sword and the Sickle*
(d) *Untouchable*

15. Anand was born in
(a) Lahore (b) Sialkot
(c) Peshawar (d) Sargodha

16. Who wrote: *Waiting for the Mahatma*?
(a) Anand (b) Narayan
(c) Raja Rao (d) Prem Chand

17. 'Din Gul' is a character in
(a) *The Village* (b) *Coolie*
(c) *Untouchable* (d) *Inquilab*

18. In which of Anand's novel does a character say, "They think we are dirt because we clean their dirt?"
(a) *The Village*
(b) *Untouchable*
(c) *Coolie*
(d) *The Sword and the Sickle*

19. Who wrote the preface to Anand's *Untouchable*?
(a) Forster (b) Eliot
(c) Virginia Woolf (d) Yeats

20. When was *Untouchable* published?
(a) 1933 (b) 1934
(c) 1935 (d) 1936

21. Raja Rao was born in
(a) 1907 (b) 1908
(c) 1909 (d) 1910

22. When did Kanthapura appear?
(a) 1935 (b) 1938
(c) 1937 (d) 1933

23. 'Ramakrishna Pai' is the hero of
(a) *Kanthapura*
(b) *The Serpent and the Rope*
(c) *The Cat and Shakespeare*
(d) None of the above

24. *The Serpent and the Rope* was published in
(a) 1960 (b) 1961
(c) 1962 (d) 1963

25. The hero of *The Serpent and the Rope* is
(a) Radhakrishna
(b) Shama
(c) Ramaswamy (in short 'Rama')
(d) Govindan Nair

26. Who is the writer of *The Man-eater of Malgudi*?

(a) Narayan (b) Raja Rao
(c) Anand (d) Anita Desai

27. Which of the following is not a sentimental comedy?
(a) *The Lying Lover*
(b) *The School for Scandal*
(c) *The Tender Husband*
(d) *The Conscious Lovers*

28. 'Joseph Surface' is a character in
(a) *Tom Jones*
(b) *Joseph Andrews*
(c) *The School for Scandal*
(d) *The Lady's Slot for Burning*

29. Who has said, "Byron is one of the most concretely objective of all our poets?"
(a) Bateson
(b) Baker
(c) Henry M. Battenhouse
(d) Abrams

30. When did Byron leave Harrow and enter Trinity College at Cambridge?
(a) 1802 (b) 1803
(c) 1804 (d) 1805

31. Byron wrote: "Maid of Athens, Ere We Part" in
(a) 1807 (b) 1810
(c) 1813 (d) 1815

32. With whom did Byron go on a long journey to Portugal, Turkey, Spain etc.?
(a) Shelley (b) Coleridge
(c) Hobhouse (d) Leigh Hunt

33. Who wrote the following Lines (in 1816):
"Every feeling hath been Shaken;
Pride, which not a world could bow,
Bows to three-by thee forsaken
Even me soul forsakes me now."
(a) Shelley (b) Keats
(c) Byron (d) Southey

34. In which work does the character Medora exist?
(a) Manfred
(b) Don Juan
(c) Childe Harold's Pilgrimage
(d) Corsair

35. Whom did Byron address when he wrote (while departing from England in April 1816):
"Here's sigh to those who love me,
And a smile to those who hate;
And whatever sky's above me,
Here's a heart for every fate!"
(a) Shelley
(b) Hobhouse
(c) (His friend) (Tom Moore)
(d) Keats

36. Who wrote the following lines on Sheridan:
"........Nature formed but one such man,
And broke the die in moulding Sheridan."
(a) Shelley in Adonais
(b) Milton in Lycidas
(c) M. Arnold in Thyrsis
(d) Byron in "Death of Sheridan" (1816)

37. Byron's Cain' is dedicated to
(a) Goethe (b) Wordsworth
(c) Scott (d) Shelley

38. Who wrote the following lines:
"I believe a leaf of grass is no less than the journey-work of the stars."
(a) Whitman in *Song of Myself*
(b) Ved Vyas in *Bhagwat Gita*
(c) Keats in *Ode to Melancholy*
(d) Yeats in *Sailing to Byzantium*

39. *Halfway House* was written by
(a) Prem Chand (b) Anand
(c) Mohan Rakesh (d) Chaman Nahal

40. Shashi Deshpande's *The Binding Vine* was published in
    (a) 1999 (b) 2000
    (c) 2001 (d) 1998
41. In which metre is Prelude written?
    (a) Ottave Rima (b) Blank Verse
    (c) Free Verse (d) Terza Rima
42. In which poem do the following lines occur:
    "Let us go then, you and I
    When the evening is spread out against the sky.
    (a) The Love Song of Alfred J. Prufrock
    (b) Sailing to Byzantium
    (c) The Last Ride Together
    (d) My Last Duchess
43. In which year did T.S. Eliot receive the Nobel Prize?
    (a) 1946 (b) 1947
    (c) 1948 (d) 1950
44. Who observed the following about Anand: ....the publication of 'The Bubble' (1984) established once again that the history of Indian English Fiction is "From Anand to Anand".
    (a) Dr. Atma Ram (b) Iyenger
    (c) Naik (d) Khushwant Singh
45. Mistress Hibbins is a character in
    (a) *The Scarlet Letter*
    (b) *Herzog*
    (c) *One Hundred Years to Solitude*
    (d) *Farewell to Arms*
46. The heroine of Tom Jones is
    (a) Estella (b) Sophia
    (c) Clara (d) Dora
47. The writer of "Pilgrimage" is
    (a) Bunyan
    (b) Milton
    (c) Dorothy Richardson
    (d) Joyce
48. Who is the writer of the following lines: "That (the story) is the highest factor common to all novels, and I wish that it was not so..."
    (a) Virginia Woolf (b) Conrad
    (c) Forster (d) Joyce
49. Who said:
    "Life is not a series of gig lamps symmetrically arranged; life is a luminous halo..."
    (a) Virginia Woolf
    (b) Joyce
    (c) Proust
    (d) Dorothy Richardson
50. Marcel Proust was
    (a) an English man
    (b) a French man
    (c) an Irish man
    (d) a German

ANSWERS

1. (b)	2. (a)	3. (c)	4. (a)
5. (b)	6. (b)	7. (b)	8. (b)
9. (a)	10. (c)	11. (a)	12. (c)
13. (b)	14. (d)	15. (c)	16. (b)
17. (a)	18. (a)	19. (a)	20. (c)
21. (b)	22. (b)	23. (c)	24. (a)
25. (c)	26. (a)	27. (b)	28. (c)
29. (c)	30. (d)	31. (b)	32. (c)
33. (c)	34. (d)	35. (c)	36. (d)
37. (c)	38. (a)	39. (c)	40. (d)
41. (b)	42. (a)	43. (c)	44. (b)
45. (a)	46. (b)	47. (c)	48. (c)
49. (a)	50. (b)		

JUNE 2007

1. Which novel has a nameless narrator?
   (a) *Moby Dick*
   (b) *Anna Karenina*
   (c) *Invisible Man*
   (d) *The Grapes of Wrath*
2. Samuel Beckett wrote
   (a) *Volpone*
   (b) *Mother Courage and Her Children*
   (c) *A Doll's House*
   (d) *Endgame*
3. Which one of the following author-book pair is correctly matched?
   (a) Elfriede Jelinek – *The Pianist*
   (b) J.M. Cootzee – *Shame*
   (c) Saul Bellow – *Herzog*
   (d) Salman Rushdie – *Disgrace*
4. *The Plough* and the *Stars* was written by
   (a) G.B. Shaw
   (b) Sean O' Casey
   (c) Lady Gregory
   (d) J.M. Synge
5. Willy Loman is a character in
   (a) *Waiting for Godot*
   (b) *A Doll's House*
   (c) *The Cherry Orchard*
   (d) *The Death of a Salesman*
6. John Evellyn and Samuel Pepys were the famous writers of
   (a) editorials (b) letters
   (c) essays (d) eiaries
7. The subtitle of Dryden's Absalom and Achitophel is
   (a) there was not Subtitle
   (b) a poem
   (c) a Satire
   (d) a Satire on the True Blue Protestant Poets
8. Who of the following is not a periodical essayist?
   (a) Richard Steele
   (b) Lancelot Andews
   (c) Joseph Addison
   (d) Jonathan Swift
9. "Did he who made the Lamb made thee" appears in
   (a) "Introduction"
   (b) "The Tyger"
   (c) "Chimney Sweeper"
   (d) "London"
10. Which of the following thinker-concept pairs is rightly matched?
    (a) I.A. Richards – Archetypal Criticism
    (b) Northrop Frye – Practical Criticism
    (c) Jacqes Devide – New Historicism
    (d) Stanley Fish – Reader Response
11. "Essays of Elia" are
    (a) economic disparity
    (b) literary criticism
    (c) political ideology
    (d) personal impressions
12. Which of the following thinker-concept pairs is rightly matched?
    (a) Mamata – Vakrokti
    (b) Abhinava Gupta – Kavya Alankar
    (c) Bharata – Natya Shastra
    (d) Vaman – Dhwanyaloka
13. Choose the correct sequence of the following schools of criticism.
    (a) Deconstruction, New Criticism, Structuralism, Reader Response.
    (b) Reader Response, Deconstruction, Structuralism, New Criticism.
    (c) New Criticism, Structuralism, Deconstruction, Reader Response.
    (d) Structuralism, New Criticism, Deconstruction, Reader Response.
14. "Peripetia" means
    (a) tragic flaw
    (b) recognition of error

(c) purgation of emotion
(d) reversal of fortune

15. "Gynocriticism" focuses on
(a) criticism of male writers by women writers
(b) criticism on women
(c) criticism by women
(d) women as writers

16. Samuel Butler's Hudibras is modelled upon
(a) Don Ouixote
(b) Endymion
(c) Annus Mirabillis
(d) Pilgrim's Progress

17. Who was the last of the Christian Humanists?
(a) John Bunyan
(b) Oliver Cromwell
(c) John Milton
(d) Richard Crashaw

18. The narrative of Raja Rao's Kanthapura is based on
(a) *The Ramayana*
(b) *The Mahabharata*
(c) *Puranas*
(d) *Shastras*

19. Which of the following author-book pair is correctly matched?
(a) Arundhati Roy – *Algebra of Infinite Justice*
(b) Shashi Tharoor – *Trotter's Name*
(c) C.L.R. James – *The English Patient*
(d) David Modouf – *The City of Djins*

20. Who wrote 'A tiger does not proclaim its tigretude'?
(a) Derek Walcott (b) Soyinka
(c) Achebe (d) Ngugi

21. "Jindiworobak" movement relates to
(a) Caribbean literature
(b) Canadian literature
(c) Australian literature
(d) New Zealand literature

22. The Montreal group of poets championed the cause of—
(a) Modernist Poetry
(b) Imagist Poetry
(c) Symbolist Poetry
(d) Nature Poetry

23. The figure of the "Abyssinian Maid" appears in
(a) *Kubla Khan*
(b) *Frost at Midnight*
(c) *Dejection: an Ode*
(d) *Christabel*

24. Coleridge's statement that "imagination "dissolves, dissipates in order to recreate" relates to
(a) secondary imagination
(b) esemplastic imagination
(c) fancy
(d) primary imagination

25. Who among the following is a writer of historical romances?
(a) Walter Savage (b) Walter Scott
(c) Jane Austen (d) Emily Bronte

26. Which of the following sequences is correct?
(a) Vanity Fair, Henry Esmond, Middlemarch, The Return of the Native.
(b) Henry Esmond, Vanity Fair, Middlemarch, The Return of the Native.
(c) Middlemarch, The Return of the Native, Vanity Fair, Henry Esmond.
(d) The Return of the Native, Middlemarch, Vanity Fair, Henry Esmond.

27. Queen Victoria's reign, after whom the Victorian period is named, spans

(a) 1833-1901 (b) 1837-1901
(c) 1840-1905 (d) 1842-1905

28. Pre-Raphaelite poetry is mainly concerned with
(a) narrative and style
(b) narrative and nature
(c) form and design
(d) form and value

29. The concept of "mad woman in the attic" can be traced to
(a) The Tenant of Wildfell Hall
(b) Villette
(c) Wuthering Heights
(d) Jane Eyre

30. Who among the Victorians is called "the prophet of modern society"?
(a) Ruskin (b) Carlyle
(c) Macaulay (d) Arnold

31. Who among the following is not pilgrim in *The Canterbury Tales*?
(a) The Haberdasher (b) The Tapyser
(c) The Blacksmith (d) The Summoner

32. Bosola is the executioner in
(a) The Spanish Tragedy
(b) The Duches of Malfi
(c) The White Devil
(d) The Jew of Malta

33. The mystery plays deal with
(a) The Life of Christ
(b) The New Testament
(c) Psalms
(d) Apocrypha

34. The Faerie Queene is based on
(a) Utopia
(b) Tottel's Miscellany
(c) Morte d' Arthur
(d) Orlando Furioso

35. Choose the correct chronological sequence of the following plays:
(a) *King Lear, Othello, Macbeth, Hamlet*
(b) *Othello, Macbeth, King Lear, Hamlet*
(c) *Hamlet, Othello, King Lear, Macbeth*
(d) *Hamlet, King Lear, Othello, Macbeth*

36. Pope's "Essay on Criticism" sums up the art of poetry as taught first by
(a) Aristotle (b) Horace
(c) Longinus (d) Plato

37. Swift's *Tale of a Tub* is a satire on
(a) science and philosophy
(b) art and morality
(c) dogma and superstition
(d) fake morals and manners

38. Dr. Johnson started
(a) The Postman (b) The Spectator
(c) The Rambler (d) The Tatler

39. Who among the following cautioned against the dangers of popular liberty?
(a) Mary Wollstonecraft
(b) Edmund Burke
(c) Thomas Hobbes
(d) John Locke

40. Which famous American classic opens with "Call me Ishmael"?
(a) Rip Van Winkle
(b) The Scarlet Letter
(c) The Grapes of Wrath
(d) Moby Dick

41. Allen Ginsberg's Vision of America is inspired by
(a) Walt Whitman
(b) Robert Frost
(c) Ralph Waldo Emerson
(d) Edgar A Poe

42. Who among the following represents the Sri Lankan diaspora?
(a) M.G. Vassanji
(b) Cyril Debydeen
(c) Michael Ondaatje
(d) Arnold H. Itwaru

43. Out of Africa is a ilm adaptation of a work by
   (a) Alice Walker
   (b) Margaret Lawrence
   (c) Margaret Atwood
   (d) Alice Munro

44. The Empire writes Back was written by
   (a) Bill Ashcroft, Helen Tiffin, Ngugi Wa Thinngo
   (b) Bill Ashcroft, Helen Tiffin, Stephen Slemon
   (c) Bill Ashcroft, Gareth Griffiths, Chinua Achebe
   (d) Bill Ashcroft, Helen Tiffin, Gareth Griffiths

45. The Theatre of Cruelty is associated with
   (a) Stanislavosky
   (b) Grotovsky
   (c) Antonin Artand
   (d) Eugino Barba

46. A particle is
   (a) a patchwork of words, sentences, passages
   (b) a satirical poem
   (c) a love song
   (d) a collection of lines from different poems

47. "Careless she is with artful Care/Affecting to seem unaffected" is an example of
   (a) Irony (b) Paradox
   (c) Simile (d) Metaphor

48. A metrical foot containing a stressed, followed by an unstressed, a syllable is
   (a) Anapaest (b) Lamb
   (c) Trochee (d) Dactyle

49. The rhyme scheme of a Spenserian sonnet is
   (a) abcb, cbch, cdcd, ee
   (b) abab, bccb, ee
   (c) aabb, bcbc, ccdd, ee
   (d) abab, bcbc, cdcd, ee

50. Using the expression "Crown" for the monarchy is an example of
   (a) Metonymy (b) Synecdoche
   (c) Irony (d) Metaphor

ANSWERS

1. (c)	2. (d)	3. (c)	4. (b)
5. (d)	6. (d)	7. (b)	8. (d)
9. (c)	10. (d)	11. (d)	12. (c)
13. (b)	14. (d)	15. (d)	16. (a)
17. (a)	18. (c)	19. (a)	20. (c)
21. (a)	22. (a)	23. (a)	24. (d)
25. (b)	26. (a)	27. (b)	28. (c)
29. (c)	30. (d)	31. (b)	32. (b)
33. (b)	34. (c)	35. (c)	36. (c)
37. (c)	38. (c)	39. (b)	40. (a)
41. (a)	42. (c)	43. (b)	44. (c)
45. (b)	46. (a)	47. (b)	48. (c)
49. (d)	50. (a)		

DECEMBER 2006

1. Who wrote "All our knowledge brings us nearer to our ignorance"?
   (a) John Milton
   (b) T.S. Eliot
   (c) William Wordsworth
   (d) Shakespeare

2. "Jacobean drama" means the drama of
   (a) The Puritan Age
   (b) The 19th Century
   (c) The Elizabethan Age
   (d) All the Ages

3. "Restoration Period" takes its name from the restoration of
   (a) Commonwealth
   (b) The Romantic spirit
   (c) The Sturat line to the English throne
   (d) None of the above

4. "Renaissance" means
   (a) a new beginning
   (b) back to nature
   (c) age is Elizabeth
   (d) rebirth
5. War and Peace is written by
   (a) Leo Tolstoy (b) Anton Tchekov
   (c) Turgenev (d) Dante
6. Voltarie is ________
   (a) a Russian novelist
   (b) a French satirist and novelist
   (c) an English novelist
   (d) None of the above
7. An exiled Russian novelist is the author of Gulag Archipelago, Gancer Ward, One day in The Life of Iron Ivorovich. Identify him from the names given below.
   (a) Leo Tolstoy
   (b) Alexander Dumas
   (c) Alexander Solyzentsin
   (d) Feodore Doestoevsky
8. Albert Camus was a French existentialist. Given below is the list of his novels. Identify the novels not written by him.
   (a) *The Trial*, *The Castle*
   (b) *The Plague*, *The Outsider*
   (c) *The Renel*, *The Myth of Sisyphus*
   (d) All of the above
9. The author of *Portrait of India* is
   (a) V.S. Naipaul (b) N.C. Chaudhary
   (c) Ved Mehta (d) E.M. Forster
10. *Revenue Stamp* is the autobiography of
    (a) Dalip Kaur Tiwana
    (b) Amrita Pritam
    (c) Shivani
    (d) Shobha De
11. Which of the following novels came under burning criticism and, even threats?
    (a) *The Suitable Boy*
    (b) *Satanic Verses*
    (c) *The Great Indian Novel*
    (d) *English August*
12. Who wrote *My True Faces*, *Azadi*, *Into Another Dawn*, *The Crown and the Lioncloth*?
    (a) Sudhir Ghose
    (b) Khushwant Singh
    (c) Manohar Malgonkar
    (d) Chaman Nahal
13. Identify the another of
    "Where is the wisdom we have lost in knowledge?
    Where is the knowledge we have lost in information?
    (a) William Wordsworth
    (b) William Shakespeare
    (c) T.S. Eliot
    (d) W.B. Yeats
14. Name the author of the *Moor's Last Sigh*.
    (a) Salman Rushdie (b) Anita Desai
    (c) Kate Atkinson (d) Vikram Seth
15. "Imagism," a poetic movement flourished in England and America between 1912-17. Who of the following was/were associated with it?
    (a) D.H. Lawrence (b) Amy Lowell
    (c) Ezra Pound (d) All of the above
16. Which of the following is not Anita Desai's work?
    (a) *In Custody*
    (b) *Voices in the City*
    (c) *A Silence of Desire*
    (d) *Clear Light of Day*
17. Who is the author of *Walden*?
    (a) E.W. Emerson (b) Thoreau
    (c) Romain Rolland (d) Nathaniel West
18. Mahatma Gandhi liked the hymn "Lead Kindly Light." Who is the author of this?

(a) Leight Hunt (b) Walter Scott
(c) William Blake (d) John Milton

19. George Meredith is a
(a) novelist (b) playwright
(c) essayist (d) dramatist

20. 'Pindaric' ode is also known as
(a) Irregular ode (b) Horatian ode
(c) Regular ode (d) Jura ode

21. 'Bacon's Essays' first appeared in
(a) 1612 (b) 1622
(c) 1580 (d) 1597

22. *The Affair* is a novel by
(a) Evelyn Waugh
(b) Joyce Cary
(c) C.P. Snow
(d) None of the above

23. Who ruled over England during the 'Georgian Age' in modern period?
(a) George III (b) George V
(c) George I (d) George VI

24. Addison wrote 51 essays for the Guardian, started by
(a) Doctor Johnson (b) Steele
(c) Swift (d) Himself

25. Name the writer of Party-Going.
(a) Graham Green (b) Hentry Green
(c) Robert Green (d) Mathew Green

26. Who is the writer of the sequence of novels entitled *A Dance to the Music of Time*?
(a) Aldous Huxley (b) Anthony Powell
(c) Kingsely Amis (d) John Barine

27. Which character in Hardy's *The Mayor of Casterbridge* sells his wife?
(a) Newson
(b) Gabriel Oak
(c) Henchard
(d) None of the above

28. Name the poet which belongs to the Victorian age but is a modern in matters of technique.
(a) Swinburne (b) Rossetti
(c) Hopkins (d) Hardy

29. Virginia Woolf belonged to a group of eminent literart figures, which was known as
(a) Angry Young Men
(b) Avant Garde
(c) Bloomsbury Group
(d) None of the above

30. All of Marlowe's plays are
(a) comedies (b) tragedies
(c) romantic (d) tragic-comedies

31. Time's Laughing Stocks is a _____ by Hardy.
(a) novel
(b) poem
(c) play
(d) collection of Poems

32. Who is the writer of *The Beggar's Opera*?
(a) Pope (b) Defoe
(c) John Gay (d) Thomas Gray

33. 'Alpha of the Plough' is the pen-name of the essayist
(a) G.K. Chesterton (b) Robert Lynd
(c) A.C. Benson (d) A.G. Gardiner

34. Pope's *An Essay on Man* is
(a) an essay (b) a short story
(c) a poem (d) None of the above

35. By whom was the critical term 'Negative Capability' introduced?
(a) Dryden (b) Coleridge
(c) John Keats (d) T.S. Eliot

36. Which of the undermentioned works is by T.S. Eliot?
(a) Little Dorrit (b) Little Gidding
(c) Little Women (d) The Little Girls

37. Christopher Isherwood has collaborated in the translation of the great Indian Classic.
    (a) *The Ramayana*
    (b) *The Bhagwat Gita*
    (c) *The Rig Veda*
    (d) *The Mahabharata*
38. Which critical work has Sidney written?
    (a) An Apologie for Poetrie
    (b) A Defence of Rhyme
    (c) The Defence of Poetry
    (d) Study of Poetry
39. Bacon has written in
    (a) French and English
    (b) Latin and French
    (c) Latin and English
    (d) Greek and Latin
40. Which of these books is not written by Swift?
    (a) *The Rape of the Lock*
    (b) *Gulliver's Travels*
    (c) *The Conduct of the Allies*
    (d) *The Battle of the Books*
41. Which of the following books is a novel by Galsworthy?
    (a) *The Man of Feeling*
    (b) *The Man of Destiny*
    (c) *The Man of Property*
    (d) *The Man of Honour*
42. Joseph Conrad was of ______ origin.
    (a) German (b) Greek
    (c) Polish (d) Lyric
43. What kind of poem is Milton's 'Lycidas'?
    (a) Elegy (b) Epic
    (c) Ode (d) Lyric
44. Which of these is not a play by Bernard Shaw?
    (a) *Arms and the Man*
    (b) *Candida*
    (c) *The Philanderer*
    (d) *The Skin Game*
45. Milton's *Paradise Lost* consists of ______ books.
    (a) ten (b) twelve
    (c) six (d) eight
46. 'The Ode to Evening' is written by
    (a) Gray (b) Collins
    (c) Pope (d) Cowper
47. Most of the novels of R.K. Narayan are set in
    (a) Madras (b) Malgudi
    (c) Trivandrum (d) Mano Majra
48. The critical essays of Walter Pater are collected in the form of a book under the title
    (a) Critical Essays
    (b) Essays in Criticism
    (c) Appreciations
    (d) Revaluations
49. Ottava Rima is a ______ stanza in Imabic pentameters.
    (a) six-lined (b) four-lined
    (c) eight-lined (d) ten-lined
50. In 1769, Coleridge started a periodical, named
    (a) The Idler (b) The Rambler
    (c) The Guardian (d) The Watchman

ANSWERS

1. (b)	2. (a)	3. (c)	4. (d)
5. (a)	6. (b)	7. (c)	8. (a)
9. (c)	10. (b)	11. (b)	12. (d)
13. (c)	14. (a)	15. (d)	16. (c)
17. (b)	18. (a)	19. (a)	20. (c)
21. (d)	22. (c)	23. (b)	24. (b)
25. (b)	26. (b)	27. (c)	28. (c)
29. (c)	30. (b)	31. (d)	32. (c)

33. (d) 34. (c) 35. (c) 36. (b)
37. (d) 38. (a) 39. (c) 40. (a)
41. (c) 42. (c) 43. (a) 44. (d)
45. (b) 46. (b) 47. (b) 48. (c)
49. (c) 50. (d)

JUNE 2006

1. Existentialism in its religious aspect goes back to
   (a) Kierkgaard (b) Satire
   (c) Camus (d) Heideggger
2. In which of his books does Carlyle discuss "the condition-of-England question"?
   (a) *Sartor Resartus*
   (b) *On Heroes, Hero-worship, and the Heroic in Poetry*
   (c) *Chartism*
   (d) *French Revolution*
3. When was the First Folio of Shakespeare's plays published?
   (a) 1623 (b) 1603
   (c) 1634 (d) 1599
4. Who said that *Hamlet* is "most certainly an aristic failure"?
   (a) Ben Jonson (b) Dr. Johnson
   (c) T.S. Eliot (d) L.C. Knights
5. Which of the following comedies was attacked by Steele in *The Spectator*?
   (a) *The Man of Mode*
   (b) *The Country Wife*
   (c) *The Double Dealer*
   (d) *The Way of the World*
6. Whose style was praised by Dr. Johnson as "elegant but not oustentatious, familiar but not ostentatious, familiar but not coarse"?
   (a) Dryden (b) Fielding
   (c) Addison (d) Goldsmith
7. Who, in Pope's Epistle to Dr. Arbuthnot, was "willing to wound but afraid to strike"?
   (a) Shaftesbury (b) Lord Harvey
   (c) Dryden (d) Addison
8. 'Surrealism' was lauched in France by
   (a) Andre Breton (b) Mallarme
   (c) Louis Aragon (d) Baudelaire
9. Who, among the following, is not one of the "The Pylin Poets"?
   (a) W.H. Auden (b) Stephen Spender
   (c) Day Lewis (d) W.B. Yeats
10. Which of the following names is associated with the controversy over the 'two cultures', scientific and literary?
    (a) Robert Lynd (b) C.P. Snow
    (c) Wilson Knight (d) Bertrand Russel
11. The Shield of Achilles is by
    (a) Homer (b) Aeschylus
    (c) W.H. Auden (d) Stephen Spender
12. "Nupital love maketh mankind: friendly love perfecteth it: but wanton love corrupteth and embaseth it". Where do these words occur?
    (a) The Old Testament
    (b) Francis Bacon
    (c) Sir Thomas Browne
    (d) John Bunyan
13. Sir Philip Sidney's Apologie for Poetrie is a rejoinder to
    (a) Plato's Symposium
    (b) Sir Leslie Stephen's An Agnostic's Apology
    (c) Stephen Gosson's Schoole of Abuse
    (d) Edmund Spenser's Complaints
14. Spenser's Astrophel is an elegy on
    (a) Sir Walter Raleigh
    (b) James I
    (c) Sir Philip Sidney
    (d) John Wyatt

15. Milton's *Comus* is
(a) an allegory (b) a masque
(c) an ode (d) a lyric

16. Dryden's *The Conquest of Granada* is a
(a) romantic tragedy
(b) heroic play
(c) romantic comedy
(d) revenge tragedy

17. "Pathetic fallacy" means
(a) building up misplaced pathos
(b) making a sad error
(c) treating inanimate objects as animate
(d) investing objects with human emotions

18. Be Produndis is
(a) a verse play
(b) a prose romance
(c) a personal letter
(d) a novel

19. *The Gates of Paradise* is by
(a) William Blake (b) Robert Southey
(c) John Milton (d) Dante Alighieri

20. Tennyson's *The Princess* deals with
(a) a moral dilemma
(b) women's education
(c) a child's dream
(d) a historical event

21. The character Subtle appears in Ben Johnson's
(a) *Everyman in His Humour*
(b) *Everyman out of His Humour*
(c) *Voepone or the Fox*
(d) *The Azchemist*

22. Who calls Shelley "a beautiful but ineffectual angel, beating in the void his huminous wings in vain"?
(a) Matthew Arnold (b) Swinburne
(c) T.S. Eliot (d) Walter Pater

23. Who said that Donne in his poetry "affected the metaphysics"?
(a) John Dryden (b) Dr. Johnson
(c) T.S. Eliot (d) H.J.C. Grierson

24. In Dryden's Absolem and Achitophel Corah stands for
(a) The Duke of Buckingham
(b) Charles II
(c) The Earl of Shaftesbury
(d) Titus Oates

25. The theme of Allegory of Love by C.S. Lewis is
(a) romantic love (b) courtly love
(c) physical love (d) divine love

26. If you say 'contagious countries' instead of 'contiguous countries', you will be making a mistake known as
(a) Euphuism (b) Spoonerism
(c) Malapropism (d) Euphemism

27. The verse in *The Canterbury Tales* consists of
(a) alliterative lines
(b) unrhymed couplets
(c) alternative lines rhyming
(d) rhymed couplets

28. The story of Sohrab and Rustum is taken from
(a) *Omar Khayyam*
(b) *Folk Literature*
(c) *The Arabian Nights*
(d) *Firdausi*

29. For Horace the most important literary value is
(a) proper diction (b) fidelity
(c) decorum (d) perspicuity

30. Eugenius in Dryden's Essay of Dramatic Poesy criticizes the Greek drama on the ground that it
(a) has conventional plot
(b) is too formal on account of the unities
(c) lacks innovation in themes
(d) is untrue to life in upholding truth

31. Identify the critic who has explained the distinction between organic form and mechanical form.
   (a) Eliot (b) Wordsworth
   (c) Lamb (d) Coleridge
32. The Oxford Movement sought to
   (a) reject the Roman Catholic Church
   (b) reinstate the Roman Catholic Church
   (c) reject the Church of England
   (d) reconcile the Church of England and the Roman Catholic Church
33. Chartist Movement was a movement for
   (a) women's rights
   (b) equal distribution of wealth
   (c) children's rights
   (d) electoral reforms
34. Who describes poetry as "the impassioned expression which is in the countenance of all science"?
   (a) Carlyle (b) Shelley
   (c) Wordsworth (d) Coleridge
35. Philistines in 'Culture and Anarchy' stand for
   (a) the English middle class
   (b) the English aristocracy
   (c) the English working class
   (d) the English Jews
36. Who attacked the Pre-Raphaelite poetry in the Fleshly School of Poetry?
   (a) Thomas Carlyle
   (b) Oliver Goldsmith
   (c) Robert Buchanan
   (d) Jeremy Collier
37. The object of imitation in drama, according to Aristotle, is
   (a) human beings
   (b) events
   (c) actions of human beings
   (d) moral excellence
38. The first English comedy was
   (a) *Ralph Roister Doister*
   (b) *Gammar Gurton's Needle*
   (c) *Euphues*
   (d) *A Midsummer Night's Dream*
39. *The Unfortunate Traveller* or *The Life of Jack Wilton* was written by
   (a) John Lyly (b) Thomas Nash
   (c) Thomas Lodge (d) Robert Greene
40. Chapman is best known for his
   (a) The Gentleman Usher
   (b) Hymns, 1624
   (c) The Admiral of France
   (d) Translations of Homer
41. English Puritanism found its first allegories in
   (a) John Bunyan
   (b) Sir Thomas Browne
   (c) Edmund Spenser
   (d) John Milton
42. Sir Gawayne and the Green Knight was written by
   (a) England
   (b) an unknown poet
   (c) Geoffrey of Monmouth
   (d) Chaucer
43. The first complete version of the Bible in English was made by
   (a) Wycliffe (b) Tyndale
   (c) Coverdale (d) King James I
44. The first example of blank verse in English is
   (a) Chaucer's Roman de ta Rose
   (b) Langland's Piers the Plowman
   (c) Surrey's Translation of the Second Aeneid
   (d) Michael Drayton's Shepherd's Garland
45. *Miracle Plays* were based on
   (a) stories from the Bible
   (b) stories from the lives of the saints

(c) marvellous happenings and events
(d) concepts of Christian theology

46. "All animals are equal, but some animals are more equal than other." This line occurs in
(a) *The Lord of the Flies*
(b) *Gulliver's Travels*
(c) *Animal Farm*
(d) *Nineteen Eighty-Four*

47. Who, among the following, is a 'materialist', according to Virginia Woolf?
(a) Thomas Hardy (b) Arnold Bennett
(c) James Joyce (d) George Eliot

48. Which novelist is primarily known for his epistolary novels?
(a) Jane Austen (b) Defoe
(c) Fielding (d) Richardson

49. Johnson's phrase, "fatal Cleopatra", refers to Shakespeare's
(a) neglect of the unities
(b) fondness for puns
(c) fondness for similes
(d) love of allusions

50. One of the sources of the symbolism of The Waste Land is
(a) Symbolist Movement in Literature
(b) The Golden Bough
(c) The Myth of Sisyphus
(d) The Road to Xanadu

ANSWERS

1. (a)	2. (c)	3. (a)	4. (c)
5. (b)	6. (c)	7. (c)	8. (a)
9. (d)	10. (b)	11. (c)	12. (b)
13. (c)	14. (c)	15. (b)	16. (b)
17. (d)	18. (c)	19. (a)	20. (b)
21. (d)	22. (a)	23. (a)	24. (d)
25. (b)	26. (c)	27. (d)	28. (d)
29. (c)	30. (b)	31. (d)	32. (d)
33. (d)	34. (c)	35. (a)	36. (c)
37. (c)	38. (a)	39. (b)	40. (d)
41. (a)	42. (b)	43. (d)	44. (c)
45. (b)	46. (c)	47. (b)	48. (d)
49. (b)	50. (b)		

DECEMBER 2005

1. The *Origin of the Species* was published in
(a) 1842 (b) 1849
(c) 1859 (d) 1855

2. The assassination of the Archduke Francis Ferdinand led to
(a) Fragmentation of the Balkans
(b) World War I
(c) World War II
(d) The Rise of Bismark

3. The notion of 'tension' in poetry was advanced by
(a) R.P. Blackmur (b) Austin Warren
(c) Cleanth Brooks (d) Allen Tate

4. 'Strong lined' poetry was a term applied in its day to
(a) Metaphysical poetry
(b) Augustan satire
(c) Hopkin's poetry
(d) Imagist poetry

5. The term 'apron stage' refers to
(a) Greek theatre
(b) Brechtion theatre
(c) Elizabethan theatre
(d) Opera

6. James Joyce's *Ulysses* was published in
(a) 1916 (b) 1922
(c) 1926 (d) 1930

7. T.S. Eliot's line "Sweet Thames run softly till I end my song" is a quotation from
(a) Shakespeare (b) Doane
(c) Wordsworth (d) Spenser

8. The group known as the Movement Poets does not include
   (a) Robert Conquest (b) Kingsley Amis
   (c) W.H. Auden (d) Philip Larkin
9. Shaw's concept of the Life Force is enunciated in
   (a) *Arms and the Man*
   (b) *Canada*
   (c) *Man and Superman*
   (d) *The Apple Cart*
10. Many of D.H. Lawrence's novels are set in
    (a) The Nottingham region
    (b) Yorkshire
    (c) Wessex
    (d) Ulster
11. Robert Frost's nature poems are chiefly set in
    (a) The Midwest (b) New Hamphire
    (c) The South (d) California
12. *The Zoo Story* is an absurdist play because
    (a) there are animal characters in it
    (b) the characters are absurd persons
    (c) mad persons appear in it
    (d) it lacks external action
13. Hester wrore the 'Scarlet letter' as
    (a) a mark of sexual transgression
    (b) a token of Dimmesdale's guilt
    (c) a momento of her relationship with the pastor
    (d) a religious observance
14. The Harikatha tradition has been extensively used in
    (a) *A River Sutra*
    (b) *The Gangaghat and Other Stories*
    (c) *Kanthapura*
    (d) *The Serpent and the Rope*
15. The poet who writes about "Whoring after the English Gods" is
    (a) A.K. Ramanujan
    (b) F. Parthasarathy
    (c) Jayanta Mahapatra
    (d) Vikram Seth
16. An Indian English novelist who is also a prominent writer of verse, is
    (a) Salman Rushdie (b) Vikram Seth
    (c) Arundhati Roy (d) Amitav Ghosh
17. The Mau May rebellion is used in a major way in
    (a) *Weep Not, Child*
    (b) *Things Fall Apart*
    (c) *Cry the Beloved Country*
    (d) *A Grain of Wheat*
18. The novel by Achebe which describes the celebration of the Uri Feast of Obierika's daughter, is
    (a) *A Man of the People*
    (b) *Things Fall Apart*
    (c) *Arrow of God*
    (d) *Anthills of the Savannath*
19. The rocks of Britanny feature in Chaucer's
    (a) *Miller's Tale*
    (b) *Franklin's Tale*
    (c) *Wife of Bath's Tale*
    (d) *Porton's Tale*
20. The first practitioner of Blank Verse was:
    (a) Chaucer (b) Marlowe
    (c) Surrey (d) Shakespeare
21. Book IV of the Faerie Queence is devoted to
    (a) holiness (b) courtesy
    (c) temperance (d) friendship
22. Sir Epicure Mammon is a character in
    (a) *The Alchemist*
    (b) *Volphone*
    (c) *Every Man in His Humour*
    (d) *Sejanus*

23. In the phrase 'O Brave New World' used by Miranda, 'brave' means
    (a) courageous (b) audacious
    (c) virtuous (d) beautiful
24. The editors of the First Folio of Shakespeare's plays were
    (a) Heminge and Condall
    (b) Beaumont and Fletcher
    (c) Johnson and Drayton
    (d) Middleton and Tourneur
25. Lycidas is an Elegy on the death of
    (a) Charles I (b) Oliver Cromwell
    (c) Edward King (d) Charles Diodati
26. The phrase "The wasp of Twicenham" is applied to
    (a) Dryden (b) Pope
    (c) Johnson (d) Swift
27. The Battle of the Books discusses the conflict between
    (a) English writers and French writers
    (b) The Ancients and the Moderns
    (c) Ben Johnson and Shakespeare
    (d) Swift and Addison
28. Wordsworth was accused of being 'the lost leader' by
    (a) Shelley (b) Byron
    (c) Arnold (d) Browning
29. A Prince of Abyssinia features in a work by
    (a) Johnson (b) Defoe
    (c) Goldsmith (d) Sheridan
30. Cain is the subject of a work by
    (a) Keats (b) Scott
    (c) Byron (d) Southey
31. Tennyson's *The Princess* deals with
    (a) enchantment
    (b) women's emanicipation
    (c) Arthurian legend
    (d) evolution
32. Dickens treats of 'the law's delay' in
    (a) *Hard Times*
    (b) *Oliver Twist*
    (c) *Little Dorrit*
    (d) *Nicholas Nickleby*
33. Hardy's title 'Far From the Madding Crowd' is taken from a poem by
    (a) Gray (b) Collins
    (c) Wordsworth (d) Keats
34. *A Fine Balance* is a novel by
    (a) M.G. Vassanji
    (b) Bharati Mukherjee
    (c) Rohinton Mistry
    (d) M.H. Kingston
35. Patrick White's 'The Solid Mandala' shares the concept of Mandala with
    (a) Freud (b) Adler
    (c) Lacan (d) Jung
36. According to Aristotle, the least essential part of tragedy is
    (a) Thought (b) Spectacle
    (c) Diction (d) Melody
37. The concept of literary 'decorum' is memorably proposed by
    (a) Longinus (b) Plato
    (c) Horace (d) Seneca
38. The observation "He invades authors like a monarch: and what would be theft in other poets, is only victory in him"—is about
    (a) Ben Jonson (b) Shakespeare
    (c) Beaumont (d) Fletcher
39. Wordsworth presents his views on the nature and function of poetry first in
    (a) the 'Preface' to the 1800 edition of the Lyrical Ballads.
    (b) the 'Advertisement' appended to the first edition of the Lyrical ballads.
    (c) a Separate Supplement.
    (d) a Letter of Dorothy.

40. The dictum that Life imitates Art is expounded by
(a) John Ruskin (b) Walter Pater
(c) Oscar Wilde (d) Matthew Arnold

41. F.R. Leavis's 'great tradition' of the English novel does not include
(a) Jane Austen (b) Thomas Hardy
(c) George Eliot (d) Joseph Conrad

42. 'Structuralism' was first employed in the study of
(a) psychoanalysis (b) anthropology
(c) literature (d) linguistics

43. The lines "Stern Daughter of the voice of God, O Duty!" illustrate
(a) synecdoche (b) antithesis
(c) apostrophe (d) interrogation

44. The lines "Bare ruined choirs, where late the sweet birds sang" contains feet that are
(a) spondaic (b) pyrrhic
(c) dactylic (d) hypermetrical

45. Information about the lives of famous Englishmen will be found in
(a) PMLA (b) DNB
(c) OED (d) NCBEL

46. The Authorized Version of the Bible appeared in the reign of
(a) Elizabeth I (b) Richard III
(c) Charles I (d) James I

47. The English writer who was imprisoned in France during the French Revolution was
(a) Byron (b) Wordsworth
(c) Tom Paine (d) Edmund Burke

48. *A Vindication of the Rights of Woman* was written by
(a) Mary Wollstonecraft
(b) Elair e Showalter
(c) Julia Kristeva
(d) Mary Shelley

49. Queen Victoria ascended the throne in
(a) 1830 (b) 1837
(c) 1832 (d) 1857

50. In Lycidas "the Pilot of the Gallean lake" refers to
(a) Jesus Christ (b) Pontius Pilate
(c) St. Peter (d) John the Baptist

ANSWERS

1. (c)	2. (b)	3. (d)	4. (c)
5. (c)	6. (b)	7. (d)	8. (c)
9. (c)	10. (a)	11. (b)	12. (b)
13. (a)	14. (c)	15. (a)	16. (b)
17. (d)	18. (b)	19. (b)	20. (c)
21. (d)	22. (a)	23. (d)	24. (a)
25. (c)	26. (b)	27. (b)	28. (d)
29. (a)	30. (c)	31. (b)	32. (c)
33. (a)	34. (c)	35. (d)	36. (d)
37. (c)	38. (b)	39. (b)	40. (a)
41. (b)	42. (b)	43. (c)	44. (d)
45. (b)	46. (d)	47. (c)	48. (a)
49. (b)	50. (c)		

JUNE 2005

1. "I speak and write in English but do not altogether share the preoccupations and perspectives of an Englishman"—was said by
(a) Rushdie (b) Conrad
(c) Walcott (d) Henry

2. Who wrote *The Inheritors*?
(a) Darwin (b) Golding
(c) Lessing (d) Woolf

3. The Future Poetry is written by
(a) Arnold (b) Aurobindo
(c) Ramanujan (d) Daruwalla

4. Which person from the following list received the Nobel Prize for literature?

(a) Winston Churchill
(b) Albert Schweitzer
(c) Graham Greene
(d) Martin Amis

5. 'The grizzly bear is huge and wild'. This line is in
(a) dactylic metre
(b) iambic metre
(c) dactylic with iambic variation
(d) iambic with dactylic variation

6. 'Venus and Adonis' is a poem written by
(a) Keats (b) Johnson
(c) Shakespeare (d) Heywood

7. Who wrote the *Cocktail Party*?
(a) Pinter (b) Eliot
(c) Greene (d) Galsworthy

8. Belinda is a character in
(a) *Absalom and Achitophel*
(b) *Paradise Lost*
(c) *The Rape of the Lock*
(d) *The Beggar's Opera*

9. Who is the author of 'The Moon And Sixpence'?
(a) Maugham (b) Pound
(c) Yeats (d) Eliot

10. Bobadill is a character in
(a) *Every Man in His Humour*
(b) *Pickwick Papers*
(c) *Roderick Random*
(d) *Moll Flanders*

11. A novel tracing the development of the artist is known as
(a) Bildungsroman
(b) Erziehungsroman
(c) Kunstleroman
(d) Graeco Roman

12. *Bhowani Junction* is written by
(a) Paul Scot
(b) John Masters
(c) Bhabani Bhattacharya
(d) Amitav Ghosh

13. *Archeology of Knowledge* is written by
(a) Aristotle
(b) Roland Barthes
(c) Jean Francois Lyotart
(d) Michel Foucault

14. "When I consider how my light is spent ...." is an example of
(a) Synecdoche (b) Hyperbole
(c) Metonymy (d) Pun

15. Who among the following is not a Marxist critic?
(a) Christopher Caudwell
(b) Raymond Williams
(c) Terry Eagleton
(d) Victor Shkolovsky

16. In An Essay of Dramatic Poesie, the views of Dryden are expressed by
(a) Crites (b) Neander
(c) Eugenius (d) Lisideus

17. Stephen Greenblatt is associated with
(a) texture and structure
(b) base and superstructure
(c) intension and extension
(d) resonance and wonder

18. Velutha, the untouchable, appears in
(a) *The God of Small Things*
(b) *Coolie*
(c) *Untouchable*
(d) *In Custody*

19. Who is considered to be the founder of the Chicago School of Criticism?
(a) C.K. Ogden (b) R.P. Blackmur
(c) R.S. Crane (d) Cleanth Brooks

20. Uncle Toby appears in
(a) *Tom Jones*
(b) *All My Sons*
(c) *Uncle Tom's Cabin*
(d) *Tristram Shandy*

21. Who wrote *Travels*?
(a) Swift (b) Mandeville
(c) Wells (d) Forster

22. Who wrote the following line
"The proper study of mankind is man?"
(a) Dryden (b) Wordsworth
(c) Arnold (d) Pope

23. Queen Victoria ascended the throne in
(a) 1830 (b) 1834
(c) 1837 (d) 1857

24. The act of Supremacy to make Henry VIII "Supreme head on earth of the Church of England" was passed in
(a) 1434 (b) 1534
(c) 1634 (d) 1734

25. Which of the following dramatists does not belong to the group called 'University Wits'?
(a) George Peele (b) Thomas Lodge
(c) John Webster (d) Thomas Nash

26. Who wrote the following line
"A hard time we had of it"?
(a) Dickens (b) Pound
(c) Arnold (d) Eliot

27. Which of the following does not belong to the Pre-Raphaelite Brotherhood?
(a) Swinburne (b) Rossetti
(c) Millais (d) Hunt

28. The phrase "dissociation of sensibility" was used by Eliot in
(a) Tradition and The Individual Talent
(b) The Metaphysical Poets
(c) Dante
(d) Baudelaire

29. The author of 'The Purloined Letter' is
(a) Poe (b) Richardson
(c) Voltaire (d) Romain Rolland

30. The phrase "Art for Art's sake" was introduced by
(a) Baudelaire (b) Mallarme
(c) Gautier (d) Wilde

31. Who wrote *Masque of Anarchy*?
(a) Godwin (b) Milton
(c) Shelley (d) Arnold

32. The *Woman in White* is written by
(a) Collins (b) Lawrence
(c) Marvell (d) Defoe

33. *The Waste Land* was published in
(a) 1911 (b) 1917
(c) 1922 (d) 1924

34. Who wrote *Troilus and Criseyde*?
(a) Shakespeare (b) Chaucer
(c) Homer (d) Dryden

35. Germaine Greer wrote
(a) *The Female Eunuch*
(b) *Sexual Politics*
(c) *Sexual/Textual Politics*
(d) *The Female Form*

36. "Honest criticism and sensitive appreciation is directed not upon the poet but upon the poetry." Who said the above sentence?
(a) Arnold (b) Eliot
(c) Ransom (d) Leavis

37. The founder of the Oxford Movement was
(a) Thomas Huxley (b) Charles Lamb
(c) John Newman (d) John Keble

38. Who is the author of 'Rosencrantz and Guildenstern Are Dead'?
(a) William Shakespeare
(b) G.B. Shaw
(c) Tom Stoppard
(d) John Osborne

39. Who wrote "The Vanity of Human Wishes"?
(a) Jonathan Swift
(b) Samuel Johnson

(c) Ben Jonson
(d) Alexander Pope

40. Who admired Ben Jonson but loved Shakespeare?
(a) Pope (b) Hazlitt
(c) Coleridge (d) Dryden

41. Who coined the term Stream of Consciousness?
(a) William James (b) Henry James
(c) James Joyce (d) J.S. Mill

42. Who among the following is also known as a lexicographer?
(a) Webster (b) Golding
(c) Johnson (d) Sterne

43. How many years did Tennyson take in composing In Memoriam?
(a) Nearly 7 years (b) Nearly 10 years
(c) Nearly 17 years (d) Nearly 20 years

44. The writer who said, "I describe not men but manners........" was
(a) Pope (b) Addison
(c) Steele (d) Swift

45. Which of the following poets has not received the Sahitya Akademi Award?
(a) Nissim Ezekiel
(b) Shiv K. Kumar
(c) A.K. Ramanujan
(d) Jayanta Mahapatra

46. When was Johnson's Dictionary published?
(a) 1756 (b) 1777
(c) 1755 (d) 1750

47. The rhyming scheme of a Shakespearean sonnet is
(a) ab ba, abba, cde, cde
(b) ab ba, ab ba, cd cd, ee
(c) ab ab, cd cd, ef ef, gg
(d) aa bb, bb ce, de, de ff

48. The first name of Marlow in Heart of Darkness, is
(a) Charlie (b) Christopher
(c) John (d) Andrew

49. Which of the following is not a bilingufal writer?
(a) Dilip Chitre (b) Kamala Das
(c) Gieve Patel (d) Vikram Seth

50. Phillip Larkin belongs to a loose group writers known as
(a) The Bloomsbury Group
(b) The Imagist Group
(c) The Movement
(d) New Generation Poets

ANSWERS

1. (b)	2. (b)	3. (b)	4. (a)
5. (b)	6. (c)	7. (b)	8. (c)
9. (a)	10. (a)	11. (c)	12. (b)
13. (d)	14. (c)	15. (d)	16. (b)
17. (d)	18. (a)	19. (c)	20. (d)
21. (a)	22. (d)	23. (c)	24. (b)
25. (c)	26. (b)	27. (d)	28. (b)
29. (a)	30. (c)	31. (c)	32. (a)
33. (c)	34. (b)	35. (a)	36. (c)
37. (d)	38. (c)	39. (b)	40. (d)
41. (a)	42. (c)	43. (c)	44. (d)
45. (d)	46. (c)	47. (c)	48. (a)
49. (d)	50. (d)		

Practice Papers

PRACTICE PAPER I

1. Point out the correct chronological sequence.
   (a) Alexander's Feast – Prelude – Rabbi Ben Ezra – Adonais
   (b) Alexander's Feast – Prelude – Adonais – Rabbi Ben Ezra
   (c) Prelude – Alexander's Feast – Adonais – Rabbi Ben Ezra
   (d) Rabbi Ben Ezra – Prelude – Adonais – Alexander's Feast
2. Of which poem is the following the opening couplet: "Sweet Spirit! Sister of that orphan one, Whose empire is the name thou weepest on?"
   (a) 'Epipsychidion' by Shelley
   (b) 'Endymion' by Keats
   (c) 'Faerie Queene' by Spenser
   (d) 'Prologue to Canterbury Tales' by Chaucer
3. 'Panthea' is a character in
   (a) Manfred
   (b) Prometheus Unbound
   (c) Candida
   (d) Waiting for Godot
4. Who says of Shakespeare: "...Sweetest Shakespeare, fancy's child. Warble his native wood—notes wild."
   (a) M. Arnold (b) Shelley
   (c) Wordsworth (d) Milton
5. Who says the following in one of Shakespeare's play (when on the point of death): "How oft when men are at the point of death. Have they been merry! Which keepers call A lightning before death?"
   (a) Julius Caesar
   (b) Romeo and Juliet
   (c) Hamlet
   (d) Brutus
6. Who said: "Shakespeare had nowhere written more than six consecutive lines of good poetry"?
   (a) Dryden (b) M. Arnold
   (c) Eliot (d) Dr. Johnson
7. Who closes one of his sonnets with the following words: "Where whenas death shall all the world subdew, Our love shall lieu, and later life renew"?
   (a) Shakespeare (b) Sidney
   (c) Spenser (d) Milton
8. Who said of Chaucer: "Here is God's Plenty"?
   (a) Dryden (b) Sidney
   (c) Shelley (d) Eliot
9. In which poem do the following lines occur : And smale fowles maken melodye, That slepen al the night with open ye?"
   (a) Pier's Plowman
   (b) L'Allegro
   (c) Prologue to Canterbury Tales
   (d) Faerie Queene
10. In which play of Shakespeare does the following lines occur: "Full many a lady I have ey'd with best regard.............O You! So perfect and so peerless are created of every creature's best."

(a) *Romeo and Juliet*
(b) *Antony and Cleopatra*
(c) *Cymbeline*
(d) *Tempest*

11. In which play of Shakespeare does the following line occur: "Uneasy lies the head that wears a crown?"
(a) *Julius Caesar* (b) *Henry V*
(c) *Henry IV* (d) *Richard III*

12. In which play of Shakespeare does the following line occur. "This land of such dear souls, this dear, dear land?"
(a) *Henry V* (b) *Julius Caesar*
(c) *Richard II* (d) *Richard III*

13. In which book of 'Paradise Lost' does Milton use the phrase 'human face divine?"
(a) Book I (b) Book II
(c) Book III (d) Book IV

14. The following lines occur in : "There is a pleasure in poetic pains which only poets know."
(a) 'Adam's Curse' by Yeats
(b) 'The Task' by Cowper
(c) 'Hellas' by Shelley
(d) 'Hollow Men' by Eliot

15. In which poem does the following line occur: "The world is poisoned at the heart?"
(a) Waste Land
(b) II Penseroso
(c) 'Dover Beach' by Arnold
(d) 'The Borderers' by Wordsworth

16. In which poem do the following lines occur: "Behold! Her bosom and half her side—A sight to dream of, not to tell?"
(a) Keats' Eve of St. Agnes
(b) Keats' Lamia
(c) Coleridge's Christabel
(d) Wordsworth's Lucy Gray

17. Who said the following lines : "The seed ye sow, another reaps, The wealth ye find, another keeps?"
(a) Goldsmith
(b) Shelley
(c) Mrs. Barret Browning
(d) Thomas Hood

18. The following lines were written by "Charm'd magic casements, opening on the foam
Of perilous seas, in faery lands forlorn."
(a) Coleridge (b) Yeats
(c) Shakespeare (d) Keats

19. Who was the king of England at the time of Battle of Norman Conquest at Hastings?
(a) Harold (b) Edgar
(c) Edward (d) Henry

20. Which king of England signed the Magna Carta?
(a) Richard I (b) Henry II
(c) John (d) None of the above

21. In which year was Magna Carta signed?
(a) 1205 (b) 1210
(c) 1215 (d) 1220

22. During which king's reign in England did the Hundred Year's war start?
(a) Henry III (b) Edward III
(c) Henry IV (d) Richard III

23. In which year did Henry V land in France?
(a) 1411 (b) 1412
(c) 1415 (d) 1416

24. Who is proverbially knonw having called Gandhi the "naked fakir"?
(a) Churchill (b) Queen Victoria
(c) Hitler (d) Stallin

25. Who was Gandhiji's mentor in Russia?
(a) Stalin (b) Lenin
(c) Gorki (d) Tolstoy

26. Who said about Vivekananda "I have gone through his words very thoroughly and after having gone through them, the love that I had my country became thousand fold?"
   (a) Tagore
   (b) Nehru
   (c) Gandhi
   (d) Subhash Chandra Bose
27. Vivekananda delivered his lectures from Colombo to Almora during
   (a) 1896-97 (b) 1897-98
   (c) 1900-01 (d) 1898-99
28. Who is the writer of "Pelican Guides of English Literature"?
   (a) Legonis (b) Fowler
   (c) Hudson (d) Boris Ford
29. Who wrote: *Theory of Literature*?
   (a) Cleanth Brooks
   (b) Hudson
   (c) Rene Wellek
   (d) Abrams
30. Which is not one of the essential characteristics of the prose drama?
   (a) Plot (b) Rhyme
   (c) Characters (d) Dialogue
31. Who is the writer of "The Anatomy of Drama"?
   (a) John Loftis (b) L.C. Knights
   (c) Majorie Boulton (d) Boris Ford
32. The author of "The Over-reacher" is
   (a) Harry Levin (b) Boris Ford
   (c) Basil Willey (d) S.W. Dawson
33. The writer of "Master of Drama" is
   (a) Walter N. King (b) John Elgon
   (c) John Gassner (d) Bradley
34. Who is the writer of the poem "Easter 1916"?
   (a) Yeats (b) Eliot
   (c) Keats (d) Milton
35. "Batter My Heart" is a sonnet by
   (a) Milton (b) Wordsworth
   (c) Donne (d) Shakespeare
36. Who is the author of *The Romantic Image*?
   (a) Bloom (b) Bowra
   (c) Fraser (d) Lewis
37. The writer of 'Towards Greek Tragedy" is
   (a) Holmes (b) Baker
   (c) Brain Wickers (d) Blackmur
38. The writer of the poem "Out of the Cradle Endlessly Rocking" is
   (a) Yeats (b) Whitman
   (c) Frost (d) Eliot
39. Who is the writer of the poem " "Meeting and Passing?"
   (a) Yeats (b) Frost
   (c) Eliot (d) Whitman
40. Who is the writer of *Who's Afraid of Virginia Woolf*?
   (a) Edward Albee
   (b) Arthur Miller
   (c) Eugene O' Neill
   (d) Tennessee Williams
41. The writer of the novel *The Power and the Glory* is
   (a) Paul Scott (b) Graham Greene
   (c) Golding (d) John Fowle
42. The writer of the novel *Brideshead Revisited* is
   (a) Evelyn Waugh (b) Golding
   (c) Conrad (d) Joyce
43. Who wrote the book: *Gentlemen and Rogues*?
   (a) Sandison (b) Alkins
   (c) G.D. Philips (d) D. Lodge
44. Who is the writer of the poem "My Cat"?
   (a) Kamala Das (b) Giene Patel
   (c) Dilip Chitre (d) Nissim Ezekiel

45. Who wrote the poem "On Killing a Tree"?
    (a) Dilip Chitre
    (b) Gieve Patel
    (c) Kolatkar
    (d) Jayanta Mahapatra
46. "Sahaja" was written by
    (a) Sri Aurobindo
    (b) Nissim Ezekiel
    (c) Ananda Coomaraswami
    (d) Tagore
47. The writer of "Culture and Imperialism" is
    (a) Bernard Lewis (b) Robert Young
    (c) Aijaz Ahmed (d) Edward Said
48. "Gao Xingjuan" who won the Nobel Prize for literature in 2000 was a
    (a) Japanese (b) Chinese
    (c) Vietnamese (d) Indonesian
49. Who is known as the "incorrigible" utopist among the following.
    (a) Shaw (b) Eliot
    (c) H.G. Wells (d) Yeats
50. In which work does the character "Rahul" exist?
    (a) Anand's 'Untouchable'
    (b) Ruskin Bond's 'The Prize'
    (c) Tagore's 'Homecoming'
    (d) Narain's 'The Doctor's Dilemma'

ANSWERS

1. (b)	2. (a)	3. (b)	4. (d)
5. (b)	6. (d)	7. (c)	8. (a)
9. (c)	10. (d)	11. (c)	12. (c)
13. (c)	14. (b)	15. (d)	16. (c)
17. (b)	18. (d)	19. (a)	20. (c)
21. (c)	22. (b)	23. (c)	24. (a)
25. (d)	26. (c)	27. (b)	28. (d)
29. (c)	30. (b)	31. (c)	32. (a)
33. (c)	34. (a)	35. (c)	36. (b)
37. (c)	38. (b)	39. (b)	40. (a)
41. (b)	42. (a)	43. (c)	44. (d)
45. (b)	46. (c)	47. (d)	48. (b)
49. (c)	50. (b)		

PRACTICE PAPER II

1. In which poem do the following lines appear. "In a land of anonymity don't look for signposts."
    (a) 'Desire' by Jayanta Mahapatra
    (b) 'Disempbarkation' by Daruwallah
    (c) 'World Malayali' by K. Ayyappa Panikkar
    (d) ONV Kurup's 'Earthen Pots'
2. "Learn hence for ancient rules a just esteem. To copy Nature is to copy them. "Who is the writer of the above lines?
    (a) Pope (b) Dryden
    (c) Dr. Johnson (d) Swift
3. Name the writer of "Descriptive Sketches."
    (a) Byon (b) Hazlitt
    (c) Wordsworth (d) Dickens
4. In which poem does the following line occur: "……nature never deserts the wise and pure?"
    (a) Wordsworth's 'Tintern Abbey'
    (b) Shelley's 'Alastor'
    (c) Coleridge's 'This Lime Three Bower'
    (d) Keats' 'Ode to a Grecian Urn'
5. In which Canto of Don Juan does the following line occur: "Men love in haste, but they detest at leisure."
    (a) I (b) II
    (c) IX (d) XII

6. Whom does Shelley call "The Pilgrim of Eternity" in his 'Adonais'?
   (a) Keats (b) Wordsworth
   (c) Byron (d) Chaucer
7. Who wrote the following lines : "Oh, lift me as a wave, a leaf, a cloud! I fall upon the thorns of life! I bleed."
   (a) Shelley (b) Keats
   (c) Robert Bridges (d) M. Arnold
8. In which poem of Shelley do the following lines occur: "That the free would stamp the impious name of KING into the dust!"
   (a) Queen Mab (b) Revolt of Islam
   (c) Ode to Liberty (d) Adonais
9. In which poem does Keats write: "Their lips touched not, but had not bade adieu?"
   (a) Ode On a Grecian Urn
   (b) Ode To a Nightingale
   (c) Hyperion
   (d) Ode to Psyche
10. Which poet is associated with the style "To load every rift with ore?"
    (a) Keats (b) Shelley
    (c) Byron (d) Wordsworth
11. In which poem does the following line occur: "Twas roses, roses, all the way?"
    (a) 'In Memorium'
    (b) 'Patriot'
    (c) 'Captain, My Captain'
    (d) 'Daffodils'
12. Who is the writer of the line: "To see the word in a grain of sand?"
    (a) Cowper (b) Goldsmith
    (c) Blake (d) Wordsworth
13. Who says, "We murder to dissect?"
    (a) Shelley (b) Yeats
    (c) Philip Larkin (d) Wordsworth
14. Who talks of "sick hurry" and "divided aims" in his poems?
    (a) Wordsworth (b) M. Arnold
    (c) Tennyson (d) Browning
15. In which work do we find the words: "I grow old, I grow old?"
    (a) 'Love Song of Prufrock'
    (b) 'Rabbi Ben Ezra'
    (c) 'Dr. Faustus'
    (d) 'The Duchess of Malfi'
16. In which play of Shakespeare do we have the lines: "Most friendship is feigning, most loving mere folly?"
    (a) *Much Ado About Nothing*
    (b) *A Midsummer Night's Dream*
    (c) *Tempest*
    (d) *As You Like It*
17. In which play of Shakespeare do the following lines occur: "Present mirth hath present laughter; What's to come is still unsure?"
    (a) *Much Ado About Nothing*
    (b) *Twelfth Night*
    (c) *As You Like It*
    (d) *Winter's Tale*
18. In which work does the following line occur: "The mountain nymph, sweet Liberty."
    (a) Byron's 'Childe Harold's Pilgrimage'
    (b) Shelley's 'Ode to the West Wind'
    (c) Milton's 'L Allegro'
    (d) Shakespeare's 'Henry V'
19. Who speaks the following word: "My fifthe housebande, god his soule blesse Which that I took for love and no richer se."
    (a) The Wife of Bath
    (b) Kamala Das
    (c) Emile Bronte
    (d) Christina Rossetti
20. In which of Spenser's poems does the following line occur: "O helpe thou my weake wit, and sharpen my dull tong?"

(a) 'Shepherd's Calendar'
(b) 'Epithalamion'
(c) 'Lament for Daphnaida'
(d) 'Invocation to the Faerie Queene'

21. Who has said, "India is simply my environment?"
(a) Nissim Ezekiel (b) Daruwallah
(c) Kamala Das (d) Shiv K. Kumar

22. In which poem of Nissim Ezekiel do we have the lines: "Only the monkeys are sad,.... Anticipating time for payment, The crowd dissolves."
(a) 'Entertainment'
(b) 'Philosophy'
(c) 'Poet, Lover, Birdswatcher'
(d) 'The Visitor'

23. In which poem of Shiv K. Kumar do the following lines occur: "Patiently they sit like empty pitchers?"
(a) 'Pilgrimage'
(b) 'Kali'
(c) 'Indian Women'
(d) 'My Co-Respondent'

24. In which period were heroic tragedies generally written?
(a) Elizabethan (b) Caroline
(c) Jacabean (d) Restoration

25. Which of the following plays of Wycherley is comparatively a satire than a piece of mere revelry?
(a) *Love in a Wood*
(b) *The Plain Dealer*
(c) *The Gentleman Dancing Master*
(d) *The Country Wife*

26. Who is the writer of "The Conquest of Garanda?"
(a) Dryden (b) Vanburgh
(c) Wycherley (d) Farquhar

27. Who said, "Man not afraid of God, afraid of me?"
(a) Dryden (b) Pope
(c) Swift (d) Byron

28. In which of Shakespeare's play is Margaret a character?
(a) *Love's Labour's Lost*
(b) *Cymbeline*
(c) *Richard III*
(d) *Tempest*

29. Who is the writer of the critical work "The Lives of the Poets"?
(a) Dryden (b) M. Arnold
(c) Eliot (d) Dr. Johnson

30. Who among the following was least affected by the French Revolution?
(a) Keats (b) Shelley
(c) Wordsworth (d) Coleridge

31. Which of Jane Austen's novel begins with the lines: "It is a truth universally acknowledged that a single man in possession of a good fortune must be in want of a wife."
(a) *Sense and Sensibility*
(b) *Emma*
(c) *Pride and Prejudice*
(d) *Persuasion*

32. Who has said about the plot of "Pride and Prejudice" that "it is as inevitable as the conclusion of a properly constructed syllogism or geometrical demonstration?" (i.e. while talking of the marriage of Elizabeth and Darcy.)
(a) Cross (b) Allen
(c) Hugh Walker (d) Barker

33. When did James Thompson die?
(a) 1880 (b) 1881
(c) 1883 (d) 1882

34. Whose death led to the writing of Arnold's elegy 'Thyrsis'?
(a) Arthur Hugh Clough
(b) Thompson

(c) Tennyson
(d) Browning

35. Who has said: "The central fact about Emile Bronte is that she is a mystic?"
(a) Cross (b) Abercrombe
(c) Walter Allen (d) Barker

36. What metre does Shakespeare apply in his plays?
(a) Blank Verse (b) Heroic Couplet
(c) Quatrains (d) Ottava Rima

37. Who generally sing songs in Shakespeare's plays like *Twelfth Night* and *As You Like It*?
(a) Heroes (b) Villains
(c) Clowns (d) Heroines

38. When was Epistle to Dr. Arbuthnot published?
(a) 1832 (b) 1833
(c) 1834 (d) 1835

39. By which of the following the Ancients are not led in *The Battle of Books*?
(a) Milton (b) Homer
(c) Pindar (d) Aristotle

40. By which of the following are the Moderns not led?
(a) Sir Temple (b) Dryden
(c) Hobbes (d) Milton

41. Who shoots an arrow at Bacon in *The Battle of Books*?
(a) Plato (b) Aristotle
(c) Milton (d) Homer

42. Who is the writer of "Mend"
(a) Kingsley (b) Newman
(c) Dickens (d) Charles Reade

43. Who is the writer of the following line:
"Cloth and alum and plaster are sold to the poor for bread."
(a) Byron (b) Tennyson
(c) Carlyle (d) Yeats

44. When did James Macpherson die?
(a) 1796 (b) 1797
(c) 1798 (d) 1799

45. Who called Addison's style "The model of middle style?"
(a) Johnson (b) Swift
(c) Pope (d) Dryden

46. Hume was the greatest philosopher of— century.
(a) sixteenth (b) seventeenth
(c) eighteenth (d) nineteenth

47. The biography of which of the following was not written by Izaac Walton?
(a) Donne (b) Johnson
(c) Wotton (d) G. Herbert

48. When was the King's Bible or the Authorized Version published?
(a) 1611 (b) 1610
(c) 1614 (d) 1608

49. King James' Bible possesses the excellence of prose of
(a) 15th century
(b) 16th century
(c) 17th century
(d) sweetness of all ages

50. Who is said to be the first to translate the Bible into English direct from original Hebrew and Greek texts?
(a) William Tyndale (b) Reynolds
(c) Crammer (d) Parker

ANSWERS

1. (b)	2. (a)	3. (c)	4. (c)
5. (d)	6. (c)	7. (a)	8. (c)
9. (d)	10. (a)	11. (b)	12. (c)
13. (d)	14. (b)	15. (a)	16. (d)
17. (b)	18. (c)	19. (a)	20. (d)
21. (a)	22. (a)	23. (c)	24. (d)
25. (b)	26. (a)	27. (b)	28. (c)

29. (d)	30. (a)	31. (c)	32. (a)
33. (d)	34. (a)	35. (c)	36. (a)
37. (c)	38. (d)	39. (a)	40. (a)
41. (b)	42. (d)	43. (b)	44. (a)
45. (a)	46. (c)	47. (b)	48. (a)
49. (d)	50. (a)		

PRACTICE PAPER III

1. In which poem of Keats do the following lines occur: "And can I ever bid these joys farewell? Yes, I must pass them for a nobler life?"
   (a) Ode on a Grecian Urn
   (b) Hymn to Intellectual Beauty
   (c) Sleep and Poetry
   (d) Ode to a Nightingale
2. In which work do the following lines occur:
   "My whole heart rises up to bless
   Your name in pride and thankfulness!"
   (a) *The Last Ride Together*
   (b) *The Ring and the Book*
   (c) *Dr. Faustus*
   (d) *Among School Children*
3. In which work do the following lines occur:
   "For who would trust the seeming sighs
   Of wife or paramour?"
   (a) *Paradise Lost*
   (b) *Samson Agonistes*
   (c) *Child Harold's Pilgrimage*
   (d) *All for Love*
4. The first edition of 'Leaves of Grass' was published in
   (a) 1850 (b) 1849
   (c) 1855 (d) 1860
5. Who wrote the following lines: "I am the poet of the body and I am the poet of the soul?"
   (a) Whitman (b) Frost
   (c) Shelley (d) Yeats
6. In which work does the character "Umbriel" exist?
   (a) *Paradise Lost*
   (b) *Tempest*
   (c) *The Rape of the Lock*
   (d) *Dunciad*
7. Which of the following characters bears the same name in *The Rape of the Lock* and *Tempest*?
   (a) Antonio (b) Ariel
   (c) Mr. Plume (d) Clarissa
8. Who among the following is the writer of "Augustan Satire"?
   (a) Jack, Ian (b) Johnson
   (c) Bower (d) Eliot
9. Who wrote *Culture and Anarchy*?
   (a) Dryden (b) M. Arnold
   (c) Eliot (d) Sidney
10. Which of the following terms is not there in *Culture and Anarchy*?
    (a) Barbarian
    (b) Philistine
    (c) Dissociation of Sensibility
    (d) Hebraism
11. Who uses the so-called "Touchstone Method" in criticism?
    (a) Sidney (b) Aristotle
    (c) Shelley (d) M. Arnold
12. What was the name of the girl whom Keats loved?
    (a) Harriet (b) Sophia
    (c) Fanny Brawne (d) Estella
13. 'Chanson de Roland' is a .... Epic.
    (a) French (b) German
    (c) Scottish (d) Roman
14. Methuselah is a .... character.
    (a) Dantian (b) Shakespearean
    (c) Shavian (d) Biblical

15. Who wrote "Imitation" in Latin?
(a) Pellison (b) Caedmon
(c) Thomas Kempis (d) Marot

16. Who wrote "Love's Riddle"?
(a) Dryden (b) Cowley
(c) Shelley (d) Byron

17. In which book of *Paradise Lost* does the following line appear: "And never to submit or yield."
(a) Book I (b) Book II
(c) Book III (d) Book IV

18. What were 'Scott-James' views regarding the line mentioned in 17 above?
(a) Great poetry
(b) Milton's best style
(c) Poetically, Milton in his weakest vein
(d) No comments

19. Which poem did Milton write in memory of his second wife Catnerine Woodcock?
(a) The Sonnet "On His Blindness"
(b) The Sonnet opening with the line "Methought I saw my late espoused saint"
(c) II Penseroso
(d) Paradise Regained

20. Who is the writer of the epic "Aeneid"?
(a) Homer (b) Dante
(c) Virgil (d) Milton

21. Mr. Whittier was
(a) an American Quaker poet
(b) a British painter
(c) a German philosopher
(d) a French courtier

22. 'Comus' by Milton is
(a) a sonnet (b) an epic
(c) a play (d) a masque

23. John Kable was a writer of ...... verses.
(a) satirical (b) descriptive
(c) sacred (d) narrative

24. Who wrote: "Ars Poetica"?
(a) Horace (b) Quid
(c) Aristotle (d) Plato

25. Pindar was a great .... lyric poet.
(a) French (b) Latin
(c) Italian (d) Greek

26. Who wrote : "Ecclesiastical Sonnets"?
(a) Milton (b) Wordsworth
(c) Sidney (d) Keats

27. Who wrote: "Irene"?
(a) Dr. Johnson (b) Shelley
(c) Yeats (d) Frost

28. Ernest Renan was
(a) a German philosopher
(b) an Italian painter
(c) a French writer and historian
(d) a Scottish poet

29. Who said the following: "The greatness of a poet lies in his powerful and beautiful application of ideas to life?"
(a) Dryden (b) M. Arnold
(c) Eliot (d) Plato

30. According to Arnold, Chaucer is
(a) greater than Dante
(b) as great as Dante
(c) not one of the great classics
(d) possessed high poetic seriousness in abundance

31. Who called poetry "The Mother of lies?"
(a) Aristotle (b) Plato
(c) Longinus (d) Sidney

32. Aristotle defines the 'ridiculous' as
(a) lazy
(b) foolish
(c) dirty
(d) a species of the ugly

33. Who wrote: *Mysteries of Udolpho*?
(a) Mrs. Radcliffe
(b) Horace Walpole

(c) Virginia Woolf
(d) Proust

34. Which of the following is a woman novelist?
(a) Hardy (b) Conrad
(c) Trollope (d) George Eliot

35. Who among the following is known as Christopher North?
(a) Francis Jeffrey (b) Lockhart
(c) John Wilson (d) Gibbon

36. By what name was Shelley called by the boys at school? .... Shelley
(a) Mad (b) Happy
(c) Redoubtable (d) Genius

37. In which of Shelley's poems do the following lines exist: "While yet a boy, I sought for ghosts, and sped Through many a listening chamber, cave and ruin."
(a) Alastor
(b) Queen Malc
(c) Revolt of Islam
(d) Hymn to Intellectual Beauty

38. Who wrote 'Heroes and Herp Worship'?
(a) Carlyle (b) Ruskin
(c) Pater (d) Eliot

39. Which of the following can be called "a tale of adventure"?
(a) 'Vanity Fair' by 'Thackeray'
(b) Cervantes 'Don Quixote'
(c) Rider Haggard's 'King Solomon's Mines'
(d) Virginia Woolf's 'To The Literature'

40. Who says, "A book should help us either to enjoy life or to endure it?"
(a) Bacon (b) Lamb
(c) Carlyle (d) Johnson

41. Who is known for his prejudicial meaning of "oats"?
(a) Horuby (b) Fowler
(c) Johnson (d) Abercrombie

42. Who wrote : "But trailing clouds of glory do we come From God, who is our home?"
(a) Shelley (b) Wordsworth
(c) Swinburne (d) Yeats

43. Which poem of Wordsworth has Emerson called "The high water-mark of poetry in the nineteenth century?"
(a) Ode on Intimations
(b) Tintern Abbey
(c) Prelude
(d) Ode to Duty

44. Malory's Morte d' Arthur is a collection of
(a) Arthurian romances
(b) Charlemaigne's campaigns in Spain
(c) Saxons' adventurous life on the sea
(d) Beowulf's adventures

45. In which work does the following line occur: "The viol, the violet, and vine?"
(a) Ode to a Nightingale
(b) 'Youth and Age' by Coleridge
(c) Edgar Allan Poe's 'The City in the Sea'
(d) Yeats 'Sailing to Byzantium'

46. Who has said: "All that we see or seem Is but a dream within a dream"?
(a) Yeats (b) Shelley
(c) Shakespeare (d) Poe

47. In which work does the following line occur: "He whom the gods favour dies young?"
(a) Dante's 'The Divine Comedy'
(b) Shakespeare's 'Romeo and Juliet'
(c) Plautus's 'Bacchides IV'
(d) Fry's 'The Lady's Not for Burning'

48. Who said: "Ye god! Annihilate but space and time, And make two lovers happy?"
(a) Pope (b) Shakespeare
(c) Webster (d) Faustus

49. Who said the following words: "Man was born free, and everywhere he is in chains?"
(a) Voltaire (b) Rousseau
(c) Alexander (d) Shakespeare

50. Who said: "Top famous men all the earth is a sepulcher?"
(a) Thuiydides (b) Euripides
(c) Ovid (d) Seneca

ANSWERS

1. (c)	2. (a)	3. (c)	4. (c)
5. (a)	6. (c)	7. (b)	8. (a)
9. (b)	10. (c)	11. (d)	12. (c)
13. (a)	14. (d)	15. (c)	16. (b)
17. (a)	18. (c)	19. (b)	20. (c)
21. (a)	22. (d)	23. (c)	24. (a)
25. (d)	26. (b)	27. (a)	28. (c)
29. (b)	30. (c)	31. (b)	32. (d)
33. (a)	34. (d)	35. (c)	36. (a)
37. (d)	38. (a)	39. (c)	40. (d)
41. (c)	42. (b)	43. (a)	44. (a)
45. (c)	46. (d)	47. (c)	48. (a)
49. (b)	50. (a)		

PRACTICE PAPER IV

1. Who translated Plutarch's lines from the French version in 1579?
(a) Marlowe (b) Chapman
(c) Thomas North (d) Golding

2. Who was the writer of 'The Civil Wars'?
(a) Drayton (b) Samuel Daniel
(c) Lodge (d) Greene

3. What type of work is mainly Samuel Pepy's "Diary"?
(a) Descriptive (b) Social
(c) Political (d) Confessional

4. Hopkins was mainly a
(a) love poet
(b) nature poet
(c) religious poet
(d) metaphysical poet

5. Maria Edgeworth's novel *Belinda* is mainly
(a) a political novel
(b) a romantic novel
(c) an educational novel
(d) a social novel

6. 'Biographia Literaria' is a critical work by
(a) Dryden (b) Wordsworth
(c) M. Arnold (d) Coleridge

7. Who among the following is the writer of absurd plays?
(a) Yeats (b) Synge
(c) Samuel Beckett (d) Lady Gregory

8. O' Henry wrote his stories when
(a) he was serving in an office
(b) he was a waiter in a restaurant
(c) he was in jail
(d) he was a businessman

9. Who among the following was not regarded as one of the "War Poets"?
(a) Frost (b) Rupert Brooke
(c) Siegfried Sasson (d) Wilfred Owen

10. Who was the inventor of "Spring Rhythm"?
(a) Yeats (b) Hopkins
(c) Spender (d) Auden

11. Who is the writer of the following line: "Go and catch a falling star"?
(a) Dryden (b) Herrick
(c) M. Arnold (d) Donne

12. Who wrote:
"The also serve who only stand and wait?"

(a) Wordsworth (b) Milton
(c) Shelley (d) Shakespeare

13. In which poem is Melancholy presented as a pensive noun "devout and pure... with even step and musing gait?"
(a) Ode To Melancholy
(b) Faery Queene
(c) She Walks in Beauty
(d) H Frnseroso

14. Who speaks the following words in Paradise Lost:
"What though the field be lost All is not lost."
(a) Satan (b) God
(c) Adam (d) Mammom

15. Where was Shakespeare born?
(a) London
(b) Lanscaster
(c) Stratford-on-Avon
(d) Dublin

16. Uriah Heep is a character in
(a) *David Copperfield*
(b) *Ivanhoe*
(c) *The Christmas Carol*
(d) *Nicholas Nickleby*

17. Which play is said to be written by Shakespeare in collaboration with (probably) Marlowe?
(a) *Tempest* (b) *Titus Andronicus*
(c) *Love's Labour's* (d) *Winter's Tale*

18. In which of the following plays of Shakespeare is a king assassinated?
(a) *Macbeth* (b) *Hamlet*
(c) *Othello* (d) *Julius Caesar*

19. Louka is a character in
(a) *The Apple Cart*
(b) *Arms and the Man*
(c) *Pygmalion*
(d) *The Devil's Disciple*

20. In one of whose sonnets does the following line appear:
"Shall I compare thee to a summer's day"?
(a) Milton (b) Sidney
(c) Shakespeare (d) Wordsworth

21. When did Kipling die?
(a) 1930 (b) 1936
(c) 1931 (d) 1940

22. On which one of the following flowers is one of Wordsworth's poem captioned?
(a) Daffodils (b) Roses
(c) Lilies (d) Lilacs

23. In which year did Paul Heyse received the Nobel Prize?
(a) 1909 (b) 1910
(c) 1911 (d) 1908

24. Who received the Nobel Prize for literature in 1995?
(a) Dario Fo (b) Wole Soyinka
(c) Seamus Heaney (d) Sartre

25. Which one among the following does not belong to "The Theatre of the Absurb"?
(a) Beckett (b) Harold Pinter
(c) Edward Albee (d) Galsworthy

26. When was Wordsworth made the poet Laureate of England?
(a) 1843 (b) 1839
(c) 1845 (d) 1849

27. When did Rushdie's 'Midnight's Children' appear?
(a) 1980 (b) 1981
(c) 1982 (d) 1984

28. When did Rushdie's 'The Moor's Last Sigh' appear?
(a) 1991 (b) 1992
(c) 1994 (d) 1995

29. Who is the writer of 'The Essays of Elia'?
(a) Lamb (b) Hazlitt
(c) De Quincey (d) Leigh Hunt

30. In which of Shaw's drama a character says, "Let us sit and talk comfortably over it like friends?"
    (a) *Candida*
    (b) *Man and Superman*
    (c) *Arms and the Man*
    (d) *The Apple Cart*
31. In which of Shakespeare's plays does the following line appear:
    "Times are out of joint?"
    (a) *Othello* (b) *Julius Caesar*
    (c) *Hamlet* (d) *Tempest*
32. Which one of the following is not a character is Hamlet?
    (a) Ophelia (b) Gonzalo
    (c) Polonius (d) Gertrude
33. When did Marx die?
    (a) 1882 (b) 1881
    (c) 1883 (d) 1885
34. When did Dylan Thomas die?
    (a) 1952 (b) 1953
    (c) 1950 (d) 1954
35. Which one among the following cannot be said to be associated with the "Surrealism" movement?
    (a) Philip Larkin (b) Herbert Read
    (c) George Barker (d) Dylan Thomas
36. In which year did Freud die?
    (a) 1938 (b) 1939
    (c) 1940 (d) 1941
37. Who wrote: "Ode on Agricourt"?
    (a) Byron (b) Drayton
    (c) Massinger (d) Herbet
38. In which poem does the following line occur: "Where youth grows pale, scepter thin and dies"?
    (a) Ode to a Skylark
    (b) Ode to the West Wind
    (c) Ode to a Nightingale
    (d) One on Indolence
39. Who was the largest contributor to the spectator?
    (a) Steele (b) Addison
    (c) Goldsmith (d) Swift
40. Marlow is a character in
    (a) Greene's 'The Heart of the Matter'
    (b) Conrad's 'Heart of Darkness'
    (c) Forster's 'A Passage to India'
    (d) Saul Below's 'Herzog'
41. In which novel is Major Scobie the central figure?
    (a) *The Grapes of Wrath*
    (b) *The Mocking Bird*
    (c) *The Lioness*
    (d) *The Heart of the Matter*
42. The writer of 'Uncle Tom's Cabin' is
    (a) Harriet Beecher Stowe
    (b) Agatha Christie
    (c) Willa Cather
    (d) Stevenson
43. *Mrs. Dalloway* is mainly a ...novel.
    (a) domestic
    (b) political
    (c) stream of consciousness
    (d) romantic
44. Who, according to George B. Smith, is "....the Shakespeare of novelists?"
    (a) Fielding (b) Richardson
    (c) Joyce (d) Saul Bellow
45. Who published 'Shamela' anonymously in 1741?
    (a) Richardson (b) Fielding
    (c) Defoe (d) Smollett
46. When was Joseph Andrews published?
    (a) 1745 (b) 1744
    (c) 1788 (d) 1742
47. Byron was born in
    (a) 1782 (b) 1784
    (c) 1788 (d) 1790

48. In which of the following this line appears? "But the triumphs of life are sung in poems of wifehood and motherhood."
    (a) A poet (b) A prose writer
    (c) A dramatist (d) A novelist
49. In which poem do the following lines appear: "But the triumphs of love are sung in poems of wifehood and motherhood?"
    (a) 'She was a Phantom of Delight'
    (b) 'She Walks in Beauty'
    (c) "In A Gondola" by Robert Browning
    (d) None of the above
50. In which work does the character "Pompilia" exist?
    (a) *Chaucer's Troilus and Cresseyda*
    (b) *The Ring and The Book*
    (c) *Merchant of Venice*
    (d) *Don Juan*

ANSWERS

1. (c)	2. (b)	3. (d)	4. (c)
5. (c)	6. (d)	7. (c)	8. (c)
9. (c)	10. (b)	11. (d)	12. (b)
13. (d)	14. (a)	15. (c)	16. (a)
17. (b)	18. (a)	19. (b)	20. (c)
21. (b)	22. (a)	23. (b)	24. (c)
25. (d)	26. (a)	27. (b)	28. (d)
29. (a)	30. (a)	31. (c)	32. (b)
33. (c)	34. (b)	35. (a)	36. (b)
37. (b)	38. (c)	39. (b)	40. (b)
41. (d)	42. (a)	43. (c)	44. (a)
45. (b)	46. (d)	47. (c)	48. (d)
49. (c)	50. (b)		

PRACTICE PAPER V

1. Which of the following is not a poem by Kamala Das?
   (a) 'The Freaks'
   (b) 'My Grandmother's House'
   (c) 'Jejuri'
   (d) 'A Hot Noon in Malabar'
2. In the mid-fifties, the magazine "Quest" was edited by
   (a) Daruwallah
   (b) Nissim Ezek lel
   (c) Jayanta Mahapatra
   (d) Kolatkar
3. Who wrote the poem "Our Casarina Tree"?
   (a) Toru Dutt
   (b) Manmohan Ghose
   (c) Tagore
   (d) Sarojini Naidu
4. When did "Savitri" appear?
   (a) 1950 (b) 1960
   (c) 1951 (d) 1961
5. In which poem do the following lines occur:
   "Lightly, O lightly, we bear her along, She sways like a flower in the wind of our song?"
   (a) 'Jejuri' by Kolatkar
   (b) 'Indian Women' by Shiv K. Kumar
   (c) 'The Freaks' by Kamala Das
   (d) 'Palanquin Bearers' by Sarojini Naidu
6. Who was the editor of the anthology "India in Song: Eastern Themes in English Verse by British and Indian poets in 1920"?
   (a) E.V. Rieu
   (b) Theodore Douglas Dunn
   (c) Nissim Ezekiel
   (d) R. Parthasarthy
7. Calcutta was the Capital of British India from
   (a) 1773 to 1911 (b) 1770 to 1910
   (c) 1770 to 1911 (d) 1773 to 1912

8. Who wrote: "Ancient Ballads and Legends of Hindustan?"
   (a) Nissim Ezekiel (b) Henry Derozio
   (c) Toru Dutt (d) Daruwallah
9. When did G.V. Desanu's "All about H. Hatterr" appear?
   (a) 1950 (b) 1951
   (c) 1953 (d) 1955
10. Who, according to Parthasarthy, is after Furtago, the only poet to have seriously considered the use of pidgin English?
   (a) Kamala Das (b) Daruwallah
   (c) Nissim Ezekiel (d) Shiv K. Kumar
11. When was the Constitution of India adopted?
   (a) 1950 (b) 1951
   (c) 1953 (d) 1955
12. Who is the writer of the following words: "Mrs. Dalloway, To the Lighthouse, are little masterpieces of atmosphere, of airy gracefulness and melancholy poetry"?
   (a) Legouis-Czamian
   (b) Allen
   (c) Crompton-Rickett
   (d) Courthope
13. When was Allen's *Reading a Novel* published?
   (a) 1950 (b) 1948
   (c) 1949 (d) 1947
14. When did Virginia Woolf die?
   (a) 1938 (b) 1939
   (c) 1940 (d) 1941
15. Which of the following is not a novel by Virginia Woolf?
   (a) *The Voyage Out* (b) *Night and Day*
   (c) *Jacob's Room* (d) *Forsyte Saga*
16. *The Dark Forest* by Hugh Walpole is a
   (a) war story
   (b) domestic novel
   (c) a metaphysical work
   (d) a travelogue
17. Somerset Maugham's first novel *Liza of Lambeth* appeared in
   (a) 1890 (b) 1892
   (c) 1897 (d) 1899
18. The novelist Arthur Morrison was born in
   (a) 1862 (b) 1863
   (c) 1861 (d) 1864
19. Shaw was born in
   (a) Dublin (b) London
   (c) Canterbury (d) Dover
20. Shaw died in
   (a) 1952 (b) 1951
   (c) 1950 (d) 1953
21. Shaw was a member of the ......society.
   (a) Fabian (b) Socialist
   (c) Psychological (d) Economic
22. Who is the writer of the poem "The Land of Heart's Desire"?
   (a) Yeats (b) Shelley
   (c) Keats (d) Ocatvio Paz
23. In which year was the Irish National Theatre Society founded?
   (a) 1901 (b) 1902
   (c) 1903 (d) 1904
24. Who were the following: "Lover" and "Lever"
   (a) Novelists of nineteenth century
   (b) Poets of sixteenth century
   (c) Dramatists of twentieth century
   (d) None of the above
25. When did Mr. T.H. Green die?
   (a) 1880 (b) 1881
   (c) 1882 (d) 1883
26. When was Hegel's 'Philosophy of Mind' published?

(a) 1890 (b) 1891
(c) 1893 (d) 1894

27. Who was Kant?
(a) A German philosopher
(b) A Russian novelist
(c) A French poet
(d) An Italian dramatist

28. Lewis Caroll died in
(a) 1872 (b) 1888
(c) 1889 (d) 1898

29. Who is the writer of "Thalaba"?
(a) Southey (b) Coleridge
(c) Byron (d) Morris

30. When was Landor born?
(a) 1770 (b) 1775
(c) 1780 (d) 1785

31. Who wrote "Lalla Rookh"?
(a) Landor (b) Peacock
(c) Thomas Moore (d) Lyly

32. Arthur Young died in
(a) 1819 (b) 1829
(c) 1818 (d) 1817

33. The writer of the novel *The Man of Feeling* is
(a) Mackenzie (b) Walpole
(c) Reeve (d) Mrs. Radcliffe

34. "Silvia" written by George Lillo in 1730 is a
(a) melodrama (b) comic opera
(c) high comedy (d) high tragedy

35. In "Splendid Shilling" (1705) John Philips imitated the style and blank verse of
(a) Marlowe (b) Shakespeare
(c) Wytt and Surrey (d) Milton

36. Lycidas appeared in
(a) 1632 (b) 1636
(c) 1637 (d) 1638

37. The following lines were written by:
"Happy those early days when I Shined in my angel infancy!"
(a) Wordsworth (b) Vaughan
(c) Herbert (d) Shelley

38. Who wrote the book of poems "The Wonder"?
(a) Shelley (b) Coleridge
(c) Thomas Traherne (d) Keats

39. The writer of 'Antheists' Tragedy is
(a) Shelley (b) Eliot
(c) Yeats (d) Tourneur

40. 'Vendice' is a character in
(a) Fry's *The Lady's Not for Burning*
(b) Shakespeare's *Much Ado About Nothing*
(c) Milton's *Comus*
(d) Cyril Tourneur's *The Revenger's Tragedy*

41. In which play does the following line occur:
"Mother come from that poisonous Woman there?"
(a) Shakespeare's *King Lear*
(b) *The Revenger's Tragedy* by Tourneur
(c) Byron's *Manfred*
(d) Beckett's *Waiting for Godot*

42. Who wrote: 'Catiline'?
(a) Lee Johnson (b) Johnson
(c) Swift (d) Pope

43. 'Livia' is a character in
(a) Shakespeare's *Twelfth Night*
(b) Johnson's *Sejanus*
(c) Barrie's *The Admirable Crichton*
(d) Shakespeare's *Much Ado About Nothing*

44. 'The Man in the Moon' is a satire by
(a) Drayton (b) Daniel
(c) Swift (d) Dryden

45. *Ideas Mirror* is a book of sonnets by

(a) Petrarch (b) Sidney
(c) Spenser (d) Drayton

46. In which play does 'Sensual Appetite" address the audience directly as under:
"For all that they be now in this hall,
They be the most part my servants all"?
(a) *Volpone* by Johnson
(b) *Dr. Faustus* by Marlowe
(c) *The Four Elements* by John Skelton
(d) *Murder in the Cathedral* by Eliot

47. Who wrote the following lines:
"When these words were spoken,
There came thinther wending,
A little boat moving,
On the waters it floated,
And two women in it,
Wondrously formed."
(a) Chaucer
(b) Gower
(c) Dunbar
(d) Layaman (regarding the story of the passing of King Arthur)

48. The romances of 'Havelok' by (by W.W. Skeat) and 'Horn' (by J. Hall) were in spired by... legends.
(a) Scandinavian (b) Danish
(c) French (d) Italian

49. The first Saxon king of England was
(a) William the Conqueror
(b) Arthur
(c) Cerdic
(d) Henry I

50. In which poem do the following lines appear:
"O young Marines,
Down to the haven
Call your companions, ..."?
(a) Coleridge's 'The Ancient Mariner'
(b) Masefield's 'Vagabond'
(c) Tennyson's 'Merlin and the Gleam'
(d) Tennyson's 'Maud'

ANSWERS

1. (c)	2. (b)	3. (a)	4. (c)
5. (d)	6. (b)	7. (a)	8. (c)
9. (c)	10. (c)	11. (a)	12. (a)
13. (c)	14. (d)	15. (d)	16. (a)
17. (c)	18. (b)	19. (a)	20. (c)
21. (a)	22. (a)	23. (c)	24. (a)
25. (c)	26. (d)	27. (a)	28. (d)
29. (a)	30. (b)	31. (c)	32. (b)
33. (a)	34. (b)	35. (d)	36. (c)
37. (b)	38. (c)	39. (d)	40. (d)
41. (b)	42. (b)	43. (c)	44. (a)
45. (d)	46. (c)	47. (d)	48. (a)
49. (c)	50. (c)		

PAPER-III

Descriptive Questions

21

Literary Comprehension

Q. 1. What do you know about Hermeneutics' and 'Deconstruction' as theories?

Ans.: 'Hermeneutics' and 'Deconstruction' are two terms that name two bodies of thought, two sets of texts, which today bear one signatures 'Gadamer' and 'Derrida': Though the express objectives of Hans-George Gadamer and Jacques Derride are divergent, there are considerable similarities between these two thinkers. "Hermeneutics" is the theory of the operation of understanding of texts. But today Hermeneutics is a discipline which is crucial not only to theology and philosophy but also to literary studies for literary hermeneutics has come of age. Though biblical and philosophical in origin, literary hermeneutics has successfully bridged the gap between theology—philosophy and literature.

Martin Heideggar and Hans-George Gadamer are colossal figures in the realm of hermeneutics and they have shaped and fashioned contemporary hermeneutics to a large extent. The two foundational texts of modern hermeneutics are Heidegger's *Sein* and *Zeit* (1927) and its English translation *Being and Time* (1962) and Gadamen's *Wahreit and Methode* (1960) and its English rendering *Truth and Method* (1975). Other key figures in contemporary hermeneutics are Paul Ricoeur and Jurgen Hebermas. Gadamer conceives hermeneutics to be dialogical wherein discourse serves as the model. He says "the logical structure of dialogue must be the guideline for any research in hermeneutics". In Gadamerian hermeneutics, the world is disclosed only in and through language. Understanding, interpretation and application, the three subtilitates constitute a unified triad in Gadamerian hermeneutics.

Deconstruction is simply a method, a way of reading texts, particularly philosophical. Deconstruction is specifically associated with J. Derrida and could be construed as 'decentring'. The other important names in deconstruction are Derrida's American associates/disciples: Paul de Man, Harold Bloom, Geoffrey Hartman and Hillis Miller.

Derrida subverts two foundational principles of Western tradition or metaphysics—phonocentrism and logocentrism. Phonocentrism, as the term signifies, suggests the primacy of speech over writing, for it believes that speech is presence and that the subject somehow inheres in his/her speech. Phonocentrism is bound up with logocentricism for the logos is presented as the Word or Being, which has ontotheological suggestions as adumbrated earlier by Heidegger in *Being and Time*. The Derridean deconstructive practice dethrones all hierarchies and subverts all binary oppositions. Deconstruction treats speech as a form of writing and also argues that writing is in fact the precondition of language and must be conceived as prior of speech. As a consequence of *difference* trace, dissemination and freeplay there are no stable and fixed meanings to a text. Meaning itself becomes slippery. Deconstruction has a strong tendency to focus on the 'marginal' elements in a text—a minor metaphor, a casual line and even punctuation marks. Its objective is to "read against the grain" and turn the text against itself.

Often a question is asked—how hermeneutical is deconstruction and how deconstructive is hermeneutics? The main point is, both hermeneutics and deconstruction, quite influential in contemporary philosophy with bearings on text interpretation, teach us to look at the text anew. Both stress linguistically and play, and reject any appeal to mens auctoris, and dismiss all kinds of dogmatic or authoritarian interpretations. But there are sharp differences between the two as well, especially with regard to meaning in the context of text interpretation. Madism is of the view that Gadamer and Derrida share a common bond a common preoccupation. This is, of course, language, writing, and textuality. And yet, they seem to inhabit uncommunicating worlds. Both brush aside the search for the authorical intentions in the explication and interpretation of texts. A significant point of departure between Gadamerian hermeneutics and Derridan deconstruction is the possibility/impossibility of meaning in text interpretation. While concluding it can be said that if hermeneutics, especially romantic hermeneutics, has anything to learn from deconstruction it is the rejection of all authoritarian interpretations with a view to highlighting the fact that texts are fluid and dynamic. On the other hand, if deconstruction can learn anything from hermeneutics, it is the warning issued by hermeneutics not to get self-enclosed and even imprisoned by language by foreclosing all reference and significations, for we speak to understand and be understood.

Q. 2. What are your views regarding the concept of "An Ideal Critic"?

Ans.: Criticism is the art or act of estimating the quality of literary or aritistic work by an analysis of its merits and defects. In the words of Cecil Day Lewis, "To say it quite simply, the critic has one pre-eminent task-the task of easing or widening or deepening our response to poetry".

From age to age, the standards of evaluation and criticism have widely varied. The term 'critic', is derived from the Greek 'critics' which means a judge. The man who judges may, therefore be called a critic. But while judging, he must substantiate his arguments, and taking the readers into his confidence, should lead them to the "realms of gold." A critic must not always pose to be an expert, who alone understands, and who thinks that the rest of humanity is a pack of fools. It means that critics often are more experienced, and have pronounced aesthetic taste, but they must not fall out with those, who poach upon what they regard as then preserves. Then again, if the critics, for instance, who belong to a particular school, feel that there are absolute standards in art and literature, they naturally become a little intolerant. They become self-opinionated, and choose to adhere to a set of formal and hide-bound rules.

If, on the other hand, a critic relies too much on personal impression, personal likes and dislikes, passions and prejudices, senses and sensibilities, he may not be an ideal critic or a safe guide either. Even Plato had his prejudices. Even in the 20th century, when people claim to be much enlightened and sophisticated, it is doubtful how many critics can rise above passions and prejudices. The existence of various schools of criticism proves beyond doubt that the exponents of each school look upon their views as sacrosanct, and those of one rival schools anathema.

An ideal critic has various duties to perform. He may be the interpreters, or the censor. He may be the artist, elucidator affording clues to the language or explaining ideas which the author has taken for granted. He may be the curious explorer. He may be the constructive historian, who tells how the history of society has affected art, and the influence of the arts has modified society. The task is colossal. Keats once said that a poet was the most unpoetical of beings, for he was like a chameleon. So is also a critic, who, in view of his multiplicity of activities, is almost a phenomenon. Conventional literary criticism can be divided into three kinds, namely, legislataive, theoretical, and descriptive. The critic is not only a judge, but also an interpreter.

It is true that many poets—ancient and modern—were critics as well e.g. Plato, Horace, Sidney, Dryden, Johnson, Wordsworth, Coleridge, Shelley, Keats, Arnold, T.S. Eliot, T.F. Hulme and Ezra Pound. Many of them were undoubtedly good critics, but to say that poets alone are the critics is bad.

Helen Gardner has made a good remark on the duty of a critic: "Elucidation or illumination, is the critic's primary task as I conceive it". He continues, "The Critic's task is to assists his readers to read for themselves, not to read for them. He is not writing to display his own ingenuity, subtlety, learning or sensitiveness; but to display the work in a manner which will enable it to exert its own power."

Criticism in the 20th century has endless ramifications. Non-literary techniques are now being extensively used; and, thus, the sphere of criticism has been considerably widened.

A large number of critics like Edmund Wilson, Kenneth Burke, David Daiches, Ralph Fox, Auden, Bateson, Cecil Day Lewis, Stephen Spender, Bernard Smith, George Lukacs and Christopher Caudwell, have appreciated poetry and literature from the sociological point of view, and yet there are readers and critics, who look upon their works as mere exercises in futility. The practitioners in practical, textual, and the New criticism look upon the study of society as a sheer waste of time.

An intensive study of the texts—their texture and structure is the primary objective of the New Critics. To the romantic critics, the dissection of the text is, what Wordsworth would say, "We murder to dissect." To a historical critic, a work of art is a historical phenomenon. While speaking of 'The Perfect Critic', he said that "he looked solely and steadfastly at the object." He thoroughly believed in the impersonality in art. And hence, according to Eliot, the critics must not seen in a work of art personal eccentricities, and oddities, and passions and prejudices of the artist. A large number of critics have been fully utilizing one knowledge derived from Psycho-analysis.

Helen Gardner believes the Torch rather than Sceptx to be the instrument of an ideal critic. Some critics themselves are of the opinion that we must abandon the idea of an ideal critic. There may be good critics, who will prove torce-bearers to the readers. Eliot says that a critic must be the whole man, a man with convictions and principles and of knowledge and experience of life. Literary criticism stands in the same relation to life as does literature. A good critic should take a synoptic view of life in its totality—life of the past, the present, and the future. We donot normally expect a critic to be as learned as George Saintsbury. But he has to be widely read in various branches, not necessarily in literature alone.

Q. 3. Write a detailed note on 'Trends in Modern Criticism'.

Ans.: George Watson once divided criticism into three types—legislative, theoretical, and descriptive. But modern criticism defries this division, and steps into frontiers, hitherto undivided. The 20th century has been called the age of interrogation. The sphere of criticism in the modern age has been unimaginably widened. Science and economics, politics and sociology, anthropology and psychology have all been laid under contribution. Marxism has of late, been made extensive use of in literary criticism. Marx and Engels formulated a systematic doctrine of literature on the basis of sociology. Literature and criticism are changing along with the changing society. The Sociologists and the Marxists, therefore, believe literature to be an expression of society. Literature is not the expression of an individual mind, but is distinctly a social phenomenon. The first critic to tackle literature from this angle is Taine, who emphasized the importance of race, milieu and the moment. Marxism wants the critics to use art and literature as effective weapons for exposing the hollowness of the traditional art and culture. Quite a number of the English critics of the 20th century were prodoundly influenced by Marx, and made specialized studies in their interpretation of literature. These writers include Edmund Wilson, Kenneth Burke, David Daiches, Ralph Fox, Auden, Cecil Day Lewis, Stephen Spender, etc.

Biographical Criticism, though not of recent origin, has become immensely popular in the modern age. Sainte-Beuve believes that no assessment of a work of art is possible without a thorough knowledge of the artist. This approach is known as biographical. Biography provides materials for a study of the Psychology of the artist. The biographer from this point of view, is as much a historian as a psychologist. With this Textual or bibliographical criticism has become quite popular in recent years. This type of criticism aims at the establishment of the correct text. A textual critic tries to reproduce what the author exactly wrote in more clear terms. In the 20th century the critics have followed a strict and often highly ingenious editorial logic that tries to take into account all ascertainable facts about the history and transmission of the text—the origin, date and comparative reliability of each separate manuscript or printing. Textual criticism have directed their attention to Shakespeare, Milton, Donne, Ben Johnson, W.B. Yeats, Anthony Trollope and Jane Austen too.

Practical criticism and textual criticism do not aim at the same objective, nor are their methods identical. And yet both are directly concerned with the texts. Some scholars of Cambridge, I.A. Richards, William Empson, F.R. Leavis with the mantle of T.S. Eliot on them, initiated a new movement known as practical criticism. F.R. Leavis promoted the cause of practical criticism in his periodical *Scrutiny*. Practical criticism consists in a personal approach to literature.

The New Criticism is a continuation of practical criticism. Though christened by J.E. Spingarn, and initiated by Richards, Eliot, Leavis, Empson, Graves and Laure Riding, the movement crossed over to America, John C Ransom, Kenneth Burke, Richard Blackman, Cleanth Brooks, Robert Penn Warren, Y. Winters, Allen Tate, and quite a few others are the New Critics, who blazed trails of glory in the sphere of criticism. The New Criticism may also be called neoclassicism in a restricted sense, for it is a positive reaction against romanticism and the expression of personality. It also tried to salvage literary, criticism from biography and history.

The New Critics demanded of poetry an intellectual texture. Wit, pun and irony were extensively explored for literary appreciation. The study of semantics—the exploration of meaning because their effective weapons. Cleanth Brooks in his Modern Poetry and the

Tradition, adopted several methods for the study of poetry viz. complexity, irony, paradox and the symbolic use of imagery.

Historical criticism, though not born in the 20th century, has its immense vogue even today. It became popular with Johnson and Thomas Warton who, while studying an artist, sought to study the historical background, the manners and customs, the state of society of the age in which the artist was born. Psychological and Psycho-analytical criticism is of recent origin, and is the rage of the day. Psychological criticism, though intimately associated today with the researches of Freud, Adler and Jung, can be traced to Plato's Ion.

Besides the schools enumerated, there are certain other schools of criticism e.g. judicial school, anthropological school, impressionistic school, linguistics and stylists, genetic school, school of comparative criticism.

Q. 4. What do you know about Eliot's theory of 'Impersonality of Poetry'?

Ans.: T.S. Eliot is the most influential of all the modern critics. He has expressed his views on almost all the aspects of literature and life—on the problem and process of creative activity, on the survival of culture and civilization, on religion and on social values. He has brought about a revolutionary change in the history of English literary criticism. He has corrected and educated the taste of his readers and has thrown a fresh light on the function of poetry and the nature of poetic process.

Eliot's classicism arose in part out of his reaction to the romantic theory which regarded poetry as the expression of the personality of the poet.

Eliot's concept of tradition and the objective correlative are important aspects of his impersonal theory of poetry, which in itself is an important aspect of his classicism. Eliot said, "Tradition is not solely, or even primarily, the maintenance of certain dogmatic beliefs. These beliefs have come to take their living form in the course of the formation of a tradition. What I mean by tradition involves all those habitual actions, habits and customs, from the most significant religious rites to our conventional way of greeting a stranger,—Tradition is the means by which the vitality of the past enriches the life of the present."

In his essay 'Tradition and the individual Talent' he takes up this problem of order by enquiring whether the works of literature coming down to us through the entire Western tradition.

The conscious or unconscious cultivation of the sense of tradition is very important both for the poet and the critic. The poet according to Eliot, must consciously try to make his work form a part of a larger and more important unit than himself, namely the whole literature of Europe to which it belongs. Eliot's idea of tradition is directly linked up with his impersonal theory of art, as he insists on the poet's duty to transcend the private self by loyalty to the tradition of European literature as a whole. He says that poetry is not the expression of the personality of the poet. Revolting against the romantic theory of poetry as the expression of self, Eliot propounds a theory of poetry which views poetic process not as an externalization of personal feelings, but as a complete surrender of personality. Poetry, according to him, is not inspiration, it is an organization. A great number of varied feelings, emotions and experiences are stored up in the mind of the poet who amalgamates them and forms a new whole out of them.

The artistic process, according to Eliot, is a process of depersonlization, the artist's continual surrender of himself as he is at the moment to something which is more valuable. He must surrender himself totally to the creative work.

Eliot believes that the greatness of a poem does not depend on the greatness or the intensity of the emotions, but on the intensity of the artistic process, the pressure under which the fusion takes place. Eliot wanted to divert the interest from the poet to the poetry, from the individual personality to the work of art itself which, he thinks, has an integrity and an existence of its own. There are three key words which Eliot has used—feeling, emotion and sensibility; and they are of fundamental importance on his theory of impersonality of poetry. Eliot's theory of the 'objective correlative' is closely associated with his idea of the impersonality of poetry. Eliot was influenced by the French symbolists and Ezra Pound in his conception of the 'objective co-relatives'. The symbolists had argued that poetry cannot express emotions directly, that emotions can only be evoked. In fact the concept of the 'objective correlative' is fully applicable to the poems of Eliot himself. He does not express the emotions directly; he evokes them by means of appropriate images and objects.

Eliot's views have, of course, been criticized and found fault with. Many critics do not agree with him and doubt if his critical concepts are valid for all ages and literatures. They feel that the exceptional quality of age made Eliot over-emphasize the value of tradition, and the absolute necessity of a conscious cultivation of the sense of tradition by the individual writer. The fact is that Eliot firmly believes to the impersonality of poetry and the concept of the 'objective correlative' puts the emphasis upon the work of art as a structure. The concern for the poem as an objective thing is the distinguishing feature of Eliot's classicism. He strongly believes that it is only through genuine impersonality that we can achieve the real end of poetry. Through his impersonal theory of poetry and his own practice, Eliot succeeded in curbing the careless, formless gush of post romantic poetry.

Q. 5. Write a detailed note on the stream of consciousness in the modern fiction.

Ans.: The stream of consciousness in modern fiction had its birth between 1913 and 1915. Those novelists who used this technique turned from external to internal reality. It was William James who first used the term 'Stream of Consciousness' in his book 'Principles of Psychology' in 1890 to describe the flux of the mind, its continuity and yet its continuous change through the human consciousness. The pioneers in this kind of fiction are Dorothy M. Richardson, James Joyce, Marcel Proust and Virginia Woolf. The past according to Bergson lives in the present in memory and in its consciousness, and it is in this manner that it shapes the future. The conscious continues only a fragment of the human 'psyche' or the 'soul'; human actions are more governed by the subconscious and the unconscious. Sexual inhibition and frustration are at the root of neurosis and abnormal behavior, according to Freud. His concepts of 'mother fixation' and 'father-fixation' influenced the novelists of the psychological novel. All these psychological theories have to be taken into consideration in dealing with the stream of consciousness novel.

The stream of consciousness novel deals with the pre-speech level of incoherence in human consciousness with a view to analyzing human nature.

The word 'interior monologue' has been used by Diaurdin the famous French novelist, for the stream of consciousness technique. This interior monologue is a technical device to enable the reader to enter the inner life of a character straightway. The reader is taken into the mind of the characters directly.

The human 'psyche', which the modern psychological novel aims at rendering faithfully and realistically, requires a special kind of technique to fulfill its design and that technique is the stream of consciousness method. The action in such novel moves backward and forward freely in time. Instead of a chronological forward movement we have a zigzag movement from the past to the present, and from the present to the past. In *Mrs. Dolloway* time has been dexterously manipulated by Virginia Woolf. The clocktime is only a single day in the life of the heroine, but we are made to move freely in Time and Space in the consciousness of *Mrs. Dolloway*, which leads to the building of her credible and rounded personality.

The first modern novelist who consciously employed the stream of consciousness was Dorothy Richardson. She came to the limelight by her novel *Pointed Roof* (1915). In this series of novels Dorothy Richardson seeks to present the adventures of a young woman, Miriam Henderson, from the feminine point of view. No woman has succeeded so well as Dorothy Richardson in presenting feminine psychology in her works. She mostly presented Miriam's Stream of consciousness in her novels. She has employed the technique of an omniscient narrator.

James Joyce used the stream of consciousness in A Portrait of the Artist as a Young Man, Ulysses and Finnegans Wake. James Joyce was influenced by Edourard Dujardin's interior monologue. His 'Portrait' is an autobiographical novel. It is the story of Joyce's own youth under the their guise of fiction. *Ulysses* points the life of a single day, June 16, 1904, in 742 pages. *Finnegans Wake* (1939) represents the dream of Finn Mac Cuinhal. The 'night language' in which it is written, and which makes it look the gibberish at a casual glance.

Virginia Woolf adopted the stream of consciousness in the *Jacob's Room,* his third novel, and went on using it in *Mrs Dolloway, To The Lighthouse, The Waves* and *Between the Acts.*

The stream of consciousness technique enjoyed its heyday from 1915 to 1941, but its influence did not come to an end with the publication of *Between the Acts* (1941). The work of the major novelists of the mid-century-Elizabeth Bowen, Graham Greene, Katherine Anne Porter, Robert Penn Warren, Delmox Schwarty and Eudora Welty—has not only accepted unuttered consciousness as a legitimate subject, but is even automatically formed in the image of the great experimental stream of consciousness novels.

Q. 6. "The Opposite of poetry is not prose but science"—Comment.

Ans.: Coleridge said: "Poetry is the antithesis of Science, having for its object pleasure, and not truth." Macaulay echoed their sentiments: "We think that as civilization advances, poetry almost necessarily declines. In proportion as men know more and think more, they make better theories but worse poems."

Aristotle and the Neo-Platonists from Plotinus to the Romantic period believe that the aim of art and poetry is truth; since science also aims at truth, there may not be much of conflict between the two. The only difference, however, is that Poetry is the result of divine inspiration, while Science owes nothing to the extra-mundane forces.

Critics have often pointed out the differences between science and poetry. Science, they maintain, obtain its knowledge by observation and experiment, the poet does not experiment, nor does he draw inferences. A poet is a seer, and his method is insight, intuition, and a vision.

The difference between Poetry and Science, and prose in general, when not itself poetical, becomes more prominent. Poetry, the Romantic poets and critics maintain, tends in the opposite direction, and seeks to express truth in the most concrete and pictorial form possible—in the form of images or pictures in which the meaning can be seen with the mind's eye, and therefore, intuitively and without the reasoning and inference peculiar to science.

The Romantics, by and large, pointed out the conflict between imaginative and scientific perception. But critics like Coleridge and Hegel maintained that 'man's highest faculty included both the emotional and rational elements'. Even the Positivist Buckley found Science and Poetry to be kindred 'simply because the emotions are a part of the mind'. Blake regarded Science as the enemy of poetry, because, to him, imagination was of supreme importance. And yet Science is a factor to reckon with even in the sphere of poetry.

But long before Aldous Huxley, Science and poetry were working in unison. Ptolemy, the great astronomer of the second century, has no difficulty in reconciling between science and poetry. John Donne started his career as a rebel against both religious and poetical orthodoxy. He used science in his poetry, for he happened to belong to an age when man had new reactions to the cosmology. George Herbert, in spite of Donne's influence, did not feel happy about science. Milton, the moral king of English literature, as Carlyle described him, attached much importance to Science in his 'Tract on Education': Milton posed a question in the eight Book of *Paradise Lost* why the firmament was revolving for the good of the earth. Raphael, the angel, explained the geocentric and heliocentric systems. Dryden in his *Essay of Dramatic Poesy* gave a faithful record of the progress of science. In the 18th century, Science made headway. Pope's couplet may be cited:

> 'Nature, and Nature's Laws lay hid in Night,
> God said, Let Newton be! And All was Light."

Addison, however, did not ignore science altogether. Dr. Johnson also thought of a happy blending of science and art: "The noblest beauties of art are those of which the effect is co-extended with rational nature, and with the whole circle of polished life."

The Romantic poets revolted not only against the neo-classicism but also against rationalism and science. They detested formal order and decorum and stressed the supreme need of emotional intensity. They could never make a compromise between reason and imagination.

Wordsworth, who in his youth welcomed the French Revolution and human progress, had no sympathy whatever for science and reason. Wordsworth wrote in the *Preface to his Lyrical Ballads* (1800)—

> "Poetry is the first and last of all knowledge—it is as immortal as the heart of man. If the labours of men of science should ever create any material revolution, direct or indirect, in our conditions and in the impressions which we habitually receive, the poetries sleep them no more than at present, he will be ready to follow the steps of the man of science, not only in those general indirect effects, but he will be at his side, carrying sensation into the midst of the objects of the science itself."

Here Wordsworth does not appear to be the sworn enemy of science. In fact, he expressed his desire to put science under poetic contribution. Shelley and Keats, in spite of their strong imagination and sensibility, remained all through susceptible to science. In the Victorian Age science is sprawling like a giant, spreading its hands in all spheres of life and activity. The Victorian Age is the age of compromise, and Tennyson had no difficulty in fusing science in his verse. Browning, though not as much influenced by science as his great contemporary, narrated the story of a young scientist in his Paracelsus. Mathew Arnold had no faith in Science, which multiplies coal as well as misery. Dr. Robert Bridges is the last of the Victorians and the first of the moderns, states his conviction how science "comforting man's animal poverty, and leisuring his toil, hath humanised manners and social temper."

In the 20th century there has been a further diffusion of knowledge in different spheres. To physical sciences was added Freudian psychology, and no branch of literature is conceivable without it. And yet there are poets who tried to avoid the tyranny of facts, intellect and science. D.H. Lawrence hated science, intellect, and mechanized civilization.

Whatever be the antagonism between science and poetry, we must remember that whether we like it or not, science has become an organic part of our life today, and cannot be detached. Arnold in his *Literature and Science* held that, 'a genuine humanism is scientific.'

PASSAGES

Passage 1 (solved)

"Another play with a political slant, Mukta-Dhara (1922), is sometimes referred to as Tagore's greatest play. The date is, perhaps, significant. Although Tagore did not share Gandhi's belief in the Spinning Wheel as the wonder solvent of India's economic maladies, he too instinctively shrank from machinery and gigantism. He saw that the machine was making terrible inroads into the human personality, and ruthless technological power frightened him. What is technology—when it is divorced from religion and even from humanity—except a throw-back on barbarism naked and unashamed, yet also a barbarism a million times more ruthless than the old barbarism of the jungle and the cave? In Satyavrata Mukherjee's words Tagore articulated in 'Mukha-Dhara' an eloquent protest against the onslaught of machinery on the ancient ramparts of man's individual freedom". At a time when steel plants and hydel schemes are being extolled as the New Temples of India's awakening nationhood, it would be a salutary experience to remember that, sometimes, human values are being sacrificed with cavalier indifference and indecent haste. 'Progress' could be a double edged sword, and one feels like asking: what price this technological 'progress'? Uttarakut and Shivtarai symbolize the exploiter and the exploited, the arrogant in power and the brave in spirit. Dhananjaya the ascetic and Abhijit the Prince who becomes the vassal of man's immortal spirit give Mukta-Dhara its spiritual and symbolic overtones and undertones.

Q. 1. What was Gandhi's belief regarding Spinning Wheel?

Ans.: Gandhiji had fixed belief that the Spinning Wheel is the wonder solvent of India's economic maladies.

Q. 2. What negative elements are attached with machinery?

Ans.: Machine was making terrible inroads into the human personality and ruthless technological power frightened many.

Q. 3. Tagore protested against whom in Mukta-Dhara?

Ans.: Tagore articulated an eloquent protest against the onslaught of machinery on the ancient ramparts of man's individual freedom.

Q. 4. Why 'Progress' has been called a double edged sword?

Ans.: In the name of progress, human values are being sacrificed with cavalier indifference and indecent haste on one hand and man's individual freedom on the other.

Q. 5. Who is exploiter and in what sense?

Ans.: The State of Utterakut was as exploiter that was exploiting the Shivtarains. Utterakutians were arrogant in power and they wanted to crush the freedom of Shivtarai.

Passage 2 (Solved)

Jane Austen worked wonders in her little bit of ivory, hardly two inches wide. Hers was a static society, more or less: at least it was recognizably a 'society'. In contrast to Jane Austen's world, post-independence Delhi defies definition and containment, and it needs all Mrs. Jhabrala's talent for resolved limitation to locate her own chunks of ivory-less than ivory and rather more than two inches wide—and execute her exquisite comedies of urban middle class life in the nineteen fifties and sixties. In Jane Austen's novels husband—hunting fills an important—almost a dominant—place in the action, in Mrs. Jhabvala's there is as much stress on wife's hunting as on husband hunting, and it is chiefly the parents who embark, on behalf of their children, on these torturously exasperating adventures. The traditional method of 'arranging' marriages after comparing the horoscopes of boy and girl, and taking into consideration family, status, caste, relative affluence and future prospects uneasily survives still, but it has had to make terms with unpredictable new forces like 'love at first sight' (that might ignore caste, class and race barriers) and the phenomenon of devil-may-care 'free love'. The pattern of emotional relationships in the Jhabvala's world of fiction is accordingly rather more confusing than in the severely inhibited world of Jane Austen.

Q. 1. Name the two major authors, discussed in the above para and the country they belong to.

Ans.: The two authors discussed are Jane Austen and Ruth Prawar Jhabvale. One is English with her two-inches ivory and the other is Indian-English depicting post-independence Delhi.

Q. 2. What is the most important element in the novels by both the novelists?

Ans. 'Marriage' is the most important element. In Jane Austen, it is husband-hunting and in Jhabvala similar stress is laid on wife hunting as on husband-hunting.

Q. 3. What is the traditional method of arranging marriages?

Ans.: The traditional method of arranging marriages after comparing the horoscopes of boy and girl, and taking into consideration family, status, caste, relative affluence and future prospects.

Q. 4. What is another factor other than arranged marriage?

Ans.: Another factor is love marriage. Love marriage takes place due to 'love at first sight'. It might ignore caste, class and race barriers.

Q. 5. Compare the element of emotional relationship in Austen and Jhabvala.

Ans.: The pattern of emotional relationships in Ruth Prawar Jhabvala's fictional world is more confusing than in the severely inhibited world of Jane Austen.

Passage 3 (Solved)

I was angry with my fried:
I told my wrath, my wrath did end.
I was angry with my foe:
I told it not, my wrath did grow.
And I watered it I fears,
Night and morning with my tears
And I sunned it with smiles,
And with soft deceitful wiles.
And I grew both day and night
Till it bore an apple bright.
And my foe beheld it shine,
And he knew that it was mine.
And into my garden stole
When the night had veiled the pole,
In the morning glad I see
My foe outstretched beneath the tree.

Q. 1. What is the subject matter of the poem?

Ans.: The poem is about the ramifications of repressed anger and hypocrisy. A parallel between the forbidden 'tree of knowledge' and the poet's 'poison tree' is rather too easy to draw.

Q. 2. What are the main themes of the poem?

Ans.: The poem discusses subtle play of Christian themes of sin and forgiveness. The tone of the narrator is mocking and ironical. Sin of anger and wrath is condemned in almost all Christian scriptures.

Q. 3. How does the poet feel at his foe's death?

Ans.: The poets happy (glad) at the death of his foe. But it was not certainly the final message. There seems an inherent irony built into the poem throughout.

Q. 4. In what way this poem is a confession of the poet's hypocrisy?

Ans.: There is mention of 'tears' and 'fears' that gives it confessional tone. The wrath consequently proves fatal to his enemy but does no harm to the narrator. This confession is different from Christian confession of sinfulness.

Q. 5. 'And I sunned it with smiles, And with soft deceitful wiles'. Can you compare these lines with any other author. Discuss its tone.

Ans.: Yes, Shakespeare also said the similar expression in different words. He said "Smile and smile, and be a villain." The tone of the poem is not repentant. It is mocking and ironical, full of truism in action.

Passage 4 (Solved)

Tyger! Tyger! Burning bright
In the forests of the night,

What immortal hand or eye,
Could frame they fearful symmetry?
In what distant deeps or skies
Burnt the fire of thine eyes?
On what wings dare he aspire?
What the hand done seize and fire?
And what shoulder, and what art
Could twist the sinews of thy heart?
And when thy heart began to beat,
What dread hand? And what dread feet?
What the hammer? What the chain?
In what furnace was thy brain?
What the anvil? What dread grasp
Dare its deadly terrors chasp?
When the stars threw down their spears,
And watered heaven with their tears,
Did he smile his work to see?
Did he who made the lamb make thee?

Q. 1. Comment on the imagery used in the above lines.

Ans.: With the help of images poet has portrayed the entire process of the tiger's creation e.g. fiery burning eyes, the fire of shine eyes' etc. The poet has called creator as a colossal winged creature.

Q. 2. Comment upon the theme of the poem.

Ans.: It is based on the Christian ideology. The tiger is a divine spark. The poet explains the objects of earth to denote that everyone is equal creation of God. Every force lies in our souls.

Q. 3. Comment upon the language used in the poem.

Ans.: The language used by poet is very simple and child like. But they are loaded with appreciable symbols and imagery. The repetition of the lines in the poem compels to contemplate about the greatest divine force.

Q. 4. What is the concept of God according to the poet?

Ans.: Poet considers God a smith and thinks that he had made the types in this workshop by the help of the same instruments. He must have flown on his powerful wings and searched the distant deeps or skies in search of fire to make the tiger.

Q. 5. Critically appreciate the poem.

Ans.: The poem is quite rich in evocative and eidetic images. It is lyrical and musical. The simple monosyllabic words produce melody in the poem.

Passage 5 (Unsolved)

The 'Preface' is remarkable as a manifesto of English Romanticism, even though Coleridge and the other Romantics had reservations about some of the positions articulated in it. There has also been considerable debate regarding the practice of the poetic principles by Wordsworth himself in his poetry. The fact that the First Edition of the Lyrical Ballads was sold out is an important commentary on its reception and the evolution of romantic 'taste'. The period of 1798-99 was one of prolific output and major poems like 'The Prelude' were written during this time. It is interesting to note that though Wordsworth lived well into the Victorian age; most of his poems were produced by 1807, with only 'The Excursion' (1814) and the collected poems of 1815 following it. Wordsworth was unable to produce the exuberance of his great period later but continued to revise some of his early works. The Prelude, one of the greatest poems in the English language, was designed as an autobiographical account, but it not only celebrates the self of the poet but also provides an interesting picture of the imagination at work. It also consists many of the themes that preoccupied Wordsworth throughout his career.

Q. 1. What do you know about writers of 'Preface'?

Q. 2. Wordsworth and his poetry belong to which age?

Q. 3. Whether 'Prelude' is an autobiographical poem or not?

Q. 4. What is the theme of 'Prelude'?

Q. 5. Comment on the expressions:
"manifesto of English romanticism"
"evolution of romantic taste"

Passage 6 (Unsolved)

It was Anold's burden to show through 'Culture and Anarchy' how the human values destroyed by materialism can be brought back to life by sweetness and light of culture. Arnold defined literature as a criticism of life. It is the function of literature, he thought, to lay bare the malaise of the age and thus reflect the conscience of the social and political life. 'Culture and Anarchy' is truly a criticism of the political and social life of the Victorian England.

Science was opening up new vistas of thought. Darwin's theory of evolution as enunciated in 'Origin of Species' shattered the deep—rooted beliefs of the English people. It came into conflict with the orthodox version of history of the world, the version according to which the world is a divine creation. Supported by this theory, the forces of darkness and materialism started playing havoc with the religious lives of the people. Arnold painfully observed how uncivilized the English had become because of the erosion of spiritual values.

The vast majority of people were ignorant, narrow-minded, and suffering from the dullness of their private lives. Yet Arnold had faith in their possibilities of perfection. He insisted upon two things to reform English social life of his time: higher education and disinterested criticism of ideas.

Q. 1. What is the function of culture?

Q. 2. Define literature according to Arnold.

Q. 3. How far science is important in this connection?

Q. 4. Name two things on which Arnold insisted.

Q. 5. Comment on the expressions:
(a) Literature as a criticism of life
(b) Darwin's theory of evolution shattered the deep-rooted beliefs.

22

Up to the Renaissance

Q. 1. How many dialects were popular during the age of Chaucer?

Ans.: There were at least four popular dialects; the Northern, the Southern, the East Midland and the West Midland dialects. Chaucer chose the London dialect, 'the King's English'. He wrote *The Canterbury Tales* and *The Prologue* to the Canterbury Tales became very popular due to its dialect.

Q. 2. How many metres are used by Chaucer in his works?

Ans.: Chaucer employed three principal metres: eight syllabic line rhyming in couplets-called Ottara Rhyma, ten syllabic lines rhyming in couplets called the heroic couplet, and the ten-syllabic line, arranged in Stanzas of seven lines each-called Rhyme Royal or Chaucerian Stanza.

Q. 3. Name the four original works of Chaucer and their dates.

Ans.: They are

(i) *The House of Fame* (1370)

(ii) *The Parliament of Fouls* (370)

(iii) *Troilus and Criseyde* (1385)

(iv) *The Canterbury Tales* (1390)

Q. 4. Comment upon the Canterbury Tales.

Ans.: The Canterbury Tales was designed in 1387. It extends to 17000 lines in prose and verse. Although incomplete, it is Chaucer's masterpiece. Prologue describes the meeting of 29 pilgrims in the Tabard Inn in Southward. In fact they add up to 31. Detailed pen-pictures are given of 21 of them.

Q. 5. Isolate some medieval and some modern features in Chaucer's poetry.

Ans.: Modernism and medievalism are both the distinctive features of Chaucer's poetry. The knight in the Canterbury Tales symbolizes the old world Chivalry, while Nun's Priest's Tale refers admiringly to Jack Straw who had raised the banner of Peasant to Revolt which was a modern trend. The ecclesiastic characters indicate the decay and corruption in religion.

Q. 6. What is your view of Chaucer as the maker of modern English?

Ans.: By shedding aside the foreign influences and by using his own native language as the medium for his poetry, Chaucer, the first national poet of England became the founder of modern English poetry. Lowel rightly said that "he found English a dialect and left it a language".

Q. 7. Comment upon the position of prose in the Age of Chaucer.

Ans.: The era saw the foundation of an English prose style in the works of Mandeville and Malory, which was both original and individual. The English tongue, now ripe for a prose style was settling to a standard unlike Latin and French.

Q. 8. What do you know about the other poets of the age of Chaucer and major trends in poetry?

Ans.: Poetry of this period more or less reveals some aspect of contemporary life and of prevailing feeling and thought. The main poets of this age are Geoffrey Chaucer (Canterbury Tales, The Legend of Good Women), William Langland (Piers the Plowman) John Wycliff, John Mandeville (Trands), John Gower (Confessio Amantis) and John Barbour (Brus).

Q. 9. Describe Renaissance

Ans.: 'Renaissance' is a French word which means 'rebirth', 'revival' or 'reawakening'. It refers to the revival of ancient classical mythology, literature, culture and also of human mind after the dark Middle Ages. It was a series of events extending over two centuries and transforming the Medieval into the Modern.

Q. 10. What do you know about Italian Renaissance?

Ans.: The Renaissance originated in Italy as early as the 14th century with Petrarch and Boccaccio. Later on, the fall of Constantinople in 1453 added much to the Renaissance movement in Italy. Many Greek Scholars took shelter to Italy with their works. As a result Italian cities became centres of Greek Study and classical culture. Florence became the centre of Italian Renaissance.

Q. 11. Comment upon Humanism and Reformation as two more aspects of Renaissance.

Ans.: Humanism refers to the classical writing. The classical authors were humanistic in outlook, which means man's concern for himself. Reformation appeared as one of the notable results of the Renaissance in the sphere of religion as church seemed to be mainly corrupt in the period of Renaissance.

Q. 12. What do you understand by 'Scholastic' impact of Renaissance?

Ans.: The first impact in England was registered by the universities. Some English scholars went to Italy and examined the manuscripts of the Greek scholar and later they organized the teaching of Greek in Oxford. Some educationists wrote their works modeled on Italian works. The above two impacts are often called the 'scholastic impact of Renaissance'.

Q. 13. William Langland is an important poet of the Age of Chaucer. Discuss.

Ans.: William Langland's (1330-31-1386) only work is Piers the Plowman, an allegorical poem, that exposes the rampant corruption in the church. It has three texts, A, B, and C, written and revised by Langland. The text is mainly divided into Visio and Vita. It tell us more about the suffering of the peasants. The poem is remarkable for its originality.

Q. 14. What do you know about the chief-prose-writers of the age?

Ans.: Chaucer's works (Tale) include a good deal of prose. Others who did more than translations were the Augustinian Canon, Walter Hilton and the great reformer John Wycliff, also known as first Prosant.

Q. 15. What do you know about Chaucer's most ambitious allegorical poem, the House of Fame?

Ans.: In this poem, Chaucer sets out to describe the caprices of fame, and the strange way in which rumour is manufactured and spread around. It is incomplete; perhaps Chaucer never finished it, finding it too artificial to satisfy his mature taste. For similar reasons Chaucer left unfinished his Legend of Good Women.

Q. 16. Comment upon the popular literature—Ballads.

Ans.: Ballads seems to have been particularly alive at that period, found all over Europe. The popular ballad is narrative, long or short, in simple verse. The word Ballad is derived from the word 'Ballare', means to dance. "A ballad differs from a lyric in being descriptive rather than impressionistic, the felling of a tale, not the expression of mood" (Compton Ricket).

Q. 17. Ballads can be divided in how many categories on the basis of metres used?

Ans.: It is possible to divide ballads into two categories. *The popular ballad*, with its simplicity, its apparent ease and artlessness, and its primitive feeling, and the '*literary ballad*, the conscious initiation of a later date of the original popular ballad.

Q. 18. 'Miracle Plays are the product of the fifteenth century.' Comment.

Ans.: Miracle Plays grew out of the liturgy itself, with its solemn rites and the chants alternating between priest and congregation. It represents the epical period. They began at short dialogues. Recited at first inside the church, these dialogues developed by degrees into little plays acted in the church porch.

Q. 19. "Their (Moral Plays) aim, like that of Miracle Plays, was primarily the teaching of the Christian faith, but they appealed more directly to the intellect". Justify.

Ans.: Moralities eliminate from allegory. Bible characters are replaced by abstract virtues and vices personified. Unlike miracles (Plays for the unlettered) morality play exacted more attention to the words, text was more important than scenery, and the construction was more artificial. It required but one fixed stage.

Q. 20. Which type of poetry was flourished during the period of 15th century?

Ans.: The poetry of the period may be divided into two classes:

(a) 'Courtly' official or Chaucerian poetry

(b) Popular or 'Folk' poetry.

Folk poetry is rich in ballad, lyric, carol etc. It is also rich in drama. The age is deficient or barren only in so far as great poetry of the first 'courtly' kind is concerned.

Q. 21. Who were Scottish Chaucerians?

Ans.: The Scottish poetry of the period also reveals the influence of Chaucer. The allegory, the dream convention and the seven lined Chaucerian stanza are also used by the poets of Scotland. But Scottish poetry reveals greater freshness, vigour and artistic beauty. Important Scottish Chaucerians' are King James I, Robert Henryson, William Dunbar and Gawin Douglas.

Q. 22. What are the 'Paston Letters'? Comment upon their importance.

Ans.: In 15th century, (the great era of letter writing) the Pastons were a well to do family of Norfolk and their letters cover three generations and give much intimate information about

English life from 1422 to 1509. They are important as they constitute a valuable social chronicle of the 15th century. The great value of the letters is that they are true and reliable social chronicles. They also reveal the gradual change, coming over the English language and grammar.

Q. 23. What do you know about John Heywood's Interludes?

Ans.: John Heywood's Interludes or forces have no other purpose but to amuse. They paved way for the artistic comedy. They are brief comic dialogues without any action or development. There is no plot but the characters are life-like and interesting. They avoid morality and practicing.

Q. 24. What do you know about Senecan tragedy?

Ans.: A senecan tragedy is an unrelieved tragedy. There is no dramatic relief. It has heaping up of crime upon crime. The motive for crime is revenge for some earlier wrong. Then there is retribution, divine punishment for that crime. It has frequent political allusion and attacks on tyrants, little action and a lot of speechifying. It abounds in maxims and sententious utterances. Language is lyrical, declamatory and highly ornamental.

Q. 25. Who was Aeropagus?

Ans.: 'Aeropagus' was a group of young men who tried to transplant classical metres into English verse. But the only imported metres that could flourish in England were the sonnet and the blank verse—the two measures associated with the names of Wyatt and Surrey.

Q. 26. What is a romantic epic? Name any romantic epic written by Spenser.

Ans.: Romantic epic has the prominent features both of a romance and an epic. The treatment of the subject must be in the grand style suitable for an epic. 'The Fairy Queen' by Spenser has been called an epic, a medieval romance, as well as a romantic epic. In it Homeric Similes have been profusely used to exalt the imagination of the readers and enlarge the range of the epic. The language too is dignified and sublime.

Q. 27. Write a brief history of the arrival of sonnet in England.

Ans.: Wyatt had imported the sonnet from Italy and Surrey had invented the English form of the sonnet. Their songs and sonnets were published together in Tottel/s Miscellany in 1556. The word 'sonnet' was used indifferently, used for any short lyric and it remained forgotten and neglected till the publication in 1591 of Sidney's Sonnets called Astrophel and Stella.

Q. 28. Write the names of famous sonnet writers of Elizabethan era.

Ans.: Sidney, Spenser and Shakespeare are the greatest sonnet writers of the Elizabethan era. Next to them stand Sammuel Daniel and Michael Drayton.

Q. 29. Who was the last of the line of Scottish poets of the fifteenth century?

Ans.: Sir David Lyndsay was the last Scottish poet. In form he belongs to the Middle Ages, but he is distinguished from his predecessors by his zeal as a social reformer. His longest poem is the 'Monarchie' (1552) based on a Sermon by Knox. To John Knox, on the contrary, may be ascribed the honour of being the first great Scottish writer in prose.

Q. 30. Comment upon the progress of the Drama after 1550.

Ans.: Not until after 1550 did the influence of the classics make itself felt, in comedy first, and, as was natural in a scholastic circle. The first comedy written in accordance with the rules of antiquity was *Ralph Roister Doister* by Nicolas Udall (1553). Farcical comedies could not contribute much to the progress of the theatre. National drama and the drama of antiquity met fully for the first time in tragedy. In 1562 a tragedy after the manners of: Gorboduc, or Ferrex and Porex was acted and paved way for the development of Drama.

Q. 31. Prove that Spenser was a great painter.

Ans.: The Faerie-Queen is, in fact, a gallery of pictures; and Spenser is a great painter who never handled a brush. Besides numerous descriptions of tapestries and pictures, a crowd of portraits, charming or grotesque, which are masterpieces of painting, are also found. The great painter was a no less great musician.

Q. 32. Comment on the Sonneteers of the Elizabethan age.

Ans.: Elizabethan Sonnet was confined within the years 1591-97. Sidney's Astrophel and Stella in 1591 was followed by Sonnets of Thomas Watson, Henry Constable and Thomas Lodge. The chief merit of the Sonnets of Daniel and Drayton lies in their style-graceful in the first, lively in the latter. But the glory of the English sonnet lies mainly in the hands of Sidney, Spenser and Shakespeare.

Q. 33. What do you know about other poetical forms of the Elizabethan time?

Ans.: Under the influence of Italy there grew up a booting of voluptuous poetry which, in spite of passages of beauty, rightly drew down upon it the reprobation of the Puritans. Marlowe's *Hero and Leander*, Shakespeare's *Venus and Adonis* and *Rape of Lucrece* are noteworthy along with the certain poems of morality and devotion by J.R. Smithwell.

Q. 34. Who are known as the Innovators of the age and why?

Ans.: In contrast with the writers live Shakespeare, Marlowe and some others who on the whole followed beaten tracks, are two poets who opened up new ways and who had the greatest influence on those of the coming age. They are Ben Jonson and John Donne.

Q. 35. Why Donne's poetry is termed as revolutionary?

Ans.: When John Donne began to write, Spenser was at the height of his fame, and the Petrarchans were producing volume after volume. Donne revolted against both. He despised convention and chivalric love, as he did smooth verse and harmonious flouring cadences. He violated all laws of rhythm in his 'Satyres', and is often perverse even in his songs and elegies. There is a unique originality in his style. Passion, sentiment, sensuality—he subordinates all to wit.

Q. 36. Discuss Ben Jonson as a poet.

Ans.: Ben Jonson was primarily a dramatist, but he has left a fair amount of poetry. It consists of miscellaneous poems included in the Epigrams and the forest and the underwoods. Satire preponderates and Jonson expresses his harsh outspokenness in lines that are often bitter. Many of his poems are in initiation of the Greek Anthology, elegies and epitaphs.

Q. 37. What kind of Prose was written from 1578 to 1625?

Ans.: Much of the prose written under Elizabeth is either Euphuistic or Arcadian. It is poetical prose, and characterizes the work of the romance—writers and the novelists. Robert Greene, Thomas Lodge, Thomas Nashe, Thomas Deloney, Thomas Dekker are few to name.

Q. 38. What do you know about 'Religious Prose'?

Ans.: Before attaining to Richard Hooker's majestic serenity the religious literature of Elizabeth's days was a succession of controversies. Their attack, in its buffoonery and virulence, appealed to the populace. These champions of orthodoxy were not inspired by religious convictions, but they loved a fight. Thomas Nashe is best known for this. But nothing in the religious prose of the Renaissance equals in beauty and importance of the authorized version of the *Bible* (1611), which was the work of fifty four scholars and inspired a thinker like Bunyan to write source of the finest English prose.

Q. 39. Comment upon the main characteristics of Shakespearean comedy.

Ans.: Shakespearean comedy is also known as Romantic comedy, which is neither based on facts nor on any set rules of literary creation.

(i) Dramatists do not care about the three Unities of Time, Place and Action.

(ii) There is a free mingling of the comic and the tragic, where comedy occupies the major portion.

(iii) The aim of romantic comedy is to produce laughter. It neither corrects nor preaches. It is free from satire and irony.

(iv) It ends with marriage bells and love at first sight is the chief element.

(v) They are known for wit, wordplay, puns, conceits and clown or court-jesters.

(vi) Love and music are their very essence.

Q. 40. What do you know about William Caxton?

Ans.: William Caxton (1422-91) is not an important creative writer. He translated Recuyell of the Historeys of Torye from French. His great contribution is the introduction of the printing press in England. He set up a Press at Westminister in 1476. The first book that he printed in 1477 was Dictes or Sayengis of the Philosophers.

Q. 41. What do you know about the writer of Morte D' Arthur?

Ans.: Sir Thomas Malory (d.1471) wrote Le Morte D' Arthur in 1470. This lengthy cycle of Arthurian legends was first published by Caxton in 1485. The important characters are Merlin, King Arthur, Queen Guinevere and the one hundred Knights. Arthur's famous sword is named Excalibur.

Q. 42. Who is William Tyndale? Write about his most important contribution.

Ans.: William Tyndale (d. 1536) was the other Reformation leader. He was the first to translate the Bible into English. He was followed by Miles Coverdale (488-1568) whose translation was superseded by the authorized version of 1611.

Q. 43. Who is known as the 'Poet's Poet'?

Ans.: The greatest poet of the Elizabethan age, known as 'Poet's Poet' and 'our serious sage Spenser (Milton) is Edmund Spenser (1552-99). He best represents the period of renaissance and reformation. His main works are The Fairy Queen, Amoretti, Prothalamim etc.

Q. 44. What do you know about the use of word 'humanitas'?

Ans.: The Latin word 'humanitas' was a programme designed to condition man both culturally and intellectually. Humanitas was an engagement that sought to elevate man to a stature that would do justice to his potential. The focus for the humanist was on a reconciliation of participation and thought which aimed to develop the individuality of man in a way that lived up to the ideal of Renaissance man.

Q. 45. Write a short note on Elizabethan Prose.

Ans.: In Elizabethan age different prose genres were not only experimented with but even developed through continuous engagement. In general terms, the prose of the period may be divided into two categories—fictional and non-fictional. The fiction of the Elizabethan period covered a diverse terrain. The variety of prose writings, from the picaresque narrative to the pamphlet, occupied the writer's mind. Many of the University Wits were prolific prose writers and wrote both fiction and non-fiction. John Lyly, Greene, Thomas Nashe, Richard Hakluyt, Richard Hooker and Francis Bacon are the chief exponents.

Q. 46. Comment upon the last plays of Shakespeare.

Ans.: Shakespeare's last plays show a much mellow orientation but nevertheless they are in keeping with the evolving character of the playwright. *Pericles* (c. 1608), probably written in collaboration with George Wilkins, introduced the quiet temper of his last plays discernible in *Cymbeline*. (c. 1610), *The Winter's Tale* (c. 1611), and *The Tempest* (c. 1611).

Q. 47. Comment upon the last plays of Ben Jonson.

Ans.: Ben Jonson (1572-1637) shows his knowledge of contemporary manners and London life in his comedies. All his plays were not successful on the stage. *The New Inn* (1629) and *A Tale of a Tub* (1633) are his last plays. Jonson is closely associated with the trend of classicism that emerged as a counterpoint to the Romantic mode epitomized by Shakespeare. He was the major Elizabethan Playwright to adhere to the idea of the 'unities' and abhorred the extravagant excesses of his contemporaries.

Q. 48. Who are the other minor poets writing in the 16th century other than Wyatt and Surrey?

Ans.: The poems of Thomas Churchyard were collected in Churchyard's Chips. He wrote pageant verses, epitaphs, etc. George Gascoigne was a dramatist and a poet whose play of mistaken identity, *Supposes* (c. 1566), anticipated Shakespeare's *The Comedy of Errors*. George Whatstone wrote a eulogy in verse praising his contemporary George Gascoigne.

Q. 49. Comment upon Philip Sidney's literary output.

Ans.: Philip Sidney's literary output covered various genres. He was a poet, writer of a romance, a dramatist, and a literary critic. In each of these genres Sidney's contribution was historically significant. He is known for his sonnets sequence, *Astrophil and Stella* (1591), *An Apology for Poetry*, *Arcadia* and *The Lady of May* (1578).

Q. 50. What do you know about the Tudor Period?

Ans.: The Tudor period was characterized by a remarkable outpouring of sonnets, both as independent poems, and also as part of sequences. The sonnet sequence was a major draw for many of the poets of the time, with Shakespeare, Spenser, Sidney, Drayton and Dower being its most famous exponents. Donne, however, did write a series of sonnets that dealt with the theme of spirituality titled Holy Sonnets.

Q. 51. Why Francis Bacon is known as the first English Philosopher in data?

Ans.: By the side of religious, there grew up a secular literature, philosophical and moral; not antagonistic too, although distinct from, the former. Francis Bacon writes of religion with respect, but his work is independent of theology, and even of Christian morality. He was one of the pioneers of that modern philosophy which is not confined within any national limits.

Q. 52. Who is the writer of 'New Atlantis' which is a scientific Utopia?

Ans.: Francis Bacon (1561-1626) wrote 'New Atlanta' which is clumsily written and is painfully didactic . He is known for 'Novum Organum', 'Advancemnt of Learning' (1605) and Historie of the Raigue of Henry VII' (1622).

Q. 53. Critically appreciate the prose-style of Bacon.

Ans.: Bacon's essays are, full of pithy aphorisms, pregnant with thought and practical wisdom. Many of his sayings have passed into proverbs. Indeed, in all Bacon's works—Latin as well as English—sentences abound as memorable for their concentrated wisdom as for their brilliance.

Q. 54. Who is the writer of 'The Anatomy of Melancholy' (1621)?

Ans.: Robert Burton (1577-1640) another prose writer of the day wrote 'The Anatomy of Melancholy', which is yet vivified by human. Burton draws on a vast canvas a picture of human frailly and folly. Crowded with Latin quotations, often redundant—for the author enjoys piling up synonyms and epithets—his style is that of the eccentric.

Q. 55. Write a brief note on Shakespearean dramatic romances.

Ans.: *Cymbeline*, *The Winter's Tale* and *The Tempest* are Shakespeare's major dramatic romances. Towards the close of his career and after his tragic period, the playwright again returned to comedy, but comedy so unlike the previous plays turned into dramatic romances. They have their own peculiar features.

Q. 56. Compare and contrast the nature of Ben Jonson's comedy with Shakespearean comedy.

Ans.: Ben's comedy is classical, while that of Shakespeare is romantic. Ben writes in accordance with the classical rules of dramatic composition. He observes the three unities, and does not mingle tragedy with comedy. Shakespeare throws all such rules to the wind and allows his imagination free play. Ben's comic aims were realistic and satiric. The plots of his comedies are all laid in London, and his characters are common London Types. His aim was to sport with human folio and affections.

Q. 57. What was Bacon's conception of the essay?

Ans.: Bacon considered the essays as a receptacle for detached thoughts. So he regarded his essays dispersed mediations. He defined his essays as 'counsels civil and moral'. In his essays he wished to give valuable guidance so his essays came to, man's business and bosom and very soon they gained immense popularity.

Q. 58. What is the most obvious quality of Bacon's style?

Ans.: The most obvious quality of Bacon's style is terseness of expression and epigrammatic shortness. Bacon possesses the power of expressing into a few words a great body of thought.

He is weighty with thought. His sentences are brief. They have terseness and brevity. His style is aphoristic.

Q. 59. Who called Bacon 'the wisest, brightest, meanest of mankind' and why?

Ans.: Bacon had a dual personality. He was the wisest and the brightest. He was a mental dwarf. He had a complex and contradictory nature. It was his complexity that Pope was forced to call him 'the wisest, the brightest and meanest of mankind'. His conduct towards the earl of essex was mean and treacherous. He had a strange mixture of intellectual strength and moral weakness.

Q. 60. Comment upon Samuel Daniel as a poet.

Ans.: Daniel is known for his most tranquil and classical poetry of the period. His longest and most characteristic work is his 'The Civil Wars' published in 1595 (a long narrative poem in eight cantos—over 7000 lines). Its subject is the Blood—Thirsty War of the Roses, and it is inspired by Daniel's patriotism.

Q. 61. Who wrote 'Polyoblion'?

Ans.: 'Polyoblion' was written by Michael Drayton. It poetises the Geography of England from one corner to another. Every hill, valley, river, even street, is personified and is made to narrate local history and legend. Drayton has used the Alexandrine, while ten or eight-syllabled lines were order of the day. He alone has poetized geography.

Q. 62. Who called Spenser 'Poet's Poet'? Give reasons.

Ans.: Charles Lamb called Spenser the 'Poet's Poet'. He has coached more poets, and many poets of 17th, 18th and 19th centuries followed him. Milton, Browne and the two Fletchers were his professed disciples. Spenser was a learned man, well-versed in literature and mythology of ancient Greece and Rome.

Q. 63. What kinds of subjects were most popular in Elizabethan lyrics?

Ans.: Love, religion and nature are the three most popular subjects of lyrics in Elizabethan times. The lyrics are in every mood, sometimes even mocking and melancholy. But the prevalent mood is gay and merry.

Q. 64. Write a brief history of the arrival of Sonnet in England.

Ans.: Wyatt had imported the sonnet from Italy and Surrey had invented the English form of the sonnet. Their songs and sonnets were published together in Tottel's Miscellany in 1556. The Sonnet remained forgotten and neglected till the publication in 1591 of Sidney's sonnet—sequence called Astrophel and Stella.

Q. 65. Name five Sonneteers of Elizabethan era.

Ans.: Sidney, Spenser, Shakespeare, Samuel Daniel and Michael Drayton are the greatest sonnet writers of the era.

Q. 66. Critically introduce Shakespeare's *The Rape of Lucrece.*

Ans.: It belongs to the category of the licentious poetry, which was quite popular in Elizabethan era. Here we get the picture of a libertine raping and debauching an innocent maiden for his pleasure.

Q. 67. What do you know about 'Silver Poets'?

Ans.: Gerald Bullet refers to Sir Thomas Wyatt, Henry Howard, Earl of Surrey, Sir Phillip Sidney, Sir Walter Raleigh and John Davies, as the Silver poets of the 16th century, for their poetry is characterized by silver-tongued eloquence. All of them wrote lyrics, sonnets, ballads, elegies, epitaph etc. All were men of breeding and culture and courtier too.

Q. 68. What do you know about 'University Wits'?

Ans.: The pre-Shakespearean dramatists, John Lyly, Robert Greene, George Peele, Thomas Kyde, Christopher Marlowe etc. are known as University Wits, for they were all university-educated man.

Q. 69. Comment upon Shakespeare's contemporaries or rivals.

Ans.: Shakespeare's chief rivals were among the humanists. The hostility shown him at the beginning by Greene and the 'University Wits' was renewed later by George Chapman and Jonson. Ben Jonson served as the antithesis of Shakespeare. Jonson, ill-tempered and arrogant, stood out against the Elizabethan drama.

Q. 70. Name some more prominent writers of the era.

Ans.: John Marston (*Antonio and Melida* (1600), East-Ward Hoe), Thomas Dekker (*The Shoemaker's Holiday*), Thomas Heywood (*The Troubles of Queen Elizabeth*), Thomas Middleton (*Michaelmas Terme*), Cyril Tourneur (*The Revenge's Tragedies*), John Webster (*Duchess of Malfi*), John Fletcher and Beaumont are the other prominent writers of the Elizabethan Era.

23

Jacobean to Restoration Periods

Q. 1. From poverty, blindness, leisure, rose his chief works: "*Paradise Lost*, *Paradise Regained* and *Samson Agonists*". Justify.

Ans.: Personal unhappiness and a nation's agony had darkened the thoughts of Milton. He felt something like disdain for the lovely rhymed verse of his youth. He wrote in blank verse only, except in some courses in Samson. At the age of 44 he became Blind and he turned his back on the Renaissance as upon trivialities, to fix his inward sight on the Bible. He sang of the creation, the fall of the angels, the fall of man, the reconquest of Paradise by Christ, or of the sacrifice of Samson.

Q. 2. What do you know about special features of Milton's greatest work, *Paradise Lost*?

Ans.: This classical epic is the fruit of a Puritan's meditation on the Bible. Milton's hell is a vast indeterminate space where, in 'darkness visible' are stretched gigantic beings, the vanquished angels changed to demand. But the arch-rebel, Satan, is the poet himself. In Satan's arrogance and revolt may be read Milton's vindictive hatred of the crown. The story of Adam and Eve is the drama of conscience, hesitating between good and evil, exposed to temptation, liable to fall.

Q. 3. '*Paradise Regained* is the complement of, and reply to, *Paradise Lost*'. Justify.

Ans.: In this epic Milton shows that Christ, after his fast of forty days, resists the three temptations of Satan and thus ends the reign on earth of the evil one Satan reappears, but he has become smaller, faded; he is no longer splendid and indomitable, but a trickster and a hypocrite. The poem is entirely human, its interest lying in the temptation of a soul. Milton saw Christ not as divine but as a Superman. In this light he describes the thoughts and mental struggles of Christ, who seeks to determine and accomplish his mission.

Q. 4. Write a brief note on Milton's descriptive power.

Ans.: Milton excels in his descriptive power. His greatness lies in even expressing the inexpressible, in the most convincing and with all, the most impressive terms. We may open Paradise Lost anywhere we please and we see the immense descriptive power at work; in the description of the lake of fire, of Satan's body rolling in it, of the dry land of hell etc., etc.

Q. 5. 'Milton is the greatest master of English music.' Do you agree?

Ans.: There is a unique musical quality in all verse from the Nativity Ode to Samson Agonists. He excels in all kinds of verse—in the Ode and Elegy, in the Lyric and Sonnet, in the Epic and Tragedy, and what is remarkable is that the various metres are well adapted to the several poetic forms. He used the stanza-form in his Ode on Christ's Nativity, and the Octo-syllabic couplet in L'Allegro and II Penseroso. In these poems he proved himself to be a master in his superb handling of rhymed verse.

Q. 6. What are the chief characteristics of the age of Milton?

Ans.: It was the age when exalted fervor of the age of Shakespeare was decaying. Passion and profundity were no more intellectual play of fancy. Prose was marked by increased activity and melancholy. Blank verse reached the climax in the age of Milton. Heroic couplet began to appear Lyrical style had increased in care and polish. There was a movement towards ornate prose style. Shorter and lyrical poems began to be written in the age of Milton and the output of poetry decreased.

Q. 7. Who has been called the Shakespeare of English prose and the Spenser of the pulpit? Justify.

Ans.: Jeremy Taylor is a prose-poet closely allied to the Elizabethans. He has been called The Shakespeare of English prose as he conceives an imaginative interest in the subjects he describes. He is not only an observer of nature but a psychologist who knows the heart of man.

Q. 8. Who served as a link between Marlowe and Dryden?

Ans.: Isaac Walton (1593-1683) holds a place apart. Due to his long life he serves as a link between Marlowe and Dryden. A plain ironmonger of Fleet Street, he had all his life a love of culture and an administration for good literature. His biographies of Donne, Wotton, Richard Hooker, George Herbert, and Sanderson are filled with intimate details and perfumed with sympathy. But his best known work is *The Compleat Angler* (1653), which is at once a technical treatise and charming idyll.

Q. 9. Who were 'Puritans'?

Ans.: Puritans were those value-based people who wanted to purify church. They rejected the charm of beauty and pleasure. Beauty in their eyes was a snare and pleasure a sin. The only mode of social intercourse which they approved was a sermon.

Q. 10. What did the term 'the New Philosophy' signify during the Puritan age?

Ans.: The term the 'New Philosophy' was used to designate experimental or empirical science. The Renaissance itself had done much to widen the mental horizons of the age, and induce newer modes of thought. The re-discovery of Greco-Roman humanistic culture, art and literature, gave a knockout blow to medieval ascetic and other worldly outlook. The medieval cosmology and philosophy were shaken by the rise of the new philosophy. The 'New Philosophy' was already catchword at the beginning of the century, and by the Restoration, scientific experiment was achieving a fashionable status.

Q. 11. What do you know about the Whigs and the Tories?

Ans.: The Restoration age witnessed the rise of the two political parties, the Whigs and the Tories, which were to play a leading role in English politics for a long time to come. The country was divided into two political parties: (1) the Whigs who sought to limit the royal power in the interests of the people and the Parliament, and (2) the Tories, who supported the 'Divine Right,' theory of King, and strove to check the growing power of the people in the interests of their hereditary rules.

Q. 12. What was the impact of the rise of the two parties (the Whigs and the Tories) on literature?

Ans.: The rise of these political parties gave fresh importance to men of literary ability, for both parties tried to enlist their support and bribed them with places and pensions. Hardly any writer of the day is free from this political bias. Dryden, for example, was a Tory and he ably advocated the cause of the monarch.

Q. 13. Comment upon the Social life in the Restoration period.

Ans.: In the social life of the Restoration period there was a marked change and the main point to be noted was the reaction against Puritanism, which suggested the wide swing of the pendulum from one extreme to the other. The atmosphere of gaiety and cheerfulness was restored. The theatres were re-opened, the bull and bearbaiting revived, and sports, dancing—a wild delight in the pleasures and varieties of this world replaced that of absorption in 'other worldliness' which characterized the extreme Puritanism.

Q. 14. Express your views regarding 'Morality in the Restoration Age'.

Ans.: The morals of the people were entirely changed. The virtues of defeated Puritanism did much to modify the reaction against the vices of the Puritan in power. There was a great reaction against the stern morality of the Puritans. A court was organized in which preferment and positions were distributed as the master desired. Licentiousness gained the upper hand. Morality was on the wane and everywhere there was laxity in life. With the collapse of the Puritan Govt., there sprang activity that had so long been suppressed. The commonwealth had insisted on gravity and decorum in all things; the Restoration encouraged the activity that often became immoral and indecent.

Q. 15. How far the Political Scene in the age of Restoration influenced literature?

Ans.: During the Restoration age politics gained the upper hand. The age was largely concerned with politics, which reflected its influence in the literature of the age. In all directions it appeared as a disposition towards conservatism and moderation. Men had learnt to fear individual enthusiasm, and therefore they tried to discourage it by setting up ideals of conduct in accordance with reason and common sense, to which all men should adapt themselves. Rules of etiquette and social conventions were established and the problem of life became that of self-expression with the narrow bounds which were thus prescribed.

Q. 16. Name the famous writers of the Restoration Age who influenced English literature.

Ans.: Pascal, Bossuet, Malherbe, Corneille, Racine, Moliere are the main French writers who influenced English literature. The French influence penetrated deeply into drama, especially into comedy, which was the most copious literary production of the Restoration. Of 'French Comedy' Moliere was the outstanding exponent, and his influence was very great. In the more formal tragedy, French and classical models were combined to produce a new type of drama called the Heroic Play. Hudson said, "As in verse pre-eminently these were now cultivated at the expense of feeling and spontaneity, the growth of an artificial type of poetry was the inevitable result".

Q. 17. What part was played by realism in the literature of the Restoration period?

Ans.: The literature of the Restoration period was marked by the tendencies of realism. The lighter literature reflects the interest of man in learning to live with one another. The Restoration literature developed realism in a marked degree. Writers sought to paint realistic pictures of a corrupt court and society, and emphasized vices rather than virtues and gave us coarse, low plays without interest or moral significance.

Q. 18. Write a short note on the prose styles during the Age of Milton (1625-60).

Ans.: During the age of Milton, the Britons were clearly divided between the Cavaliers (or Royalists) and Puritans. The practice of pamphleteering became ubiquitous and more marked and political in tone during this period. Another important feature of the prose written during this period was the Baroque style which was largely the outcome of the ornate, prolix and embellished Gothic style of the Elizabethans, much against the instructions of Bacon and character writers after him. The tide was only checked later by Dryden who pleaded for a graceful, simple and lucid style; which got perfection only in the hands of Addison, Steele and Swift.

Q. 19. Write a short note on the prose writers of the Age of Milton (1625-60).

Ans.: The important prose writers of this period were Sir Thomas Browne, Jeremy Taylor, Milton, Baxter, Thomas Fuller, Izaak Walton, Hobbes etc.

Q. 20. Write a short note on the Cavalier poets of the Age of Milton.

Ans.: It is sometimes not realized that Cavalierism arose out of the blend of the varied influence of Ben Jonson and Donne on the poetry of the period. The following were important Cavalier Poets: Thomas Carew, John Suckling, Richard Lovelace, John Cleveland and Robert Herrick.

Q. 21. Write a brief note on the Restoration Satirical Spirit.

Ans.: The most important satirical writers of the period was Samuel Butler (1612) who wrote *Hudibras* which appeared in three parts in 1663, 1664 and 1678. The work is well-known for its exceptional theme which is not only satirical but also cynical, mocking and pessimistic in the under current, even while lacking the essential unity of a consummate poem. A large host of political satirists existed in the Restoration period in the shape of Pamphleteers, etc. As for such satirists having some literary value, a few names stand out in prominence: Marvell, Oldham, Dryden and Thomas Orway.

Q. 22. Narrate the reasons behind the rise of the Heroic Play.

Ans.: Heroic play arose, first as a reaction to Shakespeare, because it was felt that nothing more could be done with the Shakespearean type of tragedy, and if they wanted really to excel and do something new, they must explore fresh fields. Secondly, it arose mainly to satisfy the social, moral and artistic needs of the age. In fact, it came into existence in response to the spiritual needs of a tired, disillusioned and decadent aristocracy.

Q. 23. Milton is known as the greatest product of Puritanism. Do you agree?

Ans.: To the extent of its power, Puritanism destroyed humane culture, and sought to confine literature within the circumscribed field of its own particular interests. This was emphatically the case with Milton. In Milton's genius and work, the moral and religions influence of Puritanism are combined with the generous culture of the Renaissance. That's why he is known as the greatest product of Puritanism.

Q. 24. What do you know about Milton's married life?

Ans.: As a pamphleteer Milton became indeed one of the great pillars of the Puritan cause, and on the establishment of the commonwealth was appointed Latin Secretary to the Committee for Foreign Affairs. In 1643, he married Mary Powell, the young daughter of a

Royalist, but the union proved a most unhappy one. Later he became blind and married again, but his wife, Catherine Woodcock, died within fifteen months. His third wife Elizabeth Minshul brought comfort to his declining years, he was greatly distressed by the unfilled conduct of his daughters by his first marriage.

Q. 25. Comment upon Milton's earlier poetry.

Ans.: Milton's earlier work falls naturally into four periods: (1) the college period, closing with the end of his Cambridge career in 1632; (2) the Horton period, closing with his departure for the Continent in 1639; (3) the period of his Prose writings, from 1640 to 1660; and (4) the late poetic period, or period of his greatest achievement.

Q. 26. Comment upon the theme of Milton's *Paradise Lost.*

Ans.: In *Paradise Lost*, Milton set forth the revolt of Satan against God, the war in heaven, the fall of the rebel angels, the creation of the world and man, the temptation of Eve and Adam, and their expulsion from Eden. Yet, while his central purpose was to show how "man's first disobedience", brought sin and death in this world, it is characteristic of him that he does not close on the note of evil triumphant, but prophetically introduces the divine work of redemption.

Q. 27. Who are known as Caroline Poets?

Ans.: Under the term Caroline Poets, we include a number of verse writers whose work may in the bulk be roughly assigned to the reign o Charles I. *Robert Herrick* (1591-1674), George Herbert, *Thomas Carew*, Sir *John Suckling* and *Richard Lovelace* are known as Caroline Poets. These poets found their main interest in religion. These are all poets in the lighter vein and made no pretence at treating their vices seriously.

Q. 28. What do you know about the Caroline Prose Writers?

Ans.: The prose literature written in Milton's age denote Caroline Prose writers such as Jeremy Taylor, Richard Baxter, Thomas Fuller, Izaak Walton, along with Sir Thomas Browne. A physician, Browne was the author of a number of books full of varied and curious erudition, but his main title of fame is his personal confession of religious faith, Religio Medici.

Q. 29. What is Restoration Theatre?

Ans.: Charles II granted William Davenant and Thomas Killigrew the monopoly to run two theatre companies in August 1660. The Restoration theatre was patronized by the court affected its audience composition as the merchant classes and the common theatre-goers. The theatre was city-based, and while the comedies made fun of the wealthy citizen and the country gentleman.

Q. 30. Write some of the qualities of the Prose of Restoration period.

Ans.: The prose writings of the Restoration period show the importance given to clarity of expression and preciseness of thought—conditions that not only reflect the temper of the Enlightment but also highlight the rationalist foundation that was behind such a philosophy.

Q. 31. Write a short not on women's writing in the Seventeenth Century.

Ans.: In the seventeenth century narratives and verses started appearing from the pen of women writers. Women writers interrogated and subsumed the ideological formations at work in contemporary society. Aphra Behn was perhaps England's first woman writer to make writing her profession for money. Though Margaret Cavendish and Katherine Philips preceded Behn. Later Anne Killingrew, another Restoration woman was scanty but nevertheless full of promise. This tradition was continued and consolidated by others like Anne Finch, Lady Mary, Eliza Haywood, Charlotte Smith and Mary Wollstonecraft.

Q. 32. Comment upon the intellectual context of the Scientific Revolution in 17th century in Europe.

Ans.: The origins of the scientific revolution are usually traced to the Copernicus questioning of the Ptolemaic model of the universe. The base provided by Copernicus, Tycho, and Kepler found in Galileo. Galileo's contribution was important, for he initiated the foundation of the modern scientific method that combined observation and experiments. Issaz Newton had a great influence on scientific experiment and philosophy.

Q. 33. What is so peculiar about the literature in Restoration Period?

Ans.: Literature ceased to soar and became pedestrian. Thus, with the Restoration we enter upon a period in which literature is intellectual rather than imaginative or emotional, and though often brilliant, is on the whole a trifle hard and unsympathetic. This is true even of poetry, which became prosaic, was made to do the work of prose, and was judged by the standards of prose.

Q. 34. Who are known as the forerunners of Dryden?

Ans.: Edmund Waller (1605-87) and Sir John Denham (1615-69) were commonly regarded as the pioneers of the so-called classic school of poetry. They were the reformers of English versification at a time when it had become insufferably rugged and harsh. Dryden said, "the excellence and dignity of rime were never fully known till Mr. Waller taught it, he first made writing easily an art." This re-shaping of the heroic couplet is Waller's principal claim to distinction.

Q. 35. Milton has been called a humanist among Puritans and a Puritan among humanists. Justify.

Ans.: Milton's mind was shaped by the twin influences of the Renaissance and the Reformation. He was a profound student both of the classical poetry and philosophy and of the Bible and the literature of the Scriptures, if he inherited the culture and humanism of the Renaissance, he had also a deeply religious temperament, he was a lover of art and music.

Q. 36. Comment upon the only two human characters of *Paradise Lost* by Milton.

Ans.: Adam and Eve, only two human characters in *Paradise Lost*, are very important for this epic. In them, Milton reveals some of the most fundamental characteristics of man and woman of all time of temptation and then her obstinate arguments with Adam who ultimately surrenders and falls in love with her, have a human touch. Milton displays in Eve all the essential weaknesses of feminine character-vanity, curiosity and willfulness. Eve is fairly a woman of this world.

Q. 37. How far it is true to say that Milton's style is that of scholar writing for a scholar?

Ans.: In general, Milton's style may be described as almost uniquely literary and intellectual. The whole treasury of poetry and whole store-house of learning are at his command. Miltonic style consists in the use of proper names which, again, shows Milton's vast erudition. It is surprising to see how Milton elevates his style by the use of monosyllables. Milton uses these tremendous monosyllables, each heavy with a sense of fate, like a bell tolling into the silence to midnight, to force our attention.

Q. 38. Why Milton is called 'a belated Elizabethan'?

Ans.: Milton is called belated Elizabethan because his poetry is a continuation as the Elizabethan tradition of poetry. His workmanship in character and temperament is largely Elizabethan. He is a belated Elizabethan because of his love for sonnets and elegies, art and music, beauty, imagination, adventure, chivalry and freedom, nationalism and patriotism and refinements.

Q. 39. What do you know about 'the Anglicans'?

Ans.: Isaac Barrow, John Tillotson, and Robert South are known as Anglicans. One finds among these Anglicans chiefly a truthful and utilitarian presentation of religious questions and a power of clear exposition, sometimes close-knit and eloquent, in correct, regular and well-balanced prose, qualities which relate them to that 'age of understanding', inaugurated by the Restoration.

Q. 40. What do you know about Samuel Butler?

Ans.: The first work of the Restoration, one which characteristically opens the new era, was the *Hudibras* of Samuel Butler (1612-80), a product of the revolt against Puritanism. In fact, Butler did not excel either in the recital of adventures or in character-drawing, as a romance his poem is of the worst. It consists wholly and solely of an account of how Hudibras one day began a campaign. But the poem is valuable for the vein of satirical comedy and fills everything, portraits, dialogues and narrative, with moral and ironic reflections.

24

Augustan Age: 18th Century Literature

Q. 1. Why do we call Augustan Age also as the Age of Peace and Prosperity?

Ans.: Albert called the eighteenth century as an age of peace and prosperity. After the succession of the house of Hanover the first half of the eighteenth century was a period of stabilization and steadily growing wealth and prosperity. It was an age of tolerance, moderation, and common sense, which in cultured circles at least, sought to refine manners and introduce into life the rule of sweet reasonableness.

Q. 2. Comment upon the Barbarity of the Augustan Age.

Ans.: Against the view of E. Albert, John Dennis and A.C. ward opine that the age showed no sign of the Augustan splendor in the eighteenth century life. It was an age of wide-spread self-indulgence and excess, an age of material greed, of speculation in the stock markets of ruinous gambling in clubs and private houses, of crime and debauchery of brutality and squalor of raves and harlots and gin-sodden poor. Roads were dangerous, police was in sufficient, Travelers had to protect themselves as they best could from the attaches of highwaymen. Readers of the 'Spectator' will remember the case of Sir Roger de Coverlet.

Q. 3. Comment upon the low status of women in the eighteenth century.

Ans.: Even Addison, while trying to instruct the 'Fair sex' as he lived to call them apparently regarded its members as an inferior order of beings. He delights to dwell on their foibles, on their dress, and on the thousand little artifices practiced by the flirt and the coquette. It was the aim of Addison and Steele to represent, and in some degree to caricature, the follies of fashionable life in the town.

Q. 4. Why this age is also termed as the classical Age?

Ans.: The word classic refers to the work of the highest order. Hence the word classic is used to designate writings that have won first rank in any nation. Every national literature has at least one period in which an unusual number of great writers are producing book and this is called the classic period of a nation's literature. The reign of Augustus is the classic or golden age of Rome; the age of Dante is the classical age of Italian literature; the age of Lewis XIV is the French classical age, and the age of Queen Anne is often called the classical age of England. It was the age of great writers in prose, poetry and drama.

Q. 5. Who called 18th century as 'the Age of Prose and Reason and why?

Ans.: It was Mathew Arnold who summed up 18th century in English literature as the Age of Prose and Reason, popularly known as our excellent and indispensable 18th century. Its literature in the main was the product of reason and intelligence; it was commonly critical, didactic and satirical. The general temper of the age may be summed up in a phrase 'The Age of Reason'. It was an age opposed to individual initiative in the arts, science and social progress.

Reason may be interpreted as good sense rationalism, intellect, wit and logicism. In fact in was opposed to excessive emotionalism, sentimentalism, extravagance, eccentricity and even imagination.

Q. 6. What do you understand by the term 'Prosaic Poetry of the Augustan age'?

Ans.: The 18th century was primarily an age of prose and not of great poetry. The poetry of the period cultivated the qualities of prose such as clarity, perspicuity and beauty of expression. It is because of this that Mathew Arnold declared, that Dryden and Pope are the classics, not of poetry but of prose. Among the great prose writers are Addison, Steele, Swift, Goldsmith and Dr. Johnson.

Q. 7. What do you know about origin of the periodical essay?

Ans.: The essay as a literary form in English originated with Francis Bacon and the periodical essay a piece of journalism was invented towards the very end of the 17th century. It reached its acme of achievement early in the work of Steele and Addison. It maintained a great popularity throughout the 18th century and disappeared about 1800 and finally withered away in 19th century.

Q. 8. Write down the causes for the popularity of the periodical essay.

Ans. Periodical essay was popular both with the writers and the readers. The basic reason is that it is the particular creation and the particular mirror of Augustan Age in England. About 90 periodicals were founded between the Tatler in 1707 and 1720. It catered all sections of the society. Men like Steele, Johnson and Goldsmith wrote some of the finest work in it. It may be said to be the only literary form used by every major writer of the century. Politics was touched. A new merchant community came into the lime–light. Its brevity was an attraction for the reading classes. It became so popular as it was a faithful reflection of 18th century society.

Q. 9. Comment upon the style of the periodical essayists.

Ans.: Most of the periodical essayists wrote in a simple, clean, conversational style to be understood by their semi-educated or unscholarly readers. They awarded individual whims, conceits, witticism and harsh words which could not be appreciated by the middle classes and the fair sex who were among the main readers of the periodical essays wherever the periodical essayist like Dr. Johnson wrote a pompous high sounding and dignified style, and he failed. 'The spectator' had great popularity, because of the style of Addison and Steele.

Q. 10. What do you know about the poetic diction in the 18th century ?

Ans.: The language of poetry became gaudy and inordinate and the common words or the ordinary language were deliberately kept out from poetic literature. The result was that the literature of the age became artificial, stilted, rational and intellectual losing all inspiration, enthusiasm and romantic favour which were the hall-marks of the literature of the Elizabethan age.

Q. 11. What is the theme of the Dryden's Plays?

Ans.: The theme of Dryden's plays resembles heroic poetry and fiction indicates conflict in human passions—love, jealousy and honour which are raised to a great height and intensity. The actions are suited to the motives and influenced by unexpected changes. Dryden in his play exhibits the immorality of the corrupted fashionable society of his time. He grows weary of the long loved mistress. His play *All For Love* is thus written in blank verse. He did not hesitate to push his characters into unnatural extravagance of passion. Critics felt it was a fault on his part.

Q. 12. Write a short note on dominance of the Heroic couplet in 18th century.

Ans.: In the form of poetry, the Heroic couplet was recognized as the only medium of expression. It was no longer possible to take a sheet of paper and write one's thought as the pen could move. In the Heroic couplet poets put all their skill and wrote with an unimaginable correctness and precision.

Q. 13. What is meant by poetic diction?

Ans.: By Poetic diction we mean the choice and arrangement of word so as to achieve the desired effect. It differs according to the subject, the literary form, and the age in which a particular work is written. In every age poets have developed their own poetic diction which markedly differs from the speech of everyday life. In good poets, poetic diction varies according to the particular character.

Q. 14. What was the status of poetic diction in the 18th century?

Ans.: The language of poetry became artificial. The common language of the common people was not used in the poetry by major poets. The result was that the literature of the age became artificial, stilted, rational and intellectual losing all inspiration, enthusiasm and romantic favour which were the hallmarks of the literature of the Elizabethan age. The Augustans were superior in other ways, notably in satire and journalism in the technical language of philosophy and science and in that great branch of modern literature, the novel, of which they were among the English pioneers.

Q. 15. What do you know about the Augustan prose writers?

Ans.: It was the great work of Richard Steele (1672-1719) and Joseph Addison (1672-1719) to bring the two England's addressed by Pope and by Defoe together by devising a form of literature acceptable and profitable to both. Though neither morality nor wit was the appendage of either side, this double aim was fairly conveyed in Addison's formulation of the purpose of the Spectator (1711-14) to enliven morality with wit, and temper wit with morality.

Q. 16. Who called 18th century 'The age of Prose' and why?

Ans.: Matthew Arnold branded the eighteenth century as the age of prose, meaning that it was poor in creative or imaginative poetry. But precisely in its prose, and the novel, the 18th century created a power surpassed only by the Elizabethans in their greatest verse.

Q. 17. What do you know about the minor Augustan poets after the death of Pope?

Ans.: English verse, from the death of Pope to 1780, must be classed, with little qualification, as either repetition or prelude. The metrical instrument which Pope had perfected continued to be used, as he had used it, for satire, exposition, and description, by great writers. Poets otherwise in the Augustan tradition used blank verse for didactic reflection for example, Robert Burns, James Thomson and Allan Ramsay. The more lyric forms of the verse especially the ode were attracting the finer poets like Thomas Gray and W. Collins.

Q. 18. Write a short note on the Gothic Novel.

Ans.: The novel of the eighteenth century from Defoe to Miss Burney was characterized by a note of realism. The novelists made attempt to portray real life and to deal with things as they saw without introducing any romantic aroma in their fictitious works. The Gothic and Oriental romancers concentrated the attention not on realistic life, but on nature, mysteries, supernaturalism and out of the way things. The interest in nature formed an important element in the novel as it was developed by Horace Walpole and Mrs. Radcliffe. Gothic novel became the ancestor of the historical novel.

Q. 19. Comment on the note of romance in Gothic fiction.

Ans.: In the Gothic novels there was an interest not in the presentation of contemporary life, but in the depiction of past life, particularly the life of the middle ages. Secondly, the scenes were invariable laid in haunted castles and ruined and dilapidated buildings. Ruins were mainly lived by the Gothic Romances. The Gothic romancers aimed to produce terror and horror by creating scenes of darkness and night, and by taking the readers to churchyards and the graves of the dead.

Q. 20. Evaluate the contribution of the Gothic novelists to the development of the novel in the eighteenth century.

Ans.: The works of Gothic novelist gave to the novel a reassurance of its poetic origins; which the first realist such as Defoe and fielding had threatened to obscure these novelists helped to make the English novel not as a dry record of every day happenings but as an interesting account of imaginative adventure and poetic thoughts. The gothic romancers saved literature from being purely utilitarian. They feel that outside the real world there is also a world of wonder and delight or to quote a phrase of Bishop Hurd 'a world of five fabling'. Gothic romancers gave special attention to plot construction and taught 19th century novelists the technique of a well made plot.

Q. 21. Write a short note on the significance of the coffee houses during Augustan period.

Ans.: Politicians are gregarious by nature and the increased activity in politics lead to a great addition to the number of political clubs and coffee-houses, which became the center of fashionable and public life. These coffee houses were entirely dominated by the party. People gathered there to show their 'wit', discuss the news of the day, and forecast the rise and fall of parties. A Whig will never go to a Tory coffee houses and vice-versa. These coffee houses gave rise to purely literary associations such as the famous scribblers and kit-cat clubs.

Q. 22. What period of 18th century is known as the age of reaction and why?

Ans.: The later half of the 18th century is known as the age of reaction and transition. In the age of Dr. Johnson, we find that there is a reaction against the self-complacency, the artificiality, the formation and intellectually of the previous age. "The emotions, long repressed were now reinstated and all life was modified in consequence" (Hudson).

Q. 23. What do you understand by picaresque novel?

Ans.: The word 'Picaresque' has been derived from the Spanish word 'Picaro' which means a 'rogue' or 'Knave'. The picaresque novel is the tale of the adventures or misadventures of a picaro or rogue who wanders from one country, to another, from one setting to another, from the town to the country, in this way the novelist gets an opportunity of introducing a variety of characters and incidents of painting society as a whole realistically. The picture may be satiric but the aim of the novelist is to delight and entertain, and not to reform or improve.

Q. 24. Comment upon the position of drama in the eighteenth-century.

Ans.: On the whole, the drama lost vitality, originality and talent. Shakespeare was being carefully re-edited by Rowe, Pope, Theobald, and Johnson. The taste for literary correctness and regularity which distinguished the reign of Queen Anne drove English drama away from the national tradition to follow the fashion of France.

Q. 25. What is the concept of Domestic Drama?

Ans.: Domestic drama is based on the idea that the destiny of ordinary men is as capable of affecting the emotions as that of heroic or legendary characters. It is of democratic origin and realistic in expression. George Lillo (1693-1739) initiated this type of play when his London Merchant or the History of George Barnwell was produced in 1731. He set out to find strong emotions, terror and pity, in prosaic life, without the help of poetry or any recourse to verse. Diderot was inspired by Lillo and Mouse in his drama and derived from their work a new dramatic system, a revolution in literature which heralded the social revolution. These domestic tragedies were edifying works. They inculcated virtue by depicting the consequences of vice.

Q. 26. What do you understand by Augustanism?

Ans.: As a term in English literary history, Augustanism refers to the dominant condition prevailing in the area of cultural production in the first half of the 18th century. Politically, Augustanism refers to the parallels drawn between the emerging structures of English society and those existing in the period of Emperor Augustus in ancient Rome. The range of Angustanism is still the subject of dispute white a consideration of the 'Augustan' age was often structured derogatorily in the early twentieth century it has remained a descriptive term indicating poetics, judgment, and taste.

Q. 27. What is 'Deism'?

Ans.: The term 'Deism' refers to a particular religious philosophy which was part of seventeenth and eighteenth century culture in England. Deism was a kind of 'natural religion' which suggested that a religious propensity is either innate in every individual or may be cultivated through the employment of reason; on the other hand, it was contrary to the view that religious understanding could come through either the agency of revelation or an institution like the church. Edward Herbert is associated with it.

Q. 28. Comment upon the 'Graveyard School of Poetry'.

Ans.: The Graveyard School of Poetry is a loosely drawn group of poets of the eighteenth century who took death, loss, and mourning as the themes of their poems. 'The Grave' (1743) by Robert Blair and Edward Young's Night thoughts (1742-45) are two representative illustrations of the group. The emergence of the Graveyard School is taken as both being a reaction to the regimentation of Neo-classicism and as foreshadowing the Romantic spirit of the early nineteenth century. Thomas Gray's Elegy written in a *Country Churchyard* (1751) is a classic representation of the ethos pursued by the Graveyard school poets.

Q. 29. Who were termed as the Pre-Romantics?

Ans.: The period 1730-70 marks the beginning of movement from one district school or convention of English poetry towards another. To the first the epithet pseudo- classical is usually applied, and to the second the epithet Romantic. From as early as 1730, there were poets, including Thomson, Cowper, Collins and Gray, who formed a bridge, as it were between the two schools, and whose works have certain characteristics of both the poets like Gray, Collins, James, Thomson, Olives Goldsmith, William Cowper, George crabbed. Robert Burns and William Blake were called Pre-romantics.

Q. 30. What do you know about Biographers and Letter writers of 18th Century England?

Ans.: The eighteenth century produced a number of biographers, autobiographers, and writers of letters. James Boswell, the biographer of Dr. Johnson, has the pride of place among them His 'Life of Johnson' is a unique work of its kind, among the autobiographers mention may also be made of Gibbon, Lord Harvey and John Wesley. Lady Mary Worley Montagu, Cowper, Chesterfield, Gilbert White, Gray and Horace Walpole were some of the famous letter—writers of the 18th century.

Q. 31. Comment upon Daniel Defoe's contribution to the Rise of the Novel.

Ans.: Defoe was a journalist by profession and his entry into the realm of the novel with novels like *Robinson Crusoe* (1719) and *Moll Flanders* (1722) was not designed. In Robinson Crusoe, which many critics consider to be the first instance of the novel prefers in English the moral and cultural specifics subtly undercut the apparently simple tale of a sailor. Historically, *Moll Flanders* is an important step in the development of the game of the novel as it focuses on characters rather than adventure. *Roxana* (1724), Defoe's next fictional experiment is more sophisticated than *Moll Flanders*.

Q. 32. What is the importance of Samuel Johnson in eighteenth century literature?

Ans.: Samuel Johnson was more important in 18th century for the influence he exerted as a man of letters and upon the cultivation of literary tastes than as a creative writer. It was mainly Johnson's image and command over the literary horizons that have overwhelmed his identity as a writer. Initially a journalist Johnson was a critic '(Lives of the Poets, Preface to Shakespeare)' a novelist (Rasselas), a poet and a lexicographer. The publication of his *Dictionary of the English Language* (1755), however brought him immediate attention and fame and—made him literary figure of the time.

Q. 33. What do you know about *Lives of the Poets*?

Ans.: *Lives of the Poets* is a major work of Samuel Johnson. His commentaries on writers, past and contemporary in this book have been referred to time and again by later writers for their insights. Johnson was writing at a transitional time and his career epitomizes the changing status of the writer in the 18th century. He marshaled the artists, writers, and thinkers of his time to form a club, which represented what is known as the Johnson circle.

Q. 34. What do you know about the origin of Coffee Houses in England?

Ans.: The first coffee house in England was started by a man called Jacobs, at Oxford, in 1650. The coffee houses soon became the centers where news was circulated and exchanged. In the middle of the 18th century there were more than five hundred coffee houses in London. Coffee houses culture impacted literary production as well especially the periodical essay; one example being the Tatler, which Steele mentioned, started functioning from St. James coffee houses.

Q. 35. What do you know about corresponding societies famous in 18th century?

Ans.: The corresponding societies were groups formed by skilled workers for the initiation of reforms towards the very end of the 18th century. One of the major influences upon these societies was the immediate example of the French Revolution. These societies had relations with one another and they 'corresponded' and had dialogues to arrive at conclusions that reflected a sense of uniformity.

Q. 36. Comment upon Methodism.

Ans.: Methodism was a religious development that began in 18th century England. The Methodists were led by John Wesley, a preacher who began his so-called religious town from 1738. These Methodists had a huge following in the nineteenth century especially in the industrial areas.

Q. 37. Who was John Gay?

Ans.: One of the most popular writers, contemporary with Pope and Swift was John Gay (1685-1732). He was known as the spoilt child of the Tory Coterie and a careless and indolent man of the world. He won popularity with his Fables (1727) in short couplets. It is by this collection and the clever songs of his Beggar's Opera (1728) that Gay is chiefly remembered now a day.

Q. 38. Name some contemporaries of Pope.

Ans.: Thomas Parnell (1679-1718), Thomas Tickell (1686-1740) and Ambrose Philips (1675-1749) belonged to the same circle. Parnell was patronized by Swift and Pope and had rather more lyrical inspiration than the rest of the group while Tickell was a member of the Whig group of which Addison was the centre. The political rivalries of the time made Philips also an adherent of Addison and therefore an enemy of Pope and the Tories.

Q. 39. Who is 'Sir Roger'?

Ans.: The creation of Sir Roger is Addison's Masterpiece. The man is not only an excellent figure of comedy with his eccentricities, his peculiar expressions, his attitudes, his mental leaps, but he is foremost among those characters who are not only loved but respected even while they are laughed at. One may thin his ideas fantastic and yet appreciate his good nature. Nothing could better inculcate tolerance and cordiality than such a portrait. By means of creating Sir Roger, Addison did more than any one to reconcile the extremes in his country and to soften the asperities of social life of 18th century England.

Q. 40. Who was John Arbuthnot?

Ans.: The physician John Arbuthnot (1667-1735) of Swift and Pope, was a scholar, a humanist, and a man of wit who devoted only a part of his activity to letters and showed no ambition for literary glory. But his moral qualities his generosity and his warm character made him the most respected of the circle of Tory writers to which he belonged. His book *The History of John bull* (1712) is an amusing allegory, which was designed to support Harley's ministry and oppose the Whigs.

25

Romantic Period

Q. 1. Define 'Romanticism'.

Ans.: The Romantic Movement is marked by a strong reaction and protest against the rules and customs and the dogmas of the new—classical writers of the 18th century Victor Hugo defined romanticism as 'Liberalism in Literature'. Romanticism is the expression of the individual genius, also known as 'The liberation of the ego'. It emphasizes the sovereignty of imagination.

Q. 2. What are the chief characteristic of romanticism?

Ans.: The chief characteristic of romanticism is the rejection of rules which became a tyranny, a fetter, an undesirable straight jacket, restraining the free play of the imagination and emotional sensibility. Individualism and subjectivity are inextricably intertwined. The romanticists stressed upon sensibility, gusto and emotion.

Q. 3. Who are the first Romantics?

Ans.: It is generally supposed that the English Romantic Movement began in 1798, with the publication of the Lyrical Ballads. In fact (according to Albert) 'the Elizabethans were our first romantics', because Elizabethan literature is essentially romantic in spirit. The romantic spirit suffered a total decline and eclipse during the Augustan age. The romantic movement in 19th century began as a reaction against the artificially of the Pseudo–classics.

Q. 4. Who are called the precursors of the Romantic Movement?

Ans.: The pre-romantics played a very prominent part in the revival of romanticism. The seed sown by Thomson in the age of pope grew and flourished in the poetry of such poets as Gray, Collins, Burns, Cowper and Crabbe. These poets, who have been rightly called the precursors of the Romantic Movement, show a genuine feeling for nature and for the simple humanity living in her lap.

Q. 5. Who are known as the Second Generation of the Romantics?

Ans.: Keats, Shelley and Byron belong to the second generation of the romantic poets. They began to compose mainly after 1815, by which date the elder romantics had given the best which they had to give. All the three were rejected by society this rejection caused them much sorrow and suffering, and people attribute their early deaths to this fact.

Q. 6. What is Hellenism?

Ans.: The word 'Hellenism' comes from 'Hellenes' meaning inhabitants of Halas or ancients Greece. Hellenism, therefore, implies a love of ancient Greek way of life, of Greek art, culture, literature and mythology, as well as the attempt to express this love in one's writings. Romantic poets such as Byron, Shelley and Keats, were mostly influenced by Hellenism.

Q. 7. What is Supernaturalism?

Ans.: Supernaturalism is another outstanding quality of romantic poetry. A sense of wonder and mystery was imparted to poetry by poets like Coleridge and Scott. It was this supernatural note that gave to romantic poetry its atmosphere wonder and mystery, unmanliness and caring feeling, and justify the title, 'The Renaissance of wonder' given to this poetic age by a critic of repute.

Q. 8. What role was played by Imagination in the Romantic Poetry?

Ans.: The romantics threw a colouring of imagination of familiar object and dealt with the light that never was on sea or land, the conservation and the poet's dream. Even romanticism has been defined as an extra- ordinary development of imaginative sensibility. The romantic poets tried to escape from actuality was attempted by different romantic poets in different ways Coleridge escaped to the world of the supernaturalism. Wordsworth threw a colouring of imagination on the common humanity and Nature. Keats took refuge in the Middle Ages and ancient Hellenic beauty.

Q. 9. Write a short note on the impact of the French Revolution on English literature of the 19th century.

Ans.: The French Revolution, which broke out in 1789, had affected not merely the political and social destiny of France, but exerted a far reaching and profound influence on English literature. The ideas, which gave birth to the French Revolution, had been seriously preached and propagated by Jean—Jacques, Rousseau and others. Rousseau impressed the romantic poets with his primitivism, individualism and romantic imagination. His advocacy of the 'stage of nature' of 'the noble savage' and of 'child life' directly influenced Wordsworth who wrote *Immortality Ode* in which he expressed Rousseau's idea of primitivism.

Q. 10. What do you know about French Encyclopaedist Movement?

Ans.: Diderot, Voltaire and Rousseau were among the inspirations behind the French Encyclopaedist Movement. In 1751 the first volume of L'—Encyclopedic was issued in Paris and the work continued till 1776. The alarm among defenders of the old order was excited by the basic assumptions, and indeed, ideas planted by L'- Encyclopedia were soon to inspire a new revolutionary phase of the romantic poetry, even if it did not originate the movement to which that title might conveniently be limited.

Q. 11. What do you know about Evangelicalism?

Ans.: Evangelicalism refers to the movement within the Church of England in the 18th and 19th centuries where the members emphasized on what they called 'vital Christianity'. The Evangelicals insisted on the adherence to a strict moral code and the importance of good work. Among the many things they insisted upon, the strict observance of Sunday is one of the more important ones. They were against the perpetuation of the slave trade and were responsible for the founding of missionary societies.

Q. 12. What is 'London Magazine'?

Ans.: Although a periodical named 'London Magazine' was published in the 18th century (1732-85) the name is more closely identified with the monthly that was in circulation from 1820 to 1829. John Scott was the editor of London Magazine. The Romantic period was one of the most successful ages in terms of magazine publication and London Magazine capitalized on the trend. Thomas De Quincy, and Charles Lamb contributed to this magazine. It also published poems by John Keats and John Clare. The Journal thrived on the rivalry with its competitors, especially Blackwood's, and Scott.

Q. 13. Discuss in brief the theory of the poetry of Wordsworth.

Ans.: Wordsworth rebelled against the poetic principles of the 18th Century. He held that the common life of the poor, simple people can serve as fit material for poetry and that the diction to be employed in poetry should be drawn from everyday speech of human beings. With this formula he led the revolt against the artificial poetry. Further, he wanted to throw a colouring of imagination over the simple material chosen for treatment in poetry. His poetry marks a complete break with the school of Pope.

Q. 14. Discuss Wordsworth as a poet of reflection and philosophic thought.

Ans.: Wordsworth's odes represent a perfect combination of profound thought and deep emotion, Wordsworth had a strong moral and didactic tendency which comes out in poems like the Ode to Duty. Wordsworth's reflective and meditative quality is seen also in 'Tintern Abbey'.

Q. 15. Write a very brief note on lyrics of Wordsworth?

Ans.: Wordsworth wrote several graceful and delicious lyrics like the 'Solitary Reaper', 'To a Skylark', 'I Wondered Lonely as a Cloud' and the 'Lucy Poems'. These lyrics convey by simple means the impression of intensity and are very melodious. It is noteworthy that Wordsworth unlike shelley is reflective rather than passionate in the lyrics. There is lack of spontaneity due to his conception of a poem as' the expression of an emotion recollected in tranquility.

Q. 16. Write in brief the influence of French Revolution on Wordsworth.

Ans.: It was the French revolution which first drew him to a love and appreciation of humanity. Being appealed by the horrible ravage and carnage of the Revolution Wordsworth turned to Nature, and Nature brought' him closer to humanity. He heard in the nature the 'sad music of humanity' and gradually he began to love common life for its own sake and for the edification of moral life.

Q. 17. Write a short note on Wordsworth as a writer of Sonnet.

Ans.: As a writer of sonnets, Wordsworth's rank is high. He wrote approximately five hundred sonnets. The particular form he chooses is not the Shakespearean form but the Miltonic form based on the traditional Italian Structure. In fact Wordsworth did valuable service to English poetry by thus reinstating the Sonnet.

Q. 18. In what sense Wordsworth can be called 'Romantic'?

Ans.: Wordsworth is a romantic in the sense that he broke away from the existing popular forms and traditions of classical poetry and broke new grounds for the expression of his ideas and sentiments. He gave great importance to imagination. His poetry is highly subjective and there is a truly romantic note in it.

Q. 19. Write in brief the influence of French Revolution on Wordsworth.

Ans.: The link between Wordsworth and French Revolution is unavoidable. It was the French Revolution which first drew him to a love and appreciation of humanity. Being appealed by the horrible ravage of the Revolution, Wordsworth turned to nature, and nature brought him closer to Humanity. He heard in the nature the 'sad music of humanity'.

Q. 20. Write a brief note on Wordsworth as a poet of man and his versatility.

Ans.: Wordsworth was a great poet of man. Man and his dignity is one of the main themes in the poetry of Wordsworth. As a poet he is versatile. Almost all forms of poetry; the epic, the ode, the sonnet and the lyric were attempted by him and he achieved great success in everything. He gave English poetry a new life and a new existence.

Q. 21. Write in brief about the Supernatural elements in Coleridge poetry.

Ans.: In his small and even fragmentary poetic achievement Coleridge remains unequalled in his treatment of Supernatural. His poem 'The Rime of the Ancient Mariner' is a wonderful example. The other two poems, dealing with supernatural element *Christabel* and *Kuble Khan* were left incomplete. He also wrote his *Biographic Literarie*, which secured his place in English literature.

Q. 22. Discuss Coleridge's conception of nature.

Ans.: Coleridge's fundamental conception of nature is that every object of nature from a simple flower to the mighty mountain is periaded by the presence of God. In the first phase he conceived that there were multitudes of spirits, by whose operation nature grew. This idea forms the basis of the Ancient Mariner. In his second phase of his conception of nature he felt that it is in our thought that we give forms to external objects and thinking. We build up the world of the nature ourselves. This idea is expressed both in The Aeolian Harp and in the Ode to Dejection.

Q. 23. Discuss Coleridge as a poet of humanitarianism.

Ans.: Coleridge upheld the French Revolution for it seemed that it would bring peace and prosperity to mankind. Later on when he found the French Revolution going against the principles of humanitarianism, he denounced it in the Ode to France. He condemns those theoretical lovers of mankind who do nothing practical for humanity.

Q. 24. Comment upon the philosophy of Coleridge.

Ans.: With an inborn taste for transcendental philosophy, Coleridge live just at the time when that philosophy took an immense spring in Germany and connected itself with an impressive literary movement. This transcendental philosophy, chiefly as systematized by mystic Schelling, Coleridge, applied with an eager, unwearied subtlety to the question of theology and poetic or artistic criticism.

Q. 25. Discuss dream quality in the poetry of S.T. Coleridge.

Ans.: The dreamy quality is an attribute of every romantic poets, but the supreme strength to use this quality lies in Coleridge. That's why he is regarded as the best dream poet; in fact the first and last of the true dream poets. His all the three great poems. 'The Ancient Mariner', 'Cristabel', and 'Kubla Khan' are the best example of dream poetry in English literature of the 19th century.

Q. 26. "There is intensity of feeling in the poetry of Shelley". Discuss this statement.

Ans.: Shelley is not only spontaneous but also intense. His poems reflect restlessness; there is no peace in them. There is a great intensity of feeling, a deep passion in Shelley's lyrics that cannot go unnoticed. In fact in ardour of passion and mystical imagination and in the witchery of music, Shelley has no equal.

Q. 27. Discuss Shelley's kinship with nature.

Ans.: Shelley used nature to startling effect showing the magnificence of the beauty all around him. He was highly observant and nature often cast a bewitching spell over him. He seems like a word painter in his poems. By the end of 1815 there was a change in Shelley's attitude towards nature. In this second stage he had started feeling a sort of kinship with nature. This attitude was fostered by his Platonism due to which he believed that the whole universe was imbued by one universal spirit. He was against the killing of animals, birds, insects etc. and used to call plants and animals his brothers and sisters.

Q. 28. Discuss ideal love in Shelley poetry.

Ans.: Shelley's life was devoted not to the pursuit of physical beauty but to his ideal idea of love and beauty for which he had aspired throughout his life. He always wanted the mingling of the two. In *Prometheus Unbound*, Shelley reached the level of thinking of Plato. Prometheus exercised the freedom of Love, the freedom of the pursuit of good. Shelley's conception of love was that of the desire of a mortal for immortality as seen through beautiful forms.

Q. 29. Discuss self-description of Shelley in his poetry.

Ans.: In the array of mourners, Shelly gives to himself an inferior position to that of Byron and Moose. He felt lonely and desolate. He projects himself as graceful and agile like a leopard with a heart filled with love for mankind. As he says in The West Wind, a heavy weight of time has chained and bowed him. critics observed that "The self-revelation of Shelly is remarkable for its accuracy. It is so detached and so exalted that he hears in it, the lyrical cry of an intellectual rather than of heart". The intensity of his thought and the anguish of his soul is well—reflected in this self-portraiture.

Q. 30. Discuss Keats' attitude towards Nature.

Ans.: Keats' attitude towards Nature is particularly Hellenic. He is a Greek also in the manner of his response to the appeal of Nature. Court-hope says "He indeed resembles the Greeks in his vivid sense of the Joyous and multitudinous life of nature, and he loved to follow them in dreaming of the powers of nature as embodied in concrete shapes of supernatural human activity and grace".

Q. 31. Discuss Pessimism in the poetry of Keats.

Ans.: Keats and Shelley both could not enjoy a happy life because of bad health and social and literary criticism that stung them deep. The poems of Keats are marked with a deep tone of melancholy and sadness. The idea of death oppressed him.

Q. 32. Discuss the occasion and origin of the poem 'Ode to a Nightingale'.

Ans.: The poem was inspired by the song of a nightingale which the poet was hearing in the garden of his friend Brown to whom he had paid a visit in 1819. The sweet melody of the nightingale singing with full throated ease sent the poet in rapture and he penned down the poem in the ecstatic mood of creativeness. Next morning Brown read, the poem and was immensely pleased with Keats efforts. He advised the poet to recast it and add touches and retouches to the poem. The poem as it stands is a fervent expression of Keats' feeling coming up to his heart as he heard the melodious song of the nightingale. The stamp of a deliberate and skilled craftsman is visible on every line of the poem.

Q. 33. "Charles Lamb is a greatest Egotist without a touch of Egotism." Evaluate.

Ans.: Lamb takes his readers entirely into confidence and conceals nothing. But due to his playful instinct and love of mystification he distorted certain facts. Charles Lamb was a warm friend, an engaging host, a gentle humorist a true companion, and a devoted and self sacrificing brother. He has given us the means to trace all these qualities in his essays.

Q. 34. Lamb's essays are 'miniature romance's wrapped in the incidents of humdrum daily life'. Evaluate the statement.

Ans.: The Essays of Elias are matchless. They are beyond the measurement through literary rules. These essays have spring out of personal impressions and memories of Charles Lamb. His vocabulary in the essays of Elia shows his wanderings among old books and his very rhythms have an echo of the 17th century. It is so quaint, so individual and idiosyncratic, that words are insufficient to describe them. Each one of them has to be read and enjoyed again and again on one's own.

Q. 35. Discuss the place of Lamb in English Literature.

Ans.: Charles Lamb is wholly bound up with the inner history of the first generation of Romanticism. He wrote poems, plays and romances. His life is full of tragic shocks. His natural taste makes his dwell in the realms of imagination and dreams, while his artistic soul belongs to the past. The main features of Lamb's genius may be analyzed as a poet, a critic, as a letter-writer, as an artist in style and as original genius.

Q. 36. Discuss blending of humour and pathos in the essays of Charles Lamb.

Ans.: Lamb's humour is inseparable from pathos. Tears and smiles mingle in his essays. His humour is so allied to pathos that it is really difficult to distinguish the one from the other. His sister Mary's condition, his visits to Asylum and other problems forced him to struggle against his misfortune. He found relief in eccentricity and freakish humour. Thus his humour was born out of suffering, a sort of defense mechanism for him.

Q. 37. Comment upon Lamb's fantastic style that makes his essays charming.

Ans.: Lamb's style is extremely quaint and mannered. His style has many conscious or unconscious reminiscences of style of Browne, Burton and fuller. The flavor of antique style is really charming. His style varies in accordance with the change in the mood of the essayist. He can be grave and brooding like the style of Thomas Browne (New year's Eve), or he can also be playfully witty like the style of fuller (A chapter on Ears). His wistful longings can be seen in the poetic prose of the essay 'Dream children'.

Q. 38. What is the significance of the term 'Gusto' in Hazlitt's Criticism?

Ans.: The term 'Gusto' possesses a great significance in the criticism of Hazlitt. It is that "amorous guest of literary beauty and rapturous enjoyment of it which has been noted as Hazlitt's great merit." We can also therefore; say that gusto is the feeling of subjective enjoyment of a work of art.

Q. 39. What do you know about mechanical art and fine art?

Ans.: The term 'Art' has philosophical and aesthetic implications side by side. Though the aesthetic sense of two term 'art' is a recent development only etymologically, art means, of course, a craft or specialized form of skill. That has none of the implications of the modern European aesthetic consciousness. Even till Renaissance, the artists believed themselves to be mere craftsmen. However, in the seventeenth century the conception of art underwent a sea change when a new term 'Fine Arts' was evolved and a sense of beauty was attached to it. A craft is something physical, where as art mental and spiritual.

Q. 40. What are the different elements of familiar style, according to Hazlitt?

Ans.: Familiar style, according to Hazlitt, is different from either a vulgar style as also from an ornate or dignified style. Familiar style demands utmost precision and purity of expression. It depends on the choice of fittest word on the part of the writer and simple structure of sentences. The writer of a familiar style should avoid meaningless pump, phrases, superfluous pedantry and sup sod references and allusions and must rather make use of the fittest idiom of Language.

Q. 41. Write any three characteristics of William Blake's poetry.

Ans.: The chief characteristics of Blake's poetry are the following:

(i) *More Romantic than classic*—That is to say the verse structure is more of the old type of poetry while his thoughts are markedly romantic revolutionary and mystic.

(ii) *Poet of Sentiment and emotional appeal*—Blake is concerned with describing feelings, instruct and emotion and therefore, his poetry is naturally full of imagination.

(iii) *He is a symbolist*—The worldly objects stood for him as mere symbols of the higher quality- namely God.

Q. 42. Discuss mysticism in Blake's poetry.

Ans.: Blake has the instinctive life of a child with love of flowers, hills, clouds and streams and the blue sky. He has spiritualized every object of nature or a common place object and has given them strangeness and wonder. Blake's mysticism is based on theology and philosophy of Sweden Borg, Boehme, Kabba and Christianity. His mysticism is blended with melancholy as he was much more dissatisfied with the show of life. But at the same time he has accepted sorrow as a necessary twin of Joy. He equates God with Mercy, Peace and Pity.

Q. 43. Do you agree with the view that Byron's Genius was not prone to satire?

Ans.: Byron was a romantic poet and his genius was not prone to satire. Intellectual analysis and social observations were not in tune with him. He would pour out romantic tunes when inspired, but in his satirical works, which he modeled on Pope, Byron was not a success. He himself acknowledged, "to say truth my satires are not playful." Byron had a paradoxical personality. He admired the classical couplet and actually used it in his first and early satires, but at the same time he found it too light to be a suitable vehicle for his own purpose, even for his social, satirical modes of thought and feeling.

Q. 44. Comment upon the influence of other poets on Byron.

Ans.: Byron frequently expressed his admiration of poets like Milton, Dryden, Pope and his irritation with Wordsworth, Coleridge and Southey. He considered the three Lake poets as political renegades. He was repelled by the obscurity of Coleridge, the plurality of Wordsworth, the dullness and porosity of Southey, and by the childish and pious sentimentality of all the three of them. He preferred the giants of the past to the fallible pretenders and rivals of the present.

Q. 45. Why do critics call Jane Austen as classical?

Ans.: Jane Austen is classical in more than one sense. Her style is classical in its simplicity, in sureness of touch and in delicacy of its spirit. Her attitude and approach to life are classical. By temperament and training, she belongs to the austere and sedate eighteenth century. She shared with the classical poets and prose writers the qualities of wit and satire. In an age which is visionary, fanciful and mystic she is worldly, matter of fact and realistic. She remains untroubled by the turmoil of French revolution and Napoleonic wars. She was called as the fine flower of the expiring 18th century, absolutory English almost Provincial.

Q. 46. Write a note on Jane Austen's attitude towards nature.

Ans.: Unlike the romantics, Jane Austen is indifferent to nature. The rocks and streams, the forests and castles which we find in the page of Scott and Wordsworth are conspicuous by their absence in her novels. Though she was very fond of the countryside, scenery plays no great part in her novels. She is closer to Cowper and Pope than to Scott, Shelley and Wordsworth. She is not a mystic or visionary like the romantics. She believes, like Pope, that 'the proper study of mankind is man.'

Q. 47. Write a note on Jane Austen's artistic detachment.

Ans.: Despite the restraints and constraints of her limited range and vision Austen has exhibited excellence in handling her material. Her art of plot construction, her art of characterization, her dramatic irony, her sarcastic humour is admirable and enviable. Besides these she also displays an impartiality and objectivity in the selection of events and delineation of characters. She could never identify herself with any of her characters, good or bad. Being a realist she never idealizes her characters to any great extent. She is not obsessed with anything in particular, although she is interested in many things and she is amused with most of the things.

Q. 48. "Her view of life is kindly, genial and free from anything like cynicism." Discuss.

Ans.: Jane Austen was absorbed with the comedy of human folly, but her humour is never malicious. It may be mischievous at times but very seldom did she intend to wound deeply. Even the cruelest shafts of her irony are feathered with the bright streamers of reformation. Her instinctive attitude is that of a humorist. The follies, and foibles, illusion and self contradictions of human nature were a joy to her for their own sake. Jane Austen's detailed gross humour may be insulting but it is smiling.

Q. 49. Discuss the treatment of marriage in Jane's novels.

Ans.: The real object of marriage according to Jane Austen is not home and housekeeping, religious or poetic but something higher. It is companionship and intellectual and emotional association between husband and wife and Jane Austen would not approve of a marriage where such an association is wanting. Marriage according to her, is a union of true minds and hearts.

Q. 50. Who called Jane Austen 'Prose Shakespeare' and Why?

Ans.: Macaulay called her 'Prose Shakespeare' because of her marvelous reality and subtle distinctive traits noticeable in her portraits. The secret of her immortality is to be found in that underlying something which is the woman herself; for, of all writers, it is she, who pursues truth with the most real and undividable devotion. Her great virtue is the solid completeness of her imaginary world, tiny though it was.

Q. 51. What is the secret of Jane Austen's popularity?

Ans.: Jane Austen was finely alive to her limitations and never touched a character or scene she did not know of. She is cool, detached, dispassionate and honest. She is a humorist. Her imagination is a comedian's imagination with a purpose to amuse the readers. This is the secret of her popularity. Nobody who reads Jane Austen with pleasure once will even find that he grows to like her less. The secret of her power lies in the complete mastery of the subject, she deals with.

Q. 52. What do you know about 'The Lady of the Lake'?

Ans.: 'The Lady of the Lake' (1819) is a great work of Sir Walter Scott, who is representative of that phase of English romanticism which goes by the name of 'The Romantic revival.' It narrates love-story of Ellen who is being loved by three persons; James, the disguised king, Roderick and Gralma. She on her side loves the last of the three. Roderick is killed in a fight sponsored by the king. Finally Ellen is married to Gralma. The poetry depicts the medieval life of Scotland. It is full of action and free from digression.

Q. 53. What do you know about 'Waverly Novels'?

Ans.: Sir Walter Scott wrote Waverly novels. He begins with Waverly in 1814 and ends with the legend of Montrose in 1819. It is known for its material which was such as to engage the deepest parts of Scott's mind, Scottish history and Scottish character. The novel as he wrote it, imposed on him no restrictions, whether of formal language, or of material. Though the extreme looseness of structure prevents any one of the Waverly novels from being an absolute success, yet these novel gave something genuinely new.

Q. 54. Comment upon Scott's genius for vitalizing the past.

Ans.: The Quality most obvious in Scott's work whether in prose and verse, is his genius for vitalizing the past. His best work has the spontaneity and ease of gossip by the fireside, for he was so saturated with old—time legends and his own associations that he exhaled them very naturally. He compels our interest by no literary trick, but by making us feel that men and women of a past age were real life human beings.

Q. 55. Find the major distinction between the words 'Romantic' and the 'Classic'.

Ans.: The distinction between the romantic and the classic may be viewed in the historical context. Both the expressions look back to the Roman Empire for their origin. The literature which was produced by classes through Latin came to be known as classical literature, which was rational at the very root. The language and literature of the masses was different from them. They generally wrote in vernacular of native language. *Langue Lative* was the language of the educated class and *Lingua Romanica* was the language of the masses. The literature which was produced by the masses through the Romance language came to be known as 'Romance'. As the masses were generally illiterate and emotional, emotion and imagination became the attributes of romantic literature.

Q. 56. Comment upon the position of 'essay' in the Romantic Age.

Ans.: Novelty of expression was adopted by the prose writers in Romantic Age. Charles Lamb and William Hazlitt, for instance, reoriented the essay form to exhibit their 'personal' inclinations and the heady mix of autobiography and a well devised imagination constituted essential features of the essay in the Romantic period.

Q. 57. Prove that Romanticism's character in England presented many faces.

Ans.: One important aspect of English Romanticism is that the writers associated with it came from a variety of social and cultural backgrounds and had very personalized themes, which weren't devised to suggest the existence or even development of a school. The perspectives offered by the situation of Romanticism, then, presents interesting counters through which interrogations of many social structures were made possible.

Q. 58. What are the factors responsible for the success of William Wordsworth as a poet?

Ans.: The poetry of William Wordsworth (1770-1850), was both popular and accessible to his contemporaries. Wordsworth inaugurated a new poetic idiom and sought to invigorate the world of poetry through a worldview that departed from and was settled against the poetics of the New—classical age. The collection of poems in 'Lyrical Ballads' is a landmark in English literary history for the 'break' it initiated with the preceding Johnsonian tradition and also because it showed the possibilities of the English language for the new philosophy that informed Romantic poetry.

Q. 59. Why did Wordsworth choose low and rustic life as his subject matter?

Ans.: Low and rustic life was generally chosen by Wordsworth, because in that condition, the essential passions of the heart find a better soil in which they can attain their maturity and are less under restraint. People speak a plainer and more emphatic language because in that condition of life the elementary feelings of people co-exist in a state of greater simplicity.

Q. 60. Write a short note on the minor novelists of the Romantic Age.

Ans.: Marie Edgeworth, Susan Edmonton Ferrier were two known women writers of the day. With men writers, meanwhile, fiction exhibited greater variety of matter and method. Charles Robert Maturin, Theodore Hook, John Galt and Thomas Love Peacock are some of the other names, which can be termed as the minor novelists of the Romantic Age.

26

Victorian and Pre-Raphaelites

Q. 1. Write a short note on the main tendencies of the Victorian era.

Ans.: From the literary point of view, Victorian age appears at first as a continuation of romanticism, but then emerged various tendencies which made it a particular age in itself. It was the period in which conflict between religious feeling and the scientific spirit, between mysticism and rationalism, became intense and widespread. Beyond any other period in our history, the Victorian Age was an age of social interests and practical ideals and it was by these that much of its literature was inspired and fed.

Q. 2. What was the effect of Victorian Age upon people-in-general?

Ans.: A vast upheaval in thought was the consequence of this rapid progress and popularization of knowledge, new theories came into conflict with old faiths; the ancient intellectual order was shaken at its foundations. Hence the Victorian Age was marked throughout by the prominence of the spirit of inquiry and criticism, by skepticism and religious uncertainty, and by spiritual struggle and unrest.

Q. 3. What was the effect of Industrial revolution upon the social structure of England?

Ans.: The old agricultural England was finally destroyed by the Industrial revolution. It shook the supremacy of the aristocratic class and brought into being a new merchant class, which desired power and prestige both, Victorian traditions and conventions were subjected to greater pressures. The two great dominant movements, in the political and social spheres, are the progress of democracy and, in the intellectual sphere, the progress of science.

Q. 4. Comment upon Democracy in the Victorian society.

Ans.: As the nineteenth century progressed, there was an increase in the reform measures initiated by the Government. The Victorian age was also the period of political stability in Great Britain. The process of democratization was not confined to the political granting of right alone. Another socially significant move was the policy of state-supported education adopted by the Government in the Victorian age. Major democratic measures introduced include the adoption of secret ballot, recognition of trade unions, educational facilities for the working class, and moves to universalize adult franchise.

Q. 5. What do you know about Victorianism and contemporary society?

Ans.: The long reign of Queen Victoria (1837-1901) saw numerous developments that shaped the culture and society of the time. The two major factors; the influence of industrialism of Darwinian theories in the social and cultural life of Britain in the nineteenth century cannot be ignored. Mechanization and growing industrialism speeded up life considerably in the Victorian age. It affected human relations, the professions, and created new opportunities for the working classes.

Q. 6. What was the condition of Religion in Victorian Society?

Ans.: The Church of England was the major religious institution in Victorian England but significant departures from the mainstream were manifested in the emergence of Methodism, the Oxford Movement, and Evangelicalism. The church functioned, at one level, as the platform for the argumentation over matters of religion and their relevance in contemporary social life. The bulk of the nation seemed to be at least nominally Christian. It was dangerous to attack religion in public except before a highly educated audience. Much public discussion was religious, or at least pietistic in tone, and popular literature and drama had a rather obtrusive, if sentimental, Christian background. Church going was an important aspect of life for a majority of Victorians.

Q. 7. "Religion and Science were two important counters in Victorian Life"—comment.

Ans.: Darwinian theories did make an impact upon the currents of thought in the Victorian age, but it is equally true that faith was far from over. People who were aware of the implications of the Darwinian position also exhibited a remarkable degree of religiosity. It is in this context of the mutual existence of opposing tendencies—of science and religion that the Victorian period is usually considered to be one fraught with contradictions. Thus, Religion and Science were important counters, but they weren't always programmed through the matrix of the either.

Q. 8. What do you know about women's lives in the Victorian Age?

Ans.: An average Victorian woman was considered to be best suited for a life of domestic activities and as the benefits of an industrial society accrued, the recruitment of domestic help may have lessened the burden of the woman but did nothing to unshackle the patriarchal structure. The man-at-work/woman-at-home binarism was evident. Along with the image of 'angel in the house,' the concept of the 'fallen woman' was also a part of the Victorian attitude towards women. In the works of many Victorian writers these images were circulated well.

Q. 9. "The growth of pessimism was further encouraged by the flow of pessimistic thought from Europe, where pessimism was much in the air at the time"—Do you agree?

Ans.: In the Victorian era old customers, belief and traditions were losing their hold on the minds of people, and the new order of things had not yet been established, as it was the age of transition. Even man started doubting God and felt orphan, miserable and helpless. David Cecil said, "Conscious, considered pessimism became a force in English literature in this age". The melancholy poems of Arnold, Fitzgerald, and Thomson along with the works of Thomas Hardy reflected the pessimistic outlook of the late Victorian era.

Q. 10. How can we call Victorian Age as the golden age of literature?

Ans.: The literature of Victorian Age was rich in literature of almost every kind. The growth of wealth gave increased leisure for the pursuit of letters, and widened the audience and readers. There were poets like Tenryson, Browning, Arnold and Macdonald. In fiction we have Dickens, Thackeray, Trolope, and in history, the third and fourth volumes of Macaulay's History. Such eminent writers as Rosette, Fitzgerald, Bronte Sisters, George Eliot, George Meredith, Ruskin, Carlyle and Mill and Newman, all made it a golden age of English literature.

Q. 11. What do you understand by Utilitarianism?

Ans.: Utilitarianism was the popular philosophy of the time, represented by commercial people, whose main aim was to achieve material progress. It appeared in the imaginative literature of the time only to be criticized.

Q. 12. What do you know about 'Victorian Complacency'?

Ans.: During the Victorian Age, the British Empire was well-established in many parts of the world and the English people were capable enough to lead a happy peaceful life. The period was marked by freedom from wars and internal strife. The calmness of the period made the Victorians, complacent and lovers of tradition, rather than those longing for revolution or any radical changes. Hence, there come the term 'Victorian Complacency'.

Q. 13. Write a brief note on the women novelists of the Victorian Period.

Ans.: Novel had become an extremely popular genre during the Victorian Period. A large number among the readers and writers were women. The major five are as follows: Mrs. Gaskell (1810-65), Charlotte Bronte (1816-55), Emily Jane Bronte (1818-48), George Eliot (1819-80) and Sarah Grand.

Q. 14. Write a brief note on 'The Victorian Novel'.

Ans.: Novel writing and reading were literally social engagements that constituted one of the more accessible forms of entertainment for the Victorian people. The main reason behind its wide-ranging popularity was its insistence on realism. The fact that Charles Dickens had to revise the ending of Great Expectations shows how deeply the sentiment of the readers was associated with the 'life' of the novel. The novelists responded to the changes taking place in contemporary society—the railways, the shifting of population because of the industrialization. The influence of mechanization, the rise of educational opportunities, urbanization etc. were all represented in the Victorian novels. Dickens, Hardy, Thackeray and many women novelists enriched this genre.

Q. 15. Write a short note on the poetry in the Victorian age.

Ans.: It became extremely difficult for the Victorian poets to respond to their world in the same way as their Romantic predecessors did. Tennyson, Browning, Elizabeth Barrett Browning, Mathew Arnold are big names for Victorian poetry. Tennyson tried his hand at a variety of forms from the elegy to the dramatic monologue. But dramatic monologue was perfected by Browning, who has been seen as an intellectual but obscure poet. Elizabeth was a bold experimenter and became very successful. Mathew Arnold through his 'Dover Beach' seems to qualify as the typical Victorian response to the inconsistencies of the age. Hardy also wrote poetry but he was more lived for his novels.

Q. 16. Comment upon the late Victorian poetic scene.

Ans.: The late Victorian poetic scene saw the emergence of the Pre-Raphaelites. This group of poets, led by Dante Gabriel Rossetti, combined mysticism with a fascination for the symbolic representation of natural elements.

Q. 17. What do you know about the Pre-Raphaelites?

Ans.: The Pre-Raphaelites were above all artists: art was their religion. It belonged at first to a group of painters who had grown enthusiastic over the Italian primitives before Raphael. It was in harmony with the aesthetic ideas of Ruskin, the scorner of the Renaissance, who hailed the beginnings of the pre-Raphaelite movement. The first and greatest of the Pre-Raphaelites, Rossetti, was a painter as well as a poet; and Morris also could use brush as well as pen.

Q. 18. Comment upon the working of Pre-Raphaelites.

Ans.: The Pre-Raphaelites worshipped beauty above everything. They echoed the American poet, Edgar Allan Poe: Keats's love of beauty as an ideal made him their great inspirer among the Romantic. They found their favourite models in the poems he wrote in the medieval setting. But they cultivated also the old Italian poets, live Dante and his contemporaries.

Q. 19. What do you know about D.G. Rossetti?

Ans.: Dante Gabriel Rossetti (1828-82), the son of an Italian refugee in England, wrote sonnets and ballads. He translated Dante's *Vita Nuova*. His work is extremely original and individual. It is distinguished in English literature by its rich Italian colouring and its warm sensuous quality. Its peculiar characteristic is the symbolic use of details to suggest a whole complex of feelings, like the emblems used by the primitive Italian Painters.

Q. 20. What was the importance of 'Rationalism' in Victorian era?

Ans.: The most original writers of the Victorian era, like Arnold, Carlyl etc. became famous because of the novelty of their point of view, midway between the predominant rationalist outlook and the still persistent Christian sentiment. Victorians loved rationalism and were against romanticism.

Q. 21. What do you know about 'The Religious Revival' in Victorian era?

Ans.: The religious revival came as the opposition of Rationalism. A purely religious revival, steeped in Romantic influences, showed itself about 1830. It was as far removed from the deism of the Broad Church as from the spirit of the Evangelicals who constituted the Low Church. The 'High Church' was favourable to mystery and miracles and appealed to the sensibility and imagination.

Q. 22. Who started 'Oxford Movement' and why?

Ans.: It was one of Wordsworth's disciples, John Keble, Professor of poetry at Oxford, who some year later started the 'Oxford Movement'. In this Oxford Movement, there were two phases. At first, there was the High Church revival in the bosom of Anglicanism. This spirit displayed itself in Oxford in the pamphlets called Tracts for the Times, where it got its name the 'tractarian movement'. Apart from Keble, it was inspired by E.B. Pusey (1800-82), who originated 'Puseyism', the form of Anglicanism which came nearest to Rome without being merged into Romanticism.

Q. 23. How far do you agree that John Henry Newman (1801-90) was the most important personality of the 'Oxford Movement'?

Ans.: John Henry Newman was its most important and well known writer. He was driven to take the decisive step by his dislike of liberalism and his indignation against political interference. He dreamt of a free and powerful church. In the course of his career, he revealed himself as a great writer in verse and prose, which was largely theological. Newman rejected liberalism. He used an extra-ordinary simple prose, supple, distinguished, essentially aristocratic and deeply imbued with the culture of oxford.

Q. 24. Comment upon Victorian Prose.

Ans.: The term 'Victorian Prose' appears inadequate in the context of the variety of prose writings, it is supposed to encompass. Carlyle, Ruskin, Macaulay and Matthew Arnold are the major prose writers of Victorian era. Carlyle's style, with its enormous wealth of vocabulary, its strangely constructed sentences, its breaks, abrupt turns, apostrophes and exclamations, is unique in our prose literature. He spoke contemptuously of art as art, and had no patience with the merely bookish side of literature. By virtue of the extent and variety of his work, his vigour and originality, his influence on art, letters and life, and the range and beauty of his style.

Q. 25. What, according to you, are the causes of the rise of the popular novel in the Victorian age?

Ans.: In the 19th century, adult literacy increases markedly, attempts to provide education by the state, and self-help schemes are partly the cause and partly the result of the popularity of the novel. Publication in installments means that works are affordable for people of modest means. The change in the reading public is reflected in a change in the subjects of novels. The great novelists wrote works which in some ways transcend their own period, but which in detail very much explore the preoccupations of their time.

Q. 26. Comment upon Bronte's Sister.

Ans.: Charlotte Bronte (1816-55) and her sisters Emily (1818-48) and Anne (1820-49) are linked together, but their work differs greatly. Charlotte is notable for several good novels, among which her masterpiece is *Jane Eyre*, in which we see the heroine, after much adversity, achieve happiness on her own terms. Emily Bronte's *Wuthering Heights* is a strange work, which enjoys almost cult status. Its concerns are more romantic, less contemporary than those of Jane Eyre—but its themes of obsessive love and self-destructive passion have proved popular with the 20th century reader.

Q. 27. Write down the style of the Victorian novel.

Ans.: The change in style in Victorian fiction was slow coming but became clear by the end of the century. Even writers of the high Victorian age were censured for their plots attacking the conventions of the day with Adam Bede being called 'the vile outpourings of a lewd woman's mind'. The cause of such fury was Hardy's frank treatment of sex, religion and his disregard for the subject of marriage, a subject close to the Victorians' heart, with the prevailing plot of the Victorian novel.

Q. 28. Comment upon Children's literature written in Victorian Era.

Ans.: The Victorians are sometimes credited with 'inventing childhood', partly via their introduction of compulsory education. As children began to be able to read, literature for young people became a growth industry, with not only established writers like Dickens, producing works for children, but also a new group of dedicated children's authors. Writers like Lewis Carroll, and Anne Sewell wrote mainly for children. Other authors such as Anthony Hope and R.L. Stevenson wrote mainly for adults, but their adventure novels are now generally classified as for children.

Q. 29. What was the position of Drama in the Victorian Age?

Ans.: In drama, farces, musical burlesques, extravaganzas and comic operas competed with Shakespeare production and serious drama by James Planche and Thomas William Robertson.

In 1855, the German Red Entertainments began a process of elevating the level of musical theatre in Britain that culminated in the famous series of Comic operas by Gilbert and Sullran. After Gilbert, Oscar Wilde became the leading poet and dramatist of the late Victorian period. Wilde's plays stand apart from the many now forgotten plays of Victorian times and have a much closer relationship to those of the Edwardian dramatists such as George Bernard Shaw.

Q. 30. Name some important translations of the period and give the reason as well.

Ans.: The interest in older works of literature led the Victorians much further afield to find new old works with a great interest in translating of literature from the farthest flung comers of their new empire and beyond. Arabic and Sanskrit literature were some of the richest bodies of work to be discovered and translated for popular consumption. *The Rubaiyat of Omar Khayyam* is one of the best works, translated by Edward Fitzgerald. The explorer Richard Francis Burtor also translated many exotic works such as *The Arabian Nights* and the *Kama Sutra*.

Q. 31. Comment upon the writing style of Carlyle.

Ans.: The passionate ideas were expressed in an eccentric and powerful style into which entered several elements borrowed from German, but which on the whole is entirely personal. His vehement style, recalling that of the Hebrew Prophets, surprises by its lyrical turn, its continual coining of new words and expressions, its personifications of abstract qualities, and its singular figure-heads. Carlyle's imaginative vision, rich in concrete details, contributes even more than his conscientious documentation to the value of his historical works. He re-creates the past. His French Revolution is perhaps his literary masterpiece.

Q. 32. Comment upon the realism of Charles Dickens.

Ans.: Dickens had been familiar with the most humble surroundings, and the most wretched districts, and he made their description his habitual subject. A new and vivid realism enters into his pictures, but it is realism, humorous and tender by turns, the opposite of that which was to triumph later in the century, gloomy, cynical and overwhelming. Dickens's realistic scenes are now lit up by laughter, now warmed by pity. The observation, which is abundant, piercing, swift, and cinematographic as we should now say, is at the same time iridescent with humour and tears.

Q. 33. How and in what respect Thackeray's realism was different from Dickens's?

Ans.: William Makepeace Thackeray (1811-63) was the penetrating analyst of both the upper middle class and aristocratic society. He brought to his pictures a realism of a very different kind from that of Dickens, more exacting and less mingled with fantasy and lyricism. The springs of action, the impulses of sentiment or egotism, are revealed with a clear sightedness impossible to Dickens. Thackeray's characters may not have all the outward vitality that Dickens could communicate, but they are studied far more deeply within.

Q. 34. Who wrote 'In Memoriam' and why?

Ans.: 'In Memoriam' is written by the great poet of Victorian era—Lord Alfred Tennyson. Moved by grief at the premature death of his friend Arthur Hallam, Tennyson sets down his thoughts on life and death, revealing the anguish of the search after grounds for belief in immortality, and the torment of the modern soul oscillating between the hopes offered by Christianity and the negation of science. Deliberately quiet and even in its tone, and made up of short stanzas all the octosyllabii quatrains (abba), it is one of the most beautiful elegies in the language.

Q. 35. Comment upon Tennyson as a dramatist.

Ans.: Tennyson, the most representative poet of the Victorian era experienced in his own being the intellectual movements of the country. He shared its aspirations, its troubles, its anxieties and reflected them in his verse. During the same period he turned to dramatic writing, and produced several plays which were well received but not triumphantly successful. They show his powers as a writer, but they lack the true dramatic inspiration.

Q. 36. Comment upon Browning as a dramatist.

Ans.: What chiefly interested Browning was the study of the human soul, he was a psychologist first of all and artist later. From the very start he discussed, in monologue or dialogue, problems of life and conscience. At intervals Browning attempted the drama proper. In 1837 he published Strafford, which was followed by other plays, six in all between then and 1846. In spite of their merits, these plays over burdened with argument, did not succeed with the public. Their action was sacrificed too much to the study of the characters.

Q. 37. Who wrote 'Pippa Passes' (1841)? Also discuss its theme.

Ans.: Robert Browning wrote 'Pippa Passes' and his limited dramatic power showed to better purpose in the isolated scenes which make up Pippa Passes. Here Browning imagined the effect of the songs of a little working-girl, strolling about during a holiday, on the destiny of the very different persons who hear them in turn. The poem reaches the height of grim tragedy in the scene of the murder of the old husband by the two lovers Sibald and Ottima.

Q. 38. Comment upon Browning's poetic style.

Ans.: It was the excess of thought over art which imperiled Browning's poetry. He had at his command a vocabulary of rare extent which included many technical terms of all descriptions. He employed blank verse with an ease that might be called excessive, and no other poet has been able to juggle so dexterously with simply, durable or triple rhymes. Thus, his verse effects are most varied, ranging from the tragic to the comic, and indeed to the grotesque. But he could restrain his exuberance on occasions, and replace it by a surprising compactness. His lyrical faculty burst forth in admirable short songs.

Q. 39. What do you know about Mrs. Elizabeth Barrett Browning?

Ans.: Elizabeth Barrett begun by writing poems which were rather old-fashioned in form, and showed a curious mingling of the influences of the Bible, the Greeks, Byron and Shelley. Her Sonnets from the Portuguese, written just before she got married, tell of her love for Browning who found her ill and lonely and cured her with his tender care. Though her diction was far from pure, and her sense of rhythm uncertain, her sonnets abound in vivid phrases, in strong new images, in trenchant brevities. Her blank verse was unequal, almost like prose. Then the verse takes wing and soars with rare ease, and with a nervous strength that is characteristic of Mrs. Browning, showing her to be not only original but an equal of the greatest.

Q. 40. Comment upon the person who started Tractarian Movement.

Ans.: The Oxford Movement formed the most important epoch in literature. The Tractarians shared with Sir Walter Scott, however, a love of medieval past and the liberalism which Scott had abhorred, they abhorred too. The Tractarians, in fact, continued the tradition of the great Caroline dinner and religious poets. It was indeed Newman who began the Tracts. He was the heart and soul of the Movement.

Q. 41. Why did Thomas Hardy become a novelist?

Ans.: Thomas Hardy became a novelist and a poet to meet the rising expenses of his first wife. He was interested in poetry by nature, but he never thought of writing novels. He never wanted to write prose novels at all, but he was forced to manufacture them, due to his wife's heavy expenses.

Q. 42. What did Hardy think about God?

Ans.: Hardy says that if there is God, he is a being who kills or ruins innocent people like Tess for free Sport. The attitude of Hardy towards God goes on changing with the passage of time. Thomas Hardy has referred to God as the first cause, the supreme power, and the president of Immortals. Hardy says that this God is coquettish because he brings rains when they are not wanted and does not give even a drop of water when it is highly urgent.

Q. 43. What is the attitude of Hardy towards women?

Ans.: Hardy's view regarding women is not advance. It is not as modern as that of Laurence. He thinks that women cannot montage an honest man. She is always attracted by unusually handsome man. That's why she suffers very much at the hands of cruel fate.

Q. 44. Was Hardy a philosopher?

Ans.: Hardy's views on life, death, man, world and God were full of pessimism. But he was not a philosopher in one sense in which Hegel and Kant were. In spite of his dislike for the title of a philosopher, his views are such as make him to look live a philosopher.

Q. 45. What is the role of fate and chance in Hardy's view?

Ans.: Fate is a character and chance is a governing agency. Man is but a toy in the hands of the cruel fate. Hardy's novels are but a study of a struggle between man and indifferent fate. Fate is a central theme and a character in Hardy's novels. Once a human being comes within the pulls of the ruthless wheels of fate, he or she is destroyed completely. Hardy saw happiness but very rare in life. Critics think that in the name of fate or chance, unusual, unexpected and unbelievable events take place.

Q. 46. Comment upon Hardy's limitations.

Ans.: Hardy's sophisticated or aristocratic characters are not convincing as he lacked proper knowledge of the upper class society. He cannot draw odious or mean characters. His wicked characters also have got the purity of heart and sincerity of action. Even his villains are ready to sacrifice their life if a suitable occasion arises. He even can't draw half length characters. He has not cared for the curiosity and interest of the readers. He has simply drawn all characters to their full length.

Q. 47. What do you know about 'Victorian Compromise'?

Ans.: Politically, Victorian compromise meant the reconciliation of the claims of liberty and progress with order. In every field the Victorians tried to uphold authority in the face of the rising tide of social change. The Victorian conflict between Faith and Science which had disturbed sensitive souls like Mathew Arnold was now resolved—mostly in favour of Science, but in few cases, in favour of Faith.

Q. 48. What was the role of journalism in the development of literature during Victorian period?

Ans.: After the great success of periodical essays in eighteenth century people could understand that to reach up to general class they need magazines and other publications that should contain good and real literature. At the same time, the proportion of the nation with a genuine interest in literature was increasing. This really helped in the development of literature.

Q. 49. What do you know about 'Naughty Nineties'?

Ans.: The last decade of the nineteenth century is referred to as 'naughty', for it was characterizes by a revolt against Victorianism, a whole sale condemnation of the ideas and values which had been cherished during the earlier decades of Victoria's reign. The revolt of the nineties has three aspects. First, it reiterates the old revolutionary formula of Liberty, Equality and Fraternity in a new setting. Secondly, it worships power rather than beauty. And thirdly, it challenges the older values of art and life.

Q. 50. Who were Aesthetes? What was their aim?

Ans.: Aesthetes are also known as The Decadents. Their main aim was to promote 'art for art's sake'. The Aesthetes liked to flout the Victorian traditions as openly and fragrantly as possible. Walter Pater was the primary figure who urged for a withdrawal of art from humanity and social problems.

Q. 51. Write a brief note on the novelists of the 'Kailyard School'.

Ans.: Certain novelists, towards the end of the nineteenth century, expressed in fiction most realistically the manners of the lowland peasant classes. The language of these novelists was coloured with Scottish dialect and they treated the subject with sympathy and humour. Ian Maclaren, G. Douglar, S.R. Crockett and Sir James Barrie belong to this Kailyard School.

27

Modern British Literature

Q. 1. Comment upon the new tendencies in the modern age.

Ans.: The period extending from 1890 to the outbreak of the First World War seems to have a fairly distinctive or unique character. It brought a profound change in the thought and outlook of the English nation. It gave birth to a new spirit, and new working class, and men spoke enthusiastically or scornfully of the 'New Woman', 'New Morality', 'New Paganism' and 'New Drama'.

Q. 2. Comment upon the social conditions of the modern age.

Ans.: Towards the close of the century, a series of crises afflicted British trade and agriculture, and the industrial supremacy of the country was seriously threatened by France, Germany and the United States. The decline in economic prosperity had serious social consequences; there was a substantial increase in unemployment and poverty, and strikes became more numerous. The middle class, having lost its superb confidence, undertook a radical criticism of its own principle and criteria.

Q. 3. Comment upon the atmosphere of unrest and anxiety in the modern age.

Ans.: The close of the century was characterized by an extraordinary social and intellectual ferment. Men were no longer satisfied with the simple security of the old orthodox assumptions. They were conscious of living in a world of rapid change and evidenced a spirit of free enquiry and criticism. A silent revolution was in progress and the age witnessed a strong reaction against the accepted standards of conduct and belief. In religion, in social relations, in domestic life men grew contemptuous of the old ideals, there was no political principle, no theological dogma, to social tradition or moral sentiment that was not challenged.

Q. 4. Comment upon the literary tendencies of the Modern Age.

Ans.: The literature of the modern age is governed more by realism than by romance. The present age is essentially the age of realism and the modern writers, instead of dealing with the times of King Arthur and the Middle Ages, have concentrated their attention on the problems of modern life. In modern age literature has been employed more for social purpose, particularly for reforming the maladies of contemporary society. The novel has become the dominant literary form and it is through the medium of this important instrument of literature that social problems have been dealt with. New experiments were tried in all branches of literature. It has considerably been influenced by foreign writers in the field of drama, poetry and fiction.

Q. 5. Comment upon the state of poetic drama in the early twentieth century.

Ans.: Stephen Philips was the earliest dramatist of poetic drama of the modern age. He wrote poetic plays between 1900 and 1908. Oscar Wilde's claim as a writer of poetic plays depends on his two plays-*Salome* and *The Duchess of Padua*. Davidson enriched poetic drama by writing The Theatocrat and Mammon Trilogy. Laurence Binyon sought to serve the old Greek world of romance and loveliness in his poetic plays. John Drinkwater wrote such famous poetic plays as *The Storm*, *A Night of the Trojan War* etc.

Q. 6. What do you know about 'The Celtic Revival' in the modern age?

Ans.: The contribution of the Irish Movement is also known as the Celtic Revival. Its great pioneers, W.B. Yeats and J.M. Synge, deprecated "the conversation of the theatre into the lecture platform and the pulpit by realistic playwrights W.H. Auden and Christopher Isherwood also collaborated in writing poetic plays".

Q. 7. Write a short note on the contribution of T.S. Eliot as a dramatist.

Ans.: The plays of T.S. Eliot are surely the most striking feature, from the literary point of view, that the English stage has had to offer since the First World War. His main plays are *Murder in the Cathedral*, *The Family Reunion*, *The Cocktail Party*, *The Confidential Clerk* and *The Statesman*. The bulk of his output is small, but its quality, and its impact on the entire course of modern English poetic drama is very deep.

Q. 8. What do you know about Christopher Fry?

Ans.: Christopher Fry, who began writing poetic plays after the Second World War, emerged as a real leader of poetic drama after T.S. Eliot. His plays include *The Firstborn*, *The Boy with a Cart*, *The Dark is Light Enough*, *Venus Observed*, *The Lady's Not for Burning* etc. He is the only modern metaphysical verse dramatist who introduced philosophical discussions in his plays.

Q. 9. What are your views regarding Modern Psychological Novel?

Ans.: Strictly speaking the modern psychological novel was born between 1913 and 1915 with the publication of Marcel Proust's Remembrance of Things Past in 1913 and Miss Dorothy Richardson's first volume of Pilgrimage in 1915. James Joyce also began publishing in 1914, in serial form, a novel entitled, *A Portrait of the Artist as a Young Man*. There was a mere coincidence that these three novelists, unknown to each other influenced English novel by turning it away from external to inner reality.

Q. 10. What is the contribution of Sigmund Freud?

Ans.: Sigmund Freud appeared on the scene with his brilliant thesis on Psycho-analysis which violently shook the foundations of human thought. Freud declared that every little action of man-even his dreams, reveries, half-expressed and unexpressed thoughts—could be traced back to his sex-instincts. People now began to look at things from a new perspective. Experiments were commenced in the light of Psycho-analysis. 'Stream of Consciousness' was one such experiment.

Q. 11. Comment upon the literary trends in modern poetry.

Ans.: Twentieth century poetry is a curious mixture of the traditional and the experimental of the old and the new. It is complex and many-sided. In fact, it is poetry of revolt against tradition, best exemplified in the poetry of T.S. Eliot. The poet sees life in its naked realism. Debris of war, the language of everyday life, delight in the sensuous beauty of nature, the humanitarian spirit and the disillusionment are other main features of modern poetry.

Q. 12. Write a short note on the Humanitarian Spirit in the modern poetry.

Ans.: Nor does the modern poet love nature alone; he also loves and feels for the lower animals living in the lap of nature. He is moved by their suffering and makes a forceful plea for a more humane treatment of the dumb creation. Indeed, humanitarianism—a deepened sense of pity for the poor and the suffering—is a leading characteristic of modern poetry. Gibson in particular is the champion of the underdog and the down trodden.

Q. 13. Write a short note on poetic techniques used in modern poetry.

Ans.: The modern poet is constantly experimenting with new verse forms and poetic techniques. The use of slang and colloquialism has became common, the language and rhythm of poetry approximate more and more of those of common speech, the bonds of metre have been loosened, and the use of verse Libra has become increasingly common.

Q. 14. Why do critics call modern age as the Age of Innovations?

Ans.: Impressionism, Imagism and Surrealism are some innovations in 20th century poetry. The impressionists seek to convey the vague, fleeting sensations passing through their minds by the use of a novel imagery and metaphor. The imagists, headed by Ezra Pound, aim at clarity of expression through the use of hard, accurate and definite images to convey their intellectual and emotional complexes. The Surrealists try to express whatever passes in the subconscious, or even the conscious, without any control or selection by the conscious. These innovations have influenced the art of poets and verse writers of the age.

Q. 15. What are the qualities of modern novel?

Ans.: A prominent feature of the modern English novel is its immense variety and complexity. It is realistic and deals with all the facts of contemporary life, the pleasant as well as the unpleasant. The theories of psychologists, like Freud and Havelock Ellis, new biological theories go far to explain the pre-occupation of the contemporary novel with sex-theories.

Q. 16. What is new in the modern novel?

Ans.: The modern novel is predominantly psychological. The impact of the new psychology on plot and character has already been noticed. There is a shift in the theme of the modern novelist. New influences, specially the Russian and the American, are daily widening its horizons and renewing its vigour and vitality. New experiments are being widening its horizons and renewing its vigour and vitality. New experiments, some temporary and fleeting, are being conducted. The caravan of the English novel goes on, every changing, becoming and growing.

Q. 17. Comment upon the Drama in the modern age.

Ans.: There is the naturalistic prose drama, dealing with contemporary social problems, just to provoke thought on these problems. Shaw and Galsworthy are the chief exponents of this realistic prose drama. Stephen Philips is important as he wrote a number of blank verse plays, including *Herod*, *Ulysses*, *The Son of David and Nero*. *Masefield*, *John Drinkwater*, *J.M. Synge*, *Lord Dunsany* and *T.S. Eliot* are important names.

Q. 18. Write down the general idea of Symbolism in the modern age.

Ans.: A symbol takes us beyond the object with the idea that it denotes to another level of significance that reaches forth to embrace that spirit. Intensity and complexity were to be achieved by condensed syntax and minor images clustered around one main metaphor, until both became symbols of the original impression.

Q. 19. What is Imagism?

Ans.: Imagism was a poetic movement that flourished in England and America between 1912 and 1917. Imagism was too restrictive to sustain long as a concerted movement, but it proved to be the beginning of modern poetry. The typical Imagist poem is written in free verse, and undertakes to render as exactly and tersely as possible, without comment or generalization, the writer's response to a visual object or scene.

Q. 20. Compare between 'new humour' and 'elder humour'.

Ans.: Wilde's Dorian Grey and the fantastic fun of J.M. Barric, contributed distinctly and originally to humorous literature; while its special characteristic lies in the self-consciousness of the jester and capricious blend of romance and reality in his method. It contains more spirit of mockery than elder humour. The humour is thinner, drier, less universal in its appeal. It belongs far more to time and to fashion than does the humour of the elder humonists.

Q. 21. What were impacts of two World Wars upon literature of twentieth century?

Ans.: In real sense, it is really from the war-period that the modern age in English literature began. A sceptical and critical attitude towards the accepted values of life had already been felt in the intense pessimism of Hardy. Poets like W.A. Auden were preoccupied with the problems of industrial civilization and borrowed imagery from mechanized life often with striking felicity.

Q. 22. What do you know about *The Stream of Consciousness Novel* in the 20th century?

Ans.: 'Stream of Consciousness Novel' is a modern development and reflects recent interest in the psycho-analytical school of Jung, Freud, Alder and the 'free association' used by psychiatry'. The novelist tries to discover a pattern in this apparently confused collection of impressions, memories and obsessive images. In 'Stream of Consciousness Novel' everything is presented through an apparently unorganized succession of images and ideals connected by association rather than by logical argument or narrative sequence. In fact, it is based on a realization of the drama that takes place in the minds of human beings.

Q. 23. Write down your views regarding the importance of Virginia Woolf as a modern novelist.

Ans.: Virginia Woolf was the first important writer who began her literary career by publishing *The Voyage Out* (1915) in the manner of H.G. Walls, and Galsworthy. Virginia Woolf wrote four remarkable Stream of Consciousness novels—*Mrs. Dalloway* (1925), *To the Lighthouse* (1927) *The Waves* (1931) and *Between the Acts* (1941).

Q. 24. What do you know about the Georgian or Pietist tradition of poetry?

Ans.: The imagists, however, extended the very technique of pictorial effects which the Georgian poets aimed at in their Quietist or Pietist tradition of poetry. Between 1912 to 1922 Edward Marsh published four anthologies called Georgian Poetry. The poems tended to be metrically conventional lyrics on rural themes. They were criticized as minor and unadventurous by those who had creaed 'modernism' like T.S. Eliot.

Q. 25. Write a short note on 'The Soldier Poets'.

Ans.: Without the poets of the two World Wars modern English poetry would have been poorer in experiments with new poetic idioms and communication of richer sensibility. War poetry communicated the shocking experience of War in an altogether new way of speaking and explored a new range of human feelings and sensibility, the key note of which was pity.

Q. 26. What do you know about 'Modernist Verse'?

Ans.: The First World War had induced a mood of depression as well as revulsion of feeling against European civilization. In this atmosphere, along with books from a dozen orthodox Georgians, were produced the poems of Eliot, Hopkins and Owen. Eliot's 'Prufrock' (1917) may be said to have inaugurated modern poetry. 'The Poems' (1918) of Hopkins were to electrify many of the younger writers.

Q. 27. In what way the modernists were influenced by The Metaphysical Revival?

Ans.: There was a very positive value in the rediscovery of the metaphysical poetry that seemed a unique answer to the poetical needs of our time. Metaphysical colloquialism of style and rhythm, realistic particularly, toughness of sensibility, the complex and often dissonant expression of tension and conflict, the resources of irony, ambiguity, paradox and wit—such qualities helped to energize and tighten the modern temper and technique, create an attitude and a medium suited to a troubled, skeptical, anti-heroic age.

Q. 28. Write a short note on the influence of Karl Marx on modern poetry.

Ans.: Marxism sees literature as an ideology that reflects the struggle between the classes and the economic conditions which are the basis of man's intellectual and social revolution. Awareness of socio-economic problems haunted the poets of Thirties. Auden, Spender and Cecil etc. wrote poetry which was largely social criticism. It was influenced by Marxism.

Q. 29. What do you know about 'The Apocalyptic Poetry'?

Ans.: The 'Apocalyptic Poetry' of the 1940's began in opposition to the political commitment of 1930s poets. The term 'Apocalyptic Poetry' came to be applied not only to the founders of 'The apocalypse'—Henry Treece, J.F. Hendry, and G.S. Fraser—but to poets such as Dylan Thomas, W.S. Graham and George Barker. The Apocalyptic poets valued myth and used surrealistic technique.

Q. 30. Comment upon the poetry in the 1960s and the 1970s.

Ans.: Since no significant poetic movements arose during the 1960s and in the 1970s, the positive disarray has continued. The poet has a multiplicity of choices open to him. The outstanding poets of this century have measured themselves not against their contemporaries but against their masters.

Q. 31. Write a short note on main characteristics of Modern Poetry.

Ans.: Beside the impact of metaphysical revival and the French symbolists some main characteristics of modern poetry may be partly attributed to both the scientific findings and the moral confusion of our time.

Q. 32. Write a short note on the most prominent features of the early twentieth century drama.

Ans.: Modern drama exhibits realistic tendencies by having a discussion about the social problems of the time. He was Henry Ibsen, the Norwegian dramatist, who popularized realism in modern drama. Ibsen's lead was followed in England by Robertson, Jones, Pinero, Shaw, Galsworthy and others. The modern drama dealing with problems of real life has become far more intellectual than ever it was before and gives us plenty of food for thought. It became more and more a drama of ideas. The problem play became essentially the drama of disillusion, for its exposed hypocrisy, pulled down old idols from their high pedestals and revealed the realities.

Q. 33. Write a note on element of romanticism in modern drama.

Ans.: The preponderating trend of realism and propaganda in modern drama was given a jolt by new trends which became perceptible with the passage of time. The first new trend against realism was romanticism in drama introduced by J.M. Baric, the Scottish dramatist. He exploited with determination and professional assurance the emotions, whims, and sentimentalism implicit in the Scottish Kailyard tradition. His plays *May Rose*, *Peter Pan*, *A Kiss for Cinderella* and *Dear Brutus* became very famous.

Q. 34. What do you know about Poetic Plays?

Ans.: Poetic Plays, as a new trend in modern drama, were another reaction to realism and naturalism in drama. It was inaugurated with great fervor by W.B. Yeats and T.S. Eliot. T.S. Eliot defended poetic plays and waged a war against realistic prose drama. Among those who gave an impetus to poetic drama in the modern age the names of Stephen Philips, J.E. Fleckin, John Drinkwater, John Masefield, W.B. Yeats, T.S. Eliot and Christopher Fry are worthy of special mention. They have produced a number of poetic plays and some of them are of first rate importance. As we go through the poetic plays we feel again closer to the romantic poets of the nineteenth century.

Q. 35. Who wrote Historical Play in 20th century?

Ans.: G.B. Shaw is at the top among the dramatists who popularized historical plays in modern times. He wrote 'Ceaser and Cleopatra' and 'St. John'. John Drinkwater penned four historical plays—*Abraham Lincoln*, *Mary Stuart*, *Oliver Cromwell* and *Robert Lee*. These historical plays of Drinkwater are not merely chronicle plays focusing attention on events and external happenings, but plays of ideas, presenting problems of human life in a dramatic form.

Q. 36. What do you know about Biographical Plays?

Ans.: Biography has been used for dramatic purposes in two plays: *Barrets of Wimpale Street* by Rudolf Besier and *The Lady with a Lamp* by Reginald Beruly. In 'Barrets' we have a picture of Robert Browning and his love affair with Elizabeth Barrett Browning, and in 'The Lady' the life-story of Florence Nightingale is presented in all vividness from the times of her youth to her glorious old age.

Q. 37. Write a short note on Impressionism and Expressionism.

Ans.: Impressionism was a movement in painting, music and literature whose aim was to force the beholder, listener or reader to participate in recreating the experience of the artist and whose method was to suggest the 'impression' or effect on the artist than to make precise and explicit events. Expressionism, an extreme reaction against naturalism, was concerned not with society but with man. It aimed to offer subjective psychological analysis using the subconscious.

The main dramatists who popularized it are Seen O'Casey, C.K. Munro, H.E. Rubinstein, J.B. Priestly and Elmer Rice.

Q. 38. What do you know about *The Comedy of Manners*?

Ans.: In contrast to these highly technical and confusing trends in modern drama, we have the light-hearted vein of social comedy popularized by Noel Coward and Somerset Maugham. During 1920's and 30s there was a revival of the comedy of manners practiced by the Restoration dramatists like Congreve and others. Though the atmosphere of the modern age did not bear a close similarity to the Restoration atmosphere, there was a general liking for the comedy of manners in which wit and sparkling dialogues played a significant part. The comedy of manners received a setback after the Second World War.

Q. 39. Write a short note on the Technique of modern drama.

Ans.: As regards the modern drama, it should be mentioned that in modern drama, the three classical unities of time, place and action are generally maintained, but there is practically no exposition in the modern plays. The modern drama opens like a Greek tragedy at the climax, dialogues are short and trenchant. In place of Soliloquies and Asides, elaborate stage directions are provided by the dramatists to add richness to their plays.

Q. 40. Write a note on trends in 20th century fiction.

Ans.: The modern age is essentially the age of the novel. In the first two decades of 20th century, the novel was mainly confined to the discussion of the problems confronting the society. The Edwardian novel was essentially a novel of ideas including in its scope a free discussion of all kinds of ideas-scientific, social, political, industrial etc. In the hands of H.G. Wells, Galsworthy, Arnold Bennett particularly concentrated on social purpose and aimed at solution.

Q. 41. Write a note on writers who presented realism in modern fiction.

Ans.: H.G. Wells realistically presented the sorrows and sufferings of a draper's assistant in Kipps and the History of Mr. Polly. George Moore, the Trish novelists, made a realistic study of the poorer classes in our society in A Modern Lover. Arnold Bennett realistically portrayed the life of the Five Towns in the Old Wives Tale and Clay Hangers. He succeeded in portraying the society, realistically the streets etc.

Q. 42. Comment upon the Treatment of Sex in modern fiction.

Ans.: During the Georgian period, a new trend began to be perceptible in English fiction, and it centered the glorification of sex and primal human emotions and passions. In this respect, the works of D.H. Lawrence, Aldous Huxley, Somerset Maugham and James Joyce are worthy of special consideration. These novelists treat of the physical side of sex in blunt matter-of-fact manner without attempting to hide facts about sex.

Q. 43. What do you know about the psychological novel?

Ans.: The twentieth century novel in the later part of the Georgian period to come under the influence of psychologists. A new technique was developed in the psychological fiction, and the new trend found its best exposition in the stream of consciousness technique, which was cultivated in all its complexity by Dorothy Richardson, James Joyce, and Virginia Woolf. Words are employed by novelists of this school not in accordance with the rules and convention of grammar, but in peculiar manner of their own using them in their original picturesque or imagistic sense.

Q. 44. In what way science has influenced the writers of 20th century fiction?

Ans.: Science has revealed to the modern novelist innumerable aspects of life, and opened new vistas of thought and imagination to be employed in fiction. The very texture of the novel has been modified by the novelist's scientific exactness of observation and scrupulous regard for details. The scientific romances of H.G. Wells such as *The Time Machine* and *The Invisible Man* are saturated in scientific lox. *The Brave New World* by Aldous Huxley is a satirical exposure of the conditions brought about by science.

Q. 45. What do you know about detective fiction?

Ans.: Detective fiction, popularized by Arthur Conan Doyle in *The Adventures of Sherlock Holmes*, was given a further impetus in the 20th century fiction by G.K. Chesterton, Edgar Wallace, Dorothy Sayers and Agatha Christie. *The Father Brown Stories* of G.K. Chesterton are very popular and so are the detective novels of Edgar Wallace.

Q. 46. "One prominent trend in modern fiction is the growth of regionalism"—Justify.

Ans.: Thomas Hardy set the trend of regional novel in twentieth century through his Wessex novels Arnold Bennett is the best exponent of the regional novel in his tales of the Five Towns in *Old Wives Tale* and *Clay Hanger Series*. Marry Webb's *Shropshire* and Sheila Kaye-Smith's *Sussex* are the best suited surroundings for then regional novels.

Q. 47. Who wrote 'Biographical novels' in modern age?

Ans.: Biographical novels and novels dealing with family life have also won recognition in our times. The World of William Classoid, *The Forsyte Sage* and *Clay Hanger* are representative novels in this direction.

Q. 48. What do you about 'Angry Young Man' in 20th century?

Ans.: In the fifties appeared a group of novelists, popularly known as 'Angry Young Men' who presented a satirical picture of the new Welfare State with something like the lower middle class of H.G. Wells' Kipps. Among these novelists names of Kingsley Amis, John Braine, and John Wain are significant.

Q. 49. Who wrote *Tristram Shandy*?

Ans.: Laurence Sterne wrote the novel *Tristram Shandy*, with no plot at all, no heroine and no action and obeying no other law than caprice and random association. Narrative consisted of episodes, conversations, perpetual digressions, excursions in learning with unfinished sentences, dashes, pages, fantastic syntax, etc. In this respect, Sterne may be called the precursor of the technique of the modern psychological novel.

Q. 50. Comment upon minimization of plot during 20th century.

Ans.: The annihilation of the tyranny of time necessitated the minimization of plot, almost complete elimination of action, and the elaborate description of characters by describing their individual appearances, gestures, circumstances and physical habits. Plot, action, character and thought are drowned in the stream of consciousness.

28

Contemporary British Literature

Q. 1. Write a short note on poetry in the twenty-first century.

Ans.: Poetry in the twenty-first century is a rich and varied genre, with poets working in traditional forms like sonnet, experimenting with the possibilities of free verse, and creating distinctive voices that will leave their mark on the English poetic tradition. Women poets are no longer sidelined but exist at the heart of a vibrant culture.

Q. 2. What is Desperado Literature?

Ans.: Desperado is an unusual term for postmodern literature. The only criterion that ought to make us point at a work as desperado is the sense of confusion it stirs up. Desperado means that all writers are desperate to use all the tricks even invented, to be different, to shock at all costs, to be their own trend.

Q. 3. Which age is known as the Desperado Age?

Ans.: The first few decades of the 20th century, the years between Henry James (at the turning point between the 19th and 20th centuries) and Joyce, Woolf, and Eliot is known as Desperado Age. In 1922, When *Ulysses* and *The Waste Land* were published almost simultaneously there was an age of denial writers who rebelled against established conventions, while apparently challenging literature, trying to replace it with life itself, with absolute periodicity. They did not aim at replacing imagination with reality, but at changing the face of literature telling a story about a past which led inevitably to present which expected a future.

Q. 4. Comment upon the plays of John Osborne.

Ans.: The plays of Osborne made their impact in the theatre by their abusive wrath and self-centeredness as well as by their shock tactics. Osborne had self-admittedly begun to be influenced by Brecht's *Epic Theatre* which meant that he concentrated more on bringing out the theatricality of the play and on discarding dramatic illusion. The play also makes much more direct references to contemporary events and persons. Look back in Anger had greater impact than any of Osborne's is other plays.

Q. 5. Write down some of the major themes of Osborne's plays.

Ans.: A number of themes can be seen to be common to Osborne's work as a whole. The most important of these themes are the relationship between the individual and society which seeks to impose its authority on him or her; the gaps and the common areas between private life and public life; the search for an adequate morality, the discrepancy between thought and action etc. also appeared as major themes of Osborne's work.

Q. 6. What is the relationship between Osborne's married life and the play *Look Back in Anger*?

Ans.: In 1951, Osborne married the actress Pamela Lane and though they divorced in 1957, it was while he was living with her that he wrote *Look Back in Anger*. The portrayal of the married couple was he himself admitted fairly accurate description of his own wedding. Like Alison, Osborne's wife left him while she was pregnant, only unlike Alison, she did not return. Her parent's disapproval of Osborne was so strong that they actually had him followed by a detective during the couple's engagement. So Jimmy's accusing Alison's parents of similar tactics is not as farfetched as it might sound.

Q. 7. Comment upon the action of *Look Back in Anger*.

Ans.: The action of *Look Back in Anger* is primarily psychological. It consists of the fluctuating thoughts, emotions and relationship of the characters and in the expression of these through word stance of gesture. In addition, there are noises or sounds other than language which help to convey the required atmosphere or emotion in performance.

Q. 8. What do you know about Osborne's dramatic language used in his plays?

Ans.: Osborne uses two kinds of stage language for two distinct purposes, self-expression through monologue and social debate through dialogue. Osborne's concern is less to allow each character to develop a distinctive voice than to find a language that can express life equally well on both the personal and the social front.

Q. 9. What do you know about the images used in *Look Back in Anger*?

Ans.: The images in *Look Back in Anger* are mainly verbal and descriptive ones. Words that form pictures and evoke scenes are also noteworthy. Animal imagery runs right though the play, and is not restricted to the 'bear and squirrel game'. In totality a set of images and symbols which, through their recurrence in the text, provide thematic and structural continuity to it.

Q. 10. Write a short note on main postmodern plays of Osborne other than *Look Back in Anger*.

Ans.: The play that followed *Look Back in Anger* was The Entertainer. The action takes places on two main settings the sea—side boarding house where the rice family live and a comedy spot where Archie Rice performs sow scenes at a microphone. It was followed by a musical play *The World of Paul Slickly* and a television play *A Subject of Scandal* and concern, and a historical play *Luther*.

Q. 11. Who wrote the event garde play *Waiting for Godot*?

Ans.: Samuel Beckett wrote *Waiting for Godot* originally in French and then translated into English and gave it the subtitle "A Tragicomedy in Two Acts".

Q. 12. What is the theatre of the Absurd?

Ans.: The Label 'Theater of the Absurd' is often applied to the plays of Engine Ionesco, Jean Genet, Arthum Adamor, Samuel Beckett and the early plays of Edward Albee. The plays by the absurdist playwrights often, start at an arbitrary point and end just as arbitrarily. The arbitrary structure of the plays reflects the arbitrary and irrational nature of life. In fact, the playwright of the absurd views life existentially, he expresses the senselessness of the human condition by abandoning rational devices. Most of the plays express a sense of wonder and incomprehension, and at times despair at the meaningless of human existence. Since they do not believe in a rational and well meaning universe, they do not see any possibility of resolution of the problems they present, either.

Q. 13. Comment on the stage setting in *Waiting for Godot.*

Ans.: Compared to the elaborate stage setting in other plays, in Waiting for Godot, the stage is almost bare and short of stage properties. This is characteristic of Beckett's plays. In this we have an open road a mound of earth and a bare tree as stage setting which is really austere.

Q. 14. Comment upon the static nature of the play *Waiting for Godot.*

Ans.: The entire action takes places at one place and the only movement is from wings to the stage and vice versa. The plot lacks linear progression. There is no basic change in the protagonist's situation. The wait seems endless. The only thing that really moves is time.

Q. 15. What do you know about different artistic forms of Godot?

Ans.: Godot has been made into an opera, a television movie and has also been adapted to two dance recitals. There is even an unauthorized sequel called *Godot Came*, written in 1966 by M. Bulatovio.

Q. 16. Do you think *Godot* is a tragicomedy?

Ans.: Yes, Beckelt himself in his English translation calls Godot a tragicomedy. It is tragic comedy because it combines tragic and comic elements. David Grossvogel speaks of 'part tragedy, part comedy' in the play.

Q. 17. In spite of a tragic scenario building up, the play *Godot* successfully avoids being a tragedy. How is it achieved by Beckett?

Ans.: It cannot be called tragic in the traditional sense as it lacks the kind of sublimity which is believed to be the common attribute of most tragedies. Beckett deals with such a tragic situation of human life comically and thus offers us a subdued form of comedy.

Q. 18. Comment upon the comedy in *Godot.*

Ans.: Its comedy is borrowed from the most direct of all forms of humour, the circus. Here wit of the dialogue, humour of character or situation or mine is note worthy. But the comedy is not unalloyed with more serious implications, so that the total atmosphere is closer to 'dark—comedy'.

Q. 19. *Waiting for Godot* fulfils Sartre's definition of an existentialist play. Justify.

Ans.: *Waiting for Godot* is also about the emptiness of modern world that does not know that it is empty. Characters like Vladimir, Estragon, Lucky and Pozzo are seen struggling with the irrationality of experience. Although Beckett himself is not aware of any such influence, his writings might be described as a literary exposition of Sartre's existentialism. There is a truly astonishing parallel between the existentialist philosophy of Sartre and the creative intuition of Beckett.

Q. 20. Comment upon the structure of *Godot.*

Ans.: The play has a 'symmetrical' structure. The play seems to have been constructed primarily on sets of binaries. This symmetry is evident in the manner Beckett conceives things in pairs; two Acts, two messenger boys and two sets of characters etc.

Q. 21. Is Godot a Christian play?

Ans.: Many commentators have interpreted *Godot* as a religious parable, although Beckett says, 'If by *Godot* I had meant God, I would have said God, not Godot'; But at the same time he uses Christian elements in the play so most critics agree that the play's religious association enliven and enrich its sense of fluidity and ambiguity.

Q. 22. Who is Douglas Adams?

Ans.: Douglas Noel Adams (1952-2001) also known as Bop Ad or Bob after his initials 'DNA' was a famous British comic radio dramatist and author. He was an environmental activist who campaigned on behalf of a number of endangered species. (The Salmon of Doubt) his another major work is Douglas Adam's starship Titanic.

Q. 23. Who is John Agard?

Ans.: A well known poet, playwright, and short-story writer, John Agard (1949) moved to England and became a lecturer for the common wealth Institute. His first book *Man to Pan* (1982) celebrated the street drums of calypso, which won him the ease de les Americas prize.

Q. 24. What do you know about Brian Aldiss?

Ans.: Popularly known as a writer of Science fiction, Brian Aldiss was also a novelist, short-story writer and critic. In 1958 he was voted the most promising new Author at the world Science fiction convention and elected President of the British Science fiction association in 1960. In 1961 he edited anthologies of science fiction entitled Penguin Science fiction.

Q. 25. What is the contribution of Kingsley Amis (1922-95) as an English writer?

Ans.: Kingsley Amis wrote his first novel Lucky Jim (1954) which remains his most popular work. Amis was associated with the social discontent of the 'angry young men' like John Osborne and Stan Barstow. Many of his later books bitingly satirize the middle class British life and its Moses. Along with many others the old Devil (1986, Booker Prize) is a humorous book at the middle-class welsh people. Amis was knighted in 1990. He is often criticized by feminists for his antagonistic representations of women.

Q. 26. How do you rate Martin Amis (1949) as a contemporary British novelist and journalist?

Ans.: He is known for a memoir entitled 'Experience' which is largely based on his relationship with his author father, Sir Kingsley Amis. At the age of 21 he wrote his first novel, *The Rachel Papers* (1973), which won him the Somerset Maugham Award in 1974.

Q. 27. Who is Edward St. Aubym?

Ans.: Edward St. Aubym is acclaimed in the U.K. as one of the most original, intelligent and witty voices of his times. His trilogy is characterized as fiction of truly rare and extra-ordinary quality. His novels are hilarious and harrowing. He wrote on a variety of subject ranging from childhood, sex, parties etc. "On the Edge" was shortlisted for the Guardian fiction prize in 1998. His writings reflect his deep and penetrating sociological and psychological insights.

Q. 28. What do you know about Beryl Bainbridge?

Ans.: Great novelist, Bainbridge, nominated several times for the Booker prize, has been described as one of the greatest living British novelists. She wrote many novels and short-stories.

Her most recent novel, *According to Queeney* (2001) is a fictionalized account of the last years of the life of Samuel Johnson.

Q. 29. Who wrote *Lord of the Flies*?

Ans.: William Golding, great novelist, recipient of the 1983 Nobel Prize for Literature, wrote his first novel Lord of the Flies, which did not appear until 1954 due to being rejected by various publishers a number of times. Later it has been translated into various languages and filmed in 1963 and 1990. This novel deals with the conflict between humanity's innate barbarism and the civilizing influence of reason. This book revealed the darkness of man's heart.

Q. 30. Write about major works of William Golding?

Ans.: Golding's Lord of the Flies was followed by the *Inheritors* (1953) which tells of man's brutal extermination. His subsequent works include the *Pyramid* (1967), *The Scorpion God* (1971), *Darkness Visible* (1979) and *Rites of Passage* (1980), which won him the Booker prize. *The Paper Men* (1984), *Fire Down Below* (1989) and the *Double Tongue* (1995) are his other notable works.

Q. 31. What do you know about Philip Larkin?

Ans.: Philip Arthur Larkin (1922-85) an English poet, novelist, critic and essayist was a prominent figure of 'The Movement' a group of British poets who joined together during the 1950 when the 'Angry young Men' also emerged on the literary scene of England. He was deeply influenced by Auden Lawrence and Yeats. In 1943 three of his poems were included in Oxford poetry.

Q. 32. Write a short note on Philip Larkin as a poet?

Ans.: As a poet, Larkin made his debut with his collection 'The Northship' in 1945. It was followed by two novels *Jill* (1946) and A Girl in Winter (1947). Later The Marvell Tress Book, initially called various poems, was published as The less deceived, which established, him thereafter in the front rank of modern British poets. A privately printed Pamphlet *xx poems* (1951), marked the emergence of his true poetic voice and its publication brought Larkin's mature work before the public for the first time. His next collection the Whitsun Weddings, which appeared in 1964, confirmed his reputation as one of the foremost figures in 20th century poetry. He edited the Oxford Books of Twentieth century English verse (1973).

Q. 33. Narrate the reasons why Doris Lessing became a prominent figure.

Ans.: A towering figure of British Literature, Doris Lessing wrote novels, short stories, science fiction, realist novel, poems and plays. Lessing's fiction is deeply autobiographical. In her writings she focuses on the clash of cultures, the gross injustice of racial inequality, and the conflict between the individual conscience and the collective good. In 1985 she published *The Good Terrorist*, which was shortlisted for the Booker Prize and won him the W.H. Smith Literary Award for 1985, and The Italian Mondello Prize.

Q. 34. Write a short note on Doris Lessing's famous novel *The Golden Notebook* (1962).

Ans.: *The Golden Notebook* is a daring narrative experiment in which the multiple selves of a contemporary woman are rendered in astonishing depth and detail. This book was hailed as a landmark by the women's movement. Undoubtedly it is Lessing's most acclaimed and innovative novel and has been translated into several languages and was awarded the Frix Prix Medicis in 1976.

Q. 35. Doris Lessing as the major contemporary British writer.

Ans.: Doris Lessing's writing spans an exceptionally wide range of genres, settings and narrative techniques, but is unified by certain persistent concerns. The analysis of contemporary culture and of social process, a sense of 20th century history as catastrophic and an attempt to link this to personal unhappiness, a mystical and sometimes utopian emphasis on higher states of consciousness, an intense anger on social injustice and an interest in sexual relations are sufficient enough to Proov Doris Lessing as the major contemporary British writer.

Q. 36. Comment upon the scholarship in Halold Pinter's drama.

Ans.: Scholarship in Pinter's drama is chiefly of three kinds; the socio-psychological approach with its emphasis on the problem of failure in communication, the symbolic—allegorical approach with emphasis on the ideas that are inherent in the plays and the theatrical approach with its concern with stage effects.

Q. 37. Comment upon the influence of Beckett and Kafka on Pinter.

Ans.: Like the works of Beckett and Kafka, Pinter's plays, in their reflections on life and death and on cosmic concept, gain positive metaphysical heights. Pinter also admits the influence and says 'when I read them (Kafka and Beckett) it rang a bell, that's all within me too'. Ben and Gus in his The Dumb Waiter, like Vladimir and Estragon know nothing of the motives or goals. They are like Kafka's characters, utterly confused and helplessly trapped.

Q. 38. Write a short note on Illusion and Reality in Pinter's Plays.

Ans.: In Pinter's plays illusion is as undefined as reality, for illusion is changed with the changing reality. Through interplay of physical realities and mental constructs Pinter's men try to circumvent the ambiguity of life. They weave the tapestry of illusions with yarns of reality.

Q. 39. Comment upon major essential Pinter-techniques used in his plays.

Ans.: One of the essential Pinter-techniques is that of game-and-role playing. Pinter's games are usually played as a flight from reality e.g. blind man's buff (The Birthday Party), the game of throwing knife between James and Bill (The Collection) improvised game of cricket (The Basement). His plays are full of images related to game playing because game offers the possibility of the release of tension and hostility. Game becomes a social ritual, enacting social intercourse.

Q. 40. Present a brief introduction of Ted Hughes and his works.

Ans.: Poet Laureate of England and one of the most controversial poets and literary figures of his time, Ted Hughes wrote fiction, plays, stories for children, and essays. He edited a number of books and translated great authors like Ovid and Aeschylus, Euripides & Racine. He married Sylvia Plath in 1956 and edited her Aerial poems during late 1960. His first collection of poems, 'The Hawk in the Rain' (1957) attracted considerable critical acclaim. He had written most of the Wodwo poems, which marked a turning point in Hughes' poetry.

Q. 41. Name the major contemporary British authors.

Ans.: Beryl Bainbridge, J.G. Ballend, A.L. Barker, Pat Barker, Julian Barnes, Peter Barnes, Nina Bawden, John Berger, Louis de Bernieru, Robert Bolt Edward, Bond, A.S Byatt, Arthen C,

Clarke, Carol Clewlow, John Michael Coelzee, William Cooper, Jim Grace, Penelope Fitzgerald, Michael Frayn, Esther Freud, Stephen Fry, David Lodge etc. are major names in the field of contemporary British Literature.

Q. 42. Establish Beryl Bainbridge as a great writer.

Ans.: Great novelist, Bainbridge, nominated several times for the Booker prize, has been described as one of the greatest living British novelists. She began her career as an actress before writing her first novel *Harriet Said* (1972). *Mum and Mr. Armitage* is a collection of her short stories. Her most recent novel *According to Queeney* (2001) is a fictionalized account of the last years of the life of Samuel Johnson.

Q. 43. What do you know about Julian Barnes?

Ans.: Reputed novelist, essayist, writer of short stories and non-fiction, and translator, Julian Barnes, is known for his debut novel *Metroland* (1980), followed by *Before She Met Me*, (1982). His next book *Flaubert's Parrot* (1984) was shortlisted for the Booker Prize for fiction and won the Geoffrey Faber memorial prize. Barnes work is witty and parodic. His preoccupation with the contemporary life is evident in the essayistic and philosophical aspects of his work, which is a constant point of reference for Julian Barnes. He is the voice of one of the most distinguished and refined intellectuals in the literary scenes of contemporary Britain.

Q. 44. Write a short note on the contemporary British writer John Berger.

Ans.: Highly acclaimed novelist, painter and art historian, John Berger became well-known as a broadcaster and journalist whose writings reflect his Marxist views. His novels reflect both his Marxism in their attention to the oppressive structures of society and his painting in their vivid realization of sensual detail *Painter of our Time* (1958), *Corker's Freedom* (1964) *Pig Barth* (1979) *The Success and Failure of Picasso* (1965) are his major works.

Q. 45. Who is known as one of the Modern Masters of Science fiction?

Ans.: Arthur C. Clarke, a British author and inventor is widely known as one of the modern masters of sciences fiction. With the release of science fiction series 2001: A Space Odyssey, Clarke became a commentator on science and technology. He penned more than 600 articles and short stories dozens of novels etc. He was knighted in 1998.

29

Literary Theory and Criticism up to T.S. Eliot

Q. 1. What is Judicial criticism?

Ans.: Criticism where the critic acts as a judge and pronounces his judgment after considering the merits and demerits or the work of the author is known as judicial criticism. Mostly it is seen that in his work he is dealing with the debate that comes first and then conclusion follows it.

Q. 2. What is Genre criticism?

Ans.: Influence of the past writers upon the present comes into genre criticism. Traditional view of point is also important in genre criticism. It places a work into definite literary setting. In it we study a literary piece in relation with the precious worries of the same kind.

Q. 3. What do you understand by the term Biographical criticism?

Ans.: To write a man's literary work in the light of his life is biographical criticism. The trouble is that sometimes we force too much of his life into his writings and make it unbelievable.

Q. 4. Explain Impressionistic criticism.

Ans.: The immediate impression left on the mind of the critic comes under Impressionistic criticism. It is quite personal and subjective. This does not tell much about the work but about the excitement, enjoyment which the critic feels. Virginia Woolf describes it in an interesting manner, "Dip yourself into the pool (Poetry) to write about it while you are still dripping." Walter Pater is also a popular impressionist critic of the modern time.

Q. 5. What do you know about New criticism?

Ans.: The belief of the new critic was to focus attention on the words on the page. Each poem is autonomous self sufficient or complete within itself. Critic feels that one should keep out biography and no psychology is required T.S. Eliot says that the function of the critic is to focus his attention not on the poet but on the poem.

Q. 6. Define feminist criticism.

Ans.: Feminist criticism has depended on the findings of modern feminists. Heavily drawing of Barthes, Lacan and Derrida, the feminist critics are more concerned with the concept 'gender' and use of language in literary texts. Helen Cixous, Julia Kristeva and Gayatry Chakravorty Kate Millett, Simone de Beauviur Spivak are the main names.

Q. 7. Define Linguistic criticism.

Ans.: Structuralism criticism comes from this linguistic criticism. The Russian Formalists, Viktor Shklovsky, Eichen Rosenbaum, Roman Jacobson and Boris Tynyanov, were the first to apply the principles of linguistics in literary Criticism. According to them the author's perception of reality is coded linguistically in the text itself.

Q. 8. Write down the points on which criticism should be studied.

Ans.: Criticism should be studied to find fault, to judge, to evaluate, to explicate, to establish rules, principles and to provide a fresh current of ideas to creative writers.

Q. 9. Give any three definitions of criticism.

Ans.: (i) "Criticism is the exercise of judgment in the province of art and literature"—Borris Worsfold.

(ii) "Criticism is the commentation and exposition of works of art by means of written words"— T.S. Eliot

(iii) "Criticism is the art of interpreting art"—Walter Pater

Q. 10. (a). Write a short note on three types of literary criticism.

Ans.: Literary criticism can be of three kinds- Legislative, theoretical and descriptive. In legislative criticism the critic assumes the role of teaching the writer how to write and of prescribing for him the rules which should guide him in literary composition. Legislative criticism often becomes magisterial or dictatorial. Theoretical criticism is concerned with the abstract question of literary aesthetics. Finally in the descriptive criticism the critic places himself in the position of a mediator between the writer and the reader.

Q. 11. Write the name of two divided groups of Psychological school of criticism along with their meanings.

Ans.: The Psychological school aspires to render criticism more scientific by an increased application of Psychological knowledge to its problems. This is divided into two groups, one of which would 'explain' works of art from a complete knowledge of the psychology of the artist. While the other finds more attractive psychological investigation of the processes of appreciation.

Q. 12. Write the main trends in psycho analytical criticism.

Ans.: In the first place there is the psychoanalytic vogue in modern criticism. The discoveries of psychoanalysis have turned out to be of immense value to literary criticism. A psychoanalytic critic is, therefore, confronted with the task of exploring the hidden motives or unconscious urges behind a work of art. The psychoanalytical criticism thus aims at 'the search for realities of the self behind social marks'.

Q. 13. What is the relationship of life, literature and criticism?

Ans.: Criticism derives its existence from Literature, as literature does form life, and it works upon what literature creates. A piece of criticism may show such insight, imagination, learning and command of language that it may be superior to the work that prompted it.

Q. 14. What do you know about qualifications of a critic?

Ans.: A critic who is to be a master of his craft needs a special equipment for his task, and his success will depend greatly upon a natural aptitude for it. He must be form in his standards but responsive to new impressions, sensitive, penetrating, and wise. Critic should be face from bias, able to pronounce on a literary question without regard to any other consideration, political, religious, or anything else.

Q. 15. What do you know about Mathew Arnold's views regarding the qualification of a critic?

Ans.: According to Mathew Arnold a critic must have "knowledge, and ever fresh knowledge", which he can pass on to his readers. A critic should have traveled widely and "every critic should try and possess one great literature, at least, besides his win".

Q. 16. What is Katharsis?

Ans.: The word 'Katharsis', or 'catharsis' has been derived from the Greek language and it is interpreted with different meanings like 'Purgation' or 'purification'. The great writer and critic, Aristotle used the word 'Katharsis' in the 'Poetics', but only at the limited places.

Q. 17. What is Aristotle's conception of Katharsis?

Ans.: In writing in the 'Poetics', about the function of tragedy, Aristotle's following words are significant "Through pity and fear effecting the proper Katharsis, or purgation of these emotions." Though Aristotle himself did not explain the term 'Katharsis' clearly and in detail, yet he indicated the significance of the term particularly for the modern critics. Aristotle relates its use only with the purification, or purgation of human feelings like those of pity and fear.

Q. 18. What do you know about 'Tragic catharsis?

Ans.: According to Aristotle, the chief aim of a true and ideal tragedy is to bring about 'tragic catharsis' through the emotional changes of pity and fear. It should be connected with soul purgation and an emotional purification. All mean feelings and ideas are automatically discarded and they give place to pity, fear and noble feelings.

Q. 19. What is the Purgation theory?

Ans.: As a medicine makes the healing effect on one's body, so 'catharsis' makes the healing effect on one's feeling or soul. A true tragedy makes the purgation or purification of the evil emotions of pity and fear from the human mind. In the neo-classical period, as an allopathic treatment 'catharsis' was adopted for curing with the unlike. It was considered to bring about purgation of other emotions like anger, pride etc. John Milton, too, discussed the idea of purgation or catharsis in the preface to 'Samson Agonists".

Q. 20. What is the meaning of purification theory?

Ans.: According to Humphrey House's 'Purification Theory', Catharsis brings about the purification of our emotions. Butcher also expresses his views on purification theory, "The tragic Katharsis involves not only the ideal of emotional relief, but the further idea of purifying, the emotions so relieved". Humphrey did not agree with the idea of purgation medically because he was the strong supporter of the 'Purification Theory'. Through that he laid stress on moral instruction and moral bearing. It may be termed as 'moral conditioning'. It helped in ideal equilibrium.

Q. 21. Write a note on poetic truth.

Ans.: Aristotle says that poetic truth is much higher and universal than other branches of literature. He says that 'it is not function of the poet to relate what has happened, but what may happen'. A poet shares one Philosophical Quest for ultimate truth. The poet aims at imparting a new shape to a universal truth.

Q. 22. Write a note on the contribution of poetics.

Ans.: The contribution of poetics to literary criticism is great. Aristotle's own logical bias enabled him to bring out the rational element of poetry. He has traced the origin and development of poetry. In chapter XXVI of 'the Poetics,' he has compared Tragedy with Epic and showed it superior. Both Epic and Tragedy initiate serious subjects in a grand kind of verse. He imparted a new concept to poetry and initiation.

Q. 23. Write an ideal theory of criticism.

Ans.: The poetry is an idealized presentation of human life. It is of immense critical value. It has given birth to various literary interpretations. Aristotle's purpose was to discuss poetry, especially tragedy and comedy and epic poetry. Aristotle's poetics is a treatise on the art of fiction. His theory of initiation applies to fiction also. He believes that all arts are based on the common principle of initiation.

Q. 24. Write a short note on Longinus as a critic.

Ans.: Longinus chose an entirely new method of criticism. Longinus turned to passion with poetry that pleases us greatly. The chief contribution of Longinus lies in the fact that it was he who re-established the imaginative and aesthetic insight of Plato. He raised totally different questions about literature from those raised earlier either by Plato or Aristotle.

Q. 25. Write a short note on Horace's perception about diction and choice of words in poetry.

Ans.: Horace emphasized that the poet must be specifically attentive in the selection of words. Poet can invent new words to create an appropriate utterance. According to him the author of the proposed poem should show taste and care in linking up his words. In reference of poetic diction, it can never be superlatively sacred.

Q. 26. What do you know about Horace's famous work 'The art of Poetry' (The Art Poetica)?

Ans.: Horace's The Art of Poetry is a statement of poetic theory as well as a frank declaration of certain values. It is a challenge to the condition of anarchies, spread in the world of art and letters. Quintus Horatius Flaecus, popularly known as Horace, has made a systematic study of poetry. In his view poetry is not a statement of absolute truth. It is, in reality, a blend of fiction, facts and fancy. Art Poetica is a skilful piece of writing, a great work of criticism.

Q. 27. How far it is correct to call Dryden as the first English critic to take criticism seriously?

Ans.: Saintsbury said rightly that Dryden set the fashion of criticizing just as Shakespeare set the fashion of dramatizing. Dryden is the first English critic who took criticism seriously and thought deeply over all the problems connected with literature like the nature and functions of poetry, dramatic art, epic, satire, translation, respective merits of rhyme and blank verse, prose and criticism itself. Besides his theoretical criticism, we have his judicial criticism also. He has given us brilliant appreciations of Chaucer, Shakespeare, Beaumont and Fletcher and Ben Jonson. Dr. Johnson is justified when he calls Dryden 'the father of English criticism'.

Q. 28. Write a note on Dryden as a father of Descriptive Criticism.

Ans.: English criticism before Dryden was either legislative or theoretical. Dryden for the first time, started the practice of writing, descriptive criticism. 'An Essay of Dramatic Poetry' and the 'Preface to the Fables' are the real fine examples of descriptive criticism in English literature. George Watson said, "The first Englishman to attempt any extended descriptive criticism was John Dryden."

Q. 29. Why do we call Dryden as the father of comparative criticism?

Ans.: Dryden is the father of comparative criticism in England. Dryden has adopted a very rational attitude, and he discarded an ancient rule when he does not find it suitable for his purpose. In his comparative method of criticism when he wanted to analyze the merits and demerits of any writer, he placed him in comparison with some other ancient or modern writer. He is the first critic in England to analyze English and foreign plays and examine their comparative merits and demerits.

Q. 30. Discuss Dryden as Pioneer of Historical Criticism.

Ans.: Dryden is the first English critic to make use of the historical method of criticism. He argues that we should judge literature in its proper historical perspective, taking into consideration all the changes that took place in a particular age. Dryden recognizes the truth that literature is not static, but a dynamic process. Saintsbury very rightly says that "Dryden is almost phenomenally able to see merits in all literary camps."

Q. 31. Discuss Dryden as Pioneer of Liberal Classicism.

Ans.: Dryden is the pioneer of liberal classicism. His liberal classicism is seen in his noble defense of the tragie-comedy. In the same way he recognizes that blind adherence to the unities often has a cramping effect and results in absurdities. That's why he prefers the irregular English plays to the more regular French plays. Dryden is most penetrating, delightful and original when he breaks free from the 'rules' and trusts to his own judgments. David Daichis appreciates Dryden's freedom from the classical rules (Aristotle etc.) and his power of independent judgment.

Q. 32. Comment upon originality in Dryden as a critic.

Ans.: Dryden did not like slavish initiation and asserted and elaborated the merits of the English drama over and above the French drama. Atkins praises Dryden's originality as a critic. T.S. Eliot also says that the great significance of Dryden's criticism is that he introduced the native element in literature.

Q. 33. Write a note on limitation of Dryden as a critic.

Ans.: It has been pointed out that Dryden is inconsistent, betrays imperfect knowledge, and sometimes gives too much concession to tradition and classical authority. Dr. Johnson pointed to the inconsistency in Dryden's attitude to rhyming plays and his lack of logic in refuting hostile critics, or in defending some license of his own. There were also occasional inaccuracies in his statements.

Q. 34. Write an introduction of Wordsworth's Poetic diction.

Ans.: Wordsworth came forward with his theory of poetic diction as a reaction against pseudo classical excesses. The ideas of distinct poetical diction developed to such an extent that the simple name of common things could not be used in poetry and paraphrases of some kind has to be invariably employed. For example, the birds became 'the plumy race' etc.

Q. 35. What is metre, according to Wordsworth?

Ans.: According to Wordsworth, metre is an additional source of pleasure, so its use is desirable, but not essential to poetry. The use of artificial poetic devices is not useless but actually harmful, when the poet speaks through his characters, the language used must be appropriate to character and situation. He comments that, "there neither is, nor can there be any essential difference between the language of prose and that of metrical composition".

Q. 36. What was the purpose of William Wordsworth in writing *The Preface to the Lyrical Ballads*?

Ans.: Wordsworth's purpose in writing The Preface was to bring about a revolution in poetic taste. His preface is in the nature of a defense of his theory that poetry must be written in a selection of the real language of men, when in a state of emotional excitement. Preface was written to explain his point of view and win recognition for his poems.

Q. 37. State the reasons why Wordsworth has chosen the various aspects of humble and rustic life?

Ans.: The reasons are as follows: (a) in humble and rustic life feelings are freely and frankly expressed (b) in rustic life feelings are more simple, and so are expressed more accurately and forcefully (c) the manners of the rustics are not sophisticated. They are simple, and so more conducive to an understanding of human nature, and (d) in rustic life, human passions are connected with the grand and noble objects of nature, and so they are more noble and permanent.

Q. 38. What are the qualifications of a Poet, according to Wordsworth?

Ans.: According to Wordsworth, a Poet is essentially a man speaking to men. A poet writes not for his pleasure alone, but for the pleasure of his readers. A poet is man who has greater and more lively sensibility, greater power of imagination, greater knowledge of human nature and greater powers of communication also.

Q. 39. Did Coleridge agree with Wordsworth's view on metre?

Ans.: No, Coleridge did not agree. In opposition to Wordsworth, S.T. Coleridge believes that meter is not something super added but an organic part of poetry. He regrets that Wordsworth has not given one independent and elaborate treatment to this subject.

Q. 40. What do you think about Coleridge's criticism of Wordsworth's theory of Poetic Diction?

Ans.: According to Coleridge, language of poetry and prose should be different to some extent. No two persons speak language alike and Coleridge writes in meter. He thinks that a poem is essentially a metrical composition.

Q. 41. Why Coleridge is known as a great dreamer of dreams?

Ans.: Coleridge took keen interest in illusions, hallucinations, magic and dreams. The dream quality of his poetry is essentially a romantic trait. He escapes from the world of reality into the mystic world of dreams. His poetry is, therefore, entirely a subjective affair; it has got nothing to do with the material world. That's why he is known as a great dreamer of dreams.

Q. 42. What is the threefold duty of the critic, according to Arnold?

Ans.: According to Arnold, the critic has a duty towards society. His task is to make best ideas prevail and make an intellectual situation of which the creative power can profitably avail itself. The critic in relation to society has a threefold function to perform. Firstly, his task is to learn and understand, to see a thing as in itself it really is. Secondly, the duty of the critic is to convert the world into an intellectual place where the best ideas prevail. And thirdly, the critic is to create an atmosphere and to promote a current of ideas in the higher degree.

Q. 43. "Arnold's criticism is wild and varied". Prove.

Ans.: The criticism of Arnold is wild and varied. Arnold's works can be divided into social and political, religious and theological writings and literary criticism. While his literary criticism directs our attention to the weaknesses of English writers, i.e. their eccentricity or arbitrariness, their complacency, their provinciality and their insensitiveness, his social criticism is the real outcome of his earlier literary criticism.

Q. 44. Write about Arnold's poetic qualities.

Ans.: Arnold was a poet turned critic. He switches over to criticism after having first tried his hand at poetry. George Watson says, "Arnold's criticism measures the distance between his ambition as a poet and his performance." Even his prose is the prose of a poet.

Q. 45. Write a note on Eliot as a great poet critic.

Ans.: T.S. Eliot is one of the long-lists of poet critics extending from Sir Philip-Sidney to our own day and including such names as Ben Jonson, Dryden, Johnson, Wordsworth, Coleridge and Arnold. Eliot's five hundred and one odd essays published as reviews and articles from time to time, have had a far-reaching influence on the course of literary criticism in the country. Eliot really made English criticism look different. His criticism is revolutionary.

Q. 46. What do you know about Eliot's essay 'Tradition and Individual Talent'?

Ans.: The essay 'Tradition and Individual Talent' was first published in 1919 in the Times Literary Supplement as a critical article. The essay may be regarded as an unofficial manifesto of Eliot's critical creed, for it contains all those critical principles from which his criticism has been derived ever since. It tells us about Eliot's concept of tradition, his theory of the impersonality of poetry and summing up of the whole discussion.

Q. 47. What is Eliot's theory of Impersonality of Poetry?

Ans.: The artist must acquire greater and greater objectivity. His emotions and passions must be depersonalized; he must be as impersonal and objective as a scientist. The personality of the artist is not important; the important thing is his sense of tradition. Poet must forget his personal joy and sorrows, and be absorbed in acquiring a sense of tradition and expressing it in his poetry.

Q. 48. Why does T.S. Eliot consider Wordsworth's formula 'emotion recollected in tranquility' as being inadequate?

Ans.: Eliot's considers Wordsworth's theory inadequate for defining the poetic process, for it's something new which emerges out of the concentration of experience within the Eliot's mind and is thus a kind of escape from his personality. Rejecting romantic subjectivism Eliot says,

"Poetry is not a twining loose of emotion, but an escape from emotion. It's not the expression of the personality, but an escape from personality."

Q. 49. Mention some faults of Eliot as a critic.

Ans.: As a critic Eliot has his faults, and some of them are quite glorious ones. Sometimes he is pontifical and instead of sympathetic understanding, his prouncements savour of a verdict. Often his criticism is marked by personal and religious prejudices, and dislike of the man comes in the way of an honest and impartial estimate. In this respect, he does not live up to his own theory of the objectivity and impersonality of poetry. Moreover, he does not judge all by the same standards of criticism.

Q. 50. What is the news of Eliot regarding the word tradition?

Ans.: T.S. Eliot began 'Tradition and Individual Talent' with the word 'Tradition', not used in the positive sense. People in his time did not consider tradition to be a positive quality but Eliot said that it should be positive. Eliot used this word in a dialectical relationship to the views of his times. He wanted to assure us that writer should be aware of the tradition and it should have desire to use it.

Q. 51. D.H. Lawrence said, "trust the tale and not the teller." In what sense it is important for criticism?

Ans.: A critic de-codes a poem, gives meaning through language. Language is a system of signs. International fallacy—the fable being that the author's intention can be found in his work, is also a matter of debate. According to Dr. Johnson, artist's intention is not available, even if it is available, it is not dependable and even if it is dependable, it is not believable. Thus Lawrence meant that the meaning of the work is in the work nor in the mind of the author, it is born in the transaction between the reader and the author.

Q. 52. Comment upon the doctrine of the objective correlative.

Ans.: T.S. Eliot along with Pound and Hulme derived this doctrine from the theory and practice of the French symbolists, who argued that poetry cannot express emotion directly, emotion can only be evoked. Objective correlative is a term introduced by T.S. Eliot in an essay on "Hamlet and his Problems" (1919).

Q. 53. What do you know about "dissociation of sensibility"?

Ans.: Dissociation of sensibility was a phrase introduced into literary criticism by T.S. Eliot in his essay "The Metaphysical Poets" (1921). Eliot's claim was that the metaphysical poets of the earlier 17th century, like the Elizabethan and Jacobean dramatists "possessed a mechanism of sensibility which could devour any kind of experience".

30

Contemporary Theory

Q. 1. Define Structuralism.

Ans.: Structuralism is complementary to formation. A structuralist critic views the work of literature as a kind of meeting place for different systems of meaning. Levi-Strauss and Barthes have given a new direction to structuralism in their practice of criticism. But a criticism of structuralism is that to discern structures and recurrent patterns. Binary oppositions in literature is not necessary to see what makes literature great or significant.

Q. 2. Who was Ferdinand de Saussure?

Ans.: Structuralism owes its origins to the Swiss linguist Ferdinand de Saussure's idea of the sign as a union of signifies and the signified. The term 'Structuralism' refers to the works of structural linguists like Saussure and Jacobson. Saussure conceived of language as a sign system that communicates in relationship or inter-dependence. According to him the relationship between the signifier and one signified is arbitrary. He is the first linguist to treat language as a system of signs.

Q. 3. Write a short note about the origin of Marxist criticism.

Ans.: Marxist criticism is a descendant of the realistic criticism of 19th century. This criticism developed as a coherent theory only after the Russian revolution. The actual Marxist movement in American literary criticism was very short-lived. The most outstanding Marxist critic is Gyorgy Luckacs. Marxist criticism is at its best when it saves as a device to expose the latest social and ideological implications of a work of art.

Q. 4. When and how the psycho-analytic criticism of literature began?

Ans.: The psycho-analytic criticism of literature began with the publication of Freud's 'Interpretation of Dreams' in 1900. Attempts at psycho-analytic criticism have been made by Cowered Aiken, Herbert Read, Trilling, Wilson, Kenneth Brown etc. I.A. Richard's great contribution lies in the evaluation of various psychological views of art and his three great books are *The Foundations of Aesthetics* (1921), *The Principles of Literary Criticism* (1924) and *Practical Criticism* (1929).

Q. 5. What do you understand by 'New Criticism'?

Ans.: Much talked about recent American criticism—the 'New Criticism' derived its title from John Crowe Ranson's *The New Criticism* (1941). The pioneers of New Criticism are T.S. Eliot and I.A. Richards. The New Critics concentrate exclusively on the language of poetry and account for its structure in terms of the layers of meaning the words are charged with. In fact, the New Critics make a twofold semantic division of language into denotation and connotation, the former being the literal or dictionary meaning which suffices. Each new critic has a basic principle to evaluate a work of art.

Q. 6. What is the aim of Myth Criticism?

Ans.: Myth Criticism aims at discovering behind all literature the original myths of mankind. G. Wilson Knight and Herbert Read have used Ingrain concepts, and C. Day Lewis explained poetic imagery in terms of the survival of mythical thinking. This Myth criticism under the influence of Frazer and Jung arose as a reaction to the New Criticism and became a great force in the 1950s in USA.

Q. 7. Who is the pioneer of Deconstruction?

Ans.: Deconstructionism emerged in late sixties and early seventies. Derrida, a philosopher by training has started deconstruction. Derrida does not distinguish between literature and other discipline like psychology, philosophy and linguistics. Deconstruction shows it clearly that the writer deconstructs whatever he constructs.

Q. 8. What is the difference between metaphysical criticism and deconstructive criticism?

Ans.: The metaphysical criticism assumes that the text has a definite meaning which the critic is supposed to highlight, whereas the deconstructive criticism believes in the indeterminacy of meaning. Deconstructionist believes that the writer at once 'affirm' and 'unaffirms' his meaning.

Q. 9. Write a short note on the Reader-response criticism.

Ans.: The Reader-response criticism centres around the elusive relationship between the text and the reader. The identity of the text and the response of the reader are crucial issues in 'reader-response criticism'. The nature of the text and the personality of the reader are vital issues that concern the critics. Some believe that the text is there before the reader takes it and will be there after the reader leaves it. Hence the text is important. Others think unless there is reader, there is no use of text.

Q. 10. Comment upon the validity of 'New Criticism'.

Ans.: Apart from emphasis on language the New Criticism has taken the organisation of a poem seriously. Influenced by Coleridge, New Criticism asserted that in a good literary work form and matter are interpenetrated. This leads the New Critics to demonstrate that each individual word in a work of art not merely contributes to the total meaning of the work, but it also derives its exact meaning from its place in the work. The validity of the New Criticism lies in the fact that it takes the poem as a work of art, a structure having an independent existence.

Q. 11. What do you know about Derrida's new concept of writing?

Ans.: Derrida's new concept of writing is based on three complex words: 'difference', 'trace' and 'arche-writing'. According to Derrida each sign performs double function differing and deferring. Hence, the structure of the sign is conditioned by differing and not by the signifier and the signified. It follows that the sign has to disappear to give meaning. Sign has no fixed meaning for its meaning is contextual. He reinterprets Saussure to establish that language is a free play without a centre and as such incapable of conveying truth. Literature is a form of writing.

Q. 12. What do you understand by 'Logocentricism' and 'Graphcentrism'?

Ans.: According to Derrida the traditional concepts of speech and writing are 'Logocentric'. Apart from 'Logocentrism', Derrida introduces another term 'graphocentricism'. It makes it clear that a unit of writing has not relevance other than simply representing a voice. Therefore graphocentricism can mean the shift in importance from speech to writing. Critics observe that Derrida is effecting a shift from logocentricism to graphocentricism.

Q. 13. What is the main strength and weakness of the theory of deconstruction?

Ans.: According to Derrida, in spite of the 'difference' (difference + deference) that the author makes between one word and another, he can never express his meaning accurately and exactly. He must always mean more than and something different from that he indicates through writing (ecriture). The critic should take the words of writers merely as 'trace' or indicator of his meaning. Here criticism becomes an endless pursuit and the critic becomes a co-creator who takes the text over from the author. The major strength and weakness of this theory is that it takes off well but it does not land us anywhere.

Q. 14. Write a short note how I.A. Richards used the word 'imagination' in six distinct senses.

Ans.: I.A. Richards said that there are at least six distinct senses in which the word 'imagination' is used. The First sense means the 'production of vivid images, usually visual images'.

Second—use of emotive language

Thirdly—word imagination is taken in an ordinary sense—plainly a necessity for communication.

Fourthly—in the sense of inventiveness, 'the bringing together of elements which are not ordinarily connected'.

Fifth—bringing relevant connection of things normally thought of as disparate.

Sixth—this is an ordering of experience in definite end or purpose.

Q. 15. What do you understand by 'Feminist Literary Criticism'?

Ans.: Feminist Literary Criticism primarily responds to the way woman is presented in literature. It has two basic premises. One, 'woman' presented in literature by male writers from their own viewpoint and two, 'woman' presented in the writings of female writers from their point of view. First is known as 'Phallocentrisism' and the second leads as to 'Gynocriticism'. Theoretical foundation of feminist criticism is said to be laid by Simone de Beauvoir's 'The Second Sex'.

Q. 16. Name three major books that deserve special mention in the field of Anglo-American Feminist Literary Criticism.

Ans.: (i) Katharine M. Roger's *The Troublesome Helpmate* (1996), (ii) Mary Ellmann's *Thinking about Women* (1968), (iii) Kate Millett's *Sexual Politics* (1969), provided a strong base for the development of Anglo-American Feminist criticism.

Q. 17. In what sense Feminism can be known as an ideology?

Ans.: Feminism is an ideology which seeks not only to understand the world but to change it to the advantage of women. Simone asserts that 'one is not born but becomes a woman'. Gynocritics seek to formulate a female frame-work for the analysis of women's literature to develop new models based on the study of female experience rather than to adopt male models and theories.

Q. 18. Comment upon working of Gynocritics.

Ans.: Gynocritics take into account the feminist research done in the field of anthropologies, history, psychology and sociology to formulate their critical principles. Working as 'gynocritics' women had tried reducing male-created texts producing a literary category as 'the women-centred' criticism. The feminist critique involves the feminist as a reader offering different interpretations of the images of women projected in the male created texts. Women critics by way of challenging and recasting the male gaze in literature, rewrite and recreate the male-created texts from the feminist perspective.

Q. 19. What do you understand by the phrase 'the absence of the author'?

Ans.: With the advent of linguistics and structuralism, the meaning itself began to disappear. Barthes goes beyond Eliot in announcing the death of the author. The absence of the author leads us to the preposition that the text does not have a fixed meaning but a plurality of meanings. Deconstructionists deny the author. New Critics, by emphasizing that the poem is on the printed page, had banished the empirical author from the text. Now by saying that the meaning is not in one text but in the mind of the reader, the Reader-Response critics indirectly subscribe to the idea of the death or the absence of the author.

Q. 20. Who speaks about the presence of the author and how?

Ans.: Michael Foucault accepts the presence of the author emphatically in his essay 'What is an Author?' Foucault states that the author's name serves to characterize a certain mode of being of discourse. The author as a person is in his work as a certain functional principle. Foucault has mentioned four author—functions by which one impedes the free circulation, the free manipulation, the free composition, decomposition and re-composition of fiction.

Q. 21. What do you know about the origin of New Historicism?

Ans.: In the 1980s came the New Historicism as a reaction against earlier schools of criticism—particularly against Formalism, Structuralism and Deconstruction to 'rehistorize' literary texts. The term 'New Historicism' was coined by Stephen Greenblatt in 1982 to describe his method of interpretation of the Renaissance texts. The term occurs in his book, *The Power of Forms and the Forms of Power in the Renaissance* (1982). Some of the leading exponents of New Historicism are Greenblatt, Jonathan Goldbers, Jean Howard, Edword Pechter and Louis Advin Montrose.

Q. 22. What is 'cultural poetics' and what is the main idea behind this school of criticism?

Ans.: After coving the term 'New Historicism', Greenblatt had second thoughts about it. He said that he used this term inadvertently and would prefer 'cultural poetics' to it. The idea behind is that history is something like a determinate text and therefore knowable. And literature reflects directly or indirectly historical reality. What is more radical about 'New Historicism' is that it recognizes a variety of competing centres of cultural power.

Q. 23. In what way New Historicists explain Shakespeare's technique of disguise?

Ans.: Shakespeare's technique of disguise his women characters in the guise of men is explained by New Historicists in terms of transvestite convention of the drama of the times. In actual life of those times girls took resort to cross-dressing. Moreover, in Elizabethan age young boys played the roles of young girls on the stage and therefore, technique of disguise well suited Shakespearean plays.

Q. 24. What is the importance of New Historicism?

Ans.: New Historicism, like earlier schools of criticism opens a new vista for the understanding of literary texts. It's emphasis on history and culture (cultural poetics) helps us to view literary texts from a new angle. This critical movement has given a new life to literary history and historical criticism. It has brought a change in the role and function of drama from knowledge or saving one's soul to an engaged socio-political and cultural form and formation.

Q. 25. What do you know about 'Introduction to Poetics' written by Tzvetan Todorov?

Ans.: Tzvetan Todorov wrote 'Introduction to Poetics' (1981) that speaks of the grammar of literature. His essay 'Definition on Poetics' presents his disagreement with the view of the New Critics. He believes that it is impossible to interpret a literary text 'for in itself' without making reference to other sources. Moreover, to interpret a literary text without taking inter-textuality into consideration, it so make a repetition of that very works under consideration. That's why, Todorov says that if we take this kind of approach to literature, we are merely making an analysis of that work without realizing it.

Q. 26. Comment upon Tzvetan Todorov as a critic.

Ans.: Todorov being a structuralist critic lays more emphasis on system or structure that produces literary texts rather than on the 'texts' proper. According to him, a literary text has a structure but is not a structure. It is true that literature is written in languages and uses language as a mode of expression but to say language is 'Literature' or literature is a mere play on language is wrong.

Q. 27. What do you know about Lukacs' perception as a critic?

Ans.: Lukacs' perception as a critic is grounded in his conception of totality in art. He lays emphasis on realism. Lukacs' has not reduced the function of literature to its publicistic or propagandist role. Lukacs criticizes modern novel because it lacks the totality of being and suffers from social and personal fragmentation.

Q. 28. What is Cultural Criticism?

Ans.: Cultural Criticism is an inter-disciplinary approach. It includes Marxist social theory, gender theory, psychoanalysis and above all, post-colonial inquiries. The diversity of popular culture-the internal differences within one culture that are class specific, age and sex specific, inflected by sexual orientation, race, ethnicity and geographical location has become the stuff upon which many cultural critics now consider culture as a source and not just a representation of art and literature. It is common knowledge that words in a language come from culture and literature exists in a language. That's why cultural critics turn to culture to explain literature in its proper context.

Q. 29. Write a short note on how do cultural critics analyze a literary work.

Ans.: Cultural critics analyze a literary work from the point of view of the means of its production. These critics posit the existence of a culture solely on the basis of a few literary works. There are three ways in which these cultural critics analyze a work of literature, British Cultural Materialism, the New Historicism and American Multiculturalism. It is closes to post-colonial criticism for both these schools take culture as the source of literature texts. There is great merit in studying literature from the standpoint of culture because a text is built and exists in a culture.

Q. 30. What do you know about Post-colonialism or Post-colonial theory?

Ans.: The new fashioned term 'post-colonialism' marks the end of 'colonialism' by giving the indigenous people, the necessary authority and political freedom to take their place and gain independence by overcoming political and cultural imperialism. Post-colonial theory is about the Third World or the twentieth century decolonized nations. Therefore, this theory is produced by authentic Third World voices and has its impact on the migrant constituencies of the First World. Edward Said, Gayatri Chakravorty Spivak, Homi Bhabha are the main proponents of postcolonial theory. It was again popularized by Bill Ashcroft, Garth Griffiths, and Helen Tiffin.

Q. 31. What do you know about Edward Said's 'Orientalism'?

Ans.: Said's contribution to postcolonial theory can be understood in its proper perspective against the backdrop of his concept of orientalism explained and developed in his major works. The term 'Orientalism' occurs in Said's 'magnum opus' Orientalism which refers to 'the historical and ideological process whereby false images of and the myths about the Eastern or the 'Oriental' world have been constructed in various Western discourses. Orientalism which is based on the cultural superiority of the West over the East paved the way for imperialism.

Q. 32. What is 'Translation Theory'?

Ans.: Modern 'Translation Theory' like modern critical theory begins with the advent of structuralism and gets proliferated in the recent years. It has developed from the linguistic approach of the nineteen sixties through the textual focus of the seventies to the culturally based approach of the eighties and after. Translation is a scholarly activity and the translator has to be instinctively bilingual.

Q. 33. What is Speech-Act theory?

Ans.: Speech-Act theory came into existence with the publication of J.L. Austin's William James Lectures. His essay 'How to Do Things with Words' gave rise to a Speech Act Theory of Translation. This theory of translation yields a topology based on the nature of the act—that is, the use of the language towards a specific end. Within the framework of a Speech-Act theory, at least two or more than two participants are involved which at least one is the Addressor and the other(s) is/are the addressee(s).

Q. 34. Write the meaning of the mirror stage.

Ans.: When we see as child looking and admiring himself in the mirror this stage is called by Lacan as mirror stage. In this child comes to know about its unified self image and tries to relate himself with it. Although his relation with this image is purely imaginary, but by this, child comes to know the existence of the subject and the object and starts to initiate the processes.

Q. 39. What do you know about Semiotics?

Ans.: The term 'Semiotic' (or semiology) is derived from the Greek word for sign. The science of signs has been in existence throughout the world, but only in recent times, it has been subjected to a systematic, principled enquiry. Semiology established a clean break from New Criticism. It applies structuralist insights to the study of sign systems. A sign system is a non-linguistic object which can be analyzed like language. Advertisements and popular cultures rely on semiotic systems. Semiotics recognizes language as the fundamental sign system, only for semiotics, sign = signifier + signified. Semiotics likens signs to symbols. The different kinds and forms of art, such as music, painting and literature, follow different sign system, and these signs are different from one another in their modes of signification.

Q. 40. What do you understand by 'The plurality of meanings'?

Ans.: Criticism consists in actively constructing a meaning for the text, and not in passively deciphering a meaning. There is no single meaning in literary works. The plurality of meanings in a text is a consequence of the absence of authorial intention in literary works. Hence, there is always an irreconcilable multiplicity of meanings. Meaning is the result of rules and conventions of different signifying systems. It is polysemic.

Q. 41. Comment upon the practice of New Historicists.

Ans.: New historicists believe that we can at best only have access to facts of the past, what we do is to interpret these facts from our own point of view, and create a history. There are only different interpretations of facts, and one interpretation is as reliable or not as another can not be said. Objective analysis of the facts is impossible. History does not progress in any linear fashion, as the old historians often believe.

Q. 42. What is Cultural Materialism? Compare it with new historicism.

Ans.: Cultural Materialism, also known as cultural criticism, as a critical method of enquiry gained currency, when it was put to use in the mid-1180s by Jonathan Dollimore, and Akan. These essays on religion, ideology and power in the drama of Shakespeare and his contemporaries provided a reading based on political commitment. This served as an alternative to the conventional, Christian framework of Shakespeare criticism which had run its course for more than four hundred years. Cultural materialism and new historicism have several affinities. The former is overtly British, and the other overtly American. Both draw upon the same sources, and in many ways, they are indistinguishable from each other. It is an outgrowth of Marxism. In fact new historicism and cultural criticism help us in many ways in strengthening our understanding of literature.

Q. 43. Comment upon parallel elements between postcolonial criticism and feminism.

Ans.: There is a lot of parallel between postcolonial criticism and feminism. A critic, Anne McClintock, observes in the book 'Colonial Discourse and Postcolonial Theory,' that in a world where women do two-third of the world's work, earn 10% of the world's income, and own less than % of the world's property, the promise of post colonialism has been a history of hopes postponed. In fact, any discussion of post colonialism cannot afford to bypass some of the following basic issues, the conception and representation of the empire, nationalization and globalization, its relationship with postmodernism and feminism, the play and place of language etc.

Q. 44. Write a short note on Reader-Response Criticism.

Ans.: I.A. Richards can be called the forerunner of reader-response (also called audience—oriented) criticism. Based on philosophic grounds, there can be another route to reader-response criticism through phenomenology. The Greek origin of this word means, 'to bring to light'. The title 'reader-response criticism' justifies what this criticism means, but the fact is that it is not just the response that matters, it is the analysis of how we respond to given text that matters. In the context of literary studies, it is still evolving, and it helps us to understand our own reading processes. It believes that work is not an achieved structure of meaning. In fact, it is the result or the outcome of the evolving process of reading. For the reader-response critics, what the text does is what matters, not so much what the text is.

Q. 45. What do you know about Transactional Reader-Response Theory?

Ans.: The theory was originally formulated by Louise Rosenblatt. The literary work is the result of the transaction between the text and the reader. As we read on, the text corrects our interpretations. Our approach should be aesthetic, and not merely focusing on the facts contained in the text. These are what are called the determinate meanings which refer to the 'gaps' in the text that force the readers to create the meanings.

Q. 46. Comment upon the theory known as 'Affective Stylistics'.

Ans.: This theory is usually associated with Stanley Fish. It is also based on the assumption that the literary text is not just an object that exists, but takes its existence from the act of reading. The text is put to a close examination to know how stylistically it affects the reader.

Q. 47. Write a short note on Reception Theory.

Ans.: It is also called the 'aesthetics of reception', meaning thereby the ways in which a text has met with its reception over a historical period of time. If reader-response theory is concerned with the microcosm of response, reception theory is concerned with the macrocosm of response. Historically, readers who come at a later point of time have an access to the response of 'the earlier generation of readers'. Thus literary history helps us in conceiving of our literary heritage in newer, and, yet newer ways.

Q. 48. What do you know about hermeneutics?

Ans.: The word 'hermeneutics' comes from a Greek word which means 'to say' or 'to explain', and thus, also 'interpretation'. The term refers both to the theory, and the practice of interpretation. The principal function of hermeneutics is to bring to light some work that is obscure and foreign to one's tongue. There is no hermeneutic school of criticism as such, nor does the term stand for any particular brand of interpretation. In the 20th century, it has to do with ontology, the essence of being. The oldest tradition in hermeneutics involves Biblical exegesis, and there are different orientations in this. Thus, there is the legal hermeneutics concerned with the understanding and interpretation of the law, and the philological preservation of classical texts. In criminal law and in legal parlance, it is a concept that is used to distinguish between the various degrees of crimes, and their relative punishment. In aesthetics and literary study, we quite often use the term to denote the intention of the author who composed a work. Heidegger, Godamer, Paul Ricoeur are some of the best thinkers associated with the epistemology of hermeneutics.

Q. 49. Define ecriture feminine.

Ans.: In broad terms, it means the feminine practice of writing. It is not possible to theorize this practice. It is form of writing that is oriented towards the female, a writing that facilitates a free play of meanings, and celebrates the female physiology.

Q. 50. Differentiate between sex and gender in gender theory.

Ans.: One has to make a distinction between gender and sex differences. Sex is biologically determined; hence we have the male and the female sex. Gender, on the other hand, is a psychological concept, and is socially/culturally constructed; hence we have the masculine and feminine gender. The difference between natural and social functions are also important. Feminist critics argue that the inequality between the sexes is produced by cultural constructions of gender differences.

Q. 51. What do you know about queer theory?

Ans.: It is a term that asserts the identity of homosexuals. It includes all 'non-straight' people. Gays and lesbians are proud to call themselves 'queer'. Sexuality, for the queer, is socially constructed; it is not controlled either by biological needs or gender roles. In literature many writers have written about such matters. Mahesh Dattani, Alice Walker, Shobha De etc. are some popular names in the field.

31

History of English Language, English Language Teaching

Q. 1. What to you know about the oral approach to language, especially English?

Ans.: The situation acts as a stimulus for the person to use language. In this case oral teaching becomes inescapable. It is therefore Psychologically sound to begin a second language orally. Many modern language teaching experts subscribe to the view that speech is the necessary starting point even for the more 'profitable' skills of reading and writing. The reason is that there is a very close correspondence between the phonological and the grammatical structures of English. When English is practiced orally with proper stress, rhythm and intonation, the learner, like the child, is exposed to these patterned units; thereby helping him to master the moulds rather than the isolated words which enable him to learn each phrase structure as a single act without interference that would inevitably occur if he were to organize consciously each phrase as well as the whole sentence. A.W. Frisby, one of the pioneers in the field observes: "Once we can say a unit of language according to the rules and so as to be really intelligible to others all the aspects of English language are really child's play."

Q. 2. What are the general principles of teaching English as Mother-Tongue (First-language)?

Ans.: Mother tongue is learnt in a natural way gradually by imitation. The general principles of teaching English as mother tongue are as follows:

1. **The Principle of Interest and Motivation.** A teacher has to use many devices for motivating the child for learning mother-tongue with interest. They should be encouraged to learn English by various ways like word—building, learning through structures, language games etc.
2. **The Principle of Activity and Task Performance.** The skills of language are developed by practicing certain activites such as speaking, writing and reading. But learning by doing is the best way of learning or developing certain skills.
3. **The Principle of Life Integration.** A child takes interest in reading and knowing subjects that are related to real life situations. Teachers should provide awareness of grammar, organization of under vocabulary etc. relating to such subjects.
4. **The Principle of Sequence and Ratio.** The ideas are expressed by speaking and writing. The receiving is through reading and listening. A language involves the following sequence:
   (a) Teacher speaks and students listen and understand.
   (b) Students imitate, speak and practice.

(c) Students read to acquire knowledge, grammar and vocabulary.

(d) Students write to express their ideas and experiences.

5. **The Principle of Conversation.** Teaching is considered a process of verbal interaction between the teacher and the students. Teaching should be child-centred rather than content centered. Therefore verbal interaction is essential for effective language teaching.

Q. 3. What are the objectives of teaching English as first language?

Ans.: English language is considered a window to the world. In English speaking countries English is used as first language and in other countries it is used as second language. The main objectives in teaching English as first language are of four types:

(a) **Skill Objectives.** Skill objectives mean the skill of speaking or pronouncing words correctly to express ideas and feelings to others alongwith the skill of writing. The skill of listening the ideas and views of others and understand them correctly alongwith the skill of reading literature and other subjects to grasp the theme is equally important.

(b) **The Cognitive Objectives.** A language is closely related to literature which is cognitive in nature. Language learning also requires knowledge of grammar and structure of sentences. Its main aims are:

(i) To develop the knowledge of grammar and application of it.

(ii) To develop the awareness of phonetics or elements or sounds and its, pronunciation in a proper way.

(iii) To develop the knowledge and understanding of morphemes.

(iv) To develop an awareness of poems, stones, novels, dramas & essays.

(c) **Attitudinal Objectives.**

(i) to develop aesthetic sense, attitudes and interest and the reptile attitude towards language and literature.

(ii) to make students participate in various activities like debate, elocution, essay writing and thus improve their language ability.

(d) **Creative Objectives.** To encourage students to develop their own style of effective writing and expressing ideas, views, feelings etc.

Q. 4. What are the problems before a learner of English as a second language, and how can he overcome it?

Ans.: In the case of a second language particularly when it happens to be a foreign like English, the natural resources are not available to the learner. Unlike the mother tongue, a second language is learnt deliberately, usually in formal classroom teaching. Therefore, the classroom activities must provide sufficient motivation and scope for practicing the language. Further, the language material presented for practice is to be carefully selected to highlight the regularities of the language so that students can make their own and adhoc rules.

The major problem before a learner is that when a child acquires his first language (mother tongue), he begins a second language the situation is quite different. Whenever he wants to express something in the second language, he has to keep the habits of the first language in check in order to produce the new sounds and structures. Further his ears have become so accustomed to the mother-tongue sounds that he doesn't easily hear the difference between the sounds of the two languages and, as a result, can not produce the distinctive sounds of the second language. This compels him to replace the sounds of the second language with the similar sounds of his mother-tongue. The same is the case with the Syntactic Structures. His conscious attempt at arranging words into syntactic patterns results in literal translation, and when the patterning in the two language differs, he produces ungrammatical structures. (known as the pull of the mother tongue). Here the learner will have to over come the pull of the mother-tongue in order to produce the sounds and the structures of the second language. It would be more fruitful if learner's attention is drawn to the peculiarities of the problematic English sounds or structures before arranging intensive practice on these items.

Q. 5. What are the various methods and techniques of teaching English as a second language?

Ans.: A method of teaching English as a second language includes all the four important components—selection, grading, presentation and repetition. The main methods of teaching English are as under:

1. **The Grammar-Translation Method.** This method also known as classical method; envisages a two pronged treatment of the language—grammatical explanation and translation of a language pattern. The mother tongue becomes the medium of instruction of teaching English. Students are required to memorize the rules of grammar and translate passages from mother tongue into English and vice-versa. Some believe that a foreign language can be required by cramming of rules of grammar. This method begins with definitions of parts of speech and memorization of grammar rules, meaning of new words, phrases and sentences.
2. **The Direct Method.** Known as 'Natural method' or the 'mother's method' is based on the philosophy of fluency in reading and facility in writing follow-fluency in speech. The central idea of the direct method is the association of words and sentences with their meaning through demonstration, dramatization and such other means and not by the use of mother-tongue. It helps to make pupil establish a bond between word and idea and think in English.
3. **Bilingual Method of Teaching.** The use of mother tongue is allowed but strictly controlled and limited to concept translation procedure of this method. It is built around situations. The focus is on the early stages, on oral or conversational proficiency. Imitation and Interpretation of basic foreign language is done alongwith FL questions-answers and conversation. It ensures accuracy, fluency and saves time and cost.
4. **West's New Method.** This method is named after its invention M.P. West. It was based on two important considerations. English should be studied from utilitarian point of view and as a means of international understanding. He believes that students should exphasize on developing reading ability and must have a control over vocabularaly.

Q. 6. What is the significance of English language in the modern world?

Ans.: Modern English, sometimes described as the first global lingua. France is the dominant international language in communications, science, business, aviation, entertainment, radio and diplomacy. It is the dominant language in the United States, whose growing economic and cultural influence and status as a global super power since World War II have significantly accelerated adoption of English has become a requirement in a number of fields, occupations and professions such as medicine and as a consequence over a billion people who speak English to at least a basic level. It is one of six official languages of the United Nations. English is a West Germanic language originating in England and is the first language for most people in the United Kingdom, the United States, Canada, Australia, New Zealand, Ireland and the Anglophone Carribbean. It is used extensively as a second language and as an official language throughout the world, especially in commonwealth countries and in many international organizations.

Approximately 375 million people speak English language as their first language. It is probably the third largest language by number of native speakers, after Mandarian Chinese and Spanish. However, when combining native and non-native speakers it is probably the most commonly spoken language in the world.

Q. 7. Write a short note on History of the English language.

Ans.: English is a West Germanic language that originated from the Anglo-Frisian and Lower-Saxon dialects brought to Britain by Germanic settlers and Roman auxiliary troops from various parts of what is now known as West Germany and the Northern Netherlands. One of there German tribes were the Angles, who may have come from Angeln, and Bede wrote that their whole nation came to Britain, leaving their former land empty. The names 'England' (or 'Aenglaland') and English are derived from the name of this tribe.

Before the Anglo-Saxons arrived in England the local language was Celtic. Although the most significant changes in dialect occurred after the Norman invasion of 1066, the language retained its name and the Pre-Norman invasion dialect is now known as Old English. Initially Old English was a diverse group of dialects. The original Old English language was then influenced by two waves of invasion. The first was by language speakers of the Scandinavian branch of the Germanic family; the second was the Normans in the 11th century, who spoke Old Norman and ultimately developed an English variety of this called Anglo-Norman. These two invasions caused English to become 'mixed' to some degree. The Norman influence entered English largely through the courts and government. Thus English developed into a 'borrowing' language of great flexibility and with a huge vocabulary.

Historically, the emergence and spread of the British Empire and the emergence of the United States as a super power helped to spread the English language around the world. Now the major branches are American, Canadian, Australian, British, Irish, Scottish and Indian English.

Q. 8. What do you know about the classification of English language and its relation with other related languages?

Ans.: The English language belongs to the western sub-branch of the Germanic branch of the Indo-European family of languages. The closest living relative of English is Scots, which is viewed by linguists as either a separate language or a group of dialects of English. Lexical differences with the other Germanic languages arise predominately because of the heavy usage of Latin and French words in English. The syntax of German and Dutch is also different form English, with different rules for setting up sentences. Semantics causes a number of false friends between English and its relatives. Phonology differences, obscure words which actually are genetically related and sometimes both semantics and phonology are different.

Many written French words are also intelligible to an English speaker because English absorbed a large vocabulary from Norman and French. As a result, a large portion of English vocabulary is derived from French, with some minor spelling differences, as well as occasional divergences in meaning of so-called false friends. The pronunciation of most French Loanwords is English has become completely anglisicized and follows a typically English pattern of stress. Some North Germanic words also entered English due to the Danish invasion shortly before them these include words such as 'Sky', Window', 'egg' and even 'they' and 'are'.

Q. 9. Write a short note on English as a global language.

Ans.: Because English is so widely spoken it has been referred to as a world language and has now inargitably global status. The lingua France of the modern world. While English is not an official language in most countries, it is currently the language most often taught as a second language around the world and used over 90 countries. Some linguistics believe that it is no longer the exclusive cultural sign of 'native English Speakers' but is rather a language that is absorbing aspects of cultures worldwide as it continues to grow. English is an official language of the United Nations and many other International Olympic Committee. English is the language most often studied as a foreign language in the European Union (by 89% of School children), followed by French (32%), German (18%) and Spanish (8%). In the EU, a large fraction of the population reports being able to converse to some extent in English. Among non-English speaking countries, a large percentage of the population claimed to be able to converse is English in one Netherlands (87%), Sweden (85%), Denmark (83%), Luxembourg (66%), Finland (60%), Slovenis (56%), Austria (53%), Belgium (52%) and Germany (51%). Norway and Lee land also have a large majority of component English speakers. Books, magazines and newspapers written in English are available in many countries around the World. English is also the most commonly used language in the sciences. In 1997, the Science Citation Index reported that 95% of its articles were written in English even though only half of them came from authors in English-Speaking countries. It is the language in which Indian parents and black Parents in South Africa wish their children to be educated. Thus underibted English has become the global language.

Q. 10. What do you know about basic and simplified versions of English language?

Ans.: To make English easier to read, there are some simplified versions of the language. One basic version is named Basic English, a constructed language with a small number of words created by Charles Kay Ogden and described in his book Basic English: *A General Introduction with Rules and Grammar* (1930). The language is based on a simplified version of English. Ogden said that it would take seven years to learn English, seven months for Esperants, and seven weeks for Basic English, comparable with Ido. Thus companies who need to make complex-books for international use employ Basic English, and by language schools that need to give some knowledge of English in a short time.

Ogden did not put any words into Basic English that could be said with a few other words and he worked to make the words work for speakers of any other language. He put his set of words through a large number of tests and adjustments. He also made the grammar simpler, but tried to keep the grammar normal for English users.

This concept gained its greatest popularity, just after the Second World War as a tool for World peace. Another Version, Simplified English, exists, which is a controlled language originally developed for aerospace industry maintenance manuals. It offers a carefully limited and standardized subset of English. Simplified English has a lexicon of approved words and those words can only be used in certain ways.

Q. 11. Give a chronological detail of the periods of the English language.

Ans.: The English language roughly can be divided into three periods:

(a) The Anglo Saxon Period (Old English Period)
(b) The Anglo-Norman Period (Medieval Period)
(c) Modern period

The Pre-Anglo-Saxon Scenario. It is believed that the common ancestor of the English and Germanic languages was the language called Proto-Indo-European. It is believed by scholars on the basis of several words of Indo-European language which have come to be known that the Indo-Europeans once live unified life around 5000-3000 B.C. in villages some where in Eastern Europe or Western Asia. It is almost certain that these people had a rural culture and they had serve knowledge of agriculture.

The Anglo-Saxon Period (449 to 1050 A.D.). The earliest known poem in (old) English literature is Beowulf which according to W.J. Long, is the earliest, and the greatest epic, or heroic poem in our literature. The authorship of Beowulf is unknown. The first to create a national identity in Britain were the Anglo-Saxons. Even the word England probably owes its origin to their language which they called English. The first usage of the word England with the spelling 'England' is said to be traceable around 1000 A.D. Alfred, the Great, was the greatest Anglo-Saxon king who ruled Wessex from 871-899 A.D. He established English as a written language and translated some Latin works into English.

The Anglo-Norman Period (1066-1350). The Anglo-Saxons were divided into tribes ruled by chieftains. But the Normans gave to the country the national idea. Anglo-Norman literature discards alliteration and adopts French endrhymes. In all literary works, religious as well as secular, French ideas are lived and respected. Instead of the melancholy-ridden mood of the Anglo-Saxon literature, there is the joy of spring in the Anglo-Norman literature which is later faithfully reflected in Chaucer's works. Chaucer found his native tongue (English) a dialect and left it a language.

Modern Period (1500—Present). The period after Chaucer is known as modern period. Language has taken a proper shape. History shows that the sound system, syntactic rules and even the semantic system of English has changed.

Q. 12. Write about the major ways by which the standard of English can be raised.

Ans.: To raise the standard of English, especially in India, the teacher should be well trained in the processes of listening, reading, writing and speaking. He should be able to describe interesting anecdotes from history, literature and life. The students should be made participants so that feel important enough to express themselves and bring out their hidden talents. Different nuances of grammar and language should be explained by the teacher in some interesting ways such as: Acting, gesturing, making students to act or indulge in some dialogues, or rhythmic words.

Teachers should attend seminars, workshops, refresher courses, meetings etc. frequently. They should as far as possible, speak good English in the classroom and encourage the students also to express themselves only in English.

Good libraries should be maintained in each school for English books. A better percentage of GDP should be spent on education in India. Experts of English language should be appointed at central, state and district level. Attention should be given to spoken language as well alongwith reading and writing. Stress should be laid on received pronunciation of Southern England as it is considered the pronunciation of standard English all over the world. Apart from giving attention to the study of grammatical elements, comprehension exercises should be done in large number to enable the student to be able to learn the method of grasping the implicit and explicit meanings and connotations.

Some system of scholarship, fee concession, appreciation certificates etc. should be started for the students, especially from the small town or village, to increase healthy competition in the learning of English.

Q. 13. How far the effective speaking skill depends upon correct pronunciation of words?

Ans.: The accuracy and effectiveness of a language depend upon correct writing or correct spelling of words and correct speaking or correct pronunciation of words and letters. The correct pronunciation of words makes the speech effective and meaningful. The effective speaking skill depends on correct pronunciation of words. Under the English language, pronunciation of words have the great variations. For example, the word 'Psychology', the sound of Letter 'P' is silent.

To acquire a correct pronunciation, prolonged practice in listening to speech sounds is needed. In the oral teaching of English it is the duty of the teacher to see that the pupil pronounces English words correctly. For good teaching of pronunciation the teacher must be acquainted with the causes of retardation in effective pronunciation among students. There may be physical disability of the child such as defective speech organs or teeth or children's habit of slurring over sounds. It is because some children have no knowledge of syllabus and consonant sounds. Pronunciation may be faulty because of the lack of knowledge of intonation and stress on all words. In English, falling intonation is used in assertive sentences and rising intonation in interrogative sentences. Even if the sentences are read with an even stress, it becomes unintelligible and ineffective. Among other reasons may be the pull of Mother-tongue and teacher's defective pronunciation.

Pronunciation deals with two inter-related skills-recognition or understanding the flow of speech, and production or fluency in the spoken language. We know that pronunciation is the sector of language where the organization of syntax and semantics is converted into motor activity which in turn produce audible sounds. The difficulties in learning to produce the sounds of English are mainly associated with the contrasts between the sound systems of the mother-tongue and those of English. Pronunciation should be taught and taught with more care and expertise than other aspects of language.

Q. 14. What do you know about the methods of English pronunciation?

Ans.: There are four main methods commonly used for teaching English pronunciation:

(1) Imitation method

(2) Phonetic method

(3) Subsidiary method

(4) Through electronic devices

1. Imitation Method—This method has four steps; perception, imitation, feedback and drill. The teacher writes the word and gives a model pronunciation; the students try to pronounce the word exactly as the teacher did. Then teacher gives feedback and either through group drill or individual drill the different aspects of pronunciation like proper sounds, stress, rhythm, intonation, fluency and pause can be taught.

It is a natural method, based on Psychological principle and takes less time. But students may imitate even the faulty pronunciation.

2. Phonetic Method—Student must acquire a knowledge of Phonetics for phonetics is the science of sounds (45 sounds) as used in Speech. Then teacher tells about how these sounds are produced by different speech organs lips, tongue, jaw, etc. Every good English dictionary gives the key to phonetic symbols comprising 12 vowels, 8 dipthongs and 24 consonants.

3. Subsidiary Method—The teacher should help the students to use the sounds in their proper places in connected speech. Pronunciation is not to be regarded as a separate area of language learning but as a number of contributory stands in the fabric of English.

4. Through Electronic Devices—These days through Audio-Video electronic gadgets like language lab, C.D., Audio cassettes etc. the right kind of pronunciation is taught. It is quite effective and students take interest in it just like a game. In this teacher can control all the students at a time.

Q. 15. What is the importance of linguistics in language teaching?

Ans.: Linguistics has different aims for language teaching. Linguistics set out to study the human language faculty, to develop theories to explain language behaviour, to provide the most efficient means for describing languages and to make the most of accurate and comprehensive descriptions of languages available. It is quite wrong to argue that developments in linguistics should cause changes in language teaching. The relationship cannot be one of cause and effect. In making language teaching decisions it is wrong to refer only to evidence drawn from linguistics. Language teaching is a pragmatic business. The very term 'applied linguistics' is open to an interpretation which suggest that language teaching is somehow derived from linguistics. Language teaching decisions have to be taken at many different levels—defining the goals of learning, determining the broad methodological approach, assessing the value of particular techniques, and organizing the language content. For the language teacher the study of linguistics is probably more rewarding in this respect than in any other. Linguistics defines the relationship between speech and writing.

Language teaching aims to be practically effective, not theoretically consistent. The study of linguistics, especially theories of language acquisition, helps to articulate the implications of many current and proposed practices in language teaching.

Q. 16. What do you know about the Audio-Lingual method of teaching English?

Ans.: The entry of the U.S. into the Second World War had a significant effect on language teaching in America. In 1939 the University of Michigan developed the first English language institute of the U.S. It specialized in the training of teachers of English as a foreign language and in teaching English as a foreign language. It became known variously as the Oral Approach, the

Aural-oral approach, and the structural approach. It advocated aural training first, then pronunciation training followed by speaking, reading and writing. It was the incorporation of the linguistic principles of the Aural-oral approach with state of the art psychological learning theory in the mid fifties that led to the method that came to be known as audio lingualisms. The term was coined by Professor Nelson Brown in 1964. Here vocabulary is introduced in a linguistic and cultural context. Audio-lingualists demanded a complete reorientation and advocated a return to speech-based instruction with the primary object of oral proficiency. It is teacher dominated method. Audio-visual aids in audio lingual method assist the teacher to develop language mastery in the learner. A language laboratory may also be considered essential.

In a typical audio-lingual lesson students first hear a model dialogue either read by the teacher or on tape containing the key structures. They repeat each live of the dialogue individually and in chorus. The teacher pays attention to pronunciation, intonation and fluency. Correction of mistakes is direct and immediate. The theoretical foundations of audio lingualism were attacked as being unsound both in terms of language theory and learning theory. Students were often found to be unable to transfer skills acquired through audio lingualism to real communication outside the classroom. Many found the experience of study through audio lingual boring and unsatisfactory.

Q. 17. What are the causes of spelling mistakes and ways of teaching spellings of English language?

Ans.: Students make spelling mistakes mainly due to faulty pronunciation, insufficient practice in writing, insufficient visual presentation of words, a general indifference to correct spelling on the part of the teacher and ignorance of the correct rules of spelling. To improve correct spelling, the teacher should have some idea of the process of acquiring correct spelling. Spelling is more a matter of reflex action than of conscious knowledge. The repeated experiences of writing a word are stored in the muscles of our fingers. When the occasion for writing word arises, the fingers, as it were, 'remember' the previous experiences and perform the required movements without our conscious effort. The experience thus stored is called vital role in all reflex actions. The other sensory aspects are visual memory and auditory memory. To have an active visual memory for spelling, the students need repeated and prolonged exposure to words. The main useful ways of teaching spellings are as under.

1. **Copying**—It is based on the kinesthetic memory through repeated transcription of a word.
2. **Delayed Copying**—Words on flash cards are shown to the students for a very short time to write out the word as soon as the card is withdrawn.
3. **Use of Mnemonics**—Mnemonics are devices which help us to remember something. Students can remember difficult spellings by memorizing short and simple formulas or sentences that highlight the troublesome part of a word.
4. **Focusing the trouble spots**—The troublesome portion of the word may be underlined or may be written in capital Letters or with coloured chalk or coloured pen.
5. **Dictation**—Dictating the correct letters of the word.
6. **Spelling Games**—There are numerous language games that can improve spellings and can be enjoyed by students.

Q. 18. Write a note on the Language Laboratory.

Ans.: Learning skills is largely a question of adequate and effective practice. Basically a language laboratory is a long classroom in which the students are isolated from each other by sound proof walls. These walls prevent the sounds made by anyone student from reaching his neighbours. This leaves him free to practice speaking without disturbing them. A whole class of students can practice speaking at the same time.

Language Lab is a powerful tool, if properly used, a waste of time and money if improperly used. There are three stages in the developing of a language lab from the simplest to the most complex. In the first stage it consists of a number of sound proof booths each containing a set of head phones connected to a microphone in front of the teacher, and carry out his instructions, copy his speech, answer his questions etc. but here teacher can not check up students work. In the second stage the teacher has earphones and is connected with a microphone in each student's booth.

The teacher and the individual student can speak to each other. The third stage of development sees the introduction in to each student's booth of a tape recorder. Now the student can record his practice efforts together with those of the model. The tape recorder back pre-recorded practice tapes. Students can play individual tapes on their dual track recorders and simultaneously record their own responses.

The language lab is for practicing aural-oral skills. These skills are more especially applied to learning language material in the fields of pronunciation and grammar. Thus procedures such as listening to, identifying, distinguishing between and copying sounds, stresses, tones and tones patterns in pronunciation and ear training are possible. But the possession of a language lab does nothing to lighter the teacher's task. The teacher cannot improvise in the lab. Nor must the teacher imagine that material prepared for one year can be used unchanged the next. It needs more energy and time from teachers. Thus the lab is one more aid, not the central component of teaching. Language labs are not meant to solve the problem of teachers' shortage. It is expensive to buy and costly to run effectively.

Q. 19. What are the various ways or methods of teaching English Grammar?

Ans.: Grammar is the theory of language and the study of organization of words into sentences. Grammar is of three types; theoretical, functional and structural. Grammar should not be taught as an intellectual exercise; attention should be paid on meaning of the structure rather than on grammatical points. The chief methods are as under.

1. **The Traditional Method**—The teacher tells a definition or a rule to the students. They memorize and solve the exercises given in the text-books on grammar.
2. **The Informal Method**—By continuous practice of using words while speaking, writing and reading, grammar is taught. This tells no rule but only correct usage informally.
3. **The Inductive-Deductive Method**—It is used to teach Science and as grammar is a science of language, it is successfully used for teaching grammar.

We should neither regard grammar as the most important part of language learning nor do away with it. We should rather adopt a moderate and practical view. Grammar should be taught as a means to an end, and not as and end in itself. It should follow the language and not precede it. It should be picked up incidentally and almost unconsciously.

Q. 20. What are the Audio-visual aids available in teaching English?

Ans.: Audio-visual aids can dispel the monotony of practice work by creating variety. They can introduce a play-element in serious work and make lessons lively and interesting. Some of the readily-available aids and their uses are as under.

1. **The Blackboard**—A traditional symbol of the classroom may be of green colour as well. The human beings have a tendency to attribute special sanctity to the written word. The teacher can write words and sentences to enable the pupils to associate the sounds with their written forms. Model sentences, cue words, questions, subscription tables, sketches can be put on the board for developing Aural-oral skills and reading and writing skills, especially teaching grammar.
2. **Charts and Tables**—Large wall-charts and tables can be used for development of all the form skills as well as for imparting the essential knowledge of structures and vocabulary. The letters should be large enough in the charts and tables to be visible.
3. **Flash Cards**—Flash cards can serve a variety of purposes. For teaching, reading by Look-and-say method they are indispensable aids. They can also be used in teaching spelling by the technique of delayed copying.
4. **Cut Outs**—Small figures of people, animals, birds etc. cut from magazines and newspapers can be excellent teaching aids.
5. **Wall Picture**—Large pictures showing a market place or a critical field can be effective for oral practice and for writing connected sentences. A series of such pictures can also be used to narrate a story in the manner of the popular comics.
6. **Flip Charts**—In a Flip Chart a series of pictures depicting a story or an incident can be pasted on card board and hurged together in this manner, and it can be shown by turning over (flipping over).
7. **Cue Sheets**— Slips of paper containing cue words and sentences are useful in group work.
8. **Sophisticated Aids**—Radio, Tape recorder, Slide Projector, Overhead Projector, Film projector, T.V., Language Lab, Video Tape or cassette recorder are useful gadgets.

Q. 21. What do you know about the use of latest Information Technology in the teaching and learning of English language?

Ans.: Besides the traditional resources blackboard and text-books as the means to acquire proficiency in the target language and improve one's communication skills, a bewildering array of technological devices have emerged under the umbrella of Information Technology and they are being used in language learning. ICT offers a wide range of language learning opportunities from radio, cassette players, VCD players, CD/DVD ROMs to the latest gadgets like mobile Phones, Personal Digital Assistant (PDA); Pod and above all computer.

Computer Assisted Language Learning drew heavily on practices with programmed institution. The development in multimedia technology, which is perhaps the most promising for language learning, is the Internet Multimedia of the World Wide Web. The Internet Multimedia does not require any special hardware in the present age as most multimedia systems already include excellent sound and video cards stereo speakers, earphones and microphones. Today development in Internet multimedia are often supplied by software called plug-ins that handles multimedia tasks via Internet browsers, such as Netscape Navigator, Microsoft Internet Explorer and Mozilla Firefox. The creation of World Wide Web (www) and Hypen Text Markup Language (HTML) have developed a new generation of technology and produced new authors. Information about the markup language and its corresponding protocol. Hypen Text Transfer Protocol (HTTP) is widely available on the www, in many books written on the subject. Besides the tools and techniques, the information available on the Web provides teachers and learners easy access to language learning resources like never before. Online journals, Newspapers and Magazines provide useful material for language learners, while teachers can find lesson plans, ideas, exercises, assessment tools and other materials for use in their classes. The World Wide Web's capability is well known, for its interactivity makes it especially exciting as a resource for language teaching and learning. The availability makes Web based language learning quite attractive to both the instructors and the learners. Teachers can even create their own interactive language learning activities on the Web, which allow them to adopt the activities to their own courses and the students.

Q. 22. How World Wide Web can be used practically to enhance the ways of English Language Teaching and Learning?

Ans.: Using Web based activities, a wide range of basic language skills can be enhanced. Vocabulary practice, grammar lessons, comprehension exercises, reading and writing tasks and pronunciation exercises can be done, and also created, on the Web and made interactive in a variety of ways. Online discussion-boards are good way to hold discussions and create reading and writing activities for the students. With discussion boards, teachers can post a question or place a subject to start discussion and every response is displayed on the board. Students can reply to the original question or to other responses, or they can create a new thread of discussion. Such discussion-boards can be created easily using a Common Gateway Interface Script and is available for download on the Web, as from Matt's Script Archive. Another site Scripts for Educators offers an array of free scripts along with the lines to several helpful online classes and tutorials on the use of scripts. Online writing assignments or discussions can also be created through a Weblog or Blog. Once created, they can use the Blog as an online journal to submit course work, to create a portfolio, or to have an online discussion.

Games and exercises designed to help students learn new vocabulary are easily put on the Web. A typical Web based vocabulary activity might be a matching exercise. In this exercise, words or phrases are matched with definitions via a pop-up menu created with a Web form. Students may click on the bottom of the page to see the correct answers. Any online form used for interactive activities. Such as quizzes and vocabulary and grammar exercises will require either a CGI script or Jawa Script, along with various activities related to language learning.

World Wide Web has the potential to serve all of the four basic language skills-reading, writing, speaking and listening. It is used as an electronic classroom for language teaching and also as a support for the traditional classroom. It is now upto the language teachers and learners to explore the remarkable potential World Wide Web Possesses.

Q. 23. Suggest some effective means of teaching English language in classroom.

Ans.: Since we need knowledge of English for different purposes, the content and character of that as well as method of imparting it have to undergo a change. English has to be taught principally as a language comprehension rather than as a literary language. In other words, the focus of ELT in India be such as it is taught as a language for functional and comprehension purposes rather than as tool for learning the nuances of English literature.

As a corollary to the functional imperative of ELT, it is also imperative to restructure the syllabus of English at school and college level so as to attain the goal of functional proficiency of English. The syllabus should be so graded that starting with the basics of English language at form of literature may be introduced in the form of interesting and instructive short stories, anecdotes, essays and poems. Writing of popular writers like Tagore, Narayan, Ruskin, Shakespeare, Dickens, Wordsworth etc. written lucidly, may be chosen to capture the imagination of the young minds. As language is an over learned skill, the prescribed literary pieces should become the spring board for the simultaneous study of language and grammar. Teaching of grammar is an important aspect of teaching/learning any language. Formal grammar presents facts/rules about a language, functional grammar illustrates their correct usage in language. Grammar does not exist in isolation or apart from a language. In a way, language is grammar.

As language is an over acquired skill, the ability in a language grows by practice-constant and consistent and not merely by knowing rules of grammar and cramming its vocabulary. So competency of teachers is also a very vital issue. UGC sponsored Orientation Programmes and refresher Courses for EL teachers to have their linguistic skills and update the knowledge of their subject are also very useful. The ELT teacher must remember that language learning is a two-way process in which involvement and participation of the students is absolutely essential. This is possible only when correct methodology of ELT is adopted. These days English Language Teachers' Association of India known as ELT@l is working hard in this direction is very helpful to all; teachers, students and scholars.

Q. 24. What do you know about Machine Translation, how it is different from natural translation?

Ans.: A typical human communication involves 'transferring' the 'mental representation' of the speaker to the listener using natural language as a vehicle. When the translation is done through machine it encounters several problems. The speaker may use more than one sentence to clarify the same concept. The problem is further compounded when the language of the speaker is different from that of the listener. A language interpreter/translator builds his/her own perception of the speaker's mental representation and is also limited by the words/ utterances and sentences used by the speakers. The translator has to map the source lexicons to equivalent target lexicons which are most appropriate to the given context and situation. In some cases, the target lexicon representing the entire original flarom and the translator has to resort to a cluster of lexicons. Therefore, it is obvious that the task of translating a natural language text requires an 'understanding' of the language. Transplanting this 'understanding' on to the machine is a hard problem. A human translator uses a number of knowledge sources, a wide variety of context and background information to arrive at a target language text as close as possible to the original source of language text.

Q. 25. Write a short note on the innovative approach to ELT in rural areas.

Ans.: The communication skills in English language are acquired through the natural stages of acquisition. The fact that is overlooked while acquiring the proficiency in English language is the role of listening skill. The acquisition of this language skill is by listening to English Speech sounds, conversation in English and exposure to English language. The exposure to listening skill is lacking in rural area because there is dearth of English listening activities. Listening is the first language mode that children acquire. It provides a foundation for all aspects and cognitive development. The first stage is not developed properly and students are expected to become efficient in the fourth stage of language skill i.e. writing. This can be developed by creating listening situations in the class. The focus should be on the remedial measures which need to be taken by providing the listening opportunities to different target levels.

Students acquire these skills gradually on a developmental continuum and need plenty of opportunities for group interactions and discussions to acquire and practice these skills. In order for students to develop the skills teachers need to:

- Promote group cohesion
- Coordinate group activities
- Enable students to explore topics creatively.

32

European Literature from Classical Age to the 20th Century

Q. 1. What do you know about 19th century European literature and the chief writers of the age?

Ans.: The entire period which encompassed the 1890s to the First World War is marked by a term which is common to most central European literature and south Slavonic literature as well—the modern a (Modernism). Although the term was taken from German literature, propinquity with that literature and its influence were at a remarkably low ebb. Only the Serbian lands under Austro-Hungarian rule at the time continued to be affected by the influence of German culture and literature.

On the literary front the new century opens with Romanticism, a movement that spread throughout Europe in reaction to 18th century rationalism. William Wordsworth and Coleridge are considered the initiators of the new school in England, while in the continent the German Sturm and Drang spreads its influence as far as Italy and Spain. The Goncourts and Emile Zola in France and Giovanni Verge in Italy produce some of the finest naturalist novels. Italian naturalist novels are especially important in that they give a social map of the new unified Italy to a people that until than had been scarcely aware of its ethnic and cultural diversity. There was a huge literary output during the 19th century. Some of the most famous writers included the Russians: Leo Tolstoy, Anton Chekov and Fyodor Dostoevsky; the English: Charles Dickens, Keats, Jane Austen, The Scottish: Sir Walter Scott, the Irish Oscar Wild; the Americans; Edgar Allen Poe, Emerson & Mark Twain, and the French: Victor Hugo, Honore de Balzac, Jules Verne and Charles Bauldelaire.

Q. 2. Write a short note on the place of Serbian Literature.

Ans.: In the transition from the nineteenth to the twentieth century, Serbian literature took on all the basic characteristics of a modern national literature. It is usually thought that the modern novel and narrative in the leading European literatures came about after the disintegration of Realism. When a transition was made from Naturalism to Impressionism. Modern lyric poetry began with the (French) Parnassians and the transition to symbolism. Literary criticism also changed, as did literary theory. Literary theory left the external interpretation of literature behind and moved to internal interpretation—to the analysis of the artistic traits of a work, and not of the circumstances under which it came into being. In Serbian literature, similar phenomenon are to be noticed not only in the appearance of the Parnassian lyric poems of Vojislav Ilic (who had a large number of followers and was a dominant figure in the 1980s), but in literary criticism as well.

In the last decade, Milorad Pavic has been one of the most often translated Serbian authors. His works have been published in twenty five languages, all over the world. L Jubomir Nedic (1858-1902) is rightfully considered to be the forerunner of the internal interpretation of literature. As early as 1893 he aimed sharp criticism at the utilitarian theory of art espoused by Svetozar Markovic, who accentuated the social role of literature in the aesthetic side of the lyric poems. Hence the place of earlier interest held primarily by those who stressed form. Thereby, the attention of the critic and the reader, and the poet himself slowly moved toward the writing of poetry as a specific artistic creation, which would have far-reaching consequences not only for re-interpreting and evaluating poetry, rather-and this is of utmost significance—for its development in the two decades to come. Of course, the changes observed in Serbian literature were stimulated by similar earlier in some of the European literatures. In the kingdom of Serbia and its capital Belgrade, the French influence suddenly grew stronger. After First World War Serbian Literature became directly involved in the powerful international movement of the literary avant garde. It is obvious that Serbian Literature in tandem with the leading literature in the other Slavic languages: Russian, Polish and Czech is simultaneously participating in the literary life of Europe, and in the general developments of the art of literature.

Q. 3. Write a note on the position of prose in Serbian literature.

Ans.: In contrast to poetry, prose changed more slowly and with greater difficulty. Moreover, the dominance of lyric poetry actually created conditions in which common characteristics appeared among prose writers, for whom J. Skerlic introduced the term 'lyrical realists'. However, the stylistic traits of Impressionism were those that came mostly to the forefront, Petar Kocic (1877-1916) was close to this, and it is often difficult to define the line between poetry in prose and in his narratives (from the mountain and under the mountain I-III, 1902-05). Beautiful and terrible in the same stroke in Kocic's works, the natural surroundings in Bosania, as an elemental force, meld with man in the resistance to the foreign, imperial rule of the Austro-Hungarian government. Kocic is the founder of the Bosnian narrative. Equally fascinating narration and impressions of the Adriatic and the Karst regions by the sea are to be found in the works of Ivo Cipiko (1869-1923). However in his novels he offered a broader picture of life in Dalmatia and its hinterlands. In his first book, seeking one's Fortune (za kruhum, 1904) the main hero departs. He is educated in another city and returns to his homeland where he then sees every mix different; in his second book, *The Spiders* (1909) he develops his portrayal of different social classes.

The Serbian modern novel and narrative actually begins with Borisav Stankovic (1867-1927). His characters are complexly constructed, with powerful internal conflicts between contradictory motives. His *Tainted Blood* (1910) is the first Serbian novel which received favourable critiques in its translations into several European Language. Almost all his narratives, and the often performed drama Kostana, are all linked to the little town of vranje in the far southern pent of Serbia.

Compelling analytical prose, all packed with carefully stylized impressions, began in that time (Fellow Travellers, 1913) under the authorship of Isidora Sekulic (1877-1958). Her works regularly use Introspection. Between the two World Wars, and even later, Isidora Sekulic was one of the best essayist and interpreters of literature. Milutin Uskokovic (1884-1915) was less apt to innovation; he wrote two novels about life in Belgrade; *The Newcomers* (1910), and

Cedomir Ilic (1914). Usko Kovic's development was ended with the World War, as was the development of an even younger author Milutin Bojic (1892-1917).

Q. 4. Write a note on 19th century Romanticism in Europe.

Ans.: Romanticism was a reactionary period of history when its seeds became planted in poetry, art work and literature. The perception that the enlightenment was destroying the natural human soul and substituting it with the mechanical, artificial heart was becoming prevalent across Europe. G.W.F. Hegal a German philosopher, rejected the rational philosophy of the 18th century because he believed in 'Idealism'. Although Romanticism was perhaps conservative in nature, every participant of this swift and silent movement could relish in his own free and glorious vision of nature. Romanticism was a time when mankind could restructure his outlook on life so that he was able to reach new heights of intellectual and political awareness.

Romanticism began in the early 19th century and radically changed the way people perceived themselves and the state of nature around them. Throughout Europe, Romanticism allowed people to get away from the constricted, rational views of life and concentrate on an emotional and sentimental side of humanity. This not only influenced political doctrines and ideology, but was also a sharp contrast from ideas and harmony featured during the Enlightment, but concentrated on human diversing and looking at life in a new way.

The romantic school had as its organ the Conciliafox established in 1818 at Milan, on the staff of which were Silvio Pelico, Lodovico di Breme, Giovile Scalvini, Tommass Grossi, Giovanni Berchet, Samucle Biava, and Alessandro Manzoni. All were influenced by the ideas that, especially in Germany, constituted the movement called Romanticism. In Italy the course of literary reform took another direction. The main instigator of the reform was Manzoni. In the Spanish Literature the early Romanticism appeared with the singular figure of Mnvel Jose Quintana. In the Romanticism important topics are, the poetry of Jose de Espronceda and other poets, the prose, (historical novel, scientific, prose, journalism, etc.) the theatre etc.

Q. 5. What do you understand by European literature? Mention the influence of Greek literature.

Ans.: European literature refers to the literature of Europe. European literature includes literature in many languages; among the most important of the modern written works are those in English, Spanish, French, Dutch, Polish, German, Italian, Modern Greek Czech and Russian and works by the Scandinavians and Irish. Important classical and medieval traditions are those in Latin, Ancient Greek, Old Norse, Medieval French and the Italian Tuscan dialect of the renaissance. In colloquial speech, European literature often is used as a synonym for Western literature. European literature is a part of world literature. Ancient Greek Literature refers to literature written in the Greek language until the 4th century A.D. This period of Greek literature structures from Homar until the 4th century BC and the rise of Alexander the Great. It is nevertheless true that the Greek world of thought was so far ranging that there is scarcely an idea discussed today not already debated by the ancient writers. At the beginning of Greek literature stand the two monumental works of Homar, the Iliad and the Odyssey. This Iliad is the famous story about the Trojan War. While the Iliad is pure tragedy, the Odyssey is a mixture of tragedy and comedy. The stories are told in language that is simple, direct and eloquent. The other great poet of the preclassical period was Hesiod. Unlike Homer Hesiod speaks of himself in his poetry. His two works were 'Works and Days' and 'Theogony': the first is the faithful depiction of the poverty stricken country life. Theogony is systematic account of creation and of the gods. Together the works of Homer and Hesiod made a kind of Bible for the Green.

Sappho and Pindar are known for their lyric poetry. Sappho has always been admired for the beauty of her writing. With Pindar the transition has been made form the preclassical to classical age. The Greeks invented the epic and lyric forms and used them skillfully. They also invented drama Ae Schylus, So Phoces and Euripides are well known writers.

Q. 6. Write a short note on Latin Literature and its chief exponents.

Ans.: By Latin literature we mean the body of Literature written in the Latin language which remains an enduring legacy of the culture of ancient Rome. The Romans produced many works of poetry, comedy, tragedy, satire, history and rhetoric, drawing heavily on the traditions of other cultures and particularly on the more matured literary tradition of Greece. Latin Literature is conventionally divided into distinct periods. The period of classical Latin, when Latin literature is widely considered to have reached its peak is divided into the Golden Age, and the Silver Age. Above all, Cicero was imitated, and his style praised as the perfect pinnacle of Latin. Medieval Latin was often discussed as 'Dog-Latin'. For most of the Medieval era, Latin was the dominant written language in use in Western Europe. The vernacular languages in the West, the languages of modern-day Western Europe, developed for centuries as spoken languages only. It was probably only after the invention of printing, people started and continued to write in Latin. Even Milton wrote many poems in Latin, or that Francis Bacon or Baruch Spinoza wrote mostly in Latin. The use of Latin as a lingua France continued smaller European lands until the 20th century. Latin scholars of the 20th and 21st centuries are R.A.B. Mynors, R.J. Ternant. L.D. Reynolds and John Brisco.

Old Latin (also known as Early Latin or Archaic Latin) refers to the Latin language in the period before the age of classical Latin. Titus Maccius Platus (C 254-184 BCE), commonly known as Plautus was a Roman playwright. His comedies are among the earliest surviving intact works in Latin literature. He wrote about 52 plays of which 20 have survived. Unlike Aristophanes, Plautus arrived current politics in his comedies one main theme of Greek New Comedy is the father son relationship. Plautine diction is distinctive in its use of archive Latin forms. Intellectual and academic critics have often judged Plautus's work as crude; yet his influence on later literature is impressive especially on two literary giants. Shakespeare and Moilere. Publius Terentius After, better known as Terence, was a playwright of the Roman Republic. All of the six plays Terence wrote have survived. Terence's plays use a convincingly 'Green' setting rather than Romanizing the characters and situations. His six plays are—*Adelphoe* (The Brothers) *Andria* (The civil from Andros), *Eunuchus*, *Heautur Timonimenos* (The Self-Tormentor), *Hecyra* (The mother in law) and *Phormio*. Marcus Porcius Cato was a historian, the first Latin prose writer of any importance and the first author of a history of Italy in Latin. His manual on running a farm is his only work that survives completely. Probably Cato's most important work 'Origines', in seven books, related the history of the Italian towns.

Q. 7. Write a short note on main writers of Italian literature.

Ans.: Italian literature is literature written in the Italian language, particularly within Italy. It may also refer to literature written by Italians or in Italy in other languages spoken in Italy.

For example, the earliest Vernacular literary tradition in Italy was not in the Italian language but rather in Occitan. The Tuscans spoke a dialect which closely resembled Latin-one which afterwards became almost exclusively the language of literature. Italian prose of the 13th century was as abundant and varied as its poetry. The oldest prose writing is a scientific book, composizine del mindo b Ristoro d Arezzo. In the year 1282 a period of new literature began. Dante the greatest of Italian poets, shows the lyrical tendencies. In 1293 he wrote La Vita Nuova, in which he idealizes live. The work which made Danteimmortal, and raised him above all other men of genius in Italy, was his Divine Commedia. Petrarch's canzoniere is also a parrionate work. Boccaccio had the same enthusiastic like of antiquity and the same worship for the new Italian literature as Petrarch. He was the first to put together a Latin translation of the Iliad and in 1375, the Odyssey. The Italian work which principally made Boccaccio famous was the Decamerone, a collection of hundred novels. Fazio was the imitators of the Divine Commedia but only in the external form. Sir Giovanni Fiorentino wrote, under the title of Pecoxone, a collection of tales. Later, names are those the Novellino and Antonio Cornezzano whose Proverbil became extremely popular.

In the field of drama Albertino Mussato of Padua wrote in Latin a history of Emperor Henry VII. Then came Lorenzo followed by Poliziano. He united with greater art, the ancient and the modern, the popular and the classical style. In his Rispelti and the plasticity form are inimitable. He wrote Italian verses with dazzling colours.

Italy never had the epic poetry, but had many poems called Cantari, because they contained stones that were sung to the people. In the 18th century the new political condition of Itlay began to improve, under Joseph II, Holy Roman Emperor and his successors. The leading figure of the literary revival of the 18th century was Giuseppe Parini.

Q. 8. Write a short note on Spanish Literature.

Ans.: Spanish literature includes Spanish poetry, prose and novels. Due to historic, geographic and generatiorial diversity, Spanish literature has known a great number of influences and it is very diverse. Medieval Spanish poets recognized the Master de Juglaria as literary form written by the Minstrels and composed of varying line length and use of assonance instead of rhyme. The Castilian narrative poetry known as the Mester de Clercia became popular in the 13th century. These poets carefully counted the number of syllables in each line and strived to achieve perfect lines.

Castile prose gained popularity in the mid-13th century when King Alfonso X el Sabio of Castilla gave support and recognition to the writing form. He, with the help of his groups of intellectuals, directed the composition of many prose works including Las sietc partidas, the first modern book of laws of the land written in the people's language. Another work was As Primera Cronica general which accerinted for the history of Spain from the creation until the end of Alfonso's father's reign, San Fernando. It is the first national history ever written. Alfonso X is called the father of Spanish Prose. His nephew, Don Juan manual is famous for his prose work El Conde Lucanor which is a frame story or short stones within an overall story. Toward the end of the Middle Ages, writer Fernando del Pulgon created a new type of prose named the verbal portrait.

The great poet Mendoze was the first to introduce the Sonnet into Spanish literature. The last great poet of the Middle Ages is Jorge Manrique. The Spanish Literature of the middle Ages concludes with the work La Calestine by Fernando de Ropis.

Three phrases in the Spanish Literature of the 18th century are line this:

- Anti Baroquism: The recreational literature is not cultivated, but they are more interested in the essay and the Satire utilizing the language with simplicity and purity.
- Neo-Classicism: It is strongly influenced by the French and Italian Classicism.
- Pre-Romanticism: This current announces the decadence of the Neo-Classicism and opens the doors to the Romantics is.

In modern Spanish Literature several current appear' parnasianism symbolism, futurism and creationism. Literary Modernism in spain was influenced by the 'disaster of '98', Regenerationism, and the free Institution of Education. The intellectual movement that thinks objectively and scientifically about the causes of the decadence of Spain as a nation between the 19th and 20th century is Regenerationism. The regernerationist intellectuals div ugled their studies in journals with a big differsion. So the movement expanded. Some important authors the Juan Roman Jimenez, Miguel de Unamuno, and Ruben Dario.

Q. 9. Give a short introduction of French Literature.

Ans.: French literature is, generally speaking, literature written in the French language, particularly by citizens of other nations such as Belgium, Switzerland, Canada, Senegal, Algeria, Morocco, etc. and is referred to as Francophone literature.

Beginning in the 11th century, literature written in medieval French was one of the oldest vernacular (non-latin) literatures in Western Europe and it became a key source of literary themes in the Middle Ages aerizs the continent. In the 18th century, French because the literary lingua France and diplomatic language of Western Europe (and America too) and French letters have had a profound impact on all European and American literary traditions. French literary developments of the 19th and 20th century have had a particular strong effect on modern world literature, including Symbolism, naturalism, the "roman-fleuves" of Balzac, Zola and Proust, Surnealism, existentialism, and the Theatre of the Absubd. French empenatisms and colouralism in the America, Africa and the far East have brought the French language to non-European cultures that are transforming and adding to the French literary experience today. Literature matters deeply to the people of France and plays an important role in their sense of identity. As of 2006, French literary people have been awarded more Nobel Prizes in Literature than novelists, poets and essayists of any other country, although writers in English have won twice as many Nobles as the French. Frederic Mistral, a poet in Occitan (1830-1914), was awarded the Nobel Prize in Literature in 1904. Under the aristocratic ideals of the ancient regime the nationalist spirit of post-revolutionary France, and the mass educational ideas of the Third Republic and modern France, the French have come to have a profound cultural attachment to their literary heritage. Today French school emphasize the study of novels, theatre and poetry. The main writers are Romain Rolland (Nobel-1915), Albert Camus (Nobel in 1957), Jean-Paul Sartre (Nobel in 1964. He declined the Prize), Samuel Beckett (Nobel in 1969, Irish, wrote to English and French), etc., Victor Hugo, Guy de Manpassant, Emile Zola, Robert-Pinget, Paul Verlaine, Francis Ponge, Raymond Queneau, Pierre Comeille, Jean Racine, Marivaux, Engene Ionesco, Jean Genet etc. are other names.

Q. 10. What do you know about German Literature?

Ans.: German literature comprises those literary texts which were written in the German language. This includes literature written in Germany itself as well as German language Swiss and Austrian literature, and to a lesser extent works of the German diaspora. German literature of the modern period is mostly in standard German, but there are some currents of literature influenced to a greater or lesser degree by dialects. Modern literature in German brings with the authors of the Enlightenment (such as Herder) and reaches its 'Classical' form at the turn of the 18th century with Weimar classicism (Goethe and Schiler).

The Boroque period (1600-1720) was one of the most fertile times in German literature. Many writers reflected the horrible experiences of the Thirty years War, and poetry and prose.

Weimar Classicism is a cultural and literary movement of Europe, and its central ideas were originally propounded by Johann Woltgarp von Goethe during the period 1788-1832.

German Romanticism was the dominant movement of the late 18th and early 19th centuries. The early German romantics tried to create a new synthesis of art, philosophy and Science, looking to integrated period. Later German Romanticism emphasized the tension between the every day world and the seemingly irrational and supernatural projections of creative genius.

The Nobel Prize in literature has been awarded to German language authors twelve times (as of 2007). Most famous are:

1902 – Theoder Mommsen
1919 – Carl Spitteler
1929 – Thomas Mann
1999 – Gunter Grass
2004 – Elfriede Jelinek

Q. 11. Give a short introduction of Austria Literature.

Ans.: Austria literature is the literature written in Austria, which is mostly, but not exclusively, written in German language. The seven volume History of Austrian literature by the editors Herbert Zeman and Friz Peter Knapp is titled History of the Literature can be divided into main divisions, namely the period up until the mid-20th century, and the period subsequent.

Austria is a country where great poets, writers and novelists lived and created their literary works. Writers like Adalbert Stifler, Arthur Schnitzler, Franz Werfel, Stefan Zweig, Fanz Kafke, and poets like George Trakl, Rose Auslander, Paul Celan etc. famous contemporary playwrights and novelists are Elfriede Jelinek and Peter Handice. Well-known essayists are Robert Manasse Karl-Marksus Gaul.

A very important centre of Austrian literature during the 20 years before the end of World War I was Prague. It was the centre of many German-speaking, mostly Jewish authors who did not only give important impulses to the entire Austrian and partly even to world literature, but represent a very important part of Austrian literature. Their influence endured until the 1930s. Authors to mention are Oskar Baum, Max Brod, Franz Kafka etc. Expressionism was presented primarily by the poet Georg Trakl and the dramatist and narrator Hugo von. The end of World

War I reduced Austria to a very small and mainly German-speaking country. The time between the two world wars gave way to a very rich literature in Austria. Robert Musil wrote the Well-known novel. The main without Qualities. A more important influence on Austrian literature resulted however from Nazi empowerment in Germany in 1933. In 1973, a new writer's association was founded in Graz, mostly as a protest against the conservatism of P.E.N. and their controlling position, e.g. concerning literature prizes. It was known as Grazer Autoreversammlung (GAV). Thomas Bernhard, Marianne fritz. Joseph Hasinger are important centers. In 1981, Elias Canetti (1905-94) and in 2004 Elfrieda Jelinek received Nobel Prize for literature.

Q. 12. What do you understand by common wealth literature as the New Literatures?

Ans.: The common wealth offers possibilities for an intelligent meeting of the East and the West. The common wealth literary studies took as their object of study literature of the viewly independent nations. Colonization in one form or the other was responsible for the use of English is these regions which already had an established tradition of literature in languages other than English. Thus the English language literature produced was a 'new' addition to the body of literature already existing like India, Kenya, Nigeria, Australia, New Zealand and Canada.

When assimilated into the existing body of English literature, seen as the repository of universal human values, the new or younger literatures in English the new or younger literatures in English are perceived as enriching or invigorating it. Bruce King in his introduction to literatures of the World in English acknowledges that there are different national literary traditions with values and histories of their own, but that each literature is a part of world English literature, and shares in the heritage of British writing. From the European perspective at least, the new literature in English deal with 'new' countries where new immigrant populations have come into existence. The new literature thus reflect par excellence the historical processes by which such societies have been created and the development of consciousness through which new lands have been inscribed in the collective imagination of emerging countries. Thus the literature of Nigeria, India and Zimbabwe are discussed because they are 'new' nations and those of Australia, Canada, New Zealand because they have been populated by 'new' immigrants but also because has recently become a nation European critics have tried to pull common wealth literature and new literature in English away from being a mere supplement to British Literature. Its main quality is that common wealth literature I is itself multicultural.

Q. 13. Write a short note on English literature from Russia.

Ans.: Russian literature refers to the literature of Russia or its émigrés. Prior to the 19th century, the seeds of the Russian literary tradition were soon by the poets, playwrights and writers as Derzhavin, Fonvizin, Sumarokov and Krylok. From around the 1830s, Russian literature underwent as astounding golden age beginning with the poet and novelist Aleksandr Pushkin and culminating in two of the greatest novelists in world literature, Leo Tolstoy and Fyoder Dostoevsky and Anton Chekhov. In the 20th century leading figures of recognized poets such as Vladimir Mayakovsky, Boris Pasternak, and Joseph Brodsky and Prose writers Maxim Gomy, Vladimir Nabokov etc.

The 19th century is traditionally referred to as me 'Golden age' of Russian novelist was Nikolai Gogol. The beginning of the 20th century ranks as the Silver age of Russian Poetry. The poets most often associated with the 'Silver age' are Anna Akhmatova, Marine. Tsvetaera, Osip Mandelstanm and Boris Pasternak. Though the Silver Age is famous mostly for its poetry, it gave some first-rate novelists and short story writers, such as Alexander Kuprin, Nobel Prize winner Ivan Bunin, Leonid Andreyer, Fedor Sologup, Dmitry Merezh Kovsky and Andrei Bely, through most of them wrote poetry as well as prose.

The end of the 20th century has proven a difficult period for Russian literature. Among the most discussed authors of these period were Victor Pelevin, who gained popularity with first short stones and then novels, novelist and playwright Viladimvi Sorokin, and the poet Dmitry Prigor. A relatively new trend in Russian literature is that female story unters. Tatyana Tolstaya and novelist Lyudmila Ulit Skays or Dina Rubine have come into provinence. Detective stories and thrillers have come proven a very successful genre of new Russians literature.

Q. 14. What is Scandinavia literature?

Ans.: Scandinavia literature or Nordic literature is the literature in the languages of the Nordic countries of Northern Europe. The Nordic countries include Denmark, Finland, Iceland Norway, Sweden and associated autonomous territories. The may only of these nations and regions use North Germanic languages. Henrik Ibsen, a Norweigian playwright, was largely responsible for the popularity of modern realistic drama in Europe, with plays him. *The Wild Dvice* and *A Doll's House*. Nobel Prizes for literature have been awarded to Selme Largerlof, Verner von Heidenstarm, Nelly Sachs, Harry Martinism etc.

The period from the 14th century upto the 19th century is considered a dark age in Norway's literature through Norweigian-born writers such as Pedon Clausson Frils and Ludvig Holbey contributed to the common literature of Denmark-Norway. With the advent of nationalism and the struggle for independence in the early 19th century a new period of national literature emerged. The dramalist Henrik Ibsen were to earn Norway an influential place of Western. European literature. In the 20th century notable Norwegian writers include the two Nobel Prize writing authors Knut Hamsun and Sirgid Undset.

33

Indian Writing in English and Indian Literature in English Translation

Q. 1. What do you understand by Indian English Literature?

Ans.: Indian English literature may be defined as literature written originally in English by authors Indian by birth, ancestry or nationality. It is clear that according to this definition neither. Anglo Indian literature, nor literal translations by others can legitimately form part of this literature. Similarly, translations from the Indian languages into English cannot also form part of Indian English literature, except when they are creative translations by the authors themselves, like Tagore's Gitanjali. K.R. Srinivasa Iyengar used the Phrase 'Indian Writing in English' for the first time. The Sahitya Academi has recently accepted 'Indian English Literature' as the most suitable appellation. For this literature constitutes one of the many streams that join the great ocean called Indian literature, which, though written in different languages, has an unmistakable unity; and secondly that it is an inevitable product of the nativization of the English language to express the Indian sensibility.

Not only Indian thought from Vedu to modern times has found its way to the West, but eminent thinkers from Ram Mohan Roy to Vivekananda, Tagore, Sri Aurobindo, Gandhi and Radhakrishnan have made themselves hard in the West. A cultural offensive rendered easier by their mastery of the English language. Prof V.K. Gokak spells out the evolution of Indian English as a 'district standard'—a standard the body of which is correct English usage, but whose soul is Indian in colour, thought and imagery, and now and then, even in the evolution of an Indian idiom which is expressive of the unique quality of the Indian mind while conforming to the correctness of English usage. Mulkraj Anand, Narayan, Raja Rao, Kamala Markandaya, Anita Desai, Shashi Deshpande, Arun Joshi, Amitabh Ghosh and Vikram Seth have their distinctive individual style and yet each style is distinctively Indian. We can divide Indian English Literature from 1930s to the end of the 20th century into two phrases; Modernist and Post-modernist, the former beginning with Raja Rao's *Kanthapura* (1938) and the latter beginning with Salman Rushdie's *Midnight Children* (1981) and Nissim Ezekiel's *Latter Day Psalms* (1982).

Q. 2. Write a short history of Indian Drama in English in the Pre-independence Period.

Ans.: Indian drama, written, both in English and translated into English from other languages, has registered a remarkable growth in recent years. The first Indian play in English *Is This Called Civilization*? was written by Michael Madhusudan Dutt in 1871. The pre-Independent era saw some major figures like R.N. Tagore, Sri Aurobindo, T.P. Kailasam, Ayyar, Lobo-Prabhu, Harindranath Chattopadhaya and Bharathi Sarabhai—who contributed substantially to the growth and development of Indian-English drama. R.N. Tagore was the first major playwright who invested Indian drama in English with lyrical excellence, symbolic overtones and allegorical significance. Sri Aurobindo inherited and carried forward the tradition of Elizabethan poetic drama of Marlowe and Shakespeare. His dramatic genius is amply revealed in his five complete plays—*Persus*, *Vasavadutta*, *Rodagune*. *The Viziers of Bassara* and *Eric*-which were written originally in English. T.P. Kailasham's English plays are inspired by puranic themes taken from the *Ramayana* and the *Mahabharata*. His play *The Purpose* (1944) dramatizes Eklavya's single-minded devotion to the art of archery.

Harindranath Chattopadhyaya added a new dimension to Indian English drama with his leftist leavings and revolutionary zeal. He has written devotional plays. He had acute awareness of social problems and his evinate sympathies for the suffering masses.

Bharati Sarabhai is the first distinguished woman dramatist, who gave a Gandhian touch to Indian English drama. Her first play *The Well of the people* (1949) followed by *Two Women* (1952) left the impression of the playwright. J.M. Lobo Prabhu is the last great name in Pre-independence Indian English drama. He has written a dozen plays. The names of a few more playwrights may be taken into account. They may be called minor dramatists. Some are Sudhindra Nath Ghose, R.K. Narayan, K.R.S. Iyengar, Balwant Gargi and Mrinalini Sarabhai. Although the pre-independence Indian English drama is notable for its poetic excellence thematic variety, technical varicosity, symbol significance and its commitment to human and moral values it was by and large not geared for actual stage production.

Q. 3. Comment upon Post-independence English Drama.

Ans.: In the Post-Independence era Indian-English drama does not make a noteworthy presence unlike poetry and fiction. The fact to be noted is that a good number of plays by Indian playwrights like Asif Currimbhoy, Pratap Sharma Gurcharan Das were successfully staged in England and USA. But no regular school of Indian-English drama was established in our country. Most of the dramas were written in prose but at the same time poetic plays also survive in the post-colonial era. M.K. Naik writes, "... the Tagore Aurobindo-Kailsam tradition of poetic drama continues, but with a difference in the hands of Manjeri Isvaran, G.V. Desani and Pritish Nandy."

Pratap Sharma wrote two prose plays: first is *A Touch of Brightness* (1968) and *The Professor Has a Warcry* (1970). His plays were staged abroad successfully but they failed to be staged in the country. Sex is the main theme of his plays.

Nissim Ezekiel's *Three Plays* are considered to be a welcome addition to the dramaturgy of Indian English drama with his short play *Sings of denovation* (1969). From 1945 onwards, one finds several dramatic organizations launched, but none devoted itself exclusively to the drama in English. In the post-independence period, performing arts were employed as an effective means of public enlightenment during 1951-54. As a result, the National School of Drama was established under the dictatorship of Alkazi. Institutions for training in dramatics were founded in big cities. The Annual Drama Festival was started in New Delhi by the Sangit Nataka Akedemi in 1954. With so much encouragement coming from so many quarters, drama begun to flourism in the regional languages, with the singular exception of the drama in English.

Q. 4. "Indian-English poetry is truly Indian"—Examine critically.

Ans.: Indian English poetry though owes its origin to Henry Derozio's Poems published in 1827, it got a local habitation and a name, with the publication of Nissim Ezekiel's *A Time to Change in London* in 1952. Between Derozio and Ezekiel, we have only a few Indian English poets such as Kashi Prasad Ghosh, Michael Madhusudan Dutt, Sri Aurobindo Ghose, Sarojini Naidu, Kamla Das, A.K. Ramanujan, Jayanta Mahapatra, R. Parthasarthi and Keki N. Daruwalla.

When Leeds University established a chair for Common- wealth Literature in 1958 and started imparting it as a course, Indian English became a part of it. Nissim Ezekiel became the first Modern Indian-English poet in the Post-Independence period and his book of Poems, *A Time to Change* can be said to herald modernism in Indian English poetry. P. Lal and his Writers' Workshop established in 1958 worked as a catalyst to further the cause of Indian-English poetry.

Nissim Ezekiel has yielded place to reality and the poet like a detached observer sees and describes what happens all around us. Indian reality has become a favourite subject of the poet for contemplation. He helped to popularize free verse in Indian-English poetry. Kamala Das's feminine sensibility finds its true and fullest expression in her love poems. Indian sensibility is transparent in her poetry and the use of Radha Krishna myth makes it more appealing to the Indian readers. Ramanujan wants to put all his experiences and visions into the texture of his poetry. Hindu consciousness is pivoted to Ramanujan's thinking. His knowledge of Indian Myths and folklore is amazing. Mahapatra's pre-occupation with the naked earth (of which Orissa forms a significant part) the favourite places such as Jagannath Puri, Cuttack, Bhubaneswar dominates his thoughts. Mahapatra has made an effort to evoke a typical Indian atmosphere by describing the Indian sky, landscape, birds and even abandoned temples in his poetry. Shiv K. Kumar's treatment of the theme of love in terms of the elements of Indian landscape has the poetic reconciliation of the spirit and the country. Images of India are handled with a consummate skill and keenness of intellectual in Kumar's poetry. Indian English poetry is incomplete without Sarojini Naidu who wrote her poetry with full of Indian colour.

Q. 5. Write a note on new Indian-English poets (poets from 1975 onwards).

Ans.: The luxuriant growth of Indian-English poetry occurred in mid-seventies with the publication of R. Parthasarthy's anthology 'Ten Twentieth Century Indian Poets' in 1976. This marked the beginning of postmodernism in Indian-English poetry. It was followed by Ezekiel's 'Hymns in Darkness' (1976), 'Ramanujan's Selected Poems' (1977), Keki N. Daruwalla's 'Crossing Parthasarthy's Rough Passage' (1976) and Shiv K. Kumar's 'Subterfuges' (1977). Indian English poetry won recognition both at home and abroad.

Sahitya Akademi, New Delhi has honoured seven Indian English poets with its Annual Award in the Post 1980 period, they are Jayanta Mahapatra for Relationship in 1981, Nissim Ezekiel for Latter Day Psalms in 1983, Keki N. Daruwalla for Keeper of the Dead in 1984, Kamala Das for Collected Poems Vol. I in 1995, Shiv K. Kumar for Trapfalls in the Sky in 1987, Dom Moraes for Sarendip in 1994 and Ramanujan for Collected Poems in 1999.

Nissim Ezekiel is to Indian-English poetry, what T.S. Eliot is to English poetry. He has given it a direction, and idiom and a sense of purpose. Kamala Das grapples with ideas and abstractions, images of men and women on several planes, the complex its of emotions centring round human activities such as love, sex, companionship and problems relating to her own art. Ramanujan combines his scholarship with poetic insight and the result is astounding. Mahapatra wants to decolonize himself and his culture so that he can be called a Post-colonial poet. Shiv K. Kumar is in favour of the subversion of tradition and rituals and therefore irony becomes a favourite mode in his poetry. Daruwalla wants to use new idiom and create new themes by writing about contemporary Indian reality, subverting the tradition so that Indian English poetry will assume an identity of its own. Other poets are O.P. Bhatnagar, A.K. Mehrotra, Gieve Patel, Eunice de souza, Arun Kolatkan, Vikram Seth, Bibhu Padhi, Shanta Acharya, Meena Alexander, Sunita Jain, Sujata Bhatt, Rukmini Bhaya Nair, Makarand Paranjape, C.P. Surendran. Nvanjan Mohanty, and R.K. Singh etc.

Q. 6. "The Indian-English writers have often used their works as vehicles of social protest or Propaganda". Discuss.

Ans.: Although the Indian fiction in English has been relatively delayed manifestation of the modern Indian imagination, it has always been instrumental in an artistic rendering of the contemporary social reality. Writers like Mulk Raj Anand did not believe that an artist should live in an ivory tower and indulged in fanciful dreams about the joys and delights of human existence. He was a believer in using art as a vehicle for the advancement and progress of human society. Anand and others like him tried and fulfilled their aims and efforts to depict the suffering and misery of the backward classes in order to bring about some kind of amelioration in their living standard. This effort made them really popular as Indian-English novelists. Women writers like Anita Desai, Shashi Deshpande, Kamala Markandaya, Kamala Das, Nissim Ezekiel, Ruth Prawar Jhabvala, Nayantara Sehgal etc. all spoke about Indian society, Indian women, their inner Psyche, their problems, man-woman relationship etc. and made people conscious about various issues affecting their lives.

Q. 7. Write a note on Pioneer of Religious and Philosophical Prose in Indian-English Literature.

Ans.: The most notable writer of religious and Philosophical prose of Indian writing in English is easily Sarvpally Radhakrishnan (1888-1975), a teacher of philosophy who rose to be President of India. Radhakrishnan's chief achievement is the recognition he won in the western world for Indian philosophy as a major system of thought. He has been accused of interpreting all Indian systems of thought in the light of his own idealistic monism, and also of offering an inadequate interpretation of Buddhist thought. He also felt the impact of Vivekananda's thought and eloquence. His M.A. dissertation on *The Ethics of the Vedanta* (1908) was a spirited reply to the Western, charged that the Vedanti has no room for Ethics. In another work *The Philosophy of Rabindranath Tagore* (1918), Radhakrishnan found support for his own views on Hindu ethics and the extremely complex doctrine of Maya, in the poetry of Tagore. Radhakrishnan's first major work, *The Reign of Religion in Contemporary Philosophy* (1920), was his earliest attempt to examine Western philosophical thought. Here he argues that the implicit pluralistic theism in the thought of many modern western philosophers demonstrates the influence of religion on philosophy. Indian Philosophy (Vols. I-II, 1923, 1927) is Radhakrishnan's magnum opus. As a comprehensive and through systematic and readable account of Indian Philosophical thought, it hardly has an equal. *The Hindu View of Life* (1926) is a forceful vindication of Hinduism as a way of life and refutes the notion that it is only a rigid set of out-moded doctrines. Other important documents are *Kalki* or the *Future of Civilization* (1929), *An Idealist View of Life* (1932), *East and West in Religion* (1933) *Eastern Religion and Western Thought* (1939) *Religion and Society* (1947), *The Principal Upanishads* (1953), and *Religion in a Changing World* (1967), *Religion and Culture* (1968), *The Present Crisis of Faith* (1970) etc. Among other significant works on religion and Philosophy may be noted P.V. Kane's *History of Dharmasastra*, S.N. Dasgupta's *History of Indian Philosophy*, R.D. Ranade's *A Constructive Survey of Upanshadic Philosophy* (1926) and *Mysticism in Maharashtra* (1930), M. Hiryann's *Outlines of Indian Philosophy* etc.

Q. 8. Comment upon Biography and Autobiography in Indian-English Literature.

Ans.: Biography and autobiography have always been forms in which Indian English Literature is rich. Of the numerous biographies of public men written during the period, a few stand out by their literary excellence. These include N.C. Kelkar's *Landmarks in Lokmanya's Life* (1924), R.P. Masani's *Dadabhai Naoroji: The Grand Old Man of India* (1939). The post-independence Indian biographer naturally found a wealth of subject, since finish had now been or was soon going to be written to the career of many a stalwart of the freedom struggle, D.K. Roy's *Among the Great* (1947) includes assessments of Gandhi, Tagore and Sri Aurobindo. Iqbal Singh's Rammohan Roy appeared in 1958. The most massive study of Mahatma Gandhi's life is by D.G. Tendulkar-*Mahatma: Life of Mohandas Karamchand Gandhi* 8 Vols. (1951-54), J.B. Kriplani's *Gandhi: His Life and Thought* (1970), and Manohar Malgonkar's *The Men Who Killed Gandhi* (1978). K.R. Srinivasa Iyengar's *Sri Aurobindo: A Biography and a History* (2 Vols., 1972) Krishna Kriplani's *Rabindranath Tagore* (1962) and Padmini Sen Gupta's *Sarojini Naidu* (1965) are worth discussing.

The Autobiographies include men and women from different walks of life. Among autobiographies by writers the earliest is Dhan Gopal Mukherji's *Caste and Outcaste* (1923) which describes his boyhood in India and his visit to Japan etc. Mulk Raj Anand's *Apology for Heroism* (1946) is much more objective analysis and remains a valuable and to the understanding of his fiction. R.K. Narayan's *My Days* (1975), K.A. Abbas's *I Write as I feel* (1948), Dom Moraes's *My Son's Father* (1968), Ved Mehta's *Face to Face* (1963) are well known autobiographies.

Of the Women autobiographers, Vijayalaxmi Pandit (So I became a Minister and Person Days 1936, 1945), Krishna Huthee Singh (With No Regrets 1944), *Prison and Chocolate Cake* (1954) by Nayantara Sehgal, *My Story by Kamala Das* (1976) etc.; Kamala Das became famous for her autobiography as it is confessional. Shobha De wrote and set a new record in the field of autobiography.

Q. 9. What do you know about The Short Story in Indian writing in English during 1920-47?

Ans.: Like the novel, the Indian English short story too came into its own during the Gandhian age. The most notable contribution here is by the leading novelists, though there are also writers who devoted themselves exclusively to this form. Shankar Ram and almost all the other notable short story writers of the period (with the exception of Mulk Raj Anand) are from South India like S.P. Ayyar, S.K. Chettur etc. The most productive of Indian English short story writers, Manjeri Isvaran, the poet, is the author of many short stories and is far more successful than some of his contemporaries in his treatment of fantasy and the supernatural element.

Isvaran, like S.K. Chettur, employs a variety of narrative strategies, including the observer's point of view and the use of journals and letters. Apart from Isvaran, the most important contribution to the short story of this period came from the three major novelists—Anand, Narayan and Raja Rao who are different in the depiction of mood and tone along with locale and characters, form and style. Narayan as the writer of *Malgudi Days* (1943) is known for his use of irony. His stories are uniformly compact and are told in his usual seemingly artless style. He sometimes uses the 'Talkative Man' as narrator. The thematic interconnections between some of his stories and novels is really interesting. Raja Rao has published only a dozen stories which are collected in the *Cow of the Barricades and Other Stories* (1947). These dozen stories exhibit considerable thematic and formal variety. Some of the other story writers of the period are K.A. Abbas, Sita Chatterjee, Dewan Sharar, A.V. Rao, T.K. Venugopal, Ela Sen and Humayun Kabir.

Q. 10. Comment upon the Indian-English story written after independence.

Ans.: The variety and fecundity of the post-Independence novel are hardly evinced in the field of Short Story, the writing of which still continues to be mostly a by-product of the novel workshop. Of the novelists, Bhavani Bhattacharya, Khushwant Singh, Manohar Malgonkan, Chaman Nahal and Joshi have produced short story collections, while among the women writers, Ruth P. Jhabvala, Anita Desai, Nergis Dalal, Attiah Hosain and Jhumpa Lahiri are prominent and well known among the masses.

Ruskin Bond has also published a number of collections of short-stories. Manoj Das, winner of the Sahitya Akademi award has published four collections of Short Stories. Anita Desai's *Games At Twilight and Diamond Dust* deal with psychology of her characters. Nergis Dalal mostly offers well—made stories with a surprise ending, or melodrama. The stories in *A Doll For the Child Prostitute* (1977) by Kamala Das generally harp upon the Sex-theme. The title story is marred by an overplus of melodrama and most of the other stories are too sketchy to present adequately realized experience. Anita Desai's *Diamond Dust*, Jhumpa Lahiri's *Unaccustomed Earth* and Aravind Adiga's *Between the Assassination* have set new landmark in the area of short fiction.

Q. 11. Write down a short history of Indian fiction in English.

Ans.: Fiction, being the most characteristic and powerful form of literary expression, has acquired a prestigious position in Indian-English literature, popularly known as Indian writing in English. It made its appearance during the nineteen twenties and thirties, when most of the vernacular literatures in India had already achieved tremendous maturity especially in the medium of fiction reflecting the universal consciousness of change. The first ever Indian novel in English was written by Bankim Chandra Chatterjee who established the novel as a major literary form in India. *His Raj Mohan's Wife* was the first and the only English novel he wrote. Then substantial and powerful fiction writers like Mulk Raj Anand, R.K. Narayan and Raja Rao began to emerge and establish their distinct identity in the domain of fiction writing. The first half of the twentieth century was governed by the trend setting solid—political and ideological events caused by the Gandhian movement which had its deep impact on the fiction writing of the era. In the post-independence era women novelists form a distinct identity of their own. Among the women fiction writers, Ruth Prawar Jhabvala, Kamala Markandaya, Nayantara Sehgal, Shanta Rama Rao, Bharati Mukherjee, Veena Nagpal, Arundhati Roy,

Shashi Deshpande, Anita Desai, Shobhaa De, Kiran Desai occupy unique place in the history of Indian English fiction.

The fiction writers were deeply affected by the radical changes which were brought about by the partition of the country. Whereas poverty, hunger, death and disease form the keynotes of the sympathy, movements like humanitarianism, socialism and liberalism spotlight the finer aspects of their dream for the future. They seem to stand between the two worlds—one dead, the other yet to be born. Major writers of the era are Sudhir Ghosh, Bhavani Bhattacharya, Ruskin Bond, Dilip Kumar Roy, Khushwant Singh, Venu Chitali, K.A. Abbas, Vikram Seth, Upmanyu Chatterjee, Amitabh Ghosh, and Man Broker Prize Winner Arvind Adiga.

Q. 12. Write a short note on Indian English Women novelists of the post-independence period.

Ans.: The very emergence of women writers during the period was of great significance. Kamala Markandaya, Ruth Prawar Jhabvala, Anita Desai, Nayantara Sehgal, Veena Paintal and Nergis Dalal have added new dimensions and depth to Indian fiction in English. The emergence of these women writers marks the birth of an era which promises a new deal for the Indian fiction in English. The battle of emancipation was taken over by a few educated women themselves who in their effort to communicate to the world their own bitter experiences as women as well as their ideals by social reform, turned writers. These women writers particularly shared experiences of Indian women in general and presented them into fictional form. Women's inner self their agonies, their pleasures are more truly depicted by the women novelists. Literature which until recently was male dominated, has started reflecting the sparks that have emanated from this struggle of woman to be herself. The women novelists of the nineteenth century tried to give their characters justice by posting various problems but it was the early experimental period. Owing to lack of experience of writing, they soon turned to didacticism, sentimentalism and romanticism which weakened their novels. But it was not so with the later women novelists who emerged in the post-independence era. The fiction of Kamala Markandaya is largely sociological in its focus. Her novels give a faithful account of contemporary Indian reality. Nayantara Sehgal, also an established political columnist, does not view her women as wives, daughter and mothers and it is in these roles that they wish to experience freedom and to become aware of themselves as individuals and to be accepted as equals. Anita Desai shows a remarkable skill in her use of highly suggestive imagery and in handling the stream of consciousness technique. There are some other notable fiction writers with an impressive corpus of fiction to their credit such as Shashi Deshpande, Attic Hussain Rama Mehta, Nergis Dalal, Bharati Mukherjee, Manju Kapoor, Shobhaa De, Kiran Desai, Namita Gokhle, Arundhati Roy etc.

Q. 13. "Through poetry of sex Kamala Das constructs a world which exposes the social reality, crime, political Lechery" etc. Comment.

Ans.: Kamala Das, the celebrated Madhavi Kutty of the Malayalam short stories, explores the murky dimensional life with a bold and uninhibited frankness. She is rich in expressing female sexuality and revealing many things about life from a woman's angle. She believes that the 'elemental fire' or sexuality, is basic to woman relationship and must be honestly accepted by every woman.

Female sexuality is a positive presence in her poems to feel valued and to boast her self esteem just as she develops the irony through a recurrent representation of selfishness, social disruption, or a disturbing detachment which begins to call into question the simplification of her sexuality. She offers a direct challenge to the fixed norms and assumptions of male sexuality just as she addresses herself to various social and Psychological problems. Through poetry of sex, she constructs a world which exposes the social reality, criminality, political lechery, fanatic waves, nightmares, terror, hypocricy and perversion that frightens the male. Through facts of sexuality and her imagery, she challenges the contemporary values and social and political mores. Her sexual reflections are sometimes like Eliot's contemplation of hooded hards. She reflects woman as a being with myriad lives and myriad sensations, a complex multiform. She is open, bold, and honest and has energy to fight discrimination, stigma, stereotype and prejudice. She challenges others and questions community norms and attitude about sexuality which defines her role and relationship with man.

Q. 14. Discuss R.N. Tagore as a dramatist.

Ans.: R.N. Tagore was an educational, social and religious reformer at par with Gandhi. He was a creative artist of incredibly abundant gifts; a writer of poetry, short stories, novels, essays and plays, a highly unorthodox painter, and a composer of songs that have completely captured not only Bengali hearts but the hearts of whole nation. Tagore as a dramatist is not much different from Tagore as a poet or a painter. His plays and poetry have universal appeal and they illuminate his complexity and his 'myraid-mindedness.' Tagore's entire creativity is permeated with the idea of the national freedom, and of the struggle for the spiritual and political liberation.

Tagore's poetic impulses deeply influence his dramatic ideas and it is rightly said of him that Tagore the playwright rarely ceases to be Tagore, the poet. In his plays he continues to superimpose his poetic expression in a subdued form. In his plays, these very ideas reflecting his philosophical attitudes and concepts are manifested. Tagore admired Shakespeare, and Ibsen but he knew his Kalidasa very well too. He was a gifted actor himself, and he wanted to give a new tone to the Bengali stage.

Tagore's dramas are divided into two classes—the earlier, non-symbolic drama such as *Sacrifice* and *The King And The Queen* and the later symbolic dramas such as *The Post Office*, *The Cycle Of Spring* and *Red Oleanders* of the non-symbolic plays some like Karna And Kunti or *Devayani* are one scene playlets. *Malini* and *The Sanyasi* are slightly larger.

In fact Tagore's symbolic dramas are better than his experiments in the field of direct dramatic representations. Krishanan Joshi and B. Shyamala Rao have divided Tagore's plays in three divisions. According to them his plays can be divided into three groups; in the plays of first group, Tagore tried to apply the elements of western tragedy to Indian materials known as dramas of conflict (*Malini*, *Sacrifice*, *King and Queen*), the second group includes plays of allegory (*The Post Office*, *Chitra*, *The King of the Dark Chambers* and *Red Oleanders*). The third group deals with plays like *Mukta Dhara*, *Natir Puja* etc. whole career by experimentation to a point of culmination by integrating the two levels if dramatic vision—those of the intellect and of experience.

Q. 15. Discuss the limitations of Tagore as a dramatist.

Ans.: Tagore's poetic impulses deeply influence his dramatic ideas and it is rightly said of him that Tagore the playwright rarely ceases to be Tagore the poet. Most of the critics have assigned his dramas a place below his poems. Thompson is inclined to give high value to his achievements as a dramatist and he regrets that Tagore did not allow his dramatic genius full development. Although there is no lack of sparkling wit in Tagore's plays, but they lack that penetrating sense of humour which enables a dramatist to understand characters of different temperaments and to identify himself equally with all of them. Tagore has never created characters like Hamlet, Iago, Cleopatra, Feste because in delineating characters, Tagore draws grand outline rather than going into subtle shades.

R.N. Tagore has the mentality of a mystic and the language barrier was always there as a major limitation. Tagore knew that his genius could blossom only through his writings in his mother tongue but to reach the world public he would have to cross the language barrier. And through him Indian literature in a new way made a triumphant entry in the map of world literature (Nobel Prize), but that was for his poetry. Some of Tagore's non-symbolic plays are so short that they may be called dramatic scenes rather than plays. (*Karna and Kunti*, *Devayani* etc.). Tagore can not be compared with Shakespeare or G.B. Shaw. His plays are not meant for the Western Stage, they are not intended to be enacted in an open air stage with practically no scenic equipment.

Tagore's larger dramas have a loose construction. They are not compact in form and the plot simply drags on the labyrinthine of digression. *Chitra* and *Malini* are exceptions. The prose dramas except *Mukta Dhara*, are also weak in construction and swift movement in them is obstructed by excessive dialogue and declamation. Theme invariably dominates over action. Thus finally we can see that Tagore has produced many great plays but his greater poems and short stories overshadow Tagore, the dramatist.

Q. 16. Comment upon Tagore's language and style in his plays.

Ans.: Tagore's plays are firmly rooted in the Indian ethos, in their themes and characters. Tagore is a master of the technique of language, he knows how to clothe the trivial happenings with the glamour of poetic fancy. He does not bother about the meaning of words; his chief aim is not to explain meanings but to knock at the door of the mind.

Tagore's witty dialogues are full of shrewed knowledge of men and women. He is interested also in the way language relates to the world: how word signify and refer, and how prepositions can be meaningful. In short, it is the logic of language that the analyst feels concerned with Tagore's concept of language is derived from his anthropology. For him, language is primarily expression, though expression entails communication. Critics believe that for Tagore language is a constant creation of alternative worlds, his concept of language offers a denial of determinism.

Tagore seems to opine that language is rooted in mystery and it is open-ended. Tagore looked at the problem of language from the aesthetic point of view. Tagore never welcomed any pre-established or enforced uniformity or standardization, because he abhorred uniformity in language.

Tagore is unique as he blended the poetic creed with the demands of drama. Language in his drama shows his great mastery over music, metaphors and symbols. K.R. Srinivasa Iyengar said, "Not the logic of careful plotting but the music of ideas and symbols is the 'soul' of the drama. Not the apparent meaning but its echoing cadence of suggestion—dhwani as the Sanskrit rhetoricians called it, in other words, the richness of the undertones is whole matters, for this alone kindles the sluggish soul to a new awareness of life's deep-magic."

Q. 17. Write a short note on the Early period of Indian-English fiction.

Ans.: The marvelous Toru Dutt, besides her many poems and her French novel, wrote in her terms and English novel also named *Bianca* or *The Young Spanish Maiden*. Romesh Chander Dutt was a gifted novelist as well. Two of his Bengali novels were also published in English *The slave girl of Agra* (1909) deals with Mogul times. Another novel *The Lake of Palms* (1902) is an intimate and reliable picture of social life in Bengal.

The various English translation of Bankim Chandra Chatterji's celebrated novels largely contributed to the literary renaissance in India during the last quarter of the nineteenth century. His novels gave at once a standing and status to the Indian novel. Among South Indian writers, the late B.R. Rajam wrote an English novel *Vasudera Sastri*. We may mention T. Ramakrishna the author of *Padmini* (1909), *The Dive for Death* (1911) and P.A. Madhvian the author of *Thillai Govidan*.

The writers from the Punjab who have attempted English fiction are Miss Sorabhi, Sir Joginder Singh and Bal Krishna. Miss Sorabhi's short stories are *Love and Life behind the Purdah, Sun Babies* and *Between the Twilights*. Sardar Joginder Singh's first two novels, *NurJahan* and *Nasrin* appeared as serials in 'The East and West'. The *Love of Kusuma* (1911) by Bal Krishna is disappointing.

Q. 18. Write a note on Middle period of Indian English Fiction and the major writers.

Ans.: Among the Indo-Anglians who came to prominence in the first decade there was: K.S. Venkataramani. His first published book *Paper Boats* gave a few vignetts of South Indian village life. Another book of prose—poem by him is "On the Sand Tunes', the form had by then been popularized by the Tagore's *Gitanjali*. After that Shankar Ram's three English publication are: *The Children of the Kaveri* (1927), *Creatures All* (1938), and *The Love of Dust* (1938).

After 1930, there came a sudden flowering in the Indian literature in English. A society compelled into self awareness like that provides a fertile soil for fiction and it is no accident that the three major Indian novelist in English viz. Mulk Raj Anand, R.K. Narayanan and Raja Rao began their career during the phase.

Dr. Mulk Raj Anand hails from the extreme North-West of India. His birth place is Peshawar. His important publications are *Across the Black Waters*, *The Coolie*, *Two Leaves and a Bud*, *The Untouchable*, and *The Village and The Big Heart*. He is an ardent believer in the doctrine of social revolution and socialistic pattern of society. His object is not merely to shock his readers by a representation of reality but to stimulate their conciousnesses, and his concern as fiction writer has always been the redemption of the poor and the oppressed.

R.K. Narayanan is little concerned with the maladies in the society and shows no desire for reforming it. All his novels are concerned in and around Malgudi, a small town in South India. His first novel is *Swami & Friends*. His *The Bachelor of Art* is a more mature work. His short stories appeared in the columns of the 'Hindu' and other journals. He is master at his own chosen grounds.

Raja Rao is deemed as the finest portrayer of Indian sensibilities. He tried to revive the ancient current of Indian creative writers in English. *Kanthapura* is his well known novel. The technique of novel is old as those of *The Ramayana* and *The Mahabharata*. The whole story is put into the mouth of an old woman of the village.

Among other novelists of the period is S. Nagarajun. His Fiction gives an enduring picture of a Maratha Brahmin family living in South India. Dewan Sharar wrote *The Gang of Shira*. It is well planned, well executed and wholly Indian Novel.

Q. 19. Account for the enduring popularity of Mulk Raj Anand as a novelist.

Ans.: Undoubtedly, Mulk Raj Anand has definite social and moral aims in the writing of his novels. Anand did not believe that an artist should live in an ivory tower and indulged in fanciful dreams about the joys and delight of human existence. Anand was no believer in art for art's sake; he was a believer in using art as a vehicle for the advancement and progress of human society known as Indian Charles Dickens. Anand described his philosophy as humanism, meaning that he was an upholder and champion of the basic rights of a human beings and a campaigner for the welfare of mankind. His novels clearly show his intense love of his fellow human beings though it has to be admitted that in those novels his attention is confined to the people of his own country. In novel after novel he revealed his concept of humanism, especially in his first three novels; *Untouchable*, *Coolie* and *Two Leaves and a Bud* give us a comprehensive picture of the miserable life led by the humble, unfortunate and disinherited classes of people in this country. Author's aim and efforts to depict the suffering and misery of the backward classes of people and to arouse the conscience of the richer classes in order to bring about same kind of amelioration in their living standard, made him really popular as an Indian English novelist.

Anand became popular among the masses as he never tried to directly lecture and sermonize to us. He conveyed his intentions and suggestions to us indirectly, through his real pictures of contemporary Indian Life.

Another reason for Anand's popularity may be his being the most prolific writer of his time. In a writing career spread over almost forty years, he produced more than a dozen novels, half a dozen collection of short stories and numerous other works, on subjects ranging from art to cosmetics and literary criticism to cookery. Most of his fictional works have been translated into several world languages. He wrote novels, short-stories, essays and criticism and poetry too. He contributed articles and review to scores of Journals.

Q. 20. How far it is correct to call M.R. Anand as 'the Charles Dickens of India?'

Ans.: Anand felt that the novel should not press the inner monologue beyond a certain point, so that the humaneness may remain a variable factor in the situation. Social awareness was always the central theme of his novels. The great novelist believed that a writer had a duty towards the society in which he lived. His creativity was with a definite purpose to serve the humanity.

Mulk Raj Anand's prolific writing career spanned more than 75 years, a rare achievement of a writer. He was widely identified with the gust for a just, equitable, and forward-looking India. He wrote extensively in areas as diverse as art and sculpture, politics, literature, novels, but also short stories and critical essays on literature and art. He was a vocal supporter of the

Gandhian non-violence movement for national liberation from British Colonial rule, although his socialist sympathies took him considerably beyond the ambit of gradualist reform favoured by the Mahatma. One of his biographers wrote: "A staunch Marxist but a Gandhian, Anand's career was launched by a family tragedy, instigated by the rigid caste system that continues to be the scourge of Indian society even today."

A man with commitment Anand was a life long crusader for the cause of have nots. If he was not branded 'a left wing writer'; opposing the British imperialists in India, he would have got the Noble Prize for literature.

In addition to exposing the social evils which were eating into the vitals of Indian society, Anand always advocated, by implication if not in explicit terms, the need of social and national integration. Anand was able to infuse life into all characters who figures in his novels; and the number and variety of the characters in his novels and multi tudinous. Here he reminds us of Charles Dickens. Almost all of Anand's characters are convincing persons. One reason for his realistic portrayal of character is that most of the persons in his novels were modeled on individuals whom he had actually known in his contemporary social life.

Q. 21. "Amitav Ghosh's singular distinction lies in his original perception of reality, which he translates through an art, which is at once intuitive, conscious and deliberate". In the light of the above comment discuss Amitav Ghosh as a novelist.

Ans.: Ghosh's engagement is with the real world. This real engagement accounts for his interest in sociology and anthropology in actual life. Amitav Ghosh is quintessentially an Indian, a Bengalee, who was born in Kolkata and raised in Dhaka and Colombo. But he came back to study at the University of Delhi and to teach in the sociology Department of Delhi School of Economics. He also taught at the universities of Virginia and Columbia, but he keeps returning to India to revive his cultural links with the country of his birth.

Ghosh has not written as a literary critic or theorist, but his art indicates that he is keenly interested in fictional form. He has used many devices to structure and organize his novel. One significant device is the trope and images 'Going away' and 'Coming there'.

Q. 22. Write down a short history of Indian English Drama.

Ans.: Girish Karnad says that the earliest extant play in India was written as early us A.D. 200. In regional language it enjoys almost an equal status along with two other major literary genres, namely fiction and poetry. But the picture proves to be rather somber and uninspiring in respect of Indian drama in English.

The first Indian English play *Persecuted* or Dramatic Scenes of the Present State of Hindu society in Calcutta, was written by Krishna Mohan Bannerji in 1831. It is a social play exposing the hypocrisy of the affluent in Hindu Society. Michael Madhusudan Dutt translated his play *Ratnavali* (1859) and *Sermista* (1859) originally written in English *Is This Called Civilization*? (1871). Ramninoo Dutt wrote his Manipuri Tragedy in 1983. Indian English drama, thus, one might venture to add, made a humble beginning in the 19th century Bengal. Nair observes that due to the lack of a firm dramatic tradition nourished on actual performance in a live theatre, early Indian English drama in Bengal as elsewhere in India, grew sporadically as mostly closet drama; and even later, only Sri Aurobindo, Rabindranath Tagore and H.N. Chattopadhyaya (known as Big Three) produced a substantial corpus of dramatic writing. Tagore wrote more than forty plays of all kinds. Though his plays have variety, there is repetition of themes and language in some of them. Sri Aurobindo wrote in all eleven verse dramas. His longest play is *Perseus the Deliverer*, inspired by his participation in Indian struggle for freedom H. Chattopadhyaya wrote devotional, social, historical and miscellaneous plays. His devotional play *Tukaram* is said to be the best Indian English play of his times in terms by characterization as well as the development of plot. His social plays are to be found in his collection *Five Plays* (1937).

Another playwright T.P. Kailasam wrote many English plays like *The Burden*, *The Brahmin's Curse,* etc. Like Shaw, Kailasam has a tendency to indulge himself in elaborate stage directions. Bharati Sarabhai as a dramatist produced her play *The Well of the People* which was a direct outcome of her association with Gandhi and Nehru.

Later it is mainly the drama in Indian languages and the drama in English translations that have registered a remarkable growth in recent decades. Several plays originally written in the regional languages, have been translated into English. It is in this context that the plays of Girish Karnad in Kannada, Mohan Rakesh in Hindi, Badar Sircar in Bengali and Vijay Tendulkar in Marathi assume significance. Since the staging of his maiden play *Housefolder* (1955) Tendulkar has come a long way.

Younger writers like Mahesh Dattani and Manjula Padamnabhan have infused new life into Indian-English Drama. Today the major place of Indian-English Drama has been occupied by translated plays, and many academicians think that it is necessary to incorporate these translations into the Corpus of Indian English Literature.

Q. 23. Comment upon the views on K.R.S. Iyengar that, "Indo-Anglican Drama; isn't it like talking about 'Snakes in Iceland'"?

Ans.: In Indian English literature we can easily witness that fiction has overshadowed drama and poetry. Picture appears more bleak, somber and uninspiring in respect of Indian drama in English. It is yet to register an appreciable growth, through several English translations of plays in the vernacular have come out. Commending on the paucity of Indian-English drama, K.R.S. Iyengar makes the natural scroll, where it is the 'Lingua franca'. He says, "Indo-Anglian Drama: isn't it like taking about 'Snakes in Iceland?' Not quite—but the problem is there, for while poetry, novels and non-fiction prose can be read in the silence of one's study, drama can come to life only in the theatre."

M.K. Naik cites a number of factors responsible for the sluggish growth of Indian English drama. He feels a playwright needs a living theatre to stage his plays, evaluate their total effects on the audience; and thereby get a chance to improve upon his performance. By and large, plays written in regional languages dominate the Indian theatre. Early Indian English playwrights could not enjoy the patronage of an English-knowing, elitist audience, and hence, the growth of Indian English drama remained, for a while, lethargic. English being a foreign language, was not intelligible to the masses, and playwright, too found it difficult to write crisp, natural and graceful dialogues in English. The dialogues proved to be somewhat stilted and artificial.

K.R.S. Iyengar just tried to draw our attention towards the paucity of originally written dramas in English by Indian playwrights. His observation is pertinent if we compare the drama with the growth of fiction in India.

Q. 24. What do you know about Sri Aurobindo as a dramatist?

Ans.: Sri Aurobindo is known as the first significant dramatist of Indian-English literature. He studied in English and French literatures, a student of Latin and Greek which necessarily calls for a study of the great dramatists like Aeschylus and Euripides, he chose the Elizabethan cast for his dramas. Like Shakespeare he worked upon themes that interested him. Five of his plays have come down in their entirety. His *Vasavadutta* is an English re-telling of Bhasa's play, *Pratijna Yaugan Dharayana*; *Rodogune* is drawn from Syrian history by Appian and inspired by the French dramatist Corneille who has written a play on the theme. The *Viziers of Bassora* takes a tale from the Arabian Nights Entertainments and reworks the story exquisitely as an Elizabethan play, *Eric* is from the Swedish Sagas; and *Perseus The Deliverer* draws from the Greek legend of Perseus and Andromeda.

In all his plays (including the unfinished one like The Prince of Edur) woman power is to the fore. Vasavadutta Anice-al-jatice, Aslang and Andromeda, are all bold figures whose romantic thoughts do not come in the way of their being achievers. Rodogune is the sole exception, just as Ophelia is the sole exception in Shakespeare's plays of a heroine who feels, looks and acts helpless and reaches a tragic end. This approach was the result of his own orientation in thought that the future of India (and the world) lay in the redemption and rise of womanhood. Sri Aurobindo writes in one of his essays: "Strength can only be created by drawing it from the internal and inexhaustible reservoirs of the Spirit, from that Adya Shakti of the Eternal which is the foundation of all new existence."

Q. 25. What is the relationship between Indian Poetics and English Studies?

Ans.: Though Indian poetics (which means practically Sanskrit poetics) is no longer a closed book to Indian scholars of English and the English Departments of some Indian universities have introduced into their courses of study. English literature is no longer a monolithic structure; it includes also Indian-English literature. Secondly, it forgets the significance of 'tradition' and fails to realize 'the presentness of the part.' While the west is firmly rooted in its tradition (beginning with Plato), we Indians are completely cut off from our Literary tradition beginning with Bharata.

Indian poetics has had along and rich tradition from Bharata to Panditoraja Jagannatha. It is full of numerous insights that are relevant. Aristotle's poetics was composed almost about the same time as Bharata's Natya-shastre. Most of the texts of Indian poetics are also available in good translation both in English and modern Indian languages. Besides there are good historics of Sanskrit poetics by S.K. De and V.P. Kane, and most of critical and expository works in English. Indian-English criticism still lacks in theoretical speculation that gives rise not only to new insights but also provides today for practical application. Most of our criticism is descriptive, and centres around the analysis of theme and characters. Indian poetics can help us in building up an infrastructure for critical inquiry. It has been primarily interested in the aesthetic appeal of literature, and can provide useful insights into the 'literaturiness' of a work. Though it may sound 'Paradoxical', Indian poetics is more practical than Western Criticism. Indian aestheticians never make a statement or propound a concept without illustrating it with suitable examples—The concept of alamiteras, Vakrokti Guna, Riti Disar (poetic blemisher) and acuity—all meant for practical application. There are English translation of the work almost all of major Sanskrit aestheticians—Bharata, Bhamaha, Dandin, Arandavanrdhana, Kuntake, Ksemendra, Masumate and Visvanathe.

Q. 26. Write a short note on themes and technique in Ezekiel's poetry.

Ans.: Nissim Ezekiel, one of the most notable poets in the Indian English tradition, had published six collections of verse. He is the most versatile poet of the country. He experimented endlessly with form and craft. In his best poetry, form and craft are deftly fused together. Versatility is the outstanding characteristic of Ezekiel's poetry. Linda Hiss says: "he is a poet of the city, Bombay, a poet of the body; and an endless explores of the labyrinths of the mind and the ceaseless attempt of man and poet to define himself and to find through all the myth and maze a way of honesty and Love." What distinguishes his poetry is the note of informality and frankness, the authencity of expression and flawless craftsmanship.

The urban theme dominates Ezekiel's poetry. He does not mivice words to expose the ugliness, dirt, wickedness, inhumanity and squalor of the metropolis. In 'A Morning Walk', Ezekiel clearly reveals the differences between dream and reality, and the wide gulf between what he wants and what he actually is. It is characteristic of Ezekiel that he finds most Bombaywallas rootless.

Ezekiel's entire poetry is suffused with Indianness. His commitment to India and to Bombay which is his chosen home, is total. Ezekiel says that the major themes of his poetry are love, personal integration, the Indian contemporary scene, modern urban life, spiritual values etc. Ezekiel's poetry is closely related with his environment. His roots lie deep in India. Ezekiel has written many poems on the subjects that immediately surround him. Ezekiel has graphically pointed in vivid picturesque words and phrases a vast gallery of portraits representing various Indian professions and ways of life. The hypocrisy of Indian gurus and saints in 'Rural Site' the exploitation of superstitions in villages is depicted. The inhibited Muslim girl appears in 'How the English Lessons Ended.' The suspected maid servant figures in 'Ganga'. Ezekiel thus succeeds in creating the authentic atmosphere of the place of the peculiar flavour of language. In this case, his use of Indian English as used by the lower middle classes is eminently successful.

Love and sex occupy a conspicuous place in his poetry. K.N. Daruwalla says, "the celebration of flesh, breakdown of married love, the transmutation of sex to blessedness, are recurring motifs in Ezekiel's poetry." Ezekiel has also centred his attention mostly on family relationship—the interaction between the poet and his immediate family—wife, children and parents. Marriage finds a prominent place in his poetry. Other themes are Alienation and Search for Identify and Religious and philosophical concerns. He is a great and gifted poetic craftsman. He uses symbols and images which are highly evocative and suggestive.

Q. 27. Write a short note on characteristics of Ramanujan's poetry.

Ans.: A.K. Ramanujan's poetic output, which consists of only two slender volumes, 'The Striders' and 'Relations', is very thin. He is a bilingual poet who composes poems in Kannada and English with equal command and mastery. He is known as a born poet who has given a new direction to Indian poetry in English. To R. Parthasarthy his poetry is the product of 'a specific culture' and his real greatness lies in his unsurpassable ability to translate this experiences 'into terms of another culture':

Ramanujan's interest in linguistics influenced his conception of poetry and poetic craftsmanship. To him words have a non verbal content. For him poetry is language that has not been used before-intense, creative, imaginative. His poetry has an undeniable stamp of authenticity of tone and treatment. His poetry is permeated with Indian experience. In fact his poetry is an expression of Indian sensibility sharpened and nourished by Western education and environment. Ramanujan's success as a poet lies in the fusion of Indian sensibility with his American experiences. The East-West or the traditional-modern conflict provides the necessary tension to his poetry and raises it to the level of the highest art. Ramanujan observes computer artistic detachment and irony to portray the Indian scene from across the Atlantic. Certain aspects of Indianness that he portrays have a universal significance.

A.K. Ramanujan has abundantly drawn upon folklore to give his 'inner forms, images and symbols.' He explores India's common heritage of myth and tradition. He is aware of the decadent social milieu of contemporary India. Ramanujan's Indian sensibility finds its superb expression in poems dealing with familial relationships. Family is the central theme in his very best poetry. Distance lends historical charm and nostalgia to his family poems. He looks across an alien culture and a vast ocean, to find his roots in Indian myth and tradition.

Ramanujan has assiduously polished and refined his poetic style. He has assigned a conspicuous place to the choice of words in poetry and to linguistic excellence. His interest in linguistics and anthropology helped his outer forms—linguistic, metrical, logical and other such ways of shaping experience. He uses simple, everyday words and observed utmost economy in the use of world. His diction is conspicuous for epigrammatic terseness, felicity of expression and classical simplicity and austerity. His poetry gains praise as it is symbolical and imagistic. His images are precise, accurate, real and highly suggestive. His technical skill remains matchless in Indian-English poetry.

Q. 28. "Kamala Das is a confessional poet." Comment with logics and examples.

Ans.: In Kamala Das's poetry we find the best expression of feminine sensibility. Her poetry is known as confessional and autobiographical. Love and sex form the main theme in her poetry. She craves for union with man for the fulfillment of love but she is disillusioned and frustrated when it degenerates into sheen lust fullness and bodily pleasures. Her poetry deals with unfulfilled love and the celebration of sex, in fact it is a record of her own unfulfilled love and her own sexual exploitation, frustration and disillusionment that she had to suffer. It is a world of dancing eunuchs. The dance of the eunuchs symbolises the dance of the sterile and, therefore, the unfulfilled and insatiable love of the woman in the poet.

Kamala Das has defly created a sterile, arid, dehumanized and exploitative world which is conspicuous by the sheer obscene of love and the predominance of sexual exploitation of women by man. She uses apt and suggestive images to visualize this world of 'vacant ecstasy'. It is a world in which extramarital relations are glorified. In poem after poem Kamala Das is preoccupied with love, sex and frustration. Love proved to be a pretention. She was tied to the tedium and monotony of sexuality. The uninhibited and frank description of sex characteristics her poetry. In writing about, love outside marriage, Kamala Das does not justify adultery and infidelity but she justifies the search for an ideal relationship which gives love, satisfaction and security. The charge of obsession with love and lust is hardly tenable because Kamala Das writes from the depth of her own experiences. No one can deny the expression of authenticity in her poetry. Without emotional involvement sex is sterile and barren for her.

Kamala Das alias Amy alias Madhvi Kutty alias Kamala Surrayya rebels against the conventions and restraints of society, which are meant to exploit womankind in a man-made world. In her poetry she is intensely conscious of herself as a woman. Feminine sensibility is badly bruised and tortured by masculine callousness, heartlessness and sexuality. There are various poems of Kamala Das which illustrate her feminine sensibility, particularly those poems which she writes in the garb of Radha waiting for Krishna to redeem her suffering love.

Her failure to realize fulfillment in love and security and her sexual exploitation, imposed on her by the time-honoured institution of marriage, disillusionment and frustrations turned her into a social rebel. She has been unconventional both in her life and poetry. She compares love beyond marriage ties with Radha's love for Krishna or Mira's love for Krishna. Her poetry also shows concern for disease, sickness, decay and death. Her confessional poetry has been compared with that of Sexton, Sylvia Plath and Judith Wright. As a true confessional poetess, she exhibits with remarkable frankness, the wrongs injustice and humiliation that she suffered.

Q. 29. Write a critical note on The Modern Indian-English Poetry.

Ans.: The poetry in Independent India is remarkable for fecundity, experimentation and the vivid presentation of contemporary reality and consciousness. The new poetry is the poetry of protest. It marks a significant departure not only in respect of the subject matter but also in the manner of expression, which involves both the choice of language and the flow of the rhythm. The eight-point poetic manifests presented by the writers' workshop Calcutta, is a manifestation of rebellion against Milton and the Romantics. The manifests summarises the aims and objectives of contemporary Indian-English poetry:

(i) We affirm our faith in a vital language as sufficient to write poetry.

(ii) We think that poetry must deal in concrete terms with concrete experience. That experience may be intellectual or emotional, but it must be precise, lucidly and tangibly expressed.

(iii) Poetry must be free from propaganda.

(iv) We commend the effort to experiment as long as it does not lead to excessive obscurity, eccentricity for eccentricity's sake, and perverse leg pulling.

(v) We claim that the phase of Indo-Anglian romanticism ended with Sarojini Naidu.

(vi) We condemn all forms of imitation.

(vii) We realize the full—time nature of the poet's vocation, if he is to do a good job.

(viii) Lastly, we emphasise the need for the private voice,—for this reason we celebrate the lyric form as the best suited for a capsule minded public, and we commend it to poets because it makes a direct appeal to that personality, and not to the mass psychology that poetry must really appeal to.

Modern Indian English poets follow these points and dismiss the obscurity of Aurobindo's poetry. K. Raghvendra Rao dismissed poets like Torn Dutt, Sarojini Naidu, and Sri Aurobindo who used the English language, not as creators but as manipulators'. Modern poets prefer originality and experiment in word craft, intensity and strength of feeling, clarity in thought structure and sense of actuality. The poets of this period have attained a fusion between substance and medium of expression. The poetry of this period ranges from personal emotion and lyricism to complex linguistic experiments, dry intellectual tone, pungent satire and nursery rhyme. Nissim Ezekiel, Dom Moraes, A.K. Ramanujan, P. Lal, Kamala Das, R. Parthasarathy, Shiv K. Kumar, Jayanta Mahapatra, K.N. Daruwalla, A.K. Mehrotra, O.P. Bhatnagar and Margaret Chatterjee have enriched modern Indian-English poetry. Women poets have deftly poetized feminine sensibility. Besides Kamala Das, Monika Verma, Gauri Deshpande, Mamta Kalia, Malathi Rao, etc. have revealed various aspects of feminine sensibility.

34

American and Other Non-British Literature

Q. 1. Write a note on the Age of Whitman as American Renaissance.

Ans.: The age of Walt Whitman is also known as American Renaissance. The term 'renaissance' signifies revival in art and learning. The English period preceded it by almost two hundred and fifty years. During the American Renaissance two domestic and foreign-influences are clearly visible. Americans of the day made respectful and deep study of ancient and contemporary foreign works. And like the people of England, who travelled to France and Italy, Americans also travelled abroad to gain knowledge and experience. At the same time proud of their native but unique democratic system and of the vast nation whose beauty and strength they were coming to know, many authors recounted the history of their land and attempted to depict accurately and faithfully native scenes and characters. As a result, these writers gave memorable expression to the ideas about which Americans were excited during the Renaissance, which was the richest period in American literary history. Walt Whitman remains the greatest literary figure of the Renaissance.

Whitman does not present his images and 'Pictures' before his readers in any logical order. He said, 'I name everything as it comes'. This is also the technique of the Stream of consciousness device as employed by Walt Whitman before William James found a name for it, Whitman's catalogue is a montage of 'pictured unrolled by stream of consciousness'.

Q. 2. Write a short note on American poetry and poets.

Ans.: In the nineteenth century the three great poets were Ralph Waldo Emerson, Walt Whitman and Emily Dickinson. Whitman's poems represent his world and his self. Of all modern poets Whitman was considered as a 'very American Poet'. He was the greatest of Bards because of the favouring circumstances of a democratic ideal and an open society. He was by birth and education a poet 'of the people'. Whitman's poetry was poetry of sweet sensations, uninhibited imagination and a violent jury in life. He encompasses within the ambit of his poems, himself and every other American, his nation, love, death, pantheistic God in every object, the future and eternity as well. As a poet Emerson was a rebel. To Emerson, poetry was a function of his own being as an individual seeking truth. For Emerson, the word as symbol was an integral part of thought, it was the vehicle of truth.

Emily Dickinson, 'the recluse of Amherest, was one of the great poets of all time, perhaps, the greatest of all American women poets.' She faced a problem to find her own integrity and her own unique mode of expression. She wrote of God, man and nature and knew love and 'death intimately', as few ever did. All her poems reveal her honest efforts at reconciling the finite with the infinite without sacrificing the integrity of the human soul or the validity of Physical nature.

In the 20th century we have Frost, Pound, Sterens, William C. Williams, Lowell, Roethke and Sylvia Plath as the most popular poets. Robert E. Spiller calls Frost, 'a 20th century transcendentalist, a latter day naturalist.' "He was a skeptical humanist, since he believed that man could defy an unreasonable deity if he had first learnt to love nature thoroughly. Lowell, Roethke and Plath are put in one group of confessional poets, because of certain qualities in their poetry. All three were subjected to internal disturbance or what the Psychoanalysts says about their poetry being an exploration of the 'unconscious materials'".

Q. 3. Give a short historical survey of the American novel.

Ans.: The first American novel was W.H. Brown's *The Power of Sympathy* (1789). The first American to devote himself wholly to novel writing was however Charles Brockden Brown, who published six novels under the influence of European romanticism, particularly, the literary genre of the 'gothu' novel which dealt with morbed emotions and sensational experiences, occurring in medieval castles, involving supernatural elements. Washington Irving exemplified the qualities of early 19th century literature and published his works from 1809 to 1859 and won recognition both in Europe and both in Europe and America. Beginning his writing career as a novelist in 1821 with the Spy, James Fenimere Cooper continual writing for thirty gears and became the first American international writer, whose novels had been translated into several languages Cooper's novels dealt with three subjects : American history, the sea and social trends in America of his own time. He became the first American novelist recording in five of his novels the exploits of the frontier hunter and good Samaritan.

Emerson with his message of self-reliance—the message that every individual shared in the divinity—progogated the kind of transcendental culture in literary writing. Thoureau, in his own way, expressed his individualism in a total rejection of organized society. How throne, unlike Emerson, was skeptical towards transcendentalism, and the central theme in his novels became the corruption of human heart by Pride and egotism. E.A. Poe believed that the function of art was the creation of ideal beauty. Mark Twain looked at life from the standpoint of the untutored frontier American and satirized human Wickedness and folly in *Huckleberry Finn* and *Tom Sawyer*. Henry James', novels—*The Ambassadors* and *The Portrait of a young Lady*—deal with Americans who are in a collision with the different traditions and values of Europe. James also popularized the 'point of view' narrative technique, which found many adherents in the 20th century. Herman Melville, whose novels were written during the last decade of the 19th century, believed in the certainly of evil. He wrote *Moby Dick*, *Billy Budd the Sailor* etc.

In 20th century American fiction, naturalism as a literary movement influenced novelists like Stephen Crane, Frank Noms, Jack London and Theodore Dreiser. The second decade of the 20th century witnessed cultural/social changes which the world war accelerated. Public interest in literature and book sales and circulation increased to fantastic proportions. The novel began to show a new vitality in the 1920s. Willa Cather was the most consistent woman novelist working through the war decade. With Sinclair Lewis fiction surged to a new importance. Earnest Hemingway handles the story of the hero's withdraw from war into love that ends in fitility. 'The Sound and the fury' and Absolom, Absalom, have been recognized for their narrative techniques—one for being the first American stream-of-consciousness novel and the other for the effective use of the point of view technique. Scott Fitzgerald attained fame in the 1920s with *The Great Gatsby*, which is a short novel of the shady and fantastically unreal career pursued by the protagonist. John Steinbeck with *The Grapes of Wrath* (1939), became a major name. Norman Mailor's *The Naked and the Dead* has a terrifying view of what war does to man. J.D. Salinger, Saul Bellow, Richard Wright, Toni Marrison. Alice Walker, Maya Angeleou are the important names.

Q. 4. Write a short note on American Drama.

Ans.: American Drama flourished in the period between the war decade and the 1920s. *O' Neill* was the first great dramatist of America. His view of man, in his plays, *O' Neill* finds fully expressive scenic and linguistic means to explore the themes of alienation, inarticulacy and dispossession.

From 1940 Arthur Miller and Tennessee Williams emerged into prominence. Tennessee's characters are victims aliented from the world. *The Glass Manageric* (1944), *A Streetcar Named Desire* and *Cat on a Hat Tin Roof*, are his major works. Arthur Milter handles the question of identify of the individual more firmly than does Wiiliams. Milter believed that tragedy brings sadness, sympathy and identification and fear, but it also brings knowledge or enlightment. Death of a Salesman is the pathetic story of Loman, the failed salesman, a genuine tragedy, of a common man. The Crucible is a dramatic representation of the witch-hunt and witch-trials. Edward Albee, a great dramatists of the latter part of the 20th century, mounts an attack on the hollowness he found in American Society. Another characteristics of his plays, is a sense of uncertainty, of doubt and even terror of the unknown. In his plays, he examines the American scene, attacks the substitution of artificial for real values in American society and condems their complacency and cruelty. *A Zoo Story* is a short play with only two characters. By combining realistic and popular dramatic techniques, Albee confronts the audience with its reluctance to become emotionally involved in a concern for others.

Q. 5. What do you know about American Literary Criticism?

Ans.: The New Critical School was the earliest critical activity in America from the 1930s to 1950s. The New Critics insisted on the autonomy of a work of art. New Criticism, it is believed, taught Americans how to read and that reading must begin with respecting the text.

Northrop Frye believed that literature is composed of archetypes and that myth is a process of intersexuality. Frye's work concided with the rise of 'Structuralism'. Hillis Miller, Paul de Man, Harold Bloom and Stanley Fish demonstrated how formalist methods of literary analysis can be enhanced by recourse to semiotics. E.D. Huisch used the word 'hermeneutics' to describe the concern of 20th century criticism as that of the interpretation of literary texts.

Jacques Derrida believed that the human agents's role in establishing meaning is limited by the shaping power of structural and semiological codes. He founded Deconstruction in the United States. Gradually the emphasis has shifted to the reader or what is known as 'reader-response', which is crucial to interpretation. Fish says, 'readers actually create the works they read. Meaning is not on the printed page; it is the experience one has while reading.' A poem is not simply a formal object in space but an experience in time; its meaning is what happens as the reader negotiated its lines.

Q. 6. Write a short note on T.S. Eliot and Modern Sensibility.

Ans.: Maxwell's statement that Eliot is 'the supreme example of the modern classicist', may be taken as representative of the early enthusiastic defenders and adulators. But recent studies on Eliot have explored the romantic element in his poetry and criticism. In fact, it was C.K. Stead who, not only in The New Poetic but also in a less well known essay 'Classical Authority and the Dark Embryo', altered the readers of the romantic heritage and mornings of Eliot. His poetry has a remarkable integrity of theme and purpose. What we learn from poems written in Early Youth is that Eliot started his poetic career under the influence of the Romantics. In the use of Poetry and the use of Criticism, Eliot speaks of the magical effect Omar Khayyam's 'Rubaiyat' had on him and of how he thereupon' went through the usual adolescent course of Byron, Shelley, Keats, Rossetti and Swinburne.

Eliot, like Romantics, displays the awareness of the need to change the idiom of poetry consonant with the changes in sensibility and our perception of reality. Eliot's advocacy of experimentation has its own logic, the need to change is in the very nature of the movement of literary history. But he also knew that experimentation has its limits beyond which the law of diminishing returns becomes operative.

The modernist like Eliot saw themselves confronted not only by the infinite complexity of life but also the inadequacy of the traditional devices of their medium. Eliot's poetry remains a classic statement of the problems of the modern man amidst the immense panorama of futility and anarchy which is contemporary history. It is but natural that Eliot, who had thought so deeply about the problems of the artist in the modern world, should have a profound influence on the later generations of poets. In fact the 'Age of anxiety' means comparison with the Waste Land as a poem dealing with spiritual drought. The technical perfection of the Sweeney quatrains affected poets as diverse as Norman Cameron, Geoffrey Grigson, and C. Day Lewis. In matter of technique also, followed by the succeeding generations of poets, Eliot's influence can be seen. Eliot has shown by his example that writing poetry is a difficult art of trying to learn to use world's requiring utmost dedication.

Q. 7. Write a note on Sylvia Plath as a powerful poetess, giving stress on the Feminine Verse in her poems.

Ans.: As a poetess Sylvia Plath appears in a self-pitying mood in most of her poems. She is a victim, she sacrifices her self, nourishing or giving life to others, but in return suffering to such an extent that she starts torturing herself and tries to accept death. The early poems attempt to transcend the terror, the later poems try to plumb the terror. She wants to accept death so readity that she is not bothered when her thumb gets cut and blood rizes out. She is reconciled that it is better to cross over to the dangerous edge of life into the external calm of death, Plath has unfolded in poem upon poem, vulnerability, regressive wish and aggressive rage, now, all is 'infolding' in death's silence. It is such a detached experience of death that sets the poetess apart from others.

Sylvia Plath is often dismissed as feminist. But in fact her themes are approximately feminine. She does not have any consistent feminist stance, nor does she harness her feminine material to a feministic mission. Her bitterest poems against the physical dominance of father, husband and the institution of marriage, are far from any feminist propaganda. She denounces these things for being agents of terror. Their being male is only an accident. She denounces with equal vehemence, mother and women also. Plath does not divide her emotional world into man and woman. Her sense of vulnerability, her concern for children, her fear of barrenness and widowhood, seem to make her more a writer with a unique 'feminine' sensibility than a feminist.

Plath in her real life also hated her mother for her neglect of the poetess after having a second child, a son, but she was fascinated by her father. They had an electra-complex relationship. After the death of her father, she felt isolated and insecure which became the major theme of the poems in 'Colossus and Daddy'. The colossus strode the fantasy world of her child hood. Her father had been her god. When the news of her death was announced, she vowed never to speak to god again. She wanted her husband to be an image of her dead father, but in vain. Unable to resurrect the father in Colossus, Plath wants to meet him in death. So she tried to kill herself every ten years, since her father's death. And finally she committed suicide.

Q. 8. Evaluate Edgar Allan Poe as a literary artist.

Ans.: Edgar Allan Poe is remembered, today, as one of the most controversial American short story writers. As a story writer, he believed that a story must be short enough for a single uninterrupted reading. Poe was one of the first to perfect the genre of short story. He set forth the basic essentials which constitute it. He thought that invention, creation, imagination and originality were requisites of any successful short story writer. He distinguishes between Truth and Beauty, saying that beauty can be better treated in a poem while truth belongs to the intellect and leaves in the mind a sense of fullest satisfaction.

Poe wrote 'The Fall of the House of Usher' in the spring or summer of 1839 in Philadelphia. It is usually admired for its atmosphere. Darrel Abel calls it an adventitious product of atmosphere. The atmosphere of gloom, suspense and tension sustains the dramatic interest of the story.

'The Gold Bug' is the most readable of the so-called metaphysical stories. The theme is old, but Poe shows his originality by making our interest centre not in the greed of finding an imense store of gold and jewels, but in the reading of captain's cryptic message, which tells where the treasure is hidden.

In poetry Poe is a master creator of moods through skillful use of internal and external rhyme, regular rhythm, carefully chosen sound, onomatopoeia and suggestively vague description. His influence through the French symbolists is still felt in American poetry.

Poe's criticism has been highly regarded because he judged by a coherent set of aesthetic and technical standards. He was not limited by American national to praise American authors.

To many Poe's metrical effects seem crude, his vocabulary meager and repetitious. Emerson called Poe the 'Jingle Man'. Detractors point out that Poe's forte is not human but abnormal Psychology. Still many critics regard Poe as a great literary artist.

Q. 9. Write a short note on style and technique of Miss Emily Dickenson.

Ans.: Miss Dickenson has used words with a creator's licence, wining with the free hand; boldly maneuvering her inherited vocabulary, springing her rhythm and standing the rhyme. She was a bold experimenter with words. She has also rearranged word-order to secure emphasis and surprise. There is hardly a line of Emily's work, however, which fails to throw out some gleam of genuine original power of imagination and of real emotional thought.

She was more or less an unlettered poet, since she does not seem to have casually and curiously read some English classics in the school or at home. She was entirely an original poet, who followed no literary tradition or poetical style. She fashioned her own poetic idiom through her limited experience and crystallized her style through her own experiments. If she uses the traditional symbols, she refurnishes and reinforces them with novel, semantic, and metaphorical connotations. Likewise, she employs words in a startlingly new sense, sometimes using their obsolete meaning or imparting them an extended meaning. In a mood of intense strong experiences she dispenses with auxiliary words freely using ellipses, dashes and interjections and capital letters to convey the whole gamut of her emotion, in the fewest possible words, e.g. the use of dashes in a single line. The adage that the 'Style is the man' is very apt to her technique since it mirrors her unique poetical character and inner self. Her tone is wholly spontaneous. The reader of Emily Dickson's poems will feel that without her extraordinary mastery of tone her achievement would have been impossible. Besides she used many aphorisms and paradoxes. She had Romantic faith in the imagination and Puriton, classical distrust of it. Her disregard for accepted forms or for regularities was incorrigible. Her works have had considerable influence on modern poetry.

Q. 10. Do you consider Bharati Mukherjee as an American writer? What are her themes?

Ans.: Bharati Mukherjee occupies the familiar privileged position of a well-bred post-colonialist—one who has been born, brought up and educated in Third World country and has achieved literary repute in the American academia. Fiercely protective of her American citizenship, Bharati Mukherjee repudiates her Indian connections. In fact she proclaims herself as an American writer and regards Indianness simply as 'a metaphor'.

Her entire corpus is replete with uneasy troubled stories about expatriates, alienation and their loss of identity. Bharati Mukherjee also brings a unique feminist perspective to the immigrant experience. Decentring dominant pactriarchal perspectives, Mukherjee revels in exploring, verbalizing and celebrating women's experiences—no longer as the mute other but as seen from within, felt and experienced. Her skillfully drawn novels and short stories are poignant renderings of her women characters' guest for their own spirituality and thus for their own identity. In her novel *Wife* (1975) she depicts the Psychological traumas of a frustrated housewife who cannot adapt herself to the cross—cultural world of the American situation in which she finds herself.

Q. 11. Give a general estimate of Frost as a poet.

Ans.: Frost is now generally recognised as the first poet of the century. He had made no systematic study of philosophy, politics, religion or even of literature as Whitman had done. But he was an extraordinary creator. Reader are attracted by his spontaneous and unsophisticated way of composing poems, which betrayed no signs of stress, strain or deliberate effort. Another quality that impressed the Americans was his transparent sincerity and truthfulness. They found in him a poet who had no passion for reform but whose main passion was to report truthfully his personal experiences. In his approach to nature he would follow neither the Wordsworthian view of intimate kinship between nature and man, nor would he subscribe to the Darwinian struggle for existence. The poetry of Frost has always a double meaning. To the simple minded he speaks like a rustic, but to the more intelligent he unfolds a different meaning, and to those who are highly intellectual he conveys a still deeper meaning. Frost had developed a Negative Capability by which he could identify himself with all sorts of people and things.

Like William Shakespeare he exhibited a rare combination of the objective and subjective approaches. Frost is a poet whose poetry is an embodiment of rich wisdom. He teaches us to look at life sympathetically, intelligently and lovingly.

As a poet he used the speech of New England but not as a vernacular intended to jolt the reader. Frost, was a farmer. The farm was a large part of himself, his anchor to reality, not local colour or a week end gesture.

Frost, though a beautiful writer is not a poet of the highest rank. A poem in his own words, begins in delight, it inclines to the impulse and it assumes direction with the first live laid down. In his aversion to poeticizing. The poet denies much of what was Witherto regarded as his material and his function. Nevertheless, Robert Frost is an important poet who has written some perfect poems—which is a rare enough commendation.

Q. 12. What do you know about Sherwood Anderson?

Ans.: Of the novelists of the modern period Sherwood Anderson was the Seceder Pan excellence. An Ohio business-man, married, he suffered a nervous break-down and walked out on both his family and his job. Establishing himself in Chicago, he began to write, and at the age of forty—with the encouragement of Carl Sandburg and the Chicago author Floyed Dell—produced *Windly Mc Pherson's Son* (1916).

As his novels and short stories were imagined variations on the theme of his own life, so in writing of his own life, he made himself express in his work. He learned from her 'Three Lives' and 'Tenda Buttons', the necessity for craftsmanship that made it a complicated process to tell the truth.

How much he managed to learn of his craft was shown by his first widely successful book, *Winesburg, Ohio* (1919). This is a collection of stories, or sketches about a small town of the kind Anderson knew from his boyhood. Some of the characters are old, crabbed, and eccentric, or borne down by failure. Anderson wrote the book in a Chicago lodging house, and said that almost every character was taken from his fellow lodgers. Many of whom had never lived in a village. The weakness in Anderson has been his inability to develop sufficiently his main theme of aspiration toward liberty.

Q. 13. What do you know about English Literature written in African countries known as African Literature?

Ans.: English Literature written in African countries like Kenya and Nigeria can not be ignored. The war of independence known as the Mau Mau was lasted from 1952 to 1960 leading to negotiations, which resulted in independence in 1963. Immediately after independence English was the official language in Kenya. In 1974 Swahili replaced English as the official language in the wake of a process which had begun in 1969. Nigeria gained independence in 1960. There are almost 400 indigenous languages in Nigeria. English and the main language of each state are the official languages; Wole Soyinki and Nigugi wa Thiong'o are major writers of these countries. Both Soyinki and Nigugi visualize the role of the writer in historical terms. Nigugi viewed literature as a means of cultural expression with reference to his native language, Kikuyu. In 1963, Obi Wali published a controversial article entitled 'The Dead End of African Literature', which Nigugi read prior to its publication in Transition. It is ironical that living in exile for over a decade now Nigugi has reverted back to using English, the colonial language he once rejected so vehemently. In fact the most significant body of Kenyan prose writing in English has come from writers whose native language is Kikuyu. Many of the works written in 1960 and 70s deal with the Mau Mau movement and its aftermath. Major novels are Nigugi's *Weep not, child* (1964), *A Grain of Wheat* (1967), Charity Waciuma's *Daughter of Mumbai* (1969) John Karoki's *The Land is Ours* (1970), Godwin Wachira's *Ordeal in the Forest* (1968) and Meja Mwangi's *Carcase for Hounds* (1974) and *Taste of Death* (1975). Prose writing in Kenye has also explored other themes. Charles Mangua and David Mailu have depicted the alienation of the educated elite, their growing disillusionment, the generation gap between parents and their children in works which have been discredited as non-serious and lacking in value because of the obscene language used. Women novelists and short story writers like Charity Waciuma and Grace Ogot voice their concern for the place of women in African society.

Theatre in Nigeria developed out of a combination of traditional rituals involving masquerades, chants, music, dancing and themes and ideas derived from the Bible under the influence of the missionaries. Hubert Ogunde, is famous for his plays like *Strike and Hunger* (1945), *Let the Yorube Think* and *Truth is Bitter* etc. E.K. Ogunmola who removed the music hall element from Ogunde's plays and substituted it by serious acting to develop Yorube Opera as a serious theatre form is famous for his plays like *The Palm Wine Drinkard*, *Comscience*, *Love of Money* etc. in fact Soyinka's dramatic theory drives from this aspect of Yoruba culture. The role of the writer in Africa is not, or rather cannot be, restricted to that of a social commentator. As Nigugi has shown through his grassroots theatrical activities it is necessary to involve the masses if literature and culture are to serve as effective tools of resistance.

Q. 14. What are the three major historical moments that have helped create a hybrid Caribbean culture?

Ans.: The Dutch, Portugese, English and French colonizers followed by Spanish and by the 18th century the entire Caribbean region was under colonial rule which by now was predominantly English. The emergence of a Caribbean literary tradition is thus an attempt at decolonizing the culture and people from the literal and literary colonization of the Britishers. Many writers critiqued the colonial educational system as a means of ideological domination that thwarted the rise of indigenous consciousness. The decade of the 1950s is very often referred to as the decade of the West Indian novel. George lamming believes that the West Indian novel was one of the important tools that facilitated the rise of national consciousness and challenged the anglocentric ideologies of colonial educational and cultural practices. According to Lamming, the West Indian novelist articulated the voice of the West Indian society and its community, some 'classics' associated with Caribbean canon, like Lamming's *In the Castle of my Skin* (1957), Naipaul's *A House for Mr. Briswas* (1961) and 'Wilson Harris *Palace of the Peacock* (1960). Influence of these writers in the creation of an aesthetic of Caribbean cannot be underestimated. Two seminal critical texts—Kenneth Ramchand's *The West Indian Novel and its Background* (1970) and Wilson Harris Tradition *The Writer and Society* (1967), firmly established the critical practice to study these writers. The practice included the notions of a separate and specific tradition relationship between writer and society, questions of audience and the responsibility of the artist, themes of alienation and isolated individual, highlighting the importance of the autobiographical novel or the novel of childhood as formative to an emerging of Caribbean literature. However, the book in literary production was largely a function of exile of a number of Caribbean writers for whom London became the literary capital. The phenomenon of exile is not peculiar to Caribbean writers of this period, but it did have significant impact on Caribbean writing.

Q. 15. Write a short note on the newly emerging literatures in English in South Asia (and the Indian novel, specifically).

Ans.: The newly emerging literatures in English in South Asia are the products of complex determinants. The colonial encounter is the formost determinant for emerging literatures in English in India and the Subcontinent. India, Pakistan, Bangladesh (erstwhile East Pakistan), Sri Lanka and Nepal are the countries covered under the rubric of South Asia. The term 'New Literatures in English' has been deemed appropriate to describe the recent literary developments in South Asian countries emerging from the experience of colonialism.

The new literature in English can be seen to develop through various stages which can be broadly classified as imitation, in the first phase, followed by a phase of protest or resistance and finally to a phase where the 'new' literature develops distinct identify of its own. This process foregrounded in the literary works of South Asian writers like Raja Rao, M.M. Dutta and James Alwis (Sri Lanka). The fiction, poetry and drama of many writers bear the imprint of the tensions of the colonial relationship while expressing an incipient nationalism and proclaiming development of a distinct identity. Different writers respond these pulls and pressures in different ways, according to diverse cultural locations and ideological positions, but certain common themes emerge in most of South Asian Literature in English: the colonial and East-West encounter, the development of a sense of pride is one's own culture, a preoccupation and experimentation with language and a, concern with issues of identity and nationhood. Some of the best South Asian fiction in English by Salman Rushdie (*Midnight's Children*, 1981), Amitav Ghosh (*The Shadow Lines*, 1988), and Michael Ondaatje (*The English Patient*, 1992) reflect and refract these urgencies and preoccupations.

The first published book in English by a South Asian was *Travels* (1794) by an Indian Muslim Sake Deen Mohammed. In the field of poetry, there was an attempt to weld South Asian epic traditions with those of Romanticism. In the 1930s, Shahid Duhrawady's poetic compositions his *Essays in Verse* (1937), drawing on the precision of Muslim art and often on English neo-classicism, could be seen as evolving a character of its own. In the field of prose writing around the same time, Ahmed Ali had introduced concepts of European realism into his Urdu literature. He then wrote *Twilight in Delhi*, the first major Muslim novel to emerge from the subcontinent. Poems of Taufia Rafat, Dand Kamal, Kaleem Omar and Maki Qureshi laid the ground work for Pakistani poetry in the 1970s and 1980s.

In the fields of novel writing, the writings of Ahmed Ali, Zulfikar Ghose, Salman Rushdie and Bapsi Sidhwa has swayed postcolonial fictional modes from realism to fantasy and metafictional language myths. Sidhwa's novels are; *The Pakistani Bride* (1983), *The Crow Eaters* (1978) and *Ice Candy Man* (1988). Notable recent novels from Pakistan include *The Thirteenth House* (1987), by Adam Zameen Zad, *Shadows of the Pomegranate Tree* (1992) by Tariq Ali and *Meathen Days* (1990) by Sara Suleri, *Season of the Rainbirds* by Nadeem Aslam, *Mothsmoke* (2000) by Mohsin Hamid etc. Short ficton and nonfiction have also been profilic genres in the hands of new writers like Aamer Hussein, Muneeza Shamsic, and Rukhsana Ahmed.

Hanif Kureshi's *My Beautiful Laundretle* deals with unemployment and racism in Britain and was followed soon after by *The Pruddha of Suburbir* which was a novel about an Asian boy growing up in Britain.

Like in other colonized areas, the early literature from Sri Lanka in English show the limitations of emulation and blind imitation. The writer in Sri Lanka faces the problem of a limited readership/overseas reader/audience. Sri Lankan poetry has evolved a vigorous local idiom of its own. The major names are Louis Nell, Ashley Halpe, Patrick Fernando, Lakdase Wikkramasinhe, Anne Ranasinghe etc. In the last two decades or so, the novels of writers like Ramesh Gunashekhara and Michael Ondaatje have enriched Sri Lankan English fiction. In recent years writings of Taslima Narreen (Bangladesh) have been accorded international recognition, but her works like *Lajja*, her autobiography and newspaper columns are note worthy not so much for their outstic merit as for their hard hitting polemic against repressive ideologies.

Q. 16. Discuss some aspects of the course Australian writing has taken.

Ans.: Australia, the smallest of continents, the largest of islands, is known for the genres of fiction and personal narratives. Writers of fiction like Patrick White, Xaviour Herbert and Randolph. Stow have been followed by renowned writers such as David Molouf, Archie Weller and Thea Astley. Sally Morgan and Ruby Langford are two Aboriginal writers whose contributions to the genre of personal narratives have not only popularized the genre, but also given a broader audience to a perspective on Aboriginal issues in Australia. Another kind of writing that finds a place today in Australia is immigrant/ diasporic writing and writers such as Judah Waten, David Martin, Dimitris Tsaloumas. Yasmine Gonneratine, Adib Khan, Satendre Nandan, Beth Yahp are just some of the representative figures in this field.

In time the very Australian canon that had been used to forge a new identity of Australia distinct from its colonial legacy by white Australian writers came to be challenged for its conceptualization and presentation of a monolithic Australian identity. The fact is that it favoured male white writers and excluded the voices of other sections of Australian society. As a reaction to this, at one level the focus started to shift to representations of Australia by women writers such as Judith Wright, Barbara Bayton and Elizabeth Jolley.

Two strong opposing impulses have been seen to pervade much of Australian literature and popular creation. Bob Hodge and Vijay Mishra in their Preface to *Dark Side of the Dream.* Australian Literature and the postcolonial mind argue that Australia's postcoloniality itself is subject to debate. In fact the term 'Australian literature' has been determined by social and political factors with different orientations to the dominant groups. Ken Goodwin in *A History of Australian Literature* feels strongly that the eleven novels of Patrick White constitute the most impressive oeuvre in Australian fiction, a judgement verified according to him by White being the only Australian writer awarded the Nobel Prize.

Q. 17. In what ways does Canada's history and geography complement its literature?

Ans.: Canada belongs to the literary common wealth of English Speaking/Writing nations. Canadian literary traditions have had their roots in England, France and United States. It is a young nation as far as its written history goes. By the early 19th century, Canadian writing has endeavoured to evolve it's a voice which bore the hallmarks of assertion and strength. In the 20th century, creative resilience and variety can be perceived in its literary enterprise.

The formation of the Canadian canon was intitated by early literary histories of the country. Most of these emerged from the extra-literary concept of the nation that involved the 'Canadian-ness' of literature written in the country. The early literary historians have looked at literature and conon-formation along with the spiritual and political development of the nation. Geography complemented history as literary creativity took off.

Canadian writing initially emerged from a colonial derivative culture and then attempted to deviate and evolve into a mature national identity. A number of Canadian writers lamented the absence of a critical approach for evaluating its writing. Geographically speaking, localized and concentrated literary activity shifted from the environs of Montreal to Toronto. The new writing exhibited a combination of simplicity, power, sympathy and intelligence as the guiding spirits especially in the field of criticism. The writers/critics laid the foundation of the emergence of Canadian Schools of criticism. One recurrent feature of Canadian life reflected in its literature is the paradoxical superimposition of vast empty spaces and the lack of privacy from prying eyes. Canadian writing was seen to incline towards metafiction or the process of creating order through myth and art. Impetus has been provided to Canada's Literary enterprise in various forms and through the encouragement given by various extra-literary sources. These include the state's cultural policy and the publishing industry and the role played by journals and little magazines. The literary milieu that now emerged, placed a premium on critical analysis and debate. Criticism had earlier favoured perspectives that were author-centered, thematic, and concerned with social matters; now it tended to focus on structural and technical commentary. Canadian writing of the 1990s focused on communicating diversity and dismembering university. Frances Brook's *The History of Emily Montague* is acclaimed as the first Canadian novel. John Richardson, Thomas Chandler Haliburton, Catherine Parr Traill and Susanna Moodie are some of the writers of the early phase Stephen Leacock, Laura Salverson, Martha, Grove, Hugh Maclennan, and deserve special mention.

The etheric fabric of Canadian society underwent a significant change in the 1970s with the opening up of borders to Asian immigrants. By the 1980s, the impact of their arrival was clearly manifest in the literature of the times. In the 1970s, native authors actually got down to recording their own history and commentating on Canadian society. Later writers wrote both prose and poetry. Margaret Atword is a well-known name. Canadian drama has lagged behind all the other literary genres in its evaluation.

Thus Canadian literature has come of age despite treading on off-beaten track. Its evolving strength has been its ability to co-exist with American culture, dominance and also by producing works that have acquired repute for quality beyond national boundaries.

35

Literary Theory and Criticism

Q. 1. Write a short note on major theorists of Deconstruction.

Ans.: 'Deconstruction' is a very knotty problem in modern philosophical thought, and in some respects, an equally naughty one. It has particularly influenced modern philosophical, social, moral, political, linguistic and literary theories. Its chief weapon is a searching analysis of language which leads to new and unexpected interpretations of facts, opinions, and theories. Derrida is usually regarded as the leader and the Chief mentor of the new trend in thought. He coins new words or phrases or uses old terms in a new context which makes comprehension very difficult. Derrida and other admirers of Deconstruction have given a special prestige to simple terms such as 'Writing', 'Presence', 'Textuality', 'Other', 'Plentitude' etc. Derrida seems to be changing his positions from time to time. He points out that dissemination ultimately has no meaning and cannot be channelized into a definition. Derrida's Style is usually allusive, elusive and evasive. Derrida dislikes the importance given to 'Speech' and the human voice-Logocentrism and Phonocentrism. He criticizes all earlier philosophers and linguisticians from Plato to Saussure for the way they relied on speech.

Other prominent thinkers connected with Deconstruction in various ways are Foucault, Barther, Harold Bloom, Lyotard, Lacan, Julia Kristeva and some others. All of them are very versatile writers, and refer frequently to language and literature. Barthers tells that literature 'signifies nothing', literature is fundamentally constitutively literature is fundamentally constitutively unrealistic, 'the text is plural' etc. J. Lacan, the famous Psychoanalyst, Julia Kristeva and many women critics turn to Freudian and Post-Freudian theories for analyzing language and literature. Women's interpretation of texts differs from male interpretation. Women deconstructionists speak of the effects of male domination on language, especially 'Patriarchal' views for determining meaning. And inter-pretation sanctioned by deconstruction gives greater scope to women to examine their own status in the civilized world.

Q. 2. What do you know about New Historicism and its future direction?

Ans.: New Historicism combines chiastically the 'textuality of history' with the 'historicity of text'. The history provides the context, for literature is an old hat which was given a fresh lease of life. The most intriguing aspect of the New Historicist reading of a text and context occupy separate spheres and are clearly distinguished from each other, in the New Historicist reading they seem to overlap and interpenetrate. The text sometimes creates its context, and the context tends to get textualized in such a way that it loses its so-called stable entity and becomes part of textual liminality. Therefore the New Historicists give so much prominence to anecdotes.

New Historicism developed as a reaction against both New criticism and Deconstruction around the 1980s, by a group of English teachers. Stephen Greenblatt, the leader of the group coined the term 'new historicism' to explain the new method they were employing in reading mainly Renaissance texts. But as the term was somewhat confusing he redefined it as 'Cultural Poetics': The conceptual basis of cultural poetics was desired from the belief that any cultural artifact cannot be examined in isolation, it can only be examined as a process of an intricate network of several intersecting traces whose cumulative energy accords the culture its inner vitality and culture dynamism.

By employing a method of reading that takes him from discursively to material conditions of existence, Derrida at one stroke joins three reading practices in one: desconstruction, new historicism, and cultural materialism. This is a happy development in critical practice and will perhaps provide a new direction to art of interpretation in the 21st century. Both new historicism and deconstruction will perhaps continue as traces of the past in the next century but they will remain as vibrant as ever as resonant voices.

Q. 3. How do you rate Aldous Huxley as a literary critic?

Ans.: T.S. Eliot says about Aldous Huxley that his place in English literature is unique and is certainly assured. There were two groups; Modern (James Joyce and T.S. Eliot) and contemporary (H.G. Wells and C.P. Snow). As a writer and critic, Huxley could not identify himself entirely with either group. Huxley lived in the house in which books were part of existence-Literature, his penetrating analysis of Wordsworth's attitude to nature seems to be influenced by Matthew Arnold, a great admirer of the poet. He maintains that tragedy 'chemically pure', is not the best form of literature. He said, "to make a tragedy the artist must isolate a singe element out of the totality of human experience and use that exclusively as his material. Tragedy is something that is separated from the whole truth, distilled from the living flower."

Huxley was aware of the fact that it is not possible to tell the whole Truth. Huxley said, 'where life in general is concerned, it is impossible to have adequate data.'

The ability to delve deep into the psyche of an artist totally different from himself makes Huxley one of the profound critics of our times. "Don't be critical; be sympathetic". Huxley followed, or tried to follow this piece of advice given by his mother. As Herbert Read points out, Huxley's essays on writers and artists should not be called 'criticism'. They should be known as 'Appreciations'. But Huxley is not a critic with 'a business'. His writing is a product of curiousity and leisure, and that its only law is sympathy. In addition, however, Huxley brings to bear on his critical writings, wide but accurate learning and his arguments are always supported by factual evidence. His approach to art and the artists based on mind-body relationship has obviously a scientific element in it, though he was not an 'academic critic'. Though a literary man, he remained close to the scientific awareness throughout his life. He was therefore, eminently qualified for the role of a bridge-builder between the two cultures.

Q. 4. Comment upon the concept of 'Teacher-critic' in India.

Ans.: The teaching of Literary criticism can easily, enjoyably and profitably become an 'applied' activity in the analysis of such actual works of literature or Criticism as are likely to facilitate demonstration of 'Principles'. Pieces of literature which allow us to actually see and show the processes of criticism in operation ought to be taken into the classroom, if teachers intend to really make the effort to 'teach' Literary criticism. This will necessitate open-eyed reading on the part of teacher-critic, exercise of imagination, some courage in venturing into unknown critical territory without any borrowable opinions to fall back on. It will necessitate reading for more carefully, seriously, adventurously, working at language in subtle and/or complicated ways, reference work to find required historical and factual date, and so on. A teacher-critic should not feel frightened by such challenges. A teacher critic should carry the Literary material into his classrooms. And instead of teaching just the theories, the more important thing is the practical applications in class room, demonstrated by teacher and followed by students. In this day and age, when so much high-flown thinking goes on regarding the presence of theories/ideologies behind practice, it is not advisable for a teacher-critic to fail to see the crucial importance of noticing the need for practice or the presence of practice behind the theories or principles.

Q. 5. What is the role of analysis in Literary studies?

Ans.: A discourse on analysis can either provide a systematic description of a specific practice from within, clarifying the assumptions and procedures which characterize that practice, or as becomes necessary in the case of literary analysis, it can stand outside the many systems of concepts which constitute the practices of the discipline, in order to theorize the enabling conditions of this plurality. The activity of ascribing properties to artifacts is necessarily linguistic, whereas the properties themselves are embodied in a specific medium, which may be non-linguistic or linguistic. When the medium is language, analysis applies itself to working, as a metalanguage, on the body of texts we call literature. When analysis addresses the entire ensemble of percepts and affects comprising language, sounds, and bodies in motion on a physical stage, the occasion of study is drama.

Analysis serves as a tool which resolves the occasion of analysis into constitutive elements. In literary study, the object which provides the occasion of analysis—the literary text, or the author as a national entity abstracted from the Oeuvre—can be broken down into many kinds of constitutive elements. The general aim of analysis is to provide understanding and literary analysis does this in many ways through exegesis, commentary, interpretation, paraphrase, explication, translation, and so on.

In fact analysis fulfil several roles in literary study: that it should inculcate reading skills which enable the meaning of a text to be understood (interpretation) aid the effective communication of that understanding (argument); and support demonstrative value judgments (evaluation). A mode of analysis concerned less with the intrinsic articulation of forms and structures within language than with the relations between the literary text and ideas, or with its social matrix, leads to various forms of ideological analysis.

Q. 6. Write a short note on the basic differences between modernism and postmodernism?

Ans.: Modernism cultivated austerity; postmodernism is interested in pleasure. Modernism tried to capture reality through individual consciousness which was equivalent of life itself. Virginia Woolf saw life as a 'semitransparent envelope', 'a luminous halo'. Eliot's objective correlative, Joyle's epiphany and the imagist doctrine offer glimpses of reality. Modernism believed that there is a centre and, in the words of Henry James 'a pattern in the carpet'. Myth and musical form were often used to give a structured unity of a chaotic material. For post-modernism. 'realism' is just an incoherent and deluding notion. Against the modernist's struggle for wholeness and unity postmodernism posits a radical indeterminacy. For post-modernism the pattern, or the centre is only a useful thinking, an imposition. The idea of a meaningful pattern is a comforting fiction at the best. The following table can make things very clear:

Modernism	Postmodernism
Form	Antiform/open
Purpose	Play
Design	Chance
Art Object	Process
Distance	Participation
Creation/Synthesis	Deconstruction/Antithesis
Presence	Absence
Determinacy	Indeterminacy

Q. 7. Write a short note on the problems faced by Indian Feminism.

Ans.: Feminism in the West could exercise its impact in developing a new female aesthetics much earlier than in our regions. In 1890s women writers in the West did write for women, about women from a woman's standpoint. This writing created new realism-feminine realism. The New women's writing consistently problematised, deconstructed, demystified or rethought 'womanliness'.

Like cultural discourse feminist discourse has multiple dimensions. These are different feminisms—English, American, French, Canadian, Black feminism, etc. No specific discourse is attempted on Indian feminism.

Indian writing in English has come of age when it comes to creative writing. But the picture is disappointing when we come to criticism; either we go to the past Indian aesthetics or directly import the Western parameters. We have neglected the area of developing new critical canon for 'new' literature. If the Western feminist critics had to 'revision' and 'reinterpret' literature against the established patriarchal literary tradition, and Indian feminist critic has to 're-revision' and 're-reinterpret' as she has to destabllish first the patriarchal then the colonial and then the local culture. With Indian feminism the thrust has to be on women's psychology which is so religio culturally bound that unless such feminine psyche is freed from this, an Indian woman will not become aware of her actual self as a separate identity. From Psycho-static she has to change to Psycho-dynamic state and this freedom should come to her not through legislation or reservation but through awakening and questioning. The syntax of her life should change from the passive voice to the active voice. In India while discussing feminism one has to take into consideration the social class of women alongwith political background, religious status and educational background of a woman.

Q. 8. What do you know about 'Spoudaios' in relation with Aristotle?

Ans.: Spoudaios (noble character) determines Aristotle's approach. For Aristotle, character is what determines moral choice. He can classifies genres using this principle. Tragedy imitates noble character, and comedy base character. Some neoclassical critics, mistake this as socially determined. Arther Miller accuses Aristotle of social snobbishness and arrogance. He chooses Willy Loman, the common man as his protagonist in *Death of a Salesman.* Aristotle never even once said that someone of the common mould cannot be a tragic hero.

It would be unfair to charge Aristotle with class-conciousness and arrogance. The nobility referred to in Poetics is morally determined and not socially construed. The protagonist is important enough to claim the attention of the audience. The life of the protagonist is worth the sacrifice he is making and we get deeply concerned with the enormity of the effect of his loss.

While describing essential factors Aristotle talks about character in detail. Character is that which reveals moral purpose and thought is the faculty of saying what is possible and pertinent in the given circumstances. Aristotle discovered that pity and fear are the two emotions which arouse tragic feelings in humans. The tragic emotions unite the other concepts, and a wholesome theory of tragedy is built. Pity and fear demand the tragic hero to be noble only then his fall from happiness to misery arouses in us these emotions.

Q. 9. What do you know about Sidneys's 'Apologie'?

Ans.: Sidneys's Apologie was probably written in 1583, though it was published in 1595, posthumously. His work was published in two separate editions. *The Defence of Poesie* by William Ponsonby and *An apology* for *Poetrie* by Henry Olney. Apologie happens to be the first English text, complete and comprehensive, propounding a set of principles on the art of Literature. Apologie is carefully crafted in the form of a rhetorical arguments and the pattern is clear for analysis.

The form or plan of Apologie confirms to the rhetorical principle of construction. Apologie falls into seven broad division:

(1) Exordium (2) Narration-describing the antiquity of poetry (3) Proposition that poetry is imitation (4) Division-religious, Philosophic, Imitative (5) Proof (6) Refutation and (7) Peroration.

Sidney offers a definition of poetry—a poet is the maker, and poetry is the art of representation. 'Poesy therefore is an art of imitation, for so Aristotle termeth it in his word *mimesis*. Sidney surveys the poetic scene in England beginning with Chaucer, and bemoans the degeneracy of drama as reflected in *Gorboduc*, which violates the essential unities so vital in dramatic composition. He discusses the function of tragedy, the comedy and the lyric. Then he goes on to discuss diction and style in poetry and prose with reference to those who do not employ a natural style, but are carried away by conceits. Sidney then discusses prosody, glorifying the English language which has both the rhymed and unrhymed facilities built into its nature and system. The treatise concludes with robust claims of the greatness of poetry as an object fit for veneration. Sidney's main objective in the treatise is to show the true value of poetry, and he does it by presenting to us a picture of the past. Apologie is in the form of a classical oration. In an age of puritan suspicion of literature, this forceful justification of poetry was a spirited defence in the truest sense of the term. Sidney's apologie is an epitome of the general Renaisance criticism.

Q. 10. What do you know about *An Essay of Dramatic Poesy*?

Ans.: John Dryden (1631-1700) was a poet, dramatist, translator, critic, all rolled into one. His most important and widely anthologised piece *An Essay of Dramatic Poesy* is the only work of criticism that Dryden published as a separate work. It deals with major issues in drama: the ancients versus the moderns, the French versus the English, blank verse versus heroic verse. The dialogue form assures an impartial enquiry. His defence of the English dramatic tradition, and his justification for his use of rhyme in his tragedies forms the clinching section of his argument.

Dryden's tolerance and impartiality are evident in the entire Essay. He favours and defends the genre tragicomedy, rejects the addiction to the unities. He says, "we have invented, increased and perfected a more pleasant way of writing for the stage than was ever known to the Ancients of Moderns of any Nation, which is Tragicomedy!" Dryden upholds the traditional view regarding the ultimate end of literature, and the force of the traditional literatures of the past as criteria for standards of judgement. Dryden's ultimate belief in literature being a mimetic art is most clearly expressed in his famous definition of the play.

Dryden's comprehensive knowledge of the tradition, and his cosmopolitanism make him a great critic. *The Essay* is the only attempt of Dryden in formal criticisms. It is said that Dryden brought criticism from the church to the coffee house. For the first time, Literary works are examined with Johnson should have called him 'the father of English criticism', for it was he who 'first taught us to determine on principles the merit of composition'. According to Sainsbury, he occupied a position shared in the history of criticism only be Dante and Goethe, the position of the greatest man of letters in his own country, and 'it is in criticism that Dryden best shows that original faculty which has often been denied him elsewhere'.

Q. 11. What do you know about the literary criticism of Wordsworth?

Ans.: The Literary criticism of Wordsworth is the manifest to the British Romantic Movement. It effects a formal break with the neo-classical tradition. He rejected the diction of 18th century poetry, and he favoured the language of prose and said that it was the same as metrical language. His naturalism and emotionalism are quite well-known. His revival of the spoken idiom for poetry has many parallels. Dryden, Eliot and Pound too have taken a similar stand with regard to their poetry. Wordsworth had specific reasons for his rejection. He dismissed elevated vocabulary, which excluded the trivial. He disliked personification, pathetic fallacy, periphrasis, inversions, antithesis, use of classical mythology, conceits, hyperbole and obscurity. He is open to charges of criticism that he employed some of these in his own poems. That was the reason why Coleridge refuted his theory and practice. Wordsworth seems to believe that there is a core language which is common to all people, and poets should employ this language. His primitivism is born out of his love for folk poetry and ballad forms of composition. Wordsworth's hope of creating 'a class of poetry...well adapted to interest mankind permanently' is not realized in terms of his own professed theory. His theory of metre also seems woefully inadequate. His 'prose' was always unsuitable to the poets who came later in time. His theory regarding the spontaneous overflow of powerful feelings is not applicable to all poets in general, and sometimes even to his own poems. It lacks the validity he claims for it, but it is a valuable statement that describes the Psychological poetic process involved in the composition of some of his most successful poems. Wordsworth's theory lacks a formal system, because it is mostly occasional, but it is original and not derivative as Shelley's Defence. In sum, the ultimate value of Wordsworth's Preface lies in the major shift it helped to effect in the emphasis from the relationship between the poem and the reader to that between poet and poem; in other words from critical evaluation and judgment to the creative process itself.

Q. 12. Evaluate Arnold as the most important critic of the latter half of the nineteenth century.

Ans.: Arnold's place as the most important critic of the latter half of the 19th century is unquestionable. Eliot and Leans among others have shown allegiance to his system of beliefs

Arnold offers us: an apology for culture; a respect for the Greek ideals, a plea for a return to the study of the humanities against the urge for Science, and utility subjects; an attack against the growing Philistinism of the middle class; and a call for improvement of criticism, and its standards. More than all, he preaches a religion devoid of dogmatism. When Arnold calls for a replacement of religion by literature, he recommends his own world new a poetic view of life in which 'morality touched by emotion' governs out being. He is a strong apologist for criticism by which he means a critical spirit; he advocates 'disinterestedness', a circulation of fresh and free ideas, freedom from British provincialism, and an acceptance of European ideas, especially drawn from Germany and France. Disinterestedness also may mean absence of prejudice and intellectual curiosity. Literary criticism, for him, is descriptive and interpretative. The function of criticism is to create an intellectual climate for the flowering of creative literature. He also firmly emphasizes the role of judicial criticism for setting the right standards in art.

Arnold's definition of poetry is that it is a criticism of life. It means that Literature is capable of interpreting life, and in this simplified sense it is a gross and didactic misrepresentation of the function of art. His didacticism in expecting high seriousness from poetry is too narrow. Again, his conviction that the Alexandrine and the couplet are inadequate for poetic expression is another fallacy. According to Arnold, grand style arises when a gifted poet treats, with simplicity or with severity, a serious subject. Infact his approach to literary criticism is moralistic.

Q. 13. Evaluate the T.S. Eliot as a critic and his ideas expressed in his essay about criticism.

Ans.: In the essay, *The Function of Criticism* Eliot says that the problem of criticism is one of establishing order. A critic must listen to his inner voice alone. He must have a highly developed sense of fact, for fact can not corrupt taste whereas Eliot's critical method are easy to identify. He practices the method of evaluatory or judicial criticism, and does not indulge in close analysis of texts as recommended by the new critics. He is a follower of Arnold. Creating an audience for him. When he discusses the writers of the past, he quickly arrives at value judgements and rates them. Eliot has the readers of his own poetry in his mind when he evaluates other poets, particularly the dead ones.

In many ways, Eliot has proved himself to be the most important critic of our century. He helped in correcting the taste of the poetry reading public; he re-evaluated the English poets. He initiated a critical theory of his own. His concept of the impersonal theory of poetry, unified sensibility, his emphasis on the perfection of the spoken idiom for poetry, and his formulae, such as the 'Objective correlative' are all invaluable aids to the understanding and appreciation of poetry. Though he had competence in abstract thinking, Eliot did not build a coherent system of aesthetics on poetry. He says that his criticism is 'workshop criticism', a by-product of my private workshop. He associated scholarship with permanent ineterst in a work and criticism with the immediate. He maintained three types of criticism. He redicules interpretation as belonging to the 'lemon-squeezer school of criticism'. Eliot's 'impersonal theory' employs a notorious metaphor of referring to the poet's mind as a platinum shred, in which case, the poet is merely a passive medium, and so, the reference to the poet's mind as a catalyst is not quite right. The major change against him is that his interest was restricted to poetry, and he turned a blind eye to American literature, and American literary tradition.

Q. 14. What is the relationship of structuralism and literature?

Ans.: For students of literature, structuralism has great significance. The medium of literature is language, and literature is a way by which the mind structures the world and explains it. Hence, there is a close relationship between literature as a field of study, and structuralism as a method of analysis. Structuralism deals mostly with the narrative domain, because narrative share many structuralist features as a plot, setting, and character. Structuralism finds out the language of literary texts, often called grammar, because of the basic rules that govern literary elements. It focuses on three areas of literary study; the classification of literary genres, the description of narrative options, and the analysis of literary interpretation.

Structuralism is sometimes described as a revolution. It evolved outside the universities, and educational institutions. A literary work is the child of the author's creative life, expressing the author's self. We enter into a communion with the author-his thoughts, his feelings-through his work.

Literature is like any other form of social or cultural activity. Literature is not only organized like language, it is made of language. Structuralism excludes both the author and reality as points of reference for interpretation. It will concentrate on signifiers at the expense of the signified. It is the type of criticism that emphasis the aspect of constructing the meaning rather than deciphering it. Structuralism refutes the Aristotelian 'mimetic' criticism that believes that literature is the imitation of reality. Structuralism rejects the Romantic 'expressive' criticism which views literature as the expression of the feelings of a creative artist.

Q. 15. What do you know about 'Affective stylistics'?

Ans.: This theory is usually associated with Stanley Fish. It is also based on the assumption that the literary text is not just an object that exists, but takes its existence from the act of reading. In his essay 'Affective Stylistics', he attacks the notion that reading is a finished activity, and substitutes a temporal view in place of a spatial view. The text is put to a close examination to know how stylistically it affects the reader, or rather how the sequence of words on a printed page gets converted to a felt experience. The results occur within the reader. Stanley Fish describes the process of the structure of the text as it occurs from moment to moment, when it undergoes the process of being read. It should not be mistaken for the impressionistic responses of the reader, but should be understood as the cognitive analysis of the reading process, resulting from specific and particular elements in the text. In the later criticism of Fish, there is a shift.

Q. 16. Write a short note on Basic Tenets of New criticism.

Ans.: Variously known as formalism, textual and ontological criticism. New criticism has brilliant practitioners both in America and in England such as John Crowe Ransom, Cleanth Brooks, Robert Penn Warren, R.P. Blackmur, Allen Tate and William Empson. The major critics whose theory and practice paved the way for the New Criticism are T.S. Eliot and I.A. Ricards. The origin of the New Criticism can be further traced back to a lecture 'The New Criticism', delivered by Joee Elias Spingarn in 1910.

The validity of the New Criticism lies in the fact that it takes the poem as a work of art, a structure having an independent existence. Biographical and sociological approaches to the poem are not favoured by the New critics. A poem is not meant to be paraphrased. But the New critics do not bother about influences on the poem, nor do they relate it to any tradition. Critics have objected against it. According to them Great works of art can not be appreciated alone.

In its attitude to language the New Criticism has anticipated both structuralism and deconstruction of the recent decades. The critical 'monism' of the New critics has its validity, though in a limited sense. However, it is to the credit of the New critics that they have taken away the importance from the author and given it to the text. The printed page 'the text' is the centre not the author, nor the reader. This is the premise of the New criticism.

Q. 17. What do you understand by Eliot's 'Objective Correlative'?

Ans.: The term 'Objective Correlative' when enunciated by Eliot in 1919 had evoked stiff opposition from critics. To them the term was ugly and the idea one of strictly local validity and it applied only to Eliot's poetry and perhaps, only to Eliot's poetry and may be to Hamlet.

It is obvious that the 'Objective Correlative' stems from Eliot's impersonal theory of poetry assumes that though the poet starts with a basic emotion, he finds for this emotion a body of expressive symbols in which emotions, feelings and thought are so extricably blended that they become the formula for the original. In his concept of the 'Objective Correlative', Eliot is seeking some definite token for the correct and artistic presentation of the personal emotions without the poet having to explain them.

Eliot's term the 'Objective Correlative' occurs in this essay *Hamlet and his Problems*. According to Eliot, *Hamlet* is an artistic failure and here Shakespeare fails to find the proper 'Objective Correlative' for Hamlet's feeling. In fact Eliot's 'Objective Correlative' comes close to ancient Indian theory of Rasa.

To Eliot the poet should occupy himself not with his emotion and personality like a Romantic but with an escape from them. What has the poet to escape into? Eliot says that the poet has only a medium to express. And this medium is 'Objective Correlative'. Eliot clarifies his concept by saying that the term 'Objective Correlative' represents what he calls 'Stimuli to the critical thinking'—conceptual symbols for an emotional bias.

Q. 18. Compare and contrast T.S. Eliot and Sri Aurobindo as critics and their views on poets and poetry.

Ans.: T.S. Eliot and Sri Aurobindo are unique personalities in literature of our century. The learnings of both of them are proverbial. Eliot's *Tradition and the Individual Talent* and Aurobindo's *The Future Poetry* are known for the identical views on poets and poetry. According to Eliot the channel of influence between the tradition of the past and individual poet of the present is not a one-way traffic. If tradition influences the individual poet, he in turn influences the tradition and the past acquires an every new meaning by virtue of the contribution which the achievements of the poets of the present make to it.

Sri Aurobindo opines that the work of the poet depends not only on himself and his age but on the mentality of the nation to which he belongs and the spiritual, intellectual, aesthetic tradition and environment which it creates for him. According to Aurobindo, "The mind of the poet sees by intuition and direct perception and brings out what they give him by a formative stress on the total image and the aspect to which he thrills is the living truth of the form, of the life that inspires it of the creative thought behind and the supporting movement of the soul and a rhythmic harmony of these things revealed to his delight in their beauty."

Eliot's impersonal theory of poetry grew out of his challenge of Wordsworth's concept of poetry as emotion recollected in tranquility. For Aurobindo poetry is neither emotion recollected in tranquility nor 'an escape from emotion', 'but something more'. To him, the poet is 'Seer', 'Kavi' and even 'Rishi'. He makes it absolutely clear when he says that "Poetry does not depend on the individual power of his age and his country, its level of thought and experience and the depth of its spiritual attainment."

In fact Eliot pleaded for poetry in language of everyday conversation.

Q. 19. What do you know about Cyberfeminism as a latest critical theory?

Ans.: Cyberfeminism is a holistic concept that has been coined and adopted to approach the burning issues of information technology, women's studies and the women's movement in the age of globalization.

Cyberfeminism popularly known as CF is a new wave of (post) feminist thinking and practice that began to contest technologically complex territories. Perhaps the most urgent issue for cyberfeminist and feminist practice and theory currently is that of seeking female affiliations that respect difference and create productive projects in solidarity with others who are working on similar issues. Cyberfeminism is theoretically and historically grounded in feminist philosophies and embedded in political, cultural and social practices. Crucially CF needs to be informed by post-colonial theories and representational politics.

The vital question is regarding the relationship of feminism and cyberfeminism. The term was coined in 1991. Cyberfeminists resist rigid definitions of their movement, but it is broadly concerned with expressing and developing feminism in the context of online interactions and online art. The term Cyberfeminism was used by the Australian collective VNS Matrix in their 1991 Cyberfeminist manifest for the 21st century.

CF is based on the idea that, with technologies it is possible to reconstruct your identity, sexuality and gender and to create new languages, programmes and myths. It focuses more on the ways in which humans and machines are intertwined and the opportunities open up by women's integration into the technology-led information society. It is connected with cyber revolution for gender equality. Cyberfeminism have the chance to create new formations of feminist theory and practice which address the complex new social conditions created by global technologies.

Q. 20. Explain deconstruction and its conditions.

Ans.: When the text is open for surface level meaning as well as for subterranial level and they are contrasted. They never go parallel, then only the text is open for deconstruction.

In one respect, deconstruction, developed by the French Philosopher Jacques Derride, has an obvious appeal for critics of various literature. Its primary source of attention, like that of the formalists and structuralists, is the way in which we tend to structure our thinking in terms of opposites such as conscious and unconscious or speech and writing. The language in a literary text is not self-contained but derives its meanings from a network of associations and relationships that can be found between the constituent parts. Many critics empty deconstruction as a tool rather than as an absolute paradigim of critical thought. Absence is more important than presence. We get traces of words which are erased. Deconstruction implies that text has two levels-one is surface and the other is deeper level. They never go parallel.

Deconstruction does not apply to all texts. It can be fruitfully applied to certain texts only. Aporia is the basis of deconstruction. It means undecidability to decide between superior and inferior, right and wrong, which direction to go etc. 'Truth is an illusion'—deconstruction always used it as quotation. It is a fact that it can be applied to romantic text than to the classical text. Derrida says, "A deconstructive reading must always aim at a certain relationship, unperceived by the writer, between what he commands and what he does not command of the patterns of language that he uses. It attempts to make the not-scene accessible to sight."

Q. 21. Write a short note on Postmodernism, its meaning, significance and limitations.

Ans.: The term postmodernism is a current term which appeared after modernism as a criticism of modernism and also as a opposition of modernism. This term was first used in 1939 by Arnold Joynbee. He coined the term in his book *A Study of History* in order to express his idea of a post-modern age in European history and since then the term gets currency, and it was very extensively used by sociologists, philosophers and anti-critics. Some think that post-modernism is a practice of style, writing which calls into question all forms of representation and all structure of interpretation. In fact post modernism is a reaction against the enlightenment project, according to which human development is based on reason, logic and use of science. It begins with Renaissance.

Essence of post-modernism is marginality, micro-politics, micro-narratives. Post-modernism divides this world into two classes. It has some strange things like 'The writer is dead' or 'the reader is co-author: Reader writes the co-text which is more important. Position of critic is more important than the creator. Critic is elevated and writer is derigated. It shares sympathy and concern with the others, with those who were marginalized for one reason or the other. It sympathizes with people who have been oppressed, exploited and suffered by the hands of others.

Limitations—Principles of post-modernism were good but in practice even their most humanitarian programmes proved anti-human and destructive. The second limitation is there which appears to be a wide gap between their words and action. Post-modernists are very serious about the problems, but they can't suggest solutions.

Q. 22. Comment upon the emergence of the stream of consciousness novel and the contribution of Bergson and Dorothy Richardson.

Ans.: The emergence of the stream of consciousness novel in contemporary fiction has provoked much controversy. Professor J.W. Beach emphasizes exploitation of the element of incoherence in our conscious process as the 'defining feature' of the new technique. The interest of all stream of consciousness novelists in the contemporary Psycho-analytical theories cannot be over-estimated, the danger lies only in exaggerating this relationship and reading their novels as were 'liberation of suppressions'. In fact, the Stream of consciousness novelists are essentially concerned with presenting individual personality and experience in terms of artistic sensibility.

The technique has also been described by some as a mere literary embellishment, a means of investing character, scene and incident with 'wise bits of philosophy', or iridescent 'flashed of beauty', lending to the entire narrative a touch of ethereality. These novelists as Herbert Muller also affirms, have in various ways adapted to fiction the technique of the impressionistic painters. The key to the emergence of the stream of consciousness novel lies in this new awareness of experience, this marked shift from a conception of personality as built round a hard and changeless core to a realization of it as a dynamic process. William James, like Bergson, believes that 'empty our minds as we may, some form of changing process remains for us to feel, and cannot be expelled'.

Our psychic kaleidoscope is perpetually forming itself into new patterns. Like Bergson again, he exposes the human doctrine that our consciousness consists of discrete fragments capable of repeating themselves. On the contrary, he observes that consciousness cannot be analysed into fragments or 'chopped up in bits'.

Elsewhere, William James refers to the halo or penumbra surrounding the image. Impact what James calls 'hals, or fringe', and Virginia Woolf 'huminous halo' is nothing else than those transitional phases of our mental processes which mark the merging of the past into the present, and the fading of the present into the future, and making experience a continuum. In James's words, 'the knowledge of some other part of the stream, past or future, near or remote, is always mixed in with our knowledge of the present thing—'.

They give that continuity to consciousness without which it could not be called a stream. It is this durational aspect of consciousness which defines the basis of the stream of consciousness novel.

Therefore, the emergence of the stream of consciousness technique as a reaction against the traditional novel may be explained through its attempt to render reality in its original aspects. Bergson says: "when we feel love or hatred, when we are gay or sad, is it really the feeling itself that reaches our consciousness with those innumerable fleeting shades of meaning and deep resounding echoes that make it something altogether our own? We should all, were it so, be novelists...."

The stream of consciousness novelists attempts to render into language some of these nuances of feeling, these innumerable, fleeting shades of meaning and deep resounding echoes, in order to capture 'The emotion, the original mood in its undefiled essence.' Bergson affirms this fact when he says: "Yes, I believe our past life is these, preserved even to the minutest details; nothing is forgotten; alive have perceived, thought willed, from the first awakening of our consciousness, persists indefinitely." Bergson believes that the novelist must take the reader below the neatly arranged surface of our consciousness and show there a multitude of secondary impressions imaging upon the present moment of experience. This is what the stream of consciousness novelist purports to achieve by employing a highly fluid form of narrative.

Dorothy Richardson, Virginia Woolf, and more particularly James Joyce, are essentially engaged in this attempt to 'realize the unrealizable' to break through the meshes of the conventional word and penetrate into the durational aspect of experience.

Dorothy Richardson, like other stream of consciousness novelists, does not attempt to regularize this life-flow into any definite channels. The stream of consciousness technique as employed by Dorothy Richardson is a novel method of representing this conception of dynamic personality and the remains its most weral exponent. But it is surprising to note that she has never taken kindly to the use of the term 'stream of conciousness'. She suggests 'fountain of consciousness' as a more appropriate Metaphor.

Time according to Dorothy is a stream and therefore cannot be divided into such pure tenses as the past, present and future. The present moment, which may outwardly appear to have an dependent identity of its own, is in truth the shadow of the past projecting itself into the future. She treats memory as a spiritual phenomenon and its offerings as revelations of a reality which normally remains buried under the think layers of habit and action. She does not suggest any formal distinction between voluntary and involuntary memory. In this respect, she differs from both Bergson and Proust. But like Proust, she believes in the power of an objet, odour, or taste to recall a past experience. It is necessary to point out that although Dorothy Richardson's. Pilgrimage has a certain historical importance in the development of the English novel, it pales into significance when compared with the novels of Virginia Woolf or James Joyce. Devoid of any dramatic interest, symbolic meaning or skilful patterning, Pilgrimage remains at best only a literal and rather uninteresting record of Miriam's stream of consciousness. Unlike Virginia or James, she does not attempt to reconcile Miriam's Stream of thought with any design or pattern. There is no attempt to create any artistic effects in Pilgrimage, nor does Dorothy Richardson ever seem to conclude' her narrative. Her novels are less successful because she goes on with the flux indefinitely till she is too tired to continue any further. She thus remains the least successful of all the stream of consciousness novelists.

Q. 23. Comment upon the contribution of Virginia Woolf towards the stream of conscious novel.

Ans.: Virginia Woolf was an exceptionally individualistic writer who had discovered her bearings at an early stage and formulated her own theories regarding the nature of reality and experience. Quite independently of any 'influence'. Was evolving a literary and philosophical outlook which has tempted many critics not unsurprisingly, into assuming, a direct relationship. In reality if she strikes one as a typical Bergsonian novelist, it is because of the marked parallelism between her use of the stream of consciousness method and the durational flux.

Of all the stream of consciousness novelist Virginia Woolf alone seems to have presented a consistent and comprehensive treatment of time. Time with her is almost a mode of perception, a filter which distils all phenomena before they are apprehended in their true significance and relationship. Her characters, like those of Proust, are 'monsters occupying a place in time infinitely more important than the restricted one reserved for them in space. Her various literary experiment are, in fact, directed towards finding a suitable medium which could render most appropriately this elusive 'sense of duration'.

Her two early novels, *The Voyage Out* (1915) and *Night and Day* (1919) are written in the traditional style and present personality in a chronological sequence of events arranged along a linear movement progressing towards a well-defined climax. *Mrs Dalloway*, published in 1925, marks another development in the evolution of Virginia's Woolf's time theme. Not only is the novel designed skillfully on a limited time pattern, covering a single day in the life of Mrs. Dalloway, but it also shows a cleaner understanding and presentation of La duree as the true essence of all aesthetic experience. *To the Lighthouse*, unlike *Mrs Dalloway*, is limited to the space of ten years. In the three sections of the novel, we have three corresponding aspects of time represented symbolically. In the first section entitled, "The Window", covering about two-thirds of the entire narrative. Virginia Woolf describes an intense human experience in a mere cross-section of a September evening from six o' clock to supper time. Therefore, whereas the clock covers only a couple of hours, it is only through La duree' that we are enabled to participate in the inner experience of various characters. The second section 'The Passes', brings into contrast with inner duration, the flow of external time ten years. When the memory of Mrs. Ramsay, after an interval of ten years, re-emerges in the mind of Lily Briscoe (third section), the former again begins to inspire her values in the minds of those who remember, love and respect her. She became like Albertine 'a mighty goddess of time'.

An acute sensibility and an almost uncanny awareness of the complexity of inner life enables her to present successfully the subjective aspect of human experience. Human life pulsates simultaneously at many levels, each corresponding to a particular ebb or flow of the psychic stream. To believe that these complex aspects of the psyche can lend themselves to a mechanically superimposed notation—the clock—would be a complete misrepresentation of reality. A stream of consciousness novelist is aware of the restrictive nature of language which can flow only in a unilateral forward movement and is incapable of representing the multi-directional nature of La duree'. This is why Virginia Woolf is inevitably compelled sometimes to state explicitly what she knows cannot be rendered symbolically.

Her next novel, *The Waves* (1931), that followed three years later, cannot be classified with any of her earlier or later novels. Exquisite in lyrical composition, rich in poetic imagery, this novel attempts to communicate an almost inexpressible fluid impulse behind all human experience. Its basic intent can again be analysed in terms of durational flux. Here Virginia Woolf has tried to project time on two different levels—the normal life-span and the diurnal movement of the sun.

Then came the novel *The Years* (1937) may be classified as a period novel, covering a span of about fifty-seven years. Although unlike Proust, Virginia Woolf is not engaged in the recapturing of lost time, nor does she expound explicitly any aesthetic theory in terms La duree, she is, none the less, basically concerned with a similar view of duration and personality. In the novels like *Mrs Dalloway* and *To the Lighthouse* memory does not exist as merely a 'residue' but is co-extensive with every perception, immanent as an all-pervasive spirit in every phenomenon. Her use of the stream of consciousness technique, in the middle phase of her literary career, marks the full realization of the importance of memory. A careful analysis of these two novels will reveal a very close resemblance between Virgina Woolf on the one hand, and Proust or Bergson on the other, in their treatment of memory. But although she, unlike Proust or Bergson does not make any clear distinction between the two forms of memory. While evoking some involuntary memories of the past, Virginia Woolf adopts the same attitude as Bergson in suggesting that once the real of memory unwinds itself, all the little details, important or unimportant, emerge from their ambush in their true pristine colour and warmth. At the same time, she believes like Bergson, in the indestructibility of the past and its power to reemerge into consciousness with all its infinite details, in the inseparableness of perception from recollection, and the power of memory to project all human experience in true perspective.

Virginia Woolf wrote in her essay on Montargue, 'movement and change are the essence of our being', rigidity is death, conformity is death'. By immersing herself in her characters' streams of consciousness, Virginia Woolf experiences under the frozen surface of their conventional ego, a state of perpetual flux of which her novels are the most faithful representation.

Q. 24. What is the role of James Joyce as a stream of consciousness novelist.

Ans.: James Joyce seems to have made an intensive study of the new time-philosophy and realized its importance to the literary artist. In presenting life as a stream 'never the same' and personality as a process of dynamic blending of psychic states, Joyce comes nearest to the Bergsonian flux. The fluid method of narrative employed in Ulysses is an attempt to represent this conception of life because the stream of consciousness along which Stephen and Bloom float are perpetually remaining their waters. Joyce is indeed really the great poet of a new phase of the human consciousness, remarks Wilson. Although Joyce, unlike Virginia Woolf, was directly acquainted with Bergson's thought, it does not necessarily imply that his literary experiments show the influence of the Philosopher's theories. Unlike Proust, Joyce makes no reference to Bergson on his letters, nor did he ever acknowledge only such affiliations with the French philosopher. What is of real importance to note is that Bergson and Joyce, together with all other stream of consciousness novelists, were manifestations of the same Zeitgeist.

Joyce's experiments with language and technique, indicating his progressive realization of character as a process, culminate in his perfection of the stream of consciousness method of narrative. In attempting to render personality as a ceaseless process of becoming, he achieves for greater success than either Dorothy Richardson or Virginia Woolf.

In fact, the development of James Joyce as an artist can be understood in terms of his increasing awareness of the free branches of the days of childhood. James Joyce suggests in Molly Blooms's monologue the fluid nature of our psychic life as 'something just like this single sentence' unbroken by full stops, not even 'interspersed with commas', in order to represent the true nature of consciousness.

James Joyce is essentially engaged in this effort to penetrate into the hard crust of the conventional word, seize it in its embryonic form and then remould it to embody nascent movements in his characters' streams of consciousness. Joyce's bold experiments with language are obviously actuated by 'an original and unique emotion'.

Memory forms in the work of Joyce, as of Proust, the basis of art. Joyce is primarily engaged in an attempt to relive his past away from the Locale and recreate it in a medium that may be called La duree. In an effort to recapture the past through his characters, Joyce only affirms the principle of continuity in all experience. To fully grasp the impulse behind Joyce's art of characterization, the reader must immerse himself in the character's stream of consciousness to realize the slow process of becoming in which he is ceaselessly involved. These 'magical' recurrences of the past images, are in fact, a permanent feature of the stream of consciousness method as employed by Joyce. These recollections come in parts, as disconnected images, half-remembered words and phrases, and float along the stream of thought. Joyce's treatment of memory is as significant as Prousts's though not as comprehensive. He is impelled by a similar urge to recognize the importance of involuntary memory in prose-fiction.

Q. 25. Write a note on plot and character in Drama.

Ans.: Plot, character, thought, language, song and spectacle are the six major elements in a tragedy. According to Aristotle, "The most important of the six is the combination of the incidents in the story. Tragedy is essentially an imitation not of persons but of action character gives us quality, but it is in our actions that we find happiness for its converable." Aristotle again says that 'the first essential, the life and soul, so to speak, of tragedy, is plot.' Plot is of primary importance, while character is of secondary importance.

Character has become more prominent today. The Shakespearean tragedies are all tragedies of characters and once the characters are taken away the plots, however, well kout, will crumble like a house of cands. As Butcher point out, 'Plot in the drama, in its fullest pense, is the artistic equivalent of 'action' in real life'. It must be clear that plot and story are not synonymous terms. In *Aspects of the Novel*, E.M. Forster says, "A story is a narrative of events arranged in time sequence. A plot is also a narrative of events arranged in time sequence. A plot is also a narrative of events, the emphasis falling on causality. The king died and then the queen died is a story. The kind died, and the queen died of grief is a plot".

According to Aristotle, "the plot must be a complete whole. It must have a beginning, middle and an end. He says, a well constructed plot must neither begin nor end haphazardly". The incidents is a plot must be linked together in a 'probable or necessary sequence.' The incidents or events must have a logical connection.

Plots may be divided into two types—simple and complex. A simple plot is one which is without reversal of intention and recognition or the revelation of truth. Shylock in *The Merchant of Venice* used bond to crush Antonio, but his own bond brought about his undoing Macbeth did not fully realize the equivocations of the witches. The reversal arisis when the action which we take to safeguard ourselves betrays us and brings about our downfall.

The Complex Plot, which according to Aristotle is the better plot, can be of two types, namely the fatal plot and the fortunate plot. These two types of plots, as a critic points out, can be further sub-divided.

There is a complex fatal plot involving the unqualified by 'good' protagonist.

There is the complex-fortune plot involving an extremely 'evil' protagonist.

There is a complex-fatal plot involving 'villainous' protagonist.

There is the complex fatal plot involving a good man who is 'between these two extremes and who makes an error through same miscalculation'.

The concept of plot has shifted for age to age in the history of literary criticism. As Preminger says: "Viewed in terms of the Principles, controlling the making of a work of art, plot has referred to action, to pattern, to structure or some variation of these elements; viewed in term of the psychological and emotional response of the audience or reader. Plot has referred to impression, to sense of unity, to purpose, or to some similar response—. In the common usage of the term plot, however, the sense of the making or shaping principle has been dominant in most criticism, and it is in that sense that this article treats the concept of plot."

If we talk about the modern concept of plot, we cannot ignore the concept of Henry James. He says, "What is character but the determination of incident? What is incident but the illustration of character?"

The element of a plot, considered from the point of view of the basic conflict, are exposition, the crisis and the falling action and the denouncement or conclusion.

No analysis of plot is considered satisfactory unless Shakespeare's plot-structures are brought into focus. Shakespeare is not credited with having any remarkable talent in the making of plots. Moreover his plots are mostly borrowed from different sources. Bentley says, "Shakespeare's plots are unappreciated precisely because they are so good because they are invisible, because at every point they town the theme and the characterizations, and we cannot discuss the without the others."

In Aristotle's opinion, characters are of secondary importance. But he emphasized that the action of a tragedy should be Spondaious, i.e. grave, novel and solemn. He also insists that the tragic characters should be appropriate. The character must not be at variance with that of the class to which the individual belongs. By 'appropriateness', Aristotle presumabley means the classification of human characters. And these characters, mostly drawn from the epics and legendary sources, must be appropriate to the traditional accounts of them. The characters should naturally be linked up with status.

Characters according to modern critics, are divided into two groups—flat and round. E.M. Forster says, "Flat characters were called 'humorous' in the 17th century and are sometimes called types, and sometimes caricatures. In this purest form, they are constructed round a single idea or quality. The test of a round character is whether it is capable of surprising in a convincing way. If it never surprises it is flat. If it does not convince it is a flat pretending to be round." For example, every comic character is a type.

One must understand the relation between plot and character, which are inextricably intertwined. We must remember that a suitable and convincing situation is necessary for the delineation of character. And hence the supreme importance of plot. It is equally true that no action is possible without characters, because action needs agents for its actualization. And hence the necessity of character. Plot and character are, therefore, interdependent.

Q. 26. What do you know about functions of criticism?

Ans.: Criticism has become an integral part of literature today. Dryden used the word 'criticism' for the first time in his Preface to *The State of Innocence*, although for over two thousand years there were excellent critics and their criteria and standards varied from age to age. Hourea was the first critic in literature, who stressed the need for inspiration writing poetry. Plato is also very important name as critic. He had little faith in the aesthetic value of art. Plato did not feel happy about the theory of poetic inspiration.

Aristotle, a direct discipte of Plato, differed from his master in his attitude to art. A systematic theorist, Aristotle is a judicial critic. Sidney, Ben Jonson, Dryden, Pope, Johnson, Mathew Arnold and T.S. Eliot are certainly not the carbon copies of each other and yet they are in a sense all judicial critics.

Creative and impressionistic criticism is an important school of literary criticism and may be distinguished from judicial criticism. The function of criticism is the healthy exercise of feelings and impression.

'Criticism' in the words of Walter Pater, 'is the art of interpreting art. It serves as an intermediary between the author and the reader by explaining the one to the other'. Carlyle said, 'criticism stands like an interpreter between the inspired and the uninspired'. The function of the criticism is to explain the full meaning and value of the work to those understand who might not their deeper import. Without the help of the critic.

Etymologically, however, the word signifies 'judgement', which tradition regards as the main function of criticism. It is clear, for example, that through a critical study by Mathew Arnold, Sir Leslie Stephen, Walter Pater, or John Morley of some author that he sincerely admires will make a more lasting addition to our understanding of literary values.

The two functions judgement and appreciation lead to an examination of the two opposed stand points from which the world has looked at Criticism. The Classical and the Romantic or the Dogmatic and the Impressionistic. But the first requisite, and the one which Arnold lays most stress in his essay on 'The Function of Criticism' in 'knowledge, and ever fresh knowledge', which he can not only use in framing his own judgement but also pass on to his readers.

Criticism, since Arnold has pursued a under course, first becoming increasingly subjective in the hands of Pater and the aesthetic critics, and then reaching to a new form of classicism.

Perhaps the basis of modern criticism is still the question: 'What has the writer proposed to himself to do, and how far has he succeeded in carrying out his own plan?'

Since the Geneva critics consider a literary work as embodying the author's unique mode of consciousness, they define the critic's task as primarily to divine the soul of the author.

Some critics believed that a work of art cannot be fully appreciated without knowing fully the life of the artist. To them, the function of criticism is to have a thorough acquaintance with the biography of the artists or the writers.

Joseph Addison is shocked to find that the business of criticism of his time is only is vilify. That is why he says, "The ancient critics are full of the praises of their contemporaries, they discover beauties which escaped the observation of the vulgar, and very often find out reasons for palliating and excusing such little slips and oversights as were committed in the writings of eminent authors. On the contrary, most of the smatterers in criticism who appear among us make it their business to vilify and depreciate every new production that gains applause, to decry imaginary blemishes, and to prove by farfetched arguments that what pass for beauties in any celebrated piece are faults and errors".

According to Coleridge, the ultimate end of criticism is much more to establish the principles of writing, than furnish the rules how to pass judgement on what has been written by other, if needed it were possible that the two could be separated. T.S. Eliot looks upon criticism as something creative. The critic should try to elucidate and illuminate a work of art through comparison and analysis. Since enjoyment is the supreme objective of art, the critic should inspire the readers to enjoy the work. If like Saintsburry, he offers too much of extraneous information and makes the critique too pedantic, bristling with the minutest details, the readers interest with flag. The critic must also remain free from passions and prejudices, which often tend to make him a propagandist, a vendor of ideas.

Illumination and exposition are, no doubt, the functions of criticism. But along with them, there should be the correction of taste. The critic may not be preceptor or a guide, but he is nevertheless an intermediary between the writer and the reader. An ideal critic is rare for his multiplicity of functions.

Q. 27. Write a short note on the salient features of the modern 20th century novel.

Ans.: Modern novel is by and large a realistic representation of the modern, social and economic life not just in the exterior visible sense, but in the inner sense with an eye on the influence of varied forces on the mind and the Psyche. Most of the modern novels represent the true complexity of life.

Modern novels as those of stream of consciousness novels such as *Ulysses*, *Mrs. Dalloway* etc. or those of Conrad and Henry James do not bother much about time and take frequent recourse of flashback and move forward. Thus in modern novels time is not divided into parts, but is deemed a continuous flow and life is not "a series of giglamps, symmetrically arranged, but a luminous halo...."

It has been greatly influenced by the Freudian Psychalogy whereby not the perceptible situation of the characters is studied but an effort is made to reach the mind and the Psyche of the characters. Their relations and actions are also studied on the psychoanalytical plane. The typical modern novel represents life as it is and does not try to moralisc, reform or guide.

In many of the modern novels we do not find the end, as life is endless, and even the characters are not elaborately drawn. Thus, there is decay of both the plot and the character in the modern novel. In the same way, we find ideas and counter-ideas, but no conclusion. Obscurity element is also there.

Science has had a great impact on the modern novel. It treats sex relationship with a freer mind. Modern novel took the modern shape in the real sense after Laurence and more particularly when Henry James, Joyce, Conrad and Virginia Woolf presented their point of view. Then there appeared a sort of cynicism, and disillusion in society, as a reset of the wars, the war looming danger of catastrophe and the all pervading cruelty and violence in society in society and apathy of the powers. In fact, all kinds of novels are popular in the modern age.

"Modern fiction is 'the ever flowering tree of truth, and of understanding.'" *Richard Church*

"Let fiction cease to lie about life, let it portray men and women as they are actuated by the motives and passions in the measure we all known". *W.D. Howells*

"The Novel is the highest example of subtle inter-relatedness that man has discovered." *D.H. Lawrence*

Henry Jones has traced unending capacity of endless accumulation of human experience in the modern English novel. Dynamism is the key-stone of the modern fiction. For H.G. Wells, "Novel is the social mediator, the vehicle of understanding the parade of morals and the exchange of manners, the factory of customs, the criticism of laws and institution of social dogmas and ideas". The chief tendencies of the modern English fiction are:

(a) The Arrival of Naturalism—During the 20th century, the tendency of Naturalism crept up into the English novel. Already through the hands of Charles Dickens, Thackeray, Meredik, George Eliot and others, the English novel has acquired enough of naturalism into fiction. In England, Arnold Bernett, John Galsworthy and H.G. Wells wrote more naturally. Henrick Ibsen, G. Hanphman and Shaw attributed a social function to the novel. Somerset Maugham, J.B. Priestly and Gissing introduced emphatically the natural tendency into English novel. Zola wrote that the novelist desires to make himself the master of phenomena so that he can control them and there lies his practical usefulness.

(b) The Study of Psycho-analysis—Sigmund Frend, Carl Gustav Jung and William Mc. Dougall unlocked the labyrinth of human consciousness by analytical methods. Many novelists tried, therefore to peep into the dark recesses of human nature. Virginia Woolf excelled herself in this respect. James Joyce set a daring precedent in the field of Psyche-analytical study. The study of Psycho-analytical literature by novelists, gave them new liberties in vocabulary and new conceptions of form.

(c) The Novel of Social Purpose—H.G. Wells, John Galsworthy, Arnold Bennett made novel as an instrument of social propaganda. They regarded that novel should serve the social purposes. The whole social life was aimed at by them and they unanimously argued that anything that concerns social life should not escape the notice of a novelist.

(d) Preponderance of Realism—Arnold Bennett, Gissing and Moore may be said to be the champions of the element of realism in English fiction. Benett's *The Old Wives' Tale* is really unprecedented in the field of new realism in modern fiction. H.G. Wells, Graham Greene, Henry James urged for 'New Realism', or 'Expressionism' in English fiction. Henry James and Jospeh Conrad stressed upon the projections of situations.

(e) The Appearance of the Regional Fiction—Hardy may be said to be the pioneer of the 'Regional Fiction', Arnold Bennett was the novelist of *Westmorland in Crumg Folk going Home*, *The Lonely Plough*, *The Splendid Fairing* and the *Trumpet in the Dust*. Eden Phillopts made Devonshire as the scene in Children of the Mist, The Human By and The Street Woman. Jane Maclaren and S.R. Brockett are also prominent regional novelists.

(f) The Technique of 'Stream of Consciousness'—One of the main trends of the modern fiction is the Stream of consciousness novel. The chief exponents are—D.H. Lawrence James Joyce, Dorothy Richardson, Virginia Woolf, A Henry James.

(g) Self-Seeking in Fiction or Autobiographical Novel—George Gissing was a consciously subjective novelist. George Eliot H.G. Wells and Henry James gave many convincing and honest personal details in their novels.

(h) Novels of Sex-Study—D.H. Lawrence made sex-study one of the chiefest themes of the modern fiction.

(i) Romantic Touches—Conrad gave a new impetus to the survival of romanticism. Kipling and Haggard popularized it.

(j) Detective Fiction—The detective writing by G.K. Chesterton and Edges Wallace popularized this form. Dorothy L. Sayers and Agatha Christie are more chiseled and more popular detective novelists of the modern novels.

Q. 28. Write a detailed note on Feminism in the poetry of contemporary Indian English Women poets.

Ans.: Feminism is attached to assertion of female identify and implies radical reorientation of life, culture and literature. Its focus is on woman, major Indian-English poets mainly, Kamala Das, Imtiaz Dharkar, Charmayne D' Souza and Tara Patel, Kamala Das's poetry reveals conflicting situations and emotions. 'Kamala Das alias Kamala Surayyia' spoke a lot about women and their lot in the patriarchal set up. In Dharkar's *Purdah*, an element of protest against the Muslim treatment of women and a strong critique of patriarchy is evident. D' Souza holds extreme views on love, marriage and the man-woman nexus. Tara Patel's *Single Woman* maps out the Psychology of a single woman whose life with all her freedom has its own pains and anxieties.

Modern Indian women poets tread the middle path. Sometimes they show the position of women in India and the various ways by which women are being suppressed, which always pushes the female self into the position of marginality. These poets discard the conventional notion of Indian womanhood. The body is the central metaphor in their confessional poetry. They do not-altogether reject men and marriage. They talk about their need of love, man and companionship.

These poets have a wonderful gift of articulation. Writing for them becomes a means of self-discovery and the three stages of articulation, analysis and protest laid down by Elaine Showalter are clearly visible in their works. I call them real feminists because they not only attack patriarchy and its bad elements but make their writing an exercise an 'Psychic striplease' and present themselves 'gynocentric'.

These modern poets are away from virgin syndrome and talk freely about women's sexual needs in their poetry. Kamala Das, one of the pioneers in modern feminist poetry, finds writing an instrument of catharsis and protest. She craves for a relationship which could provide them both emotional and sexual gratification. Due to which she was branded as 'promiscuous', 'nymphomanial' or 'a girl with vast sexual hungers', though she does not advocate adultery in her poems. She frankly says, 'I always wanted love, and if you don't get it within your home, you stray a little'. Her life seems meaningless without love, 'a barren wasteland'.

Dharkar can be compared with Kamala Das as far as expression is concerned. Dharkar also talks of how women become a viction of patriarchal gaze.

The new Hajji
There was nothing holy in the look
Hands that prayed at Mecca
Dropped a shy flower on your Book

Dharkar in her poems complains about the restrictions and prescriptions imposed on Indian woman.

D'Souza in her first book *A Spelling Guide to Woman* (1990), talks about the situation of women. Her view of the man-woman nexin, love and marriage is unromantic to the point of bordering on the cynical. She often writes about the attractions of insecurity, the fun of anxieties, as security though attractive, is at the same time also a trap, an illusion. A Maiden's Prayer, amusingly contrasts the real desires of the maiden's heart with the imagined peace of a night alone 'without a man'. Hugging a pillow the maiden desires what she lacks.

Another poet Tara Patel in her collection *Single Woman* (1991) maps out the Psychology of a single women. A Single woman's mind is replete with contradictions, humiliations and defeats. There is longing for love, aim and companionship as Tara Patel believes that a woman can feed herself but 'Love begins with a man'. However, the love she longs for is not just ethereal emotion. In her poem, 'Calangute Beach, Goa', the single woman turns down the invitation of an American to go swimming naked and this becomes 'a growing regret' for her. In one of her poems, she frankly tells us, 'I want to touch a man', and in another the woman's cry is 'Touch me, touch, touch me somewhere/give me permission to touch you'. Because Tara Patel feels that touch speaks a language which communicates for more effectively than mere words, 'once touched silence is articulation':

The single woman living alone, without the security of husband or family, works for a anchor in another woman's man,' but then realize, it is a temporary one as he is always another woman's man.

Tara also talks about woman's feeling of growing old. At places existential element also enters her poetry, with a sense of purposelessness and loneliness as in her poem.

All these poets in their poems are expressive their feelings of exhilaration and sorrow at the gender injustices in society, in terms of other bodies. The unique method of responding to a women's experience in the face of patriarchy has been advocated by these feminist poets.

These poets share a common belief of the fallacy of masculinist thought. According to them, men are responsible for the prevalent binary system of meaning: male/female, active/passive, nature/culture, reason/chaos. But these feminist poets differ in their way of expressions. Cixous wrote 'write yourself. Your body must be heard'. These women proved may to continue that to achieve selfhood, a women must speak. Despite being very different, there are several similarity in the poems by these feminist poets, particularly their emphasis on the female body. They write personal poetry (most of them in confessional mode) breaking all conventional norms. They all write about their incessant search for true love, their repeated failures and the pain and the intense loneliness she experiences some of Kamala Das's poems voice social concerns and some explore her childhood, her love for Ghanshyam but the major theme of her poetry remains the search for fulfillment as a woman.

Q. 29. Write a detailed note on Historical survey of Indian Drama in English.

Ans.: A Short Historical Survey of Indian-drama in English Indian drama in English is a link in the continuation of its rich heritage. Indian drama, written both in English and translated into English from other languages, has registered a remarkable growth in recent years. As Krishna Kriplani points out, the modern Indian drama "owned its first flowering to foreign grafting." Furthermore, English education gave an impetus and a momentum to the critical study of not only western drama, but also classical Indian drama. The western impact also quickened the drying roots of Indian native tradition with the sap of a new life, thereby opening the exciting chapter of modern Indian drama written originally in the vernaculars and at times translated into English.

The first Indian play in English. "*Is This Called Civilization?*" was written by Michael Madhusudan Dutt in 1871. But no sustainable creative effort appeared for decades thereafter. The growth of Indian-English drama was arrested for many years due to some plausible reasons like English being the learnt or the second language; absence of Professional stage; Complex structure of contemporary Indian theatre and mainly because no regular school of Indian English drama was established in our country. To route H.M. Williams, the English speaking theatre in Indian anxiously awaits a writer of Narayan's or Raja Rao's Stature one who might perhaps combine the poetic vision of a Sri Aurobindo or a Dom Moracs with the professional craftsmanship of an Asif currimbnoy.... There is intense interest in avant-grade western plays and films in literary and theatrical circles in Indu but the quality achieved by Satyajit Rai has yet to be seen in the English-speaking Indian theatre. (Indo-Anglian Literature A Survey) Unlike poetry and novel, drama is a composite art involving the dramatist, the actor and the audience in a commonly shared artistic experience. Moreover, since the normal medium of conversation in India was the mother tongue, it was difficult then to make a dialogue between Indians in English. This may sound natural and convincing but this difficulty has been overcome by some talented Indian. English dramatists by carefully choosing the situations and language that transcend time and place, and the convincing characters.

The pre-Independent era saw some major figures like Rabindranath Tagore, Sri Aurobindo, T.P. Kailsama, A.S.P. Ayyar, Lobo-Prabhu, Harindranath Chattopadhyaya and Bharathi Sarabhai—who contributed substantially to the growth and development of Indian English drama. Rabindranath Tagore was the first major playwright who invested Indian drama in English with lyrical excellence, symbolic overtones and allegorical significance. His best known plays—*Sacrifice, Chitra, Mukta Dhara, The Post Office, The King Of The Dark Chamber* and *Red Oleanders*—display a unique blend of simplicity and complexity as also conventionality and modernity. Though his plays abound in great variety and richness they tend to be too suggestive and symbolic thereby lacking in dramatic action. In the words of Thompson they are "vehicles of thought rather than expressions of action". However, Tagore's plays though rendered into English often by the author himself, belong properly to Bengali drama.

Sri Aurobindo inherited and carried forward the tradition of Elizabethan poetic drama and Shakespeare. His dramatic genius is amply revealed in his five complete plays—*Persus, Vasavadutta, Rodogune*, The *Viziers Of Bassara* and *Eric*— which were written originally in English. A study of the five plays of Sri Aurobindo reveals that he is a highly competent dramatist and an accomplished craftsman in verse. His plays reveal Aurobindo's exquisite skill in the portrayal of characters. The most notable thing is that Sri Aurobindo opened up new vistas in Indian English drama displaying his robust optimism about the future of mankind.

T.P. Kailasam's English plays are inspired by puranic themes taken from the Ramayana and the Mahabharata. His first play, *The Burden* (1933), is derived from the *Ramayana* and deals with the predicament in which Bharata is placed at the death of his father, Dasaratha. His another play *Fulfilment* is a play that recounts Ekalavya's decision to join the Kauravas against the Pandavas. His play *The Purpose* (1944) dramatizes Ekalavya's single-minded devotion to the art of archery.

Harindranath Chattopadhyaya added a new dimension to Indian English drama with the leftist leanings and revolutionary zeal. He has written devotional plays like *Radias*, *Chokha Mela*, *Pundalik*, *Saku Bai*, *Tuka Ram*, etc. He has also written some social play like *The Window*, *The Parrot*, *The Coffin*, *The Evening Lamp*, etc. He had acute awareness of social problems and his innate sympathics for the suffering masses.

Bharati Sarabhai is the first, most distinguished Woman Dramatist, who gave a Gandhian touch to Indian English drama. Her first play, *The Well of the People* (1949), followed by *Two Women* (1952) left the impression of the playwright. After Harindranath, we have a few playwright who proceeded on the lines suggested in his social plays, thereby making Indian-English drama more and more realistic and purposeful.

J.M. Lobo Prabhu is the last great name in pre-independence Indian English drama. He has written over a dozen play but only, Mother of New India: *A Play of the Indian Village in Three Acts* (1944) and *Death Adbicate* (1945) appeared before Independence. His *Collected Plays* was published in 1956.

The names of a few more playwrights may be taken into account. They may be called minor dramatists. Some are Subhindra Nath Ghose, R.K. Narayan, K.R.S. Iyengar, Balwant Gargi and Mrinalini Sarabhai.

Although the pre-independence Indian English drama is notable for its poetic excellence, thematic variety, technical virtuosity, symbolic significance and its commitment to human and moral values, it was by and large not geared for actual stage production.

Post-Independence Indian English Drama. In the post-Independence era Indian-English drama does not make a noteworthy presence unlike poetry and fiction. The fact to be noted is that a good number of plays by Indian playwrights like Asif Currimbhoy, Pratap Sharma Gurucharan Das were successfully' staged in England and U.S.A. but no regular school of Indian-English drama was established in our country. Most of the dramas were written in prose but at the same time poetic plays also survive in the post-colonial era. M.K. Naik writes, "...the Tagore Aurobindo-Kailsam tradition of poetic drama continues, but with a difference in the hands of Manjeri Isvaran, G.V. Desani and Pritish Nandy."

Pratap Sharma wrote two prose plays; first is *A Touch of Brightness* (1968) and *The Professor Has a Warcry* (1970). His plays were staged abroad successfully but they failed to be staged in the country. Sex is the main theme of his plays.

Nissim Ezekiel's three plays are considered to be a welcome addition to the dramaturgy of Indian-English drama with his short play *Songs of Denovation* (1969).

Modern Indian-English Drama. From 1945 onwards, one finds several dramatic organizations launched, but none devoted itself exclusively to the drama in English. In the post-Independence period, performing art were employed as an effective means of public enlightenment during 1951-54. As a result, the National School of Drama was established under the directorship of Alkazi. Institutions for training in dramatics were founded in big cities. The Annual Drama Festival was started in New Delhi by the Sangeet Nataka Akademi in 1954. With so much encouragement coming from so many quarters, drama begun to flourish in the regional languages, with the singular exception of the drama in English. In this context, M.K. Naik points to the distinct native trend emerging in the modern English drama in India:

> "But during recent years vernacular Indian drama has increasingly been turning to folk forms and tapping their springs of vitality with splendid results."

Girish Karnad, a recipient of the Jyanpith Award, is a living legend in the arena of contemporary Indian-English drama. His journey from 'Yayati' to 'The Fire And The Rain' holds a mirror to the very evolution of Indian theatre during nearly four decades. He represents a synthesis of cultures and his formal experiments have been for more conceived and have certainly been for more successful than those of his contemporaries. "The likes of Girish Karnad enable us to pretend that there is such a thing as a truly 'Indian' theatre which can be true to its traditions and at the same time responsive to contemporary concerns."

Tughlaq, *Hayavadane, Tale-Dande* and *Naga-Mandala* are some of his wonderful dramatic creations.

Apart from these major plays by major authors; we can find some plays of interest by various writers of this era which can be categorized as follows:

Play	Writer
The Goddess Speaks	V.K. Gokak
Prometheus Rebound	B.S. Mardhkar
Chidambram: A Chronicle Play	K. Nagarjan
A Passage to India	Santha Rama Rau
Line of Mars	Manohar Malgonkar
The Last Wedding Anniversary	Shiv K. Kumar
Anarkali	Ahmed Akhtar
The Myth Makers	Dina Mehta
Gandhiji's Sadhana	K.S. Rangappa
To Anchor a Cloud	Dilip Hiro
Lord Ravan of Lanka	P.S. Vasudev
Princes	Greve Patel
The King Who Sold his Wife	Syed Amanuddin
Apply, Apply, No Reply	Dilip Hiro

Indian English Drama in Post Modern Era. The term 'Post-modern' refers to various other trends like structuralism, modernism, deconstruction, social realism and socio-psycho analytical criticism. In the sociological and structural analysis it can be argued that social realism and psychological conflict have become the chief vehicles of literary expression and Indian drama in English is no exception to it.

The form and facets of post-modern drama have crystallized and have become galvanized because of the overwhelming impact of G.B. Shaw, Ibsen, Eliot, Yeats, etc. But strangely enough, Indian English drama could neither strike roots in the Indian soil, nor it could succeed in envisaging the origin and growth of Indian English theatre movement. Theoretically, it is assumed that the theatre (stage) is a laboratory where dramas are experimented and examined. H.M. Williams, a reputed literary critic, examines Indian English drama within his critical frame work and writes "The English speaking theatre in India anxiously awaits a writer of Narayan's or Raja Rao's stature, one who might perhaps combine the poetic vision of a Sri Aurobindo or a Dom Moraes with the professional craftsmanship of an Asif Currimbhoy.... There is intense interest in avante-garde western plays and films in literary and theatrical circles in India but the quality achieved by Satyajit Ray in his Bengali films has yet to be seen in the English speaking Indian theatre." In comparison to other literary genres, Indian English drama has achieved a little but, in the changing perspective, the realm is full of fruit-bearing possibilities. As Dr. R.K. Dhawan observes, "very recently Indian English drama shot into prominence. Younger writers like Mahesh Dattani and Manjula Padmanabhan have infused new life into this branch of writing."

Mahesh Dattani, a young man of only thirty eight, is a promising playwright. Some of his worth-staging plays are *Where There Is A Will*, *Final Solution*, *Dance Like a Man* and *Tara*. Acclaimed as a leading playwright in English, he has now bagged the Sahitya Academy Award for English Literature for his play, *Final Solutions*.

Manjula Padmanabhan is the next great voice in the recent Indian English drama. Her pioneering play *Harvest* bagged *Onassis* Award and got tremendous popularity throughout the world. She portrays a mean and *morbund* world where mothers sell their children for the price of rice: Her play *Harvest* deals with a miserable family dwelling in a single room in a chawl of Mumbai.

Indian English drama, moreover, has registered a remarkable growth and maturity through English translation of Hindi, Marathi, Bengali and Kannada plays in the 1980s. A study of Vijay Tendulkar, Mohan Rakesh, Muktibodh, Badal Sircar and Girish Karnad amply reveals that they have added a new dimension to Indian drama through their substantial contributions.

Vijay Tendulkar is today well-known for his contribution to Indian Theatre and ranked as a front-line playwright in contemporary Indian theatre along with Mohan Rakesh. Since the staging of his maiden play *Householder*, Tendulkar has come a long way. His works have such a wide ambit that it reveals the multifacetedness of Tendulkar's creative genius. His 'Silence! The Court is in Session' earned him a special place among leading Indian dramatists, while his *Ghasiram Kotwal* won him international fame in the mid-seventies.

Thus it is mainly the drama in Indian languages and the drama in English translations that have registered a remarkable growth in recent decades. During the last few years, several plays, originally written in the regional languages, have been translated into English. Today many academicians are of the view that it is necessary to incorporate these translations into the corpus of Indian English literature.

Solved Papers*

DECEMBER 2008

Directions: Read the following poem and answer the questions given under it from Questions 1 to 5 in 30 words each:

Life is real! Life is earnest!
And the grave is not its goal!
'Dust thou art, to dust returnest',
Was not spoken of the soul.
Not enjoyment, and not sorrow,
Is our destined end or way;
But to act, that each tomorrow
Find us farther than today.
Art is long and Time is fleeting.
And our hearts, though stout and brave,
Still, like muffled drums, are beating
Funeral marches to the grave.

Q. 1. What is the truth about human body and soul?

Ans.: Human body and Soul are two different entities. While human body is perishable, soul is immortal.

Q. 2. What is the goal of life according to this passage?

Ans.: The goal of life is neither enjoyment not sorrow. Joy and sorrow come alternately and pass. The goal of life is action. Man must act and every tomorrow should take us farther than today. This march should go on.

Q. 3. What does the poet say about the Past, Present and Future?

Ans.: The poet makes very striking observations about the Past, Present and Future. He says that Past has passed and cannot be recalled; the Future is unseen and uncertain. The most important is the Present which we must make the best use of.

Q. 4. What can we learn from the lives of great men?

Ans.: We must learn from the lives of great men who we can also make our lives sublime and memorable and leave the prints of our feet on the stands of time.

---

* This paper is as per the old pattern. The new pattern has been implemented from June 2010 onwards.

Q. 5. What is the poet's advice to man?

Ans.: The poet's advice is that we must work ceaselessly, with heart and soul. Act and act and wait for the result with patience and hope. Result will come sooner or later.

Directions: Write the answer of the question no. 6 to 20 in 30 words.

Q. 6. What is meant by Renaissance?

Ans.: Renaissance means 'revival' or 'rebirth' of Greek learning, art, literature and culture of the Middle Ages in Europe. In England it came through Italy and flourished in the Elizabethan Age in the works of Shakespeare, Spenser, Marlowe and Ben Jonson.

Q. 7. What is meant by Reformation?

Ans.: Reformation was a religious Movement led by Martin Luther in the fifteenth century. It protested against the practices of the Roman Catholic Church. It advocated complete faith in the Bible and in one's own soul for salvation.

Q. 8. What is the relationship between Poverty, Life and Morality according to Mathew Arnold?

Ans.: According to Arnold, poetry consoles and sustains us. "A poetry of revolt against moral ideas is a poetry of revolt against life; a poetry of indifference towards moral ideas is a poetry of indifference towards life."

Q. 9. What does Keats mean by "Negative Capability"?

Ans.: Keats means to say that a poet has no personality of his own; he assumes the personality of the character he creates. "The poet has none, no identify—he is certainly the most unpoetical of all god's creatures."

Q. 10. What is a Lyric?

Ans.: A Lyric is a short musical composition meant too be sung to the accompaniment of a lyre by a single singer. Now the term is used for any short non-narrative poem expressing a single thought or feeling of the poet.

Q. 11. Comment on the addressee in Shakespeare's Sonnets.

Ans.: The sonnets of Shakespeare are addressed to two unidentified persons—a Dark Lady and a certain friend addressed as Mr. W.H. Thus these sonnets express Shakespeare's frustrated love and broken friendship. The addresses are wrapped in mystery.

Q. 12. What is *Comedy of Manners*?

Ans.: The *Comedy of Manners* exhibited the artificial manners and low moral values of the high class society of the Restoration Age. They largely displayed the intrigues, witty remarks, sparkling dialogues and verbal fencings between gentleman and sophisticated ladies.

Q. 13. What is *Pastoral Elegy*?

Ans.: The *Pastoral Elegy* is an elegy cast into the conventional pastoral form. It is presumed that the poet is a shephered mourning the death of a fellow shepherd. The whole imagery of goats/sheep, pastures and pastoral gods and goddesss is drawn into it.

Q. 14. Explain Victorian Dilemma.

Ans.: The term Victorian Dilemma suggests the conflict between science and religion that raged in the Victorian Age. The traditional religion, beliefs and conventions of Christianity were challenged by the discoveries and explorations of science.

Q. 15. Justify the title *Songs of Innocence.*

Ans.: The Songs of Innocence is a volume of songs written by William Blake. The soul of a Child is absolutely innocent and is, therefore, protected by God. Worldly experience tarnished the human soul.

Q. 16. Define Keats's concept of 'Negative Capability'.

Ans.: By 'Negative Capability' Keats meant that the poet must completely identify and submerge his own identify with that of his subject of poetry. The poet has no personality of his own.

Q. 17. What does 'Unicorn' symbolize in the play *The Glass Menageries* by Tencese William?

Ans.: The glass unicorn is a symbol of uniqueness. Like the glass unicorn Amanada is unique. She is not a normal girl. Amanada is set apart from the rest of her humanity due to her mental and physical illness. Like the unicorn is extinct, similarly she is also extinct only as a piece.

Q. 18. Who were the 'University Wits'?

Ans.: The University Wits were writers who had training in Oxford or Cambridge. They were members of learned societies and rather liberal in their view concerning God and morality. They were all reckless bohemians. In their intellectualism they were true embodiments of the impact of the Renaissance an English author and sensibility.

Q. 19. Write a brief note on Synge's impact on Irish Dramatic Writing.

Ans.: The minor dramatist echoes his age; but the dramatist of genius is one who stands outside his age or creates his age Synge came close to creating an age in Ireland. He more than any other changed the shape of Irish dramatic writing; he more than any other showed Ireland to the world. If Ireland choose to misunderstand him in the very moment of applauding him, the loss is not his but that of Ireland.

Q. 20. How did Renaissance influence poetry?

Ans.: Sir Thomas Wyatt and the goal of Surrey were the pioneers of poetry in England. They gave poetry a new sense of grace, dignity, delicacy, and harmony which was found lacking. Wyatt introduced sonnet into English literature, and Surrey to have written blank verse.

Directions: Write the answers of the question no. 21 to 25. Each Question carries 12 marks and has to be answered in about 200 words.

Q. 21. Summarise the views of Sidney on the use of verse and metre in poetry.

Ans.: In the use of verse and metre in poetry Sidney oscillated between the classical concept and Elizabethan practices. According to the classical concept, verse or metre is not indispensable for poetry, but according to Elizabethan practices metre was desirable, if not indispensable. Sidney seems to reconcile the two extremes. Holding the classical view he says that metre is "but an ornament and no cause to poetry, sith there have been many most excellent poets that never versified, and now swarm many versifiers that need never answer to the name of poets". He further says, "It is not rhyming and versing that maketh a poet, no more than a long gown maketh an advocate, who though he pleaded in armour should be an advocate and no soldier". Invention is the soul of poetry, and in this sense if prose is inventive, it should be classed with poetry.

Then comes on him the Elizabethan influence. This attracts him to favour the use of verse or metre in poetry, though on other grounds. He says that verse being sweeter and more appealing to our aesthetic sense should be used in poetry. Verse is a superior form of expression to ordinary prose. He says, "The senate of poets hath chosen verse as their fittest raiment, weighing each syllable of each word by just proportion according to the dignity of the subject". He further says than on account of its sweetness and orderliness verse is fittest for memory, and memory is the treasure-house of knowledge. Musical verse can be more easily remembered and retained in the mind than prose. Therefore it is advisable to write poetry in verse and metre.

Q. 22. Which is more important between plot and character in the Tragedy, according to Aristotle?

Ans.: A question is often asked whether plot is more important or character in the Tragedy. According to Aristotle, Plot is the very soul of the tragedy and therefore far more important than character. In his definition of the tragedy Aristotle says that "Tragedy is an imitation of an action that is serious, complete, and of a certain magnitude". Here he does not say that tragedy is an imitation of 'characters'. Again, in the same definition he says, "in the form of action, not of narration". Clearly enough, 'action' in his definition means 'plot'. Characters are merely agents of the action or the plot, and therefore subordinate to it.

From the above definition it follows that 'Tragedy is an imitation, not of men, but of an action and of life, and life consists in action'. To the question whether plot makes a tragedy or character, Aristotle replies that "without action there cannot be a tragedy: there may be without character". It is, of course, a riddle which is not easy to solve because action themselves issue from characters. Resolving this riddle Aristotle say, "character determines men's qualities, but it is by their actions that they are happy or the reverse". A plot imitates action, and character men. A tragedy is a representation of men in action. Sometimes action can occur even without men or characters. A huge natural calamity like earthquake, flood or storm may occur, causing incalculable devastation without any role of men or characters. Hence it is the deeds or actions (or incidents woven into a plot) which make the tragedy, and not merely men or characters in their inactive or passive state.

Q. 23. Briefly discuss Horace's observation on Poetry.

Ans.: Horace was the leading Roman critic whose observations on poetry and drama have their relevance to the present day. In this observations on Poetry he begins with discussing what should be the proper subject-matter for greater poetry. He says, "I would advise the well-instructed *imitator* (poet) to take the model from life and customs." But this imitation should be enriched with imagination or even with some "believable false." Then he passes on to defining the function or poetry. He says that poets should inculcate a love of all that is nobel in life "so that our young men, like persons who live in a healthy place, may be perpetually influenced for good." He goes on to say, "Poets desire either to improve or to please, or to unite the agreeable and the profitable, with what pleases and at once delight and instruct the reader." "It is not enough", he further says, "for poems to have beauty, they must also be pleasing and lead the listener's soul whether they will." Horace goes on to say, "He who chooses his subject wisely will find that neither words nor lucid arrangement will fail him." Passing on to metre he says that there is a fixed appropriate metre for each kind of poetry whether epic, lyric, elegiac, pastoral and so on. In the use of language for poetry, Horace accepts the verdict of Homer. A poet is free to use both familiar words and new ones provided they give clearness and effectiveness to the poem. The poets should remember that words also grow old and die in course of time, and many dead words come back to life. The poet should be conscious of his fact while writing his poetry, His language should have "taste, beauty and charm."

Q. 24. Briefly analyse Dr. Johnson's views on Drama and its art.

Ans.: In his analysis of dramatic art, Dr. Johnson has given his views on all debatable points such as the dramatic unities, dramatic pleasure, and the tragicomedies. First of all he says that drama must be "a faithful mirror of manners and of life." It should present human sentiments in human language. The story of drama must be true to life, but it must not be the story of one man or a few men, but of a wide section of humanity. Shakespeare's plays are great because each play is miniature picture of any one aspect of the whole of humanity.

So far as Dramatic Unities are concerned, Dr. Johnson approved of only one unity—the unity of Action. This is necessary to make the plot complete and one whole. There would be utter chaos if there were many action leading to different ends. In a good play all the actions should join together and lead to one desired end. So far as the unities of Time and Place are concerned, he finds them unnecessary and highly undesirable. The stage in a play is an imaginary platform. It is neither a real Rome nor a real Alexandria, and therefore the shifting of scenes from one place to another is also an imaginative process. So is the case with the passage of time. The audience imaginatively travels from place to place, and passes days and years through the same process of imagination. After all, a play is not a literal picture but an imaginative recreation of life. In the same way he defends tragic comedy. Life itself is a mingling of tragic and comic occurrences. Moreover, tragic and comic scenes throw each other into greater relief by contrast. Therefore there is nothing unnatural or inartistic in a tragic-comedy.

Q. 25. Which, according to Aristotle, is a higher and nobler literary work between an Epic and a Tragedy?

Ans.: To the questions whether the Epic or the Tragedy is the better and nobler form of art, Aristotle gives preference to the Tragedy. Those who hold the plea in favour of the Epic argue that is appeals to a more refined class of society, the cultured few, and that it achieves its effect without the aid of any external paraphernalia such as the theatrical stage and the spectacle and that its action is more varied. Aristotle concedes all these points and still boldes the view that tragedy is the better form of art. He argue that the tragedy equally appeals to the more refined class, and that it can be appreciated and enjoyed in reading as well as in witnessing on the stage. Therefore it appeals to a wider section of society—to the section of reading class as well as to the spectator or audience class. Theatrical performance is an additional accessory and no compulsory equipment of its literary craft. On the contrary, its performance on the stage makes its appeal deeper and wider. As for the varied action of the Epic, it is a drawback rather than a strong point because unity of tone and action makes a more concentrated effect than the varied one. The effect on a larger and more varied scale dilutes the totality of effect. Therefore Aristotle holds the Tragedy on the higher level than the Epic.

Direction: Write an essay of about 1000 words on any of the following topics:

Q. 26. Discuss your view about the Drama in both literature and theatre.

Ans.: Originally Dr. Rama was known as Dramatic Poesy. Dryden entitled his famous treatise on Drama as an Essay Dramatic Poesy. The term Dramatic Poesy points to the fact that Drama is as much an intrinsic part of literature as Poetry. It is not essential that drama must be acted on the stage in a theatre. In fact, drama has a double advantage. It can be enjoyed as a distinct genre of literature both on the stage as well as in one's study room. Great works of Drama are equally successful on the stage as well as in the study parlour.

However, earliest drama were written only for the stage. They were *Miracle plays*, *Mystery plays*, *Morality plays*, and *Interludes*. These plays were basically religious and didactic and were meant to teach the largely illiterate English public principles, teaching and tenets of Christianity by staging them at public places. Since there were no regular public theatres in those days, these plays were staged under the open sky or on public platforms. The *Miracle plays* presented the lives and martyrdom of the great Christian saints. The *Mystery plays* staged the theme of the Bible in a chronological order beginning with Nativity, Crucifixion, Resurrection of Christ and the last Judgment. The *Morality plays* presented on the stage personified Virtues, Vices, and Death as the Reward of Sin. The *Interludes* just entertained the public to relieve them from boredom. Since the larger section of the public could not read them, they were staged on the artificially created platforms. Sometimes, they were also staged in the Halls of Dukes, Barons and other royal personalities. They were all rudimentary plays and had very little literary value.

Shakespeare's plays touch the highest watermark as literature as well as stage plays. He is the greatest dramatist the world has ever produced. His plays are held to be as important today as they were when they were written more than four centuries ago. The fact that several of his plays are still prescribed in the syllabi or universities in many countries of the world goes to prove that his plays are highly and widely recognized works of literature. They are equally popular as theatrical plays. His important tragedies are *Hamlet, Othello, Macbeth* and *King Lear*. His famous comedies are *As You Like It, Twelfth Night, A Midsummer Night's Dream. Merchant of Venice. Much Ado About Nothing,* and several more. His Historical Plays and Romances are in no way less important. In all he has written thirty-seven plays, and all of them have been celebrated both as literary works and theatrical plays. A great admirer of Shakespeare, M. Henry Cochin, praises the genius of Shakespeare in these words: "Shakespeare is the King of poetic rhythm and style as well as the king of realm of thought, along with his dazzling prose. Shakespeare has succeeded in giving us the most varied, the most harmonious verse which has ever sounded upon the human ear since the verse of the Greeks."

There are many more dramatists whose dramas are remarkably literary as well as fit for the stage. Their plays can be read as works of literature in one's parlour, but they would be equally successful on the stage. These dramatists include Marlowe, Ben Jonson, Dryden Congreve, Vanbrugh, Farquhar, Sheridan, Goldsmith and a few others. They present the sociocultural life of the age in which they lived and wrote. Ben Jonson's plays are called *Comedies of Humours*.

They caricature human foibles and eccentrics in good humour. Sheridan, Congreve, Farquhar present the falling morals and foppish fashions of the Restoration Age. They largely display the intrigues, foppish manners, witty remarks, sparkling dialogues, and verbal fencing between aristocratic ladies and lords. The Restoration Age was known for these characteristic. Presenting the true picture of the Restoration Age, these plays deal with the relations and intrigues of gentlemen and ladies living in a polished and sophisticated society, and rely for comic effect in great part on the wit and sparkle of the dialogues, leading to a kind of verbal fencing match. Excellent examples of such plays are Congreve's *The Way of the World,* and Wycherley's *The Country Wife*. These plays were repeatedly acted on the stage and appreciated by the public. But they were equally good and enjoyable as master pieces of literature in their own areas. People read them for pleasure in their parlours.

There is one more distinctly different type of drama which is known as Poetic Play or Lyrical Play. These plays are actually long poems of epical dimensions split up into Acts and Scenes. They are avowedly written for reading as purely literary works and not for acting on the stage. In fact, it is a long poem cast into the dramatic form and meant to be read as a poem. The poetic play is also called a Closet play. The normal stage play is not complete in itself. It requires a complex external paraphernalia such as a theatre, a stage, actors and audience, and its success depends upon their performance on the stage. Against it, the poetic play is complete in itself. It can be read and enjoyed by the reader in his own closet or study-room without any external aid. The reader can enjoy it all by himself as he can enjoy an epic or a novel. The poetic play is normally written in blank verse. It is generally written on some classical, mythological or legendary theme. The poetic plays came to be written in the Romantic Age. The principal writers of the poetic plays were practically all the Romantic poets including Wordsworth, Southey, Coleridge, Shelley, Keats, Byron and later on Tennyson and Browning. However, the earliest poetic plays were *Comus* and *Samson Agonistes* written by Milton. T.S. Eliot's *Murder in the Cathedral* is also a famous poetic play. Hardy's *The Dynasts* is also a very long play not meant to be acted. It is an epic-drama.

Thus there are two principal types of plays—those which are both literature as well as stage plays, and those which are only literature not designed to be acted.

JUNE 2008

Directions: Read the following passage carefully and write the answers of the questions no. 1 to 5 in 30 words.

When you look at the historical side, at all times it had many races, many languages and many religions. There was never any question of saying that this group is the biggest or that is not the biggest. The idea was to accommodate all, and to harmonise all faiths. Even a very conservative legislator like Manu tells us that all the people should learn their own particular traditions. We never believed that we are a chosen race. We never believed that ours is a chosen religion or a chosen tribe. The historical traditions of each race, of each community, of each tribe, were preserved and taught to them. It was this attitude of acknowledging every path, rejecting none, trying to find something of value in each tribe and in each community, that has been the tradition which governed the history of our country. You find something similar in the

Koran. There it is said: "O mankind, we created you from a single pair of a male and a female, and made you into nations and tribes that you may know each other, not that you may despise each other." So, it was a question of what may be regarded as "*Sarvamata-samanvaya*"—integration of all religions or faiths.

In the greatest periods of our history, when we were able to make a mark, we adopted this attitude of toleration and goodwill. Ashoka sent missionaries to far countries. He had his great principles cut out in rock: *Samanvaya Sudha*—conrad alone is meritorious. In the next great empire of the country, the Golden Age of the Guptas, Fa Hien, a Chinese traveller, who spent ten years in India, was impressed by the toleration of the people. He testifies that he was allowed to go and do whatever he wanted, and that the people of India never believed in the superiority of their own religion. Harsha Vardhana also followed the religion of freedom.

Q. 1. What is the true spirit of national unity in India?

Ans.: India is a country of many races, many languages and religions. Indian culture believes in harmonizing all of them in the true national spirit. Indian culture seeks to develop true national unity amidst all this diversity.

Q. 2. What tradition has governed the history of India?

Ans.: The tradition that governs Indian history is that of tolerating and accommodating all religions, faiths, customs and manners in a spirit of equality and harmony. We believe in finding and accepting something good in every faith and concept.

Q. 3. What does Koran teach us?

Ans.: Koran teaches us that Allah created all human beings out of single pair of a male and female. They grew into many tribes and nations. Therefore they should not despise each other.

Q. 4. Why is the Age of Guptas called the Golden Age in the history of India?

Ans.: The Age of the Guptas is called the Golden Age because there prevailed the spirit of toleration and accommodation between all faiths and religions in the Age. All were equally bound in bonds of mutual respect and appreciation.

Q. 5. What is the message of Indian culture according to this passage?

Ans.: The message of Indian culture is that of mutual respect and appreciation of all faith, beliefs and concepts. India discovers something good in each of them and accepts it. Our culture is all assimilating.

Directions: Write the answers of the question no. 6 to 20 in 30 words.

Q. 6. What is a Problem Play?

Ans.: The Problem Play is a newly developed dramatic genre. It is so called because its central theme is a social, economic, legal, political or humanitarian problem. This problem is dramatically presented.

Q. 7. What is a One-Act Play?

Ans.: A One-Act Play is short dramatic composition in one Act only. It can have several scenes in the same Act. It is now a complete dramatic genre in itself. It generally deals with a contemporary problem.

Q. 8. What was Caroline Age?

Ans.: The reign of Charles I (in Latin 'Carolus') from 1625 to 1649 is called Caroline Age. It was the period of the English Civil War which led to the murder of Charles I and establishment of Commonwealth under Cromwell.

Q. 9. What was Resotration Age?

Ans.: The Restoration implies the restoration of Charles II to the throne in 1660 at the end of the Commonwealth. This Age was characterized by high fashions, artificial manners and low morals which Charles had brought from France.

Q. 10. What is a Short Story?

Ans.: A Short Story is a novel in a miniature form. All the compenent parts which we find in a novel are found in the short story also, but they are found on a smaller scale in a compact form.

Q. 11. What is a Biography?

Ans.: A Biography is the life-history of a person from the birth to death, judiciously highlighting his failings and achievements, artistically written in prose by one of his admirers. It is now a distinct literary genre.

Q. 12. What is an Autobiography?

Ans.: An Autobiography is the life-history of an individual written by himself. A good autobiography should be a judicious and dispassionate self-assessment, which is indeed a difficult task.

Q. 13. What is a Memoir?

Ans.: In the Memoir the writer does not write out his own life, but he recollects his personal contacts with various people he meets in this personal or professional life.

Q. 14. What are Periodical Essay?

Ans.: The Periodical Essays are journalistic essays which appear in local Dailies, Weeklies or Monthlies. These essays are written on contemporary, social or political problems. They are often written in humorous or satirical vein.

Q. 15. What is a Novel?

Ans.: A Novel is a long prose fiction having a plot, a number of characters, and the plot developing and coming to a logical conclusion through the characters' interaction with one another.

Q. 16. What are Prose Romances?

Ans.: Prose Romances, like Verse Romances, are simply fantasies in which the authors make the fullest use of their imagination and fancy and create an ideal world which bears little or no semblance with real life.

Q. 17. What is meant by Recognition in a tragedy?

Ans.: In a tragedy the hero remains in a state of deception or illusion to a great extent. Gradually he emerges from this state of illusions, but by then it is too late to rectify his error. This realization of real facts is called Recognition.

Q. 18. What is Soliloquy?

Ans.: Soliloquy means 'talking to one's ownself' or 'loud thinking'. A character expresses his secret thoughts and feelings so loudly that the audience can hear him, but other characters are supposed not to hear him.

Q. 19. What is a Melodrama?

Ans.: Melodrama or Horror play is a crude type of tragedy. In this type of tragedy sensational scenes of violence, cruelty, murders, bloodshed, and physical atrocities predominate.

Q. 20. What is the special feature of New Criticism?

Ans.: New Criticism lays emphasis upon the close study and appreciation of the text of a literary work. It seeks to discover and expose its symbolical, allegorical, emotional, or interpretative implications as an independent complete unit.

Directions: Write the answers of the question no. 21 to 25 in 200 words.

Q. 21. Briefly discuss Horace's observation on Poetry.

Ans.: Horace was the leading Roman critic whose observations on poetry and drama have their relevance to the present day. In this observations on Poetry he begins with discussing what should be the proper subject-matter for greater poetry. He says, "I would advise the well-instructed *imitator* (poet) to take the model from life and customs." But this imitation should be enriched with imagination or even with some "believable false." Then he passes on to defining the function of poetry. He says that poets should inculcate a love of all that is noble in life "so that our young men, like persons who live in a healthy place, may be perpetually influenced for good." He goes on to say, "Poets desire either to improve or to please, or to unite the agreeable and the profitable, with what pleases and at once delight and instruct the reader." "It is not enough", he further says, "for poems to have beauty, they must also be pleasing and lead the listener's soul whether they will." Horace goes on to say, "He who chooses his subject wisely will find that neither words nor lucid arrangement will fail him." Passing on to metre he says that there is a fixed appropriate metre for each kind of poetry whether epic, lyric, elegiac, pastoral and so on. In the use of language for poetry, Horace accepts the verdict of Homer. A poet is free to use both familiar words and new ones provided they give clearness and effectiveness to the poem. The poets should remember that words also grow old and die in course of time, and many dead words come back to life. The poet should be conscious of his fact while writing his poetry, His language should have "taste, beauty and charm."

Q. 22. What was F.R. Leavis's Concept of Literature and its function?

Ans.: Literature, for F.R. Leavis, is not merely an aesthetically written work of art designed to give pleasure to the reader. It is not simply a document of 'language charged with meaning to the utmost possible degree'. According to Leavis, 'it is the storehouse of recorded values.' It is the writer's exploration of the cultural tradition of his age. It is a record of all that the age habitually thinks, feels, and acts upon. Literature keeps the healthy moral and cultural traditions alive. Great literature does something more too—it enriches a nation's cultural heritage and tradition in several ways. Great literature age after age forms the literary of a nation. Is in literature that the best of the nation's culture, both of the past and the present, is kept alive and communicated to the future. It appeals to and elevates not only the smaller section of educated people but also refines the masses. It exercises a pervasive influence upon feelings, thought, culture, and standard of living. In brief, literature is not just an aesthetic experience but a faithful record of the author's an aesthetic experience but a faithful record of the author's profoundest interests in life. Leavis says, "Aesthetic is a term the literary critic would do well to deny himself. Opposed to moral, it certainly doesn't generate light." Leavis also says that literature is higher than history even in preserving the culture of the past. History only maintains the record of the past; literature infuses life into it. Literature *relives* the life and culture of the past for us. Leavis calls it 'the exploratory-creative use of words upon experience."

Q. 23. Give Wordsworth's definition of Poetry. How would you reconcile the two apparent contradictions in it?

Ans.: In the *Preface to the Lyrical Ballads,* Wordsworth defines Poetry thus: "Poetry is the spontaneous overflow of powerful feelings; it takes its origin from emotion recollected in tranquility" on the other side are apparently two contradictory statements. "Spontaneous overflow" must be immediate and unrestricted without any interval of time between feeling and its expression. The expression "recollected in tranquility" would suggest intervention of time between feeling and its expression. "Recollection" means remembering some impression after some lapse of time. Wordsworth himself has tried to reconcile this apparent contradiction in his further elucidation of his definition. Immediate impression has a blending of both important and unimportant impressions. When they are allowed to rest for some time, only the important impressions remain in the memory, and the unimportant ones wash away. The poet would then express those powerful impressions spontaneously with ease and felicity without any imposition of restriction in point of language or poetic diction. The poet's expression of those powerful feelings must be easy, smooth and natural.

Q. 24. What is Ben Jonson's concept of Humours? How does he apply them in his comedies?

Ans.: The term 'Humour' as used by Ben Jonson is based on an ancient physiological theory of four fluids found in human body. According to this theory there are four fluids in human body which determine a man's temperament and mental state. These four humours are Blood, Phlegm, Choler (or yellow bile) and Melancholy (or black bile). A normal man has these four humours in a balanced proportion. But the excess of any one of these humours makes him eccentric in one way or the other. He becomes abnormal and develops some kind of oddity in his temperament or behavior and thus becomes an object of fun and ridicule. The humour of Blood makes a man excessively optimistic or sanguine even without the slightest chance of hope or success. Phlegm makes one excessively calm and docile, choler makes one highly ill-tempered, and black bile makes one excessively melancholy and morbid. Ben Jonson explains the theory of Humours in the induction to his play *Every Man in His Humour*. Ben Jonson's comedies are called Comedies of Humours because the principal characters in all his comedies are victims of one humour or the other. Bobadil, for example, is characterized by his decorous manners, uttering improbable boasts. As per in *Every Man Out of His Humor* is a harsh and pitiless judge. Deliro is an idolizing husband consistently rebuffed by his wife. There is a stream of satire in all Ben Jonson's principal characters.

Q. 25. How does Sidney defend poetry against the major charges leveled against it by Gosson?

Ans.: Gosson scandalously condemned poets and poetry in his notorious treatise entitled Schoole of Abuse. He placed poets, pipers, player and jesters into one group and called them "caterpillars of a commonwealth." He called the poets "fathers of lies, pipes of Vanities, and Schooles of Abuse." Principally he inducted poetry on four major grounds: one, that a man could employ his time more usefully than in poetry; second, that is the mother of lies; third, that it is the nurse of abuse; and fourth that Plato had very justly banished the poets from his ideal Republic. Sidney defends poetry against all these charges in his *Apologie for Poetrie* in a very logical and scholarly way. He takes up his defence point by point. Defending poetry against the first charge he says that man could not employ his time more usefully than in poetry. He says that "no learning is so good as that which teacheth and moveth to virtue, and that none can both teach and move thereto so much as poetry, then is the conclusion manifest and ink and paper cannot be to a more profitable purpose employed." Next, Sidney rebuts the charge of lying leveled against it. He who does not seek to established any fact, past or present, can never lie. The poet creates something by emotion or imagination against which no charge of lying can be brought. The question of truth of falsehood would arise only when a person insists on telling a fact. The poet does not do so. He only probes into the human heart and pours out human feelings which can never be false. A true poet can never be a liar even if he seeks to be one. The third charge that 'it abuses men's unit, training it to wanton sinfulness and histful love' may be partly justified, but for this a particular poem may be blamed but not poetry. This charge may be levelled against comedy, lyric, sonnet or the epic into which the element of love enters. But even if it is true, it is the poet and not the form of poetry that can be inducted. It is not poetry that abuses man's wit, but man's wit that abuses poetry. A thing cannot be blamed if it is misused by man, for poetry can be written without resorting to sinful love. The fourth charge that a great philosopher like Plato proposed to banish the poets from his ideal Republic is also not tenable because Plato sought to banish some bad poets of his times and not poetry itself. Plato himself believed that poetry is divinely inspired. Sidney concludes: "So as Plato, banishing the abuse, not the thing, not banishing it, but giving due honour unto it, shall be our patron and hot adversary."

Directions: Write the answer of the question no. 26 in 1000 words.

Q. 26. Write an essay on Shakespeare's Historical or Chronicle Plays.

Ans.: An Important Group of Plays: Shakespeare's Historical or Chronicle plays form an important group of his plays. Shakespeare wrote them in difference stages of his dramatic career. But taken together they form a group of nine plays. They are: *King John, King Richard the Second, King Henry the Fourth, Part I, King Henry the Fourth, Part II, King Henry the Fifth, King Henry the Sixth, Part I, King Henry the Sixth, Part II, King Henry the Sixth, Part III, King Richard the Third,* and *King Henry the Eighth*. These plays were not written in historical sequence, but they cover a long period of British history from the middle of the eleventh century to the middle of the sixteenth century. King Henry the Eighth was the father of Queen Elizabeth. During these centuries England passed through so many internal riots internal riots and feuds which led to the dethronmene execution of several monarchs. Therefore Shakespeare's historical plays are important both historically as well as artistically.

Shakespeare's Sources: There was no consistent history of England when Shakespeare wrote his historical plays. He derives his sources from the random writings of antiquarians and chroniclers. They were not equal to the task they had taken up. They largely wrote anecdotes of history rather than regular history. Therefore Shakespeare had to weave these anecdotes into history by his art and imagination. The first Tudor Chronicler was Edward Hall. He was supremely patriotic, holding Henry to be the greatest of English monarchs. Therefore he could not be historically objective. However, Shakespeare had to use his chronicles as one of his important sources. Raphael Holinshed's *Chronicles of England, Scotland and Ireland* (1577, enlarged 1586) were much wider in scope and more authentic. They were Shakespeare's principal source for his historical plays. Harrison's *Description of England* was also there. With William Camden the chronicles reached their point of climax. Shakespeare made use of all these sources, using them judiciously for his subject matter. There was also Marlowe's *Edward II* which could serve as a model for Shakespeare.

Some Common Characteristics: The historical plays of Shakespeare have some common characteristics. They deal with the medieval period of the British history, roughly from the eleventh to the fifteenth century. They are all largely tragic plays striking the great irony of kingship. With the exception of Henry V, they all end tragically. Each begins with the display of the magnificence and autocratic rule of the monrach, and each ends with the imprisonment and murder of the king. In each, the base is the historical fact, but the event to history are suitably moulded and even changed to suit the demands of the stage and dramatic effect. The queen plays an important role in each day, generally in bringing about the tragic end of the monarch. Each play displays the magnificence and grandeur of medieval England, and very effectively creates on old-world atmosphere. Each play is, thus, a product of the patriotic spirit that ruled supreme in the Elizabethan England.

Two Types of Kings: The historical plays fall into two distinct groups, the one presenting studies of kingly weakness, the other of kingly strength. To the first group belong *King John, King Richard II,* and *King Henry VI;* to the second group belong *King Henry IV, King Henry V,* and *King Richard III,* a royal saint, is weak in his saintliness. King Richard II, a graceful, sentimental monarch, is too feeble to assert his authority and impose his will on his nobles. On the other hand, Henry IV, who usurps the throne of Richard II, is a man of resolution and action, and knows how to take advantage of political sagacity, and his ability to dominate over both men and circumstances. Lastly, Richard III, though a criminal, is strong in his criminality, and is, in this respect, an antithesis to King John.

Predominance of Action: The underlying thought in all the historical plays of Shakespeare is the predominance of action in life. It is man's action that brings success or failure in life. He presents the problem of success or failure in life. "The characters in the historical plays are conceived chiefly with reference to action." "The world represented in these plays is not so much the world of feeling or of thought, as the limited world of the practicable. Shakespeare studies in them not what man is but what he does. It is his success or failure in the world which determines his worth for him." King Henry V is a great king, because he achieves great victories, because he is the hero of Agincourt. He is gifted with those qualities which enable him to subdue his enemies both at home and abroad. Henry V is great because of this great actions and achievements.

Patriotic Note: Every historical play of Shakespeare is deeply instilled with patriotic passion. The feeling of patriotism is particularly notable in *Richard II, Henry IV* and *Henry V.*

DECEMBER 2007

Directions: Read the following poem and answer the questions given under it from Questions 1 to 5 in 30 words each:

I will arise and go now, and go to Innisfree,
And a small cabin build there, of clay and wattles made,
Nine-been rows will I have there, a hive for the honey-bee,
And live alone in the bee-loud glade.
And I shall have some peace there, for peace comes dropping slow,
Dropping from the veils of the morning to where the cricket sings;
There midnight's all a glimmer, and noon a purple glow,
And evening full of the linnet's wings.
I will arise and go now, for always night and day
I hear lake water lapping with low sounds by the shore;
While I stand on the roadway, or on the pavements grey,
I hear it in the deep heart's core.

Q. 1. Where is the Lake Isle of Innisfree? Is it a real or an imaginary island?

Ans.: The Lake Isle of Innisfree is a real island. It is situated on the shore of Scotland. The beauty of the island as described by the poet is imaginary.

Q. 2. How does the poet want to live there?

Ans.: The poet wants to live in peace and natural beauty on the island. The poet would make a small cottage, sow some bean plants and make a hive for honey-bees and live there in peace and beauty of nature.

Q. 3. Describe the beauty and peace that prevail in the Island of Innisfree.

Ans.: The Isle of Innisfree is very peaceful, colourful and beautiful. Even the midnight has glimmering light there and noons have purple glow. Birds and linnets sing their songs.

Q. 4. How does the poet feel the fascination of the island?

Ans.: The poet is so fascinated with the beauty and peaceful atmosphere of the island that he remembers it and hears its song even on the roadways and pavements of his city.

Q. 5. Why do you feel the poet wants to go and live in the Island of Innisfree?

Ans.: The poet wants to go and live on the Lake Isle of Innisfree because he is tired of the noise and hurry and worry of city life. He wants to live amidst natural beauty and peace.

Directions: Write the answer of the question no. 6 to 20. Each Question carries five marks and each to be answered in about 30 words.

Q. 6. What is a Personal Essay?

Ans.: True essay, according to Hudson, is essentially personal. Montaigne says, "I am myself the subject of my book". In the Personal essay the author gives his own experiences, impressions of reactions about the subjects taken up for writing his essays.

Q. 7. What is an Aphoristic Essay?

Ans.: Aphoristic Essays are impersonal essays. They are pithy and short essays pactful of the author's knowledge, wisdom and philosophy of life. They are rugged and abrupt and difficult to understand on account of their depth of thought.

Q. 8. What is Descriptive Criticism or Practical Criticism?

Ans.: Descriptive Criticism is a study or evaluation of individual works or authors. The critic evaluates their aims, methods and effects, and brings out their aesthetic beauty, emotional effect and literary significance by whatever criteria he deems fit.

Q. 9. What is Impressionistic Criticism?

Ans.: Impressionistic Criticism is that branch of criticism in which the critic evaluates a work by the impressions it makes upon his own mind. He expresses the attitudes and feelingful responses the work evokes in him as an individual.

Q. 10. On what basis does Shelley call the poets "unacknowledged legislators of the world"?

Ans.: Shelly calls the poets legislators of the world on account of the profound wisdom contained in their poetry. "A great poem is a fountain forever overflowing with the waters of wisdom and delight—an unconceived delight".

Q. 11. What is meant by 'Poetic Justice'?

Ans.: The term 'Poetic Justice' was coined by Thomas Rhymer. It means exact reward or punishment given to a character according to his good or bad deeds. This exactness of justice is possible only in the world of poetry.

Q. 12. What is Drama?

Ans.: Drama is a long literary composition in prose or verse, developed through dialogues and action to be presented on the stage. While every other form of literature is complete in itself; drama remains incomplete without a stage.

Q. 13. What is a Miracle Play?

Ans.: A Miracle play is basically a religious play. They deal with the lives of saints and the miracles performed by them. The life and martyrdom of a saint formed the central theme of a Miracle play.

Q. 14. What is a Chronicle or Historical Play?

Ans.: A Chronicle or Historical play deals with the life of a king or with some important historical event. However, the dramatist weaves an imaginative or highly emotional garb around it to make it appealing to the spectators sitting in the theatre.

Q. 15. What is a Dramatic Monologue?

Ans.: 'Monologue' literally means 'Dialogue with the self'. In the Dramatic Monologue there is only one character who expresses out his own innermost feelings and thoughts through a long poetic speech. It offers a psychological analysis of the solo-speaker.

Q. 16. Write the meaning of the term Metaphysical.

Ans.: The term 'metaphysical' was first used of Dryden in his assessment of the poetry of John Done. The metaphysical poets were men of learning, and to show their learning was their whole endeavour.

Q. 17. What do you mean by Comedy of Humours?

Ans.: Ben Jonson was the principal exponent of the Comedy of Humours. The Comedy of Humours was actually satirical comedy based on the classical concept of humours.

Q. 18. What is Comedy?

Ans.: Comedy, in general, is a play of love, romance and marriage, joy and delight, wit and humour, light satire and irony exposing the follies and foibles of man good humouredly. It deals with the light and trivial occurrences of life which are treated in such a manner that the ludicrous and comic element predominates.

Q. 19. What is the meaning of Renaissance?

Ans.: The term Renaissance literally means re-birth on revival. In Art and Literature it meant the rebirth or revival of Greek art, literature, culture and pattern of life which had been partly or largely destroyed by the repeated invasions of the Turks.

Q. 20. Define the term Romanticism.

Ans.: Romanticism has been variously defined by various critics and scholars. According to Walter Pater, "Romanticism is the addition of curiosity to the desire of beauty."

Directions: Write the answer of the question no. 21 to 25. Each Question carries 12 marks and has to be answered in about 200 words.

Q. 21. Which is more important between plot and character in the Tragedy, according to Aristotle?

Ans.: A question is often asked whether plot is more important or character in the Tragedy. According to Aristotle, Plot is the very soul of the tragedy and therefore far more important than character. In his definition of the tragedy Aristotle says that "Tragedy is an imitation of an action that is serious, complete, and of a certain magnitude". Here he does not say that tragedy is an imitation of 'characters'. Again, in the same definition he says, "in the form of action, not of narration". Clearly enough, 'Action' in this definition means 'plot'. Characters are merely agents of the action or the plot, and therefore subordinate to it.

From the above definition it follows that 'Tragedy is an imitation, not of men, but of an action and of life, and life consists in action'. To the question whether plot makes a tragedy or character, Aristotle replies that "without action there cannot be a tragedy: there may be without character". It is, of course, a riddle which is not easy to solve because actions themselves issue from characters. Resolving this riddle Aristotle says, "character determines men's qualities, but it is by their actions that they are happy or the reverse". A plot imitates action, and character men. A tragedy is a representation of men in action. Sometimes action can occur even without men or characters. A huge natural calamity like earthquake, flood or storm may occur, causing incalculable devastation without any role of men or characters. Hence it is the deeds or actions (or incidents woven into a plot) which make the tragedy, and not merely men or characters in their inactive or passive state.

Q. 22. Discuss T.S. Eliot's views about Impressionistic or Aesthetic School of Criticism.

Ans.: T.S. Eliot did not approve of the Impressionistic School of Criticism because it was purely subjective without any definite norms or principles to evaluate a literary work. Mr. Symons initiated this approach, which was further supported by Pater and Swinburne. T.S.Eliot called it "Imperfect Criticism". Explaining his approach, Symons says that "it is a faithful record of the impressions, more numerous or more refined than our own, upon a mind more sensitive than our own. These impressions are as much created as transmitted by the criticism".

T.S. Eliot's objection is that an individual's personal impressions can neither be universal nor unbiased nor unprejudiced. They cannot set a standard or evaluation for others. They would differ from person to person according to one's taste, level of sensitivity, and power of discrimination. Eliot says that a critic is concerned only with the principles and precepts of poetic communication, not with the man behind a work of art. The main objective of criticism is 'the common pursuit of true judgement', unconditioned by any 'personal prejudices or cranks'. A true critic encounters in a work of art its intrinsic vision, embodied in at well-organised system. In brief, T.S. Eliot launches a violent attack on all impressionistic critics who seek a kind of "self-gratification through their subjective pronouncements on writers and their works".

Q. 23. On what grounds does Crites defend the ancient Greek and Roman poets and dramatists?

Ans.: Crites begins defending the ancient Greek and Roman poets and dramatists by observing at the very outset that "it is our greatest praise to have imitated them well; for we do not only build upon their foundations, but by their models". He goes on to say that "all the rules by which we practice the drama of this day were delivered to us from the observations which Aristotle made of those poets who either lived before him, or were his contemporaries". Horace's Ars Poetica is an excellent comment on the art of poetry which our poets follow and feel honoured. Aristotle also laid down the principles of the three dramatic unities - the Unities of Time, Place and Action. By the unity of time he meant that the action of a play should not exceed "the compass of a natural day". If the action is limited within this compass "it would be thought the nearest imitation of nature". It is unnatural to shift the action from one place to another, specially to distant places. This will give the greatest likelihood to untruth. By the unity of action he meant that there should be only one action, great and complete enough, to cover the whole plot. Two or more actions should not go side by side in the play. In this respect "both the best and worst of the modern poets will equally instruct you to admire the ancients". The ancients observed the three dramatic unities faithfully, and the Romans, the French, and the English dramatists tried their best to observe them, though not always successfully. Thus the ancients are our first law-givers as well as models for the moderns to follow.

Q. 24. What are the qualifications of an ideal critic according to Pope?

Ans.: Discussing the qualifications of an ideal critic, Pope begins with the remark that only a poet can be an ideal critic:

"Let such teach others who themselves excel,
And censure freely who have written well".

He further says about a poet and a critic:

"Both must alike from heaven derive their light,
Those born to judge, as well as those to write".

Divine inspiration is essential equally to the critic and the poet:

"A perfect judge will reach each work of Wit
With the same spirit that its author writ".

The critic and the poet should both have wit, taste and judgement in equal measure.

All the same, the ideal critic is aware of his limitations. He knows "how far his genius, taste, and learning go". He will not launch "beyond his depth".

Furthermore, the ideal critic would not be guided only by the prescribed rules. He should have an instinctive sense to feel and understand the nameless graces which no methods or principles can teach. He has the taste to notice "a grace beyond the reach of art". His judgments are well nourished and developed. He is not satisfied with a "little learning" which is "a dangerous thing". He is blessed with an exact taste and has a knowledge of books and humanity in right proportions. He is:

"Generous to converse, a soul exempt from pride,
And love to praise, with reason on his side".

The ideal critic's duty is to give advice. He is pleased to teach and he ought to be proud of his knowledge yet he should be unbiased and unprejudiced. In the true spirit of literary criti cism there are no friends or foes. So Pope says:

> "Modestly bold, and humanely severe, Who to a friend his faults can freely show, And gladly praise the merit of foe".

Q. 25. Summarise the views of Sidney on the use of verse and metre in poetry.

Ans.: In the use of verse and metre in poetry Sidney oscillated between the classical concept and Elizabethan practices. According to the classical concept, verse or metre is not indispensable for poetry, but according to Elizabethan practices metre was desirable, if not indispensable. Sidney seems to reconcile the two extremes. Holding the classical view he says that metre is "but an ornament and no cause to poetry, sith there have been many most excellent poets that never versified, and now swarm many versifiers that need never answer to the name of poets". He further says, "It is not rhyming and versing that maketh a poet, no more than a long gown maketh an advocate, who though he pleaded in armour should be an advocate and no soldier". Invention is the soul of poetry, and in this sense if prose is inventive, it should be classed with poetry.

Then comes on him the Elizabethan influence. This attracts him to favour the use of verse or metre in poetry, though on other grounds. He says that verse being sweeter and more appealing to our aesthetic sense should be used in poetry. Verse is a superior form of expression to ordinary prose. He says, "The senate of poets hath chosen verse as their fittest raiment, weighing each syllable of each word by just proportion according to the dignity of the subject". He further says that on account of its sweetness and orderliness verse is fittest for memory, and memory is the treasure-house of knowledge. Musical verse can be more easily remembered and retained in the mind than prose. Therefore, it is advisable to write poetry in verse and metre.

Direction: Write an essay of about 1000 words on any of the following topics:

Q. 26. Write an essay on The Augustan Age in English Literature.

Ans.: The Classical or the Augustan Age historically refers to the glorious period of Emperor Augustus of Rome. The roots of Roman literature can be traced back to Greek literature through the Renaissance. Their principles and ideals in literature were adopted and practiced by English authors of the eighteenth century, roughly from Dryden to Dr. Johnson. Strictly speaking, therefore, in English literature this Age should be called Neo-Classical or Neo-Augustan Age. It covers the whole of our 'Indispensable Eighteenth Century'.

Adherence to Classical Rules: The most important factor of the literature of the Neo-Classical School is its adherence to the original classical rules and models in all forms of literature. The authors of this period had great respect for rules and discipline both in inspiration and form. Classical conventions governed every variety of literature—drama, poetry, epic, satire, ode or pastoral. They laid more emphasis on form than on thought or emotion. Seneca provided the model for tragedy, Terence for comedy, Virgil for epic and pastoral, Juvenal for satire, and Horace for literary taste and criticism. They laid more emphasis on intellectual and artistic craftsmanship than on imaginative or emotional fervour. Dryden's Prefaces to his plays and Fables, Pope's Essay on Poetry, several of Addison's literary essays and Dr. Johnson's Lives and Preface to Shakespeare enunciate these classical principles for the guidance of the English classical authors.

Satirical and Didactic Spirit: The literature of the classical school is basically satirical or didactic. Pope's Dunciad, *An Essay on Man, Satires and Epistles*; Dr. Johnson's *The Vanity of Human Wishes*; Gray's Elegy *Written in a Country Churchyard*; *The Poetry of the Churchyard School* and of the *Metaphysical School*, and Dryden's *Mac Flecknoe* are all typical Neoclassical poems and plays.

Intellectual Quality: Classical literature was predominantly intellectual rather than emotional or imaginative. These authors avoided all extravagance and emotionalism. They laid emphasis on correctness, or what Pope called 'nature methodized'. The ideals of order and restraint were so over-emphasised that art degenerated into artifice. Poetry of love, beauty, emotional fervour and humanism which flourished in the Elizabethan Age was rigorously suppressed. In their place satirical poetry flourished. The poetry of these poets was bred more in the head than in the heart, and was addressed to the intellectual, not to the feelings. Even the drama of Dryden which might have roused deep emotions was chilled down by classical discipline and sharp intellect. Wit was their strongest point. These poets had a gift for pregnant and memorable phrases and critical and philosophical terms.

Use of Poetic Diction: According to the classical poets, the language of everyday life is not a language fit for poetry. They wrote their poetry in what is called Poetic Diction. Their concept was that the farther the language of poetry is removed from the language of real life, the better it is. Dr. Johnson defined Poetic Diction thus:

"A system of words at once refined from the grossness of domestic use, and free from the harshness of terms appropriate to particular arts". As such the language of poetry tended to be stilted and standardized.

Use of Heroic Couplet: The Heroic couplet was the standard verse form and stanza for the classical poets. The Heroic couplet was a two-line stanza written in Iambic Pentameter. It was believed to be suitable for all types of literature, epic, drama, and satire. The Heroic couplet was initiated by Waller and Denham, and systematized by Dryden and Pope. It ousted all other verse forms, metres and stanza forms which were so popular in the Elizabethan Age. Even the Blank Verse of such mighty poets and dramatists as Marlowe and Shakespeare was replaced by it. Even the Spenserian stanza had become outdated. The Heroic couplet came to be recognized as the natural expression of the intellectual mood of the author.

Treatment of Aristocratic Life: The classical literature, specially poetry, primarily dealt with town life. It presented the aristocratic life of big cities, highlighting their fashions, manners, morals and outlandish style of living: London became the centre for all poets and authors. Fashionable clubs and coffee-houses became the haunts of all literary figures. Men of different tastes, temperaments and professions assembled there. They usually discussed literary problems on the coffee tables. At one time there were as many as three thousand coffee houses in London alone. These coffee-houses served to establish contact not only between the author and the reader, but also between author and author. Dryden and Pope, for example, met for the first time at a coffee-house. As a result, life of the common men was completely neglected by the classical authors. Nature was also no proper subject for their poetry. There is no first hand description of any object of nature or any landscape. Satire on aristocratic life became the stock subject for poetry. Pope's *Rape of the Lock* is the representative example of the Classical School of poetry. The major engagements of the aristocratic lords and ladies were display of fashions, playing cards, flirting with women, and passing their time in clubs. Here is a graphic description of Belinda's Toilet:

> "The inferior Priestess, at her altar's side, Trembling begins the sacred rites of Pride. Unnumber'd treasures ope at once, and here The various off rings of the world appear; From each she nicely culls with curious toil, And decks the Goddess with the glitt'ring spoil, This casket India's golden gems unlocks, And all Arabia breathes from yonder box. Puffs, Powders, Patches, Bibles, Billet-doux Now awful Beauty puts on all its charms".

Imitation of the Classics as their Creed: The neo-classical poets measured their success in proportions as they succeeded in imitating the great classical poets. They sought to adhere to their principles, their styles, their mannerisms, their themes and even their thoughts and sentiments. This is what Pope advised his contemporary authors to follow the ancients slavishly. In the Essay on Criticism he advises every poet and every critic thus:

> "Know well each Ancient's proper character; His fable, subject, scope in e'ry page; Religion, country, genius of his Age: Without all these at once before your eyes, Cavil you may, but never criticize. Be Homer's works your study and delight, Read them by

day, and meditate by night; Thence your judgements, thence your maxims bring, And trace the Muses upwards to their spring".

These were the major characteristics of the Neo-Classical authors of the eighteenth century. But because of the basic fact that their poetry and plays were satirical and intellectual exercises, shorn of emotion and imagination, their vogue could not last long. Their decline started in the latter half of the eighteenth century and with the publication of Wordsworth and Coleridge's Lyrical Ballads, the Neo-Classical poetry was totally replaced by Romantic poetry.

Or

Q. Write an essay on the Metaphysical School of Poets.

Ans.: Meaning of the Term 'Metaphysical': The term 'Metaphysical' was first used by Dryden in his assessment of the poetry of John Donne. Later on the term was popularized by Dr. Johnson when he applied it to a group of poets who are now known as the poets of the Metaphysical School. Explaining the term 'Metaphysical Poets', Dr. Johnson says, "The metaphysical poets were men of learning, and to show their learning was their whole endeavour. They neither copied nature nor life. Their thoughts are often new, but seldom natural; they are not obvious, but neither are they just; and the reader, far from wondering that he missed them, wonders more frequently by what perverseness of industry they were ever found". Their poetry was deeply religious, spiritual, philosophical and symbolic which they tried to make as difficult and unintelligible as possible.

Characteristics of Metaphysical Poetry: The central creed of the Metaphysical poets is that they tried their best to make their poetry as obscure, deep and mysterious as possible. Their primary aim was to startle the reader by their obscure and unpredictable imagery and conceit. Their poetry is packed with affectations and conceits. In their effort to surprise the reader by the boldness and novelty of their images, they indulged in strained metaphors, far-fetched similes, and the most extravagant hyperboles. They cultivated ingenuity at any cost. They substituted philosophical subtleties and logical hair-splitting against the natural expression of feeling. They employed their vast out-of-the-way learning without the slightest regard to propriety or naturalness. As a result, they are in general violent, harsh, cold, and obscure. Their poems are hard nuts to crack. Their poetry was misled 'by voluntary deviation from nature in pursuit of something new and strange'. Sir Walter Scott said: "They played with thoughts as the Elizabethans had played with words". They carried the Elizabethan freedom of imagination and delight in verbal fancies to a point at which it became difficult for the average reader to grasp their meaning. A comparison is often instituted between objects that have ostensibly little in common with each other. Cowley, for example, compares being in love with different women to traveling through different countries:

"Hast thou not found each woman's breast
(The land where thou hast travell'd)
Either by savages possesset,
Or wild, and uninhabited?
What joy could'st take, or what repose
In countries so uncivilized as those?"

John Donne (1573-1631): John Donne was the first poet to whom the epithet 'Metaphysical' was first applied by Dryden. Donne wrote many types of poems—lyrics, elegies, satires, and religious and philosophical poems. But we are concerned here only with his religious and philosophical poems. His religious and philosophical poems are marked with subtlety, conceits, odd imagery, and obscure allusions which make them beyond the comprehension of the reader. They are an amalgam of writ, vagueness, obscurity and incongruity. But they have a remarkable depth of meaning if they can be explored with labour and insight. Ben Jonson esteemed him to be the first poet in the world, but he was not likely to be remembered long for not being understood by the common reader. Leisman observes in his book *The Monarch of Wit*: "Donne had, above all, wit; often deliberately outrageous and impudent and coat-trailing, often breath-taking, ingenious in the discovery of comparisons and analogies, but nearly always, in one way or another, argumentative whether in defence of preposterous paradoxes or in the mock-serious devising of hyperbolic compliments". Here is a typical example:

"Go, and catch a falling star,
Get with child a mandrake root,
Tell me, where all past years are,
Or who cleft the Devil's foot".

It is difficult to understand what the poet wants to convey through these lines.

Abraham Cowley (1618-67): Abraham Cowley is regarded as the chief representative poet of the Metaphysical School. In his own day he was considered to be the greatest of English poets. He influenced a large number of poets, specially three important metaphysical poets—Crashaw, Herbert and Vaughan. Cowley started as a typical metaphysical poet with highly intricate conceits, symbols and imagery. But in his later poetry he discarded much of his former extravagance and wrote in restrained and sober style. Here is a sample of his poetic art:

"Gentle Henrietta then,
And a third Mary next began;
Then Joan and Jane and Audria,
And then a pretty Thomasine
And then a another Katharine,
And then a long et cetera".

Richard Crashaw (1613-49): The religious and sacred poetry of Crashaw has greater fire and passion, though it is sometimes ruined by highly intricate conceits. He was influenced by Spanish mystic poets and he wrote much of his poetry after their fashion. He published his religious poems in a volume entitled 'The Step to the Temple'. His poetry is marked with the typical conceits, symbols, imagery and extravagances of the Metaphysical School. Here is a sample of his religious spirit:

"Still live in me this loving strife.
Of living Death and dying life,
For while Thou sweetly slayest me,
Dead to myself, I live in thee".

George Herbert (1593-1633): Herbert's collection of lyrics entitled *The Temple* breathes the spirit of purest poetry. Herbert is called the saint of the Metaphysical School. By profession also he was a priest, and he believed that a man should dedicate all his gifts to the service of God. A poem entitled *Pilgrimage,* which was included in his collection *The Temple,* is probably the best of his lyrics. He describes his poetry as "a picture of the many spiritual conflicts that have passed betwixt God and soul, before I could subject mine, to the will of Jesus, my Master, in whose service I have now found perfect freedom". In spite of his perfect sincerity and devotion to religion, he could not liberate himself from the prevailing conceits, oddities, quaints and crabbed metaphors which characterized the poetry of the Metaphysical School. At times, of course, his poetry is simply appealing to the reader:

"Judge not the preacher; for He is thy Judge:
If thou mislike him, thou conceiv'st him not,
God calleth preaching folly. Do not grudge
To pick out treasures from an earthen pot.
The worst speak something good; if all want sense,
God takes a text, and preacheth patience".

Henry Vaughan (1622-95): Vaughan was greatly influenced by Herbert. Even sometimes he copies Herbert directly. Vaughan was basically a mystic. His piety is much more mystical and his thoughts deeper. He is meditative to the level of dullness. His most famous and successful poem is "They are all gone into a world of light":

"They are all gone into the world of light!
And I along site lingering here;
Their very memory is fair and bright
And my sad thoughts doth clear".

Another of his famous poems is The World with its wonderful opening:

"I saw Eternity the other night
Like a great ring of pure and endless light
All calm as it was bright".

The great age of the Church of England finds in Vaughan its best poetical exponent.

Andrew Marvell (1621-78): Andrew Marvell was the only Puritan among the Metaphysical poets. Yet, strangely enough, he was a passionate lyrical poet of love and nature. Though a poet of the Metaphysical School, he does not share the quaintness and obscurity of his fellow poets. He is a Metaphysical poet only in the sense that there is religious ardour in his poetry. Even his religious poetry has a touch of humanism. Even his poems of love have the streak of mysticism:

"Thy beauty shall no more be found;
Nor in thy marble vault, shall sound
My echoing song: then worms shall try
That long preserved virginity:
....
The grave's a fine and private place,
But none I think do there embrace".

Thomas Traherne (1637-74): Traherne was the last of the Metaphysical poets. He was a mystic, and it is his mysticism that links him with the Metaphysicals. His poetry had remained lost for more than two hundred years, and was recovered and published in 1903. Then he was at once recognized as one of the greatest religious and metaphysical poets. Although Traherne's work presents much of the difficulty common to the metaphysicals, it has also much beauty and eloquence as well as profundity of thought and spiritual insight.

JUNE 2007

Directions: Read the following poem carefully and write the answer of the questions from 1 to 5 in 30 words.

"Givd on thy sword, O man, thy strength endure,
In fair desire thine earth-born joy renew,
Live thous thy life beneath the making sun,
Till Beauty, Truth, and Love in thee are one,
Thro' thousand ages hath thy childhood run :
On timeless ruin hath the glory been:
From the forgotten night of loves foredone,
Though risest in the dawn of hopes unseen.
Higher and higher shall thy thoughts aspire,
Unto the stars of heaven, and pass away,
And earth renew the buds of the desire
In fleeting blooms of everlasting day,
Thy work with beauty crown, thy life with love;
Thy mind with truth uplift God above:
For whom all is, from whom was all begun,
In whom all Beauty, Truth, and Love are one."

Q.1. Is the poem idealistic, visionary or inspirational? Explain how?

Ans.: This poems basically an inspirational poem. The title *Gird On Thy Sword* means 'Be prepared to fight out the battle of life.' Man must collect all this courage and strength to render some valuable service to mankind.

Q2. In what kind of stanza form is this poem written? Give the rhyme scheme of each stanza.

Ans.: The poem is written in irregular fourline stanza form. The rhyme-scheme in the first and fourth stanzas is—

a a b b

The second and third stanzas have the rhyme-scheme:

a b a b

Q. 3. The poem invokes a celebrated Trinity. What is this Trinity?

Ans.: The celebrated trinity in this poem is the Trinity of the three great ideals of life. These ideals are Beauty, Truth and Love. This Trinity is the emblem of God.

Q. 4. What is the message of the poem?

Ans.: The message of this poem is that one should remain undaunted against the problems and difficulties of life. One should undauntedly strive to achieve the Trinity of Beauty, Truth and Love in life.

Q. 5. Why is the Trinity of Beauty, Truth and Love important in life?

Ans.: Beauty, Truth and Love are the three great ideals of perfect life. There should be Beauty in one's actions, Love in one's life, and Truth in ones faith in God.

Directions: Write the answer of the question no. 6 to 20 in 30 words.

Q. 6. What is a Prophetic Novel?

Ans.: The Prophetic Novels try to forecast what the future would be like. They do not claim to be absolutely correct. They only give a tentative picture of the future on the basis of the tendencies prevailing in the present.

Q. 7. What is Psychological Novel?

Ans.: The Psychological Novels are also known as the 'Stream of Consciousness Novels'. These novels probe into the working of human psychology at the conscious, subconscious and unconscious levels. The plot is developed on these psychological levels.

Q. 8. What is a Burlesque?

Ans.: Burlesque is defined as 'an incongruous imitation.' It imitates the matter or manner of a serious literary work, or literary genre, but makes the imitations funny and amusing by a ridiculous disparity.

Q. 9. Who are known as Cavalier Poets?

Ans.: The Cavalier Poets were associated with the Court of Charles I. They wrote witty and polished lyrics of live and gallantry. The group included Richard Lovelace, John Suckling, Thomas Carew and Robert Herrick.

Q. 10. What is Metaphysical School of Poetry?

Ans.: The term 'Metaphysical' was first used by Dryden and further extended by Dr. Johnson. It refers to a group of seventeenth century poets who employed far-fetched imagery, abstruse arguments, scholastic philosophical terms, and subtle logic.

Q. 11. What is meant by 'Poetic Licence'?

Ans.: By 'Poetic Licence' is meant a certain amount of liberty enjoyed by the poets in the use of grammar, word-order or coinage of words in order to produce greater poetic effect.

Q. 12. What is an Epic?

Ans.: The Epic is the greatest and most sublime form of poetry. The Epic is a long poem, divided into several books, celebrating the life, heroic deeds and achievements of national hero, whether historical of legendary.

Q. 13. What is a Patoral Elegy?

Ans.: It is an elegy cast into the conventional pastoral form. It is presumed that the poet is a shepherd mourning the death of a fellow shepherd. The whole imagery of goats, sheep, postures and pastoral gods and goddesses is drawn into it.

Q. 14. What is a Ballad?

Ans.: The word 'Ballad' literary means 'a dance-song'. They generally sang of the brave deeds and heroic exploits of historically or legendary heroes and knights.

Q. 15. Define a Satire.

Ans.: Dryden defines the Satire as "a literary composition whose principal aim is to ridicule folly or vice. The true end of satire is the amendment of vices by correction." A healthy satire good-humouredly exposes one's folly or vice.

Q. 16. What is Hamartia?

Ans.: Hamartia is the 'tragic flaw' in the character of the tragic hero who is basically a good and great man. This 'tragic flaw' becomes the cause of his fall, doom and death.

Q. 17. What is meant by Peripetetia?

Ans.: Peripetetia means sudden change in the fortune or position of the hero from good to bad, or high to low. This reversal of fortune happens due to Hamartia in the character of the hero.

Q. 18. What is meant by Catastrophe?

Ans.: The final end of the tragedy is called catastrophe. At this point the hero or the heroine or both meet their tragic death. The tragic end comes through Hamartia and Perpheteia.

Q. 19. What was the Neo-Classical or Augustan Age?

Ans.: The eighteenth century in England is called Neo-classical or Augustan Age because the leading writers of this period followed the literary principles and models of the great Roman and Greek authors of the Age of Emperor Augustus.

Q. 20. What is meant by the Romantic Movement?

Ans.: The Romantic Movement in English Literature came in the nineteenth century. The literature of this period is characterized by love of nature, love of humanity, full display of the writer's imaginative and emotional faculty.

Directions: Write the answer of the question no. 21 to 25 in 200 words.

Q. 21. What are the sources of Sublimity in literature according to Loginus?

Ans.: There are five sources of sublimity according to Longinus. They are : (1) Grandeur of thought, (2) Capacity for strong emotion, (3) Appropriate use of Figures, (4) Nobility of diction, and (5) Dignity of Composition. The first two of these five sources are gifts of nature, and the last three can be cultivate by art.

Grand thoughts and strong emotions emanate from the lofty soul. "Sublimity is the echo of greatness of soul." It is impossible for those whose thoughts are mean and acts servile to produce anything worth universal respect and admiration. Lofty thoughts and noble emotions belong to the noble soul and lofty mind. Meanness and sublimity cannot dwell together. Great accents fall from the lips of those whose thoughts have always been deep enriched by proper discipline and emulation of great men. Sublimity of expression is linked with sublimity of thought. A mean thought is too low to be expressed through sublime diction. There is a natural synthesis between noble thoughts and sentiments with appropriate use of figures, nobility of diction and dignity of composition. Figures of speech add to the dignity of expression. But they should be used judiciously so that they may not become coumbersome. Sweet and suitable words add to the grandeur, beauty and dignity of expression. A proper arrangement of all these elements would impart subline harmony and grandeur to the whole work.

Q. 22. What is the value of Poetry according to I.A. Richards?

Ans.: Thomas Love Peacock denounced poets and poetry in his notorious booklet *The Four Ages of Poetry*. He wrote that poets were only exploring myths and legends and were thus "wallowing in the rubbish of departed ignorance. He further wrote, "A poet in our times is a semibarbarian in a civilized community. He lives in the ways that are past. His ideas, thoughts, feelings, associations, are all with barbarious manners, obsolete customs, and exploded superstitions. The march of his intellect is like that of a crab, backward." Keeping these absurd allegations in his mind Richards pleaded that even in the age of science, scepticism and interrogation, poetry has its great value. It enlivens, ennobles and regenerates our benevolent and humanitarian feelings and emotions. Thus it plays a vital role in the life of the individual and society. In the mind and heart so enlightened by poetry there lies the hope of civilization.

Explaining his point of view, Richards says that experiences of life may be both good and bad. The poet responds to and communicates only the good and pleasurable ones through the medium of his poetry. Normally, in routine life, mind receives all kinds of experiences, impressions, and reactions. In course of time the weaker and unpleasant impressions are washed away, and only the deeper, pleasurable and benevolent ones get imprinted in the mind the poet. The poet enshrines these deeper and noble experiences in his poetry and unconsciously communicates them to society. Thus poetic experiences and impulses take the form of highest moral values. They create and spread currents of hope, delight, refinement, and highest moral values in human environment. Nothing can be nobler than poetic experience and its dissemination.

Q. 23. Why did Wordsworth write such along Preface to his *Lyrical Ballads?*

Or

Wordsworth lays down the basic tenets of his poetry in the *Preface to the Lyrical Ballads*. Discuss.

Ans.: When the first edition of Wordsworth's *Lyrical Ballads* was published, it was discovered that Wordsworth's poem were diametrically opposite to the standard poetical norms as preached and practiced by the Neo-classical poets like Ben Jonson, Dryden, Pope, Gray, and Dr. Johnson. There was a sort of uproar in literary circles. Thereupon some of Wordsworth's friends advised me to prefix a systematic defence of the theory upon which the Poems were written. Hence he published a detailed preface to the second edition of his *Lyrical Ballads*.

In the Preface, Wordsworth begins with the percent that poetry should be a spontaneous overflow' of powerful feelings, not a laboured exercise. Secondly, the subject matter of poetry should be the life of the common men, because poets do not write their poetry for poets only but for the common public to read and enjoy. For the same reason, poetry should be written, as far as possible, in the language of the common men really used by them, and not in the highly artificial and stilted 'Poetic diction'. There should be no difference between the language of prose and that of poetry. These are the basic tenets of Wordsworth's theory of poetry.

Q. 24. "To judge of poets is only the faculty of poets." Examine the qualifications of a good critic on the basis of this remark by Ben Jonson.

Ans.: Discussing the qualification of a good critic. Ben Jonson says, "To judge of poets is only the faculty of poets, and not of all poets but the best...such was Horace, an excellent and true judge upon cause and reason, not because he thought so, but because he knew so, out of use and experience." This assertion of Ben Jonson should not be taken in its literal sense but in its essential spirit. For there have been many great critics who have never been actually poets. The most important of them have been Plato and Aristotle themselves. Plato and Aristotle have been universally recognized as the first and the greatest critics, but they were not poets by vocation. Therefore what Ben Jonson means to say is that a good critic must have poetic sensibilities, if not practicing as a poet. He must be a great scholar possessing deep understanding of the poetic art. Deep scholarship is the basic condition for being a critic. Horace was "an excellent and true judge upon cause and reason, not because he thought so, but because he knew so, out of use and experience." Jonson means to say that there must be 'solid and perfect learning' in a critic and he should be a poet by perception if not by vocation. Further, a good critic must exercise discipline and control upon his expression in awarding his judgment on a literary work. He must follow a code of conduct in his literary judgements. He can be an adviser or a guide, but not a commander or a hanging judge.

Q. 25. On what grounds does Gosson condemn poets and dramatists?

Ans.: All forms of literature blossomed and flourished luxuriantly in the Elizabethan Age. But detractors and abusers of poetry and drama were also there. The leader of these abusers and detractors was Stepher Gosson, accompanied by his Puritan companions. Gosson wrote a highly malicious treatise, *The Schoole of Abuse,* and mischievously dedicated it to Sir Philip Sidney who was at that time the most celebrated literary figure. He called this mischievous treatise "a pleasant invective against poets, Pipers, players, jesters and such like caterpillars of commonwealth." It denounces the poets as the "fathers of lies, pipes of vanities and schools of Abuse." He goes on to say. These are the cuppes of Circes that turn reasonable creatures into brute beasts." He even more maliciously condemns drama and says that it has abused "Greeces of gluttony. Italy of wantonness. Spain of pride, France of deceit, and Dutchland of quaffing." Gosson further says, "I accuse the poets of bringing their cunning into theatres, that they have willfully left, or with ignorance lost those warlike tunes which were used in ancient times to stir up in us a manly motion...and rocke us a sleepe in all ungodliness." He sides with Plato and justifies his stand in banishing all poets from his ideal Republic.

Gosson's Schoole of Abuse evoked two replies—one from Thomas Lodge titled A Defence of Poetry, Music, and Stage-Play, and the other from Sidney entitled An Apologie for Poetrie, Sidney's Apologie has become a landmark in the history of English criticism.

Direction: Write the answer of the question no. 26 in 1000 words.

Q. 26. Write an essay of The Oxford Movement.

Ans.: The Oxford Movement was basically a religious Movement. It was an outcome of a long controversy and ideological conflicts amongst different Christian sects and churches. Since the battle-ground of these controverse was Oxford, this Movement came to be known as Oxford Movement. Again, since these controversies were carried through tracts and pamphlets, this Movement was also called the Tractarian Movement. It was in the course of its development that it took a literary turn too. This happened because some of its development that it took a literary turn too. This happened because some of its leaders were poets and prose-writers too. These literary men supported the cause of the English church and the Prayer Book through their writings. But this Movement did not remain confined to Oxford city only. Soon it spread out over the whole country. So Sampson says, "Viewed from afar the Oxford Movement appeared to be a theological dispute among the local cleagy in a university city; in the course of a few years it was to shake the whole church of England and change the very nature of its being." The aim of the Movement was to rehabilitate the dignity of the church, to defend the church against the interference of the State, to fight against liberalism, to defend the church against the interference of the State, to fight against liberalism, to defend the religion against the onslaught of scientific discoveries, and to preserve faith against rationalism.

Opposition of Religion by Science: The scientific discoveries challenged the age-old institutions, Divine laws and faith in religion. In science every fact is proved by reason, experiment and factual observation. The traditional religious beliefs and theories of the creation of the world and living species and branches of science. The most powerful of these scientific discoveries which shook the very foundations of religion was Darwin's *Origin of Species*. This discovery challenged the very basis of Divine Order and that God created the universe. Several other scientists including Wallace, Herbert Spencer, T.H. Huxley, and John Tundall threw similar challenges to religion in other fields. Religion had to be saved because man cannot live without faith in some higher power. This challenge was accepted by the leaders of the Oxford Movement.

Literary Figures Associated with the Oxford Movement: We shall now consider only the literary figures who were associated with the Oxford Movement. Though the most influential of them was John Henry Newman, the originator of the Movement was John Keble. Other important literary figures were two brothers Richard Hurrell Froude and James Anthony Froude. Edward Pusey, Isaac Williams, Richard William Church, and a few more. We shall consider the contribution of the more important of them.

John Keble: John Keble was the originator of the Oxford Movement. The most popular of his books of verses was *The Christian Year* published anonymously in two volumes in 1827. It bore the sub-title *Thoughts in Verse for the Sundays* and *Holidays Throughout the Year*. These verges embody something of the spirit of the English Book of Common Prayer.

John Henry Newman: Newman was the most notable figure in the Oxford Movement. He was a talented writer. He had no great learning, but he had remarkable charm and grace. His first important work was *Essay on the Development of Christian Doctrine* published in 1845.

He wrote several *Tracts,* but his *Tract No. 90* raised a storm against him. This storm compelled him to join the Roman Catholic Church. His famous literary works include *Apologia pro Vita Sua, Sermons Preached Before the University of Oxford, Sermons Bearing upon the subjects of the Day, Discourses Addressed to Mixed Congregations. Sermons Preached on Various Occasions. The idea of a University,* and *Discourses on the Scope and Nature of University Education.* His writings present Newman at his best, polished, urbane, persuasive, and delicately humorous. Newman wrote verses too. The Collections of his verses and *Verses on Various Occasions, Lyra Apostolica* and *Dream of Gerontius.* However, his poems are not of high quality.

Froude Brothers: Richard Hurrell Froude and James Anthony Froude were two poet brothers. James Froude took orders. He wrote *History of Henry VIII.* The elder brother, Richard Froude was glowing with religious ardour. He published a volume of poems called *Lyra Apostalica.* The collection of his tracts was called *Tracts for the Times.* After his death was published his *remains* in two volumes. Mr. J.L. May said about him, "Froude's part in the Movement was brief, but it was all important. He was the match that fired the train. He brought Keble and Neman to understand each other, and that was an achievement pregnant with consequences."

Edward Pusey: Edward Pussey originated Puseyism. It was a form of Anglicanism which was akin to Roman Catholicism. He was a learned man and a great protagonist of the Movement. Comparing him to Newman, Compton-Rickett says, "He is far less attractive as a personality, more questionable in his craftsman." He published *The Library of the Fathers of the Holy Catholic church.*

W.G. Ward and R.W. Church: They were the followers of Newman. They attained much celebrity in literature. Church was dean of St. Paul's W.G. Ward wrote *Idea of Christian Church* and Church wrote *A History of Oxford Movement.* Both of them were among the pillars of the *Oxford Movement.*

The Religious and Literary Importance of the Oxford Movement: The Oxford Movement has a great importance in the religious as well as literary sense. During the eighteenth century the church had sunk into stagnation. Its liturgy was reduced to the minimum. The church had lost its life and vitality. The Oxford Movement rejuvenated it. Concluding his observations on the value of the Oxford Movement. Sampson says: "the chief aim of the Oxford Movement was to make plain to the Englishmen the historical continuity of the national church. The glamour of the Oxford Movement touched many who were far from the time and place of conflict. In the poetry of Christina Rossetti it kindled a new life exuberant and a flame. To Christina Rossetti the Catholic theology of the English Church was the very breath of life, and she accepted its sternness without dispute. The real teaching of the Church would be found if you went back to the right sources."

DECEMBER 2006

Directions: Read the following passage carefully and write the answer of the question no. 1 to 5 in 30 words.

It is your duty to train and develop your Mind and acquire knowledge, as much knowledge as you possibly can obtain. Knowledge is like a deep well, fed by perennial springs, and your Mind is the little bucket that you drop into it: you will get as much as you can assimilate. The Brain, which is the physical organ of the Mind, really distinguishes you from the animals. Many animals have very powerful sense organs: the eagle, the ant, and the dog have keener senses than Man. But no animal has a more evolved Brain and a higher intelligence. If you do not develop and use this Brain to the utmost of your power, you are more akin to the beast than to *Homo sapiens*.

Knowledge and mental self-culture will confer untold blessings upon you. You will not be the victim of superstition and demagogy in religion and politics. You will know your duty and do it. To be wise and independent in your religion and your politics, not to be doped and duped by the selfish priests and the scheming politicians, is this not a noble aim worth striving for? Most men and women today are not free and wise: They are fleeced and fooled on account of their ignorance of Science, History, Economics, and other subjects. Half the ills of mankind are due to Ignorance, the other half arise from Egotism. Knowledge is fully as important as Ethics: they are really interdependent. As Lessing says: "The aim of knowledge is Truth, and Truth is a need of the soul." The Persian poet Shaadi exhorts all to acquire knowledge with unremitting zeal: "Like a taper, one should melt in pursuit of knowledge. This is thy duty, even if thou hast to travel over the whole earth."

Q. 1. What distinguishes man from animals according to this passage?

Ans.: Man differs from animals in one respect only. Man has a more developed mind and higher intelligence. A man who does not make the fullest use of his mind and intelligence is no way different from animals.

Q.2. Why should one try to acquire as much knowledge as possible?

Ans.: One should try to acquire as much knowledge as possible because this will bring untold blessings to him. He will be free from all superstitious and religious and political dogmas. He will not be duped by anyone.

Q. 3. What would one gain by acquiring mental self-culture?

Ans.: Mental self-culture will make one free from all superstitions and false faiths. He will not be under the unwanted control of priests and politicians. He will not be fleeced by any one on account of his ignorance.

Q. 4. What ills would Ignorance bring to man according to this passage?

Ans.: Ignorance will make one a slave to priests and politicians. His thoughts and actions would be controlled by them. He would be an easy prey to and fleeced by any clever man.

Q. 5. "One should melt in pursuit of knowledge." What does this statement imply?

Ans.: The statement means that one should pursue knowledge to the last point of his faculty, because without knowledge one is in no sense different from animals. One should go to the farthest limit in pursuit of knowledge.

Directions: Write the answer of the question no. 6 to 20 in about 30 words.

Q. 6. Enumerate Wordsworth's theory of poetry.

Ans.: In the preface of the second edition of the Lyrical Ballads Wordsworth sets out his theory of poetry. It reveals a lofty conception of the dignity of that art which is the breath and finer spirit of all knowledge, and which is the product of the spontaneous overflow of powerful feelings taking its origin from emotion recollected in tranquility. The qualifications of the poet are on a level with the dignity of his art. To Wordsworth, he is a man possessed of more than usual organic sensibility, and one who has also brought long deeply.

Q. 7. What picture of India does Raja Rao portray in *Kanthapura*?

Ans.: In *Kanthapura*, Raja Rao evokes the 'idea' of India that appealed to European-ancient history, religion, landscape and the life of the Kanthapura village community-without, however, evading a realistic stance, Gandhi's ethics, Moorthy's Marxism', the mythology of the 'Harikatha'. Raja Rao offers interpretations of the place of nationalism and good and evil in Indian life. Kanthapura symbolizes India, its capacity to absorb influences yet remain essentially unchanged.

Q. 8. How did the scientific development effect the Victorian age?

Ans.: The rapid development of science transformed the entire environment. It created lot of

Ireland. He more than any other changed the shape of Irish dramatic writing; he more than any other showed Ireland to the world. If Ireland choose to misunderstand him in the very moment of applauding him, the loss is not his but that of Ireland.

Q. 14. What is a 'Jucture' in Linguistic?

Ans.: The process of keeping words apart of the manner of transaction from one vowel consonant to another is called juncture. When we write English, the boundaries between words are symbolized by leaving a space between them. But when we speak English grammatical boundaries are indicated by features of the sound system itself. The ways of getting from one speech sound to another may contrast in the same environments and as such this feature which is known as juncture is also given the name phoneme and it belongs to category of suprasegmental phonemes.

Q. 15. What are the salient characteristics of the Pre-Raphaelite poetry?

Ans.: Firstly, like the Romantics, the pre-Raphaelities were inspired by the Middle Ages by the their romance, chivalry, superstition, and strange combination of the material and mystrical. Secondly, the Pre-Raphaelites where above all artists. Art was their religion. They were for the most part as free from any moral or didactic purpose as Keats, who came closest to them among the Romantics. In poetry, as in painting, they aimed at perfect from and finish. Thirdly, as was natural in the work of writers who often were also painters, Pre-Raphaelite poetry was full of picture sequences and vividity.

Q. 16. Comment on the quest for self in The Bachelor of Arts.

Ans.: R.K. Narayan's protagonist in The Bachelor of Arts, Chandran, purses both Western and Indian ideals, but finds both inappropriate. While learning, mysticism and romantic love may all be good, they appear self-centered in his case. Here even modest fulfillment has to be achieved within a social context while adherence to the traditional ways imposes a limit on ambition. Though Kalias and prof. Raghavachar Chandran attains' a life freed from distracting illusions and hysterics. Ultimately moral insight borings to Chandran a gracious acceptance of life.

Q. 17. What was the State of English language in the age of Chaucer?

Ans.: The period of transition is now over. The English language has shaken down to a kind average-to the standard of the East Midland speech, the language of the capital city and of the universities. The other dialects, with the exception of the Scottish branch, rapidly melt away from literature, till they become quite exiguous, French and English have amalgamated to form the standard English tongue, which attains to its first full expression in the works of Chaucer.

Q. 18. How did Renaissance influence poetry?

Ans.: Sir Thomas Wyatt and the goal of Surrey were the pioneers of poetry in England. They gave poetry a new sense of grace, dignity, delicacy, and harmony which was found lacking. Wyatt introduced sonnet into English literature, and Surrey to have written blank verse.

Q. 19. What is the Role of Nature in J.M. Synge's play *Deirdre of the Sorrows*?

Ans.: In *Deirdre of the Sorrows*, nature is an intimate a poet of the people's life and speech as ever, but there is perhaps more definition, almost more consciousness in Synge's perception. For in the ancient Irish legends from which he drew for this play, he found an experience like his own. In this play, the nature experience of his life, time seems to meet and join hands with that ending tradition of Irish thought and poetry. It is no ornament. It is waven deep.

Q. 20. Write a note on weakness in the play *Anna Cheistic* by O'Neill.

Ans.: There is a fatal weakness in this play. For purposes of dramatic effect Anna is at first shown to be a vulgos, cynical street walker. At the proper moment she breaks down and confesses to her lover and after it has been asserted that she is really pure in soul, she is ready to marry her man. In this way the author has tried to do more than he legitimately could do. He first shocks us by the spectacle of conventional sin and then asks us to forget it. No, Anna is by no means consistent. Human nature and dramatic technique are not quite reconciled.

Direction: Write the answer of the question no. 21 to 25 in about 200 words each.

Q. 21. Write a note on the Eighteenth Century Periodical essay?

Ans.: The periodical essay as a piece of journalism began towards the end of the seventeenth century. The periodical essay reached its acme of achievement early in the works of Steele and Addison. In the eighteenth century it was a popular genre and even more popular than the mock-heroic and the novel. The periodical essay was popular both with the writers and the readers. About its in a style wholly individual. He was fearless in the poetic proclamation of his ideals of liberty and justice, and fireless in the metrical ingenuity with which he fashioned his astonishing fluency into poetic forms with musical and memorable.

In conclusion, it will perhaps be quite appropriate to observe here that the first number of The Germ contained as well as Rossetti's My Sister's Sleep, two lyrics by his sister Christina Georgia Rossetti (1830-94), which gave evidence of clear and original genius. However, unlike her brother, whose sympathy with religion was merely artistic, and still more unlike Swinburne, whose attitude was openly hostile, Christina Rossetti was, to the end of her life, a devout Christian, finding the highest inspiration in her faith and investing Anglican ideals of worship with mystical beauty. Her volumes of verse, beginning with Goblin Market and Other Poems in 1862 and ending with New Poems collected in 1896 by her brother William Michael, are rich in devotional feeling. It is perhaps difficult to find any who can contest her claim to be the finest of English poetesses.

Q. 22. Elaborate Coleridge's skill in making the unreal real, in 'The Ancient Mariner'.

Ans.: The great charm and power of the poem lies in the skill with which the unreal is made to look real. Description of natural phenomena are given with such minuteness and detail, and dovetailed on to the imaginative and supernatural parts with such nicety, as to make the whole story look quite probable. The dreadful silence of the far seas; the hot stagnant waters with the intolerable blasting sun overhead, and the vast unknown furnish a background of reality on which the emotions of sensitive human soul may be portrayed with absolute human freedom and yet carry conviction with them, "I never met", writes Stopford Brooke, "a sailor whose ship had been among the lonely places of the sea, who did not know of their haunting, who would be surprised to see the phantom ship, who did not hear in the air that signed in the rigging the voices of the creatures that are half of the water and half of the air above them".

Q. 23. What was the development in the art of fiction in The Romantic Age?

Ans.: Of the different kinds of prose composition, the novel showed in this period the most marked development. This was largely due to the work of Scott and domestic types of novel. With regard to the work of Scott, we can here only briefly summarize what was already-been said. He raised the historical novel to the rank of one of the major kinds of literate; he brought to it knowledge, and through the divine gift of knowledge made it true to life; he fired historical characters with living energy; he set on foot the device of the unhistorical hero-that he, is made the chief character purely fictitious, and caused the historical persons to rotate about it; he established a style that suited many periods of history; and pervading all these advances was a great and genial personality that transformed what might have been mere lumber into an artistic product of truth and beauty. Jane Austen's achievement was of a different kind. She revealed the beauty and interest that underlie ordinary affairs; she displayed the infinite variety of common life, and so she opened an enexhaustible vein that her successors were assiduously to develop.

Q. 24. Examine the chief characteristics of Tennysons' poetry.

Ans.: First, Tennyson's poetry is not so much to be studied as to be read and appreciated : he is a poet to have open to one's table, and to enjoy as one enjoys his daily exercise. And second, we should by all means begin to get acquainted by more mature minds. Tennyson is for enjoyment, for inspiration, rather than for instruction. Only youth can fully appreciate him; and youth, unfortunately, except in a few rare, beautiful cases, is something which does not dwell with us long after our school days. The secrets of poetry, especially of Tennyson's poetry, is to be eternally young, and, like Adam, in Paradise, to find every morning a new world, fresh, wonderful, inspiring, as if just form the hands of God. Thirdly, his style is marked by a wonderful combination of simplicity and ornateness; he is always absolutely clear and is rarely merely plain, finally, his lyrical measures have often supreme beauty.

Q. 25. Do you agree that in his own day Browning was overrated as a thinker and underrated as a poet?

Ans.: It is an admitted fact that critical appreciation of Browning's poetry was hampered because the public opinion was prejudiced against him. He was admired by a few devotees in his own age. Both critics and laymen persistently sneered at him. His works were not properly assessed or adequately valued in his life time. While Tennyson was regarded as a great artist and highly eulozed in his age. Browning met with much scathing criticism, misunderstanding and even contempt. In his life-time, the Browning society was formed in order to arouse public interest, and also to remove the cobwebs surrounding his personality and talent. In spite of the magnitude and importance of work, his opponents chose to ridicule him and even suggested that he was a poet at all but he is a philosopher.

Direction: Write an essay of about 1000 words on the following topics.

Q. 26. The Objectives of English Teaching in India Today.

Ans.: The Objectives of English Teaching in India Today:

"One has to convey in a language that is not one's own. The spirit is one's own. One has to convey the various shades and omissions of a certain though movement that looks maltreated in an alien language.... We are instinctively bilingual. We cannot write like the English. We should not. We cannot write only as IndiAns.: We have grown to look at the large world as part of us. Our method of expression therefore has to be a dialect which will some day prove to be as distinctive and colourful as the Irish or the American. Times alone will justify it." (Raja Rao)

Macaulay might have thought that the knowledge of English was essential for civilizing Indians, earlier generations might have thought English was necessary for the shaping of character or the development of the aesthetic sense. But the present generation is convinced that English is needed for nobility and social and economic development. English is the language of opportunities because it takes one outside one's own community to places where more opportunities are available for professional growth and economic advancement. Indeed English has a lot of 'surrender value' and learners rightly want to cash in it. So there is a great demand for English.

Today English is the language not of Westernization, but of modernization. That is why, for instance, English is the language of our agricultural universities even though it is not that our agriculture. Unfortunately, while our learners are fully aware of this modernizing role of English in India and would like to speed up the 'lab to the land' process, our curriculum designers and teachers are not. The latter must change first if English is indeed to become an agent of change and modernization.

Students of English in India have realized that English is necessary if they are to talk about their identity, their languages, their literature, their science and technology, their society and economy and polity, their values and culture so that the world outside will know that they are. For example, we have to talk about Panini, Nagarjuna, et al., in English so that the world outside may know that there is a rich tradition of language philosophy in India that can engage the latest in modern thought. We must be in a position to talk about our ancient writers, like Valmiki and Tulsidas, or our contemporary writers, like Premchand and Shakti Chattopadhyay, or our filmmakers, like Shyam Benegal and Satyajit Ray, or about our achievements in the industrial and economic spheres or about our sociolinguistic paradise and our unity in diversity.

Moreover, we need to translate; there is a big market-for quality translations and adaptations of Indian books, classical as well as contemporary, in English. Good translations in English are to be attempted in the India with the help and cooperation of other language departments, and a meaningful interaction between Indian languages and English must be encouraged.

'The existing system of English teaching in India promotes neither critical thinking nor even an attempt at original writing on the part of the students. Therefore a new approach should be envisaged that will look beyond the classroom, the text book & the examination based on 'prescribed books'. A different kind of text book that will be more of a pretext than a text—something that can leave the students to drive confidently outside the protected area where they will learn how to drive in crowded places and in actual traffic conditions. Moreover, the texts selected or written for the purpose must be so opened that no crib-writer can predict probably questions and answers, in order to encourage students to read intelligently, respond critically and write creatively so that the ability to use the language in situations other than the ones in which it was learned can be tested in a meaningful way.

As part of our preparation for the future, language learning should be integrated with the art and science of intellectual self-discipline, of critical thinking and of reasoning competently. The aims of language teaching are not just the four skills: listening, speaking, reading and writing. We should evolve a model, based on the principle of recitation and revelation, an inherent property of texts, thinking and enquiring, silence and contemplation, that will capture the synergic processes of language learning. The myth of the ESL or English as second language must also be examined. The conclude with proper professionalism and better perceptions., an indigenous approach to the teaching of English in India can be arrived at.

JUNE 2006

Directions: Read the following poem and answer the questions given under it from Questions 1 to 5 in 30 words each.

Animals bring us tranquility; Cats sleep through a war;
Dogs ignore your sister concern, forgive betrayals and nations;
While all morning a man cannot bear his own betrayal.
After sleeping with two women.
But a dog will not mount one bitch after another.
Nor want to kill himself for being a Cat.
And quails are monogamous, says the encyclopedia.
The baboon has a harem but he is not tormented by claims for equal time.
But then I forget how troubled I was when at seventeen,
After quarreling with my father about my mother's rights.
A female ape with a blank stripped snout.
Sorted out patiently with her long hands.
Sniff and lick lattice leaves clean for her lord,
And master while he growled all the time.

Q. 1. Comment on the ironic implications of betrayal in the poem.

Ans.: Human beings alone are guilty of betrayal. They betray their spouses, feel guilty, repeat, and yet commit acts of betrayal. Animals and birds commit no such acts of betrayal. The irony is that animals are better than men.

Q. 2. Identify the antithetical elements projected in the poem.

Ans.: The poem is largely antithetical. Men and animals are brought to comparison on the issue of betrayal, and the poem concludes that many kinds of animals and birds are more faithful to their spouses than men.

Q. 3. Discuss the narrator's position on female rights.

Ans.: The narrator pleads for equal rights to women. He remembers that at the age of seventeen he quarreled with his father for defending the rights of his mother. Females, whether human or of animals, are usually submissive to their male partners.

Q. 4. How does the poem address the issue of sexuality?

Ans.: On the issue of sexuality the narrator says that males and females should be faithful to their partners. They should not betray their spouses. Some animals and birds are more faithful than human beings.

Q. 5. What is the implication of 'growing' at the end of the poem?

Ans.: The male ape keeps on 'growling' at the female ape all the time, even though she tries to keep him as happy as possible. This is, more or less, the position of all females, whether human or of animals.

Directions: Write the answer of the question no. 6 to 20. Each Question carries five marks and each to be answered in about 30 words.

Q. 6. Comment on the addressee in Shakespeare's Sonnets.

Ans.: The Sonnets of Shakespeare are addressed to two unidentified persons—a Dark Lady and a certain friend addressed as Mr. W.H. Thus these sonnets express Shakespeare's frustated love and broken friendship. The addresses are wrapped in mystery.

Q. 7. What is *Comedy of Manners?*

Ans.: The Comedy of Manners exhibited the artificial manners and low moral values of the high class society of the Restoration Age. They largely displayed the intrigues, witty remarks, sparkling dialogues and verbal fencings between gentleman and sophisticated ladies.

Q. 8. What is *Pastoral Elegy?*

Ans.: The Pastoral Elegy is an elegy cast into the conventional pastoral form. It is presumed that the poet is a shepherd mourning the death of a fellow shepherd. The whole imagery of goats / sheep, pastures and pastoral gods and goddesses is drawn into it.

Q. 9. Explain Victorian Dilemma

Ans.: The term Victorian Dilemma suggests the conflict between science and religion that raged in the Victorian Age. The traditional religion, beliefs and conventions of Christianity were challenged by the discoveries and explorations of science.

Q. 10. Justify the title *Songs of Innocence.*

Ans.: The *Songs of Innocence* is a volume of songs written by William Blake. The soul of a child is absolutely innocent and is, therefore, protected by God. Worldly experience tarnishes the human soul.

Q. 11. Define Keat's concept of 'Negative Capability'.

Ans.: By 'Negative Capability' Keats meant that the poet must completely identity and submerge his own identity with that of his subject of poetry. The poet has no personality of his own.

Q. 12. Comment on the intersection of human and the natural world with reference to any one novel of Hardy.

Ans.: There is a deep intersection between human life and nature in all the novels of Hardy, but it is particularly so in *The Return of the Native.* Egdan Heath is the permanent natural background for human actions in this novel.

Q. 13. What does the Thunder say in the *Wasteland?*

Ans.: The Thunder says that the world is like a barren track of mountains. The mountains have no drop of water to quench the first of mankind. Mankind needs for peace Datta, Dayadhvam, Damayata (*i.e.* Giving, Sympathy, Self-Control).

Q. 14. What is the significance of the cave in *A Passage to India?*

Ans.: *A Passage to India* by E.M. Forster is a symbolic novel representing racial tensions and antagonism between the Britishers and the Indians. The caves symbolize different kinds of traps to torment the natives.

Q. 15. What is Rushdie's Concept of Imaginary Homelands?

Ans.: Salman Rushdie's *Imaginary Homelands* is a volume of Essays and Criticism. In this volume Rushdie described the plight and mental and spirtitual agony of those people who migrate from their homeland to other countries.

Q. 16. Define the Campus Novel.

Ans.: The Campus Novels deal with the life and problems of students in colleges and universities. They highlight the problems of education and careers of students during this formative period.

Q. 17. Identify the elements of Sublimity as defined by Longinus

Ans.: Longinus has identified five principal elements of Sublimity. Sublimity in literature depends upon the sublimity of theme and sublimity of style and expression. Its five elements are (1) Grandeur of thought, (2) Strong Emotions, (3) Proper use of Fingers, (4) Nobility of Diction, (5) Dignity of Compostion.

Q. 18. What is an Auto suggestive text?

Ans.: The texts of certain very ancient books are not found in their authentic forms. Different editors or publishers modify them in their own way. Efforts should be made to discover their real or authentic form.

Q. 19. What are the hallmarks of Anglo-American feminism?

Ans.: Anglo-American feminism refers to the new spirit of awakening amongst women for their rights and privileges. Women are rising up for equality with men in all fields of life.

Q. 20. Differentiate between a 'Readerly' and a 'Writerly' text.

Ans.: 'Readerly' text is written keeping in mind the interests of the reading public. It should attract more and more reading public. 'Writerly' text concentrates upon the interests of the writer rather than those of the reader.

Directions: Write the answer of the question no. 21 to 25. Each Question carries 12 marks and has to be answered in about 200 words.

Q. 21. What are the major trends in Romantic criticism? Explain with reference to any critic.

Ans.: Romantic criticism is diametrically opposed to Neo-classical criticism both in its concept and execution. Whereas the Neo-classical criticism valued literature on the basis of reason, aristocracy, satire and adherence to classical rules. Romantic criticism laid emphasis on emotion, imagination, aesthetic pleasure, humanitarianism and spontaneity in feeling and expression. Wordsworth Coleridge and Shelley were the most powerful Romantic poets as well as critics. Though Wordsworth was the founder of Romantic Criticism, Coleridge was a better and greater critic. Coleridge held imagination to be the soul of poetry. Poetry is the product of imagination working on the objects of human life and nature. It is this power of imagination that infuses life and spark and beauty into the objects of the world. The next essential element is the presence of sublime thought and emotion. The poet should have a large heart enlivened with love, compassion and humanitarian zeal. Romantic criticism also disapproves of the eighteenth century Poetic Diction. Wordsworth holds that poetry should be written in a language really spoken by men. Romantic criticism also liberates poetry from the fetters of Heroic couplet. Great poetry can be written in any stanza form or in Blank Verse. The vogue of Romantic criticism continues to prevail to the present day.

Q. 22. Bring out the contribution made by Alexander Pope in theorizing English Criticism.

Ans.: Pope was a champion of the classical school of criticism in English. He laid down the classical theories of criticism and advocated that English critics must follow them and evaluate a literary work in the light of those theories. Aristotle, Plato, Virgil, Longinus were his literary gods and he advocated blind adherence to them both in concept and practice. The classical critics were moralities who believed in the didactic, reformatory, and moral functions of literature. As such Pope also advocated that literature must teach high moral values. Mere emotional or imaginative pleasure was not the end of great literature. According to him reason overpowers imagination, logic must replace fancy and good sense must prevail over sentiment. For all these values be travelled back to the ancients. He advocated:

"Know well each Ancient's proper character:
His fable, subject, scope in every page:
Religion, country, genius of every age:
....
Be Homer's works your study and delight,
Read them by day, and mediate by night,
Thence form your judgement, thence your maxims bring.
And trace the Muses upward to their spring."

The ideal critic's duty is to give advice. He is pleased to teach and he ought to give advice. He is pleased to teach and he ought to proud of his knowledge, yet he should be unbiased and unprejudiced. In the true spirit of literary criticism there are not friends or foes. So Pope says:

"Modestly bold, and humanely severe,
Who to a friend his faults can freely show,
And gladly praise the merit of a foe."

Q. 23. Attempt a critique of the notion of Euphuism?

Ans.: The term Euphuism is derived from John Lyly's prose romance Euphues. The full title of Euphues is Euphues, the Anatomy of Wit. It also has a sequel entitled Euphues and His England. It is a love romance. It enjoyed extra-ordinary popularity in its times and went through ten editions within a few years. It became a guide to polite behavior and elegance is speech and writings. However, in literature it is known for its typical style of writing. Its style is characterized by extreme elaboration and artifice. It is further distinguished by a number of rhetorical devices which give it a quality of its own. It is its typical style on account of which it has retained its fame through so many centuries. The most outstanding feature of its style is excessive use of balanced antithesis. We quote hero a typical sentence : "As you may suspect me of idleness in giving ear to your talk, so you may convince me of lightness in answering such toys." In this sentence there is a series of contrary expressions: "suspect me" and "convince me"; giving ear" and "answering"; "idleness" and "lightness", "talk" and "toys". These are contrasting pairs. Lyly also freely uses all Figures of Speech. Therefore Euphuism has been accepted as a literary term.

Q. 24. How does Marxion ideology influence literary studies?

Ans.: The Marxist Theory of Criticism is based on the sociological theory of Marx and Lenin. It is based on the concept that every work of art and literature is the product of the social and political conditions of the age of which it is produced. It believes that literature is inseparably related with the social, political and economic background of the period: "This sociological approach to literature is particularly cultivated by those who profess a specific social philosophy. Marxist critics not only study those relations between literature and society, but also have their clearly defined conception of what these relations should be both in our present society and in a future classless society. They tell us not only what were and are the social conditions and implications of an author's work, but what they should have been or ought to be. They are not only students of literature and society but also prophets of the future, monitors, propagandists and they have no difficulty in keeping these two functions separate." (Rene Wellek) Some important critics who belong to this School are Edmund Wilson, F.O. Mathiessen, Christopher Caudwell, and H.B. Parkes. All these critics believe that no author can deep himself detached from those broad currents of thought and feeling which are shared by the other members of contemporary society. A work of literature and contemporary society. A work of literature and contemporary society are interdependent on each other.

Q. 25. Account for the broadening of literary studies and their merger with cultural studies.

Ans.: Literature and contemporary social values and ideologies are inseparably interdependent on each other. Literature and cultural awakening go side by side. There is a kind of second Renaissance in our present age. There is a new educational, cultural, scientific, economic, and national and international awakening in the world today. The narrow regional, racial, religious, cultural and linguistic barriers and breaking down. A sort of international fraternity is growing up. Naturally there is an ever-widening public interested in literary studies. The literary authors, both in prose and verse, come up to meet the demand of the fast increasing reading public. Millions of books, magazines, journals and periodicals are being published and widely circulated in the world today. Correspondingly, new and amazingly fast methods of printing are coming up. The invention of preserving the original texts in the form of computer C.D.'s and Floppies has further facilitated and preserving and reprinting of the books. Huge libraries can now be safely preserved in a single almirah. As a result, literature and culture have merged into each other. This new awakening has led to the fast growth of the public interested in literary studies. And as literature and culture cannot be separated today, cultural awakening has accompanied literary studies.

Direction: Write an essay of about 1000 words on any of the following topics:

Q. 26. Drama in both literature and theatre.

Ans.: Drama and Poetry: Originally Dr. Rama was known as Dramatic Poesy. Dryden entitled his famous treatise on Drama as an Essay Dramatic Poesy. The term Dramatic Poesy points to the fact that Drama is as much an intrinsic part of literature as Poetry. It is not essential that drama must be acted on the stage in a theatre. In fact, drama has a double advantage. It can be enjoyed as a distinct genre of literature both on the stage as well as in one's study room. Great works of Drama are equally successful on the stage as well as in the study parlour.

Early Dramas only for the Stage: However, earliest drama were written only for the stage. They were Miracle plays, Mystery plays, Morality plays, and Interludes. These plays were basically religious and didactic and were meant to teach the largely illiterate English public principles, teachings and tenets of Christianity by staging them at public places. Since there were no regular public theatres in those days, these plays were staged under the open sky or on public platforms. The Miracle plays presented the lives and martyrdom of the great Christian saints. The Mystery plays staged the theme of the Bible in a chronological order beginning with Nativity, Crucifixion, Resurrection of Christ and the last Judgement. The Morality plays presented on the stage personified Virtues, Vices, and Death as the Reward of Sin. The Interludes just entertained the public to relieve them from boredom. Since the larger section of the public could not read them, they were staged on the artificially created platforms. Sometimes, they were also staged in the Halls of Dukes, Barons and other royal personalities. They were all rudimentary plays and had very little literary value.

Shakespeare's Plays: Shakespeare's plays touch the highest watermark as literature as well as stage plays. He is the greatest dramatist the world has ever produced. His plays are held to be as important today as they were when they were written more than four centuries ago. The fact that several of his plays are still prescribed in the syllabi of universities in many countries of the world goes to prove that his plays are highly and widely recognized works of literature. They are equally popular as theatrical plays. His important tragedies are *Hamlet, Othello, Macbeth* and *King Lear*. His famous comedies are *As You Like It. Twelfth Night, A Midsummer Night's Dream. Merchant of Venice, Much Ado Nothing,* and several more. His Historical Plays and Romances are in no way less important. In all he has written thirty-seven plays, and all of them have been celebrated both as literary works and theatrical plays. A great admirer of Shakespeare, M. Henry Cochin, praises the genius of Shakespeare in these words: "Shakespeare is the king of poetic rhythm and style as well as the king of realm of thought, along with his dazzling prose. Shakespeare has succeeded in giving us the most varied, the most harmonious verse which has ever sounded upon the human ear since the verse of the Greeks."

Other Stage Dramatists: There are many more dramatists whose dramas are remarkably literary as well as fit for the stage. Their plays can be read as works of literature in one's parlour, but they would be equally successful on the stage. These dramatists include Marlowe. Ben Jonson, Dryden, Congreve, Vanbrugh, Farquhar, Sheridan, Goldsmith and a few others. They present the socio-cultural life of the age in which they lived and wrote. Ben Jonson's plays are called Comedies of Humours. They caricature human foibles and eccentrics in good humours. Sheridan, Congreve, Farquhar present the falling morals and foppish fashions of the Restoration Age. They largely display the intrigues, foppish manners, witty remarks, sparkling dialogues, and verbal fencing between aristocratic ladies and lords. The Restoration Age was known for these characteristics Presenting the true picture of the Restoration Age, these plays deal with the relations and intrigues of gentlemen and ladies living in a polished and sophisticated society, and rely for comic effect in great part on the wit and sparkle of the dialogues, leading to a kind of verbal fencing match. Excellent examples of such plays are Congreve's *The Way of the World,* and Wycherley's *The Country Wife*. These plays were repeatedly acted on the stage and appreciated by the public. But they were equally good and enjoyable as master pieces of literature in their own areas. People read them for pleasure in their parlours.

Purely Literary Dramas: There is one more distinctly different type of drama which is known as Poetic Play or Lyrical Play. These plays are actually long poems of epical dimensions split up into Acts and Scenes. They are avowedly written for reading as purely literary works and not for acting on the stage. In fact, it is a long poem cast into the dramatic form and meant to be read as a poem. The poetic play is also called a Closet play. The normal stage play is not complete in itself. It requires a complex external paraphernalia such as a theatre, a stage, actors and audience, and its success depends upon their performance on the stage. Against it, the poetic play is complete in itself. It can be read and enjoyed by the reader in his own closet or study-room without any external aid. The reader can enjoy it all by himself as he can enjoy an epic or a novel. The poetic play is normally written on some classical, mythological or legendary theme. The poetic plays came to be written in the Romantic Age. The principal writers of the poetic plays were practically all the Romantic poets including Wordsworth, Southey, Coleridge, Shelley, Keats, Byron and later on Tennyson and Browning. However, the earliest poetic plays were *Comus* and *Samson Agonistes* written by Milton. T.S. Eliot's *Murder in the Cathedral* is also a famous poetic play. Hardy's *The Dynasts* is also a very long play not meant to be acted. It is an epic drama.

Thus there are two principal types of plays—those which are both literature as well as stage plays, and those which are only literature not designed to be acted.

DECEMBER 2005

Directions: Read the following poem and answer the questions given under it from Questions 1 to 5 in 30 words each:

The sea of faith
Was once, too, at the full, and round earth's shore
Lay like the folds of a bright girdle furl'd;
But now I only hear
Its melancholy, long, withdrawing roar
Retreating to the breath
Of the night-wind down the vast edges drear
And naked shingles of the world.
Ah, love, let us be true
To one another! for the world, which seems
To lie before us like a land of dreams.
So various, so beautiful, so ner,
Hath really neither joy, nor love, nor light,
Nor certitude, nor peach, nor help for pain;
And we are here as on a darkling plain
Swept with confused alarms of struggle and fight,
Where ignorant armies clash by night.

Q. 1. Why does the poet say that the sea of faith is retreating with a melancholy roar?

Ans.: There was a serious conflict between science and faith in the Victorian Age. The force of science proved stronger, with the result that the sea of faith had to recede back painfully.

Q. 2. Why does the poet say that the world has really 'neither joy, nor love, nor light'?

Ans.: With the recession of faith, man was left with no shelter or succour in his hour of grief, hopelessness or despondency. Man wandered in the desert of darkness without peace within or calm around.

Q. 3. What is the central idea of the poem?

Ans.: The central idea of the poem is that having lost faith in God and religion, man is wandering helplessly in the desert in the desert of disbelief all around him. He has neither hope, nor love, nor peace within him.

Q. 4. What figure of speech is suggested by the lines:

"But now I only fear
Its melancholy, long, withdrawing roar."

Ans.: The figure of speech used in these lines is Onomatopoeia, because the sound of words used in these lines expresses the sense of the receding sea. The sound of words expresses their meaning.

Q. 5. Explain the meaning of the line:

"Where ignorant armies clash by night."

Ans.: By 'ignorant armies' the poet means "large crowds of people who have lost faith in God and religion." The word 'darkness' here means 'scepticism'. The world has become a dark arena where blind-fold people are fighting aimlessly.

Directions: Write the answer of the question no. 6 to 20. Each Question carries five marks and each to be answered in about 30 words.

Q. 6. What is a Historical Novel?

Ans.: The Historical Novel draws its theme from some important historical event. But around this historical event the novelist weaves some imaginative and artistic environment to make it an interesting and arresting theme for a novel.

Q. 7. What is a Regional Novel?

Ans.: The Regional Novel is a novel which describes the social and family life, customs and manners, language and dress, occupations and professions of the people of a particular region. The entire novel is woven around these factors of the region.

Q. 8. What was the Pre-Raphaelite School of Poets?

Ans.: A group of painter-poets led by D.G. Rossetti founded the Pre-Raphalite School of poetry. Other poets of this school were Christina Rosetti, Swinburne, and William Morris. They wrote highly sensuous, pictorial and symbolical poems which could be painted with equal effect.

Q. 9. What was Oxford Movement?

Ans.: The Oxford Movement was essentially a religious Movement started to reform the English Church, the clergy and theology, Kebic's sermons and poems started the reformatory Movement. However, its greatest champion was Henry Newman.

Q. 10. What is Didactic Literature?

Ans.: Didactic Literature is that form of literature that directly seeks to teach some moral or religious lesson. Allegorical works like Sonser's *Faerte Queene* or Bunyan's *Pilgrim's Progress* are didactic literature. Most of the eighteenth-century literature is didactic.

Q. 11. What is meant by Renaissance?

Ans.: Renaissance means 'revival' or 'rebirth' of Greek learning, art, literature and culture of the Middle Ages in Europe. In England it came through Italy and flourished in the Elizabethan Age in the works of Shakespeare, Spenser, Marlowe and Ben Jonson.

Q. 12. What is meant by Reformation?

Ans.: Reformation was a religious Movement led by Martin Luthur in the fifteenth century. It protested against the practices of the Roman Catholic Church. It advocated complete faith in the Bible and in one's own soul for salvation.

Q. 13. What is the relationship between Poetry, Life and Morality according to Mathew Arnold?

Ans.: According to Arnold, poetry consoles and sustains us. "A poetry of revolt against moral ideas is a poetry of revolt against life; a poetry of indifference towards moral ideas is a poetry of indifference towards life."

Q. 14. What does Keats mean by "Negative Capability"?

Ans.: Keats means to say that a poet has no personality of his own; he assumes the personality of the character he creates. "The poet has none, no identify—he is certainly the most unpoetical of all god's creatures."

Q. 15. What is a Lyric?

Ans.: A Lyric is a short musical composition meant too be sung to the accompaniment of a lyre by a single singer. Now the term issued for any short non-narrative poem expressing a single thought or feeling of the poet.

Q. 16. What is an Idyll?

Ans.: The Origin of Idylls may be traced back to the Greek poet Theocritus, Idylls are small lyrical poems generally describing the scenes and pleasures of rural countryside. They depict country life as realistically and pictorically as possible.

Q. 17. What are called Interludes?

Ans.: The interludes were generally short entertainments inserted within a longer play or amidst some other festivities or festivals. Their primary function was to entertain the audience by humour or even by farce.

Q. 18. What is a Tragedy?

Ans.: The Tragedy is the tragic story of a good and great man who, on account of a slight flaw in his character, passes through a harrowing emotional and spiritual crisis, and finally meets his doom and death.

Q. 19. How is the Victorian Age characterized in literature?

Ans.: The Victorian Age covers the period from 1837 to 1901. Most of the literature of this period deals with the current social, economic, industrial and intellectual problems including the conflict between science and religion.

Q. 20. How is the literature of the Modern Age characterized?

Ans.: The term 'Modern' is generally applied to the literature produced since the beginning of the World War I. Since then so many experiments have been made both in the subject matter and form in all the genres of literature.

Directions: Write the answer of the question no. 21 to 25. Each Question carries 12 marks and has to be answered in about 200 words.

Q. 21. Which, according to Aristotle, is a higher and nobler literary work between an Epic and a Tragedy?

Ans.: To the questions whether the Epic or the Tragedy is the better and nobler form of art, Aristotle gives preference to the Tragedy. Those who hold the plea in favour of the Epic argue that is appeals to a more refined class of society, the cultured few, and that it achieves its effect without the aid of any external paraphernalia such as the theatrical stage and the spectacle and that its action is more varied. Aristotle concedes all these points and still boldes the view that tragedy is the better form of art. He argue that the tragedy equally appeals to the more refined class, and that it can be appreciated and enjoyed in reading as well as in witnessing on the stage. Therefore it appeals to a wider section of society—to the section of reading class as well as to the spectator or audience class. Theatrical performance is an additional accessory and no compulsory equipment of its literary craft. On the contrary, its performance on the stage makes its appeal deeper and wider. As for the varied action of the Epic, it is a drawback rather than a strong point because unity of tone and action makes a more concentrated effect than the varied one. The effect on a larger and more varied scale dilutes the totality of effect. Therefore Aristotle holds the Tragedy on the higher level than the Epic.

Q. 22. Discuss I.A. Richards' concept of Poetry and poetic composition.

Ans.: I.A. Richards is the most influential literary theorist of the twentieth century. He is the pioneer of what has come to be known as New Criticism. He judges every literary and aesthetic activity in the light of the latest discoveries in the field of psychology and working of human mind. It is in the same light of human psychology and working of human mind that he gives his theory of Poetry and poetic composition. He says that poetry is a 'system of impulses' produced in the mind by some stimulus leading to the production of poetry. When the stimulus first occurs, it produces a large number of mixed impulses which pull the mind in different directions. Gradually these impulses organize themselves in a state of poise poetry germinates. But it should be remembered that by poetry Richards means not only verse but all imaginative literature. The poet simply records the happy play of impulses on a particular occasion. The reader of poetry should not seek any thought from a poem: he should only share the experience, the happy play of impulses working in the mind of the poet. However, much that goes to produce a poem is, of course, unconscious. It should be remembered, as the modern psychologists says, that the unconscious processes are more important than the conscious ones. It is these unconscious impulses that lead the poet or any artist to produce a poetical work or any other work of art.

Q. 23. Discuss Dr. Johnson's Historical approach to criticism.

Ans.: Rising above the classical approach to criticism, Dr. Johnson also developed and practiced historical approach to criticism. This does not in any way mean that Dr. Johnson overruled the classical principles : it only means that he added historical approach wherever this led to the better evaluation of a literary work. He holds that every literary work is conditioned by the historical background and the author's age and environment. No literary work can be correctly evaluated without taking into consideration "the genius of the age and nation in which the author lived." Dr. Johnson says, "To judge rightly of an author, we must transport ourselves to his time, and examine what were the wants of his contemporaries, and what were his means of supplying them." What may be essential at one time may become superfluous at another time. The author's biographical conditions, his opportunities and limitations are essential to consider in order to form a correct estimate of his performance. In other words, the historical estimate is an important factor in the real estimate of an author. If we examine Chaucer's *Prologue to the Canterbury Tales* without taking into consideration the socio-religious conditions of fourteenth century England, our evaluation of Chaucer would be grossly wrong. In the same way, we cannot correctly evaluate the literature of the Restoration Age without placing it in the age of Charles II and the morals he brought in from France. While evaluating Milton, we must know his handicaps, his blindness, his opposition on religious and political grounds and how he overcame them simply by his genius. Then only we would know his real greatness as a poet.

Q. 24. Discuss the plan of Dryden's *Essay of Dramatic Poesy*.

Ans.: Dryden developed a very ingenious plan for writing his *Essay of Dramatic Poesy*. In 1665 great plague broke out in London. In order to escape from the infection of the plague, many people left London and moved out to the countryside. Dryden takes this situation and develops a plan to write a great treatise on the theory and practice of dramatic poesy. He imagines that he had his three friends sail out of London in a boat on the river Thames. The journey is long and tedious. Therefore in order to avoid the boredom of the journey, the four friends decide to hold some useful discourse on the theory and practice of Drama in different ages in Greece, Rome, France and England. The four friends by mutual agreement decide to allot one country or one age to each of the four friends. Thus there are four interlocutors, each taking up the defence of dramatic literature of one country or one age. Crites speaks for the Greek and Roman dramatists and their principles. Lisideius defends the French, and Eugenius the English drama of the last age in England and Neander (or Dryden himself) pleads for England and liberty. This ingenious device helps Dryden in developing historical, comparative, descriptive, and independent methods of criticism. In final conclusion, Dryden holds that ancient principles should be respected but they should not be followed slavishly.

Q. 25. How does Sidney establish the superiority of poetry over all other branches of learning?

Ans.: Sidney says that poetry is the first and most ancient source of learning and wisdom. It is "the first light giver to ignorance, and first Nurse, whose milk by little and little enabled them to feed afterwards of rougher knowledge." Poetry is the better and nobler source of wisdom than even history and philosophy which are believed to be the richest sources of knowledge and wisdom. Even philosophy was first taught in verse. Wise Solomon was directly a poet. Plato's *Dialogues* are in spirit poetical prose and its saying are called verses. All the ancient; philosophers "walked into Apollo's Garden". In the like manner, the historians too, imitate poetic methods. Sidney says: "And even Historiographers, although their lips sound of things done, and verities be written in their foreheads, have been glad to borrow both fashion and perchance weight of poets." So Sidney finally says: "Truly, neither philosopher nor historiographer could at the first have entered into the gates of popular judgments, if they had no taken a great passport of Poetry." The Romans called the poets *Vates* meaning thereby 'creators' and believed that poets were the only creators after God. Even the barbarous races such as Turks, Danes, Normans and Saxons admired their poets. The poet even transcends nature and makes more beautiful than it is. So poetry is the mother and nurse of all knowledge and wisdom. Even Plato said that poetry is divinely inspired. In the end Sidney says. "The philosopher teacheth them who are already taught, the Poet is indeed the right popular philosopher."

Direction: Write an essay of about 500 words on the following topics.

Q. 26. Write an essay on 'The Comedy of Humours'.

The Concept of 'Humours'. Ben Jonson was the principal exponent of the Comedy of Humours. The Comedy of Humours was actually satirical comedy based on the classical concept of Humours. According to the ancient or classical theory, the 'Humours' were held to be the four primary fluids-blood, phlegm, choler (or yellow bile), and melancholy (or black bile) found in human psychology. These 'humours' are normally held in a balance in a normal human being. Their admixture determines both a man's physical state and his character type. An imbalance of one or another humour in a temperament produced one of the four kinds of disposition. The excess of the humour of 'blood' makes one too optimistic, the excess of 'melancholy' makes one too morbid and depressed. In Ben Jonson comedies of 'humours' each of the major characters, instead of being a balanced individual, has a characteristic distortion or eccentricity of disposition. Jonson expounds his theory in the 'Induction' to his play *Every Man in His Humour*. In Jonson's own words:

"When some one peculiar quality
Doth so possess a man, that it doth draw
All his affects, his spirits and his powers
In their confluctions, all to run one way;
This may be truly said to be a humour.'

As such all his major characters are caricatures or satirical character portraits who amuse us without offending any one. So in the same 'Induction' to *Every Man in His Humour,* Ben Jonson says:

"But deeds, and language, such as men do use;
And persons, such as Comaedie would chuse,
When she would shew an Image of the times, and sport with humane follies, not with crimes."

Eccentric Characters: Ben Jonson's comedies present "a gallery of sixteenth century oddities. He was a profound scholar of human nature to stop at such a superficial stage. He knew the point at which eccentricity shades off into vice, and discerned the subtle links whereby crime is connected with moral weakness. Therefore in the noblest of his plays dominant passions tower above the undergrowth of 'humours'. Lust, hunger for gold, jealousy, brutal egotism, vulgar ambition, and control asway the multiform prism of minor aberrations brought before our notice in bewildering profusion. The robust power of characterization and of maintaining the gradations of dramatic interest is Jonson's highest quality." Therefore Ben Jonson's characters tend to be 'types' rather than individuals. There are no varieties, but only types or patterns. However, Ben Jonson's plays begin a new chapter in the history of English drama. A satirical representation of life on the stage was, of course, no new thing. The earlier drama was full of it, though never so systematized as here. But this simplification of complex human nature to leading typical trait was only a part of the poet's more general theory.

Ben Jonson's 'Humorous' Comedies: Ben Jonson's most important humorous comedy is *Every Man in His Humour*. This play established his reputation as a dramatist. It was considered to be an epoch-making play, for it was this play in comedy leis in the conception of the characters, each governed by some salient trait or characteristic, Brainworm with his passion for "gulling everybody" is gulled in the end himself. Bobadil, eager to appear the supreme duelist, is at heart a coward. Knowell, Downright often betray themselves by their names. Jonson's characters largely reveal themselves by their names. Kitley is a jealous young lady, jealous even of her sister.

Every Man Out of His Humour is a continuation of *Every Man in His Humour*. Here we have a vainglorious knight, a public jester, an affected courtier, a doting husband and others who all exhibit their humours, and are finally forced out of their affectations through the agency of Macilente, who, also, is cured of his besetting envy. Sampson says, "*Every Man Out of His Humour* is long-winded, didactic, and over-changed with satirical criticism of his contemporaries." Its characters, Deliro, Fallace, Asper, and their rest bear Italian names which are teasing to the reader.

The Cynthia's Revells completes the trio of this famous plays with the above named two plays. It resembles *Every Man Out of His Humour* in its general plan of a group of would be gallants and ladies whose follies ae exposed to ridicule and shame through the efforts of a censor representing the author's attitude. Its song *Queen and Huntress* is highly appreciated. His censor of contemporaries ridiculed in this play brought a storm of opposition against him.

This was followed by four comedies. They are *Volpone or the Foxe, The Salient Woman, The Alchemist,* and the *Bortholomew Fayre*. The chief character of *Volpone* is Volpone himself. He is a miser and sensualist. He works on the greed of his acquaintances, and exposes their hypocrisy. Its plot, characters, and blank verse are unusuallay vigorous and flowing, which show Jonson at his best. *The Silent Woman* is less intent on moral castigation and therefore most agrreable. In *The Alchemist* Jonson brings a larger canvas of trickseters and gulls. The entire play is in blank verse, which is most carefully adapted to rapid dialogue and orations. The important characters, specially Sir Epicure Mammon and the two Puritans are masterly sketched. The satire on alchemistry flavours the fun without destroying it, and the picture of Elizabethan London is without an equal in its graphic presentation. In the presentation of manners and characters, *Bortholomew Fayre* outranks even *The Alchemist*. It has all the fun of the fair, its bustle and disorder. The principal characters are drawn with remarkable exactness and unflagging animation. It is all written in remarkable prose.

Some Other Writers of Comedies of Humours: Jonson set the vogue of writing 'Humour' comedies. A few other Elizabethan dramatists also tried their hand at Humour Comedies. In fact, even Shakespeare drew some of his characters on the same theory. The notable amongst such characters are Falstaff, Jaques, Touchstone., Malvolio, Shakespeare's *Merry Wives of Windsor* is written on the pattern of 'humour' comedies. Chapman's *Humorous Day's Mirth,* Day's *Humour Out of Breath,* an anonymous play *Every Woman in Her Humour,* Marston' *The Scourge of Villatny* are some of the Elizabethan plays written on the theory of Humours. The vogue of Humour Comedies ended with Ben Jonson and some of his contemporaries.

JUNE 2005

Directions: Read the following poem and answer the questions given under it from Questions 1 to 5 in 30 words each:

Tell me not, in mournful numbers,
Life is but an empty dream!
For the soul is dead that slumbers,
And things are not what they seem.
Life is real! Life is earnest!
And the grave is not its goal!
'Dust thou art, to dust returnest',
Was not spoken of the soul.
Not enjoyment, and not sorrow,
Is our destined end or way;
Find us farther than today.
Art is long and Time is fleeting.
And our hearts, though stout and brave,
Still, like muffled drums, are beating
Funeral marches to the grave.

Q. 1. What is the truth about human body and soul?

Ans: Human body and soul are two different entities. While human body is perishable, Soul is immortal.

Q. 2. What is the goal of life according to this passage?

Ans: The goal of life is neither enjoyment nor sorrow. Joy and sorrow come alternately and pass. The goal of life is action. Man must act and every tomorrow should take us farther than today. This march should go on.

Q. 3. What does the poet say about the Past, Present and Future ?

Ans.: The poet makes very striking observations about the Past, Present and Future. He says that Past has passed and cannot be recalled; the Future is unseen and uncertain. The most important is the Present which we must make the best use of.

Q. 4. What can we learn from the lives of great men?

Ans.: We must learn from the lives of great men how we can also make our lives sublime and memorable and leave the prints of our feet on the sands of time.

Q. 5. What is the poet's advice to man?

Ans.: The poet's advice is that we must work ceaselessly, with heart and soul. Act and act and wait for the result with patience and hope. Result will come sooner or later.

Directions: Write the answer of the question no. 6 to 20. Each Question carries five marks and each to be answered in about 30 words.

Q. 6. What does Matthew Arnold say about the future of poetry?

Ans.: According to Matthew Arnold, "The future of poetry is immense, because in poetry, where it is worthy of its high destinies, our race, as time goes on, will find an ever surer and surer stay."

Q. 7. How does Wordsworth define poetry?

Ans.: According to Wordsworth, "Poetry is a criticism of life under the laws of poetic truth and poetic beauty. Poetry is a spontaneous overflow of powerful feelings, taking its origin from emotions recollected in tranquility."

Q. 8. Define an ode.

Ans.: An Ode is a long lyrical poem, serious in subject, elevated in style and elaborate in its stanzaic structure. It is in the form of an address to the object or the person about whom it is written.

Q. 9. What is a Pindaric Ode?

Ans.: The Pindaric Odes are written on the model of the odes written by Pindar, the great Greek poet. They are choric in character and designed to be sung by a troupe of dancers in churnes or public halls.

Q. 10. What is a Mystery Play?

Ans.: The Mystery Plays basically deal with the themes taken from the Bible. They present in chronological order major events from the creation and fall of man through Nativity, Crucifixation, Resurrection of Christ to the last Judgement.

Q. 11. What are Morality Plays?

Ans.: Morality Plays are allegorical plays. They present on the stage personified Virtues and Vices. Everyman is presented as the Hero. Satan personified as Vice, God or Christ as Virtue, and Death as the Reward of Sin.

Q. 12. What is a Tragi-Comedy?

Ans.: A Tragi-Comedy is an artistic combination of both tragedy and comedy. It develops as a tragedy to the point of climax, and then takes a happy turn and finally ends into a happy denouement.

Q. 13. What is meant by Denouement?

Ans.: The conclusion of a comedy is called denouement. Here all the obstacles and tangles that came in the path of true love are resolved and the lovers get happily married.

Q. 14. What is Heroic Drama?

Ans.: Heroic drama was mainly written in the Restoration Age principally by Dryden. It tried to emulate the dimensions of Epic or Heroic poetry. Its hero was a great warrior whose fate affected the fate of an empire, such as Dryden's *All For Love*.

Q. 15. What is a Chorus?

Ans.: The term Chorus is taken from Greek drama. In English drama it is applied to a character who speaks the Prologue and Epilogue and also communicates to the audience the exposition, setting and offstage events in the play.

Q. 16. What is a Comedy?

Ans.: The Comedy is a type of drama characterized by romantic love, humour, pleasantry, light satire and cross love finally leading to a happy denouement. Though fortune may be unkind to some stage, all ends happily at last.

Q. 17. What is Romantic Comedy?

Ans.: The Romantic Comedy is basically a love comedy. There is usually a story of triangular love with two heroes and one heroine, or two heroines and one hero, but finally the play ends in happy marriage.

Q. 18. What is a Comedy of Humours?

Ans.: The Comedy of Humours is a classical satirical comedy developed on the concept of four 'Humours' found in human physiology. The hero develops into a caricature or eccentric figure due to the excess of any one of these Humours.

Q. 19. What is an Epistolary Novel?

Ans.: The Epistolary Novel is a novel of which the plot develops through the medium of letters. The characters exchange their thoughts and views through letters there is very little dialogue face to face.

Q. 20. What is a Domestic Novel?

Ans.: The domestic novels present the day-to-day domestic life of the middle-class families and their friends and relations. The festivals and festivities, functions and celebrations, birthdays and marriage are graphically described in them.

Directions: Write the answer of the question no. 21 to 25. Each Question carries 12 marks and has to be answered in about 200 words.

Q. 21. What are the characteristics of a good Plot in a Tragedy?

Ans.: Artistic Arrangement: The Plot is 'the soul of a tragedy'. Therefore it should have a very effective artistic arrangement. It should have, first, unity of action. No action should be presented on the stage which may not help in the development of the plot towards its conclusion. Broadly speaking, the plot is divisible into two parts—complication and catastrophe. The first part is called rising action, and the second falling action ending into catastrophe.

Simple or Complex Plot: The plot may be simple or complex. A simple plot has no complications, surprise or suspense. Therefore it falls flat on the spectator without arresting his attention. A good plot is a complex plot. Its complications, sudden turns of events, and situations of suspense keep the spectator spell-bound. The occurrence of *Peripeteia* and *anagnorisis* is possible only in a complex plot. Peripeteia is reversal of fortune from good to bad, or from high to low. Anagnorisis is recognition of the cause of his fall. These two elements arouse the emotions of pity and fear which constitute the real spirit of the tragedy. Therefore a 'perfect tragedy' should be constructed not on the simple but on the complex plot. So Aristotle says: "For the plot ought to be so constructed that, even without the aid of the eye, he who hears the tale told will thrill with horror and melt to pity at what takes place."

Q. 22. Discuss I.A. Richards' theory of Poetic Communication.

Ans.: Poetic Communication, for Richards, is an implied, not vocal, dialogue between the poet and the reader. He says, "The arts are the supreme form of the communicative activity, since any attempt to harness psychology to the service of criticism is bound to insist upon poetry as a strictly analyzable human activity." However, communication is not the primary function of the poet. Communication of his experience is no part of the poet's work. Eliot says, "Communication is an irrelevant or at best a minor issue, and that what he is making is something which is beautiful in itself, or satisfying to him personally; or something expressive of his emotions, or of himself, something personal and individual. That other people are going to study it, and to receive experiences from it may seem to him a merely accidental, inessential circumstances." But his conscious neglect of communication does not in the least diminish the importance of the communicative power. The extent to which his work accords with his experience can be known only by the extent to which it arouses the same experience in others. If it fails to do so, the experience has not been accurately embodied in the work. To that extent the poet has failed in his mission. Man being accustomed to communication from infancy, each experience of his takes a communicative form. Eliot says, "The emphasis which natural selection has put upon communicative ability is overwhelming." The poet uses 'emotive language' i.e. language of emotions, and communicates his experiences 'with his heart on fire.' Thus communication is inseparable from his poetic experience.

Q. 23. Briefly analyse Dr. Johnson's views on Drama and its art.

Ans.: In his analysis of dramatic art, Dr. Johnson has given his vies on all debatable points such as the dramatic unities, dramatic pleasure, and the tragicomedies. First of all the says that drama must be "a faithful mirror of manners and of life." It should present human sentiments in human language. The story of drama must be true to life, but it must not be the story of one man or a few men, but of a wide section of humanity. Shakespeare's plays are great because each play is a miniature picture of any one aspect of the whole of humanity.

So far as Dramatic Unities are concerned, Dr. Johnson approved of only one unity—the unity of Action. This is necessary to make the plot complete and one whole. There would be utter chaos if there were many actions leading to different ends. In a good play all the actions should join together and lead to one desired end. So far as the unities of Time and Place are concerned, he finds them unnecessary and highly undesirable. The stage in a play is an imaginary platform. It is neither a real Rome nor a real Alexandria, and therefore the shifting of scenes from one place to another is also an imaginative process. So is the case with the passage of time. The audience imaginatively travels from place to place, and passes days and years through the same process of imagination. After all, a play is not a literal picture but an imaginative recreation of life. In the same way he defends tragic-comedy. Life itself is a mingling of tragic and comic occurrences. Moreover, tragic comic scenes throw each other into greater relief by contrast. Therefore there is nothing unnatural or inartistic in a tragic-comedy.

Q. 24. Why is Dryden called "the Father of English Criticism"?

Ans.: Dr. Johnson called Dryden "the father of English Criticism who first taught us to determine upon principles the merit of composition." Dr. Johnson was very correct in giving

Dryden this honour because before him there was no Consistent critic in England. Sidney and Ben Jonson were, of course, there but they only made occasional observations without producing any consistent critical work or establishing any critical theory. Dryden's principal critical work is his *Essay of Dramatic Poesy*, though his critical observations are also found in the prefaces to several of his works, specially in the *Preface to the Fables*. The *Essay of Dramatic Poesy* establishes him as the first historical critic, first comparatives critic, first descriptive critic, and the first independent English critic. The *Essay of Dramatic Poesy* is developed in the form of dialogues amongst four interlocutors representing four different literatures or literary ages. Crites speaks for the ancient Greek and Roman authors, Lisideius for the French, Eugenius for the English literature of the last age, and Neander for England and liberty. In this way he develops historical comparative, and descriptive forms of criticism, and finally gives his own independent views through the replies of Neander. He respects the ancient Greek and Roman principles but he refuses to adhere to them slavishly, specially in respect of Tragi-comedy and observance of the three dramatic unities. Thus Dryden began a great regular era of criticism, and showed the way to his countrymen how to be great as creative authors as well as critical evaluators and what makes great literature. Thus he is indeed "the father of English Criticism."

Q. 25. Evaluate Sidney's views on the three Dramatic Unities.

Ans.: Sidney was a strong advocate of the three dramatic Unities of Time, Place and Action. These three unities must be observed if a play is believed to be a true copy of life. Sidney regretted that none of the English plays, except *Gorboduck* to some extent, observed the three Dramatic unities.

The Unity of Time requires that the plot or action of a play should not exceed the limit of one natural day of twenty-four hours. If the action exceeds this time limit, the play would appear to be highly unnatural. But English dramatists have most hideously violated this unity. "For ordinary it is", he says, "that two young princes fall in love, after many traverses, she is got with child, delivered of a fair boy; he is lost growth a man, falls in love, and is ready to get another child, and all this in two hours space." Nothing could be more absurd than this. Such an absurd situation should be avoided.

The Unity of Place require that the action of the play should not shift frequently from on distant place to another. The English dramatists violated the unity of place equally grossly. "You shall have Asia of the one side, and Africa of the other, and so many other under-kingdoms, that the player must ever begin with telling where he is, or else the tale will not be conceived." Also the same stage has to be taken for a garden, a graveyard, a palace or an island where there is a shipwreck, or a battle field. This is straining the imagination of the spectator to the breaking point. This should be equally avoided.

The Unity of Action required that there should be no admixture of the comic and the tragic scenes in the most unnatural way. A comedy should be a comedy, and a tragedy should be a tragedy from the beginning to the end. The tragic and comic scenes and situations should not be mixed up. The king and the clown should not be mixed up on the stage. It is on this ground that Sidney harshly condemns the vogue of tragic-comedies coming up in English drama.

Direction: Write an essay of about 1000 words on the following topics.

Q. 26. Write an essay on the Graveyard School of Poetry.

Ans.: The Graveyard School of Poetry: The term 'Graveyard School of Poetry' is applied to a group of eighteenth-century poets who wrote meditative poems, usually set in the background of a graveyard, on the theme of human mortality and in moods which ranged from elegiac pensiveness to profound grief and gloom. These poets were the forerunners of romantic melancholy that appeared in the poets of the next generation. To some poets these poems were a king of safely valves to escape from the agonies and sorrows of life. Their poems ranged from melancholy to the mortality of life, inevitability of death, and vanity of human wishes and ambitions. These poems are different from elegies, for elegies are written on the death of some particular person, but the graveyard poems deal with the mortality of human life in general. The poems of this School have the tone of despair, the odour of the charnel house, meditation of the shortness of life, and inevitability of death. They are steeped in what we call 'melancholy pleasure' or 'pleasing gloom.' There are four important poets who belong to this School. They are Thomas Parnell, Robert Blair, Edward Young, and Thomas Gray.

Let us consider them one by one.

Thomas Parnell (1679-1718): The Graveyard School was initiated by Thomas Parnell with his well-known poem *A Night Piece on Death*. With this poem set in the vogue of Graveyard or Churchyard poems. Parnell deeply mediated on life and death in this meditative mood:

"Those graves, with bending osier bound
That nameless have the crumbled ground."
In the same poem. Parnell cautions man
Against the inevitable approach of Death:
"Ha! while I gaze, pale Cynthia fades,
The bursting Earth unveils the Shades!
All slow, and won, and wrap'd with Shrouds,
They rise in visionary Clouds,
And all with sober Accent cry,
Think, Mortal, what it is to die."

The poet further calls man to hear the subdued groans of the dead from their tombs:

"Now from yon black and fun'ral yew.
That bathes the Charnel House with dew,
Methinks I hear a voice begin:
(Ye Ravens, cease your croaking Din,
Ye tolling clocks, no Time resound
O'er the long lake and midnight Ground)
It sends a Peal of hollow Groans,
Thus speaking from among the Bones."

These lines draw an eerie image the Graveyard in the night. Words like *Yew, Charnel House, ravens, hollow groans,* and *bones* create an uncanny atmosphere in the mind of the reader.

Robert Blair (1699-1746): Robert Blair, a Scottish poet, also joined the group of the Graveyard poets. His long poem, *The Grave,* is a meditation on death. This is the only poem that Blair wrote. It is written in blank verse in the Elizabethan style. This poem has the deep spirit of the Graveyard School. The following lines may be quoted to illustrated this eerie tone of the poem:

"Tell us, ye dead! will none of you, in pity
To those you left behind, disclose the secret?
Oh! That some courteous ghost would blab it out
What 'tis you are, and we must shortly be.
I've heard that souls departed have sometimes
Forewarned men of their death.
'Twas kindly done
To knock and give the alarm,
Bt what means
This stinted charity? 'Tis but lame kindness
That does its work by halves. Why might you not
Tell us what 'tis to die? Do the strict laws
Of your society forbid your speaking
Upon a point so nice? I'll ask no more."

Edward Young (1683-1765): With Edward Young we come to a poet of greater originality and force. He is primarily remembered for his *Night-Thoughts.* Its central theme is mortality of man. Its unbroken gloom tires one to the extreme degree. Its moral is more apparent than real. Young reflects on the death of his wife and of his step daughter and her husband during nine nights, and in each one gloom is expressed with all the artistry of an amorist stroking a shroud. He pours his broodings in the gloomy context of night:

"Night, sable goddess! from her above throne.
In rayless majesty now stretches forth
Her leaden scepter o'er a slumbering world.
Silence, how dead! and darkness, how profound!
Nor eye nor listening ear an object finds;
Creation sleeps."

In the darkness of the night, there is darkness of the grave. In this darkness of the grave man is a helpless creature:

"How poor, how rich, how abject, how august,
How complicate, how wonderful is man!"

In these circumstances the only consoling force it religion.

Thomas Gray (1716-71): By far the most important poet belonging to the Graveyard School of Poetry was Thomas Gray. His representative poem, *An Elegy Written in a Country Churchyard* was believed to be the greatest poem of the century of its class. In the opinion of some critics it is the most powerful elegiac poem in the world. Its influence was felt immediately, not only in England but all over Europe. Edmund Gosse says, "*The Elegy* has exercised an influence on all the poetry of Europe, from Denmark to Italy, from France to Russia. With the exception of certain works of Byron and Shakespeare, no English poem has been so widely admired and imitated abroad." It is the most widely quoted poem in English.

Its Melancholy Setting: The *Elegy* is set in a highly uncanny and melancholy atmosphere at dusk hour in a country Churchyard. It is believed that in order to instill in himself the real atmosphere of the Churchyard while writing this poem, Gray placed a human skull on his table and stuck two burning candles in the eyeholes of the skull and wrote in their light. W.H. Hudson says, "There is the Churchyard scene, the twilight atmosphere, and the brooding melancholy of the poem, which at once connect it with one side of the romantic movement. The contrast drawn between the country and the town—the peasants' simple life and 'the madding crowd's ignoble strife' needs to be noted. The tender feelings shown for 'the rude forefathers of the hamlet' and 'the short simple annals of the poor' reach out to include humble aspects of life hitherto ignored by the neoclassicists.

Mortality and Vanity of Human Life:

The *Elegy* exposes the mortality and vanity of human life:

"The boast of heraldry, the pomp of power,
And all that beauty, all that wealth e'er gave,
Awaits alike th' inevitable hour:
The paths of glory lead but to the grave."

Therefore there is no use building memorial monuments or inscribing tales of one's glories on them. None of these can call back the departed soul:

"Can stories urn or animated bust
Back to its mansion call the fleeting breath?
Can Honour's voice invoke the silent dust.
Or flattery soothe the dull cold ear of Death?"

Therefore the rich and the proud should not deride the poor commoners because Death, the leveler, makes them all equal in the grave:

"Let not Ambition mock their useful toil,
Their homely joys, and destiny obscure;
Nor Grandeur hear with a disdainful obscure;
The short and simple annals of the poor."

Death is a fearful but inevitable end of life. Nobody likes to leave his dear and near ones and sink into the grave:

"For' who, to dumb forgetfulness a prey,
This pleasing anxious being e'er resign'd,
Left the warm precincts of the cheerful day,

Nor cast one longing lingering look behind?"

This is the whole story of life. We all come and play our part on the stage of the world, and then depart without leaving even the foot-prints on the sands of time.

This is the melancholy, morbid, and vain glorious, but absolutely true story of life, which the poets of the Graveyard School presented.

Appendix

Appendix

GENERAL SECTION
TYPICAL FORMS OF LITERATURE

Allegory: A figurative narrative in which some hidden meaning is to be read in between the lines. The underlying idea is usually moral or ethical. The notable examples of allegory in English are Spenser's *The Faerie Queene* and Bunyan's *Pilgrims's Progress*.

Autobiography: The story of a man's life written by himself. It is a literature of personal revelation. Nehru's *My Autobiography*, Churchills's *My Early Life*, *My Story* etc. are examples.

Ballad: A simple story in verse, generally dealing with some patriotic or romantic theme, full of deeds of prowess and supernatural happenings. Its special characteristic is a refrain at the end of a stanza. Others are repetition, swift movement, and forceful narration.

Biography: A deliberate history of the life of a particular individual. The earliest biography in English is, perhaps, Asser's Alfred. Boswell's *Life of Johnson* is the first biography in the modern sense of the term. But the cut of biography changed in the hands of Lytton Strachey, whose *Queen Victoria* gave a new they to the art of biographies.

Burlesque: Derived from the Italian word burla meaning ridicule or mockery. In its wider sinse it is used for any literary composition or dramatic representation which aims at producing laughter by the comic treatment of a serious subject or the ridiculous imitation of a serious work. For example—Chaucer's Sir Topas, Fieldieng's Tom Thumb the Great, etc.

Carol: A jouous song, generally, accompanying the dance, and more particularly a Christmas hymn sung at the celebration of the nativity. The first collection of Christmas carols was printed in 1521 by Wynkyn de Worde.

Chronicle Play: A chronicle play means a play dealing with some historical facts and personages. The type reached its culmination in the historical plays of Shakespeare, e.g. Henry V, Richard II and Julius Caesar. Shaw's St. Joan and Caesar and Cleopatra are also included in it.

Closet Play: Primarily a play meant to be enjoyed in private and not to be staged for public. It is doubtful whether any play has been written for that purpose alone Milton's Samson Agonists, Shelley's Prometheus Unbound and Swinburne's Atalante in Calydon are notable examples. Some plays by J.M. Barrie and G.B. Shaw are also of these type.

Comedy: The play with happy ending that emokes thoughtful laughter is called comedy. It differs from tragedy in that they have a happy ending and from force in that they contain some sublity and character drawing. Shakespeare's *Twelfth Night*, *As You Like it*, or Shaw's *Condida* are well known examples. There are various groups of comedy; such as Comedy of Manners, Comedy of Character, of Humours Comedy of Intrigue and Comedy of Morals. The first

English comedy is Ralph Reister Doister. Modern comedy turns mainly upon the trivial complications of sex, and has lost both its robust humour its wit.

Comedy of Humours: Generally associated with Ben Jonson. It is based on an old medical theory that a man's temperament was determined by the proportion of four bodily fluids or humours. The comedy of Humours depicts persons marked with some strong humours (characteristics) and subjects them to criticism for their abviormality. Jonson's: *Every Man in His Humour*, *Every Man Out of his Humour*, *The Alchemist*, and *Volpone* are the best examples of this type.

Comedy of Intrigne: Subordinates character to plot, originated in Spain, and was practiced in England by Mrs. Aphra Behn. Her famous comedies are *The Rovir* and *The City Hevirs*.

Comedy of Manners: Originated in France with Moliere's Les Preciuses ridicules (1658) and Moliere himself defined it when he said 'correction of social absurdities must at all times be the matter of true comedy': In English literature the term is generally associated with the Restoration; with Congreve and Wycherley. It seeks to present the superficial side of social life and is remarkable for its humour, wit and polish. It is sometimes called Artificial comedy. In the eighteenth century it was revived by Goldsmith and Sheridan.

Diary: Diary is a daily record of events, generally personal in character. Diaries of great public men, explosers, statesmen, and soldiers are particularly interesting for ther comments on contemporary events as for the revelation of their own character. The notable English Diaries are those of Pepys and Evelyn (17th Century)

Dirge: A funeral song, composed to commemorate the dead and sung in Roman funeral processions or at funeral banquets. (Shakespeare's *Cymberline*)

Domestic Tragedy: Drama of a serious nature dealing with the thoughts and actions of ordinary people rather than men of great fortune and status. E.g. O' Neill's Desire Under the Elms, Synge's Riders to the Sea etc.

Elegy: Generally speaking, the term denotes a poem of mourining or lamenting. It may be objective like Gray's Elegy written in a country churchyard or subjective like Shelley's Adonais. The Pastoral Elegy follows the tradition set by the Greek poets, Theocritus, and imitated by the Roman poet, Virgil. In it grief is conventionalized, the dead man is referred to as a shepherd, a pastoral setting is given to the poem, pagon mythology is introduced and all nature participates in the mourning. The notable English examples of this type are Milton's Lycidas, Shelley's Adonais and Arnold's Thyrsis.

Epic: A long narrative poem dealing with heroic figures and written in an elevated style. Homer's 'Iliad' and the 'Odyssey' serve as the chief models of epic poetry. *The Mahabharata* and the *Ramayana* are Indian epics. The best epic in English poetry is Milton's *Paradise Lost and Paradise Regained.*

Epistle: Originally a formal alternative for letter; now reserved mainly for certain Biblical writings. The Epistles of Paul. Some English poets, Drayton, Burns, and Shelley have written verse in the form of epistles.

Epithalami: A marriage song or hymeneal, sung by choruse of young men and women before the bridal chamber after the bride and groom have retired. A book of Sappho's poetry in devoted to Epithalamia.

Essay: First used by Michel de Montaigne in 1580. Under the title *Essai*. The meaning of the word Essai is 'attempt', which indicates its incompleteness and tentativeness. In its broader sense it means a prose composition characterized by brevity and restricted topic. The subject matter is not so important as the style of the essay. It should bear the stamp of the writer's personality and it should be thoroughly readable and light enough to be enjoyed.

Fable: A short allegorical tale, in prose or verse, having a moral lesson. C.F. Fables, Ancient and Modern, by Dryden.

Fantasy: It represents a picture of life as it could never be. It includes action, characters, or setting, things that are impossible under ordinary conditions or in the normal course of human events. E.g. Shakespeare's *A Midsummer Night's Dream* and Huxley's *Brave New World.*

Farce: Generally means low comedy, intended to excite laughter by means of buffoonery and exaggeration. The term is often used in a derogatory sense to indicate an inferior variety of entertainment. Shakespeare's *Comedy of Errors* is an example.

Heroic Drama: A type of the English Restoration drama written mamily in heroic couplets. Its main emphasis was on volour, beauty and love. It was written in a bombastic style and was spectacular in production. It was originated by Devenant but its main exponent was John Dryden.

Historical Romance: A particular type of romantic fiction dealing with some remote period of history in an imaginative manner. Sir Walter Scott is perhaps the greatest writer of such romances.

Hymn: A lyric poem expressing religions emotion and generally intended to be sung by a chorus. Some notable hymn writers of England were Wesley, Coupler, Watts and Newman.

Edyll: A lyrical poem giving a little picture of everyday life amid natural surroundings, generally rural or pastoral. Originally the term was applied to the odes of Pindar. Later examples are Tennyson's Idylls of the king and Browning's Dramatic Idylls of the king and Browning's Dramatic Idylls.

Interlude: A short dramatic piece or musical performance given between the parts of an independent play or musical entertainment. John Heywood wrote a number of Interludes of whlich the most famous is The Four P's.

Lampoon: Popular in the 17th and 18th centuries Lampoon is a violent satire or personal attack in prose or verse, generally on some prominent individual. Its chief motive is to satisfy personal malice.

Lay: A short romantic tale of adventure is called Lay. Like the ballad, it was intended for singing. The notable examples are Scott's Lay of the Last Ministrel and Macaulay's Lays of Ancient Rome.

Letters: Personal literature, not meant for publication. The letters of great men are usually published after their death. The letters of Horacle Walpole, Lady Mary W. Montague, and Lord Chesterfield are well known. A Brunch of Old letters by Nehru is a notable Indian example.

Limerick: A popular type of nonsense verse, popularized by Edward Lear in his Book of Nonsense.

Lyric: Originally a poem to be sung to the lyre; but now understand to be a short, personal poem of spontaneous over flow, usually turning on a single thought, emotion or situation. The special features of a lyric are thus music, subjectivity, unity, spontaneity and brevity Shelley is regarded as a lyrical poet par excellence.

Madrigal: It is a lyric, song of Italian origin. Originally it meant a pastoral, but now it comes for any short love song. e.g. Shakespeare's *Crabbed Age and Youth*.

Masque: A sort of dramatic entertainment is which originally the performers work master of peculiar forms suggestive of the allegorical character assumed. It flourished mainly in England during the career of Ben Jonson. The real charm of these masques Lay in songs, dances and elaborate costumes. The dancers were known as 'Masquers'.

Melodrama: Originally, a play with music; now a play of a very sentimental nature, marked by rapid and incessant action, violently expressed emotion, blood and murder. The conventional characters are the hero, the heroic and the villain.

Memoirs: The autobiography of a person in the form of recollections, often laying emphasis on events external to the writer's own life. They give some prominence to personalities and actions other than writer's own.

Miracle Plays: Medieval religious dramas in which divine miracle played a part. They dealt either with stories from the Bible or with the lives of the saints. The miracle plays were further classified into Mysteries and Miracles. The Mysteries Miracles dealt the lives of saints and Martyrs.

Monodrama: A dramatic piece for one player. The term is also applied to an extended poetic soliloquy such as Tennyson's Mand. Some of the dramatic monologues of Browning e.g. Fra Lippo Lippi, also come in the category.

Monody: A mourning poem, an elegy presented by one person. Arnold calls Thyrsis a monody.

Monologue: A monologue is a speech by one person. The plays of Shakespeare abrind in monologues. Browning is the famous writer of dramatic monologues used in his poetry.

Morality Plays: It is a type of medieval drama. Morality plays are sermons in disguise. Their main theme is the struggle between the forces of good and evil. The characters are abstract, allegorical or symbolical, bearing the names of virtues and vices they represent.

Mystery Plays: A type of medieval religious drama, dealing with biblical stories. In recent years the term has sometimes been used for plays dealing with crime and detection.

Myth: Essentially a religious term. Myth in literature stands for a folk tale of ancient or primitive people, usually involving their religious beliefs. Of late the term stands for a product of the poetic faculty, complete in itself and without any ulterior purpose.

Nonsense Verse: An exhibition of 'folly for folly's sake': The two masters of nonsense verse were Lewis Carroll and Edward Lear.

Novella: An Italian term meaning a short story and exemplified by the tales of Boccaccio's Decameron.

Ode: Ode is a poem intended to be sung to music, often in the form of an address, generally dignified or exalted in subject, feeling and style. It is of two types—classical and modern.

One-Act Play: Comparatively of recent origin, it came into prominence with the growth of the experimental movement. It is to the full-length play what the short story is to the novel. It can stress but one aspect, character, or action, or background, or emotion. It occupies roughly half-an-hour in presentation. Some famous one act plays are W.W. Jacob's *The Monkey's Paw*, A.A. Milne's *Wurxel Flummery* and Alfred Sutro's *A Marriage Has Been Arranged.*

Opera: A drama whose language is song, and whose action is performed to the accompaniment of musical instruments. It was first adopted in Italy. Later Dryden, Addison, Fielding, Garrick and Sheridan contributed to it.

Pamphlet: A small tract, containing one or more folded printed sheets stitched or stapled together. It is especially of some topical interest. Swift made it a weapon of political controversy. Some other pamphlet writers were Robert Greene, Nash and Milton.

Parable: A short tale intended to convey some moral. Its characters are usually human beings and not animals or plants as in a fable. The best examples of parables are those of Jesus in the New Testament.

Parody: A composition in which the manner and spirit of another author is consciously imitated so as to make him appear ridiculous. Fielding's novel *Joseph Andrews* was initially an attempt to parody Richardson's Pamela. But it turned out to be a great novel.

Pastoral: The term is applied to writings about Shepherds and simple country life. The genre ordinate with the Greek poet, Theocritus. Spenser was the first exponent of pastoral poetry in England. Sidney's Arcadia is a pastoral romance in prose and Shakespeare's *As You Like It* is a pastoral play.

Pastoral Elegy: A conventionalized expression of grief on the model of 'Theocritus's The Lament for Daphnis. Here all the objects of nature participate in the mourning and ultimately the sorrow changes to joy when it is realized that the departed soul has joined the immortals. Milton's Lycidas, Shelley's Adonais and Arnold's Thyrisi are example.

Picaresque: From the Spanish word picaro meaning a rogue, the term was originally applies to a novel which told the life story of a rogue or knave. Fielding popularized this type of novel with Tom Jones.

Pindoric: A type of ode, popularized by the Greek poet, Pindar. It is regular and observes a definite structural scheme in the verse arrangement.

Propaganda Play: A play with a purpose, designed to spread a specific idea or a particular belief. Most of the modern realistic plays dealing with contemporary, social, economic and political problems are propaganda play. Ibsen and Shaw are the notable writers of such plays. Even Galsworthy's plays *Jistic* and *Loyaltiest* may be termed as propaganda play.

Radio Play: Drama specially written to suit the requirements of the radio. While it relies for its effects almost entirely on words, sound effects and musical accompaniments are often used. As spoken word is all important.

Restoration Comedy: The Comedy of Manners which originated in France and proved fertile in Restoration England, gave us the plays of Congreve. This is also called Artificial comedy or old comedy. At its best this comedy is delicate and disarming, at its worst equivocal and indecent, but always witty and intellectually remote from reality.

Revenge Play: A type of drama which flourished in the Elizabethan age under the influence of the Roman dramatist, Seneca. Its main theme was revenge for murder. Kyd's Spanish Tragedy is the example. The typical characteristics of a revenge play are: *Blood and Murder*, *Horror and Terror*, *Ghosts*, *Real or Feigned Madness*, *Episodes of a Sensational Nature* and *A Language Full of Conceits and Ephuism*.

Review: A short article published in some magazine or newspaper, aiming at a critical appraisal of a literary work. Its main emphasis is on information. The importance of a review, in modern times, can not be underestimated as the public reception to a new work largely depends on it. A thoroughly satisfactory review should present clearly and as interestingly as possible, the scope and theme of the work in question.

Romance: Originally a long, fictions narrative in verse or prose, written in the Middle Ages, dealing with Chivlric ideals and depending largely for its interest on strange adventures and the love of ladies, now used for any work of fiction in which imagination is given free play and which is not based on reality. Many romances were written about king Arthur and his knights.

Romantic Comedy: The term is generally assigned to the Shakespearean comedy. It generally deals with strange, remote and unreal happenings. Love, humour and music are its key notes. The most notable examples of romantic comedy are *Twelfth Night*, *Much Ado About Nothing*, *As You Like It* by Shakespeare.

Rubaiyat: From the Arabic, plural of rubai meaning a quatrain. Most of the Urdu and Persian poets are find of writing Rubaiyat. *Fitzgerald* has translated into English the *Rubaiyat of Oman Khayyam*.

Satire: A composition in prose or verse, conveying sensorious criticism of human frailty. Its chief purpose is ethically or aesthetically corrective. It is generally motivated by a desire to reform. Dryden, Pope, Addison, Steele and Swift were the great masters of satire.

Sencecan Tragedy: A term applied to the tragedies of the Roman dramatist, Seneca and to later imitations of them in the Elizabethan age by Kyd Chapman, Marston, Webster and Shakespeare. The Revenge play can be directly attributed to the influence of Seneca.

Sentimental Comedy: A type of pathetic play which reflected the false sensibility of the rising 18th century middle class. It presented the weaknesses of mankind in such a way as to enlist the sympathy of the audience and to appeal to their better instincts and nobility of heart. It was first introduced by stele and developed by Colley Cibber, John Kelly and Comberland.

Sentimental Novel: A popular novel in the 18th century, started by Richardson's Pamela and Sir Charles Grandism. It was full of didacticism and emotionalism. It rested upon a belief in the goodness of average human nature and in the benevolence of man's original instincts.

Short Story: A prose-narrative, with a definite technique of its own, emerged in the 19th century. It is short in length; presents a slice of life and complete in itself and provides aesthetic satisfaction to the reader. Rudyard Kipling was the first Englishman who was acclaimed as a great writer of short stories.

Soliloguy: Literally solus, alone + logui, to speak. A solioguy is spoken by one person that is alone or acts as though he were alone. It is a kind of talking to oneself not intended to affect others. It was a favourite device with the Elizabethan dramatists. They introduced soliloquies in order to convey to the audience the internal conflict of a character or to give information regarding the fourtherance of the plot e.g. To be or not to be (Hamlet).

Song: A poem in particular, or poetry in general. It is a musical composition in regular metrical form. Songs are frequent in the drama, especially in the Elizabethans. The comedies of Shakespeare are rich in it. Sometimes he introduced songs in his tragedies (mad Ophelia's song in Hamlet) to enhance the dramatic effects.

Sonnet: Originally a poem to be sung to music now a lyric of fourteen lines, with a formal rhyme scheme. Its of two kinds. English and Italian. It was introduced into England in the sixteenth century by the poets Wyatt and Survey. Shakespeare, Sidney, Spenser, Wordsworth, Keats, Rossetti and Arnold are main exponents.

Sonnet Sequence: A form which exists for prolonged lyrical meditation. It is a collection or sequence of sonnets, which despite their value as isolated lyrical pieces, if read in a connected link, reveal a fanciful story of the author's life.

Tale: A story in prose or verse. The Canterbury Tales of Chaucer serve as a good example of tales in verse. Lamb's Tales from Shakespeare are well known in the field of prose.

Thesis Play: Also known as problem play. A play in which a social problem is presented with the dramatists solution. Ibsen, Shaw, Henry James etc. have written many such plays.

Threnody: A Greek lyric, usually a Choral durge for singing in praise of the dead.

Thriller: A story or play depicting an atmosphere of fear, excitement or suspense.

Tragedy: Aristotle said, 'tragedy is an imitation of an action that is serious, complete and of certain magniture'. The important characteristics of tragedy are: seriousness, magnitude, unity, conflity, suffering.

Tragic-Comedy: An off-shoot of pure tragedy, tragedy containing a blend of tragedy and comedy. The story of a tragic-comedy is inherently tragic, but some how or other the tragedy is averted and the concussion is happy. The last plays of Shakespeare are tragic-comedies. *Cymberline* is the best example of a tragic-comedy.

Treatise: Originally a narrative or any literary work; now a work mehodically analyzing the organization or expounding the principles of a subject. An example of treatise is Hume's Philosophical Work, Treatise of Human Nature.

SOME MORE LITERARY TERMS

Addisonian: It is generally used in connection with the style of a prose author. The term usually stands for a balanced and judicial style and approach.

Affection: It is generally used in a bad sense. It suggests a style that does not fit the person, subject or occasion.

Anachorism: Anachronism is related with time, whereas Anachorism is related with space. It means locating something where it does not belong to; it say, for example, the seas of Tiber or the mountains of Sahara.

Aphorism: The term is generally applied to sharp and pointing saying. It is derived from the Greek word 'Aphorismos', which means definition.

Apollonian-Dionysian: These terms were used by Nietzsche in The Birth of Tragedy out of the spirit of Music. Nietzsche seeks to describe through these words the opposition between reason and instinct, culture and primitive nature.

Archaism: The deliberate use of words or expressions appropriate to an older period. The writings of Edmund Spenser and Charles Lamb are replete with examples of archaism.

Architectonics: The principle on which a work of art is given its unity. The best known examples of Architectonics in English poetry is Milton's *Paradise Lost*.

Aside: A remark which is not meant to be heard by the other present on the stage. It is meant for the audience only.

Association of Ideas: This theory is supposed to have been formulated for the first time by Hume. It is a psychological process through which a link is established between two mental states.

Attic: Intellectual Sharpness; refined but stinging wit.

Atticism: Of style; simple direct and devoid of rhetorical adornment.

Boroque: Boroque's style in literature is one that deliberately rejects the finite for the infinite and the indefinite, that sacrifices harmony and proportion to dynamism. That chooses the antithetical and the explosive, the playful and the obscure.

Belles-Letters: A French word meaning literature in general.

Blue-Book: Short tales written after the Gothic romances.

Blue-Stocking: Used a female literature Blue stocking clubs substituted conversation for cards and literature for lackadaisy.

Bourgeois: Middle class. Mathew Arnold speaks of them as Philistines.

Catastrophe: The unhappy end of a tragedy.

Catharsis: It means the ignition of the excessive emotions of pity and fear.

Cavalier: A group of court poets-Suckling; Lovelace and Carew-who wrote lyrics of love and beauty is generally known as Cavalier poets.

Classic: A work that merits lasting interest.

Cockney-Rhymes: False rhymes

Comic–Relief: The Psychological relaxation and relief offered by a comic scent in a serious play which serves to purposes:

To provide relief and to relax mental tension.

To prepare the spectator for more tragic things to come. E.g. Porter scene in Shakespeares *Macbeth*.

Consonance: Harmony of sound, idea or style.

Crisis: The point at which the opposite forces in a play or a story interlock for the last time, moving towards the decisive moment.

Dadaism: A school of art and literature which seeks to do away with the ordinary logical links between thought and expression-thoroughly iconoclastic. Later on it took the shape of Surrealism.

Decadence: The decadents believed that art is superior to nature and that living itself is an art; amounting to artificiality. Deeply co-related with 'art for art sake' movement called 'fin de siecle' also.

Denouncement: Also known as Anti-climax; the unraveling of the complications of a plot.

Diabolism: Works dealing with what is called Satanism:

(i) Books that deal with theory and practice of black magic

(ii) Books about diabolism, mainly histories:

(iii) Creative literature which shows a concern with diabolism.

It also includes blasphemy and an unsuinpassable revolt against morality.

Doric: Opposed to Attic: rustic, unrefined, simple.

Epigram: Generally a short poem ending with a pointed turn or thought. According to Coleridge its body is brevity, and wit its soul.

Epistolary Fiction: Narratives told through letters (Richardsons Pamel).

Euphuism: Generally used for a style which is balanced and rhetorical; replete with antithesis and alliteration and full of question marks and dashes, commas and semi-colons, e.g. prose style of John Lyly.

Expressionism: An aesthetic doctrine which seeks to establish that the only aim of the literary artist is to express the intrinsic worth of his deeply felt emotions. The expressionists remember what they have to express but forget those whom they are going to express to the audience, it causes obscurity.

Fancy: Generally considered with synonymous with wit, fancy is differentiated from imagination by S.T. Coleridge in his Biographia Literaria Fancy seeks to juxtapose opposite images without synthesizing them.

Farcical: Derived from farce, suggesting a lack of versisimilitude and a serious purpose.

Genre: Literary kinds; such as the epic, the sonnet, the ballad, the lyric and so on. The Classical theory of genres is that there are only fixed kinds which were invented by nature and not by individual authors or poets.

Georgic: A poem dealing with rural life, agriculture in particular.

Gothic: The general characteristics of the Gothic novel are best summed up by words like horror, terror, revenge, bloodshed, darkness, skeletons and beneak. Also known as the novel of terror. e.g. Horace Walpole and Mrs Radcliffe's novels.

Grand Style: It arisis in poetry when a novel nature poetically gifted treats with simplicity or with severity a serious subject.

Hamartia: The some error in the character of good hero is hamartia. It may be an error of judgement or a moral fault or an inherent human weakness.

Hellenism: The governing idea of Hellenism is Spontaneity of Consciousness. (Used with Greek spirit)

Hybris: Overweening pride, breach of divine command due to ambition or lust or other passions.

Introjection: Empathy

Irony: The frequent employment of the various devices of irony implies an attitude of detachment and a tendency to perceive life in terms of the incongruities that occur between occurrences and reality.

Ivory Tower: The Shelter of the escapists. Generally used in the derogatory sense, irony tower suggests the isolated position from which certain artists contemplate the world. Generally used in connection with the pre-Raphaelites and the decadents.

Leitmotif: Leaving motif. Applied to an expression that as a unit bears a particular significance – e.g. the repeated phrases in a ballad.

Local Colour: The use of picturesque details of the environment in which a novel, a play or a story is set e.g. Novels of Thomas Hardy.

Macaronic: A mixture of two or more languages in a poem. e.g. T.S. Eliot's *The Wasteland* and *The Cantos* of Ezra Pound.

Melapropism: Named after Mrs. Malaprop in Sheridern's *The Rivals* who mispronounces words so as to produce a ludiorous incongruity.

Medievalism: Love for the Middle Ages. e.g. Keats, the pre-Raphaelites, Ruskin.

Milier: The environment of the age.

Naturalism: The term has been used in three different ways:

(i) as a synonym for realism

(ii) love of natural beauty

(iii) used in the historical sense for the works of zola and his followers. The naturalists believe that the strength of external forces limit human rationality and moral responsibility.

Neo-Classicism: A movement to recapture the spirit of classical literature, generally applied to the Augustan age.

Objective-Correlative: T.S. Eliot defines it as the only way of expressing emotion in art by finding an 'objective correlative'. He criticizes Shakespeare's *Hamlet* in the plea that Hamlet's madness has no objective correlative.

Pathetic Fallacy: The transfer of subjective emotions to objects of nature.

Plagiarism: Literary theft; borrowing from other people's work without proper acknowledgement.

Poetic Diction: The use of a dignified and nobler vocabulary used in poetry.

Poetic Justice: A belief that in works or art the good must be rewarded, the evil punished.

Poetic Licence: The liberty that a poet takes and that can be justified on the ground that they add to the total effect of his work.

Polyphonic Prose: Poetic prose. The idea was derived from the French poet Paul Fort who wrote verse printed as prose.

Pseudo: Alleged, supposed, unreal.

Regionalism: A tendency to set works of art in a particular locality. Examples the Wenex of Hardy and the five towns of Arnold Bennett and Malgudi of R.K. Narayana.

Semantics: The study of the relation between words and things; study of the relations between language, thought and behaviour.

Slice of Law: Uncoloured life in the raw; applied to the works of naturalism writers.

Verisimilitude: Correspondence to the objective data. Truth may be stranger than fiction but fiction must not be stranger than truth.